DAVID BUSCH'S

Nikon® Z5

GUIDE TO
DIGITAL PHOTOGRAPHY

DAVID D. BUSCH

David Busch's Nikon® Z5 Guide to Digital Photography
David D. Busch

Project Manager: Jenny Davidson
Series Technical Editor: Michael D. Sullivan
Layout: Bill Hartman
Cover Design: Mike Tanamachi
Indexer: Valerie Haynes Perry
Proofreader: Mike Beady

ISBN: 978-1-68198-711-8
1st Edition (1st printing, February 2021)

© 2021 David D. Busch

All images © David D. Busch unless otherwise noted

Rocky Nook, Inc.
1010 B Street, Suite 350
San Rafael, CA 94901
USA
www.rockynook.com

Distributed in the UK and Europe by Publishers Group UK
Distributed in the U.S. and all other territories by Ingram Publisher Services

Library of Congress Control Number: 2020942764

This book is printed on acid-free paper.
Printed in Korea

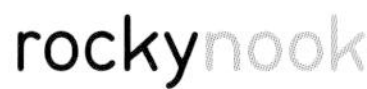

For Cathy

Acknowledgments

Thanks to everyone at Rocky Nook, including Scott Cowlin, managing director and publisher, for the freedom to let me explore the amazing capabilities of the Nikon Z5 in depth. I couldn't do it without my veteran production team, including project manager, Jenny Davidson and series technical editor, Mike Sullivan. Also, thanks to Bill Hartman, layout; Valerie Haynes Perry, indexing; Mike Beady, proofreading; Mike Tanamachi, cover design; and my agent, Carole Jelen, who has the amazing ability to keep both publishers and authors happy.

About the Author

With more than 3 million books in print, **David D. Busch** is the world's #1 selling digital camera guide author, and the originator of popular digital photography series like *David Busch's Pro Secrets* and *David Busch's Quick Snap Guides.* He has written more than four dozen hugely successful guidebooks and compact guides for Nikon digital cameras, several dozen additional user guides for other camera models, as well as many popular books devoted to dSLRs, including *Mastering Digital SLR Photography, Fourth Edition* and *Digital SLR Pro Secrets.* As a roving photojournalist for more than 20 years, he illustrated his books, magazine articles, and newspaper reports with award-winning images. He's operated his own commercial studio, suffocated in formal dress while shooting weddings, and shot sports for a daily newspaper and an upstate New York college. His photos and articles have been published in magazines as diverse as *Popular Photography, Rangefinder, Professional Photographer,* and hundreds of other publications. He's also reviewed dozens of digital cameras for CNet Networks and other CBS publications. His advice has been featured on National Public Radio's *All Tech Considered.*

When About.com named its top five books on Beginning Digital Photography, debuting at the #1 and #2 slots were Busch's *Digital Photography All-In-One Desk Reference for Dummies* and *Mastering Digital Photography.* He's had as many as five of his books listed in the Top 20 of Amazon.com's Digital Photography Bestseller list—simultaneously! Busch's 300-plus other books published since 1983 include bestsellers like *Digital SLR Cameras and Photography for Dummies.*

Busch is a member of the Cleveland Photographic Society (www.clevelandphoto.org), which has operated continuously since 1887. Visit his website at http://www.nikonguides.com or his Facebook group *David D. Busch Photography Guides.*

Contents

CHAPTER 6

Advanced Techniques   143

CHAPTER 7

Focus on Lenses   187

CHAPTER 8

Mastering Light   237

CHAPTER 12

The Custom Settings Menu   371

CHAPTER 16
Troubleshooting and Prevention 475

Preface

The new Nikon Z5 is proof that a mirrorless full-frame camera can be highly affordable, without sacrificing sophisticated features. This 24-megapixel camera packs a surprising number of high-end capabilities into a compact body, including dual memory card slots, five-axis image stabilization, and an advanced hybrid autofocus system. The Z5 looks and handles like a Nikon, with controls and menus that veteran Nikon owners will find comfortably familiar and new users will grow to love as they explore its exciting enhancements. Every photo enthusiast will easily master the Z5's capabilities, even though the sheer number of features and options can be daunting. The only thing standing between you and pixel proficiency is the fat, but confusing book included in the box as a manual.

Everything you need to know is in there, somewhere, but you don't know where to start, nor how to find the information you really need to master your camera. In addition, the Z5 camera manual doesn't offer much guidance on the principles that will help you master digital photography. Nor does it really tell you much about how mirrorless shooting might differ from the kinds of digital photography you may already be used to. If you're like most enthusiasts, you're probably not interested in spending hours or days studying a comprehensive book on digital photography that doesn't necessarily apply directly to the enhanced features of your Z5.

What you really need is a guide that explains the purpose and function of the Z5's basic controls, available lens options, and most essential accessories from the perspective of mirrorless cameras. It should tell you how you should use them, and *why*. Ideally, there should be information about the exciting features at your disposal, how to optimize image quality, when to use exposure modes like Aperture- or Shutter-priority, and the use of special autofocus modes. In many cases, you'd prefer to read about those topics only after you've had the chance to go out and take a few hundred great pictures with your new camera. Why isn't there a book that summarizes the most important information in its first two or three chapters, with lots of illustrations showing what your results will look like when you use this setting or that? This is that book.

If you can't decide on what basic settings to use with your camera because you can't figure out how changing ISO or white balance or focus defaults will affect your pictures, you need this guide. I won't talk down to you, either; this book isn't padded with dozens of pages of checklists telling you how to take a travel picture, a sports photo, or how to take a snapshot of your kids in overly simplistic terms. There are no special sections devoted to "real-world" recipes here. All of us do 100 percent of our shooting in the real world! So, I give you all the information you need to cook up great photos on your own!

Introduction

In the short time since Nikon's advanced mirrorless Z-mount cameras and accessories were introduced in August 2018, the Z-system has blossomed into a full-fledged alternative to traditional digital SLRs (chiefly those offered by Canon and Nikon itself) and mirrorless models from a variety of vendors. As I write this, Nikon offers 16 different lenses and two tele-converters in your Z5's native Z-mount, with an additional eight more optics scheduled on the company's "lens map' projections. If you add in the dozens of existing original F-mount lenses that can be used on the Z5 with the optional FTZ adapter, and full line of electronic flash units and accessories compatible with both Z-mount and F-mount cameras, you'll see the company has built a formidable (and comprehensive) Z system quite quickly.

The Z5 occupies one of two "entry-level" slots in the Z-series lineup, as Nikon's lowest-cost full-frame mirrorless camera, priced just a few hundred dollars more than its APS-C ("crop sensor") sibling, the Z50. It's an affordable option for those who feel they don't need all the advanced features of the more upscale Z7 and Z6. As such, your new Nikon Z5 has to be one of the top photographic bargains on the market today.

Although priced at introduction at an affordable $1,400 for the body alone, the Z5 has nearly all the killer features found in the Z7 II and Z6 II. Indeed, it *matches* the more expensive models by including *two* (count 'em) memory card slots—the single most-wanted "missing" feature among photo enthusiasts. If you've been delaying your jump to the mirrorless world waiting for Nikon to introduce a worthy, affordable offering, your wait is over. For most of us on a budget, the Z5 is the dream mirrorless camera we've been hoping for.

Of course, despite what you might read elsewhere, the Nikon Z-series cameras are not the first mirrorless interchangeable-lens cameras Nikon has offered. That distinction belongs to the company's Nikon 1 product line, a series of consumer-oriented cameras that were truly small in size, and which used small 1-inch sensors. Those cameras, targeted at amateur snapshooters, allowed Nikon to develop considerable expertise in mirrorless technology. Your Z5 builds on what the company learned in carefully designing a new platform that fully meets the needs of a much different group: dedicated photo enthusiasts, semi-professionals, and, even, professional photographers.

Despite what I said earlier, I hesitate to call the Z5 an "entry-level" full-frame camera, although even the rawest beginner will find it easy to learn and simple to use with a little practice. Nikon's APS-C ("crop sensor") model, the Z50, which lacks an in-body image stabilization (anti-shake) feature is a better fit for the entry-level label. With *this* camera you're not giving up much, other than a mirror, bulky optical viewfinder, and weight of traditional dSLRs.

Indeed, the Z5 is, in many respects, Nikon's mirrorless "do-everything" camera. It has enough resolution—at 24MP—to satisfy the needs of landscape and fine-art photographers. Its 4.5 frames per second continuous shooting is fast enough for all but the most frenetic sports action. A built-in intervalometer effortlessly captures the beauty of an unfolding blossom and can shoot time-lapse movies.

Still, you may be asking yourself—*how do I use this thing?* Nikon's manual is mind-numbingly dense, and online tutorials from ad-supported YouTube click-bait sites can't cover all these features in depth. Who wants to learn how to use a camera by sitting in front of a television or computer screen? Do you want to watch a movie or click on HTML links, or do you want to go out and take photos with your camera?

The included manual is thick and filled with information, but there's really very little about *why* you should use particular settings or features. Its organization makes it difficult to find what you need. Multiple cross-references send you searching back and forth between two or three sections of the book to find what you want to know. The basic manual is also hobbled by black-and-white line drawings and tiny monochrome pictures that aren't very good examples of what you can do.

I've tried to make *David Busch's Nikon Z5 Guide to Digital Photography* different from your other Z5 learn-up options. The roadmap sections use larger, color pictures to show you where all the buttons and dials are, and the explanations of what they do are longer and more comprehensive. I've tried to avoid overly general advice, including the two-page checklists on how to take a "sports picture" or a "portrait picture" or a "travel picture." You won't find half the content of this book taken up by generic chapters that tell you how to shoot landscapes, portraits, or product photographs. Instead, you'll find tips and techniques for using all the features of your Nikon Z5 to take *any kind of picture* you want. If you want to know where you should stand to take a picture of a quarterback dropping back to unleash a pass, there are plenty of books that will tell you that. This one concentrates on teaching you how to select the best autofocus mode, shutter speed, f/stop, or flash capability to take, say, a great sports picture under any conditions.

This book is not a lame rewriting of the manual that came with the camera. Some folks spend five minutes with a book like this one, spot some information that also appears in the original manual, and decide "Rehash!" without really understanding the differences. Yes, you'll find information here that is also in the owner's manual, such as the parameters you can enter when changing your Z5's operation in the various menus. Basic descriptions—before I dig in and start providing in-depth tips and information—may also be vaguely similar. There are only so many ways you can say, for example, "Hold the shutter release down halfway to lock in exposure." But not *everything* in the manual is included in this book. If you need advice on when and how to use the most important functions, you'll find the information here.

David Busch's Nikon Z5 Guide to Digital Photography is aimed at both Nikon and dSLR veterans as well those who have used other mirrorless cameras and those who are total newcomers to digital or mirrorless photography. Both groups can be overwhelmed by the options the Z5 offers, while underwhelmed by the explanations they receive in their user's manual. The manuals are great if you already know what you don't know, and you can find an answer somewhere in a booklet arranged by menu listings and written by a camera vendor employee who last threw together instructions on how to operate a camcorder.

Family Resemblance

If you've owned previous models in the Nikon digital camera line, and copies of my books for those cameras, you're bound to notice a certain family resemblance. Nikon has been very crafty in introducing upgraded cameras that share the best features of the models they replace, while adding new capabilities and options. You benefit in two ways. If you used a previous Nikon camera prior to switching to this latest Z5 model, you'll find that the parts that haven't changed have a certain familiarity for you, making it easy to make the transition to the newest model. There are lots of features and menu choices of the Z5 that are exactly the same as those in the most recent models. This family resemblance will help level the learning curve for you.

Similarly, when writing books for each new model, I try to retain the easy-to-understand explanations that worked for previous books dedicated to earlier camera models, and concentrate on expanded descriptions of things readers have told me they want to know more about, a solid helping of fresh sample photos, and lots of details about the latest and greatest new features. Rest assured, this book was written expressly for you, and tailored especially for the Z5.

Who Am I?

After spending many years as the world's most successful unknown author, I've become slightly less obscure in the past few years, thanks to a horde of camera guidebooks and other photographically oriented tomes. You may have seen my photography articles in the late, lamented *Popular Photography* magazine. I've also written about 2,000 articles for magazines like *Rangefinder*, *Professional Photographer*, and dozens of other photographic publications. But, first, and foremost, I'm a photojournalist who made my living in the field until I began devoting most of my time to writing books. Although I love writing, I'm happiest when I'm out taking pictures, which is why I spend four to six weeks in Florida each winter as a base of operations for photographing the wildlife, wild natural settings, and wild people in the Sunshine State. In recent years, I've spent a lot of time overseas, too, photographing people and monuments. You'll find photos of some of these visual treasures within the pages of this book.

Like all my digital photography books, this one was written by a Nikon devotee with an incurable photography bug who has used Nikon cameras professionally for longer than I care to admit. Over the years, I've worked as a sports photographer for an Ohio newspaper and for an upstate New York college. I've operated my own commercial studio and photo lab, cranking out product shots on demand and then printing a few hundred glossy 8 × 10s on a tight deadline for a press kit. I've served as a photo-posing instructor for a modeling agency. People have actually paid me to shoot their weddings and immortalize them with portraits. I even prepared press kits and articles on photography as a PR consultant for a large Rochester, NY company, which older readers may recall as an industry giant. My trials and travails with imaging and computer technology have made their way into print in book form an alarming number of times, including a few dozen on scanners and photography.

Like you, I love photography for its own merits, and I view technology as just another tool to help me get the images I see in my mind's eye. But, also like you, I had to master this technology before I could apply it to my work. This book is the result of what I've learned, and I hope it will help you master your Nikon Z5, too.

Some readers who visit my blog have told me that the Nikon Z5 is such an advanced camera that few people really need the kind of basics that so many camera guides concentrate on. "Leave out all the basic photography information!" On the other hand, I've had many pleas from those who are trying to master digital photography as they learn to use their Z5, and they've asked me to help them climb the steep learning curve.

Rather than write a book for just one of those two audiences, I've tried to meet the needs of both. You veterans will find plenty of information on getting the most from the Z5's features and may even learn something from an old hand's photo secrets. I'll bet there was a time when you needed a helping hand with some confusing photographic topic.

In closing, I'd like to ask a special favor: let me know what you think of this book. If you have any recommendations about how I can make it better, visit my website at www.nikonguides.com, click on the E-Mail Me tab, and send your comments, suggestions on topics that should be explained in more detail, or, especially, any typos. (The latter will be compiled on the Errata page you'll also find on my website.) I really value your ideas and appreciate it when you take the time to tell me what you think! Most of the organization and some of the content of the book you hold in your hands came from suggestions I received from readers like yourself. If you found this book especially useful, tell others about it. Visit http://www.amazon.com/dp/1681987112 and leave a positive review. Your feedback is what spurs me to make each one of these books better than the last. Thanks!

Thinking Outside the Box 1

If you're like me, the first thing you probably did when you extracted your Z5 from the box, was attach a lens, power up the beast, and begin taking photos through a tentative trial-and-error process. Who has time to even scan a manual when you're holding some of the most exciting technology Nikon has ever offered in your hands? If you're a veteran Nikon shooter, you probably found many of the controls and menus very similar to what you're used to, even though the camera itself is much more compact and lighter in weight than its Nikon dSLR counterparts.

But now that you've taken a few hundred (or thousand) photos with your new Nikon Z5, you're ready to learn more. You've noted some intriguing features and adjustments that you need to master. Goodies inside your Z5 include diffraction correction, in-body five-axis vibration reduction, totally silent shooting, a high-resolution *electronic* viewfinder, and other enhanced capabilities.

Of course, on the other hand, you may be *new* to the Nikon world, or the Z5 may be your first advanced digital camera, and you need some guidance in learning to use all the creative options this camera has to offer. In either case, despite your surging creative juices, I recommend a more considered approach to learning how to operate the Nikon Z5. This chapter and the next are designed to get your camera fired up and ready for shooting as quickly as possible. And while it boasts both Auto and sophisticated Programmed Auto modes, the Z5 is not a point-and-shoot model; to get the most out of your camera, you'll want to explore its capabilities fully.

So, to help you begin shooting as quickly as possible, I'm going to first provide a basic pre-flight checklist that you need to complete before you really spread your wings and take off. You won't find a lot of detail in these initial two chapters. Indeed, I'm going to tell you just what you absolutely *must* understand, accompanied by some interesting tidbits that will help you become acclimated to your Z5. I'll go into more depth and even repeat a little of what I explain here in the chapters that follow, so you don't have to memorize everything you see. Just relax, follow a few easy steps, and then go out and begin taking your best shots—ever.

I hope that even long-time Nikon owners won't be tempted to skip this chapter or the next one. No matter how extensive your experience level is with dSLRs, your new mirrorless camera has a lot of differences from what you may be used to. Yet, I realize you don't want to wade through a manual to find out what you must know to take those first few tentative snaps. I'm going to help you hit the ground running with this chapter, which will help you set up your camera and begin shooting in minutes. Because some of you may already have experience with previous Nikon cameras, each of the major sections in this chapter will begin with a brief description of what is covered in that section, so you can easily jump ahead to the next if you are in a hurry to get started.

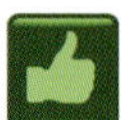

TIP In this book you'll find short tips labeled **My recommendation** or **My preference**, each intended to help you sort through the available options for a feature, control, or menu entry. I'll provide my preference, suitable for most people in most situations. I don't provide these recommendations for every single feature, and you should consider your own needs before adopting any of them.

First Things First

This section helps get you oriented with all the things that come in the box with your Nikon Z5, including what they do. I'll also describe some optional equipment you might want to have. If you want to get started immediately, skim through this section and jump ahead to "Initial Setup" later in the chapter.

The Nikon Z5 comes in an impressive black and Nikon-yellow box filled with stuff, including lots of paperwork. The most important components are the camera and lens (if you purchased your Z5 with a lens), battery, battery charger, and, if you're the nervous type, the neck strap. You'll also need an SD memory card or two, plus spares, as they are not included.

The first thing to do is carefully unpack the camera and double-check the contents. While this level of setup detail may seem as superfluous as the instructions on a bottle of shampoo, checking the contents *first* is always a good idea. No matter who sells a camera, it's common to open boxes, use a particular camera for a demonstration, and then repack the box without replacing all the pieces and parts afterward. Someone might have helpfully checked out your camera on your behalf—and then mispacked the box. It's better to know *now* that something is missing so you can seek redress immediately, rather than discover two months from now that the USB cable you thought you'd never use (but now *must* have for an important video project) was never in the box.

In the Box

At a minimum, the box should contain the following components:

- **Nikon Z5 digital camera.** It almost goes without saying that you should check out the camera immediately, making sure the back-panel LCD monitor isn't scratched or cracked, the memory card and battery doors open properly, and, when a charged battery is inserted and lens mounted, the camera powers up and reports for duty. Out-of-the-box defects like these are very rare, but they can happen. It's more common that your dealer played with the camera or, perhaps, it was a customer return. That's why it's best to buy your Z5 from a retailer you trust to supply a factory-fresh camera.

- **Lens (optional).** At its introduction, the Z5 was available *only* as an unadorned body or in a kit with either the Nikkor 24-50mm f/4-6.3 Z or the Nikkor 24-200mm f/4-6.3 Z lenses. Both are great lenses, priced to keep the Z5 package at an affordable price. If you buy your lens in a kit with the Z5, the super-compact 24-50mm lens adds only $300 to the price of the body alone, while the versatile 24-200mm optic comes at just an $800 premium. Both figures are somewhat less than the MSRP for each lens if purchased separately.

  Nikon may offer *other* lenses as part of a kit in the future, and most retailers will readily package this camera with the lens of your choice, often at a savings over buying them individually.

- **USB cable UC-E24.** This is a Type-C cable (the easy-insert kind that doesn't require a specific orientation). You can use this cable to transfer photos from the camera to your computer (I don't recommend that because direct transfer uses a lot of battery power), to upload and download settings between the camera and your computer (highly recommended), and to operate your camera remotely using Nikon Camera Control Pro software (optional, and not included in the box).

  My recommendation: This cable is a standard USB Type-C cord that works with a few other digital cameras that have adopted the USB Type-C interface. If you already own such a cable, you can use it as a spare. If you need a cable that's longer than this two-foot connector, you can find them for much lower than this unit's $34.95 list price online. I've tried several third-party cables and they work fine.

- **Rechargeable Li-ion battery EN-EL15c.** You'll need to charge this 7.0V, 2280mAh (milliampere hour) battery before use, and then navigate immediately to the Setup menu's Battery Info entry to make sure the battery accepted the juice and is showing a 100 percent charge. (You'll find more on accessing this menu item in Chapter 13.) You'll want a second EN-EL15c battery (about $70) as a spare (trust me), so buy one as soon as possible.

- **Quick charger MH-25a.** This charger comes with both a power cable and a power adapter that can be used instead of the cable to plug the charger directly into a wall outlet.

- **AN-DC19 neck strap.** Nikon provides you with a neck strap emblazoned with the Nikon Z logo. It's not very adjustable, and, while useful for showing off to your friends exactly which nifty new camera you bought, the Nikon strap also can serve to alert observant unsavory types that you're sporting a higher-end model that's worthy of their attention.

  My recommendation: I never attach the Nikon strap to my cameras, and instead opt for a more serviceable strap like the one shown in Figure 1.1. I strongly prefer this type over holsters, slings, chest straps, or any support that dangles my camera upside down from the tripod socket and allows it to swing around too freely when I'm on the run. Give me a strap I can hang over either shoulder, or sling around my neck, and I am happy.

I use the UPstrap shown in the figure, with a patented non-slip pad that keeps your Z5 on your shoulder, and not crashing to the ground. Inventor-photographer Al Stegmeyer (www.journeycamera.com) can help you choose the right strap for you.

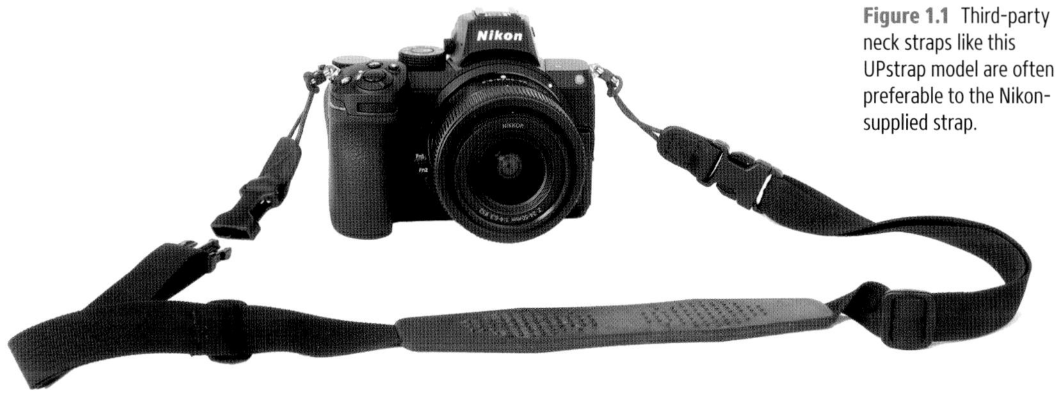

Figure 1.1 Third-party neck straps like this UPstrap model are often preferable to the Nikon-supplied strap.

- **BF-N1 body cap.** The body cap keeps dust from infiltrating your camera when a lens is not mounted. Always carry a body cap (and rear lens cap) in your camera bag for those times when you need to have the camera bare of optics for more than a minute or two. (That usually happens when repacking a bag efficiently for transport, or when you are carrying an extra body or two for backup.) The body cap/lens cap nest together for compact storage.

- **DK-29 rubber eyecup.** This is the round rubber eyepiece that comes installed on the viewfinder of the Z5. It slides on and off the viewfinder. If you prefer, you can augment it or replace it with several accessories discussed in the next section.

- **BS-1 accessory shoe cover.** This little piece of plastic protects the electrical contacts of the "hot" shoe on top of the Z5. You can remove it when mounting an electronic flash, Nikon GP-1/1a GPS device, or other accessory, and then safely leave it off for the rest of your life. I've never had an accessory shoe receive damage in normal use, even when not protected. The paranoid among you who use accessories frequently can keep removing/mounting the shoe cover as required. Note that Nikon also offers a BS-3 shoe cover ($10) with better weather sealing to protect the hot shoe if you're working in damp environments.

  My recommendation: Find a safe place to keep it between uses, or purchase replacements for this easily mislaid item. The previous low-cost source for these covers has gone out of business, so I've imported a stock of them, in both standard and bubble-level versions, which I'll send you for a few bucks. (Visit www.laserfairepress.com for more details.) I also can supply spare rear lens caps and body caps in vivid Nikon yellow hues if you need one.

- **User's manual.** Even if you have this book, you'll probably want to check the user's 170-page printed guide that Nikon provides, if only to check the actual nomenclature for some obscure accessory, or to double-check an error code.

  My recommendation: If you lose your printed book, just Google "Nikon Z5 manual PDF" to find a downloadable version that you can store on your laptop, on a USB stick, or other media in case you want to access this reference when the paper version isn't handy. You'll then be able to access the reference anywhere you are because you can always find someone with a computer that has a USB port and Adobe Acrobat Reader available.

- **Warranty and registration card.** Don't lose these! You can register your Nikon Z5 by mail or online (in the USA, the URL is www.nikonusa.com/register), and you may need the information in this paperwork (plus the purchase receipt/invoice from your retailer) should you require Nikon service support.

Optional and Non-Optional Add-Ons

Don't bother rooting around in the box for anything beyond what I've listed. There are a few things Nikon classifies as optional accessories, even though you (and I) might consider some of them essential. Here's a list of what you *don't* get in the box but might want to think about as an impending purchase.

I'll list them roughly in the order of importance:

- **Memory card.** As I mentioned, the Z5 does *not* come with a memory card. If you want to take advantage of the camera's dual memory card slots, you'll need at least two. Cards are an "optional" accessory because Nikon doesn't have the slightest idea of what capacity or speed card you prefer, so why charge you for one or more? The Nikon Z5 is likely to be purchased by photographers who have quite definite ideas about their ideal card. Perhaps you're a wedding photographer who prefers to use 32GB cards (generally the smallest available in the Secure Digital—SD—form factor these days) as a safety measure when capturing a nuptial event. Other photographers, especially sports shooters, instead prefer larger cards to minimize swapping during non-stop action. If you are shooting continuously, or transfer lots of photos to your computer with a speedy card reader, you might opt for the speediest possible memory card. The Z5 supports UHS-II transfer for both slots, currently the fastest class for SD cards.

  My recommendation: The Z5's 24-megapixel image files each amount to roughly 10.2MB for JPEG Fine to 241MB for Compressed 14-bit NEF (RAW) files. I use 64GB SanDisk cards and Sony G-series cards as the best price/capacity compromise, although I also own 128GB and 256GB media. It's better to have two 64GB cards available (one for overflow or backup) than depend on a single 128GB or 256GB SD card.

- **Extra EN-EL15c battery.** As a mirrorless model, the Z5's sensor and electronic viewfinder and/or LCD monitor are energized anytime you are using the camera, so you may note that you are getting fewer shots per charge than you may be used to. Nikon says that if you shoot with the viewfinder only, you can expect to get as many as 390 images before you'll need to swap batteries; if using the less energy-hungry LCD monitor, up to 470 shots should be possible. You should be able to capture 115 to 120 minutes of video with either display.

  As a result, at least one extra battery is virtually mandatory. Fortunately, you can use the previous model EN-EL15, EN-EL15a, and EN-EL15b batteries used in many older and current Nikon models, with one caveat. The older versions of the EN-EL15 battery, marked with a *Li-ion 01* designation to the left of the hologram on the cell's bottom, are not fully compatible with the Z5, and will, in fact, show less capacity than they really contain when used. The newer EN-EL15 version (marked *Li-ion 20*) and latest EN-EL15a/b/c batteries do not have this problem. In addition, I have not found *any* third-party EN-EL15/EN-EL15a/b batteries that will work in the Z5 at all. (The camera reports a "dead" battery even if it's fully charged.)

  My recommendation: Buy an extra EN-EL15c or two. They have slightly higher capacity than the older versions and are the only batteries that can be charged while in the camera using a USB-C cable connected to a power supply. Keep all your batteries charged, and free your mind from worry. Even though you might get 470 or more shots from a single battery, it's easy to exceed that figure in a few hours of shooting sports at 4.5 fps. Batteries can unexpectedly fail, too, or simply lose their charge from sitting around unused for a week or two. Although third-party vendors may eventually reverse engineer the encoding required to allow their batteries to function in the Z5, I don't recommend using them simply to save $70 or so with a camera that costs around $1,400 for the body alone.

- **EH-7P charging AC adapter.** Plug this small, square "wall wart" into an AC outlet and connect its non-removable Type-C USB connector cable to the USB port of the Z5 and you can recharge the EN-EL15c battery of the camera internally while the camera is turned off. It can be used to supply power to the camera for taking pictures, if you set USB Power Delivery to Enable in the Setup menu, as described in Chapter 13. It is an optional accessory priced at about $50.

  My recommendation: You can pick up one of these if you feel the need, but you can do the same thing with any Type-C USB cable and an external USB power source that supplies 5V/3A juice. Nikon has tested and recommends the Anker PowerCore+ 26800 PD 45-watt power bank, which is estimated to provide three full battery charges and up to 2,120 shots.

- **Nikon Capture NX-D or Nikon ViewNX-i software.** You can download a free copy of these software utilities from Nikon's website. Nikon no longer packs a CD-ROM with its cameras.

- **Camera Control Pro 2 software.** This is the utility you'll use to operate your camera remotely from your computer. Nikon charges extra for this software, but you'll find it invaluable if you're hiding near a tethered, tripod-mounted camera while shooting, say, close-ups of hummingbirds. There are lots of applications for remote shooting, and you'll need Camera Control Pro to operate your camera.

  My recommendation: You may already own Adobe Lightroom, which does an excellent job for tethered shooting, or DxO Labs' Capture One. Buy a suitably longer USB-C cable, too.

- **Add-on Speedlight.** Like all Nikon's full-frame Z-mount cameras to date, the Z5 does not have a built-in electronic flash. If you do much flash photography at all, consider an add-on Speedlight as an important accessory.

  My recommendation: An add-on flash can serve as the main illumination for your picture, diffused or bounced and used as a fill light, or, if you own several Speedlights, serve as a remote trigger for an off-camera unit. At around $250, the Nikon SB-500 has the most affordable combination of reasonable power, compact size, and features, including a built-in LED video light. If you need more power, the Speedlight SB-700, SB-910, or SB-5000 also offer more flexibility. For example, the SB-5000 can be triggered by radio control using another radio-compatible flash, or the WR-R10 transmitter. I'll provide more information on electronic flash in Chapters 9 and 10.

- **Remote control cable MC-DC2.** You can plug this one-meter-long electronic release cable accessory into the accessory port on the side of the Z5, and then fire off the camera without the need to touch the camera itself. In a pinch, you can use the Z5's self-timer to minimize vibration when triggering the camera. But when you want to take a photo at the exact moment you desire (and not when the self-timer happens to trip) or need to eliminate all possibility of human-induced camera shake, you need this release cord.

  My recommendation: These sometimes get lost in a camera bag or are accidentally removed. I bought an extra MC-DC2 cable and keep it in a small box in the trunk of my car, along with an extra memory card. There are many third-party equivalent cables, but the Nikon-brand release costs only about $30 and sometimes it's wise not to pinch pennies.

- **HDMI audio/video cable.** The Z5 can be connected to a high-definition television and can export its video output to an external recorder. You'll need to buy a mini-HDMI C (high-definition multimedia interface) cable to do that. No HDMI cable is included with the camera.

- **AC adapter EH-5d/EH-5c, EP-5b adapters.** There are several typical situations where this AC adapter set for your Z5 can come in handy, such as when in the studio shooting product photos, portraits, class pictures, and so forth for hours on end; when using your Z5 for remote shooting as well as time-lapse photography; for extensive review of images on your standard-definition or high-definition television; or for file transfer to your computer. These all use significant amounts of power. The EH-5d/5c and EH-5b power supplies each require the EP-5B adapter to connect to the camera.

  My recommendation: Unless you regularly do time-lapse or interval photography for long periods of time, you can probably skip these expensive accessories.

- **Multi-power battery pack MB-N10.** This battery/grip fits on the Z5 as well as the Z6 and Z7. Lots of photographers consider a battery pack/vertical grip to be an essential item. The pack holds two EN-EL15c batteries and increase the number of shots and video recording time by approximately 1.8X. It will provide the same level of environmental sealing as the Z5, and its internal batteries can be recharged using an external adapter. While many find a grip of this sort makes a small camera like the Z5 more comfortable in their hands, it doesn't offer separate vertical controls; you still must use the shutter release button and dials built into the camera itself. Your Z5 already has a removable battery door and two mounting holes on the bottom to accept it. You can bet that third-party suppliers are busy designing compatible grips, too.

  My recommendation: Hold out for the MB-N10. Many people love third-party grips from Meike, Neewer, Vivitar, and others, at a cost somewhat less than the roughly $200 Nikon asks for its MB-N10. I expect similar units will be available for the Z5 by the time this book is published. However, most people like to clamp their add-on grips onto the camera and remove them only rarely. If you intend to make a battery grip part of your permanent setup, the Nikon model will be better made, more rugged, and guaranteed to work seamlessly with your camera.

- **SC-28 TTL flash cord.** Allows using Nikon Speedlights off-camera, while retaining all the automated features.

- **SC-29 TTL flash cord.** Similar to the SC-28, this unit has its own AF-assist lamp, which can provide extra illumination for the Z5's autofocus system in dim light (which, not coincidentally, is when you'll probably be using an electronic flash).

  My recommendation: If you intend to work with an external flash extensively, you'll definitely want to use it off camera. Either of these cables will give you that flexibility. Wireless flash operation (described in Chapter 10) is more versatile but requires more setup and has a steeper learning curve. With a flash cord, you just connect the cable to your camera and flash and fire away.

Your Memory Cards

One of the early "controversies" (if you can call it that) when the original Z7 and Z6 were introduced was that each had only a single card slot. Apparently, all professional or semi-professional cameras must have the ability to use two card slots, for overflow or backup purposes, and the lack of such was roundly condemned by many. The Z5 solves that problem, offering two UHS-II slots for SD cards. The fix was a relatively easy one, as SD cards have a much thinner form factor than the XQD and CFexpress Type B (CFE-B) cards used in the Z7 and Z6. While smaller CFexpress Type A cards are available, they are not compatible with any Nikon cameras as I write this.

Dual memory cards in overflow mode come in especially handy for spot news and sports, as a photojournalist will frequent swap out a card that's 80 percent (or slightly more) full for a fresh one to avoid missing something important during an inopportune trade. But most of the time I simply store my images on my fastest or largest memory card and treat the second slot as convenient insurance.

Secure Digital cards have a lower top-speed ceiling than XQD or CFexpress cards and typically don't have the ruggedness and comforting larger size afforded by XQD/CFE that many advanced enthusiasts and professionals prefer. However, SD cards, including the latest SDXC cards are available in speeds up to 300Mbs transfer rates with UHS-II-compliant cameras like the Z5. Keep in mind that different vendors use different specifications for speed (both "X" factors and megabytes per second), and that *write* speed means how fast the device can transfer an image file to storage, while *read* speed (which may be emphasized because it is faster) represents how quickly the image can be transferred to your computer though a sufficiently fast connection (such as a USB 3.0 card reader).

My recommendation: I suggest sticking with Sony's G-series memory cards, rather than their slower M series, because the Z5 can benefit from fast transfer. Sony has also introduced a more expensive "tough" version that resists bending, x-rays, magnetic fields, and other hazards. I have standardized on Sony SF-G SDXC memory cards for my Z5. Unlike many other memory cards, their read and write speeds are roughly comparable. The SDXC card boasts 300Mbs/read and 299Mbs/write speeds. Both are fast enough to suck up images as quickly as the Z5's buffer is able to deliver them. In read mode, the cards can feed images to my computer as fast as my Windows or Mac machines can receive them. (I use Sony USB 3.0 card readers to transfer images.)

SanDisk, owned by Western Digital, also makes popular memory cards, but their popularity has led to widespread counterfeiting, with the fakes even slipping into the distribution channels of some major retailers. Although original parent company Micron shut down production of Lexar cards, new owner Longsys has resumed production, and I haven't had the chance to test their latest offerings. I have used several ProGrade in other form factors and find them first-rate but have not tried out their SDXC offerings. Delkin Devices Power series are also highly regarded among pro users.

USB 3 FLUX

The conglomerate of corporations in charge of promoting the current USB specification (Hewlett-Packard, Intel, Microsoft, and NEC, among others, and cleverly named the USB 3.0 Promoter Group) keep meddling with the nomenclature, first merging the original USB 3.0 moniker with its successor the USB 3.1 (as USB 3.1 Gen 1 and Gen 2). There is now a USB 3.2 spec to accommodate the USB Type-C connector found on the Z5. Don't panic; devices labeled with these variations are all compatible, differing only by top theoretical transfer speed and type of connector at the end that plugs into your device. If you see a card reader or other add-on labeled USB 3.0, it will work fine in any USB slot, even though, officially, USB 3.0 (as a name) no longer exists.

Initial Setup

This section familiarizes you with the three important controls most used to make adjustments: the multi selector and the main and sub-command dials. You'll also find information on setting the clock, charging the battery, mounting a lens, making diopter vision adjustments, and inserting a memory card.

Once you've unpacked and inspected your camera, the initial setup of your Nikon Z5 is fast and easy. Basically, you just need to set the clock, charge the battery, attach a lens, make diopter adjustments, and insert a memory card. If you already are confident you can manage these setup tasks without further instructions, feel free to skip this section entirely. While many buyers of a Z5 are experienced photographers, I realize that some readers are ambitious, if inexperienced, and should, at a minimum, skim the contents of this section, because I'm going to list a few options that you might not be aware of.

Mastering the Multi Selector and Command Dials

I'll be saving descriptions of most of the other controls used with the Nikon Z5 until Chapter 3, which provides a complete "roadmap" of the camera's buttons and dials and switches. However, you may need to perform a few tasks during this initial setup process, and most of them will require the MENU button and the multi/sub-selector buttons and pad. (See Figure 1.2.)

- **MENU button.** It requires almost no explanation; when you want to access a menu, press it. To exit most menus or to confirm and exit in some cases, press it again.
- **Multi selector pad/Directional buttons.** This pad may remind you of the similar control found on many point-and-shoot cameras, and other digital cameras. It consists of a thumbpad-sized button with notches at the up, down, left, right, and diagonal positions.

  The multi selector is used extensively for navigation, for example, to navigate among menus; to advance or reverse display of a series of images during picture review; or to change the kind of photo information displayed on the screen. It can also be used interchangeably with the sub-selector "joystick" (described below) to choose one of the user-selectable focus areas on the viewfinder and LCD monitor displays.

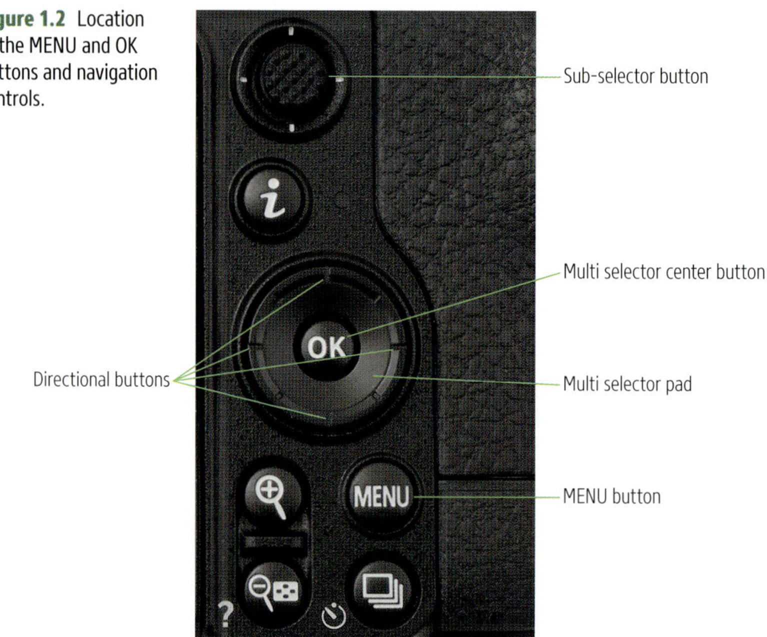

Figure 1.2 Location of the MENU and OK buttons and navigation controls.

- **Multi selector center button.** The center button (as well as the right directional button) can be used to select a highlighted item from a menu. (I find pressing the right directional button faster and easier.) The center button also can function as an OK/Enter key.

- **Sub-selector button.** The sub-selector can be moved like a joystick or pressed as if it were a button. As a navigational control, the sub-selector joystick's default function is a convenient control for selecting the focus point *only*, as I'll explain in Chapters 3 and 5. If you also want to use the joystick for menu navigation scrolling or playback functions, you can add those behaviors using Custom Setting f2: Custom Controls, as described in Chapter 12.

  The sub-selector center button, by default, can be pressed to lock focus or exposure (as an AE/AF lock button), but it can also be redefined to other behaviors with Custom Setting f2.

The main command dial and sub-command dial are located on the rear and front of the Z5, respectively. The main command dial is used to change settings such as shutter speed, while the sub-command dial adjusts an alternate or secondary setting. For example, in Manual exposure mode, you'd use the sub-command dial to change the aperture, while the main command dial is used to change the shutter speed. (In both cases, the dial is "active" for these adjustments only when the Z5's exposure meter is on.) The meter will automatically go to sleep after an interval (you'll learn how to specify the length of time in Chapter 12), and you must wake the camera (just tap the shutter release button) to switch the meter back on and activate the main and sub-command dials.

Touch Screen

The tilting LCD monitor supports a number of touch operations. For example, you can use it to navigate menus or make many settings. However, the touch screen can be especially useful during image playback and when shooting in live view.

Here's a list of things you can do:

- **In Playback mode:**
  - **Navigate among images.** You can flick the screen to advance to other images during playback. (I'll explain all the touch screen gestures shortly.)
  - **Zoom in or out.** Double-tap on the touch screen to zoom in or out of an image under review.
  - **Relocate zoomed area.** You can slide a finger around the monitor to reposition the zoomed area.
  - **View thumbnails and movies.** You can navigate among index thumbnails and movies.
- **In Photo shooting mode (when using the LCD monitor):**
  - **Take pictures.** In Photo mode, when the monitor is active you can tap the touch screen to take a picture without pressing the shutter release. (However, you can't begin video capture with a tap.)
  - **Select a focus point.** In both Photo and Movie modes, you can tap a location on the touch screen to specify a focus point.
  - **Navigate menus.** Personally, I find the touch screen clumsy for navigating menus. The menu bars and icons are a bit too small on the 3.2-inch screen to be tapped with precision. You still must press the MENU button to produce the menus, tap the main menu tab at the left of the screen, then tap the specific item, and then choose among its options. Most of the time the multi selector directional buttons are a lot faster.
  - **Enter text.** When working with a text-entry screen (for example, to enter copyright information in the Setup menu), you can tap the on-screen keyboard to enter your text. That's *much* faster than the alternative—using the directional buttons to tediously move the highlighting from one character to another.

You can disable touch functions entirely or enable them for Playback functions only (and thus disabling touch menu navigation) in the Setup menu, as described in Chapter 13. You can also specify direction for full-frame playback "flicks" (left/right or right/left) using the Touch Controls entry. In addition, you can turn the Touch Shutter/AF feature off by tapping an icon that appears at the left side of the screen during live view and movie shooting.

When adjustments are available, a white rectangle is drawn around the indicator that can be accessed by touch. You will see up/down and left/right triangles used to adjust increments, or other icons for various functions. Available gestures include:

- **Flick.** Move a single finger a short distance from side to side across the monitor. Note that if a second finger or other object is also touching the monitor, it may not respond. During playback, a flick to the right or left advances to the next or previous image.
- **Slide.** Move a single finger across the screen in left, right, up, or down directions. You can use this gesture during playback to rapidly move among subsequent or previous images in full-frame view, or to scroll around within a zoomed image. (See Figure 1.3, top left.)
- **Stretch/pinch.** Spread apart two fingers to zoom into an image during playback or pinch them together to zoom out. (See Figure 1.3, bottom left.)

- **Tap.** Touch the screen with a single finger to make a menu adjustment. (See Figure 1.3, right.) For example, you can tap an up/down or left/right triangle to increment or decrement a setting, such as monitor brightness. When Touch Shutter is activated, tapping the screen locates the focus point at the tapped location and takes a picture when you remove your finger from the screen. When Touch Shutter is deactivated, tapping the screen simply relocates the focus point. (You'll find a Touch Shutter on/off icon at the left side of the LCD monitor screen, as explained in Chapter 14.)

A TOUCH OF SCREEN

Throughout this book, when telling you how to use a touch-compatible feature, I'm going to stick to referring to the physical buttons and dials, for the benefit of those who prefer to use the traditional controls. From time to time I'll remind you that a particular function can also be accessed using the touch screen.

Nikon really needs to redesign the camera interface to take full advantage of the touch-screen capabilities. Cameras from other vendors, for example, use more slider controls instead of left/right touch arrows to make many adjustments. While some may find Nikon's implementation helpful, it's best when used with the Touch Shutter/AF feature, zooming in/out of a playback image, or, especially, when "typing" text rather than scrolling around with the directional buttons. Those functions are perfect for touch control.

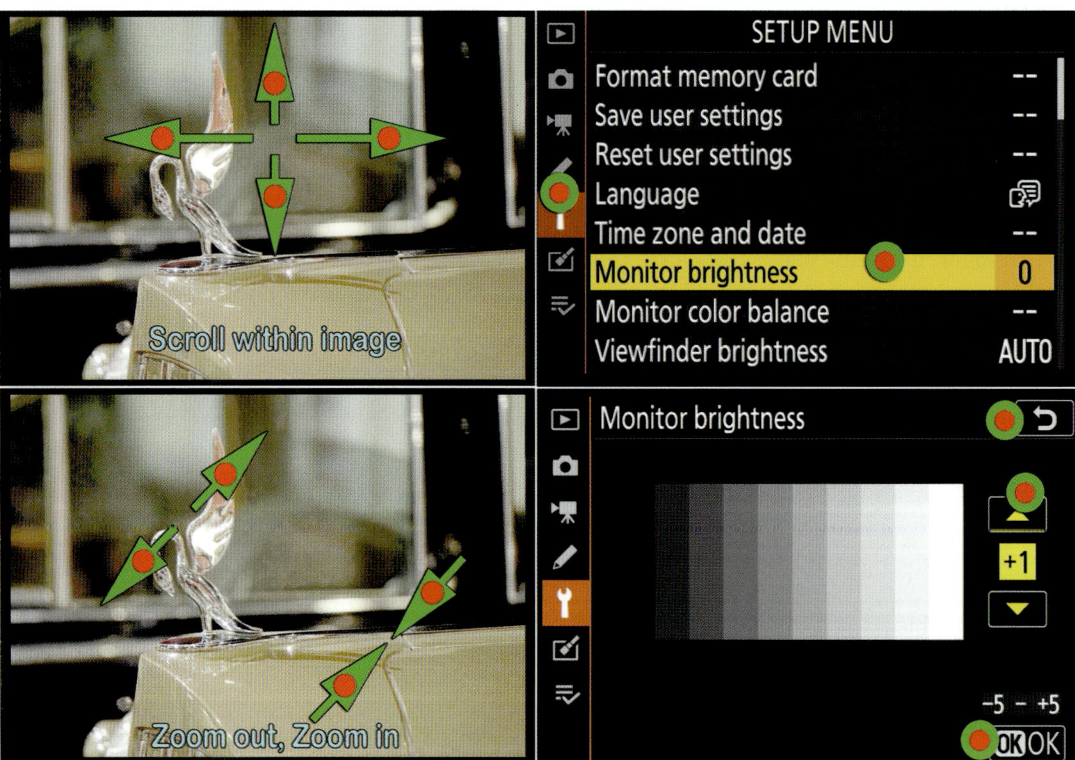

Figure 1.3 Slide your finger across the touch screen to scroll from side to side or up or down (top left), pinch or spread two fingers to zoom in and out (bottom left). Tap menu tabs, entries, and settings to make adjustments (right).

Because the screen uses static electricity, it may not respond when touched with gloved hands, fingernails, or when covered with a protective film. I have a GGS glass screen over my Z5's monitor and it works just fine; your experience may vary, depending on the covering you use. Don't use a stylus, pen, or sharp object instead of a finger; if your fingers are too large, stick to the physical controls such as the buttons or dials. As you'll learn in Chapter 13, you can enable or disable the touch controls or enable them only during playback, using an option in the Setup menu.

Setting the Clock

The Z5's clock settings are stored in internal memory powered by a rechargeable battery that's not accessible to the user. It is recharged whenever a removable battery is installed in the battery compartment, and two days of normal use will recharge the internal battery enough to power the clock for about a month. The Z5 is normally sold without its main battery installed, so you'll probably see a Clock Not Set icon the first time you power it up. In addition, if you store your Z5 for a long period without a charged main battery, the "clock" battery may go dead and "forget" your time/date/zone settings. It will recharge when a fresh EN-EL15c battery is inserted, and you'll need to set the clock again.

So, when you receive your camera, it's likely that its internal clock hasn't been set to your local time, so you may need to do that first. You'll find complete instructions for setting the four options for the date/time (time zone, actual date and time, the date format, and whether you want the Z5 to conform to Daylight Savings Time) in Chapter 13. However, if you think you can handle this step without instruction, press the MENU button, use the multi selector (that thumb-friendly button I just described, located to the immediate right of the back-panel LCD monitor) to scroll down to the Setup menu, press the multi selector button to the right, and scroll down to Time Zone and Date choice, and press right again. The options will appear on the screen that appears next. Keep in mind that you'll need to reset your camera's internal clock from time to time, as it is not 100 percent accurate.

Battery Included

Your Nikon Z5 is a sophisticated hunk of machinery and electronics, but it needs a charged battery to function, so rejuvenating the EN-EL15c lithium-ion battery pack furnished with the camera, an EN-EL15a/b pack, or EN-EL15 battery (Li-ion 20 version, if you're using an older EN-EL15 battery, please!) should be your first step. A fully charged power source should be good for approximately 390 shots, based on standard tests defined by the Camera & Imaging Products Association (CIPA) document DC-002. In the real world, of course, the life of the battery will depend on how much image review you do, and many other factors. You'll want to keep track of how many pictures *you* are able to take in your own typical circumstances, and use that figure as a guideline, instead.

All rechargeable batteries undergo some degree of self-discharge just sitting idle in the camera or in the original packaging. Lithium-ion power packs of this type typically lose a few percent of their charge every few days, even when the camera isn't turned on. Li-ion cells lose their power through a chemical reaction that continues when the camera is switched off. So, it's very likely that the battery purchased with your camera is at least partially pooped out, so you'll want to revive it before going out for some serious shooting.

Charging the Battery

When the battery is inserted into the MH-25a charger properly (it's impossible to insert it incorrectly), a Charge light begins flashing, and remains flashing until the status lamp glows steadily indicating that charging is finished, in about 2.5 hours. You can use the supplied connector cable or attach a handy included plug adapter that allows connecting the charger directly to a wall outlet (both shown at top left in Figure 1.4). When the battery is charged, flip the lever on the bottom of the camera and slide the battery in, as shown at top right in Figure 1.4. As noted earlier, when the camera is powered down, you can also charge the battery in the camera using the EH-7P AC adapter (Figure 1.4, bottom). Check the Setup menu's Battery Info entry to make sure the battery is fully

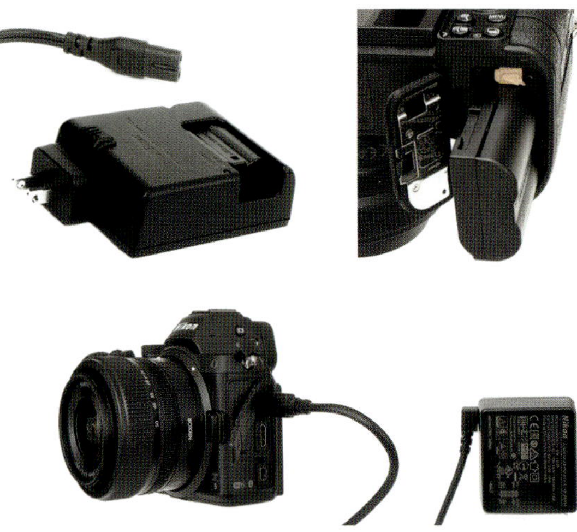

Figure 1.4 Charge the battery before use, and then insert the battery in the camera; it only fits one way.

charged. If not, try putting it in the charger again. One of three things may be the culprit: a.) the actual charging cycle sometimes takes longer than you (or the charger) expected; b.) the battery is new and needs to be "seasoned" for a few charging cycles, after which it will accept a full charge and deliver more shots; c.) you've got a defective battery. The last is fairly rare, but before you start counting on getting a particular number of exposures from a battery, it's best to make sure it's fully charged, seasoned, and ready to deliver.

My recommendation: Because Li-ion batteries don't have a memory, you can top them up at any time. However, their capacity when fully charged will eventually change over time. Once in a while, it's a good idea to use a battery until it is fully discharged, and then recharge it beyond the normal charging time. (Don't remove the battery from the charger until the light has gone out *and* the battery has fully cooled down.) It's also best to not store a battery for long periods either fully discharged or completely charged in order to maintain its longevity. If you own several (as you should), you'll probably want to rotate them to even the electronic wear and tear. I'll show you how to monitor battery use in Chapter 13.

Final Steps

Your Nikon Z5 is almost ready to fire up and shoot. You'll need to select and mount a lens, adjust the viewfinder for your vision, and insert a memory card. Each of these steps is easy, and if you've used any Nikon before, you already know exactly what to do. I'm going to provide a little extra detail for those of you who are new to the Nikon or digital camera worlds.

Mounting the Lens

As you'll see, my recommended lens mounting procedure emphasizes protecting your equipment from accidental damage and minimizing the intrusion of dust. If your Z5 has no lens attached, select the lens you want to use and loosen (but do not remove) the rear lens cap. I generally place the lens I am planning to mount vertically in a slot in my camera bag, where it's protected from mishaps, but ready to pick up quickly. By loosening the rear lens cap, you'll be able to lift it off the back of the lens at the last instant, so the rear element of the lens is covered until then.

After that, remove the body cap by rotating the cap away from the release button. You should always mount the body cap when there is no lens on the camera because it helps keep dust out of the interior of the camera. (Although the Z5's sensor cleaning mechanism works fine, the less dust it has to contend with, the better.) The body cap also protects the sensor from damage caused by intruding objects (including your fingers, if you're not cautious).

Once the body cap has been removed, remove the rear lens cap from the lens, set it aside, and then mount the lens on the camera by matching the alignment indicator on the lens barrel with the raised white bump on the camera's lens mount. Rotate the lens toward the shutter release until it seats securely.

Set the focus mode switch on the lens to A (autofocus). If the lens hood is bayoneted on the lens in the reversed position (which makes the lens/hood combination more compact for transport), twist it off and remount with the "petals" (found on virtually all lens hoods for newer Nikon optics) facing outward. (See Figure 1.5.) A lens hood protects the front of the lens from accidental bumps, and reduces flare caused by extraneous light arriving at the front element of the lens from outside the picture area.

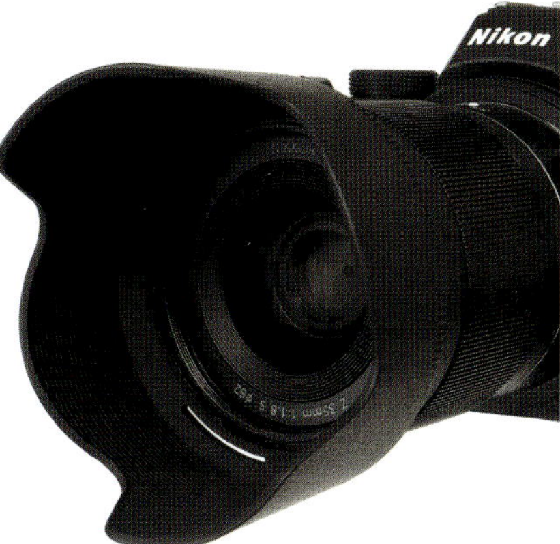

Figure 1.5 A lens hood protects the lens from extraneous light and accidental bumps.

DEALING WITH ERRORS

After you've mounted your lens properly (or *think* you have), you might find various error codes appearing on the control panel, viewfinder, and back-panel color LCD monitor. Here are the most common error codes, and what you should do next:

- **F --.** Lens not mounted. Make sure the lens is securely seated.
- **[-E-].** No memory card inserted.
- **∗Card Err (flashing).** Some error has taken place with your memory card.
- **Err.** A camera malfunction. Release the shutter, turn off the camera, remove the lens, and remount it. Try another lens. If the message persists, then there is a problem unrelated to your lens, and your Z5 may need service.
- **∗ For (flashing).** Card has not been formatted.

Adjusting Diopter Correction

Those of us with less than perfect eyesight can often benefit from a little optical correction in the viewfinder. Your contact lenses or glasses may provide all the correction you need, but if you are a glasses wearer and want to use the Z5 without your glasses, you can take advantage of the camera's built-in diopter adjustment, which can be varied from −4 to +2 correction. Pull out, then rotate the diopter adjustment control next to the viewfinder (see Figure 1.6) while looking through the viewfinder until the image of your subject is sharp. (The focus screen where your subject appears, and the indicators outside the image area are at slightly different "distances" optically, so you should use an actual image rather than the status indicators if you want to be able to evaluate focus through the viewfinder accurately.)

If more than one person uses your Z5, and each requires a different diopter setting on the camera itself, you can save a little time by noting the number of clicks and direction (clockwise to increase the diopter power; counterclockwise to decrease the diopter value) required to change from one user to the other.

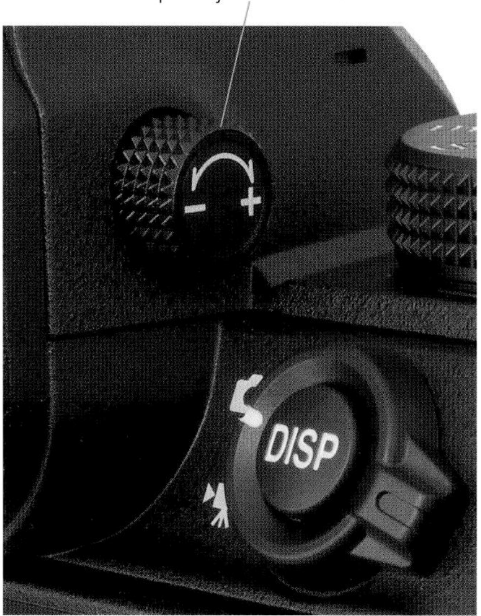

Figure 1.6 Viewfinder diopter correction from −4 to +2 can be dialed in.

Inserting a Memory Card

You've probably set up your Z5 so you can't take photos without a memory card inserted. (There is a Slot Empty Release Lock entry in the Setup menu that enables/disables shutter release functions when a memory card is absent—learn about that in Chapter 13.) So, your final step will be to insert a memory card. Slide the door on the back-right edge of the body toward the back of the camera to release the cover, and then open it. (You should only remove a memory card when the camera is switched off, or, at the very least, the yellow-green memory access light that indicates the camera is writing to the card is not illuminated.)

Inside, you'll find two card slots. You can use one card, or two. The camera will operate even if only one of the slots is occupied, and regardless of how you have set your Primary Slot Selection option in the Photo Shooting menu. Insert the memory card with the label facing the back of the camera, oriented so the edge with the contacts goes into the slot first. (See Figure 1.7.) Close the door, and, if necessary, format the card. Either card can be removed just by pressing it inward; it will pop out far enough that you can extract it.

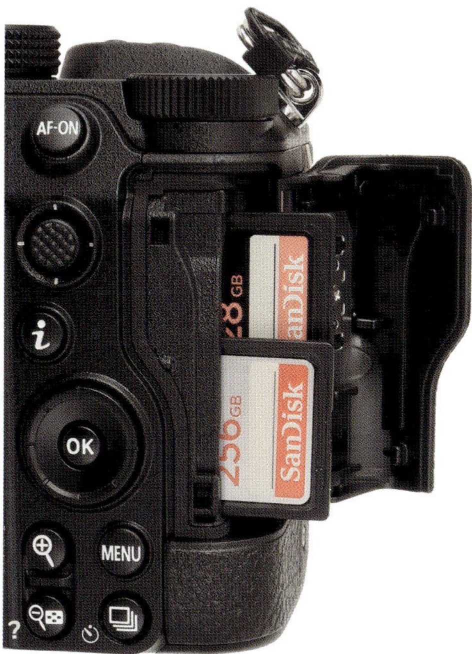

Figure 1.7 The memory card is always inserted with the label facing the back of the camera.

Formatting a Memory Card

There are three ways to create a blank memory card for your Z5, and two of them are wrong. Here are your options, both correct and incorrect:

- **Transfer (move) files to your computer.** When you transfer (rather than copy) all the image files to your computer from the memory card (either using a direct cable transfer or with a card reader), the old image files are erased from the card, leaving the card blank. Theoretically. Unfortunately, this method does *not* remove files that you've labeled as Protected (by pressing the *i* button during Playback and selecting Protect from the screen that pops up), nor does it identify and lock out parts of your memory card that have become corrupted or unusable since the last time you formatted the card. Therefore, I recommend always formatting the card, rather than simply moving the image files, each time you want to make a blank card. The only exception is when you *want* to leave the protected/unerased images on the card for a while longer, say, to share with friends, family, and colleagues.

- **(Don't) Format in your computer.** With the memory card inserted in a card reader or card slot in your computer, you *can* use Windows or Mac OS to reformat the memory card. Don't! The operating system won't necessarily install the correct file system. The only way to ensure that the card has been properly formatted for your camera is to perform the format in the camera itself. The only exception to this rule is when you have a seriously munged memory card that your camera refuses to format. Sometimes it is possible to revive such a corrupted card by allowing the operating system to reformat it first, then trying again in the camera.

- **Setup menu format.** To use the recommended method to format a memory card, press the MENU button, use the up/down buttons of the multi selector to choose the Setup menu (which is represented by a wrench icon), navigate to the Format Memory Card entry with the right button of the multi selector, and select Yes from the screen that appears. Press OK to begin the format process.

  My recommendation: I always use the Setup menu format before each shoot, as long as the images thereon have already been transferred to my computer. Nothing is worse than beginning a session and discovering that your memory card is almost full and contains images you don't want to delete to make room for new shots. If you neglected to bring along an extra memory card, you may have some difficult decisions to make.

Nikon Z5 Quick Start

2

You'll find that it takes only a few minutes to learn the basics of operating your new Nikon Z5, and I'll give you everything you need to begin taking great pictures in this chapter. If you've mounted a lens and inserted a fresh, fully charged battery as I explained in the last chapter, you're ready to begin. Power your camera up—the On/Off switch is on the right side, concentric with the shutter release button. All you need to do next is select a release mode, exposure mode, metering mode, and focus mode.

The Z5 has a sensor located just above the viewfinder window. When it detects you've brought the camera up to your eye, the Z5 switches its display from the LCD monitor to the viewfinder, and then back again when you remove the camera from your eye. You can change this default behavior, as I'll explain in Chapter 3, or manually switch between them using the Monitor Mode button located on the left side of the viewfinder "pentaprism" hump.

Selecting a Release Mode

This section shows you how to choose from Single frame, Continuous (low speed or high speed), and Self-timer. Unless you have need of burst shooting or the self-timer, you can set your camera to Single frame mode and skip ahead to "Selecting an Exposure Mode" (next). Just press the release mode button at the lower-right corner of the back of the camera and when the selection screen pops up, use the left/right directional buttons on the multi selector (the pad with the OK button in the center) to highlight the S setting, if it's been changed to something else. (See Figure 2.1.)

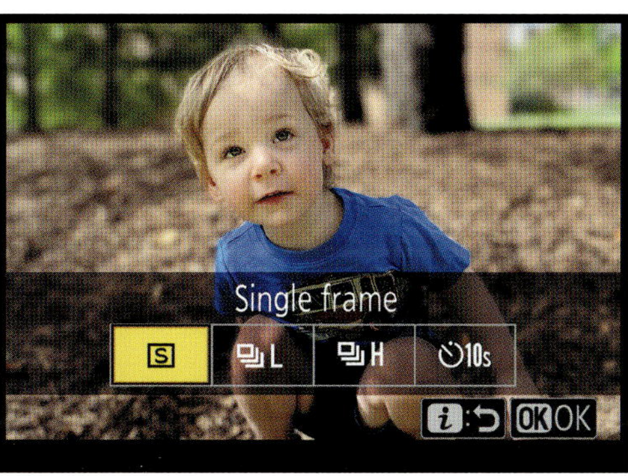

Figure 2.1 Using the release mode button.

The shooting mode determines when (and how often) the Z5 makes an exposure. If you're a late-comer moving to the interchangeable-lens camera world from a point-and-shoot camera, you might have used a model that labels these options as *drive modes*, a term that dates back to the film era when cameras could be set for single shot or "motor drive" (continuous) shooting modes. Your Z5 release (shooting) modes are described below. I'll explain all these modes in more detail and provide tips for using them in particular situations in Chapter 4.

The shooting modes are as follows:

- **Single frame.** In single-frame mode, the Z5 takes one picture each time you press the shutter release button down all the way. If you press the shutter and nothing happens (which is very frustrating!), you may be using a focus mode that requires sharp focus to be achieved before a picture can be taken. This is called *focus-priority* and is discussed in more detail under "Choosing a Focus Mode," later in this chapter.

- **Continuous L.** This "low-speed" shooting mode can be set to produce bursts of from 1 to 4 frames per second, at your option. When Continuous L is highlighted, press the down directional button on the multi selector to select your frame rate. You can also set a *default* for Continuous L in Custom Setting d1.

  I use this setting when slicing a scene into tiny fragments of time isn't necessary or desirable (say, I'm bracketing in multi-shot bursts, or don't want a zillion versions of a scene that really isn't changing that fast). Custom Settings are explained in more detail in Chapter 12. In continuous low-speed and high-speed mode (described below), the viewfinder and LCD monitor update in real time while shooting is underway, so you are always looking at the actual image you are capturing.

  My recommendation: I find continuous low speed, set to 2 fps, to be particularly useful for street photography and photojournalism applications. Because the speed is so slow, you can use it like single frame most of the time and capture a single image by pressing the shutter release once and then lifting your finger. But if you find a subject that merits a more rapid-fire approach, you can keep the shutter release pressed down, and fire off several shots sequentially. That's faster than switching from single to continuous mode, and you can avoid the intrusive, distracting "machine gun" approach.

- **Continuous H.** This mode fires off shots at *up to* 4.5 fps, and you can't change this frame rate to some other value, as you can with the continuous low-speed setting. However, the frame rate can slow down as your Z5's memory buffer fills, which forces the camera to wait until some of the pictures you have already taken are written to the memory card, freeing up more space in the buffer. The frame rate may also decrease when you're using the Z5's electronic shutter, or mechanical shutter speeds slower than 1/250th second, when using high ISO or Auto sensitivity settings or small apertures, when vibration reduction is active, or when some other operations force the Z5 to work at a slightly slower interval.

- **Self-timer.** If you want to set a short delay before your picture is taken, you can use the self-timer. When self-timer is highlighted, you can press the down directional button and choose delays of 2s, 5s, 10s, or 20s, as well as the number of shots taken after the delay. You can also choose these parameters in the Self-timer entry of the Photo Shooting menu (as described in Chapter 11).

Once the self-timer has been selected as the release mode, press the shutter release to lock focus and start the timer. The self-timer lamp on the front of the camera will blink and the beeper will sound (unless you've silenced it in the menus) until the final two seconds, when the lamp remains on and the beeper beeps more rapidly.

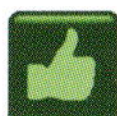

TIP If you plan to dash in front of the camera to join the scene when working with the self-timer, consider using manual focus so the Z5 won't refocus on your fleeing form and produce unintended results. (Nikon really needs to offer an option to autofocus at the *end* of the self-timer cycle.) An alternative is to use one of the optional wireless remotes, including the WR-R10/WR-T10, because the camera focuses when you press the button (after you've ensconced yourself safely in the frame). The SnapBridge feature of the Z5 also allows you to control your camera remotely from a smart device app running on your iOS or Android phone. I have a special section on using SnapBridge in Chapter 6.

SHOOTING MOVIES

You'll learn more about shooting HDTV movie clips with your Z5 later in Chapter 15. But if you want to get started right away, it's easy. Just rotate the Photo/Movie selector switch (located on the back of the camera to the immediate right of the viewfinder window) to the Movie position and press the button with the red dot on the top-right panel, southwest of the shutter release button. Press the button again to stop shooting. That's it!

Selecting an Exposure Mode

This section shows you how to choose an exposure mode, rotating the mode dial on the top-right shoulder of the camera. If you already understand exposure modes, jump to the next section on choosing a metering mode.

The Nikon Z5 has one full Auto mode (marked with a green camera icon on the mode dial located on the right shoulder of the camera). It's more likely you'll be working with the four manual and semi-automatic modes including Programmed auto (or Program mode), Shutter-priority auto, Aperture-priority auto, and Manual exposure mode. These modes allow you to specify how the camera chooses its settings when making an exposure, for greater creative control. (The other three positions on the mode dial, marked U1, U2, and U3 are not exposure modes, but, rather User Setting memory registers to store preferred settings for quick recall.)

If you're very new to digital photography, you might want to set the camera to P (Program mode) and start snapping away. That mode will make all the appropriate settings for you for many shooting situations. If you have more photographic experience, you might want to opt for one of the semi-automatic modes. These, too, are described in more detail in Chapter 4. These modes all let you apply

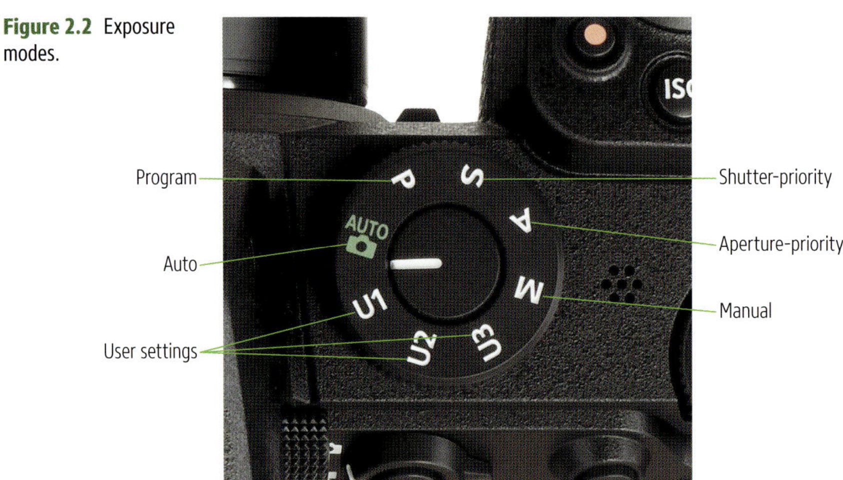

Figure 2.2 Exposure modes.

a little more creativity to your camera's settings. To set the exposure mode, just rotate the mode dial. (See Figure 2.2.)

- **P (Program).** This mode allows the Z5 to select the basic exposure settings, but you can still override the camera's choices to fine-tune your image, while maintaining metered exposure, as I'll explain in Chapter 4.

- **S (Shutter-priority).** This mode is useful when you want to use a particular shutter speed to stop action or produce creative blur effects. Choose your preferred shutter speed by rotating the main command dial when the meter is active, and the Z5 will select the appropriate f/stop for you.

- **A (Aperture-priority).** Choose when you want to use a particular lens opening, especially to control sharpness or how much of your image is in focus. Specify the f/stop you want using the sub-command dial when the meter is "awake" (tap the shutter release to activate the meter, if necessary), and the Z5 will select the appropriate shutter speed for you.

- **M (Manual).** Select when you want full control over the shutter speed and lens opening, either for creative effects or because you are using a studio flash or other flash unit not compatible with the Z5's automatic metering when using an attached electronic flash. Use the main command dial and sub-command dial when the exposure meter is active to specify the shutter speed and f/stop (respectively).

Choosing a Metering Mode

This section shows you how to choose the area the Z5 will use to measure exposure, giving emphasis to the center of the frame or to highlight areas; evaluating many different areas of the frame; or measuring light from a small spot in the center of the frame.

The metering mode you select determines how the Z5 calculates exposure. You might want to select a particular metering mode for your first shots, although the default Matrix metering is probably the best choice as you get to know your camera. I'll explain when and how to use each of the four metering modes later. To change metering modes, press the *i* button (located to the right of the LCD monitor) and use the multi selector directional buttons to navigate to the Metering icon, third from the left in the bottom row. When it's highlighted, you can rotate either command dial to select one of the choices listed below. I'll discuss selection of all types of metering in Chapter 4 (see Figure 2.3):

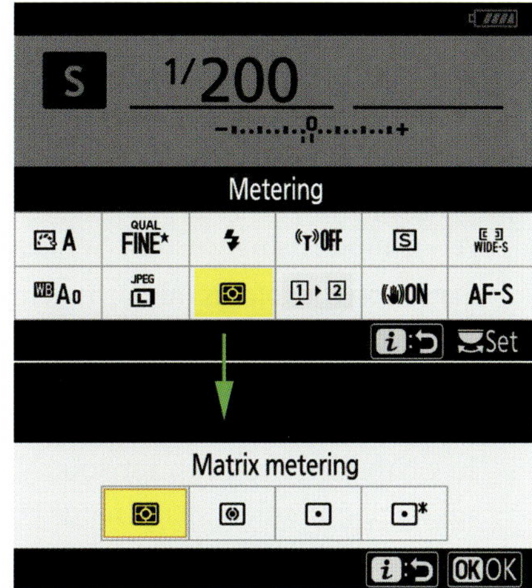

Figure 2.3 Choose a metering mode from the *i* menu. Left to right: Matrix, Center-weighted, Spot, and Highlight-weighted metering.

- **Matrix metering.** The standard metering mode; the Z5 attempts to intelligently classify your image and choose the best exposure based on readings from the sensor.
- **Center-weighted metering.** The Z5 meters the entire scene, but weights 75 percent of the exposure to the central area of the frame, measuring about 12mm (by default; you can choose full-frame averaging instead, Custom Setting b3, as I'll describe in Chapter 12).
- **Spot metering.** Exposure is calculated from a smaller 4mm central spot, about 1.5 percent of the image area, centered on the current focus point.
- **Highlight-weighted metering.** Despite its icon (a "spot" accompanied by an asterisk), this is not a spot metering variation. Highlight-weighted metering uses a matrix measuring system to emphasize the highlights of an image, retaining detail in the brightest areas.

You'll find a detailed description of each of these modes in Chapter 4.

Choosing a Focus Mode

This section shows how to select *when* the Z5 calculates focus: all the time (continuously), only once when you press a control like the shutter release button (single autofocus), or manually when you rotate a focus ring on the lens.

You can easily switch between automatic and manual focus by moving the AF/MF or M-AF/MF switch on the lens mounted on your camera. You can select the autofocus mode (*when* the Z5 measures and locks in focus) and autofocus pattern (*which* of the available autofocus points are used to interpret correct focus). To specify when the Z5 locks in focus, follow these steps:

1. **Activate autofocus.** Make sure the camera is set for autofocus mode by sliding any A/M switch on the lens (if present) to the A position.
2. **Enter setting mode.** Access the *i* menu. Press the *i* button and navigate to the Focus Mode label, located at far right in the bottom row.
3. **Choose AF mode.** Rotate either command dial until AF-S or AF-C (or M if you want Manual focus) is shown on the display when the information screen is visible. (Press the button labeled DISP, located to the right of the LCD monitor, to produce it.) If you haven't activated autofocus mode, as described in Step 1, you can select AF-S or AF-C, but the focus mode will not change until you set the switch on the lens to A (if your lens has a focus mode switch). The focus modes are described in more detail next.

The two autofocus modes available in still shooting mode are as follows:

- **Continuous-servo autofocus (AF-C).** This mode, sometimes called *continuous autofocus*, sets focus when you partially depress the shutter button (or other autofocus activation button), but continues to monitor the frame and refocuses if the camera or subject is moved. This is a useful mode for photographing sports and moving subjects. Focus- or release-priority can be specified for AF-C mode using Custom Setting a1.
- **Single-servo autofocus (AF-S).** This mode, sometimes called *single autofocus*, locks in a focus point when the shutter button is pressed down halfway (there are other autofocus activation button options, described in Chapter 13). The focus will remain locked until you release the button or take the picture. This mode is best when your subject is relatively motionless. As you'll learn in Chapter 13, you can set your Nikon Z5 using Custom Setting a2 so that the camera will not take a photo unless sharp focus is achieved (*focus-priority*), or so that it will go ahead and snap a photo while still adjusting focus (*release-priority*).

Choosing the Focus Area Mode

The Nikon Z5 uses up to 273 different focus points to calculate correct focus, using one or more points selected automatically by the camera, or chosen by you. I'll show you exactly where these focus areas are located in Chapter 5. To choose a focus area mode, follow these steps:

1. **Enter setting mode.** Access the *i* menu and navigate to the AF-area label, located at the far right of the top row.
2. **Rotate either command dial.** Rotate either command dial to highlight Pinpoint-AF (available in AF-S focus mode only), Single-point AF, Dynamic-area AF (available in AF-C focus mode only), Wide-area AF (Small), Wide-area AF (Large), or Auto-area AF.
3. **Choose AF-area mode.** For now, you should set to Auto-area AF (Auto) and allow the Z5 to choose the focus zone for you. Press OK to confirm and exit.

The AF-area modes are as follows. You'll find more information in Chapter 5.

- **Pinpoint-AF (AF-S only).** The camera uses a small point to calculate focus. Use this for precise focus on a specific area.
- **Single-point (AF-S or AF-C).** The camera focuses on a point you select, using the multi selector directional buttons or sub-selector joystick. This mode is good for non-moving subjects.
- **Dynamic-area (AF-C only).** You select the focus point, but if the subject moves from the selected area, it will use information from the surrounding points. It's often the best AF-area mode for moving subjects.
- **Wide-area AF (Small) (AF-S or AF-C).** Calculates focus from a larger area than Single-point AF and is best for stationary subjects that occupy more space in the frame.
- **Wide-area AF (Large) (AF-S or AF-C).** Calculates focus from an even larger zone and can achieve accurate focus on subjects that may be located in a wider area of the frame.
- **Auto-area AF (AF-S or AF-C).** The Z5 chooses a focus point without input from you, rapidly detecting likely subject matter, especially humans. If a portrait subject is detected, faces will be indicated by a yellow border. You can automatically track them by pressing the OK button.

Adjusting White Balance and ISO

If you like, you can custom-tailor your white balance (color balance) and ISO sensitivity settings. To start out, it's best to set white balance (WB) to $Auto_0$, and ISO to ISO 200 for daylight photos, and to ISO 400 for pictures in dimmer light. (Don't be afraid of ISO 1600 or even higher, however; the Z5 does a *much* better job of producing low-noise photos at higher ISOs than earlier generations.) You can adjust white balance now by pressing and holding down Fn1, the default White Balance button on the front of the camera to the right of the lens and rotating the main command dial until A_0, A_1, or A_2 appear. Then, with the button still held down, rotate the sub-command dial, if necessary, to select A_0 (Keep White/Reduce Warm Colors), which is the default auto white balance setting. (The other two partially or fully preserve the warm color cast produced by incandescent lighting, as I'll explain in Chapter 11.)

To set ISO, press the ISO button on the top-right shoulder just aft of the On/Off switch, and rotate the main command dial until the setting you want is displayed in the viewfinder or monitor.

Reviewing the Images You've Taken

Read this section when you're ready to take a closer look at the images you've taken, and you want to know how to review pictures and zoom in.

The Nikon Z5 has a broad range of playback and image review options, and I'll cover them in more detail in Chapter 11. For now, you'll want to learn just the basics. Here is all you really need to know at this time, as seen in Figure 2.4.

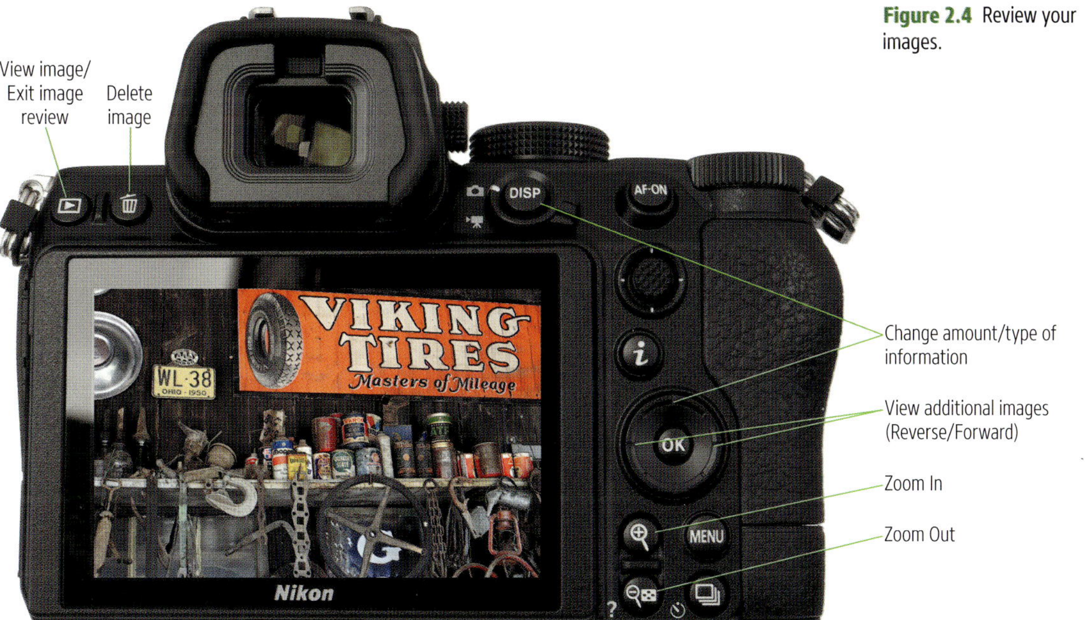

Figure 2.4 Review your images.

Here are your options:

- **View image.** Press the Playback button (marked with a white right-pointing triangle) at the extreme left corner of the back of the camera to display the most recent image on the LCD monitor.

- **View additional images (Reverse/Forward).** Press the multi selector left or right to review additional images. Press right to advance to the next image or left to go back to a previous image.

- **Change amount/type of information.** Press the multi selector button up or down or the DISP button to change among overlays of basic image information or detailed shooting information.

- **Zoom In/Zoom Out.** Press the Zoom In button repeatedly to zoom in on the image displayed; the Zoom Out button reduces the image. (Both buttons are located to the right of the color LCD monitor.) A thumbnail representation of the whole image appears in the lower-right corner with a yellow rectangle showing the relative level of zoom. At intermediate zoom positions, the yellow rectangle can be moved around within the frame using the multi selector.

- **Delete image.** Like a doctor, you *can* bury your mistakes. Press the Trash button when you spot an unwanted image and confirm to delete it forever.

- **Exit image review.** Press the Playback button again, or just tap the shutter release button to exit playback view.

Transferring Photos to Your Computer

The final step in your picture-taking session will be to transfer the photos you've taken to your computer for printing, further review, or image editing. Your Z5 allows you to print directly to PictBridge-compatible printers and to create print orders right in the camera, plus you can select which images to transfer to your computer. I'll outline those options in Chapter 11.

I always recommend using a card reader attached to your computer to transfer files, because that process is generally a lot faster and doesn't drain the Z5's battery. However, you can also use a cable for direct transfer, which may be your only option when you have the cable and a computer, but no card reader (perhaps you're using the computer of a friend or colleague, or at an Internet café).

To transfer images from the camera to a Mac or PC computer using the USB cable:

1. Turn off the camera.

2. Pry back the rubber cover that protects the Z5's USB port on the left side of the camera and plug the USB cable furnished with the camera into the USB port. (See Figure 2.5.)

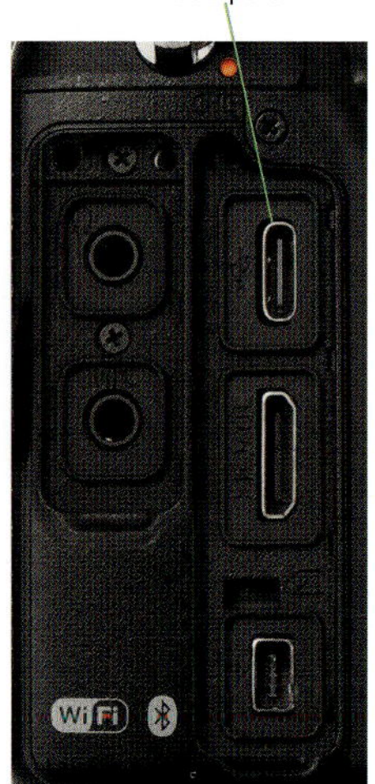

Figure 2.5 Images can be transferred to your computer using a USB cable connected to this port.

3. Connect the other end of the USB cable to a USB port on your computer.

4. Turn on the camera. The operating system itself or installed software such as Nikon Transfer or Adobe Photoshop Elements Transfer, usually detects the camera and offers to copy or move the pictures. Or, the camera appears on your desktop as a mass storage device, enabling you to drag and drop the files to your computer.

To transfer images from a memory card to the computer using a card reader:

1. Turn off the camera.

2. Open the memory card door and extract the memory card containing your photos.

3. Insert the memory card into your memory card reader. Your installed software detects the files on the card and offers to transfer them. The card can also appear as a mass storage device on your desktop, which you can open and then drag and drop the files to your computer.

Changing Default Settings

This section is purely optional, especially for true beginners, who should skip it entirely for now, and return when they've gained some experience with this full-featured camera. This section is for the benefit of those who want to know *now* some of the most common changes I recommend to the default settings of your Z5. Nikon has excellent reasons for using these settings as a default, covered earlier in the chapter; I have better reasons for changing them.

Even if this is your first experience with a Nikon interchangeable-lens digital camera, you can easily make a few changes to the default settings that I'm going to recommend, and then take your time learning *why* I suggest these changes when they're explained in the more detailed chapters of this book. I'm not going to provide step-by-step instructions for changing settings here; I'll give you an overview of how to make any setting adjustment and leave you to navigate through the fairly intuitive Z5 menu system to make the changes yourself.

Resetting the Nikon Z5

If you want to change from the factory default values, you might think that it would be a good idea to make sure that the Nikon Z5 is set to the factory defaults in the first place. After all, even a brand-new camera might have had its settings changed at the retailer, or during a demo. Unfortunately, Nikon doesn't make it easy to reset *all* settings in the camera to their factory defaults. In fact, there are no fewer than *four* different menu resetting options, each of which does slightly different things. Those ways include:

- **Photo Shooting/Movie Shooting menu reset.** The Photo Shooting and Movie Shooting menus each have a reset entry as their first listing. You'll zero out the changes you've made to the default options. You can view the settings and their defaults in Chapter 11.

- **Custom Settings menu reset.** The Custom Settings menu also has a separate Reset Custom Settings option that zeroes out most of the changes you've made to the default options to Custom Settings menu entries. The default values are listed in Chapter 12.

- **Setup menu reset.** The Reset All Settings entry in the Setup menu (described in Chapter 13), will restore almost all the camera's settings to their factory defaults, including Copyright information and IPTC presets, but *not* Language or Time Zone/Date information. Before doing this type of reset, it's a good idea to save your settings to a memory card using the Save/Load Settings entry in the Setup menu. As most Setup menu entries are camera configuration items rather than operational options, I won't be recommending preference changes for them in this chapter. The default Setup menu settings can be found in Chapter 13.

Photo Shooting Menu/Movie Shooting Menu/Custom Settings Menu Reset

If you'd like to reset all the options in the Photo Shooting, Movie Shooting, or Custom Settings menus, follow these steps:

1. **Access menus.** Press the MENU button located on the right back panel of the Z5.
2. **Choose Photo Shooting, Movie Shooting, or Custom Settings menus.** Press the multi selector down button to scroll down to the Photo Shooting menu (represented by a still camera), the Movie Shooting menu (represented by a movie camera icon), or the Custom Settings menu (represented by a pencil icon). Press the right multi selector button to reveal the Photo Shooting, Movie Shooting, or Custom Settings menus.
3. **Access Reset.** Use the down button to scroll to the entries labeled Reset Photo Shooting Menu, Reset Movie Shooting Menu, or Reset Custom Settings, then press the right button.
4. **Reset.** You'll be presented immediately with the option of choosing Yes or No to reset the respective menu. Highlight Yes and press OK.
5. **Repeat.** If you want to reset other menus, repeat steps 3 and 4.
6. **Exit.** When finished, press MENU or tap the shutter release to exit.

Recommended Default Changes

Although I won't be explaining how to use the Nikon Z5's menu system in detail until Chapter 11, you can make some simple changes now. These general instructions will serve you to make any of the default setting changes I recommend next. To change any menu setting, follow these steps:

1. **Access menus.** Press the MENU button located below the multi selector on the back-panel LCD monitor.
2. **Choose the main menu you need to access.** Press the multi selector down button to scroll down to the menu containing the entry you want to change. The available menus include (from top to bottom in the left column of the menu screen): Playback menu (right-pointing triangle icon); Photo Shooting menu (still camera icon); Movie Shooting menu (movie camera icon); Custom Settings menu (pencil icon); Setup menu (wrench icon); Retouch menu (paintbrush icon); My Menu (text page/text page with checkmark icon).
3. **Select main menu.** Press the right multi selector button to choose the menu heading containing the submenu entry you want to change.
4. **Choose menu entry.** Press the down multi selector button to move within the main menu to the entry you want to change. A scroll bar at the right side shows your progress through the menu,

as all the main menus except for the Custom Settings menu and My Menu (if it contains fewer than five custom entries) have more items than can fit on a single screen.

5. **Choose options.** Press the right multi selector button to choose the highlighted menu entry and view a screen with options. Select the options you want and press OK to confirm. Some menus allow you to confirm by pressing the right button again or require you to select and confirm Done before exiting.

6. **Exit menus.** Usually you can exit the menu system by pressing the MENU button. If an option has variations, I'll explain them when I discuss each of the menu choices in Chapters 11, 12, and 13.

Nikon does an excellent job with specifying default values, but here are some of the changes I recommend you make to the defaults that Nikon sets up for you. There are only a few, and I have no changes to recommend for the Playback, Setup, and My Menu settings, which are fine the way they are for most people, nor for the Retouch menu (which doesn't have parameters that can be stored).

Here are my suggestions for the Photo Shooting menu entries listed:

- **Image Quality.** Change from JPEG Normal to JPEG Fine *, to produce better image quality. (The star indicates least compression, and best quality.)

- **High ISO NR.** The default setting is Normal. I prefer Off. Wait until you've had a chance to evaluate whether the Z5 performs to your liking at high sensitivity settings. Off produces the least amount of noise reduction, but also doesn't degrade the amount of detail as much as any of the On settings.

- **Auto ISO sensitivity control: Maximum sensitivity.** The default value for the Z5 is a lofty 51200. You should lower it to ISO 6400 or below. New users of this camera shouldn't want to allow the camera to select a higher value until they've had a chance to decide if images at settings higher than ISO 6400 are acceptable to them. It's better to be unable to take pictures at all in very dim light than to end up with excessively grainy images when the Z5 chooses an ISO setting automatically that isn't acceptable.

Recommendations for the Movie Shooting menu:

- **Auto ISO sensitivity control: Maximum sensitivity.** The default value for movie shooting is 25600. You should lower it to ISO 6400 or below, for the reasons described above.

- **High ISO NR.** The default value for movie shooting is Normal. Nikon reasons that noise reduction, with an accompanying loss of detail, is more acceptable with video because each frame is viewed for only a fraction of a second. While that is true, I do recommend you turn it off, at least temporarily, and shoot some test video and then compare to video with noise reduction set to Normal to see which best suits your needs.

Make these changes to the Custom Settings and Setup menu entries listed:

- **Custom Setting c3: Power off delay: Standby timer.** If you shoot sports or other events where you don't want the camera going to sleep and delaying your ability to snap off a shot *now*, change from the default 30 seconds to 5 minutes or 10 minutes. You'll use more power but won't lose a shot from a split-second delay while the camera wakes up.

- **Setup menu: Slot empty release lock.** This controls what happens when you press the shutter release while no memory card is loaded in the camera. Change from the default OK: Enable Release to LOCK: Release Locked. Why would you want to be able to take pictures with no memory card in the camera, other than to demonstrate the camera or a few other reasons? Even though a DEMO label appears on the LCD monitor when you "take" pictures with no memory card inserted, it's easy to overlook. Turn this capability to LOCK.

Shooting Tips

I'm ending this chapter with some tips on settings to use for different kinds of shooting, including recommended settings for some Photo Shooting and Custom Settings menu options. You can set up your camera to shoot the main type of scenes you work with, then use the tables that follow to make changes for other kinds of images. Most will set up their Z5 for my basic settings and adjust from there. I'm not going to provide recommendations for *every* menu setting, as many are simply personal preferences that don't apply to everyone. If you see a listing missing, it's because the setting should be made to your preference. Chapters 11, 12, and 13 provide more detailed recommendations.

Photo Shooting Menu Recommendations

I'll list my Photo Shooting menu suggestions first, in Tables 2.1 and 2.2. The Custom Settings menu recommendations are divided into the exact same categories but, of course, deal with different options. In Table 2.1, the second column shows the default settings, as the Z5 comes from the factory. (I have no specific recommendations for the Movie Shooting or Setup menus.)

TABLE 2.1 Photo Shooting Menu Recommendations #1

OPTION	CAMERA DEFAULT	BASIC SETTING	STUDIO FLASH	PORTRAIT
File Naming	DSC/_DSC	NZ5/_NZ5 or your choice	NZ5/_NZ5 or your choice	NZ5/_NZ5 or your choice
Image Quality	JPEG Normal	JPEG Fine*	NEF	NEF+JPEG Fine*
Image Size:				
> JPEG/TIFF	Large	Large	Large	Large
NEF (RAW) Recording:				
> Type	Lossless compressed	Lossless compressed	Lossless compressed	Lossless compressed
> NEF (RAW) bit depth	14 bit	14 bit	14 bit	14 bit
ISO Sensitivity Settings:				
> ISO sensitivity	100	100	100	100
> Auto ISO sensitivity control:	On	On	Off	Off
Maximum sensitivity	51200	6200	1600	1600
Maximum sensitivity/ flash	25600	1600	800	800
Minimum shutter speed	Auto	1/60 sec.	1/60 sec.	1/60 sec.

TABLE 2.1 Photo Shooting Menu Recommendations #1 *continued*

OPTION	CAMERA DEFAULT	BASIC SETTING	STUDIO FLASH	PORTRAIT
White Balance	Auto 0	Auto 0	Preset Manual	Preset Manual
Set Picture Control	Auto	Save as C-1 (Standard + Sharp 7)	Standard	Save as C-3 (Neutral + Sharp −2)
Color Space	sRGB	Adobe RGB	Adobe RGB	Adobe RGB
Active D-Lighting	Off	Off	Off	Off
Long Exp. NR	Off	Off	Off	Off
High ISO NR	Normal	Low	Low	Low
Auto Distortion Control	On	Off	Off	Off

TABLE 2.2 Photo Shooting Menu Recommendations #2

OPTION	LONG EXPOSURE	SPORTS OUTDOORS	SPORTS INDOORS	LANDSCAPE
File Naming	NZ5/_NZ5 or your choice	NZ5/_NZ5 or your choice	NZ5/_NZ5 or your choice	NZ5/_NZ5 or your choice
Image Format/Quality	NEF	JPEG Fine	JPEG Fine	NEF+JPEG Fine*
Image Size:				
> JPEG/TIFF	Large	Large	Large	Large
> NEF (RAW)	RAW Large	RAW Large	RAW Large	RAW Large
NEF (RAW) Recording:				
> Type	Lossless compressed	Lossless compressed	Lossless compressed	Lossless compressed
> NEF (RAW) bit depth	14 bit	14 bit	14 bit	14 bit
ISO Sensitivity Settings:				
> ISO sensitivity	100	400	1600	100
> Auto ISO sensitivity control:	Off	On	Off	Off
Maximum sensitivity	25600	3200	1600	1600
Maximum sensitivity/ flash	25600	1600	800	800
Minimum shutter speed	Auto	1/60 sec.	1/60 sec.	1/60 sec.
White Balance	Auto 0	Auto 0	Auto 0	Auto 0
Set Picture Control	Standard	Standard	Standard	Landscape
Color Space	sRGB	Adobe RGB	Adobe RGB	Adobe RGB
Active D-Lighting	Off	Off	Off	Auto
Long Exp. NR	Off	Off	Off	Off
High ISO NR	Normal	Low	Low	Low
Auto Distortion Control	Off	Off	Off	Off

Custom Settings Menu Recommendations

Next come the Custom Settings menu recommendations—Tables 2.3 and 2.4. I don't have any recommendations for CSM g: Movie Settings, which assigns functions for movie shooting only; your preferences will depend entirely on what kind of video you capture.

TABLE 2.3 Custom Settings Menu Recommendations #1

ITEM	OPTION	CAMERA DEFAULT	BASIC SETTING	STUDIO FLASH	PORTRAIT	LONG EXPOSURE
AUTOFOCUS						
a1	AF-C priority selection	Release	Release	Release	Release	Release
a2	AF-S priority selection	Focus	Focus	Focus	Focus	Focus
a3	Focus tracking with lock-on	3	3	3	3	3
a4	Auto-area face/eye detection	Face and Eye Detection	Face and Eye Detection	Face and Eye Detection	Face and Eye Detection	Off
a5	Focus points used	All points	All points	All points	All points	All points
a6	Store points by orientation	No	No	Yes	Yes	No
a7	AF activation	Shutter/AF-ON	Shutter/AF-ON	Shutter/AF-ON	Shutter/AF-ON	Shutter/AF-ON
a8	Limit AF-area mode selection	All Available	All Available	All Available	All Available	All Available
a9	Focus point wrap-around	No wrap (OFF)	No wrap (OFF)	No wrap (OFF)	No wrap (OFF)	No wrap (OFF)
a10	Focus point options:					
	> Manual focus mode	On	On	On	On	On
	> Dynamic-area AF assist	On	On	On	On	On
a11	Low-light AF	On	Off	Off	Off	On
a12	Built-in AF assist illuminator	On	On	Off	Off	Off
a13	Manual focus ring in AF mode (with supported lenses only)	Enable	Enable	Enable	Enable	Enable
METERING/EXPOSURE						
b1	EV steps for exposure control	1/3 step	1/3 step	1/3 step	1/3 step	1/3 step
b2	Easy exposure compensation	Off	Off	Off	Off	Off
b3	Center-weighted area	12mm	12mm	12mm	12mm	12mm

TABLE 2.3 Custom Settings Menu Recommendations #1 *continued*

ITEM	OPTION	CAMERA DEFAULT	BASIC SETTING	STUDIO FLASH	PORTRAIT	LONG EXPOSURE
METERING/EXPOSURE *continued*						
b4	Fine-tune optimal exposure:					
	> Matrix metering	0	0	0	0	0
	> Center-weighted	0	0	0	0	0
	> Spot metering	0	0	0	0	0
	> Highlight-weighted metering	0	0	0	0	0
TIMERS/AE LOCK						
c1	Shutter-release button AE-L	Off	Off	Off	On (Half-press)	Off
c2	Self-timer:	10 sec.	20 sec.	10 sec.	10 sec.	2 sec.
	> Self-timer delay	10 sec.	10 sec.	10 sec.	20 sec.	10 sec.
	> Number of shots	1	1	1	3	1
	> Interval between shots	0.5 sec.	0.5 sec.	3 sec.	0.5 sec.	0.5 sec.
c3	Power off delay:					
	> Playback	10 sec.	10 sec.	10 sec.	10 sec.	20 sec.
	> Menus	1 min.	20 sec.	20 sec.	20 sec.	20 sec.
	> Image review	4 sec.	10 sec.	4 sec.	4 sec.	4 sec.
	> Standby timer	30 sec.	10 sec.	20 sec.	20 sec.	20 sec.
SHOOTING/DISPLAY						
d1	CL mode shooting speed	3 fps	2 fps	2 fps	2 fps	2 fps
d2	Max. continuous release	100	100	100	100	100
d3	Sync. release mode options	Sync	Sync	Sync	Sync	Sync
d4	Exposure delay mode	Off	Off	Off	Off	3 sec.
d5	Shutter type	Auto	Auto	Mechanical	Mechanical	Mechanical
d6	File No. sequence	On	On	On	On	On
d7	Apply settings to live view	On	On	On	On	Off
d8	Framing grid display	Off	Off	Off	Off	On
d9	Peaking highlights	Off/Red	3/Yellow	3/Color contrasting with subject	3/Color contrasting with subject	3/Color contrasting with subject
d10	View all in continuous mode	On	On	On	On	Off

TABLE 2.3 Custom Settings Menu Recommendations #1 *continued*

ITEM	OPTION	CAMERA DEFAULT	BASIC SETTING	STUDIO FLASH	PORTRAIT	LONG EXPOSURE
BRACKETING/FLASH						
e1	Flash sync speed	1/200	1/250	1/250	1/250	1/250
e2	Flash shutter speed	1/60	1/60	1/60	1/60	1/60
e3	Exposure comp. for flash	Entire frame	Entire frame	Entire frame	Background only	Entire frame
e4	Auto flash ISO sensitivity control	Subject and background	Subject and background	Subject and background	Subject only	Subject only
e5	Modeling flash	ON	ON	OFF	ON	ON
e6	Auto bracketing (Mode M)	Flash/speed	Flash/speed	Flash/aperture	Flash/aperture	Flash only
e7	Bracketing order	Normal: Meter> Under>Over	Normal: Meter> Under>Over	Under> Meter>Over	Under> Meter>Over	Under> Meter>Over
CONTROLS						
f1	Customize *i* menu	Set Picture Control; White balance; Image quality; Image Size; Flash Mode; Metering; Wi-Fi connection; Active D-Lighting; Release mode; Vibration Reduction; AF-area mode; Focus Mode	Replace Wi-Fi and Vibration Reduction with your preference	Replace Wi-Fi and Vibration Reduction with your preference	Replace Wi-Fi and Vibration Reduction with your preference	Replace Wi-Fi and Vibration Reduction with your preference
f2	Custom control assignment	Multiple defaults	Multiple defaults	See Chapter 12	See Chapter 12	See Chapter 12
f3	OK button:					
	> Shooting mode	Reset to center focus point	Reset to center focus point	Reset to center focus point	Reset to center focus point	Reset to center focus point
	> Playback mode	Zoom on/off	Zoom on/off	Zoom on/off	View histograms	View histograms
	> Live view	Reset to center focus point	Reset to center focus point	Reset to center focus point	Zoom on/off	Zoom on/off
f4	Shutter speed and aperture lock (S, A, and M modes only)	Shutter/Aperture both off	Shutter/Aperture both off	Shutter/Aperture both on	Shutter/Aperture both on	Shutter/Aperture both on

TABLE 2.3 Custom Settings Menu Recommendations #1 *continued*

ITEM	OPTION	CAMERA DEFAULT	BASIC SETTING	STUDIO FLASH	PORTRAIT	LONG EXPOSURE
CONTROLS *continued*						
f5	Customize command dials:					
	> Reverse rotation	Exposure compensation and Shutter speed/Aperture both off	Exposure compensation and Shutter speed/Aperture both off	Exposure compensation and Shutter speed/Aperture both off	Exposure compensation and Shutter speed/Aperture both off	Exposure compensation and Shutter speed/Aperture both off
	> Change main/sub	Exposure/Autofocus setting both off	Exposure/Autofocus setting both off	Exposure/Autofocus setting both off	Exposure/Autofocus setting both off	Exposure/Autofocus setting both off
	> Menus and playback	Off	Off	Off	Off	Off
	> Sub-dial frame advance	10 frames	10 frames	10 frames	10 frames	10 frames
f6	Release button to use dial	No (OFF)	No (OFF)	No (OFF)	No (OFF)	No (OFF)
f7	Reverse indicators	-0+	-0+	-0+	-0+	-0+

TABLE 2.4 Custom Setting Menu Recommendations #2

ITEM	OPTION	SPORTS INDOORS	SPORTS OUTDOORS	LANDSCAPE	BRACKETING
AUTOFOCUS					
a1	AF-C priority selection	Release	Release	Focus	Focus
a2	AF-S priority selection	Release	Release	Focus	Focus
a3	Focus tracking with lock-on	+4	+4	3	3
a4	Auto-area face/eye detection	Face and Eye Detection	Face and Eye Detection	Off	Off
a5	Focus points used	Every other point	Every other point	All points	All points
a6	Store points by orientation	Yes	Yes	No	No
a7	AF activation	AF ON only	AF ON only	Shutter/AF-ON	Shutter/AF-ON
a8	Limit AF-area mode selection	Unmark Pinpoint-area and Wide-area Large	Unmark Pinpoint-area and Wide-area Large	Unmark Pinpoint-area and Wide-area Large	All Available
a9	Focus point wrap-around	No wrap (OFF)	No wrap (OFF)	No wrap (OFF)	No wrap (OFF)
a10	Focus point options:				
	> Manual focus mode	On	On	On	On
	> Dynamic-area AF assist	On	On	On	On

TABLE 2.4 Custom Setting Menu Recommendations #2 *continued*

ITEM	OPTION	SPORTS INDOORS	SPORTS OUTDOORS	LANDSCAPE	BRACKETING
AUTOFOCUS *continued*					
a11	Low-light AF	Off	Off	Off	Off
a12	Built-in AF-assist illuminator	Off	Off	Off	Off
a13	Manual focus ring in AF mode (with supported lenses only)	Enable	Enable	Enable	Enable
METERING/EXPOSURE					
b1	EV steps for exposure control	1/3 step	1/3 step	1/3 step	1/3 step
b2	Easy exposure compensation	Off	Off	Off	Off
b3	Center-weighted area	12mm	12mm	12mm	12mm
b4	Fine-tune optimal exposure:				
	> Matrix metering	0	0	0	0
	> Center-weighted	0	0	0	0
	> Spot metering	0	0	0	0
	> Highlight-weighted metering	0	0	0	0
TIMERS/AE LOCK					
c1	Shutter-release button AE-L	On (Half-press)	On (Half-press)	Off	On (Half-press)
c2	Self-timer:	10 sec.	20 sec.	10 sec.	10 sec.
	> Self-timer delay	10 sec.	10 sec.	10 sec.	20 sec.
	> Number of shots	1	1	1	3
	> Interval between shots	0.5 sec.	0.5 sec.	3 sec.	0.5 sec.
c3	Power off delay:				
	> Playback	10 sec.	10 sec.	10 sec.	10 sec.
	> Menus	1 min.	20 sec.	20 sec.	20 sec.
	> Image review	2 sec.	2 sec.	4 sec.	4 sec.
	> Standby timer	5 min.	5 min.	1 min.	1 min.
SHOOTING/DISPLAY					
d1	CL mode shooting speed	2 fps	2 fps	2 fps	2 fps
d2	Max. continuous release	75	75	200	200
d3	Sync. release mode options	Sync	Sync	Sync	Sync
d4	Exposure delay mode	Off	Off	Off	Off
d5	Electronic front-curtain shutter	Off	Off	Off	Off
d6	File No. Sequence	On	On	On	On

TABLE 2.4 **Custom Setting Menu Recommendations #2** *continued*

ITEM	OPTION	SPORTS INDOORS	SPORTS OUTDOORS	LANDSCAPE	BRACKETING
SHOOTING/DISPLAY *continued*					
d7	Apply settings to live view	On	On	On	On
d8	Framing grid display	Off	Off	On	Off
d9	Peaking highlight color	Off/Red	Off/Red	Off/Red	Off/Red
d10	View all in continuous mode	Off	Off	On	On
BRACKETING/FLASH					
e1	Flash sync speed	1/250	1/250	1/250	1/250
e2	Flash shutter speed	1/60	1/60	1/60	1/60
e3	Exposure comp. for flash	Entire frame	Entire frame	Entire frame	Background only
e4	Auto flash ISO sensitivity control	Subject and background	Subject and background	Subject and background	Subject only
e5	Modeling flash	ON	ON	OFF	ON
e6	Auto bracketing (Mode M)	Flash/speed	Flash/speed	Flash/aperture	Flash/aperture
e7	Bracketing order	Normal: Meter>Under>Over	Normal: Meter>Under>Over	Under>Meter>Over	Under>Meter>Over
CONTROLS					
f1	Customize *i* menu	Set Picture Control; White balance; Image quality; Image Size; Flash Mode; Metering; Wi-Fi connection; Active D-Lighting; Release mode; Vibration Reduction; AF-area mode; Focus Mode	Replace Wi-Fi and Vibration Reduction with your preference	Replace Wi-Fi and Vibration Reduction with your preference	Replace Wi-Fi and Vibration Reduction with your preference
f2	Custom control assignment	Multiple defaults	Multiple defaults	See Chapter 12	See Chapter 12
f3	Multi selector center button:				
	> Shooting mode	Reset to center focus point	Reset to center focus point	Reset to center focus point	Reset to center focus point
	> Playback mode	Zoom on/off	Zoom on/off	Zoom on/off	View histograms
	> Live view	Reset to center focus point	Reset to center focus point	Reset to center focus point	Zoom on/off
f4	Shutter speed and aperture lock (S, A, and M modes only)	Shutter/Aperture both off	Shutter/Aperture both off	Shutter/Aperture both on	Shutter/Aperture both on

TABLE 2.4 Custom Setting Menu Recommendations #2 *continued*

ITEM	OPTION	SPORTS INDOORS	SPORTS OUTDOORS	LANDSCAPE	BRACKETING
CONTROLS *continued*					
f5	Customize command dials:				
	> Reverse rotation	Exposure compensation and Shutter speed/Aperture both off	Exposure compensation and Shutter speed/Aperture both off	Exposure compensation and Shutter speed/Aperture both off	Exposure compensation and Shutter speed/Aperture both off
	> Change main/sub	Exposure/Autofocus setting both off	Exposure/Autofocus setting both off	Exposure/Autofocus setting both off	Exposure/Autofocus setting both off
	> Menus and playback	Off	Off	Off	Off
	> Sub-dial frame advance	10 frames	10 frames	10 frames	10 frames
f6	Release button to use dial	No (OFF)	No (OFF)	No (OFF)	No (OFF)
f7	Reverse indicators	-0+	-0+	-0+	-0+

Nikon Z5 Roadmap 3

For some of us, shooting with the Z5 mirrorless camera is like working with an old friend. Some-one who has used virtually any previous Nikon dSLR will find the Z5 mirrorless camera comfortably familiar in shape and placement of the controls. The only things missing are the mirror and quite a bit of weight and bulk. The Z5 has been right-sized to fit in your hand, with all the buttons, dials, and knobs needed for the most frequently adjusted functions arranged for easy access. Another 12 settings can be adjusted from the *i* menu, and you can substitute other options for any of the dozen default *i* menu settings to suit your own working habits. (I'll show you how to personalize the *i* menu in Chapter 12.) With so many control choices available, you'll find that the bulk of your shooting won't be slowed down by a visit to the vast thicket of text options called Menu-land.

As a bonus, if you're a photographer who likes (or needs) to work with multiple bodies, the Z5 and its upscale siblings the Z7 and Z6 make perfect companions, as the bodies are in many respects very similar. So, if you need a camera with speedy continuous shooting, say, for sports photography, and a higher resolution model for landscapes or for capturing portraits suitable for printing in large sizes, the Z7 with the Z5 can make an excellent tandem. Pro photographers may rely on two (or more bodies) for backup purposes, and it's a definite plus if both cameras have virtually the same controls and menus.

Of course, if you want to operate your Z5 efficiently, you'll need to learn the location, function, and application of all these controls. What you really need is a street-level roadmap that shows where everything is, and how it's used. But what Nikon gives you in the user's manual is akin to a world globe with an overall view and many cross-references to the pages that will tell you what you really need to know. Check out the "Getting to Know the Camera" section, primarily pages 1 through 4, in Nikon's manual, which offers four tiny black-and-white line drawings of the camera body that show front, back, two sides, and the top and bottom of the Z5. There are about six dozen callouts pointing to various buttons and dials. If you can find the control you want in this cramped layout, you'll still need to flip back and forth among multiple pages (individual buttons can have several different cross-references!) to locate the information.

Most other third-party books follow this format, featuring black-and-white photos or line drawings of front, back, and top views, and many labels. I originated the up-close-and-personal, full-color, street-level roadmap (rather than a satellite view) that I use in this book and my previous camera guidebooks. I provide you with many different views and lots of explanation accompanying each zone of the camera, so that by the time you finish this chapter, you'll have a basic understanding of every control and what it does. I'm not going to delve into menu functions here—you'll find a discussion of your Playback, Photo Shooting, Movie Shooting, Custom Settings, and Setup options in Chapters 11, 12, and 13. Everything here is devoted to the button pusher and dial twirler in you.

You'll also find this "roadmap" chapter a good guide to the rest of the book, as well. I'll try to provide as much detail here about the use of the main controls as I can, but some topics (such as autofocus and exposure) are too complex to address in depth right away. So, I'll point you to the relevant chapters that discuss things like setup options, exposure, use of electronic flash, and working with lenses with the occasional cross-reference.

Nikon Z5: Up Front

This is the side seen by your subjects as you snap away. For the photographer, though, the front is the surface your fingers curl around as you hold the camera, and there are really only a few buttons to press, all within easy reach of the fingers of your left and right hands. There are additional controls on the lens itself. You'll need to look at several different views to see everything. Figure 3.1 shows the front of the camera with the lens removed. The components are as follows:

- **Sub-command dial.** This dial is used to change shooting settings. When settings are available in pairs (such as shutter speed/aperture), this dial will be used to make one type of setting, such as aperture, while the main command dial (on the back of the camera) will be used to make the other, such as shutter speed. Using the Custom Setting f5 menu adjustments, you can reverse the default rotational direction, swap the functions of the sub-command and main command dials, control how the sub-command dial is used to set aperture, and tell the Z5 that you want to use the main command dial to scroll through menus and images. All these options are discussed in more detail in Chapter 12.

Figure 3.1

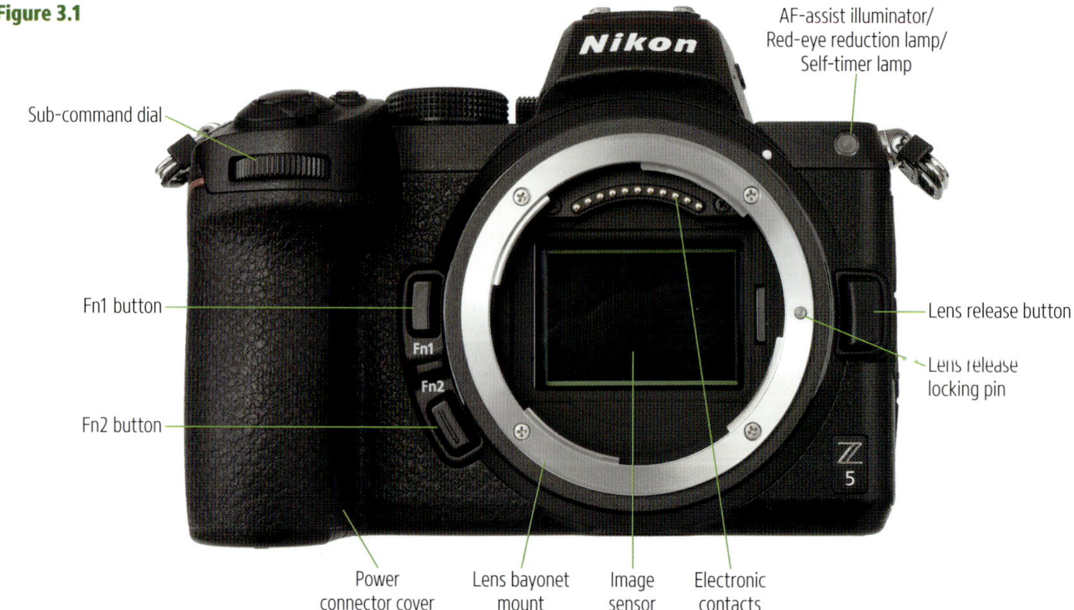

- **Electronic contacts.** These 11 contact points mate with matching points on the bayonet mount of the lens itself and allow two-way communication between the camera and lens for functions like aperture size and autofocus information.

- **Image sensor.** The Z5's 24MP sensor is fully exposed when the lens is removed. You should be careful and never touch or press against it, to avoid damaging the in-body image stabilization system or the protective surface of the sensor itself.

- **Function 1 (Fn1) button.** This conveniently located button has the White Balance function assigned by default. (Just hold down the button and rotate either command dial.) However, using Custom Setting f2, it can be programmed to perform other actions, ranging from metering modes (Matrix, Center-weighted, Highlight-weighted, or Spot) to flash off or bracketing bursts. I'll explain how to define a function in Chapter 12.

- **Function 2 (Fn2) button.** By default, this button adjusts Focus-area mode when you hold it and rotate the sub-command dial and Focus mode when held while you spin the main command dial. This button can be redefined using the same functions offered for the Fn1 button, as discussed in Chapter 12.

- **Lens bayonet mount.** This precision bayonet mount mates with the matching mount on the back of each compatible lens. The Z-mount is held on the camera using four screws that provide a secure attachment to the body, but not *too* secure. Their mounting holes are shallow enough to allow the bayonet mount to pop off if you drop the camera on the lens (which avoids even worse damage to the camera body itself). But don't worry, the mount is more than secure enough for everyday use, even with the heaviest lenses.

- **Lens release button.** Press this button to retract the locking pin on the lens mount so a lens can be rotated to remove it from the camera.

- **Lens release locking pin.** This pin slides inside a matching hole in the lens to keep it from rotating until the lens release button is pressed.

- **AF-assist illuminator/Red-eye reduction lamp/Self-timer lamp.** This lamp lights up when needed to help the camera autofocus in low-light conditions. During flash photography, the lamp provides a burst of light that can help reduce red-eye effects. Some flashes are able to emit a stronger burst than the lamp can provide and are used instead. When using the self-timer, the lamp flashes to mark the countdown until the photo is taken and will stop two seconds before the timer expires.

- **Power connector cover.** This little door flips open to allow plugging a cable from the AC/DC adapter into the battery compartment in the hand grip.

Figure 3.2 shows a view of the left side of the Nikon Z5, as seen from the front. The main components you need to know about are as follows:

- **Memory card door.** Your memory card can be inserted here when you slide the door toward the rear of the camera to open it.

- **Shutter release button.** Angled on top of the hand grip is the shutter release button, which has multiple functions. Press this button down halfway to lock exposure and focus. Press it down all the way to actually take a photo or sequence of photos if you've set the release mode to any of the continuous shooting modes, or if you've defined the behavior of the self-timer to take 1 to 9 exposures when its delay has expired. (I'll show you how to take multiple shots with the

Figure 3.2

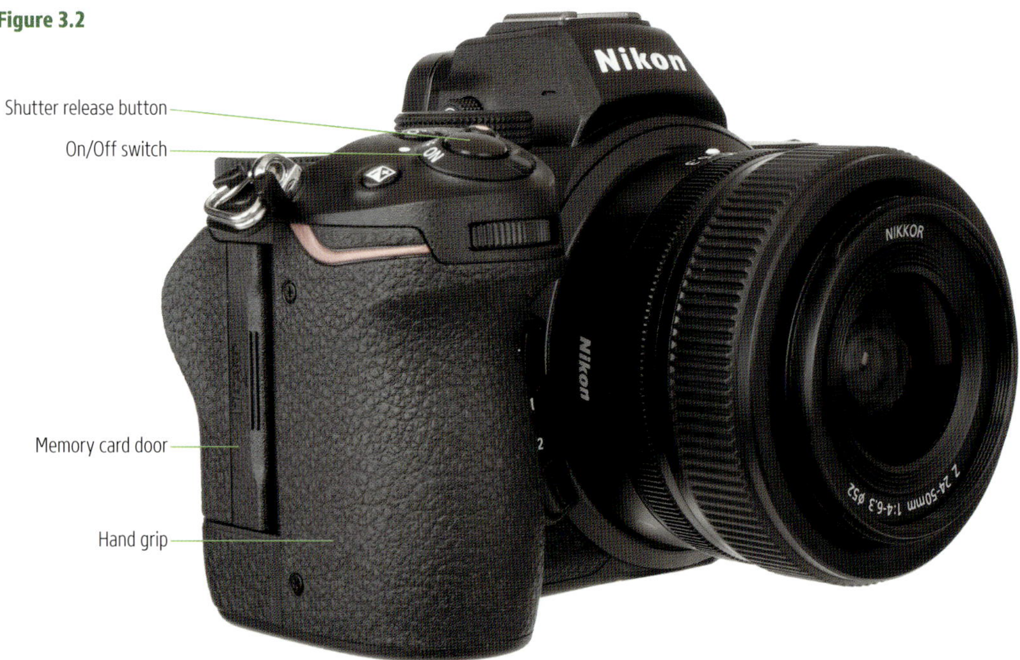

self-timer in Chapter 11.) Tapping the shutter button when the Z5's exposure meters have turned themselves off reactivates them, and a tap can be used to remove the display of a menu or image from the rear color LCD monitor.

- **On/Off switch.** Rotating this switch to the detent turns the camera on.
- **Hand grip.** This provides a comfortable handhold, and also contains the Z5's battery.

You'll find more controls on the other side of the Z5, shown in Figure 3.3, which shows the rubber covers on the side that protect the camera's USB, HDMI, headphone, and microphone connectors, and accessory terminal. You can see the actual connectors in Figure 3.4. The main points of interest shown include:

- **Covers.** These two rubber covers protect the USB, HDMI, microphone, and headphone connectors, and accessory terminal when not in use.
- **Headphone connector.** Plug in your headphones or other audio device here using a stereo miniplug to monitor your sound as you record, or to listen to the audio when playing back a video clip.
- **Microphone connector.** Although the Z5 has built-in microphones on top, if you want better quality (and want to shield your video clip soundtracks from noises emanating from the camera and/or your handling of it), you can plug in an accessory mic, such as the Nikon ME-1, here.
- **USB connector.** Plug in the USB cable furnished with your Nikon Z5 and connect the other end to a USB port in your computer to transfer photos, to upload Picture Control settings, or to upload/download other settings between your camera and computer. This USB 3 Type-C connector is also used for charging the battery and powering the camera.

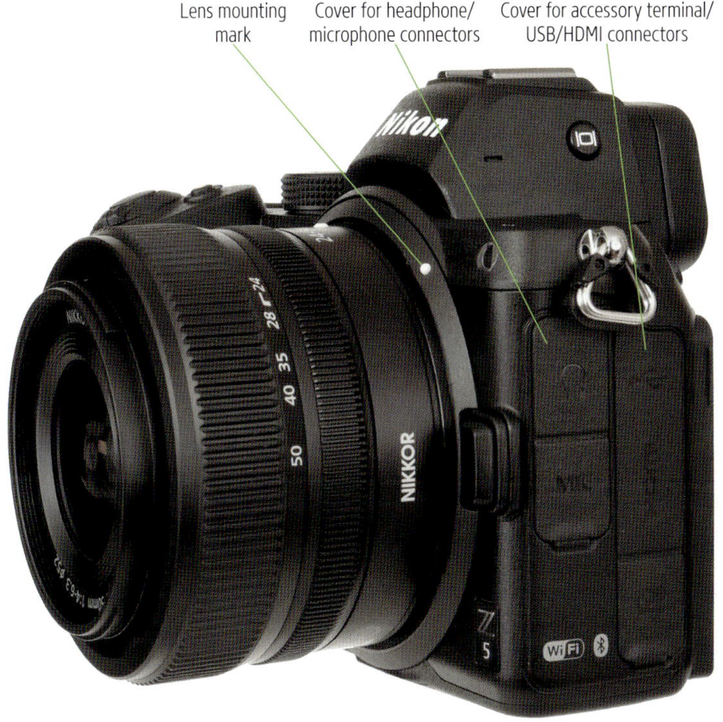

Figure 3.3

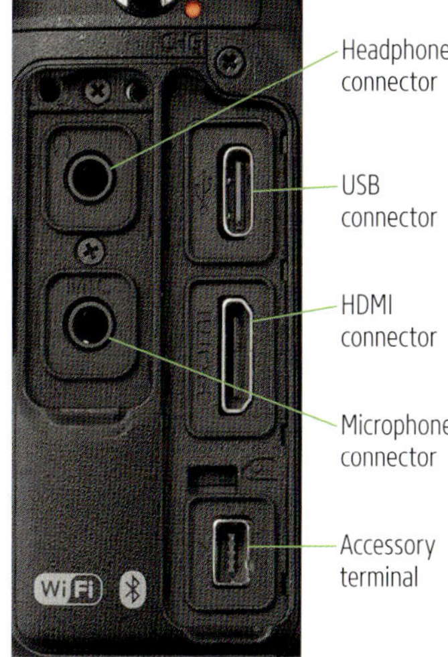

Figure 3.4 Headphone, microphone, USB, and HDMI connectors and accessory terminal.

- **HDMI connector.** You need to buy an accessory HDMI mini-C cable to connect your Z5 to an HDTV or video recorder, as one to fit this port is not provided with the camera. If you have a high-resolution television, it's worth the expenditure to be able to view your camera's output in all its glory, and this connector is essential for serious videographers who want to use an external monitor or recorder.

- **Accessory terminal.** Accessories including the DC-MC2 remote release, GP1a GPS unit, and WR-R10 wireless remote transceiver can be plugged in here.

The Nikon Z5's Business End

The back panel of the Nikon Z5 bristles with more than a dozen different controls, buttons, and knobs. That might seem like a lot of controls to learn, but you'll find, as I noted earlier, that it's a lot easier to press a dedicated button and spin a dial than to jump to a menu every time you want to change a setting. You can see the controls clustered along the top edge of the back panel in Figure 3.5. The key buttons and components and their functions are as follows:

- **Playback button.** Press this button to review images you've taken, using the controls Rand options I'll explain in the next section. To remove the image display, press the Playback button again, or simply tap the shutter release button.

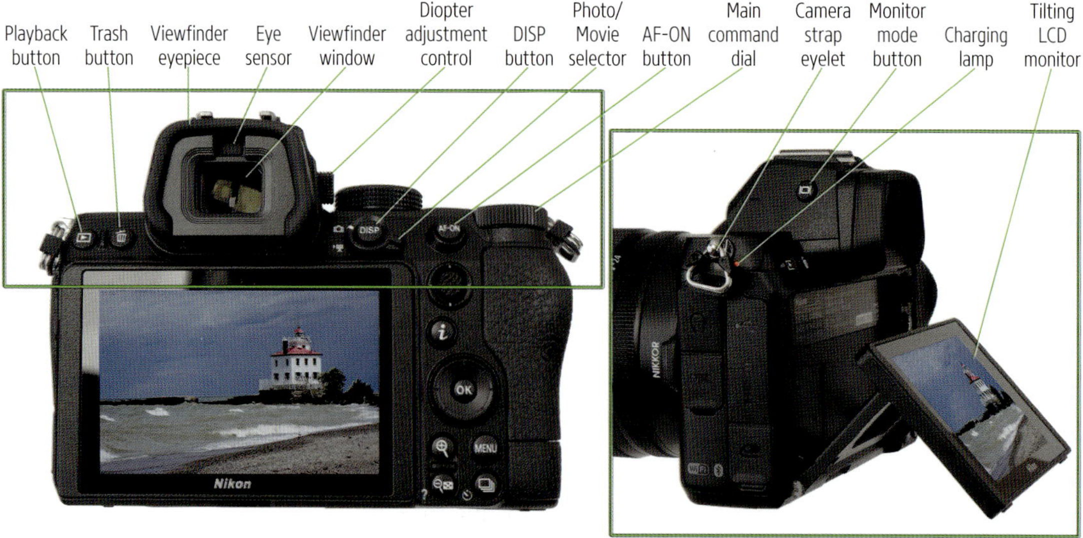

Figure 3.5

- **Trash button.** Press to erase the image shown on the LCD monitor. A display will pop up on the LCD monitor asking you to press the Trash button once more to delete the photo or press the Playback button to cancel.

- **Viewfinder eyepiece/Viewfinder window.** You can frame your composition by peering into the 3,690,000-pixel (Quad-VGA) OLED electronic viewfinder, which shows 100 percent of your image frame at a generous 0.8 percent magnification. It's surrounded by a soft rubber frame that seals out extraneous light when pressing your eye tightly up to the viewfinder, and it also protects your eyeglass lenses (if worn) from scratching. Your eye can be up to 21mm away from the viewfinder window (the "eyepoint") and still view the entire focus screen area.

- **Eye sensor.** Detects when your eye (or anything else) approaches the viewfinder window (anything closer than about three inches in my tests).

- **Diopter adjustment control.** Pull this knob out, and then rotate it to adjust the diopter correction for your eyesight; then push it in to lock the setting. Adjustments are available from −4 to +2.

- **DISP button.** Shows or hides informational displays in the LCD monitor or viewfinder. Press to cycle among the available displays in Photo, Movie, and Playback modes.

- **Photo/movie selector.** Switches the camera from Photo shooting mode to Movie mode.

- **AF-ON button.** Press this button to activate the autofocus system without needing to partially depress the shutter release. This control, used with other buttons, allows you to lock exposure and focus separately: Lock exposure by pressing the shutter release halfway; autofocus by pressing the shutter release halfway, or by pressing the AF-ON button. There are lots of cool ways you can use the AF-ON button, and I'll explain them in detail in Chapter 12.

- **Main command dial.** This is the main control dial of the Z5, used to set or adjust most functions, such as shutter speed, bracketing sequence, white balance, ISO, and so forth, either alone or when another button is depressed simultaneously. It is often used in conjunction with the sub-command dial on the front of the camera when pairs of settings can be made, such as image formats (main command dial: image format; sub-command dial: resolution); exposure (main: shutter speed; sub: aperture); flash (main: flash mode; sub: flash compensation); or white balance (main: WB preset; sub: fine-tune WB). You can swap functions of the main and sub-command dials, reverse the rotation direction, choose whether the aperture ring on the lens or the sub-command dial will be used to set the f/stop, and activate the main command dials to navigate menus and images. You'll learn about these Custom Settings menu options in Chapter 12.

- **Tilting LCD monitor.** The 3.2-inch LCD monitor has a 1,040,000-dot TFT touch-sensitive screen with a 170-degree viewing angle that allows you to see the screen clearly even from the side or slightly above. It provides a 100 percent view of what the sensor sees. It swivels so you can position the camera down low (say, for macro shots of flowers) or up high for a periscope view.

- **Charging lamp.** This LED glows amber while charging the camera's EN-EL15c battery when an external USB power adapter (not supplied with the Z5) and Type-C cable is plugged into the USB port. The lamp turns off when charging is complete. External power supplied to the USB port can be used to operate the camera for long periods, say, when shooting time-lapse photography over the course of several hours. That's a less expensive option than the AC adapter EH-5b/EH-5c or EP-5b. Remember that EN-EL15 and EN-EL15a batteries cannot be charged at all through the USB connector; only the EN-EL15b and EN-EL15c batteries can be charged internally.

- **Camera strap eyelet.** It comes with a split-ring attached that can be used to fasten a neck strap to the Z5.

- **Monitor mode button.** Press this button to cycle among the four LCD monitor modes. You can disable unwanted modes in the Setup menu's Limit Monitor Mode Selection entry.
  - **Automatic display switch.** Alternates between viewfinder and monitor as your eye approaches the eye sensor or is moved away.
  - **Viewfinder only.** Displays in the viewfinder only.
  - **Monitor only.** Displays on the monitor only.
  - **Prioritize viewfinder.** The viewfinder is turned on and off by the eye sensor, but the monitor does not illuminate in Photo mode.

On the lower right of the back panel of the Z5 you'll find a cluster of essential controls (see Figure 3.6):

- **Sub-selector.** In shooting mode, this joystick-like control can be pressed sideways instead of the multi selector (described soon) to select a focus point (autofocus is covered in Chapter 5), whereas pressing the sub-selector down (as if it were a button) locks focus and exposure while it's held down. In playback mode, it behaves the same as the multi selector to scroll around within a zoomed image. Or, you can reprogram it to display the next or previous image instead, using Custom Setting f2, as I'll explain in Chapter 12.

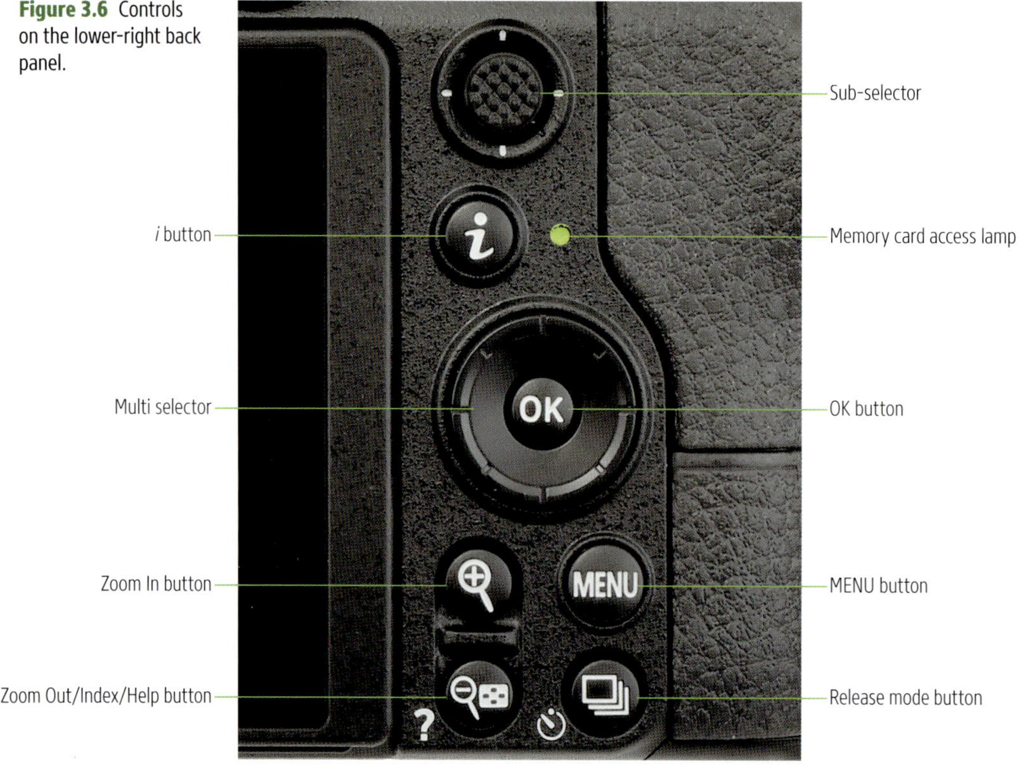

Figure 3.6 Controls on the lower-right back panel.

- ***i* button.** Pressing this button in Photo or Movie shooting modes summons the *i* menu, which I first showed you in Figure 2.1 in the previous chapter. A total of 12 adjustments can be accessed from the *i* menu, but you can replace any entry you don't use much with another function of your choice, using Custom Setting f1: Customize *i* Menu, as described in Chapter 12.

  In Playback mode, the *i* button has a different function. When reviewing a still image, press the *i* button and choose Rating, Select to Send/Deselect (Smart Device), Retouch, Jump to Copy on Other Card, Choose Folder, Protect, or Unprotect All, plus Side-by-Side comparison. (You'll need to scroll down to see the last entry, which is available only when viewing a retouched copy or the copy's source.) When a movie clip is displayed during Playback mode, your choices are Rating, Volume Control, Trim Movie, Choose Slot and Folder, Protect, and Unprotect All. (See Figure 3.7.)

- **Memory card access lamp.** When lit or blinking, this lamp indicates that a memory card is being accessed.

- **Multi selector.** This joypad-like button can be shifted up, down, side to side, and diagonally for a total of eight directions. It can be used for several functions, including AF point selection, scrolling around a magnified image, trimming a photo, or setting white balance bias along the green/magenta and blue/yellow axes. Within menus, pressing the up/down arrows moves the on-screen cursor up or down; pressing toward the right selects the highlighted item and displays its options; pressing left cancels and returns to the previous menu.

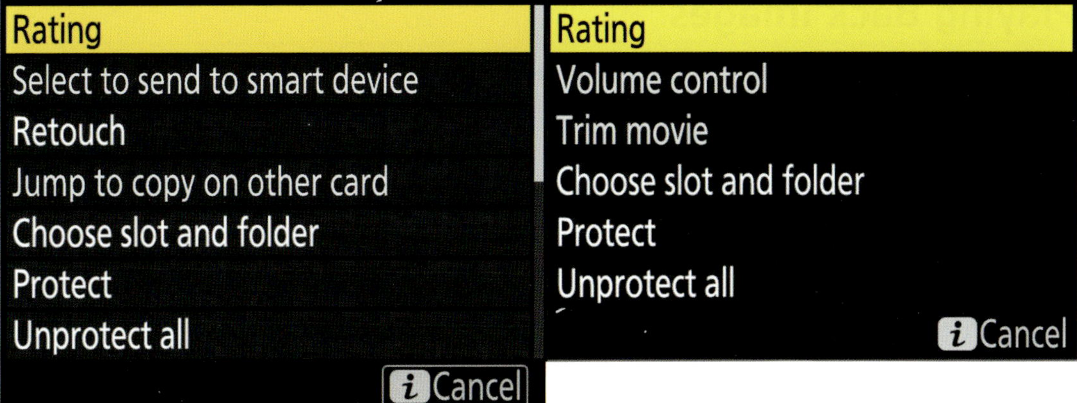

Figure 3.7 Left: In Playback mode, the *i* button allows you to select a rating, send an image to a smart device, retouch a still image, jump to copy on other card, choose a slot and folder, or protect/unprotect an image from erasure. You must scroll down to see the side-by-side comparison choice when it's available. An additional option, Quick Crop, appears when the image is magnified. Right: For video clips, your choices are Rating, Volume Control, Trim Movie, Choose Slot and Folder, Protect, and Unprotect All.

- **OK button.** The OK button in the center of the multi selector can be pressed to activate several different default functions, depending on your current mode. Like many other controls, it can be redefined; in this case use Custom Setting f3. I'll explain those options in Chapter 12. The default behaviors vary by mode:
  - **Shooting mode.** Resets the focus point to the center of the frame.
  - **Playback mode.** Turns zoom on/off.
  - **Menu mode.** Selects highlighted menu option (same as right arrow button).
- **MENU button.** Summons/exits the menu display. When you're working with submenus, this button also serves to exit a submenu and return to the main menu.
- **Zoom In button.** Used exclusively in Playback mode. Press to zoom in on an image when in full-screen view, or to decrease the number of thumbnails when in index view (described next). **Note:** you can also zoom in and out in Playback mode using "squeeze" and "stretch" gestures on the touch screen, similarly to the techniques used with smartphones. I'll explain zooming and other playback options in the next section.
- **Zoom Out/Index/Help button.** This button has separate Playback and Shooting mode functions:
  - **Playback mode.** Use this button to change from full-screen view to 4, 9, or 72 thumbnails. Press the Zoom In button to go the other way back to full-screen and magnified views.
  - **Shooting mode.** When viewing most menu items on the monitor, if a ? icon appears in the bottom-left corner of the screen, pressing this button produces a concise Help screen with tips on how to make the relevant setting. You can scroll through the screen using the up/down buttons or press this button again to return to the menus.
- **Release mode button.** Allows choosing the Z5's release modes: Single frame, Continuous L, Continuous H, and Self-timer, using the command dials as described in Chapter 2.

Playing Back Images

Reviewing images is a joy, whether you use the big 3.2-inch color LCD monitor or the viewfinder (which is especially handy for viewing images in bright light under which the monitor may tend to wash out).

Here are the basics involved in reviewing images on the Z5's displays (or on a screen you have connected with an HDMI cable). You'll find more details about some of these functions later in this chapter, or, for more complex capabilities, in the chapters that I point you to. This section just lists the must-know information.

- **Start review.** To begin review, press the Playback button at the upper-left corner of the back of the Z5. The most recently viewed image will appear on the display.

- **Playback slot/folder.** You can select which slot and folder is used for playback by starting playback with the Playback button, and then pressing the *i* button and selecting Choose Slot and Folder. Press the directional buttons to first choose which slot to use, and then to select from a list of available folders. Press the right button again to activate that slot/folder.

    You can also select the active folder using the Playback Folder option (choose NZ5 folders, All, or Current Folder) in the Playback menu. You can create and activate a *new* folder using the Storage Folder entry in the Photo Shooting menu. See Chapter 11 for more information on both options.

- **View thumbnail images.** To change the view from a single image to 4, 9, or 72 thumbnails, plus calendar view, follow the instructions in the "Viewing Thumbnails" section.

- **Zoom in and out.** To zoom in or out, press the Zoom In or Zoom Out buttons, following the instructions in the next section. (It also shows you how to move the zoomed area around using the multi selector keypad.)

- **Move back and forth.** To advance to the next image, press the right edge of the multi selector pad; to go back to a previous shot, press the left edge. When you reach the beginning/end of the photos in your folder, the display "wraps around" to the end/beginning of the available shots. **Note:** You can assign a special behavior to the sub-command dial such that rotating it skips ahead either 10 or 50 images, or advance by other parameters, such as rating. See the discussion of Custom Setting f5 (Customize Command Dials > Sub-dial Frame Advance) in Chapter 12 for more information.

- **See different types of data.** To change the type of information about the displayed image that is shown, press the up and down portions of the multi selector pad. You must first select which combination of seven informational screens appear, using the Playback Options entry in the Playback menu (described in Chapter 11).

- **Remove images.** To delete an image that's currently on display, press the Trash button once, then press it again to confirm the deletion. To select and delete a group of images, use the Delete option in the Playback menu to specify particular photos to remove, as described in more detail in Chapter 11.

- **Cancel playback.** To cancel image review, press the Playback button again, or simply tap the shutter release button.

Zooming the Nikon Z5 Playback Display

The Nikon Z5 zooms in and out of preview images using the procedure that follows:

1. **Zoom in.** When an image is displayed (use the Playback button to start), press the Zoom In button to fill the screen with a slightly magnified version of the image. When viewing on the monitor, you can also press the multi selector center button, tap the touch screen twice, or touch two fingers to the LCD monitor and spread them apart to enlarge the image.

2. **Continue zooming.** A navigation window appears in the lower-right corner of the LCD monitor showing the entire image. Keep pressing to continue zooming in to the maximum of 33X enlargement (with a full-resolution large image in FX format). (Medium and Small images can be enlarged up to 25X and 17X, respectively.)

3. **Zoomed area indicated.** A yellow box in the navigation window shows the zoomed area within the full image. (See Figure 3.8.) The entire navigation window vanishes from the screen after a few seconds, leaving you with a full-screen view of the zoomed portion of the image.

4. **Move zoomed area around.** Use the multi selector buttons to move the zoomed area around within the image. The navigation window will reappear for reference when zooming or scrolling around within the display. You can also slide one finger around the touch screen to move the zoomed area.

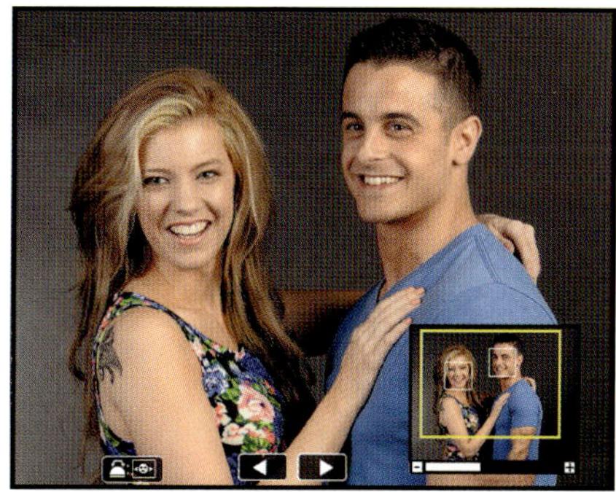

Figure 3.8 The Nikon Z5 incorporates a small thumbnail image with a yellow box showing the current zoom area.

5. **Find faces.** To detect faces, rotate the sub-command dial while an image is zoomed. Up to 35 faces will be detected by the Z5, indicated by white borders in the navigation window. Rotate the sub-command dial or tap the on-screen guide (seen at the lower-right bottom edge in the figure) to move highlighting to the individual faces.

6. **Quick Crop (optional).** While the image is magnified during Playback, you can press the *i* button and choose Quick Crop. The Z5 will save a new file cropped to that image size. Your original image is untouched.

7. **Review same area on another image.** Use the main command dial or tap the left/right triangles at the bottom of the touch screen to move to the same zoomed area of the next/previous image. This allows you to compare a detail in a series of similar shots. I often use the capability to see if a spot in an image is a dust spot (it shows up in the same place in other images) or just an artifact found in a single image.

8. **Zoom out.** Use the Zoom Out button to zoom back out of the image.

9. **Exit.** To exit zoom in/zoom out display, keep pressing the Zoom Out button until the full-screen/full-image/information display appears again. Or just tap the shutter release halfway or press the Playback button to exit playback entirely.

Viewing Thumbnails

The Nikon Z5 provides other options for reviewing images in addition to zooming in and out. You can switch between single-image view and 4, 9, or 72 reduced-size thumbnail images on a single LCD monitor screen. You can also see a calendar view in which images are arranged by the date on which they were taken.

Pages of thumbnail images offer a quick way to scroll through a large number of pictures quickly to find the one you want to examine in more detail. The Z5 lets you switch quickly with a scroll bar displayed at the right side of the screen to show you the relative position of the displayed thumbnails within the full collection of images in the active folder on your memory card. Figure 3.9 offers a comparison between the three levels of thumbnail views. The Zoom In and Zoom Out/Thumbnail buttons are used, or you can use the pinch and spread gestures with two fingers on the touch screen to increase or decrease the number of thumbnail indexes shown.

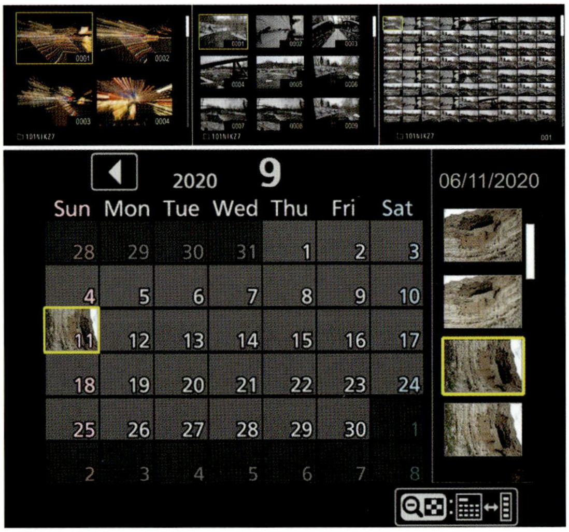

Figure 3.9 Top: Switch between 4 thumbnails (left), 9 thumbnails (center), or 72 thumbnails (right), by pressing the Zoom Out and Zoom In buttons or using pinch and spread gestures on the touch screen. Bottom: Calendar view allows you to browse through all images on your memory card taken on a certain date.

- **Add thumbnails.** To increase the number of thumbnails on the screen, press the Zoom Out button or pinch the touch screen. The Z5 will switch from single image to 4 thumbnails to 9 thumbnails to 72 thumbnails. An additional press brings up the calendar view, which I'll explain shortly. (The display doesn't cycle back to single image again once you've reached calendar view.)

- **Reduce number of thumbnails.** To decrease the number of thumbnails on the screen, press the Zoom In button or use the spread gesture on the touch screen to change from calendar view to 72 thumbnails to 9 thumbnails to 4 thumbnails, or from 4 to single-image display. Continuing once you've returned to single-image display starts the zoom process described in the previous section.

- **Change slot and folder.** When viewing images, if two memory cards are installed in the Z5, press the *i* button to produce the dialog box (shown earlier in Figure 3.7) that includes an option to choose the playback slot and folder of the memory card that contains the images you want to view.

- **Switch between thumbnails and full image.** When viewing thumbnails, you can quickly switch between thumbnail view and full-image display by pressing the OK button in the center of the multi selector, or by tapping the thumbnail image on the touch screen.

- **Retouch an image/thumbnail.** When an image or thumbnail is viewed, press the *i* button to access the options screen that includes a Retouch option for that image (described in Chapter 13).

- **Change highlighted thumbnail area.** Use the multi selector to move the yellow highlight box around among the thumbnails, or, preferably, use a single finger on the touch screen to scroll back and forth or to select a particular thumbnail. Note that *touching* a thumbnail moves the highlighting to that thumbnail, while *tapping* the thumbnail produces a full-screen view of the image.

- **Protect and delete images.** When viewing thumbnails or a single-page image, press the *i* button and select the Protect function to preserve the highlighted image against accidental deletion (a key icon is overlaid over the thumbnail image; press Protect again to remove protection). (You can also define a button to perform this function using Custom Setting f2: Custom Controls, as I'll explain in Chapter 12.)

- **Exit image review.** Tap the shutter release button or press the Playback button to exit image review. You don't have to worry about missing a shot because you were reviewing images; a half-press of the shutter release automatically brings back the Z5's exposure meters, the autofocus system, and, unless you've redefined your controls or are using manual focus, cancels image review.

Working with Calendar View

When you're in 72 thumbnail mode, pressing the Zoom Out button one more time takes you to calendar view, where you can sort through images arranged by the date they were taken. This feature is especially useful when you're traveling and want to see only the pictures you took in, say, a particular city on a certain day.

- **View dates and images taken on that date.** A yellow highlight box appears around a selected date in the date list calendar, as shown at the bottom of in Figure 3.9. When there are images available that were taken on that date, a scrolling thumbnail column appears at the right of the screen. The thumbnail column disappears if there are no photos taken on the highlighted date.

- **Change dates.** Use the multi selector keys to move through the date list.

- **View a date's images.** Press the Zoom Out/Index button to toggle between the date list and the scrolling thumbnail list of images taken on that date at the right of the screen. When viewing the thumbnail list, you can use the multi selector up/down keys to scroll through the available images. Press the Zoom Out/Index button again to return to the date list calendar when you want to select a different date.

- **Preview an image.** In the thumbnail list, when you've highlighted an image you want to look at, press the OK button to see an enlarged view of that image without leaving calendar view. The zoomed image replaces the date list. Press OK again to return to calendar view.

- **Delete images.** Pressing the Trash button deletes a highlighted image in the thumbnail list. In the date list view, pressing the Trash button removes all the images taken on that date (use with caution!). If you press Trash by accident, press the Playback button to cancel.

- **Protect images.** Press the WB button to protect a highlighted image. Some Wi-Fi cards can be set to upload only images marked with Protect, so you can use this feature to define the photos that will be uploaded.

- **Exit calendar view.** In thumbnail list view, if you highlight an image and press the OK button, you'll exit calendar view and the highlighted image will be shown on the LCD monitor in the display mode you've chosen. In date list view, pressing the Zoom In button exits calendar view and returns to 72 thumbnails view. You can also exit calendar view by tapping the shutter release (to turn off the LCD monitor to ready the camera for shooting) or by pressing the MENU button.

Using the Photo Data Displays

When reviewing an image on the viewfinder or monitor displays, your Z5 can supplement the image itself with a variety of shooting data, ranging from basic information presented at the bottom of the display, to a series of text overlays that detail virtually every shooting option you've selected. There is also a display for GPS data if you're using a GPS device, and two views of histograms. I'll explain how to work with histograms in the discussion on achieving optimum exposure in Chapter 4. However, this is a good place to provide an overview of the kind of information you can view when playing back your photos.

You can change the *types* of information displayed using the Playback Display Options entry in the Playback menu. There you will find checkboxes you can mark for both basic photo information (over-exposed highlights and the focus point used when the image was captured) and detailed photo information (which includes an RGB histogram and various data screens). You must mark any unchecked box to enable that type of information display. I'll show you how to activate these info options in Chapter 11 and provide more detailed reasons why you might want to see each type of data when you review your pictures. This section will simply show you the type of information available. Most of the data is self-explanatory, so the labels in the accompanying figures should tell you most of what you need to know. To change to any of these views while an image is on the screen in Playback mode, press the DISP or up buttons.

- **File information screen.** The basic full-image review display is officially called the file information screen and looks like Figure 3.10. Press the multi selector down button to advance to the next information screen (or the up button to cycle in the other direction).

- **Highlights.** When highlights display is active (after being chosen in the Display Mode entry of the Playback menu, as described in Chapter 11), any overexposed areas will be indicated by a flashing black border. As I am unable to make the printed page flash, you'll have to check out this effect for yourself. You can visualize what these "blinkies" look like in Figure 3.11, as they are most easily discerned as the black splotches in the sky.

- **RGB histogram.** Another optional screen is the RGB histogram, which you can see in Figure 3.12. I'm going to leave the discussion of histograms for Chapter 4.

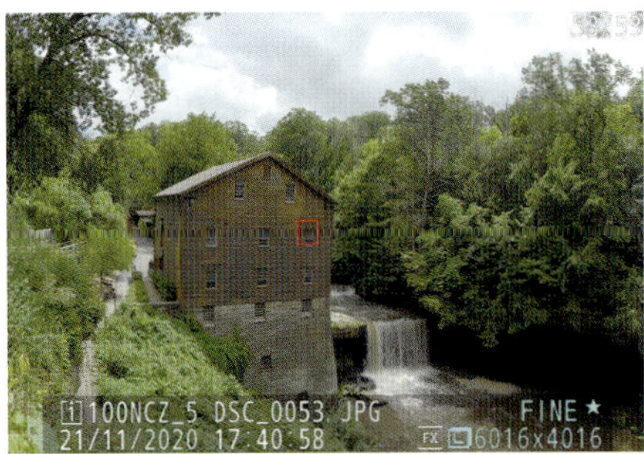

Figure 3.10 File information screen.

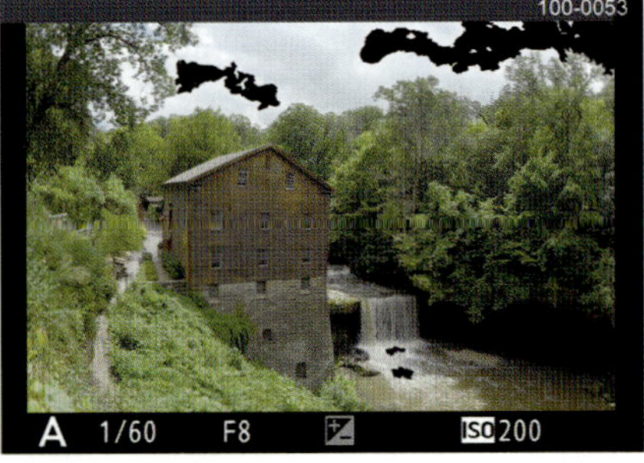

Figure 3.11 Highlights screen.

■ **Shooting data 1–6.** These are a series of screens that collectively provide everything else you might want to know about a picture you've taken. Note that each screen may not show all the information that can be displayed on that screen, and that all the screens may not appear. Only the data and screens that apply to your image will be shown. For example, the GPS screen appears only if a picture has GPS information embedded in it; the Artist/Copyright screen is shown only if you have chosen to embed that information in your image file using the Image Comment entry in the Setup menu. (I'll show you how to do that in Chapter 13.) The six screens are shown in Figures 3.13 to 3.18.

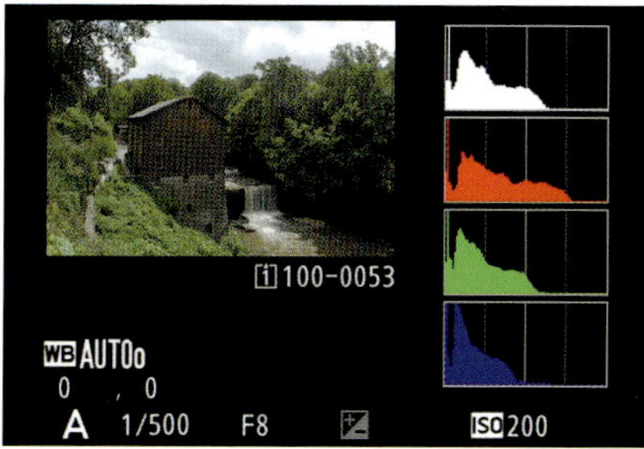

Figure 3.12 RGB histogram screen.

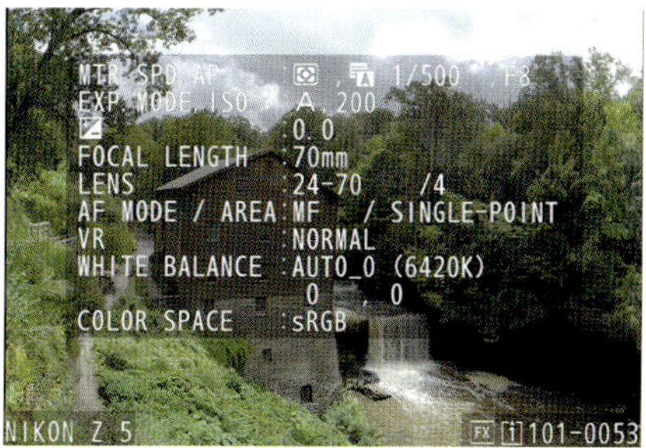

Figure 3.13 Exposure, lens, and autofocus/VR information appears here.

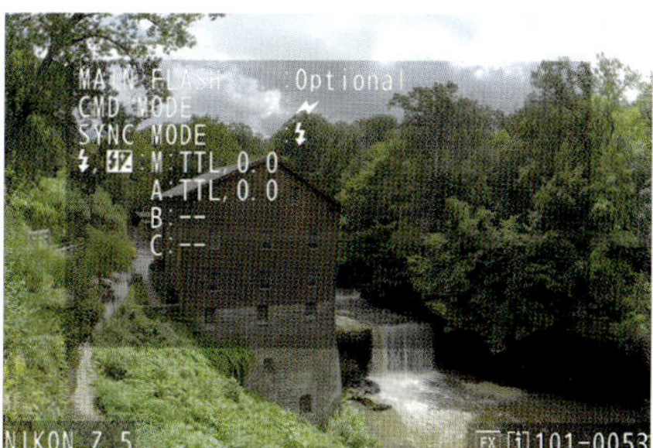

Figure 3.14 Information about flash exposures are shown on this screen.

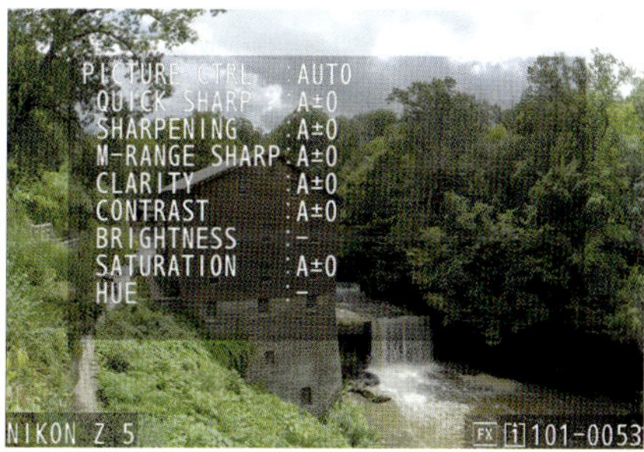

Figure 3.15 Picture Control adjustments appear here.

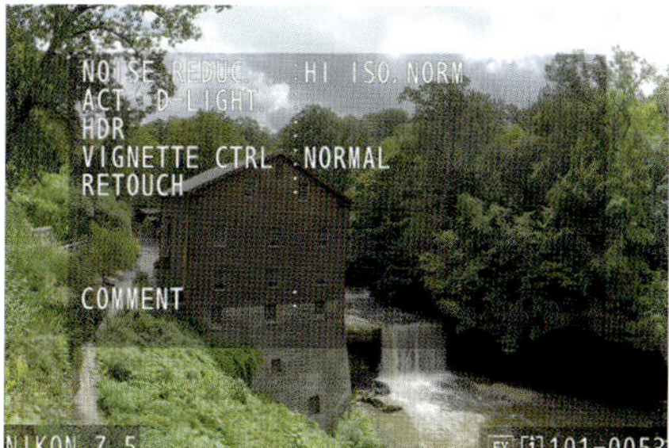

Figure 3.16 Noise reduction, Active D-Lighting, HDR, Vignette Control, Retouching, and other information are shown here.

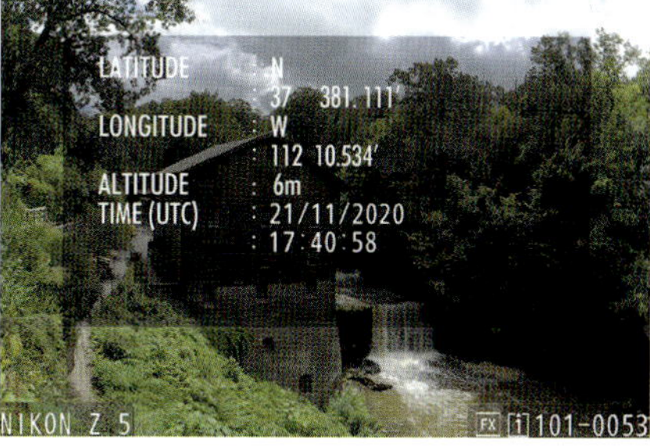

Figure 3.17 GPS data is displayed if the image was taken using a GPS device.

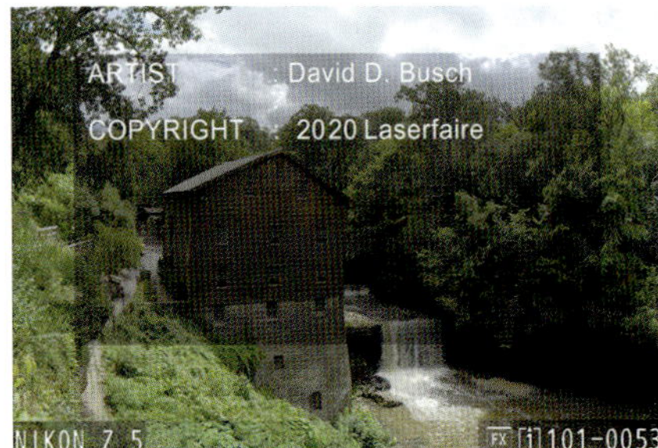

Figure 3.18 Artist information and copyright notices, if enabled, are shown.

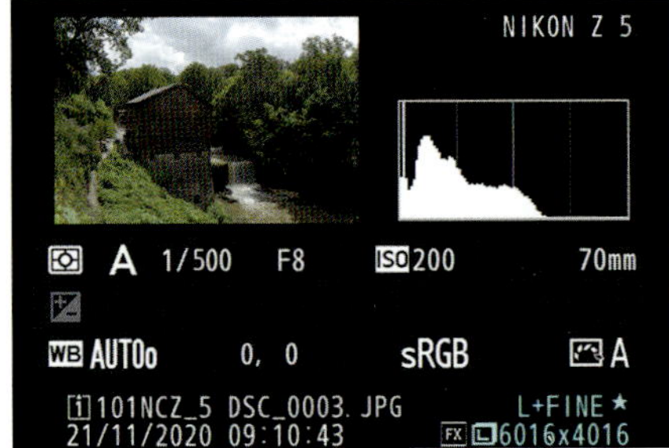

Figure 3.19 This overview screen includes a brightness histogram and basic information about the image.

- **Overview data.** This screen, shown in Figure 3.19, provides a smaller image of your photo, but offers more information, including a luminance (brightness) histogram, metering mode used, lens focal length, exposure compensation, flash compensation, and lots of other data that's self-explanatory.

Going Topside

The top surface of the Nikon Z5 has its own set of frequently accessed controls. (See Figure 3.20.)

- **Accessory shoe.** Slide an electronic flash into this mount when you need a more powerful Speedlight. A dedicated flash unit, like the Nikon SB-5000, can use the multiple contact points shown to communicate exposure, zoom setting, white balance information, and other data between the flash and the camera. There's more on using electronic flash in Chapters 9 and 10. You can also mount other accessories on this shoe, such as the Nikon GP-1a GPS adapter or Nikon ME-1 microphone.

- **Stereo microphones.** This pair captures sounds when shooting video.

- **Power switch.** Rotate this switch clockwise to turn on the Nikon Z5 (and virtually all other Nikon interchangeable-lens digital cameras).

- **Shutter release button.** Partially depress this button to activate the exposure meter (and the main and sub-command dials that adjust metering settings), lock in exposure, and focus (unless you've redefined the focus activation button, as outlined in Chapter 12). Press all the way to take the picture. Tapping the shutter release when the camera has turned off the autoexposure and autofocus mechanisms reactivates both. When a review image is displayed on the back-panel color monitor, tapping this button removes the image from the display and reactivates the autoexposure and autofocus mechanisms. You can also tap the button to exit image review and menus, readying the camera to take a picture.

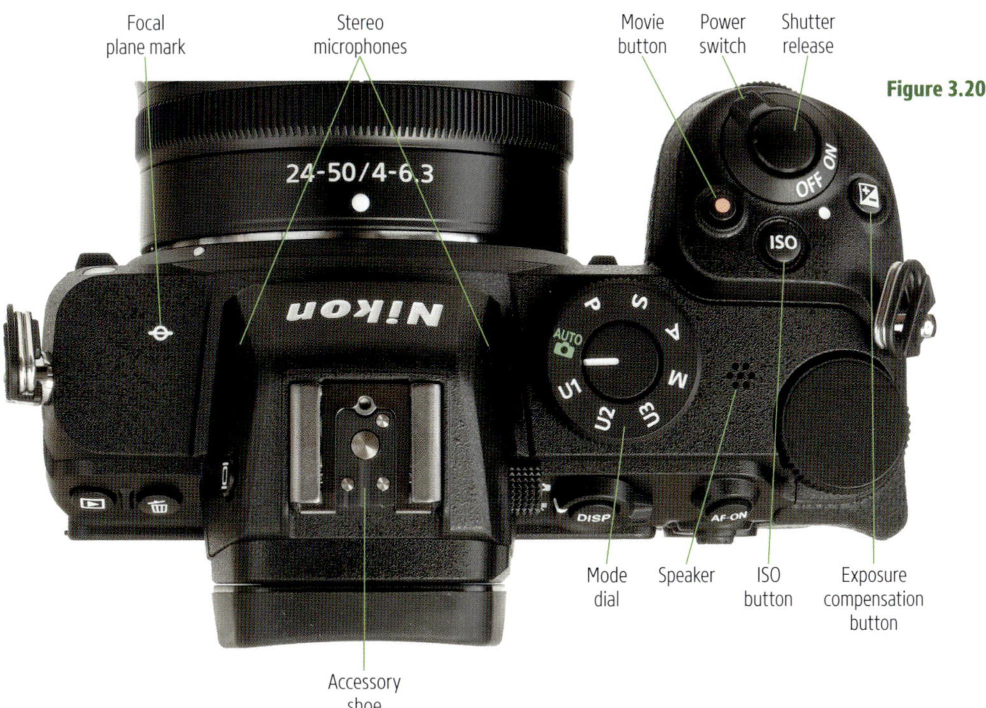

- **Exposure compensation button.** Hold down this button and spin the main command dial to add or subtract exposure when using Program, Aperture-priority, or Shutter-priority modes. (In Manual mode, the exposure remains the same, but the "ideal" exposure shown in the electronic analog display is modified to reflect the extra/reduced exposure you're calling for.) The exposure compensation amount is shown on the display as plus or minus values.

- **Focal plane mark.** This indicator shows the *plane* of the sensor, for use in applications where exact measurement of the distance from the focal plane to the subject is necessary. (These are mostly scientific/close-up applications.)

- **Movie button.** Press to begin video capture; press a second time to stop.

- **ISO button.** Hold this button and rotate the main command dial until the ISO value you want is shown on the top control panel, in the viewfinder, and on the monitor.

- **Mode dial.** Rotate to select shooting mode or one of the three user settings.

- **Speaker.** Sounds emitted by your Z5 emanate from this speaker.

Lens Components

Not all Nikon lenses include all of the features shown in Figure 3.21. For example, G-series lenses (learn about different lens types in Chapter 7) do not have an aperture ring. Components shown in the figure include:

- **Filter thread.** Most lenses have a thread on the front for attaching filters and other add-ons. Some, generally older F-mount lenses, also use this thread for attaching a lens hood (you screw on the filter first, and then attach the hood to the screw thread on the front of the filter). Some F-mount lenses, such as the AF-S Nikkor 14-24mm f/2.8G ED lens, have no front filter thread, either because their front elements are too curved to allow mounting a filter and/or because the front element is so large that huge filters would be prohibitively expensive. Some of these front-filter-hostile lenses allow using smaller filters that drop into a slot at the back of the lens.

- **Lens hood bayonet.** Lenses use this bayonet to mount the lens hood. Such lenses generally will have a *lens hood alignment indicator,* a dot on the edge showing how to align the lens hood with the bayonet mount.

- **Focus/control ring.** This is the ring you turn when you manually focus the lens, or fine-tune auto-focus adjustment. It's a narrow ring at the very front of the lens on some lenses, or a wider ring located somewhere else. The function of the focus/control ring (on Z-mount lenses only) can be redefined, as I'll explain in Chapter 12.

- **Zoom ring.** Turn this ring to change the zoom setting.

- **Autofocus/Manual focus switch.** Allows you to change from automatic focus to manual focus.

- **Electronic contacts.** These metal contacts pass information to matching contacts located in the camera body, allowing a firm electrical connection so that exposure, distance, and other information can be exchanged between the camera and lens.

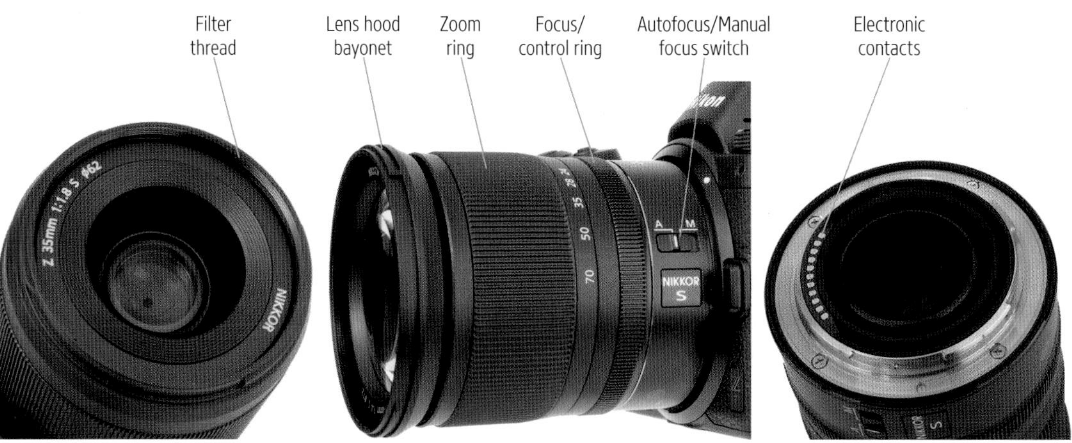

Figure 3.21

Underneath Your Nikon Z5

There's not a lot going on with the bottom panel of your Nikon Z5. You'll find the battery compartment access door and a tripod socket, which secures the camera to a tripod. The socket accepts other accessories, such as quick-release plates that allow rapid attaching and detaching the Z5 from a matching platform affixed to your tripod. The socket is also used to secure the optional MB-N10 battery grip, which provides more juice to run your camera to take more exposures with a single charge. Figure 3.22 shows the underside view of the camera.

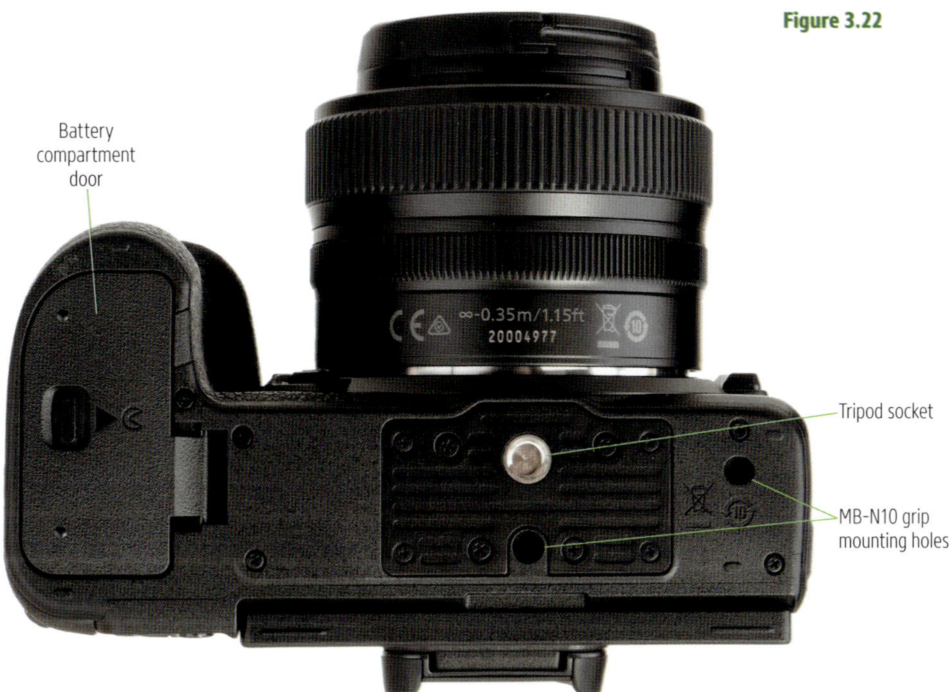

Figure 3.22

The Viewfinder/Monitor Displays

Much of the important shooting status information is shown inside the electronic viewfinder and LCD monitor of the Nikon Z5. In shooting mode, you can press the DISP button to cycle through the available views. The shooting information display appears only on the monitor (still photo) and can be shown in dark-on-light or light-on-dark color schemes. (See Figure 3.23.) Choose your scheme using the Information Display entry in the Setup menu, as explained in Chapter 13. One additional Information Display is available when an SB-300, SB-400, SB-500, or SB-5000 flash unit is attached and powered up, or a WR-R10 wireless remote controller is commanding a flash using radio control. (See Figure 3.24.)

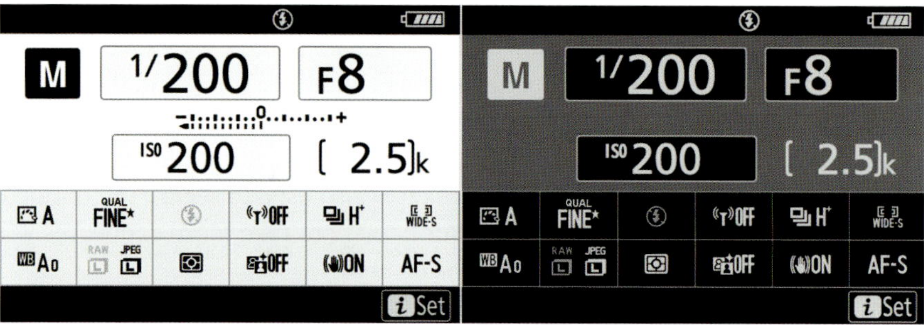

Figure 3.23 Photo information displays can be shown in light and dark color schemes.

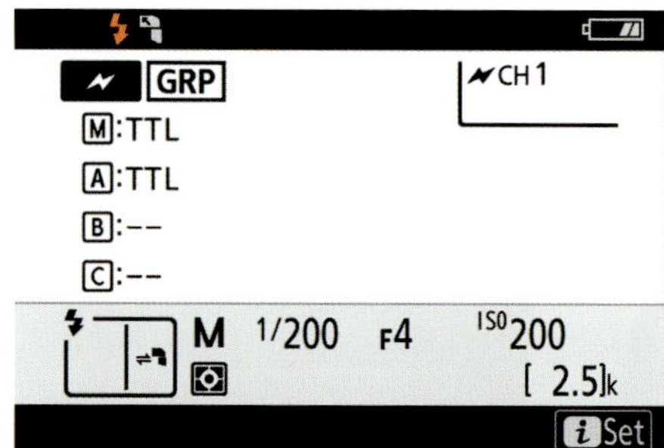

Figure 3.24 Flash information appears when a compatible flash is mounted and powered up.

The other displays show information overlaid on the frame. Not all of this information will be shown at any one time. Figure 3.25 shows what you can expect to see on the LCD monitor. The viewfinder display is similar, but the icons are arrayed along the top and bottom instead of overlaid along the sides of the frame. The histogram is not displayed when Overlay Shooting is used in multiple exposure mode (see Chapter 11) or Custom Setting d7: Apply Settings to Live View is set to Off (see Chapter 12).

In addition to the features shown, a framing grid can be applied. This optional grid (it can be turned on and off in Custom Setting d8) can be useful when aligning horizontal or vertical shapes as you compose your image. The virtual horizon, shown in Figure 3.26, shows rotational and front/back tilt.

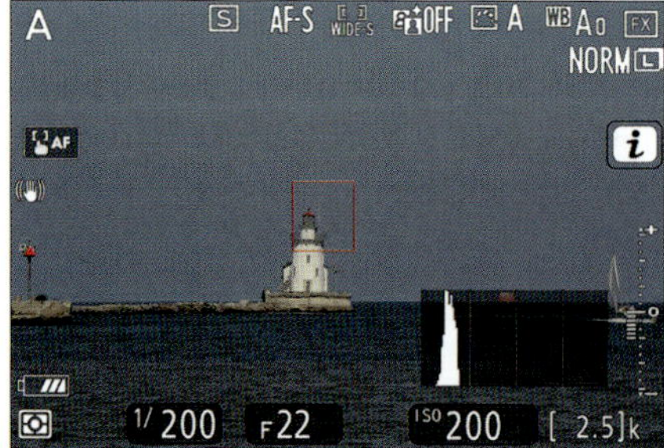

Figure 3.25 Overlaid information on the monitor screen.

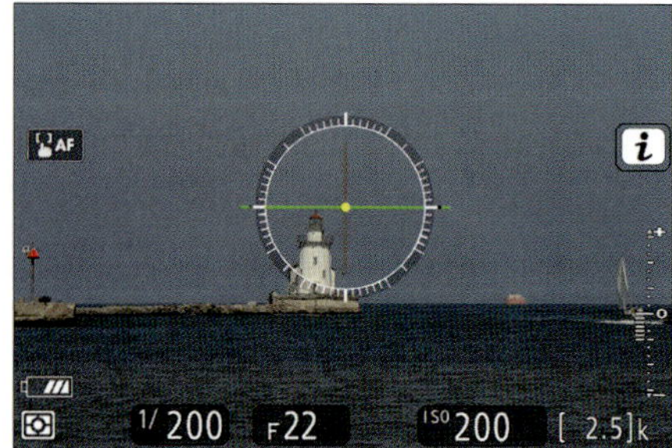

Figure 3.26 The virtual horizon display is useful for correcting side to side and front/back tilt.

Nailing the Right Exposure 4

If you consider the qualities that constitute the most important tools for creating an outstanding image, an appropriate exposure is easily in the top three, along with picture sharpness/focus, and framing/composition. Within this triumvirate, exposure potentially involves the largest number of variables and can improve (or hinder) the impact of your image in a variety of ways. That's particularly true because *how* you achieve a particular exposure setting can have as much impact as *what* settings you select.

Think about it. Incorrect exposure can affect the tonal values in your image in a detrimental way, obscuring detail in shadows or washing out the highlights. But even exposure that's *theoretically* satisfactory can still produce an image that is objectionably blurry because the shutter speed is too slow or objectionably grainy looking because the ISO sensitivity has been set too high or lacks sufficient detail in some areas because depth-of-field is lacking. Nailing the right exposure involves more than just appropriate settings. You also need to understand how the elements of exposure affect your final photograph.

Your Z5 has an exceptional amount of intelligence when it comes to calculating a proper exposure for a wide variety of scenes. Even so, you are smarter—and have creative vision the camera lacks. The more you shoot, the more ways you'll discover how to improve on your camera's picture-taking decisions and, even when to *ignore* them when you want to create a particular look or effect. For example, when you shoot with the main light source behind the subject, you end up with *backlighting*, which can result in an overexposed background and/or an underexposed subject. The Nikon Z5 recognizes backlit situations nicely, and, in most cases, can properly base exposure on the main subject using the default Matrix metering mode, producing a decent photo.

But, as an inventive photographer, there will be many instances where you would rather *not* have automatic correction for backlighting. What if you *want* to underexpose the subject, to produce a silhouette effect? The Z5 does a poor job of exposing intentional silhouettes and will end up producing unwanted detail in what should have been inky black areas of your image. Fortunately, the camera has metering modes and other exposure options that allow you to produce the image you are looking for. If you're looking for an extensive exposure range, features like the Z5's built-in HDR and Active D-Lighting can fine-tune your exposure as you take photos, preserving detail in the highlights and shadows as required. Your Nikon Z5 also has the capability of *fine-tuning* exposure separately for each of the metering modes, so you can consistently add or subtract a little exposure to suit your creative tastes.

In the next few pages, I'm going to give you a grounding in exposure concepts, either as an introduction or as a refresher course, depending on your current level of expertise. When you finish this chapter, you'll understand most of what you need to know to take well-exposed photographs creatively in a broad range of situations.

Getting a Handle on Exposure

This section explains the fundamental concepts that go into creating an exposure. If you already know about the role of f/stops, shutter speeds, and sensor sensitivity in determining an exposure, you might want to skip to the next section, which explains how the Z5 calculates exposure.

In the most basic sense, exposure is all about light. Correct exposure brings out the detail in the areas you want to picture, providing the range of tones and colors you need to create the desired image. Poor exposure can cloak important details in shadow or wash them out in glare-filled featureless expanses of white. However, getting the perfect exposure requires some intelligence—either that built into the camera or the smarts in your head—because digital sensors can't capture all the tones we are able to see. If the range of tones in an image is extensive, embracing both inky black shadows and bright highlights, we often must settle for an exposure that renders most of those tones—but not all—in a way that best suits the photo we want to produce.

As the owner of a Nikon Z5, you're probably well aware of the traditional "exposure triangle" of aperture (quantity of light, light passed by the lens), shutter speed (the amount of time the shutter is open), and the ISO sensitivity of the sensor—all working proportionately and reciprocally to produce an exposure. The trio is itself affected by the amount of illumination that is available to work with. So, if you double the amount of light, increase the aperture by one stop, make the shutter speed twice as long, or boost the ISO setting 2X, you'll get twice as much exposure. Similarly, you can increase any of these factors while decreasing one of the others by a similar amount to keep the *same* exposure.

Working with any of the three controls always involves trade-offs. Larger f/stops provide less depth-of-field, while smaller f/stops increase depth-of-field and decrease sharpness through a phenomenon called diffraction. Shorter shutter speeds do a better job of reducing the effects of camera/subject motion, while longer shutter speeds make that motion blur more likely. Higher ISO settings increase the amount of visual noise and artifacts in your image, while lower ISO settings reduce the effects of noise. (See Figure 4.1.)

To further understand exposure, you need to understand the six aspects of light that combine to produce an image. Start with a light source—the sun, an interior lamp, electronic flash, or the glow from a campfire—and trace its path to your camera, through the lens, and finally to the sensor that captures the illumination.

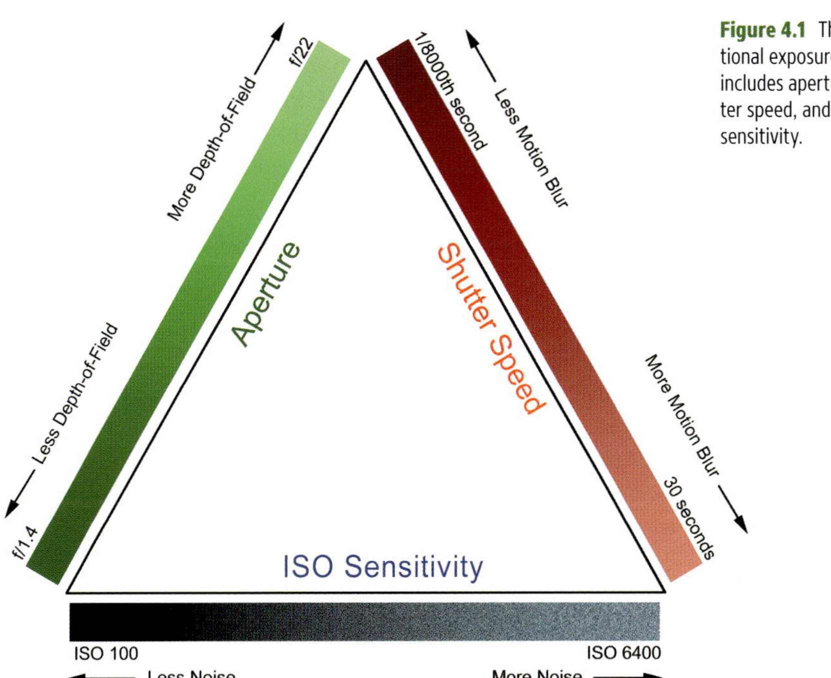

Figure 4.1 The traditional exposure triangle includes aperture, shutter speed, and ISO sensitivity.

Here's a brief review of the things within our control that affect exposure, listed in "chronological" order (that is, as the light moves from the subject to the sensor):

- **Light at its source.** Our eyes and our cameras—film or digital—are most sensitive to that portion of the electromagnetic spectrum we call *visible light.* That light has several important aspects that are relevant to photography, such as color and harshness (which is determined primarily by the apparent size of the light source as it illuminates a subject). But, in terms of exposure, the important attribute of a light source is its *intensity.* We may have direct control over intensity, which might be the case with an interior light that can be brightened or dimmed, or electronic flash output that can be increased or decreased manually or automatically. In other cases, we might have only indirect control over intensity, as with sunlight, which can be made to appear dimmer by introducing translucent light-absorbing or reflective materials in its path.

- **Light's duration.** We tend to think of most light sources as continuous. But, as you'll learn in Chapter 8, the duration of light can change quickly enough to modify the exposure, as when the main illumination in a photograph comes from an intermittent source, such as an electronic flash.

- **Light reflected, transmitted, or emitted.** Once light is produced by its source, either continuously or in a brief burst, we are able to see and photograph objects by the light that is reflected from our subjects toward the camera lens; transmitted (say, from translucent objects that are lit from behind); or emitted (by a candle or television screen). When more or less light reaches the lens from the subject, we need to adjust the exposure. This part of the equation is under our control to the extent we can increase the amount of light falling on or passing through the subject (by adding extra light sources or using reflectors), or by pumping up the light that's emitted (by increasing the brightness of the glowing object).

- **Light passed by the lens.** Not all the illumination that reaches the front of the lens makes it all the way through. Filters can remove some of the light before it enters the lens. Inside the lens barrel is a variable-sized diaphragm that produces an opening called an *aperture* that dilates and contracts to control the amount of light that enters the lens. You, or the Z5's autoexposure system, can control exposure by varying the size of the aperture. The relative size of the aperture is called the *f/stop*. (See Figure 4.2.)

- **Light passing through the shutter.** Once light passes through the lens, the amount of time the sensor receives it is determined by the Z5's shutter, which can remain open for as briefly as 1/8000th of a second, or, for as long as 30 seconds—or even longer if you use the Bulb or Time settings (located past the 30-second speed as you rotate the command dial, and available only in Manual exposure mode).

- **Light captured by the sensor.** Not all the light falling onto the sensor is captured. If the number of photons reaching a particular photosite doesn't pass a set threshold, no information is recorded. Similarly, if too much light illuminates a pixel in the sensor, then the excess isn't recorded or, worse, spills over to contaminate adjacent pixels. We can modify the minimum and maximum number of pixels that contribute to image detail by adjusting the ISO setting. At higher ISOs, the incoming light is amplified to boost the effective sensitivity of the sensor.

Four of these factors—quantity of light, light passed by the lens, the amount of time the shutter is open, and the sensitivity of the sensor—all work proportionately and reciprocally to produce an exposure. That is, as I mentioned, if you double the amount of light, increase the aperture size by one stop, make the shutter speed twice as long, or double the ISO sensitivity, you'll get twice as much exposure. Similarly, you can reduce any of these and reduce the exposure when that is preferable.

As we'll see however, changing any of those aspects in P, A, or S mode does not change the exposure; that's because the camera also makes adjustments when you do so, in order to maintain the same exposure. That's why Nikon provides other methods for modifying the exposure in those modes.

Figure 4.2 Top row (left to right): f/4, f/5.6, f/8; bottom row: f/11, f/16.

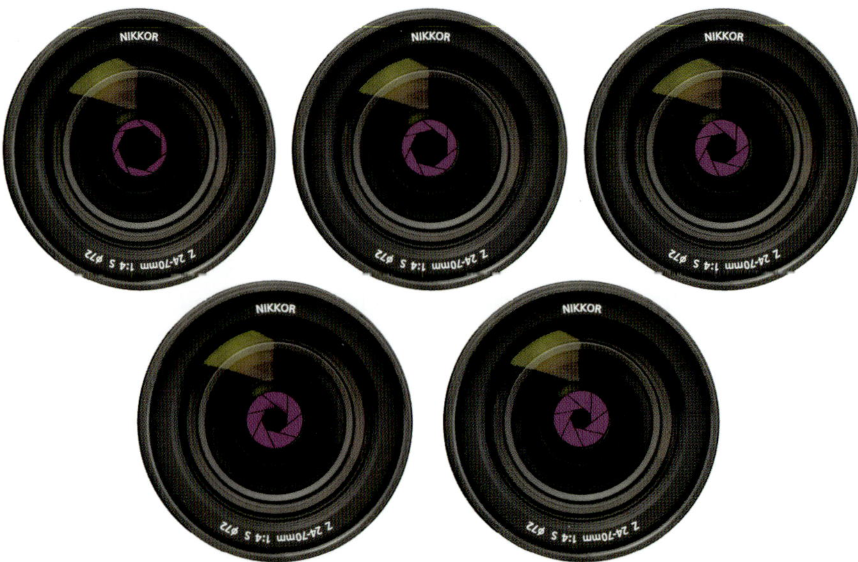

F/STOPS AND SHUTTER SPEEDS

If you're *really* new to more advanced cameras (and I realize that a few ambitious amateurs do purchase the Z5 as their first serious camera), you might need to know that the lens aperture, or f/stop, is a ratio, much like a fraction, which is why f/2 is larger than f/4, just as 1/2 is larger than 1/4. However, f/2 is actually *four times* as large as f/4. (If you remember your high school geometry, you'll know that to double the area of a circle, you multiply its diameter by the square root of two: 1.4.)

Lenses are usually marked with intermediate f/stops that represent a size that's twice as much/half as much as the previous aperture. So, a lens might be marked: f/4, f/5.6, f/8, f/11, f/16, with each larger number representing an aperture that admits half as much light as the one before, as shown in Figure 4.2. Of course, you can also set *intermediate* apertures with the Nikon Z5, such as f/6.3 and f/7.1, which fall between f/5.6 and f/8.

Shutter speeds are actual fractions (of a second), but the numerator is omitted, so that 60, 125, 250, 500, 1,000, and so forth represent 1/60th, 1/125th, 1/250th, 1/500th, and 1/1000th second. To avoid confusion, Nikon uses quotation marks to signify longer exposures: 2", 2"5, 4", and so forth representing 2.0-, 2.5-, and 4.0-second exposures, respectively.

Equivalent Exposure

Most commonly, exposure settings are made using the aperture and shutter speed, followed by adjusting the ISO sensitivity, if it's not possible to get the preferred exposure (that is, the one that uses the "best" f/stop or shutter speed for the depth-of-field or action stopping we want).

One of the most important aspects in this discussion is the concept of *equivalent exposure*. This term means that exactly the same amount of light will reach the sensor at various combinations of aperture and shutter speed. Whether we use a small aperture (large f/number) with a long shutter speed or a wide aperture (small f/number) with a fast shutter speed, the amount of light reaching the sensor can be exactly the same. Table 4.1 shows equivalent exposure settings using various shutter speeds and f/stops; in other words, any of the combination of settings listed will produce exactly the same exposure.

When the Z5 is set for P mode, the metering system selects the correct exposure for you automatically, but you can change quickly to an equivalent exposure by spinning the main command dial until the desired equivalent exposure combination is displayed, with an asterisk appearing next to the P when you're using this "Flexible Program" feature. You can make Flexible Program adjustments more easily if you remember that you need to rotate the command dial toward the left when

TABLE 4.1 Equivalent Exposures

SHUTTER SPEED	F/STOP	SHUTTER SPEED	F/STOP
1/30th second	f/22	1/1000th second	f/4
1/60th second	f/16	1/2000th second	f/2.8
1/125th second	f/11	1/4000th second	f/2
1/250th second	f/8	1/8000th second	f/1.4
1/500th second	f/5.6		

you want to increase the amount of depth-of-field or use a slower shutter speed; rotate to the right when you want to reduce the depth-of-field or use a faster shutter speed. The need for more/less DOF and slower/faster shutter speed are the primary reasons you'd want to use Flexible Program. This program shift mode does not work when you're using flash.

In Aperture-priority (A) and Shutter-priority (S) modes, you can change to an equivalent exposure, but only by either adjusting the aperture with the sub-command dial in A mode (the camera chooses the shutter speed) or shutter speed with the main command dial in S mode (the camera selects the aperture). I'll cover all these exposure modes later in the chapter.

F/STOPS VERSUS STOPS

In photography parlance, *f/stop* always means the aperture or lens opening. However, for lack of a current commonly used word for one exposure increment, the term *stop* is often used. In the past, EV (Exposure Value) served this purpose, and was used as a measure of the total sensitivity range of a device such as a light meter, but exposure value and its abbreviation have since been inextricably intertwined with its use in describing exposure compensation. In this book, when I say "stop" by itself (no *f/*), I mean one whole unit of exposure, and am not necessarily referring to an actual f/stop or lens aperture. So, adjusting the exposure by "one stop" can mean changing to the next shutter speed increment (say, from 1/125th second to 1/200th second) or the next aperture (such as f/4 to f/5.6). Similarly, 1/3-stop or 1/2-stop increments can mean either shutter speed or aperture changes, depending on the context. Be forewarned.

How the Z5 Calculates Exposure

Although it can make some good guesses based on how the brightness levels vary within a scene, your Z5 has no way of knowing for sure what it's pointed at. So, it must make some assumptions and calculate the correct exposure based on its internal rules. One parameter is that the brightness of all—or part—of a scene will average down to a so-called middle-gray tone. The conventional wisdom is that this tone is roughly 18 percent gray. Unfortunately, while the traditional 18 percent value is a middle gray in terms of what the eye sees, the Z5 is actually calibrated for a slightly darker tone. This section explains how your Z5 decides on an exposure in one of its semi-automatic (non-manual) modes.

The exposure is measured using a specific pattern of exposure measuring areas that you can select (more on that later). Exposure is calculated based on the assumption that each area being measured reflects about the same amount of light as a neutral gray card that reflects a "middle" gray of about 12 to 18 percent reflectance. (The photographic "gray cards" you buy at a camera store have an 18 percent gray tone. Your camera is calibrated to interpret a somewhat darker 12 percent gray; I'll explain more about this later, too.) That "average" 12 to 18 percent gray assumption is necessary, because different subjects reflect different amounts of light. In a photo containing, say, a white cat and a dark gray cat, the white cat might reflect five times as much light as the gray cat. An exposure based on the white cat will cause the gray cat to appear to be black, while an exposure based only on the gray cat will make the white cat appear to be washed out.

This is more easily understood if you look at some photos of subjects that are dark (they reflect little light), those that have predominantly middle tones, and subjects that are highly reflective. The next few figures show a simplified scale with a middle gray 18 percent tone, plus black and white patches, along with a human figure (not a cat) to illustrate how different exposure measurements actually do affect an exposure.

Correctly Exposed

The image shown in Figure 4.3, left, represents how a photograph might appear if you inserted the patches shown at the bottom, and then calculated exposure by measuring the light reflecting from the middle gray patch, which, for the sake of illustration, we'll assume reflects approximately 12 to 18 percent of the light that strikes it. The exposure meter in the Z5 sees an object that it thinks is a middle gray, calculates an exposure based on that, and the patch in the center of the strip is rendered at its proper tonal value. Best of all, because the resulting exposure is correct, the black patch at left and white patch at right are rendered properly as well.

When you're shooting pictures with your Z5, and the meter happens to base its exposure on a subject that averages that "ideal" middle gray, then you'll end up with similar (accurate) results. The camera's exposure algorithms are concocted to ensure this kind of result as often as possible, barring any unusual subjects (that is, those that are backlit, or have uneven illumination). The Z5 has four metering modes (described shortly), each of which is equipped to handle certain types of unusual subjects, as I'll outline.

Overexposed

At center in Figure 4.3 you can see would happen if the exposure were calculated based on metering the leftmost, black patch. The light meter sees less light reflecting from the black square than it would see from a gray middle-tone subject, and so figures, "Aha! I need to add exposure to brighten this subject up to a middle gray!" That lightens the "black" patch, so it now appears to be gray.

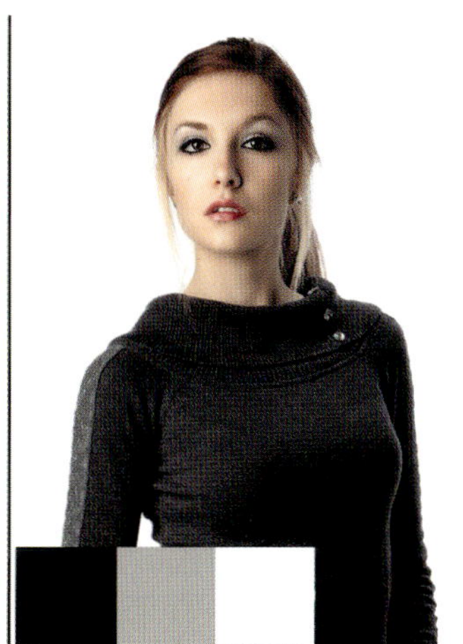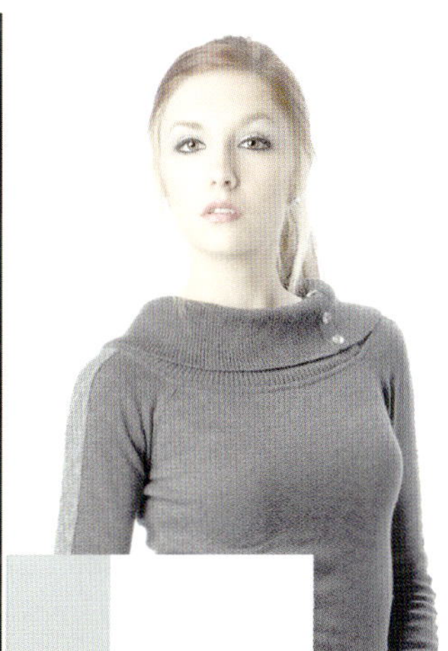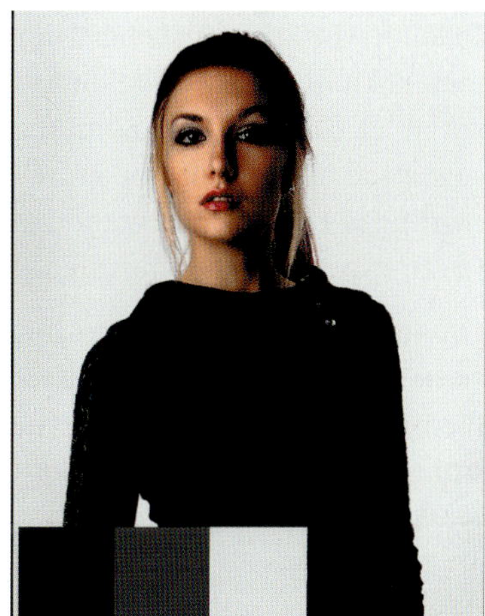

Figure 4.3 Exposure based on the middle-gray tone in the center of the card is accurate (left). Metering the black square, the black patch looks gray, the gray patch appears to be a light gray, and the white square is seriously overexposed (center). With exposure calculated from the white patch, the photo is underexposed (right).

But now the patch in the middle that was *originally* middle gray is overexposed and becomes light gray. And the white square at right is now seriously overexposed and loses detail in the highlights, which have become a featureless white. Our human subject is similarly overexposed. You should always be *aware* when overexposure occurs but note that it's not *always* a bad thing. Some slight overexposures add a dreamy look to an image; once you know how the rules are derived, you'll know how and when to break them.

Underexposed

The third possibility in this simplified scenario is that the light meter might measure the illumination bouncing off the white patch and try to render *that* tone as a middle gray. A lot of light is reflected by the white square, so the exposure is *reduced*, bringing that patch closer to a middle gray tone. The patches that were originally gray and black are now rendered too dark, as you can see at right in Figure 4.3. Clearly, measuring the gray card—or a substitute that reflects about the same amount of light—is the only way to ensure that the exposure is precisely correct.

Metering Mid-Tones

As you can see, the ideal way to measure exposure is to meter from a subject that reflects 12 to 18 percent of the light that reaches it. If you want the most precise exposure calculations, the solution is to use a stand-in, such as the evenly illuminated gray card I mentioned. But, because the standard Kodak gray card reflects 18 percent of the light that reaches it and, as I said, your camera is calibrated for a somewhat lighter 12 percent tone, you would need to add about one-half stop *more* exposure than the value metered from the card. Of course, in most situations, it's not necessary to do this. Your camera's light meter will do a good job of calculating the right exposure, especially if you use the exposure tips in the next section. But I felt that explaining exactly what is going on during exposure calculation would help you understand how your camera's metering system works.

In some very bright scenes (like a snowy landscape or a lava field), you won't have a mid-tone to meter. Another substitute for a gray card is the palm of a human hand (the backside of the hand is too variable). But a human palm, regardless of ethnic group, is even brighter than a standard gray card, so instead of one-half stop more exposure, you need to add one additional stop. That is, if your meter reading is 1/500th of a second at f/11, use 1/500th second at f/8 or 1/200th second at f/11 instead. (Both exposures are equivalent.)

Or, you might want to resort to using an evenly illuminated gray card mentioned earlier. Small versions are available that can be tucked in a camera bag. Place it in your frame near your main subject, facing the camera, and with the exact same even illumination falling on it that is falling on your subject. Then, use the Spot metering function (described in the next section) to calculate exposure.

But the standard Kodak gray card reflects 18 percent of the light while, as I noted, your camera is calibrated for a somewhat darker 12 percent tone. If you insisted on getting a perfect exposure, you would need to add about one-half stop more exposure than the value provided by taking the light meter reading from the card. Of course, in most situations, it's not necessary to do this.

Your camera's light meter will do a good job of calculating the right exposure, especially if you use the exposure tips in the next section. But I felt that explaining exactly what is going on during exposure calculation would help you understand how your Z5's metering system works.

In serious photography, you'll want to choose the *metering mode* (the pattern that determines how brightness is evaluated) and the *exposure mode* (determines how the appropriate shutter speed and aperture is set). I'll describe both aspects in later sections.

ORIGIN OF THE 18 PERCENT "MYTH"

Why are so many photographers under the impression that camera light meters are calibrated to the 18 percent "standard," rather than the true value, which may be 12 to 14 percent, depending on the vendor? You'll find this misinformation in an alarming number of places. I've seen the 18 percent "myth" taught in camera classes; I've found it in books, and even been given this wrong information from the technical staff of camera vendors. (They should know better—the same vendors' engineers who design and calibrate the cameras have the right figure.)

The most common explanation is that during a revision of Kodak's instructions for its gray cards in 1977, the advice to open up an extra half stop was omitted, and a whole generation of shooters grew up thinking that a measurement off a gray card could be used as-is. Kodak restored the proviso in 1997, it's said, but by then it was too late.

EXTERNAL METERS CAN BE CALIBRATED

The light meters built into your Z5 are calibrated at the factory and can only be changed using the Fine Tune Optimal Exposure option (Custom Setting b4). But if you use a hand-held incident or reflective light meter, you *can* calibrate it, using the instructions supplied with your meter. Because a hand-held meter *can* be calibrated to the 18 percent gray standard (or any other value you choose), my rant about the myth of the 18 percent gray card doesn't apply.

MODES, MODES, AND MORE MODES

Call them modes or methods, the Nikon Z5 seems to have a lot of different sets of options that are described using similar terms. Here's how to sort them out:

- **Metering method.** These modes determine the *parts of the image* within the sensor that are examined in order to calculate exposure. The Z5 may look at many different points within the image, segregating them by zone (Matrix metering); examining the same number of points, but giving greater weight to those located in the middle of the frame (Center-weighted metering); evaluating only a limited number of points in a limited area (Spot metering); or adjusting exposure to preserve detail in highlights (Highlight-weighted metering).

- **Exposure method.** These modes (Program, Aperture-priority, Shutter-priority, or Manual) determine *which* settings are used to expose the image. The Z5 may adjust the shutter speed, the aperture, or both, or even ISO setting (if Auto ISO is active), depending on the method you choose.

Choosing a Metering Method

The Z5 has four different schemes for evaluating the light received by its exposure sensors: Matrix, Center-weighted, Spot, and Highlight-weighted metering. Select the mode you want from the *i* menu (or you can assign the metering adjustment function to a custom control using Custom Setting f2, as noted in the sidebar below).

INSTANT SWITCHING

If you frequently use one metering method, but occasionally like to switch to another method on the fly, you can redefine the Z5's Fn1 or Fn2 buttons to shift to your alternate mode instantly. The buttons can be programmed to provide Matrix metering, Center-weighted metering, Spot metering, or Highlight-weighted metering (as well as other functions discussed in Chapter 12), using Custom Setting f2.

The really cool thing is that you can define one button for, say, Center-weighted metering, another one for Spot metering, and then set the main metering mode switch to Matrix, and thus be able to switch among those three on a whim. I've done this as a way to compare the exposure settings of the three metering methods while composing a single image in the viewfinder. I've also found the capability useful when I'm, say, working with Matrix metering and want to zero in on a particular area of the frame temporarily using Spot metering. The indicators in the viewfinder will help you remember what metering mode you've switched to. (See Figure 4.4.)

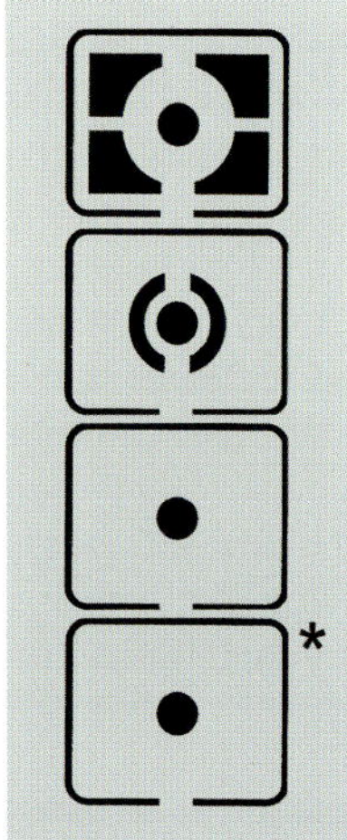

Figure 4.4 Top to bottom: Matrix, Center-weighted, Spot, and Highlight-weighted metering icons.

Your Z5 calculates exposure by measuring the light that passes through the lens and strikes the sensor. These pixels are said to be able to detect light over a range of –4 to +17 EV at ISO 100. That translates into exposures from sixteen minutes at f/16 to 1/2000th second at f/16.

In everyday terms, 0 EV represents the illumination you might see outdoors at night under a full moon, while the brightest daytime scene you're likely to encounter (a snow scene in full daylight) would be 16 EV. Your Z5 is able to *detect* photons under an extremely broad EV span—two stops dimmer than full moonlight, and one stop brighter than a daylight snow scene. However, your camera's ability to *capture* images is limited to a much smaller range. Note that the sensor's dynamic range (the tones it can preserve in your final image) is less than the full range of tones it can *detect*. It's easy to get these two separate aspects confused.

Matrix Metering

For Matrix metering mode, the Z5 reads the light falling on the sensor and compares the brightness of many areas using a matrix array. When Matrix metering is active, an icon indicator appears in the photo information screen, which you can summon by pressing the DISP button until it's shown. Then, the Z5 evaluates the differences between the many zones, and compares them with a built-in database of 30,000 actual images to make an educated guess about what kind of picture you're taking. For example, if the top sections of a picture are much lighter than the bottom portions, the algorithm can assume that the scene is a landscape photo with lots of sky. However, if there is a lighter area in the center of the frame, and the camera detects skin tones, the Z5 will assume that you're shooting a portrait and not a landscape photo and expose for the human subject. A typical image suitable for Matrix metering is shown in Figure 4.5. (The Matrix Metering icon is shown at upper left for reference; it does not appear overlaid on your image or in the viewfinder/monitor display!)

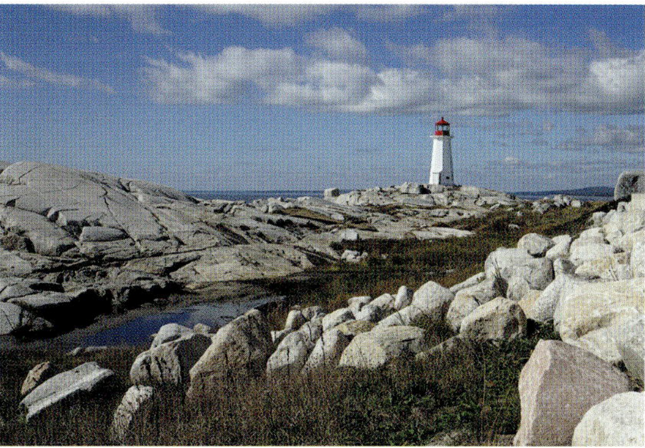

Figure 4.5 Complex scenes, like the one at right, lend themselves to the exposure interpretation provided by Matrix metering.

Matrix metering mode can often recognize many types of bright scenes and automatically increase the exposure to reduce the risk of a dark photo. This will be useful when your subject is a snow-covered landscape or a close-up of a bride in white. Granted, you may occasionally need to use a bit of exposure compensation, but often, the exposure will be close to accurate even without it. In my experience, Matrix metering is most successful with light-toned scenes on bright days and is especially good when humans are in the frame. When shooting in dark, overcast conditions, it's more likely to underexpose a scene of that type.

Exposure meters have long used brightness to calculate correct exposure. The Nikon Z5's advanced technology uses other information to make more intelligent settings. These factors include:

- **Patterns.** As mentioned earlier, the camera compares exposure across the entire sensor with a database of tens of thousands of picture types, looking for differences among pixels, and similarities to images in the database. When it finds a match, it uses that information as a basis for its recommended exposure. If the contrast in a scene is high enough that the sensor probably won't be able to preserve detail in both highlights and shadows, in most cases, the Z5 will favor the highlights. As you'll learn later in this chapter, once highlights are lost, they are gone forever, but it is sometimes possible to retrieve data in shadow areas. If you are shooting RAW, the exposure setting and other adjustments can often boost information in darker areas.

- **Colors.** The camera can enhance its readings based on the colors detected in the frame. Large areas of blue in the upper part of the image can be deemed to be sky, greens, or foliage, while skin tones may indicate human beings.

- **Autofocus area.** Whether you or the camera selects which autofocus zone is used, the exposure system assumes, logically, that the part of the image that is in focus contains your subject matter.

- **Distance and focal length.** The Z5 is able to use the distance and focal length supplied by your Z-mount lenses to better calculate what kind of scene you have framed. For example, if you're shooting a portrait with a longer focal-length lens focused to about 5 to 12 feet from the camera, and the upper half of the scene is very bright, the camera assumes you would prefer to meter for the rest of the image, and will discount the bright area. However, if the camera has a wide-angle lens attached and is focused at infinity, the Z5 can assume you're taking a landscape photo and take the bright upper area into account to produce better looking sky and clouds.

Matrix metering is best for most general subjects, because it is able to intelligently analyze a scene and make an excellent guess of what kind of subject you're shooting a great deal of the time. The camera can tell the difference between low-contrast and high-contrast subjects by looking at the range of differences in brightness across the scene. Because the Z5 has a fairly good idea about what kind of subject matter you are shooting, it can underexpose slightly when appropriate to preserve highlight detail when image contrast is high. (It's often possible to pull detail out of shadows that are too dark using an image editor, but once highlights are converted to white pixels, they are gone forever.)

CAUTION If you're using a strong filter, including a polarizing filter, split-color filter, or neutral-density filter (particularly a graduated neutral-density filter), you should switch from Matrix metering to Center-weighted, because the filter can affect the relationships between the different areas of the frame used to calculate a Matrix exposure. For example, a polarizing filter produces a sky that is darker than usual, hindering the Matrix algorithm's recognition of a landscape photo. Extra-dark or colored filters disturb the color relationships used for color Matrix metering, too.

Center-weighted Metering

In this mode, the exposure meter emphasizes a zone measuring 12mm in the center of the frame to calculate exposure. This type of metering was the only available option with cameras some decades ago, and was considered an upgrade from averaging, which simply based exposure on an average of the illumination of the entire frame.

With Center-weighted metering, you end up with conventional metering without any "intelligent" scene evaluation. The light meter considers brightness in the entire frame but places the greatest emphasis on a large area in the center of the frame (shown in blue in Figure 4.6, left), on the theory that, for most pictures, the main subject will not be located far off-center.

About 75 percent of the exposure is based on the selected 12mm central area, and the remaining 25 percent of the exposure is based on the rest of the frame. So, if the Z5 reads the center portion and determines that the exposure for that region should be f/4 at 1/250th second, while the outer area, which is a bit darker, calls for f/16 at 1/250th second, the camera will give the center portion the most weight and arrive at a final exposure on the order of f/5.6 at 1/250th second.

Of course, Center-weighted metering is most effective when the subject in the central area is a mid-tone. Even then, if your main subject is surrounded by large, extremely bright or very dark areas, the exposure might not be exactly right. (You might need to use exposure compensation, a feature discussed shortly.) However, this scheme works well in many situations if you don't want to use one of the other modes, for scenes like the one shown in Figure 4.6. This mode can be useful for close-ups of subjects like flowers, or for portraits. You can adjust the size of the area assigned the greatest

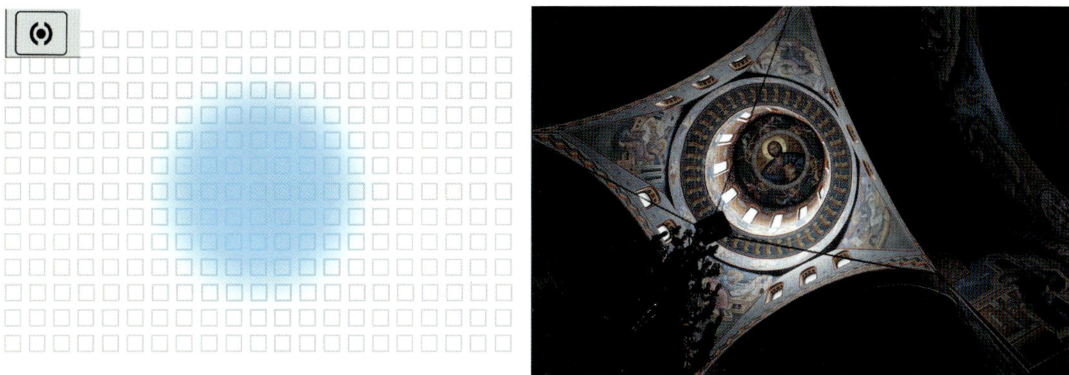

Figure 4.6 Scenes with the main subject in the center, surrounded by areas that are significantly darker or lighter, are perfect for Center-weighted metering.

weight using Custom Setting b3, as described in Chapter 12. You can select the default 12mm circle, or choose "Average" (which in effect, covers the entire screen to produce what is called Average metering). Since Center-weighted metering is "fuzzy" anyway, I find the default 12mm to be the best compromise.

Spot Metering

Spot metering is favored by those of us who have used a hand-held light meter to measure exposure at various points (such as metering highlights and shadows separately). However, you can use Spot metering in any situation where you want to individually measure the light reflecting from light, midtone, or dark areas of your subject—or any combination of areas.

This mode confines the reading to a limited 4mm area in the viewfinder, making up only 1.5 percent of the image, as shown by the blue circle in Figure 4.7. The circle is centered on the *current focus point* (which can be *any* of the available focus points, *not* just the center one shown in the figure), *but is larger than the focus point*, so don't fall into the trap of believing that exposure is being measured only within the viewfinder indicators that represent the active focus point. This is the only metering method you can use to tell the Z5 exactly where to measure exposure. However, if you have selected Auto-area AF, only the center focus point is used to spot meter.

You'll find Spot metering useful when you want to base exposure on a small area in the frame. If that area is in the center of the frame, so much the better. If not, you'll have to make your meter reading for an off-center subject using an appropriate focus point, and then lock exposure by pressing the shutter release halfway, or by pressing an AE-L/AF-L button you may have defined using Custom Setting f2. This mode is best for subjects where the background is significantly brighter or darker.

If you Spot meter a very light-toned area or a dark-toned area, you will get underexposure or over-exposure, respectively; you would need to use an override for more accurate results. On the other hand, you can Spot meter a small mid-tone subject surrounded by a sky with big white clouds or by an indigo blue wall and get a good exposure. (The light meter ignores the subject's surroundings so they do not affect the exposure setting.) That would not be possible with Center-weighted metering, which considers brightness in a much larger area.

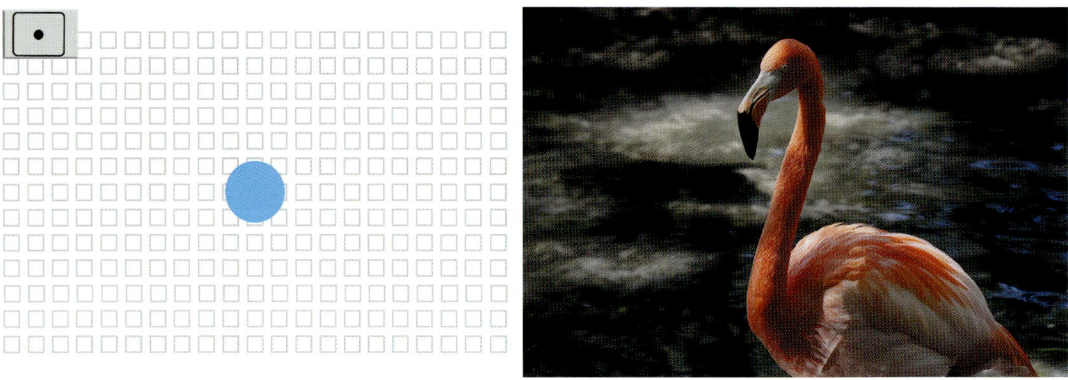

Figure 4.7 Spot metering calculates exposure based on a center spot that's only 1.5 percent of the image area, centered around the current focus point.

Using Spot Metering

Matrix and Center-weighted metering basically have few options to worry about. They are both affected by exposure compensation changes and Custom Setting b4: Fine-Tune Optimal Exposure adjustments. Spot metering, on the other hand, can benefit from your input in selecting the spot used. Here are some considerations to keep in mind:

- **Moving the spot.** Remember that you don't move the metering spot itself; the Z5 uses the current *focus* spot. So, you must be using an AF-area mode that allows changing the AF spot, which happens to be any of the AF-area modes *except* Auto-area AF. In that mode the center focus point is *always* used as the metering spot, and you cannot change it.

- **Choosing a compatible AF-area mode.** Use the *i* menu to cycle among the available AF areas, which differ depending on the focus mode you've chosen. All these AF-area modes will allow you to switch the AF point to any of the available focus areas in the display:

  - **AF-S focus mode:** Pinpoint AF, Single-point-AF, Wide-area AF (Small), or Wide-area AF (Large). (**Note:** Dynamic-area AF is not available.)

  - **AF-C focus mode:** Single-point-AF, Dynamic-area AF, Wide-area AF (Small), or Wide-area AF (Large). (**Note:** Pinpoint-AF is not available.)

  - **Manual focus mode:** Only Single-point selection is available. **Note:** With Manual focus, the Z5 does not autofocus, of course; the position of the focus point is used only for the electronic rangefinder and Spot metering functions. You can find information on all the focus and AF-area modes in Chapter 5.

- **Wrap around.** You'll use the sub-selector joystick or the multi selector's directional buttons to move the AF point around within the display—and the metering spot with it. The focus point's movement will stop at the left/right/top/bottom edges *unless* you've turned on focus point wrap-around in Custom Setting a9.

- **When using Auto-area AF.** If you've selected Auto-area AF, the center focus point will always be used—*even if the camera selects a different point for the autofocus function*. That's actually a positive: since in Auto-area AF mode you don't know what the focus spot will be until you press the shutter release halfway, it's *good* to know that the Z5 will be using the center spot. While Spot metering is most useful when not using Auto-area AF, it still functions, albeit in a less flexible way.

- **Reminder: when the focus point moves, the spot metering point moves, too.** If you're using Dynamic-area AF and continuous autofocus (AF-C, described in Chapter 5), the Z5 may move the focus point you originally selected and base focus on the surrounding focus points. *The metering area will tag along.*

A good example of a scene where you might want to use Spot metering is shown in Figure 4.7, which shows an egret surrounded by very dark foliage. The illumination might have fooled both Matrix and Center-weighted metering (although Center-weighted might have come close), but Spot metering allowed taking a reading directly from the bird's plumage. While I preferred Spot metering in this case, another option might have been Highlight-weighted metering, described next.

Highlight-weighted Metering

In this metering mode, the Z5 examines your entire scene, just as it does using Matrix metering. It is *not* a spot metering mode, despite its icon, which is the same as the Spot icon, with an asterisk added. With this mode, the camera's Expeed 6 processor seeks out highlight areas of your image and bases exposure on a setting that will keep those highlights from being overexposed. Less emphasis ("weight") is given to non-highlight areas. That's why Highlight-weighted *might* have worked for the egret image above, but it's actually better suited for images in which the highlights are spread over a larger area of the frame.

So, if you're shooting spotlit performers on-stage at a concert or play, the Z5 is able to calculate the correct exposure using the performers, and ignoring, for the most part, the dark surroundings. You'd have your choice of measuring exposure in Spot mode, as described in the previous section, placing the metering spot on the dancer's face or shirt, or, you could select Highlight-weighted metering and allow the camera to identify the performer when figuring exposure. Your results might be similar with either, depending on how well you "placed" the Spot area and how cleverly the Z5 sorts out your subject from the background. I tend to use Spot mode when the area I want to meter is clearly defined, and Highlight-weighted when there is a range of highlights that I'd like to preserve, as in the photo of Billy Zoom, from the LA punk band X, shown in Figure 4.8.

LOCKING EXPOSURE

An important tool when using any metering method is the ability to *lock* exposure once you've set shutter speed, aperture, and ISO to your satisfaction, allowing you to reframe your image before taking a picture. The default behavior of the sub-selector center button is AE-L/AF-L, which locks both exposure and autofocus. However, you can define another control for that function using Custom Setting f2: Custom Controls, described in Chapter 12.

Your defined control can be set to function as an AE/AF lock or AE Lock Only (which is useful if you're using back-button focus, described in the next chapter). The same Custom Setting can also be used to define a Shutter Speed and Aperture Lock button, which effectively locks exposure by freezing the shutter speed in Aperture-priority mode and aperture in Shutter-priority mode.

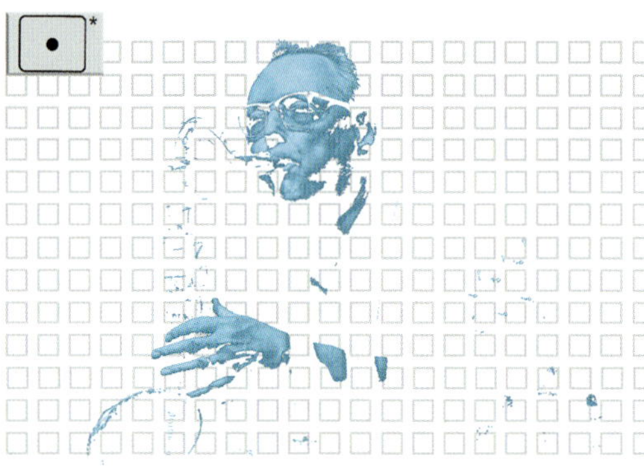

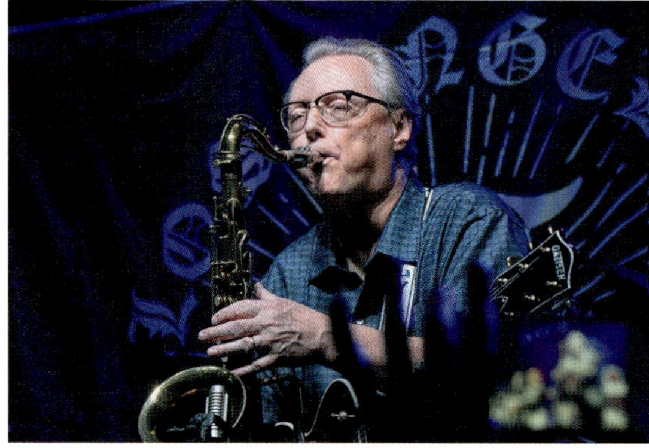

Figure 4.8 Highlight-weighted metering is especially useful for stage performances.

Choosing an Exposure Method

You'll find four methods for choosing the appropriate shutter speed and aperture when using the semi-automatic/manual modes. You can choose among Aperture-priority, Shutter-priority, Program, or Manual options by rotating the mode dial on the top-right shoulder of the camera. Your decision on which is best for a given shooting situation will depend on things like your need for lots of (or less) depth-of-field, a desire to freeze action or allow motion blur, or how much noise you find acceptable in an image. Each of the Z5's exposure methods emphasize one aspect of image capture or another. This section introduces you to all four.

Aperture-Priority

In Aperture-priority (A) mode, you specify the lens opening used, and the Z5 will set a suitable shutter speed appropriate for the aperture and the ISO sensitivity in use. If you change the aperture, from f/5.6 to f/11, for example, the camera will automatically set a longer shutter speed to maintain the same exposure, using guidance from the built-in light meter. (I discussed the concept of equivalent exposure earlier in this chapter and provided the equivalent exposure table.)

Aperture-priority is especially good when you want to use a particular lens opening to achieve a desired effect. Perhaps you'd like to use the smallest f/stop possible (such as f/22) to maximize depth-of-field (DOF) in a close-up picture. Or, you might want to work with a large f/stop to throw everything except your main subject out of focus, as in Figure 4.9. Maybe you'd just like to "lock in" a particular f/stop because it's the sharpest available aperture with that lens. Or, you might prefer to use, say, f/2.8 on a lens with a maximum aperture of f/1.4, because you want the best compromise between shutter speed and sharpness.

Aperture-priority can even be used to specify a *range* of shutter speeds you want to use under varying lighting conditions, which seems almost contradictory. But think about it. You're shooting a soccer game outdoors with a telephoto lens and want a relatively high shutter speed, but you don't care if the speed changes a little should the sun duck behind a cloud. Set your Z5 to A, and adjust the aperture until a shutter speed of, say, 1/1000th second is selected at your current ISO setting. (In bright sunlight at ISO 400, that aperture is likely to be around f/11.) Then, go ahead and shoot,

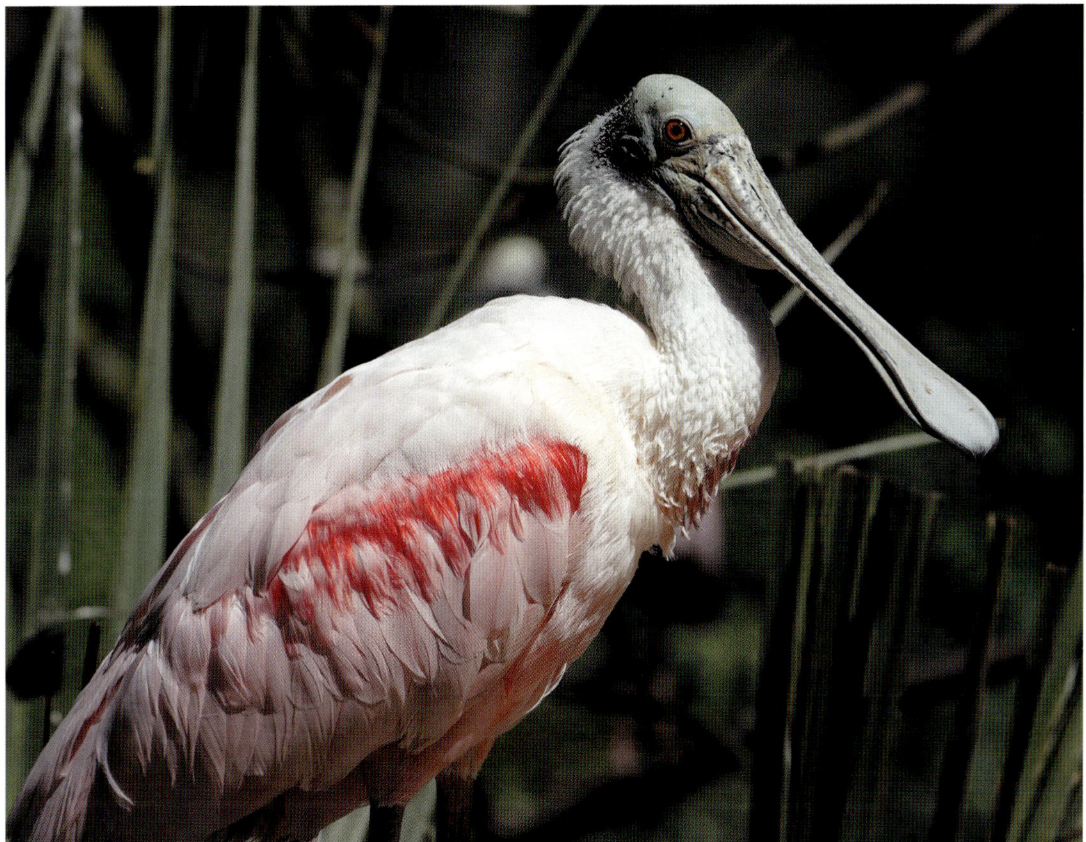

Figure 4.9 Use Aperture-priority to "lock in" a large f/stop when you want to blur distracting elements, or emphasize the main subject in the photo, in this case a roseate spoonbill.

knowing that your Z5 will maintain that f/11 aperture (for sufficient depth-of-field as the soccer players move about the field), but will drop down to 1/640th or 1/500th second if necessary should the lighting change a little.

When the shutter speed indicator in the viewfinder and the top-panel monochrome LCD blink, that indicates that the Z5 is unable to select an appropriate shutter speed at the selected aperture and that over- or underexposure will occur at the current ISO setting. That's the major pitfall of using A: you might select an f/stop that is too small or too large to allow an optimal exposure with the available shutter speeds. For example, if you choose f/2.8 as your aperture and the illumination is quite bright (say, at the beach or in snow), even your camera's fastest shutter speed might not be able to cut down the amount of light reaching the sensor to provide the right exposure. Or, if you select f/8 in a dimly lit room, you might find yourself shooting with a very slow shutter speed that can cause blurring from subject movement or camera shake. Aperture-priority is best used by those with a bit of experience in choosing settings. Many seasoned photographers leave their Z5 set on A all the time. The exposure indicator scale in the display indicate the amount of under- or overexposure.

When to use Aperture-priority:

- **General landscape photography.** The Z5 is a great camera for landscape photography, of course, because its 24MP resolution allows making huge, gorgeous prints, as well as smaller prints that are filled with eye-popping detail. Aperture-priority is a good tool for ensuring that your landscape is sharp from foreground to infinity, if you select an f/stop that provides maximum depth-of-field, as shown in Figure 4.10.

  If you use A mode and select an aperture like f/11 or f/16, it's your responsibility to make sure the shutter speed selected is fast enough to avoid losing detail to camera shake, or that the Z5 is mounted on a tripod. One thing that new landscape photographers fail to account for is the movement of distant leaves and tree branches. When seeking the ultimate in sharpness, go ahead and use Aperture-priority, but boost ISO sensitivity a bit, if necessary, to provide a sufficiently fast shutter speed, whether shooting hand-held or with a tripod.

- **Specific landscape situations.** Aperture-priority is also useful when you have no objection to using a long shutter speed, or, particularly, *want* the Z5 to select one. Waterfalls are a perfect example. You can use A mode, set your camera to ISO 100, use a small f/stop, and let the camera select a longer shutter speed that will allow the water to blur as it flows. Indeed, you might need to use a neutral-density filter to get a sufficiently long shutter speed. But Aperture-priority mode is a good start.

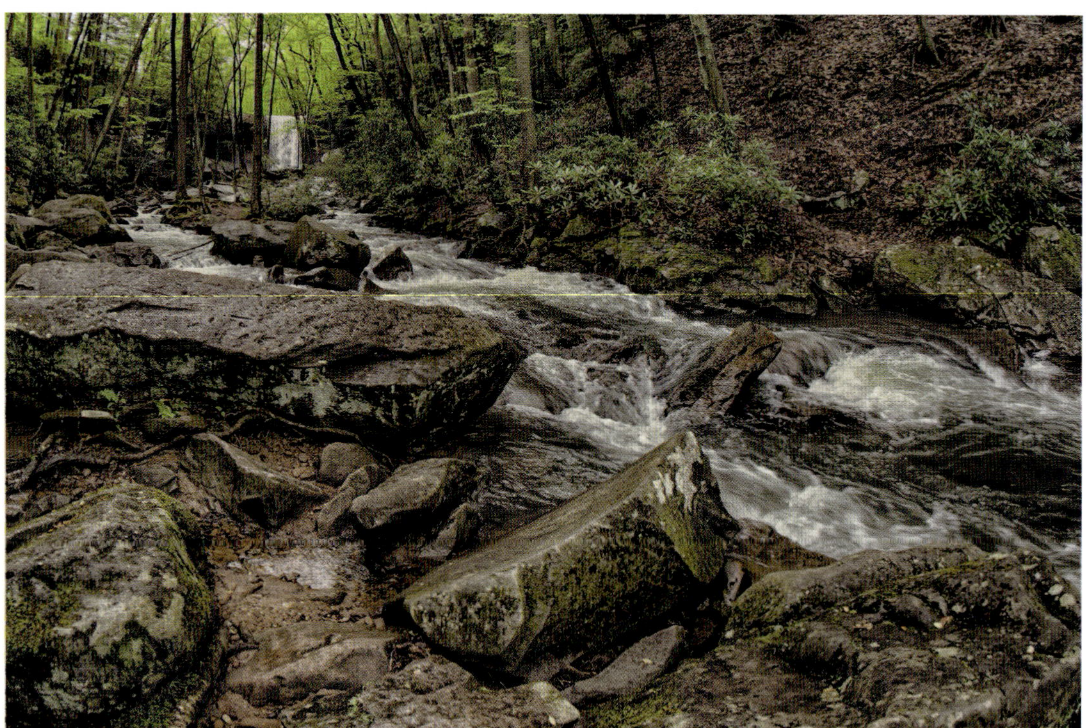

Figure 4.10 Extra depth-of-field came in handy when shooting Cucumber Falls in Ohiopyle, Pennsylvania.

- **Portrait photography.** Portraits are the most common applications of selective focus. A medium-large aperture (say, f/5.6 or f/8) with a longer lens/zoom setting (in the 85mm-135mm range) will allow the background behind your portrait subject to blur. A *very* large aperture (I frequently shoot wide open with my 85mm f/1.4G Nikkor) lets you apply selective focus to your subject's *face*. With a three-quarters view of your subject, as long as his or her eyes are sharp, it's okay if the far ear or her hair is out of focus.

- **When you want to ensure optimal sharpness.** All lenses have an aperture or two at which they perform best, providing the level of sharpness you expect from a camera with the resolution of the Z5. That's usually about two stops down from wide open, and thus will vary depending on the maximum aperture of the lens.

- **Close-up/Macro photography.** Depth-of-field is typically very shallow when shooting macro photos, and you'll want to choose your f/stop carefully. Perhaps you might want to use a wider stop to emphasize your subject. Or, you might need the smallest aperture you can get away with to maximize depth-of-field. Aperture-priority mode comes in very useful when shooting close-up pictures, too. Because macro work is frequently done with the Z5 mounted on a tripod, and your close-up subjects, if not living creatures, may not be moving much, a longer shutter speed isn't a problem. Aperture-priority can be your preferred choice.

Shutter-Priority

Shutter-priority (S) is the inverse of Aperture-priority: you choose the shutter speed you'd like to use, and the camera's metering system selects the appropriate f/stop. Perhaps you're shooting action photos and you want to use the absolute fastest shutter speed available with your camera; in other cases, you might want to use a slow shutter speed to add some blur to an action photo that would be mundane if the action were completely frozen. Shutter-priority mode gives you some control over how much action-freezing capability your digital camera brings to bear in a particular situation.

Take care when using a slow shutter speed such as 1/8th second or slower, because you'll get blurring from camera shake unless you're using a lens with vibration reduction (described in Chapter 7), or have mounted the Z5 on a tripod or other firm support.

You'll also encounter the same problem as with Aperture-priority when you select a shutter speed that's too long or too short for correct exposure under some conditions. As in A mode, it's possible to choose an inappropriate shutter speed. If that's the case, the shutter speed indicator in the display will blink.

When to use Shutter-priority:

- **To reduce blur from subject motion.** Set the shutter speed of the Z5 to a higher value to reduce the amount of blur from subjects that are moving. The exact speed will vary depending on how fast your subject is moving and how much blur is acceptable. You might want to freeze a basketball player in mid-dunk with a 1/1000th second shutter speed or use 1/200th second to allow the spinning wheels of a motocross racer to blur a tiny bit to add the feeling of motion.

- **To add blur from subject motion.** There are times when you want a subject to blur, say, when shooting waterfalls with the camera set for a one- or two-second exposure in Shutter-priority mode.

- **To add blur from camera motion when *you* are moving.** Say you're panning to follow a pair of relay runners. You might want to use Shutter-priority mode and set the Z5 for 1/60th second, so that the background will blur as you pan with the runners. The shutter speed will be fast enough to provide a sharp image of the athletes, while reducing their distracting background to a blur. (See Figure 4.11.)

- **To reduce blur from camera motion when *you* are moving.** In other situations, the camera may be in motion, say, because you're shooting from a moving train or auto, and you want to minimize the amount of blur caused by the motion of the camera. Shutter-priority is a good choice here, too.

- **Landscape photography hand-held.** If you can't use a tripod for your landscape shots, you'll still probably want the sharpest image possible. Shutter-priority can allow you to specify a shutter speed that's fast enough to reduce or eliminate the effects of camera shake. Just make sure that your ISO setting is high enough that the Z5 will select an aperture with sufficient depth-of-field, too.

- **Concerts and stage performances.** I shoot a lot of concerts with my 70-200mm f/2.8 VR Nikkor lens, using the FTZ adapter if I elect to work with my Z5, and have discovered that, when vibration reduction is taken into account, a shutter speed of 1/160th second is fast enough—along with vibration reduction—to eliminate camera shake that can result from hand-holding the Z5 with this lens, and also to avoid blur from the movement of all but the most energetic performers. I use Shutter-priority and set the ISO so the camera will select an aperture in the f/4–5.6 range.

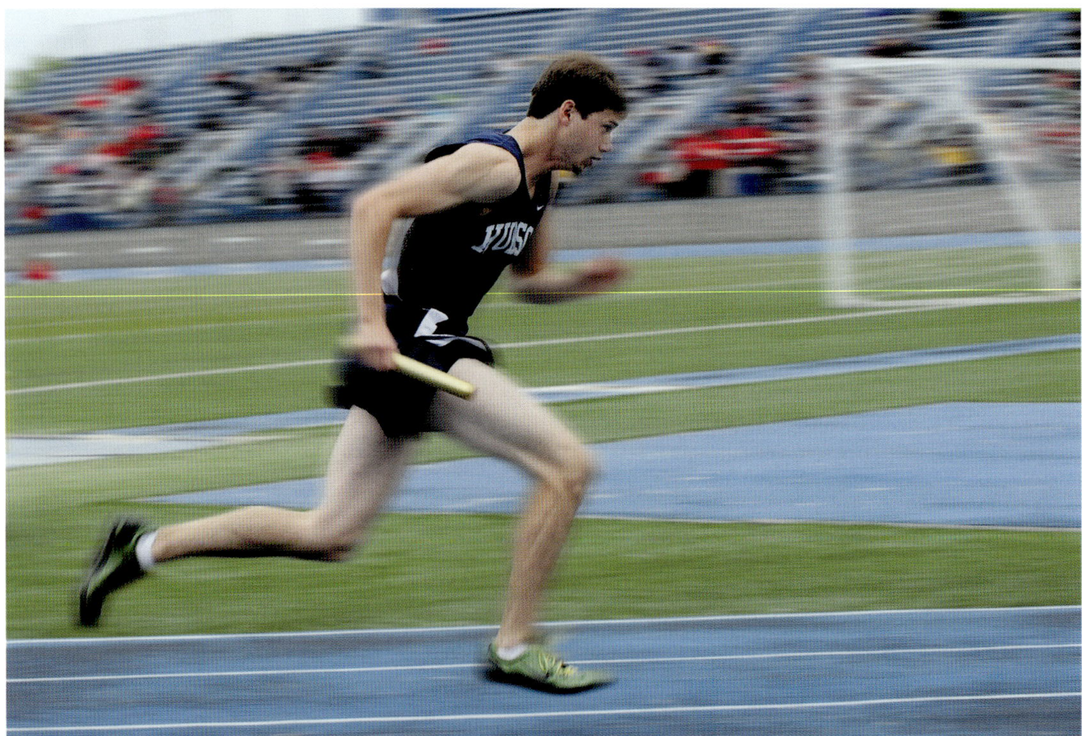

Figure 4.11 Shutter-priority allows you to specify a speed that will render a moving subject like this relay runner reasonably sharp as you pan.

Program Mode

Program mode (P) uses the Z5's built-in smarts to select the correct f/stop and shutter speed using a database of picture information that tells it which combination of shutter speed and aperture will work best for a particular photo. If the correct exposure cannot be achieved at the current ISO setting, the shutter speed and aperture will blink in the display. You can then boost or reduce the ISO to increase or decrease sensitivity.

The Z5's recommended exposure can be overridden if you want. Use the EV (exposure value) setting feature (described later, because it also applies to S and A modes) to add or subtract exposure from the metered value. And, as I mentioned earlier in this chapter, in Program mode you can rotate the main command dial to change from the recommended setting to an equivalent setting (as shown previously in Table 4.1) that produces the same exposure, but using a different combination of f/stop and shutter speed.

This is called *Flexible Program* by Nikon. Rotate the main command dial left to reduce the size of the aperture (going from, say, f/4 to f/5.6), so that the Z5 will automatically use a slower shutter speed (going from, say, 1/200th second to 1/125th second). Rotate the main command dial right to use a larger f/stop, while automatically producing a shorter shutter speed that provides the same equivalent exposure as metered in P mode. An asterisk appears next to the P in the viewfinder/monitor display, so you'll know you've overridden the Z5's default program setting. Your adjustment remains in force until you rotate the main command dial until the asterisk disappears, or you switch to a different exposure mode, or turn the Z5 off.

MAKING EV CHANGES

Sometimes you'll want more or less exposure than indicated by the Z5's metering system. Perhaps you want to underexpose to create a silhouette effect or overexpose to produce a high-key look. It's easy to use the Z5's exposure compensation system to override the exposure recommendations. Press the exposure compensation (EV) button on the top of the camera (just southeast of the shutter release). Then rotate the main command dial left to add exposure, and right to subtract exposure. The EV change you've made remains for the exposures that follow, until you manually zero out the EV setting. The EV plus/minus icon appears in the display to warn you that an exposure compensation change has been entered. You can increase or decrease exposure over a range of plus or minus five stops. (If you've activated Easy Exposure Compensation using Custom Setting b2, as described in Chapter 12, you don't have to hold down the EV button; rotating the main or sub-command dials alone changes the EV value when using Program, Aperture-priority, Shutter-priority, or Manual exposure modes.)

When to use Program mode:

- **When you're in a hurry to get a grab shot.** The Z5 will do a pretty good job of calculating an appropriate exposure for you, without any input from you.
- **When you hand your camera to a novice.** Set the Z5 to P, hand the camera to your friend, relative, or *trustworthy* stranger you meet in front of the Eiffel Tower, point to the shutter release button and viewfinder, and say, "Look through here, and press this button." I like this option more than using Auto mode, because I can make slight adjustments to suit before handing over my camera.

- **When no special shutter speed or aperture settings are needed.** If your subject doesn't require special anti- or pro-blur techniques, and depth-of-field or selective focus aren't important, use P as a general-purpose setting. You can still make adjustments to increase/decrease depth-of-field or add/reduce motion blur with a minimum of fuss.

Manual Exposure

Part of being an experienced photographer comes from knowing when to rely on your Z5's automation (with P mode), when to go semi-automatic (with S or A), and when to set exposure manually (using M). Some photographers actually prefer to set their exposure manually, as the Z5 will be happy to provide an indication of when its metering system judges your manual settings provide the proper exposure, using the analog exposure scale at the bottom of the viewfinder.

Manual exposure can come in handy in some situations. You might be taking a silhouette photo and find that none of the exposure modes or EV correction features give you exactly the effect you want. Set the exposure manually to use the exact shutter speed and f/stop you need. Or, you might be working in a studio environment using multiple flash units. The additional flash are triggered by slave devices (gadgets that set off the flash when they sense the light from another flash unit, or, perhaps from a radio or infrared remote control). Your camera's exposure meter doesn't compensate for the extra illumination, so you need to set the aperture manually.

Because, depending on your proclivities, you might not need to set exposure manually very often, you should still make sure you understand how it works. Fortunately, the Z5 makes setting exposure manually very easy. Just press the mode dial lock release and rotate the mode dial to M to change to Manual mode, and then turn the main command dial to set the shutter speed, and the sub-command dial to adjust the aperture. Press the shutter release halfway or press your defined AE lock button, and the exposure scale in the viewfinder shows you how far your chosen setting diverges from the metered exposure.

When to use Manual exposure:

- **When working in the studio.** If you're working in a studio environment, you generally have total control over the lighting and can set exposure exactly as you want. The last thing you need is for the Z5 to interpret the scene and make adjustments of its own. Use M, and shutter speed, aperture, and (as long as you don't use ISO-Auto) the ISO setting are totally up to you.

- **When using non-dedicated flash.** The Nikon Creative Lighting System (CLS) and the new Advanced Lighting System (ALS, introduced with the SB-5000) are cool, and can even be used to coordinate use of your Z5 with external compatible dedicated flash units, like the SB-5000 or SB-910. But if you're working with non-CLS flash units, particularly studio flash plugged into the PC/X adapter attached to the Z5's accessory shoe, the camera has no clue about the intensity of the flash, so you'll have to dial in the appropriate aperture manually.

- **If you're using a hand-held light meter.** The appropriate aperture, both for flash exposures and shots taken under continuous lighting, can be determined by a hand-held light meter, flash meter, or combo meter that measures both ambient illumination and flash. With an external meter, you can measure highlights, shadows, backgrounds, or additional subjects separately, and use Manual exposure to make your settings.

- **When you want to outsmart the metering system.** Your Z5's metering system is "trained" to react to unusual lighting situations, such as backlighting, extra-bright illumination, or low-key images with murky shadows. In many cases, it can counter these "problems" and produce a well-exposed image. But what if you don't *want* a well-exposed image? Manual exposure allows you to produce silhouettes in backlit situations, wash out all the middle tones to produce a luminous look, or underexpose to create a moody or ominous dark-toned photograph.

- **When you want to select shutter speed and aperture.** Aperture- and Shutter-priority give you autoexposure while allowing you to lock in a preferred shutter speed or aperture—but not both at the same time. Manual exposure makes it possible to specify both and *retain* autoexposure capabilities. All you have to do is activate ISO Auto. The Z5 will keep the shutter speed and aperture you want but raise or lower the sensitivity setting to provide an appropriate exposure.

- **When you want extra-long exposures.** None of the semi-automatic modes will give you an exposure longer than 30 seconds. In Manual mode, however, you can spin the command dial past 30 seconds to Time or Bulb and achieve exposures as long as you want. For example, I used a three-minute exposure (and an Aurora Aperture PowerND 16-stop neutral-density filter) to capture the scene shown in Figure 4.12. I'll give you some more uses for time and bulb exposures in Chapter 6.

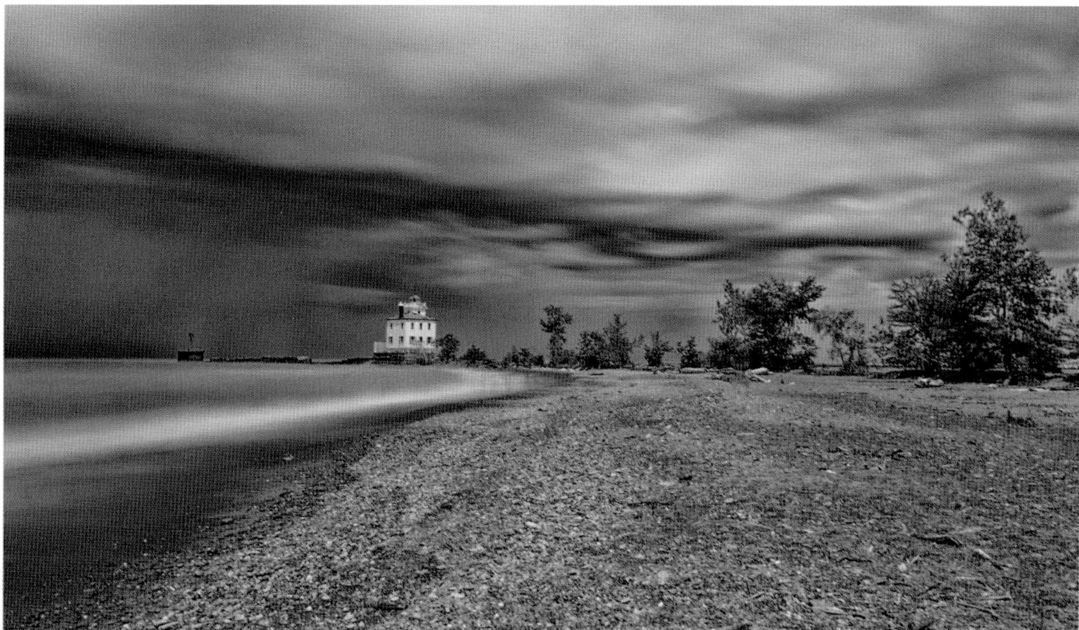

Figure 4.12 A three-minute exposure (using a neutral-density filter) yielded this unusual shot.

Adjusting Exposure with ISO Settings

As I mentioned above, another way of adjusting exposures is by changing the ISO sensitivity setting. Sometimes photographers forget about this option, because the common practice is to set the ISO once for a particular shooting session (say, at ISO 100 for bright sunlight outdoors, or ISO 800 when shooting indoors) and then forget about ISO. ISOs higher than 400 are seen as "bad" or "necessary evils." However, changing the ISO is a valid way of adjusting exposure settings, particularly with the Nikon Z5, which produces good results at ISO settings that create grainy, unusable pictures with some other camera models.

Indeed, I find myself using ISO adjustment as a convenient alternate way of adding or subtracting EV when shooting in Manual mode, and as a quick way of choosing equivalent exposures when in Program or Shutter-priority or Aperture-priority modes. For example, I've selected a Manual exposure with both f/stop and shutter speed suitable for my image using, say, ISO 200. I can change the exposure in 1/3-stop increments by holding down the ISO button located on the top-right shoulder of the camera, and spinning the main command dial one click at a time. The difference in image quality/noise at ISO 200 is negligible if I dial in ISO 160 or ISO 125 to reduce exposure a little or change to ISO 250 or 320 to increase exposure. I keep my preferred f/stop and shutter speed, but still adjust the exposure. (And, as I noted earlier, if ISO Auto is active, I can even allow the Z5 to set the exposure automatically using the f/stop and shutter speed I want.)

Or, perhaps, I am using S mode and the metered exposure at ISO 200 is 1/500th second at f/11. If I decide on the spur of the moment I'd rather use 1/500th second at f/8, I can press the ISO button and spin the main command dial to switch to ISO 100. Of course, it's a good idea to monitor your ISO changes, so you don't end up at ISO 6400 accidentally. An ISO indicator appears in the display to remind you what sensitivity setting has been dialed in.

ISO settings can, of course, also be used to boost or reduce sensitivity in particular shooting situations. The Z5 can use ISO settings from Auto to Lo 1 (ISO 50 equivalent) and thence to ISO 100 up to ISO 51200, plus Hi 1 (equivalent to ISO 102400). The camera can also adjust the ISO automatically as appropriate for various lighting conditions. When you choose the Auto ISO setting in the Photo Shooting menu, as described in Chapter 11, the Z5 adjusts the sensitivity dynamically to suit the subject matter, based on minimum shutter speed and ISO limits you have prescribed. As I note in Chapter 13, you should use Auto ISO cautiously if you don't want the Z5 to use an ISO higher than you might otherwise have selected.

Fortunately, the Z5 includes several useful wrinkles in its Auto ISO arsenal. You can set limits, specifying both a *maximum sensitivity* (for both ambient exposures and flash) and a *minimum* shutter speed. If Auto ISO is active (it will be indicated in the display), the camera will never select an ISO you deem to be too high. Moreover, if your exposure will result in a speed slower than the minimum you set (thereby risking blur from subject motion and/or camera movement), the Z5 will switch to a higher ISO setting to allow using the minimum shutter speed or faster.

However, as I'll explain in Chapter 13, buried in the Photo Shooting menu within the Minimum Shutter Speed option in the Auto ISO settings is an additional Auto setting that allows you to specify how quickly the camera reacts to counter that longer shutter speed. Select Slower, and the Z5 will delay raising the ISO (useful if you want to keep a constant shutter speed, even if slow, to maintain a consistent "look" in a series of photos). Choose Faster, and the camera responds more quickly to reduce the possibility of image blur. Nikon has given enthusiast photographers a useful tool that allows you to fine-tune your Z5's behavior so it works the way you want it to in a wider variety of circumstances.

Dealing with Noise

Visual image noise is that random grainy effect that some like to use as a special effect, but which, most of the time, is objectionable because it robs your image of detail even as it adds that "interesting" texture. Noise is caused by two different phenomena: high ISO settings and long exposures.

High ISO noise commonly appears as you increase your camera's ISO setting, which causes the Z5 to amplify the base signal (captured at ISO 100). In the other direction, you can easily capture relatively low-noise images at ISO 800 and above. However, some noise may become visible at ISO 1600, and is often fairly noticeable at ISO 6400. At ISO 25600 and above, noise is often quite bothersome, although I have used ISO 25600 when photographing subjects that are fairly low in contrast. Nikon tips you off that settings higher than ISO 104400 may be tools used in special circumstances only by labeling them Hi 0.3 through Hi 2. You can expect noise and increase in contrast in any pictures taken at these lofty ratings.

High ISO noise appears as a result of the amplification needed to increase the sensitivity of the sensor. While higher ISOs do pull details out of dark areas, they also amplify non-signal information randomly, creating noise. You'll find a High ISO NR choice in the Photo Shooting menu, where you can specify High, Normal, or Low noise reduction, or turn the feature off entirely. Because noise reduction tends to soften the grainy look while robbing an image of detail, you may want to disable the feature if you're willing to accept a little noise in exchange for more details.

A similar noisy phenomenon occurs during long time exposures, which allow more photons to reach the sensor, increasing your ability to capture a picture under low-light conditions. However, the longer exposures also increase the likelihood that some pixels will register random phantom photons, often because the longer an imager is "hot," the warmer it gets, and that heat can be mistaken for photons. There's also a special kind of noise that CMOS sensors like the one used in the Z5 are potentially susceptible to. CMOS imagers contain millions of individual amplifiers and A/D converters, all working in unison. Because these circuits don't necessarily all process in precisely the same way all the time, they can introduce something called fixed-pattern noise into the image data.

Fortunately, Nikon's electronics geniuses have done an exceptional job minimizing noise from all causes in the Z5. Even so, you might still want to apply the optional long exposure noise reduction that can be activated using Long Exp. NR in the Photo Shooting menu, where the feature can be turned On or Off. This type of noise reduction involves the Z5 taking a second, blank exposure, and comparing the random pixels in that image with the photograph you just took. Pixels that coincide in the two represent noise and can safely be suppressed. This noise reduction system, called *dark-frame subtraction,* effectively doubles the amount of time required to take a picture, and is used only for exposures longer than one second. Noise reduction can reduce the amount of detail in your picture, as some image information may be removed along with the noise. So, you might want to use this feature with moderation.

You can also apply noise reduction to a lesser extent using Photoshop, and when converting RAW files to some other format, using your favorite RAW converter, or an industrial-strength product like Noise Ninja (www.picturecode.com) to wipe out noise after you've already taken the picture.

Bracketing

Bracketing is a method for shooting several consecutive exposures using different settings, as a way of improving the odds that one will be exactly right. Alternatively, bracketing can be used to create a series of photos with slightly different exposures (or white balances) in anticipation that one of the exposures will be "better" from a creative standpoint. For example, bracketing can supply you with a normal exposure of a backlit subject, one that's "underexposed," producing a silhouette effect, and a third that's "overexposed" to create still another look.

Before digital cameras took over the universe, it was common to bracket exposures, shooting, say, a series of three photos at 1/125th second, but varying the f/stop from f/8 to f/11 to f/16. In practice, smaller than whole-stop increments were used for greater precision, and lenses with apertures that were set manually commonly had half-stop detents on their aperture rings or could easily be set to a mid-way position between whole f/stops. It was just as common to keep the same aperture and vary the shutter speed, although in the days before electronic shutters, film cameras often had only whole increment shutter speeds available.

Today, cameras like the Z5 can bracket exposures much more precisely, and bracket white balance and Active D-Lighting (described later in this chapter) as well. While WB bracketing is sometimes used when getting color absolutely correct in the camera is important, autoexposure bracketing is used much more often. When this feature is activated, the Z5 takes a series of consecutive photos: starting with the metered "correct" exposure, then progressing to shots with less exposure, and additional shots with more exposure, using an increment of your choice up to +3/−3 stops. In A mode, the shutter speed will change, while in S mode, the aperture will change as the bracketed exposures are made.

Setting up autoexposure bracketing parameters is trickier than it needs to be, but you can follow these steps:

1. **Choose type of bracketing.** First, select the type of bracketing you want to do, using Auto Bracketing Set within the Auto Bracketing entry in the Photo Shooting menu, as explained in Chapter 11. You can select autoexposure and flash, autoexposure only, flash only, white balance only, and ADL bracketing.

   If you plan on shooting in Manual exposure mode, you can specify how bracketing is performed using Custom Setting e6. Your choices there are flash+shutter speed, flash+shutter speed+aperture, flash+aperture, or flash only. White balance and ADL bracketing are not available in Manual exposure mode.

2. **Choose bracketing order.** With Custom Setting e7 you can select MTR > Under > Over or Under > MTR > Over bracket orders. I prefer the latter order, as it makes it easier to have the frames of certain types of manual HDR exposures in order of increasing exposure.

3. **Select number of bracketed exposures.** In the Auto Bracketing entry of the Photo Shooting menu, select Number of Shots and use the multi selector left/right buttons or touch screen, pressing left to choose the number of shots in the sequence, 0 (which turns bracketing off), –2, +2, –3, or +3. Press the right button to specify 3-, 5-, 7-, or 9-shot bracket sets centered around the metered exposure.

4. **Choose bracket increment.** Next, select Increment, and use the left/right buttons or touch screen to choose the exposure increment: 1/3, 2/3, 1, 2, or 3 EV. **Note:** If you select an increment of 2 EV or 3 EV, then the number of shots in the bracketed set that you specified in Step 3 is limited to 5. If you had chosen 7 or 9 shots in Step 3, the Z5 will automatically change the setting to 5 shots.

5. **Frame and shoot.** As you take your photos, the camera will vary exposure, flash level, or white balance for each image, based on the bracketing "program" you selected, and in the order you specified in Custom Setting e7. In Single-frame mode, you'll need to press the shutter release button the number of times you specified for the exposures in your bracketed burst. I've found it easy to forget that I am shooting bracketed pictures, stop taking my sequence, and then wonder why the remaining pictures in my defined burst are "incorrectly" exposed. To avoid that, I often set the Z5 to one of the two continuous shooting modes, so that all my bracketed pictures are taken at once.

6. **Turn bracketing off.** When you're finished bracketing shots, remember to return to the Auto Bracketing entry and change Number of Shots to 0, and the BKT indicator is no longer displayed, as the setting remains in effect when you power down the camera and subsequently turn it on again.

ACTIVATING BRACKETING

Once you've set up the type of bracketing you want to use, as described next, taking a bracketed set of exposures is easy. When bracketing is active, to initiate exposing a set, just press the Bracketing Burst button. (Use Custom Setting f2 as described in Chapter 12 to assign the Bracketing Burst behavior to a button.) Once the button is pressed, all shots in the set will be taken each time you press the shutter release button once.

White Balance Bracketing

When you choose white balance bracketing, the Z5 does not take three different exposures (even if you've defined a Bracketing Burst button, only one shot will be taken). There's no need if you think about it. The camera always takes a RAW exposure first, no matter whether the camera is set to JPEG, RAW, or RAW+JPEG. If you've selected JPEG-only mode, the camera converts the initial RAW exposure to JPEG format using the settings you've opted for in the camera, and then discards the RAW data. In RAW mode, the camera stores the RAW data as a NEF file, and also creates a Basic

JPEG version of the image that is embedded in the RAW file as a thumbnail. That thumbnail is what you're actually looking at on the back-panel LCD monitor when you review your pictures; you never actually see the RAW file itself until you import it into your image editor. Your computer may also use the embedded JPEG file when it displays a RAW image. Finally, if you save in RAW+JPEG, you end up with two files: the NEF RAW file (with its embedded JPEG image) and a separate JPEG file at the quality level you specify (Fine, Normal, or Basic).

Since the RAW file that the camera initially captures contains all the digital information captured during exposure, when you specify white balance bracketing, the Z5 needs to take only one picture—and then save a JPEG file at each of the required white balance settings. One snap, and you get either two or three JPEG files at the quality level you specified, bracketed as you directed. Very slick. As you might guess, WB bracketing is applied only to JPEG files; you can't specify WB bracketing if you've chosen RAW or RAW+JPEG. RAW files created are always unmodified and will be converted according to the white balance settings you opted for in the camera when the photo is imported into your image editor (if you make no white balance changes during importation).

White balance bracketing produces JPEG files that vary, not by f/stops (which is the case with exposure bracketing), but by units called *mireds* (micro reciprocal degrees) that are used to specify color temperature. You don't really need to understand mireds at all, other than to know that WB bracketing varies the color temperature of your images by 5 mireds for each shot taken in the bracket set. Changes are made only in the amber-blue range; bracketing isn't applied to the green-magenta color bias.

To activate White Balance bracketing, just follow these steps:

1. **JPEG only.** Make sure you've selected a JPEG-only setting in the Image Quality entry of the Photo Shooting menu.

2. **Specify WB Bracketing.** In the Auto Bracketing entry of the Photo Shooting menu, choose WB Bracketing as your bracketing set.

3. **Choose number of shots.** In the Auto Bracketing screen, after you've chosen WB Bracketing, scroll down to Number of Shots and select how many bracketed exposures you want. You can choose two different ways:

   - Select 0, 3, 5, 7, or 9 (use the right directional button) and the Z5 will take the specified number of shots, in the amber and blue directions, equally spread on either side of the zero point of the amber-blue scale. For example, if you choose 5 as your number of shots, the sequence will include one neutral shot, plus two biased by 5 and 10 mireds in both amber and blue directions. With 0 as your number of shots, bracketing is disabled, just as it is with exposure bracketing.

   - Select B2, A2, B3, A3 bias (using the left directional button) and the Z5 will take either two or three shots biased in the blue or amber directions. For example, B3 would include shots biased 5, 10, and 15 mireds *only* in the blue direction.

ADL Bracketing

To initiate Active D-Lighting bracketing, select it from the Photo Shooting menu's Auto Bracketing Set menu entry and select number of shots and amount, as described next. As with exposure bracketing, you can trigger a burst with one press of the shutter release if you've defined a Bracketing Burst button.

- **0 (Number of shots).** Active D-Lighting bracketing is disabled. Only *bracketing* is turned off. If you've turned basic Active D-Lighting on in the Shooting menu, then each shot you take will have the amount of ADL applied that you specified (Auto, Extra High, High, Normal, or Low).
- **2 (Number of shots).** Only two shots will be taken, one Off (ADL turned Off, your control, so to speak) and one at the setting you specify. Scroll down to the Amount box. You can select OFF/Auto (No ADL, plus Auto ADL), Off/Extra High, Off/High, Off/Normal, or Off/Low.
- **3–5 (Number of shots).** You can choose 3, 4, or 5 shots. One will be Off (ADL disabled) and the others will be taken at the settings indicated in the Amount box. (You cannot choose the ADL settings in the Amount box when 3, 4, or 5 shots are taken.)
  - **3 shots:** Off, plus Low and Normal.
  - **4 shots:** Off, plus Low, Normal, and High.
  - **5 shots:** Off, plus Low, Normal, High, and Extra High.

As with exposure, flash, and WB bracketing, remember to turn off ADL bracketing when you no longer want to use it. Once set, it is automatically invoked each time you take a picture until disabled.

Working with HDR

High Dynamic Range (HDR) photography is quite the rage these days, and entire books have been written on the subject. It's not really a new technique—film photographers have been combining multiple exposures for ages to produce a single image of, say, an interior room while maintaining detail in the scene visible through the windows.

It's the same deal in the digital age. Suppose you wanted to photograph a dimly lit room that had a bright window showing an outdoors scene. Proper exposure for the room might be on the order of 1/60th second at f/2.8 at ISO 200, while the outdoors scene probably would require f/11 at 1/400th second. That's almost a 7 EV step difference (approximately 7 f/stops) and well beyond the dynamic range of any digital camera, including the Nikon Z5.

Until camera sensors gain much higher dynamic ranges (which may not be as far into the distant future as we think), special tricks like Active D-Lighting and HDR photography will remain basic tools. With the Nikon Z5, you can create in-camera HDR exposures, or shoot HDR the old-fashioned way—with separate bracketed exposures that are later combined in a tool like Photomatix or Adobe's Merge to HDR image-editing feature. I'm going to show you how to use both.

Auto HDR

The Z5's in-camera HDR feature is simple, not particularly flexible, but still surprisingly effective in creating high dynamic range images. It's also remarkably easy to use. Although it combines only two images to create a single HDR photograph, in some ways it's as good as the manual HDR method I'll describe in the section after this one. For example, it allows you to specify an exposure differential of three stops/EV between the two shots, the same as when shooting bracketed exposures.

As I noted, with digital camera sensors, it's often tricky to capture detail in both highlights and shadows in a single image, because the number of tones, the *dynamic range* of the sensor, is limited. The solution, in this particular case, was to resort to the Z5's Auto HDR feature, in which the two exposures were combined in the camera to produce a final image.

Figure 4.13 illustrates how the two shots that the Z5's HDR feature merges might look. There is a three-stop differential between the underexposed image at left, and the overexposed image at center. The in-camera HDR processing is able to combine the two to derive an image similar to the one shown in Figure 4.13, right, which has a much fuller range of tones.

To use the Z5's HDR feature, just follow these steps. The feature does not work if you have selected RAW or RAW+JPEG formats, and cannot be used simultaneously with bracketing features, multiple exposure, or time-lapse photography.

1. **Activate the menu.** Press the MENU button and navigate to the Photo Shooting menu, represented by a camera icon. (If you need more help using the Z5's menu system, you'll find an introduction at the beginning of Chapter 11.)

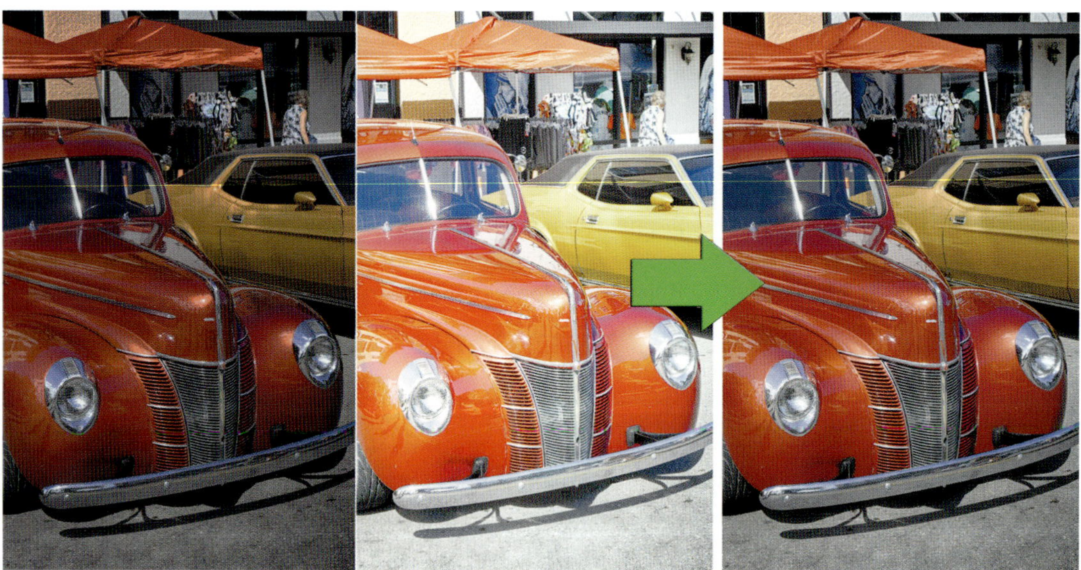

Figure 4.13 The underexposed image (left) can be combined with the overexposed image (center) to produce the merged HDR image (right).

2. **Scroll down to HDR.** Press the right multi selector button. A screen appears with four choices: HDR Mode, Exposure Differential, Smoothing, and Save Individual Images (NEF). (See Figure 4.14, upper left.)

3. **Turn on HDR.** Choose HDR Mode, press right, and select either On (series) if you want to shoot multiple HDR photos consecutively or On (single photo) to take a single HDR image and then shut the feature off. Choose OFF to disable the feature. Press OK to confirm. (See Figure 4.14, upper right.)

4. **Set amount.** Choose Exposure Differential, press the right button, and select Auto (the Z5 chooses the differential based on how contrasty it deems your scene to be), 1 EV, 2 EV, or 3 EV. Auto is a good choice for your initial experiments. Or select a higher EV strength for higher-contrast subjects, and a lower value for lower-contrast subjects. Press OK to confirm. (See Figure 4.14, lower left.)

5. **Choose smoothing.** HDR can cause haloing around the boundaries of areas within an image. You can control the effect by choosing a Smoothing value of High, Normal, or Low. (See Figure 4.14, lower right.)

6. **Save Individual Images (optional).** Ordinarily, the Z5 captures two images, combines them to produce an HDR shot, and then deletes the individual images. Turn Save Individual Images (NEF) on, and the camera will store a Large RAW version of each shot (even if you have not selected RAW or Large image quality/size). You'll have the intermediate images available for editing/tweaking on your computer.

7. **Set Aperture-priority mode.** You want the camera to adjust the exposure by changing the f/stop, rather than using a different aperture, in order to keep your depth-of-field the same for each shot.

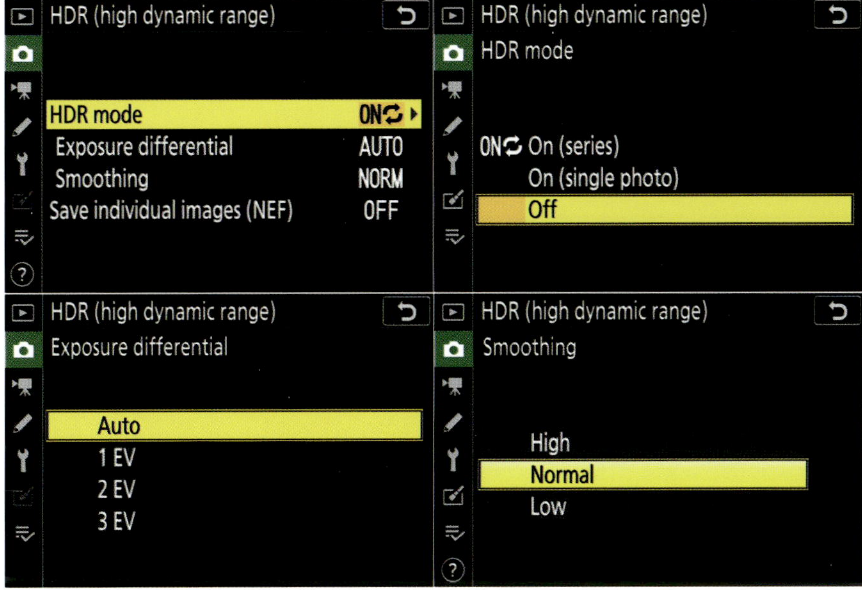

Figure 4.14 Choose HDR parameters.

8. **Take your shot.** Set your camera to Aperture-priority mode. Although you can shoot HDR hand-held, you'll get the best results with the Z5 mounted on a tripod, and with subjects that don't display a lot of motion. Waterfalls are a poor choice. Note that because the camera tries to align shots, even if there is slight camera movement, some portion of the images at the edges will be cropped out. You're better off using a tripod for Auto HDR, even though it does a decent job handheld.

Bracketing and Merge to HDR

If your credo is "If you want something done right, do it yourself," you can also shoot HDR manually, without resorting to the Z5's HDR mode. Instead, you can shoot individual images either by manually bracketing or using the Z5's auto bracketing modes, described earlier in this chapter.

While my goal in this book is to show you how to take great photos *in the camera* rather than how to fix your errors in Photoshop, the Merge to HDR Pro feature in Adobe's flagship image editor is too cool to ignore. The ability to have a bracketed set of exposures that are identical except for exposure is key to getting good results with this Photoshop feature, which allows you to produce images with a full, rich dynamic range that includes a level of detail in the highlights and shadows that is almost impossible to achieve with digital cameras.

When you're using Merge to HDR Pro, you take several pictures, some exposed for the shadows, some for the middle tones, and some for the highlights. The exact number of images to combine is up to you. Four to seven is a good number. Then, use the Merge to HDR Pro command to combine all of the images into one HDR image that integrates the well-exposed sections of each version. Here's how.

The images should be as identical as possible, except for exposure. So, it's a good idea to mount the Z5 on a tripod, use a remote release like the MC-DC2, and take all the exposures in one burst. Just follow these steps:

1. **Set up the camera.** Mount the Z5 on a tripod.
2. **Set the camera to shoot a bracketed burst with an increment of 2 EV or 3 EV.** This was described earlier in this chapter.

DETERMINING THE BEST EXPOSURE DIFFERENTIAL

How do you choose the number of EV/stops to separate your exposures? You can use histograms, described at the end of this chapter, to determine the correct bracketing range. Take a test shot and examine the histogram. Reduce the exposure until dark tones are clipped off at the left of the resulting histogram. Then, increase the exposure until the lighter tones are clipped off at the right of the histogram. The number of stops between the two is the range that should be covered using your bracketed exposures. You can learn more about histograms in the section following this one.

3. **Choose an f/stop.** Set the camera for Aperture-priority and select an aperture that will provide a correct exposure at your initial settings for the series of manually bracketed shots. *And then leave this adjustment alone!* As I noted earlier, you don't want the aperture to change for your series, as that would change the depth-of-field. You want the Z5 to adjust exposure *only* using the shutter speed.

4. **Choose manual focus.** You don't want the focus to change between shots, so set the Z5 to manual focus, and carefully focus your shot.

5. **Choose RAW exposures.** Set the camera to take RAW files, which will give you the widest range of tones in your images.

6. **Take your bracketed set.** Press the button on the remote (or carefully press the shutter release or use the self-timer) and take the set of bracketed exposures.

7. **Continue with the Merge to HDR Pro steps listed next.** You can also use a different program, such as Photomatix, if you know how to use it.

The next steps show you how to combine the separate exposures into one merged HDR image. The sample images in Figure 4.15 (left) show the results you can get from a three-shot bracketed sequence.

1. **Copy your images to your computer.** If you use an application to transfer the files to your computer, make sure it does not make any adjustments to brightness, contrast, or exposure. You want the real raw information for Merge to HDR Pro to work with.

2. **Activate Merge to HDR Pro.** Choose File > Automate > Merge to HDR Pro.

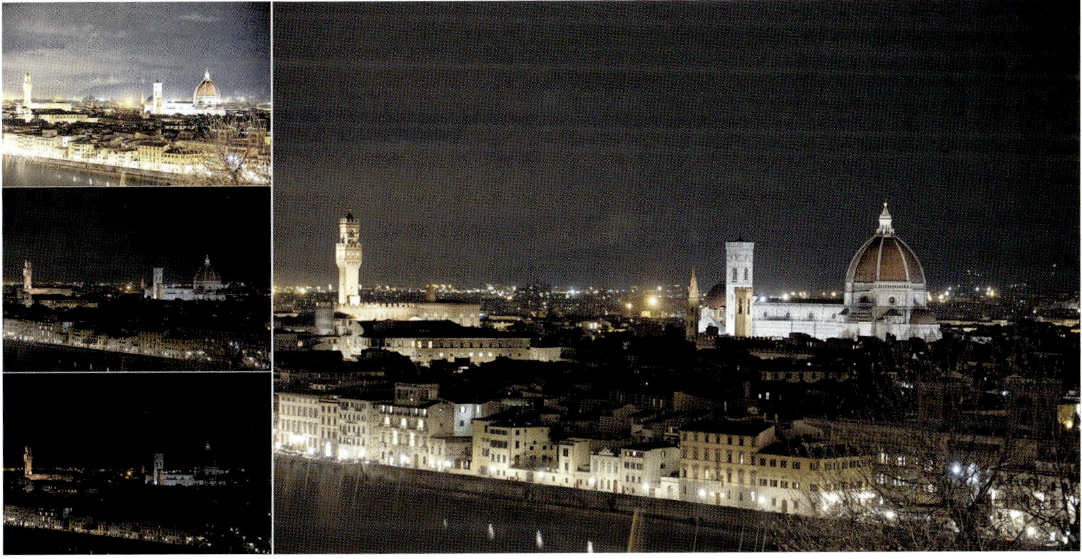

Figure 4.15 Left: Three bracketed photos should look like this. Right: You'll end up with an extended dynamic range photo like this one.

3. **Select the photos to be merged.** Use the Browse feature to locate and select your photos to be merged. You'll note a check box that can be used to automatically align the images if they were not taken with the camera mounted on a rock-steady support. This will adjust for any slight movement of the camera that might have occurred when you changed exposure settings.

4. **Choose parameters (optional).** The first time you use Merge to HDR Pro, you can let the program work with its default parameters. Once you've played with the feature a few times, you can read the Adobe help files and learn more about the options than I can present in this non-software-oriented camera guide.

5. **Click OK.** The merger begins.

6. **Save.** Once HDR merge has done its thing, save the file to your computer.

If you do everything correctly, you'll end up with a photo like the one shown in Figure 4.15 (right).

What if you don't have the opportunity, inclination, or skills to create several images at different exposures, as described? If you shoot in RAW format, you can still use Merge to HDR, working with a *single* original image file. What you do is import the image into Photoshop several times, using Adobe Camera Raw to create multiple copies of the file at different exposure levels.

For example, you'd create one copy that's too dark, so the shadows lose detail, but the highlights are preserved. Create another copy with the shadows intact and allow the highlights to wash out. Then, you can use Merge to HDR to combine the two and end up with a finished image that has the extended dynamic range you're looking for. (This concludes the image-editing portion of the chapter. We now return you to our alternate sponsor: photography.)

Fixing Exposures with Histograms

While you can often recover poorly exposed photos in your image editor, your best bet is to arrive at the correct exposure in the camera, minimizing the tweaks that you have to make in post-processing. However, you can't always judge exposure just by simply looking at the preview image on your Z5's display before the shot is made, nor the review image in Playback. Ambient light may make the monitor difficult to see, and the brightness level you've set for the monitor and viewfinder in the Setup menu can affect the appearance of the image.

Instead, you can use a histogram, which is a chart shown on the Z5's display that shows the number of tones that have been captured at each brightness level. Histograms are available in real time on your display as you shoot and in the review image during playback, but they are available only when enabled. To view histograms in Live View or Playback mode, press the DISP button until a screen with the histogram appears.

- **Photo and Movie modes.** For still and movie shooting, the histogram can be activated by choosing On for Custom Setting d7: Apply Settings to Live View (see Chapter 12). In addition, if you're capturing multiple exposures, you must choose On for Overlay Shooting in the Multiple Exposure entry in the Photo Shooting menu (as discussed in Chapter 11). The histogram appears at lower right, as seen in Figure 4.16.

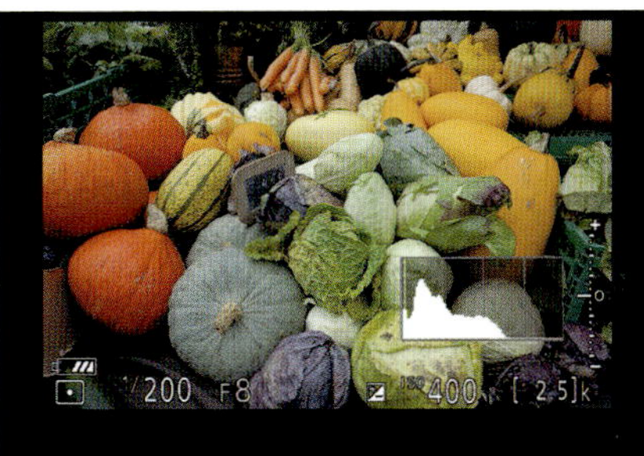

Figure 4.16 In Photo and Movie shooting modes the histogram appears in your live view image when enabled.

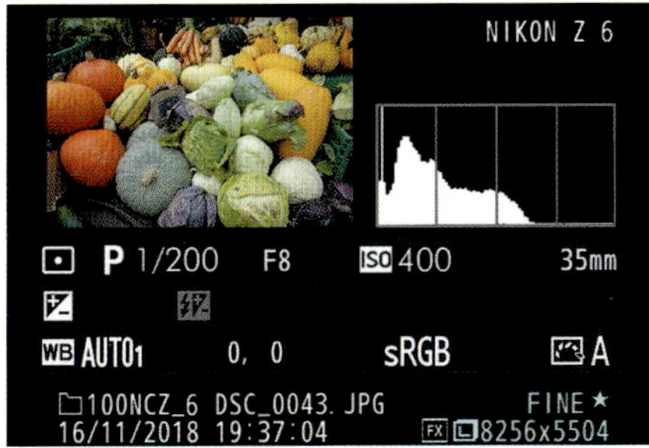

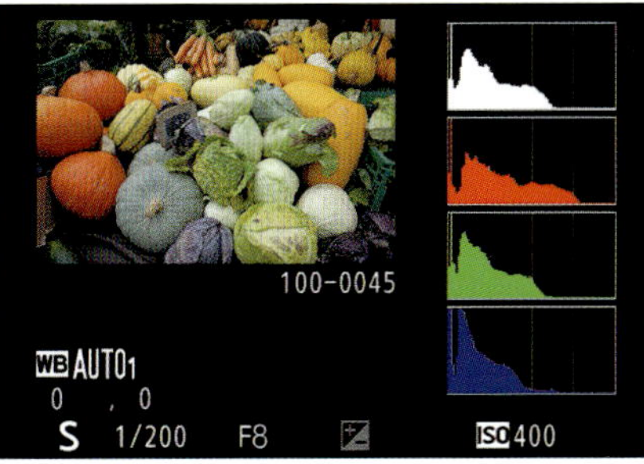

Figure 4.17 Histograms are available on two different screens during playback.

- **Playback.** To see histograms during image review, check the Histogram box in the Playback Display Options entry of the Playback menu (discussed in Chapter 11). The Z5 offers four histogram variations in two screens: one histogram that shows overall brightness levels for an image (see Figure 4.17, left) and an alternate version that also shows brightness (also called *luminance*), but offers additional histograms that separate the red, green, and blue channels of your image into separate graphs (see Figure 4.17, right).

Tonal Range

Histograms help you adjust the tonal range of an image, the span of dark to light tones, from a complete absence of brightness (black) to the brightest possible tone (white), and all the middle tones in between. Because all values for tones fall into a continuous spectrum between black and white, it's easiest to think of a photo's tonality in terms of a black-and-white or grayscale image, even though you're capturing those tones in three separate color layers of red, green, and blue.

Because your images are digital, the tonal "spectrum" isn't really continuous: it's divided into discrete steps that represent the different tones that can be captured. Figure 4.18 may help you understand this concept. The gray steps shown range from 100 percent gray (black) at the left, to 0 percent gray (white) at the right, with 20 gray steps in all (plus white).

Along the bottom of the chart are the digital values from 0 to 255 recorded by your sensor for an image with 8 bits per channel (8 bits of red, 8 bits of green, and 8 bits of blue equal a 24-bit, full-color image). Any black captured would be represented by a value of 0, the brightest white by 255, and the midtones would be clustered around the 128 marker. The actual information captured may be

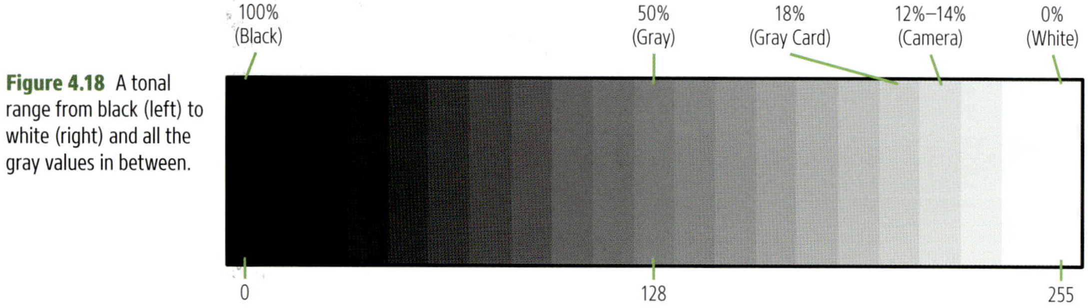

Figure 4.18 A tonal range from black (left) to white (right) and all the gray values in between.

"finer" and record say, 0 to 4,094 for an image captured when the Z5 is set to 14 bits per channel in the NEF (RAW) Recording Bit Depth setting of the Photo Shooting menu (see Chapter 11 for more detail on that option).

Grayscale images (which we call black-and-white photos) are easy to understand. Or, at least, that's what we think. When we look at a black-and-white image, we think we're seeing a continuous range of tones from black to white, and all the grays in between. But that's not exactly true. The blackest black in any photo isn't a true black, because *some* light is always reflected from the surface of the print, and if viewed on a screen, the deepest black is only as dark as the least-reflective area a computer monitor can produce. The whitest white isn't a true white, either, because even the lightest areas of a print absorb some light (only a mirror reflects close to all the light that strikes it), and, when viewing on a computer monitor, the whites are limited by the brightness of the display's LCD or LED picture elements. Lacking darker blacks and brighter, whiter whites, that continuous set of tones doesn't cover the full grayscale tonal range.

The full scale of tones becomes useful when you have an image that has large expanses of shades that change gradually from one level to the next, such as areas of sky, water, or walls. Think of a picture taken of a group of campers around a campfire. Since the light from the fire is striking them directly in the face, there aren't many shadows on the campers' faces. All the tones that make up the *features* of the people around the fire are compressed into one end of the brightness spectrum—the lighter end.

Yet, there's more to this scene than faces. Behind the campers are trees, rocks, and perhaps a few animals that have emerged from the shadows to see what is going on. These are illuminated by the softer light that bounces off the surrounding surfaces. If your eyes become accustomed to the reduced illumination, you'll find that there is a wealth of detail in these shadow images.

This campfire scene would be a nightmare to reproduce faithfully under any circumstances. If you are an experienced photographer, you are probably already wincing at what is called a *high-contrast* lighting situation. Some photos may be high in contrast when there are fewer tones and they are all bunched up at limited points in the scale. In a low-contrast image, there are more tones, but they are spread out so widely that the image looks flat. Your digital camera can show you the relationship between these tones using a *histogram*.

Histogram Basics

Your Z5's histograms are a simplified display of the numbers of pixels at each of 256 brightness levels, producing an interesting "mountain range" shape in the graph. Although separate charts may be provided for brightness and the red, green, and blue channels, when you first start using histograms, you'll want to concentrate on the brightness histogram.

Each vertical line in the graph represents the number of pixels in the image for each brightness value, from 0 (black) on the left to 255 (white) on the right. The vertical axis measures that number of pixels at each level.

Although histograms are most often used to fine-tune exposure, you can glean other information from them, such as the relative contrast of the image. Figure 4.19, top, is a simplified rendition of the upper half of the Overview screen, with an image having normal contrast. In such an image, most of the pixels are spread across the image, with a healthy distribution of tones throughout the midtone section of the graph. That large peak at the right side of the graph represents all those light tones in the sky. A normal-contrast image you shoot may have less sky area, and less of a peak at the right side, but notice that very few pixels hug the right edge of the histogram, indicating that the lightest tones are not being clipped because they are off the chart.

With a lower-contrast image, like the one shown in Figure 4.19, center, the basic shape of the previous histogram will remain recognizable, but gradually will be compressed together to cover a smaller area of the gray spectrum. The squished shape of the histogram is caused by all the grays in the original image being represented by a limited number of gray tones in a smaller range of the scale.

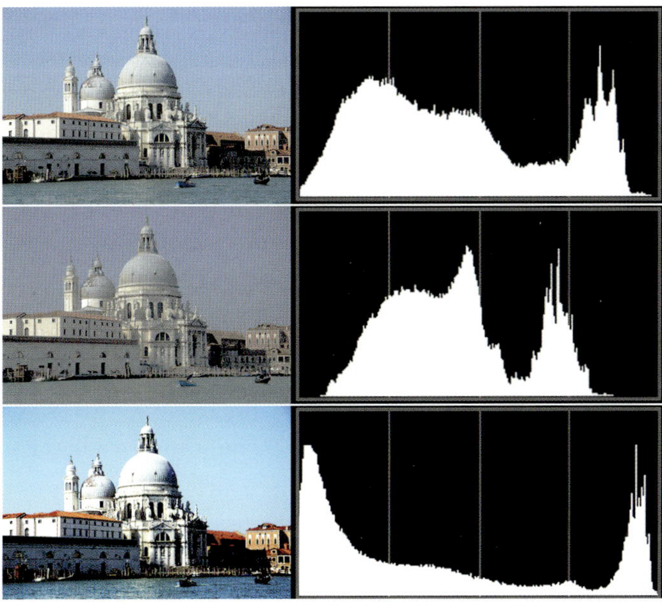

Figure 4.19 Top: This image has fairly normal contrast, even though there is a peak of light tones at the right side representing the sky. Center: This low-contrast image has all the tones squished into one section of the grayscale. Bottom: A high-contrast image produces a histogram in which the tones are spread out.

Instead of the darkest tones of the image reaching into the black end of the spectrum and the whitest tones extending to the lightest end, the blackest areas of the scene are now represented by a light gray, and the whites by a somewhat lighter gray. The overall contrast of the image is reduced. Because all the darker tones are actually a middle gray or lighter, the scene in this version of the photo appears lighter as well.

Going in the other direction, increasing the contrast of an image produces a histogram like the one shown in Figure 4.19, bottom. In this case, the tonal range is now spread over the entire width of the chart, but, except for the bright sky, there is not much variation in the middle tones; the mountain "peaks" are not very high. When you stretch the grayscale in both directions like this, the darkest tones become darker (that may not be possible) and the lightest tones become lighter (ditto). In fact, shades that might have been gray before can change to black or white as they are moved toward either end of the scale.

The effect of increasing contrast may be to move some tones off either end of the scale altogether, while spreading the remaining grays over a smaller number of locations on the spectrum. That's exactly the case in the example shown. The number of possible tones is smaller, and the image appears harsher.

Understanding Histograms

The important thing to remember when working with the histogram display in your Z5 is that changing the exposure does *not* change the contrast of an image. The curves illustrated in the previous three examples remain exactly the same shape when you increase or decrease exposure. I repeat: The proportional distribution of grays shown in the histogram doesn't change when exposure changes; it is neither stretched nor compressed. However, the tones as a whole are moved toward one end of the scale or the other, depending on whether you're increasing or decreasing exposure. You'll be able to see that in some illustrations that follow.

So, as you reduce exposure, tones gradually move to the black end (and off the scale), while the reverse is true when you increase exposure. The contrast within the image is changed only to the extent that some of the tones can no longer be represented when they are moved off the scale.

To change the *contrast* of an image, you must do one of four things:

- **Change the Z5's contrast setting** using the menu system. You'll find these adjustments in your camera's Picture Controls menus, as explained in Chapter 11.
- **Use your camera's shadow-tone "booster."** As previously discussed, Active D-Lighting (or plain old D-Lighting applied after the fact from the Retouch menu) can also adjust contrast.
- **Alter the contrast of the scene itself,** for example, by using a fill light or reflectors to add illumination to shadows that are too dark.
- **Attempt to adjust contrast in post-processing** using your image editor or RAW file converter. You may use features such as Levels or Curves (in Photoshop, Photoshop Elements, and many other image editors), or work with HDR software to cherry-pick the best values in shadows and highlights from multiple images.

Of the four of these, the third—changing the contrast of the scene—is the most desirable, because attempting to fix contrast by fiddling with the tonal values is unlikely to be a perfect remedy. However, adding a little contrast can be successful because you can discard some tones to make the image more contrasty. However, the opposite is much more difficult. An overly contrasty image rarely can be fixed because you can't add information that isn't there in the first place.

What you *can* do is adjust the exposure so that the tones *that are already present in the scene* are captured correctly. Figure 4.20, top, shows the histogram for an image that is badly underexposed. You can guess from the shape of the histogram that many of the dark tones to the left of the graph have been clipped off. There's plenty of room on the right side for additional pixels to reside without having them become overexposed. So, you can increase the exposure (either by changing the f/stop or shutter speed, or by adding an EV value) to produce the corrected histogram shown in Figure 4.20, center.

Conversely, if your histogram looks like the one shown in Figure 4.20, bottom, with bright tones pushed off the right edge of the chart, you have an overexposed image, and you can correct it by reducing exposure. In addition to the histogram, the Z5 has its Highlights option, which, when activated, shows areas that are overexposed with flashing tones (often called "blinkies") in the review screen. Depending on the importance of this "clipped" detail, you can adjust exposure or leave it alone. For example, if all the dark-coded areas in the review are in a background that you care little about, you can forget about them and not change the exposure, but if such areas appear in facial details of your subject, you may want to make some adjustments.

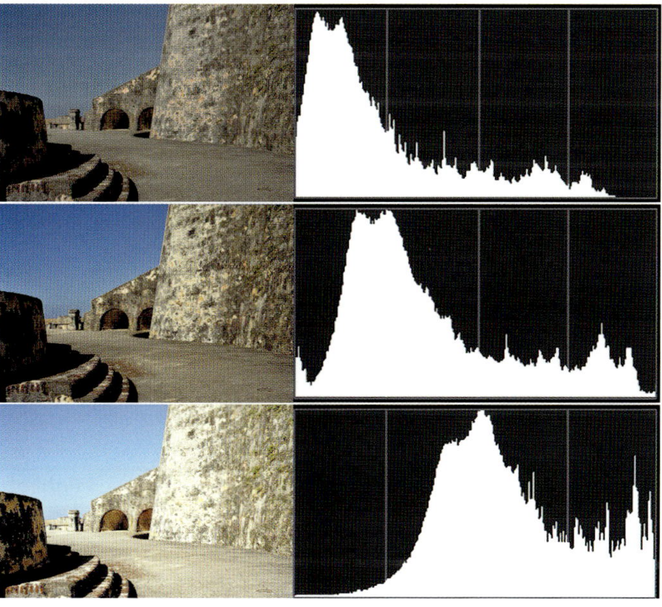

Figure 4.20 Top: A histogram of an under-exposed image may look like this. Center: Adding exposure will produce a histogram like this one. Bottom: A histogram of an overexposed image will show clipping at the right side.

In working with histograms, your goal should be to have all the tones in an image spread out between the edges, with none clipped off at the left and right sides. Underexposing (to preserve highlights) should be done only as a last resort, because retrieving the underexposed shadows in your image editor will frequently increase the noise, even if you're working with RAW files. A better course of action is to expose for the highlights, but, when the subject matter makes it practical, fill in the shadows with additional light, using reflectors, fill flash, or other techniques rather than allowing them to be seriously underexposed.

A traditional technique for optimizing exposure is called "expose to the right" (ETTR), which involves adding exposure to push the histogram's curve toward the right side *but not far enough to clip off highlights.* The rationale for this method is that extra shadow detail will be produced with a minimum increase in noise, especially in the shadow areas. It's said that half of a digital sensor's response lies in the brightest areas of an image, and so require the least amount of amplification (which is one way to increase digital noise). ETTR can work, as long as you're able to capture a satisfactory amount of information in the shadows.

Exposing to the Right

It's easier to understand exposing to the right if you mentally divide the histogram into fifths (unfortunately, the Z5's histogram uses quarters instead). And, for the sake of simplicity and smaller numbers, assume you're shooting in 14-bit RAW. Any 14-bit image can record a maximum of 16,383 different tones per channel. However, each fifth of the histogram does *not* encompass 3,277 tones (one-fifth of 16,383).

Figure 4.21 Tones are not evenly allocated throughout a histogram.

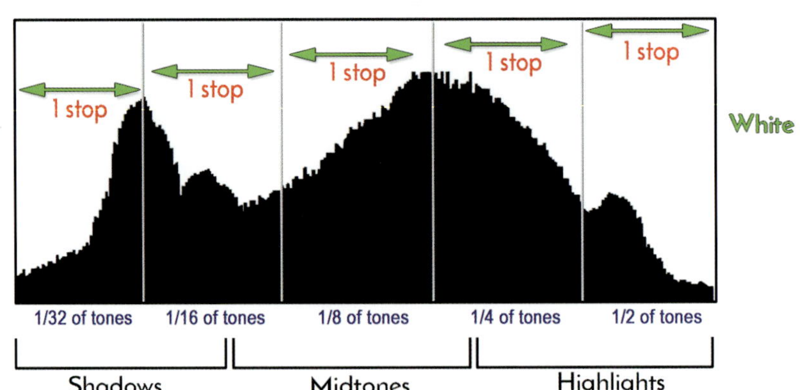

Instead, the right-most fifth, the highlights, shown in Figure 4.21, accounts for half of the available tones. Moving toward the left, the next fifth represents 1/4 of the available tones, followed by 1/8th, 1/16th levels, and, in the left-most section where the deepest shadows reside, only 1/32nd of the different tones are captured. When processing your RAW file, there are roughly 500 tones to recover in the shadows, which is why boosting/amplifying them increases noise. (The effect is most noticeable in the red and blue channels; your sensor's Bayer array has twice as many green-sensitive pixels as red or blue.)

Instead, you want to add exposure—as long as you don't push highlights off the right edge of the histogram—to brighten the shadows. Because there are more than 8,000 tones available in the highlights, even if the RAW image *looks* overexposed, it's possible to use your RAW converter's Exposure slider (such as the one found in Adobe Camera Raw) to bring back detail captured in that surplus of tones in the highlights. This procedure is the exact opposite of what was recommended for film of the transparency variety—it was fairly easy to retrieve detail from shadows by pumping more light through them when processing the image, while even small amounts of extra exposure blew out highlights. You'll often find that the range of tones in your image is so great that there is no way to keep your histogram from spilling over into the left and right edges, costing you both highlight and shadow detail. Exposing to the right may not work in such situations. A second school of thought recommends *reducing* exposure to bring back the highlights, or "exposing to the left." You would then attempt to recover shadow detail in an image editor, using tools like Adobe Camera Raw's Exposure slider. But remember, above all, that this procedure will also boost noise in the shadows, and so the technique should be used with caution. In most cases, exposing to the right is your best bet.

Dealing with Channels

The more you work with histograms, the more useful they become. One of the first things that histogram veterans notice is that it's possible to overexpose one channel even if the overall exposure appears to be correct. For example, flower photographers soon discover that it's really, really difficult to get a good picture of a red rose, like the one shown at left in Figure 4.22. The exposure looks okay—but there's no detail in the rose's petals. Looking at the histogram (see Figure 4.22, right) shows why: the red channel is blown out. If you look at the red histogram, there's a peak at the right edge that indicates that highlight information has been lost. In fact, the green channel has been blown, too, and so the green parts of the flower also lack detail. Only the blue channel's histogram is entirely contained within the boundaries of the chart, and, on first glance, the white luminance histogram at top of the column of graphs seems fairly normal.

Any of the primary channels—red, green, or blue—can blow out all by themselves, although bright reds seem to be the most common problem area. More difficult to diagnose are overexposed tones in one of the "in-between" hues on the color wheel. Overexposed yellows (which are very common) will be shown by blowouts in *both* the red and green channels. Too-bright cyans will manifest as excessive blue and green highlights, while overexposure in the red and blue channels reduces detail in magenta colors. As you gain experience, you'll be able to see exactly how anomalies in the RGB channels translate into poor highlights and murky shadows.

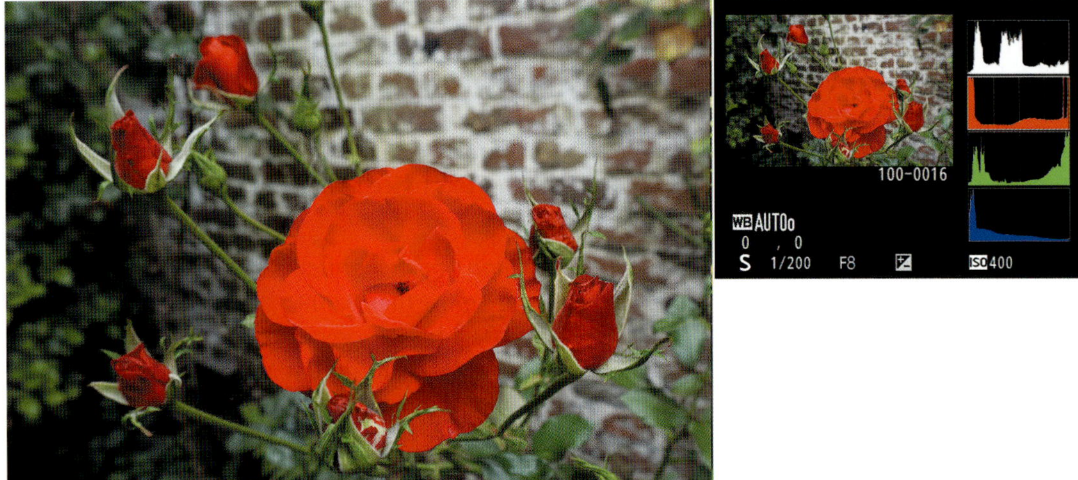

Figure 4.22 It's common to lose detail in bright red flowers because the red channel becomes overexposed even when the other channels are properly exposed (left). The RGB histograms show that both the red and green channels are overexposed, with tones extending past the right edge of the chart (right).

The only way to correct for color channel blowouts is to reduce exposure. As I mentioned earlier, you might want to consider filling in the shadows with additional light to keep them from becoming too dark when you decrease exposure. In practice, you'll want to monitor the red channel most closely, followed by the blue channel, and slightly decrease exposure to see if that helps. Because of the way our eyes perceive color, we are more sensitive to variations in green, so green channel blowouts are less of a problem, unless your main subject is heavily colored in that hue. If you plan on photographing a frog hopping around on your front lawn, you'll want to be extra careful to preserve detail in the green channel, using bracketing or other exposure techniques outlined in this chapter.

Fine-Tuning Exposure

When all else fails—that is, when you find your camera *consistently* over- or underexposes when using a particular exposure mode—you can recalibrate the Z5 to produce images more to your liking. This setting is a powerful adjustment that allows you to dial in a specific amount of exposure adjustment that will be applied, invisibly, to every photo you take using each of the three metering modes. No more can you complain, "My Z5 always underexposes by 1/3 stop!" If that is actually the case, and the phenomenon is consistent, you can use Custom Setting b4: Fine Tune Optimal Exposure to compensate.

Exposure compensation is usually a better idea (does your camera *really* underexpose that consistently?), but this setting does allow you to adjust your Z5's behavior yourself. However, you have no indication that fine-tuning has been made, so you'll need to remember what you've done. After all, you someday might discover that your camera is consistently *over*exposing images by 1/3 stop, not remembering that you've made the adjustment.

In practice, it's rare that the Nikon Z5 will *consistently* provide the wrong exposure in any of the three metering modes, especially Matrix metering, which can alter exposure dramatically based on the Z5's internal database of typical scenes. This feature may be most useful for Spot metering, if you always take a reading off the same type of subject, such as a human face or gray card. Should you find that the gray card readings, for example, always differ from what you would prefer, go ahead and fine-tune optimal exposure for Spot metering, and use that to read your gray cards.

I explain how to use the Z5's menus at the beginning of Chapter 11 and won't repeat those instructions here. You can jump ahead to that explanation, or, if you're comfortable working with the camera's menu system, you can fine-tune your exposure now:

1. **Select fine-tuning.** Choose Custom Setting b4: Fine-Tune Optimal Exposure from the Custom Settings menu.

2. **Consider yourself warned.** In the screen that appears, choose Yes after carefully reading the warning that Nikon insists on showing you each and every time this option is activated. The screen shown in Figure 4.23, left, appears.

3. **Select metering mode to correct.** Choose Matrix metering, Center-weighted metering, Spot metering, or Highlight-weighted metering by highlighting your choice and pressing the multi selector right button.

4. **Specify amount of correction.** Press the up/down buttons to dial in the exposure compensation you want to apply (see Figure 4.23, right). You can specify compensation in increments of 1/6 stop, half as large a change as conventional exposure compensation. This is truly *fine-tuning*.

5. **Confirm your change.** Press OK when finished. You can repeat the action to fine-tune the other two exposure modes if you wish. To return your settings to your defaults, simply repeat the process and dial in 0 correction for the desired mode.

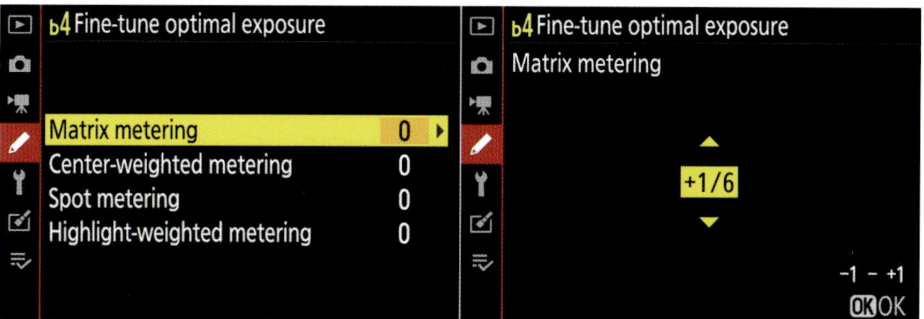

Figure 4.23 Fine-tune optimal exposure.

Mastering the Mysteries of Focus

5

How far we've come! My first professional job was as a reporter/sportswriter/photographer for a daily newspaper (back when a backslash really *meant* something), and focusing to achieve a sharp image was a manual process accomplished by turning a ring or knob on the camera or lens until, in one's highly trained professional judgment, the image was satisfactorily in focus. Manual focus was particularly challenging when shooting sports.

Today, modern digital cameras like the Z5 can identify potential subject matter, lock in on human faces, if present, and automatically focus faster than the blink of an eye. Usually. Of course, sometimes a camera's AF will zero in on the *wrong* subject, become confused by a background pattern, or be totally unable to follow a fast-moving target like a bird in flight. While autofocus *has* come a long way in the last 30-plus years, it's still a work-in-progress that relies heavily on input from the photographer.

One key problem is that the camera doesn't have any way of determining, for certain, what subject you want to be in sharp focus. It may select an object and lock in focus with lightning speed—even though the subject is not the one that's the center of interest of your photograph. Or, the camera may lock focus too soon, or too late. While Nikon has given us faster and more precise autofocus systems, with many more choices, it's common for the sheer number of options to confuse even the most advanced photographers.

So, even though your Nikon Z5 has the potential to calculate and set focus for you quickly and with a high degree of accuracy, you still need to make a few settings that provide guidance on three Ws of autofocus: *what, where,* and *when.* Your decisions in how you apply those choices supplies the fourth W: *why.* This chapter will provide you with everything you need to put all four to work.

Auto or Manual Focus?

Your first step is to decide whether you want to use automatic or manual focus—or *combine* the two by using the Z5's AF system to perform the initial focus task for you, followed by manual fine-tuning. Remember that while manual focus is, relatively speaking, an ancient technology, modern cameras like the Z5 supply you with powerful focusing aids. You can zoom into your subject to manually focus on an enlarged image, view color-coded cues that show you which parts of the image actually *are* in focus, or check an electronic "rangefinder" that alerts you when a given subject is in focus.

These manual focus aids are great features. Although Nikon added autofocus capabilities in the 1980s, in the film era, such assists were much more primitive and focusing was always done manually. Honest. Even though optical viewfinders were big and bright, special focusing screens, magnifiers, and other gadgets were the only tools available to help the photographer achieve correct focus. Imagine what it must have been like to focus manually under demanding, fast-moving conditions such as sports photography!

Advances in autofocus technology have given photographers the confidence to rely on AF most of the time and use manual focus only for those special applications. For the average subject, a camera like the Z5 will do an excellent job of evaluating your scene and quickly focusing on an appropriate subject. Interestingly enough, however, the switch to mirrorless technology has actually revived interest in old-school manual focus. Here are five reasons why manual focus is being used more by creative photographers.

- **WYSIWYG.** What you see (in the viewfinder or LCD monitor) is what you get, in terms of sharp focus. When focusing manually with the Z5, you're evaluating the exact same sensor image that will be captured when you press the shutter release. Traditional single-lens reflex (SLR) cameras use a mirror to direct the image to a separate focusing screen (when not in live view), which can be coarser, not as bright, and possibly out of alignment.

- **WYSIWYW.** Focusing manually can mean that *what you see is what you want,* that is, *you* can select the precise plane of focus you desire for, say, a macro photo or portrait, rather than settle for what the camera *thinks* you want. Your camera doesn't have any way of determining, for certain, what subject you *want* to be in sharp focus. It can't read your mind (at least, not yet). Left to its own devices, the Z5 may select a likely object—often the one nearest the camera—and lock in focus with lightning speed, even though the subject is not the one that's the center of interest of your photograph.

- **Less confusion.** Nikon has given us faster and more precise autofocus systems, with many more options, and it's common for the sheer number of these choices to confuse even the most advanced photographers. If you'd rather not wade through the AF alternatives for a given shot, switch to manual focus and shoot. You won't have to worry about whether the camera locks focus too soon, or too late.

- **Focus aids.** As I noted earlier, you can zoom in on the sensor image as you focus manually and use a feature called *focus peaking* to accentuate in-focus areas with distinct colored outlines. I'll explain all these options later.

- **More lenses.** All mirrorless cameras—and not just the Nikon Z-series—had a limited number of lenses available when they were originally introduced. Happily, Nikon has been filling in the gaps quickly. Meanwhile, the reduced flange-to-sensor distance (which I'll explain in more detail in Chapter 7) offers plenty of room to insert an adapter that allows mounting an extensive number of existing lenses, including those from manufacturers other than Nikon. Many of those third-party optics are inexpensive manual focus lenses, or lenses intended for other camera platforms which function only in manual focus on the Z-series models. A whole generation of photographers who grew up using nothing but autofocus have discovered that focusing manually is a reasonable tradeoff for access to this wide range of optics.

How Focus Works

Simply put, focus is the process of adjusting the camera so that parts of our subject that we want to be sharp and clear are, in fact, sharp and clear. We allow the camera to focus for us, automatically, or we can rotate the lens's focus ring manually to achieve the desired focus. Manual focusing is especially problematic because our eyes and brains have poor memory for correct focus. That's why your eye doctor conducting a refraction test must shift back and forth between pairs of lenses and ask, "Does that look sharper—or was it sharper before?" in determining your correct prescription. Too often, the slight differences are such that the lens pairs must be swapped multiple times.

Similarly, manual focusing involves jogging the focus ring back and forth as you go from almost in focus, to sharp focus, to almost focused again. The little clockwise and counterclockwise arcs decrease in size until you've zeroed in on the point of correct focus. What you're looking for is the image with the most contrast between the edges of elements in the image.

The Nikon Z5's autofocus mechanism, like all such systems found in modern cameras, also evaluates these increases and decreases in sharpness, but it is able to remember the progression perfectly, so that autofocus can lock in much more quickly and, with an image that has sufficient contrast, more precisely. Unfortunately, while the camera's focus system finds it easy to measure degrees of apparent focus at each of the focus points in the viewfinder, it doesn't really know with any certainty *which object* should be in sharpest focus. Is it the closest object? The subject in the center? Something lurking *behind* the closest subject? A person standing over at the side of the picture? Using autofocus effectively involves telling the Z5 exactly what it should be focusing on.

Learning to use the Z5's modern autofocus system is easy, but you do need to fully understand how the system works to get the most benefit from it. Once you're comfortable with autofocus, you'll know when it's appropriate to use the manual focus option, too.

As the camera collects focus information from the sensors, it then evaluates it to determine whether the desired sharp focus has been achieved. The calculations may include whether the subject is moving, and whether the camera needs to "predict" where the subject will be when the shutter release button is fully depressed and the picture is taken. The speed with which the camera is able to evaluate focus and then move the lens elements into the proper position to achieve the sharpest focus determines how fast the autofocus mechanism is. Although your Z5 will almost always focus more quickly than a human eye, there are types of shooting situations where that's not fast enough. For example, if you're having problems shooting a sport with many fast-moving players because the Z5's autofocus system manically follows each moving subject, a better choice might be to switch Autofocus modes, or shift into Manual and prefocus on a spot where you anticipate the action will be, such as a goal line or soccer net.

The Z5 has a hybrid autofocus system, using two technologies called contrast-detection autofocus (CDAF) and phase-detection autofocus (PDAF). I'm going to provide a quick overview of contrast detection first, and then devote much of the rest of this chapter to the complexities of phase detection.

Contrast Detection

This is a slower, but potentially more accurate mode, best suited for static subjects, and was originally the only kind of autofocus available for mirrorless cameras and for dSLRs when shooting in their Live View and Movie modes. The recent innovation of adding phase-detection abilities to the sensor itself (as I'll describe shortly) made contrast detection a fine-tuning option for hybrid autofocus systems that combined CDAF and PDAF.

Contrast detection is very easy to understand, and is illustrated by Figure 5.1, a close-up of some weathered wood. At top in the figure, the transitions between the edges found in the image are soft and blurred because of the low contrast between them. Whether the edges are horizontal, vertical, or diagonal doesn't matter in the least; the focus system looks only for contrast between edges, and those edges can run in any direction at all.

At the bottom of Figure 5.1, the image has been brought into sharp focus, and the edges have much more contrast; the transitions are sharp and clear. Although this example is a bit exaggerated so you can see the results on the printed page, it's easy to understand that when maximum contrast in a subject is achieved, it can be deemed to be in sharp focus. Although achieving focus with contrast detection is generally quite a bit slower, there are several advantages—and disadvantages—to this method:

- **Works with more image types.** Any subject that has edges will work with CDAF.
- **Focus on any point.** With contrast detection, any portion of the image can be used to focus: you don't need dedicated AF sensors. Focus is achieved with the actual sensor image, so focus point selection is simply a matter of choosing which part of the sensor image to use. It's easy to move the focus point around to virtually any location. Because a smaller area of the sensor can be used to focus, the Z5 uses contrast detection when the autofocus area mode is set to Pinpoint AF. (I'll explain AF-area modes later in this chapter.)
- **Potentially more accurate.** Contrast detection is clear-cut. The camera can clearly see when the highest contrast has been achieved, as long as there is sufficient light to allow the camera to examine the image produced by the sensor. However, some "hunting" may be necessary. As the camera seeks the ideal plane of focus, it may overshoot and have to back up a little, then re-correct if the new focus plane is not optimal. However, once CDAF settles on the ideal focus plane, the results are generally very accurate. Contrast detection is an excellent way of fine-tuning focus that has been achieved through PDAF.

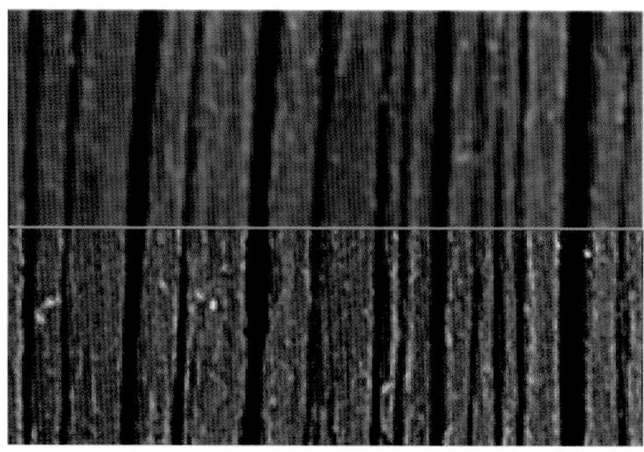

Figure 5.1 Focus in contrast-detection mode evaluates the increase in contrast in the edges of subjects, starting with a blurry image (top) and producing a sharp, contrasty image (bottom).

Phase Detection

Phase detection is easily much more rapid than contrast detection. The challenge is to make its operation as accurate as possible. Digital SLRs, like the Z5's sibling the D780, have always used PDAF. Such dSLR systems include an array of tiny autofocus sensors, located in the "floor" of the mirror box, with a small portion of the illumination directed downward to the autofocus sensor array.

In the Z5, that separate AF sensor is replaced by 273 phase-detect autofocus points embedded in the camera's imaging sensor. These points are located in the center of the boxes shown in Figure 5.2. The boxes represent the positions you can individually select as your AF area in Single-point AF-area mode—not the size of the PDAF pixels themselves, which are much smaller.

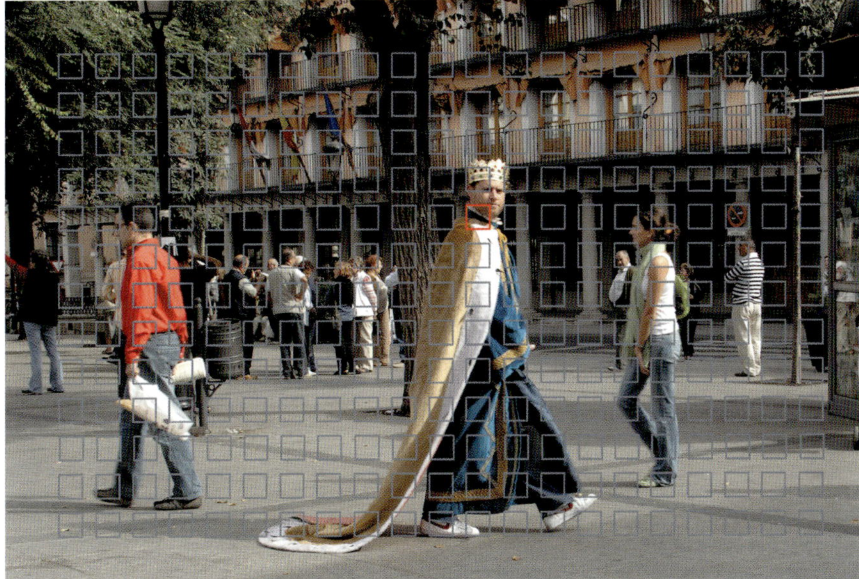

Figure 5.2 The boxes represent the 273 selectable AF areas when using Single-point autofocus.

The phase-detection pixels in the Z5's sensor have a mask covering half of the pixel on one side, with a nearby laterally displaced phase-detection pixel masked on the opposite side. The effect is to create two different "views," each arriving from opposite sides of the lens. This pair of images functions exactly like the rangefinders used for surveying and in rangefinder-focusing cameras like the venerable Leica M series. The dual images are separated when out of focus, and then gradually brought together to achieve sharp focus, as shown from top to bottom in Figure 5.3. **Note:** Using some photosites as AF sensors doesn't rob your Z5 of resolution; the camera has 24 *million* pixels available to create an image; assigning a few hundred to the AF task is a minor cost to pay.

This process tells the camera when the image pair are "in phase" and aligned. The rangefinder approach of phase detection tells the Z5 exactly how out of focus the image is, and in which direction (focus is too near, or too far) thanks to the amount and direction of the displacement of the split image. The camera can quickly and precisely snap the image into sharp focus and match the lines.

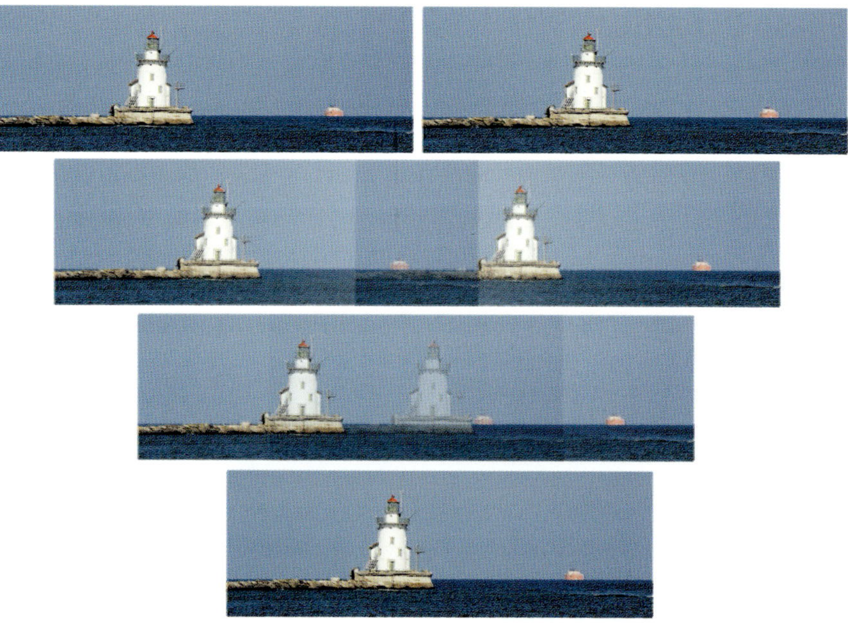

Figure 5.3 In phase detection, parts of an image are split in two and compared (top). When the image is in focus, the two halves of the image align, as with a rangefinder (bottom).

The PDAF sensors in the Z5 are all *line sensors,* which means they work best with features that transect the sensor either perpendicularly or at an angle, as visualized in Figure 5.3, top left and right. It's easy to detect when the two halves of the vertical lines of the weathered wood—actually a 19th century lighthouse—are aligned. However, when the same sensor is asked to measure focus for, say, horizontal lines that don't split up quite so conveniently, or, in the worst case, subjects such as the sky (which may have neither vertical nor horizontal lines), focus can slow down drastically, or even become impossible. One such scenario is pictured in Figure 5.4, bottom left. A possible solution is to incorporate vertically oriented AF sensors, which can easily focus horizontal subject matter (Figure 5.4, bottom right). The line sensors arranged perpendicularly to each other are called "cross-type" sensors.

However, the Z5 has no cross sensors, as such PDAF pixels are difficult (expensive, actually) to embed in today's image sensors. Nikon uses a different approach. Once the focus plane has been achieved using the line sensors of the phase-detect system, the Z5 is able to use contrast detection to fine-tune focus, if necessary. The combination provides the speed of PDAF with the accuracy of CDAF.

As with any rangefinder-like function, phase-detection accuracy is better when the "base length" between the two images is larger. (Think back to your high school trigonometry; you could calculate a distance more accurately when the separation between the two points where the angles were measured was greater.) For that reason, phase-detection autofocus is more accurate with larger (wider) lens openings—especially those with maximum f/stops of f/2.8 or better—than with smaller lens openings, and may not work at all when the f/stop is smaller than f/8. As I noted, the Z5 is able to perform these comparisons very quickly.

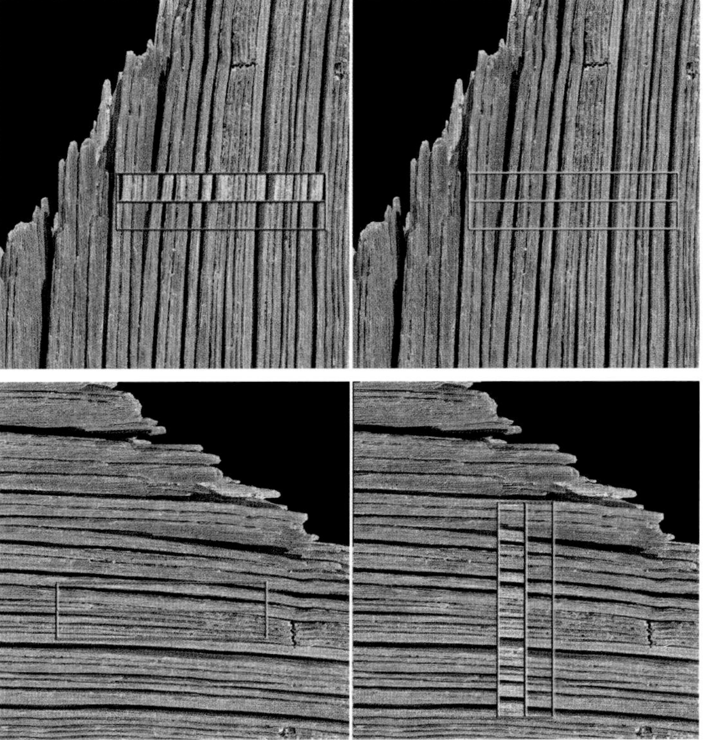

Figure 5.4 When an image is out of focus, the split lines don't align precisely (top left). Using phase detection, the Z5 is able to align the features of the image and achieve sharp focus quickly (top right). Horizontal lines aren't ideal for horizontally oriented sensors (bottom left) and require vertically oriented AF sensors (bottom right).

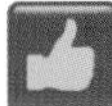

TIP If you find your Z5's horizontal line AF sensors (which are most sensitive to vertical lines) have difficulties focusing on a subject that is predominated by horizontal features, rotate the camera at least 45 degrees and lock focus, then return to your previous orientation. Obviously, this works best with subjects that aren't moving.

Adding Circles of Confusion

But there are other factors in play, as well. You know that increased depth-of-field brings more of your subject into focus. But more depth-of-field also makes autofocusing (or manual focusing) more difficult because the contrast is lower between objects at different distances. So, autofocus with a 200mm lens (or zoom setting) may be easier than at a 28mm focal length (or zoom setting) because the longer lens has less apparent depth-of-field. By the same token, a lens with a maximum aperture of f/1.8, such as the Z-mount 50mm f/1.8 and 35mm f/1.8 optics, will be easier to autofocus (or manually focus) than one of the same focal length with an f/4 maximum aperture, such as the Nikkor Z 24-70mm f/4 zoom, because the f/4 lens has more depth-of-field *and* a dimmer view at a particular focal length.

To make things even more complicated, many subjects aren't polite enough to remain still. They move around in the frame, so that even if the Z5 is sharply focused on your main subject, it may change position and require refocusing. An intervening subject may pop into the frame and pass between you and the subject you meant to photograph. You (or the Z5) have to decide whether to lock focus on this new subject or remain focused on the original subject. Finally, there are some kinds of subjects that are difficult to bring into sharp focus because they lack enough contrast to allow the Z5's AF system (or our eyes) to lock in. Blank walls, a clear blue sky, birds-in-flight, or other subject matter may make focusing difficult.

If you find all these focus factors confusing, you're on the right track. Focus is, in fact, measured using something called a *circle of confusion*. An ideal image consists of zillions of tiny little points, which, like all points, theoretically have no height or width. There is perfect contrast between the point and its surroundings. You can think of each point as a pinpoint of light in a darkened room. When a given point is out of focus, its edges decrease in contrast and it changes from a perfect point to a tiny disc with blurry edges (remember, blur is the lack of contrast between boundaries in an image). (See Figure 5.5.)

If this blurry disc—the circle of confusion—is small enough, our eye still perceives it as a point. It's only when the disc grows large enough that we can see it as a blur rather than a sharp point that a given point is viewed as out of focus. You can see, then, that enlarging an image, either by displaying it larger on your computer monitor or by making a large print, also enlarges the size of each circle of confusion. Moving closer to the image does the same thing. So, parts of an image that may look perfectly sharp in a 5 × 7–inch print viewed at arm's length, might appear blurry when blown up to 11 × 14 and examined at the same distance. Take a few steps back, however, and it may look sharp again.

To a lesser extent, the viewer also affects the apparent size of these circles of confusion. Some people see details better at a given distance and may perceive smaller circles of confusion than someone standing next to them. For the most part, however, such differences are small. Truly blurry images will look blurry to just about everyone under the same conditions.

Technically, there is just one plane within your picture area, parallel to the back of the camera (or sensor, in the case of a digital camera), that is in sharp focus. That's the plane in which the points of the image are rendered as precise points. At every other plane in front of or behind the focus plane, the points show up as discs that range from slightly blurry to extremely blurry. In practice, the discs in many of these planes will still be so small that we see them as points, and that's where we get depth-of-field. Depth-of-field is just the range of planes that include discs that we perceive as points rather than blurred splotches. The size of this range increases as the aperture is reduced in size and is allocated roughly one-third in front of the plane of sharpest focus, and two-thirds behind it. The range of sharp focus is always greater behind your subject than in front of it. (See Figure 5.6.)

Figure 5.5 When a pinpoint of light (left) goes out of focus, its blurry edges form a circle of confusion (center and right).

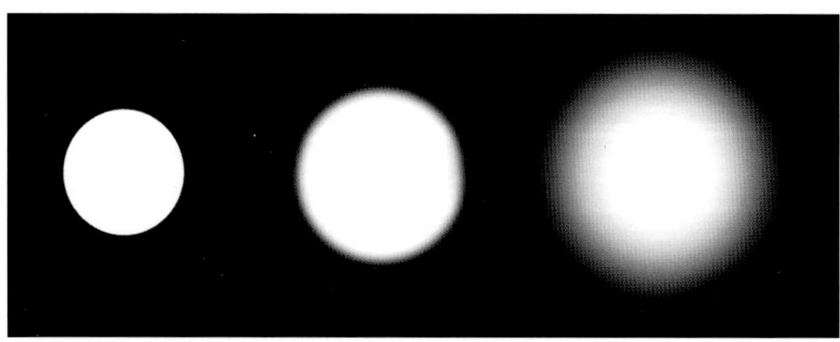

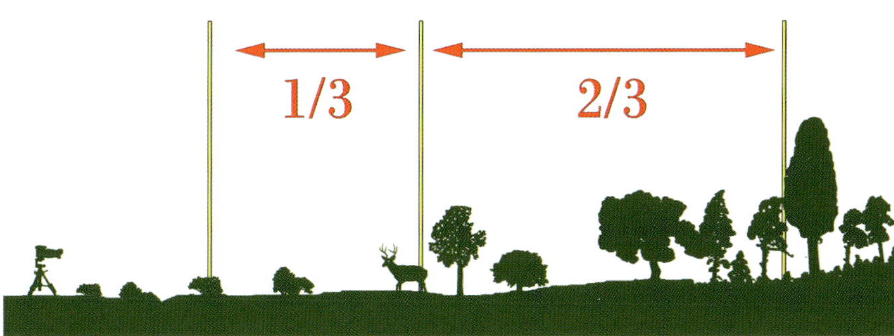

Figure 5.6 The range of sharp focus is greater behind your subject than in front of it.

Using Autofocus with the Nikon Z5

Autofocus can sometimes be frustrating for the new digital photographer, especially those coming from the point-and-shoot world. That's because correct focus plays a greater role among your creative options with a digital camera, even when photographing the same subjects. Most point-and-shoot digital cameras and smartphones have sensors that are much tinier than the sensor in the Z5. Those smaller sensors require shorter focal length lenses and zoom settings, which have, effectively, more depth-of-field.

The bottom line is that with the average point-and-shoot camera or smartphone, *everything* is in focus from about one foot to infinity and at virtually every f/stop. Unless you're shooting close-up photos a few inches from the camera, the depth-of-field is prodigious, and autofocus is almost a non-factor. The Z5, on the other hand, is a full-frame camera that uses longer focal length lenses to achieve the same field of view with its larger sensor, so there is less depth-of-field. That's a *good* thing, creatively, because you have the choice to use selective focus to isolate subjects. But it does make the correct use of autofocus more critical. To maintain the most creative control, you have to choose three attributes:

- **How much is in focus.** Generally, by choosing the f/stop used, you'll determine the *range* of sharpness/amount of depth-of-field. The more extensive the DOF, the "easier" it is for the autofocus system's locked-in focus point to be appropriate (even though, strictly speaking, there is only one actual plane of sharp focus). With less depth-of-field, the accuracy of the focus point becomes more critical, because even a small error will result in an out-of-focus shot.

- **What subject is in focus.** The portion of your subject that is zeroed in for autofocus is determined by the autofocus zone that is active, and which is chosen either by you or by the Nikon Z5 (as described next). For example, when shooting portraits, it's actually okay for part of the subject— or even part of the subject's face—to be slightly out of focus as long as the eyes (or even just the *nearest* eye) appear sharp.

- **When focus is applied.** For static shots of objects that aren't moving, *when* focus is applied doesn't matter much. But when you're shooting sports, or birds in flight, or children, the subject may move within the viewfinder as you're framing the image. Whether that movement is across the frame or headed right toward you, timing the instant when autofocus is applied can be important.

Bringing the Z5's AF System into Focus

I've explained individual bits and pieces of the Nikon Z5's autofocus system earlier in this book, particularly in the "roadmap" sections that showed you where all the controls were located, and the "setup" chapters that explained the key autofocus options. Now it's time to round out the coverage as we tie everything together. There are three aspects of autofocus that you need to understand to use this essential feature productively. They apply—in slightly different ways—to both autofocus when using the optical viewfinder, and in Photo/Movie shooting modes. For now, we're going to concentrate on the system's most important features:

- **Autofocus mode and priority.** This governs *when* during the framing and shooting process autofocus is achieved. Should the camera focus once when activated, or continue to monitor your subject and refocus should the subject move? Is it okay to take a picture even if sharp focus isn't yet achieved, or should the camera lock out the shutter release until the image is sharp?

- **Autofocus point selection.** This aspect controls how the Z5 selects which areas of the frame are used to evaluate focus. Point selection allows the camera (or you) to specify a subject and lock focus in on that subject.

- **Autofocus activation.** When should the autofocus process *begin*, and when should it be locked? This aspect is related to the autofocus mode but uses controls that you can specify to activate and/or lock the autofocus process.

As the camera collects information from the sensors, it then evaluates the data to determine whether the desired sharp focus has been achieved. The calculations may include whether the subject is moving, and whether the camera needs to "predict" where the subject will be when the shutter release button is fully depressed and the picture is taken.

The speed with which the camera is able to evaluate focus and then move the lens elements into the proper position to achieve the sharpest focus determines how fast the autofocus mechanism is. Although your Z5 will almost always focus more quickly than a human, there are types of shooting situations where that's not fast enough. For example, as I mentioned, if you're having problems shooting sports because the Z5's autofocus system follows each moving subject, a better choice might be to switch autofocus modes or shift into manual and prefocus on a spot where you anticipate the action will be, such as a goal line. At night football games, for example, when I am shooting with a telephoto lens almost wide open, I often focus manually on one of the referees who happens to be standing where I expect the action to be taking place (say, a halfback run or a pass reception).

Focus Mode and Priority

Choosing the right focus mode (AF-S, AF-C, or Manual) is another key to focusing success. (Your Z5 also has an additional focus mode, AF-F—full-time autofocus in Movie mode, as explained in Chapter 14.) To save battery power, when shooting stills, your Z5 doesn't start to focus the lens until you partially depress the shutter release or press the AF-ON button on the back of the camera (unless you've reprogrammed the button for some other function or have specified another control to activate autofocus, as described in Chapter 12). But, autofocus isn't some mindless beast out there snapping your pictures in and out of focus with no feedback from you after you press that button.

There are several settings you can modify that return at least a modicum of control to you. Your first decisions should be whether you set the Z5 to AF-S, AF-C, or manual focus; and whether to use focus-priority or release-priority.

You can easily specify AF-S, AF-C, or Manual focus: just press Fn2 and rotate the main command dial (unless you've redefined the button for some other behavior). Or press the *i* button and access Focus Mode, located by default at the far right in the bottom row of the *i* menu. If you have a lot of time on your hands, use the Focus Mode entry in the Photo or Movie Shooting menus. The AF mode appears at the top of the viewfinder or on the monitor screen as you make the adjustments.

Autofocus Mode

This choice determines *when* your Z5 starts to autofocus, and what it does when focus is achieved. In still photo mode, automatic focus is not something that happens all the time when your camera is turned on. As I mentioned, to save battery power, your Z5 generally doesn't start to focus the lens until you partially depress the shutter release. (You can also use the sub-selector center button or substitute a defined AE/AL Lock button instead to start autofocus, as described under Custom Setting f2 in Chapter 12.)

Single-Servo Autofocus (AF-S)

In this mode, also called *Single Autofocus* or *AF-S*, focus is set once and remains at that setting until the button is fully depressed, taking the picture, or until you release the shutter button without taking a shot. For non-action photography, this setting may be your best choice, as it minimizes out-of-focus pictures (at the expense of spontaneity). The drawback here is that you might not be able to take a picture at all while the camera is seeking focus; you're locked out until the autofocus mechanism is happy with the current setting. As described in Chapter 12, you can set AF-S mode to use either focus-priority (the default) or release-priority using Custom Setting a2.

A red indicator shows the user-selected focus area, which you can move around within the frame using the directional controls. In Auto-area AF mode, red brackets (which you cannot move) are displayed representing the location of the 273 individual PDAF focus points. When sharp focus is achieved, the user-specified focus point (or the points selected by the camera in Auto-area AF mode) will turn green. You'll hear a beep (if not disabled using Beep Options in the Setup menu, as described in Chapter 13) and the camera is set to focus-priority. By keeping the shutter button depressed halfway, you'll find you can reframe the image while retaining the focus (and exposure) that's been set. You can also use your AE-L/AF-L button (such as the sub-selector button). If the camera is unable to focus, the focus point will flash red. Because of the small delay while the camera zeroes in on correct focus, you might experience slightly more shutter lag. This mode uses less battery power.

Using the directional controls, you can select any of the 273 focus areas in this AF mode when your Autofocus Area setting (described shortly) is set to Single-point AF, large and small zones when Wide (S) or Wide (L) focus area modes are enabled, or virtually anywhere within the focus area encompassed by the boxes in Figure 5.2 when Pinpoint-area AF is active. AF-S is the mode to use if you want to place the focus point within your frame with accuracy.

Before the introduction of mirrorless cameras, AF-S was the most convenient way of locking in focus precisely on a subject not located in the center of the frame. Although dSLRs generally have multiple available focus points, they are all concentrated in a region around the center area and may cover only 25 to 30 percent of the frame. To lock focus on areas outside that coverage area, it's necessary to frame an image so the subject is within the AF area, using the AF-S focus mode. You can then press the shutter release halfway to lock focus, and then reframe.

You can do the same thing in AF-S with the Z5 if you like, but it isn't actually necessary, as the available focus points cover virtually all of the frame, and you can easily relocate a user-selectable active focus point or zone anywhere you like. So, AF-S isn't as useful as it was with non-mirrorless cameras.

LOW-LIGHT AF

All digital cameras find autofocusing in low-light environments a challenge. The Z5's abundant PDAF pixels slightly reduce the area of the sensor available to capture photons, and some report the bands or stripes that can appear in darker areas of an image. You may be able to improve autofocus performance for subjects that are within the range of about three feet to nearly 10 feet (1 to 3 meters) with the built-in AF-assist illuminator lamp on the front of the camera, which is activated by default but may be disabled using Custom Setting a12. You can also activate Custom Setting a11: Low-Light AF, which works in any still photo shooting mode other than Auto. Autofocus may take longer in Low-Light mode, so a warning appears on the display. Both settings operate only when using the AF-S focus mode.

Continuous-Servo Autofocus (AF-C)

This mode, also known as *AF-C*, is the mode to use for sports and other types of photography with fast-moving subjects. In this mode, once the shutter release is partially depressed, the camera sets the focus but continues to monitor the subject, so that if it moves or you move, the lens will be refocused to suit. Focus and exposure aren't really locked until you press the shutter release down all the way to take the picture. You'll find that AF-C produces the least amount of shutter lag of any autofocus mode when set to release-priority: press the button and the camera fires, even if sharp focus has not quite been achieved. It also uses the most battery power, because the autofocus system operates as long as the shutter release button is partially depressed.

When using AF-C, the active focus areas are shown in red, as with AF-S mode. However, when you press the shutter release halfway down (or press a defined AE-L/AF-L button), when the camera achieves sharp focus, you won't see a green box or hear a beep as confirmation. That's a *good* thing. If that were the case, since AF-C constantly refocuses as long as the shutter release is held down halfway (or AE-L/AF-L button is depressed), you'd be treated by a barrage of beeps and constantly flickering green indicator until the picture is taken. If you see your subject has gone out of focus and the Z5 doesn't quickly recover, just release the button and press again to restart the focusing process.

Continuous-servo autofocus uses a technology called *predictive tracking AF*, which allows the Z5 to calculate the correct focus if the subject is moving toward or away from the camera at a constant rate. It uses either the automatically selected AF point (in Auto-area AF mode) or the point you select manually to set focus. As described in Chapter 12, you can set AF-C mode to use release-priority (the default), or focus-priority using Custom Setting a1.

Focus-Priority versus Release-Priority

One autofocus aspect that's often misunderstood is the concept of *priority*. The Z5 allows you to choose either focus-priority or release-priority, which determine whether the camera delays taking a picture until sharp focus is achieved when the shutter release is pressed down all the way, or whether it takes a picture immediately. You can use Custom Settings a1: AF-C Priority Selection and a2: AF-S Priority Selection to specify your choice.

- **Focus-priority.** This is the default setting for the AF-S autofocus mode. When enabled, the Z5 will not take a picture when you press the shutter release down all the way until focus is confirmed. This may cause a slight delay, *but only if the Z5 has not yet finished the autofocus process.* In practice, there are three possibilities:
  - **In AF-S mode:** if you've already pressed the shutter release halfway to lock in focus, the camera will go ahead and take your photo with no further delay.
  - **In AF-S mode:** if you haven't pressed the shutter release halfway—say you press down all the way in one continuous motion—there may be a delay until the camera confirms focus. This delay may be very short if your subject can be easily focused using your current AF-area mode, or somewhat longer if achieving sharp focus (say, with a subject that's low in contrast against its background) is problematic. Note that focus-priority can reduce continuous shooting frame rates while the Z5 waits for the AF system.
  - **In AF-C mode:** if you've set AF-C mode to focus-priority (which I don't recommend), the camera will continuously focus and refocus as long as the shutter release is held down halfway. That will usually translate into only a minimal delay when the shutter button is finally fully depressed to take the picture.
- **Release-priority.** This is the default setting for AF-C autofocus mode. When active, the Z5 will take a picture as soon as the shutter release is pressed down all the way, *even if sharp autofocus has not been confirmed.* Sports, action, and wildlife photographers use release-priority almost exclusively, because capturing the decisive moment takes precedence over getting the sharpest possible photo. But don't make the mistake of thinking that release-priority will produce a large number of slightly out-of-focus photos. The majority of the time, this setting will produce sharp photos even though the AF system has not yet been able to *confirm* focus.

  I like to stick with release-priority for AF-C mode, because it has less impact on continuous shooting speeds. In general, AF-C will lock in focus for the first shot in a continuous sequence and subsequent exposures in the series won't really require much adjustment of focus. You could use focus-priority in AF-C mode when *not* shooting continuously and the sharpest focus possible was required. Release-priority provides no special advantages for AF-S mode (especially if you prefocus by pressing the shutter button halfway), so I don't use it.

Full-time Autofocus (AF-F) (Movie Mode Only)

This mode, also known as *AF-F*, is available only in Movie mode. You don't need to activate focus with a button: the camera adjusts focus continually as your subject moves. Focus locks only when the shutter release is pressed halfway. Obviously, this mode uses the most juice.

Manual Focus

Set manual focus by sliding the focus mode switch on a lens to the M position (if it has such a switch), or by using the Fn2 button, *i* menu, or Photo/Movie Shooting menu options. (F-mount lenses attached to the Z5 using the FTZ adapter may use a variation on the M position, which I'll explain later.) There are some advantages and disadvantages to using Manual focus. While your batteries will last longer in manual focus mode, it will take you longer to focus the camera for each photo, a process that can be difficult. Modern digital cameras depend so much on autofocus that the viewfinders are no longer designed for optimum manual focus. Pick up any film camera and you'll see a bigger, brighter viewfinder with a focusing screen that's a joy to focus on manually. I'll tell you more about manual focus later in this chapter.

Choosing an Autofocus Area Mode

If your Z5 isn't focusing on the correct subject, autofocus speed and activation are pretty much wasted effort. As you've learned, the Z5 has up to 273 different points on the screen that can be individually selected to determine the active focus zone. You can choose which of those points is used by selecting an AF-area mode. As with AF mode, you can select the AF-area mode from the *i* menu, Photo/Movie Shooting menus, or by holding down the Fn2 button and rotating the sub-command dial. The Z5 has six different focus point selection modes. I'm going to describe each of the modes and explain how to use them.

Pinpoint AF

This mode is available only in Single AF (AF-S) focus mode. In this mode, you always select the focus point manually, using the sub-selector joystick *or* the multi selector (which, helpfully, will respond to your thumb presses not only in the left/right and up/down directions, but diagonally, as well). Return the focus point to the center at any time by pressing the OK button.

The focus point is represented by the tiny box shown in Figure 5.7. You have an extraordinary amount of freedom in placing the focus area, which is roughly one-quarter the size of that used for Single-Point AF (described next). Pinpoint AF uses contrast detection within the selected area; it's not limited by the position of the fixed PDAF pixels represented by the larger boxes.

Obviously, selecting an AF point so precisely can be time-consuming, so Pinpoint AF is best suited for subjects that don't move. It's especially good for macro work and any photography undertaken with the camera mounted on a tripod.

Single-Point AF

As with the other user-selectable area modes, you can select the focus point manually, using the sub-selector joystick *or* the multi selector. The Z5 evaluates focus based solely on the point you select, making this another good choice for subjects that don't move much. You can choose Custom Setting a5: Focus Points Used, to select whether the focus point resides within the 273-area array by choosing ALL (see Figure 5.8) or a more widely spaced distribution (Every Other Point) which activates only one-quarter of the focus areas, 77 in an 11 × 7 array (see Figure 5.9). The alternate point mode allows much faster positioning of your focus zone. I use Every Other Point a lot for sports, because

I plan on filling as much of the frame as possible with players and can usually estimate where they will appear in the frame. (That's usually off center, closer to the edge where I expect them to enter the frame.) Single-Point AF is excellent for achieving focus on a subject that might otherwise blend in with its background.

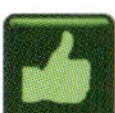 **TIP** The Every Other Point setting does not affect the number of focus points used with Wide-area AF (Small or Large), which I'll describe shortly.

Dynamic-Area AF

In this mode, available only when AF-C is active, you still select the *primary* focus point yourself from among the 273 available using the multi selector or sub-selector controls (see Figure 5.10). The camera will focus on that point in most cases, but if the subject departs from the selected area, the Z5 uses information from the surrounding areas. However, if the user-selected primary focus point isn't suitable for focusing, the Z5 will use one of the secondary focus points instead. That might be

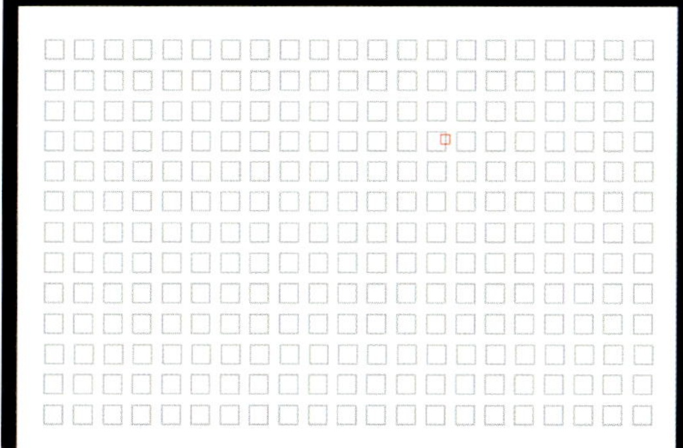

Figure 5.7 The Pinpoint AF selection box can be moved in tiny increments virtually anywhere within the area represented by the 273 AF point boxes.

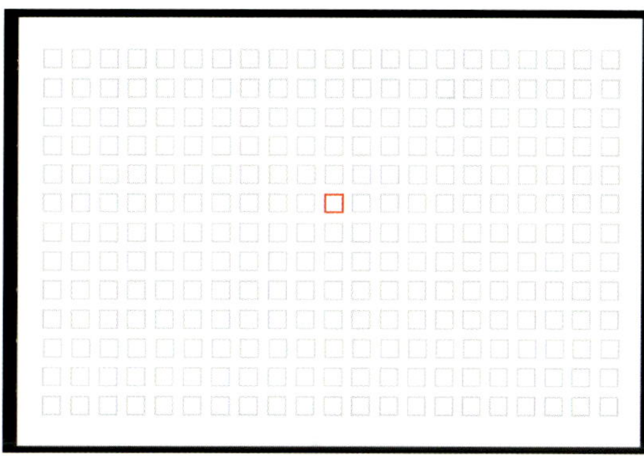

Figure 5.8 By default, Single-point AF allows you to choose from all 273 focus zones.

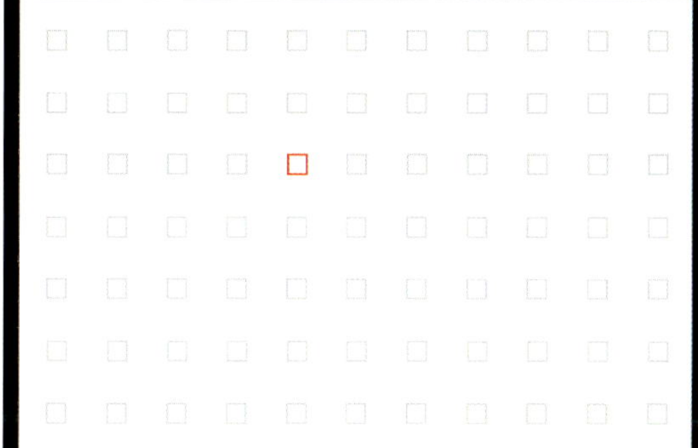

Figure 5.9 The number of focus points is reduced by three-quarters when you specify Every Other Point with Custom Setting a5.

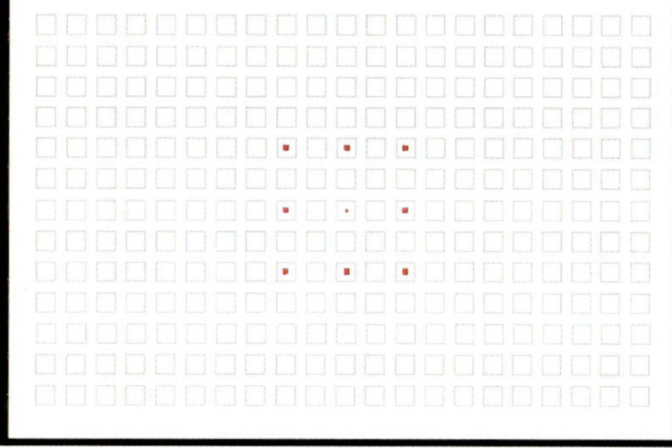

Figure 5.10 You can select a primary focus point with Dynamic-area AF, but adjacent points will also be used if your subject moves outside the primary area.

the case if the selected focus point is on an area of low contrast, such as the sky, or the subject is too small (perhaps a distant object).

The red-highlighted points in the middle of Figure 5.10 show the active focus points when the dynamic area is centered in the frame. You can move the grouping to any of the other points, but when the grouping reaches the top border or corners (as shown in the corners of the figure), some of the potential points are outside the array, effectively giving you fewer points to work with.

Dynamic-area AF is a more sophisticated version of Single-point AF. You can select the *initial* focus point, and then trust the Z5's smarts to continue focusing on a moving subject. That frees you to concentrate on framing your composition rather than worrying about whether your subject remains in focus.

This setting is excellent for slow-moving subjects, as seen in Figure 5.11, left, but flexible enough to follow subjects that move erratically from side to side (say, a child at play or a basketball player moving around the court on defense), because the camera can use the distance information to differentiate the original subject from objects that are closer or farther away, especially human subjects (see Figure 5.11, right). However, many photographers also use this setting for birds in flight. Very rapid motion may call for the Z5's tracking feature, described shortly.

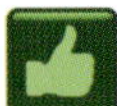 **TIP** In Pinpoint AF, Single-point AF, or Dynamic-area AF, if you want to lock the focus point you've selected for a series of shots, you can temporarily lock the focus point by partially depressing and holding the shutter release, or pressing and holding the AE-L/AF-L button (by default the sub-selector button). Press the multi selector center button to move the single focus point back to the center of the frame quickly.

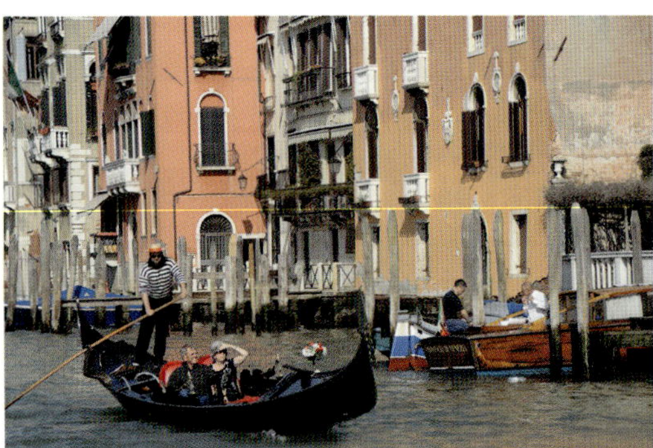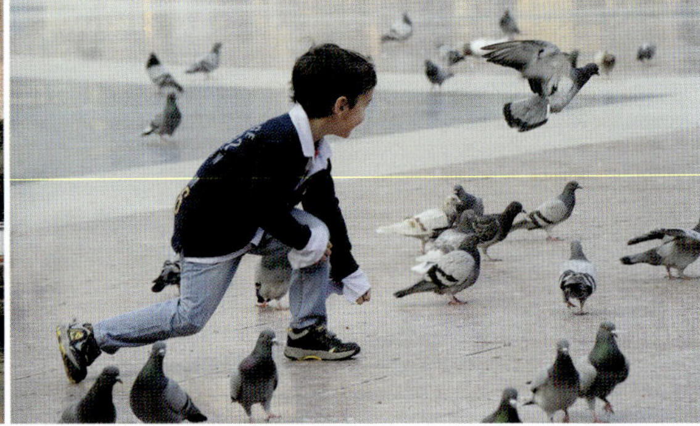

Figure 5.11 Focus on slow-moving subjects with Dynamic-area AF (left). More erratic subjects (right) can work, too, but may require using the Z5's tracking feature.

Wide-Area AF (Small and Large)

This mode uses the focus points within zones you can move around the display. You can choose the smaller of the wide-area zones (one is shown outlined in red in Figure 5.12, or even larger zones, like the one seen outlined in red in Figure 5.13). I don't use these much, especially Wide-area (L), because they each encompass so much of the frame that they're best suited for large subjects that will reside in a predictable area, and those are often handled quite efficiently with Single-point AF. The Wide-area AF settings try to focus on the closest object within the zone, so you can end up having the Z5 focus on the nose of a long-snouted animal (or person with a prominent schnozzola) instead of the eyes. However, when I do use either of these, I prefer the Small version. The Wide-area AF (Large) option can often inappropriately focus on the background even if your main subject is the closest object.

Automatic-Area AF

In this mode, autofocus point selection is out of your hands; the Z5 performs the task for you using its own intelligence. The camera can even work with the distance information supplied by the lens and its face detection technology to distinguish humans from their background, so a person standing at the side of the frame will be detected and used to evaluate focus, while the camera ignores the background area in the frame.

In AF-S mode, the active focus points, all located within the red brackets shown in Figure 5.14, are highlighted with an array of green boxes that illuminate as you hold the shutter release down halfway; until that happens, you have no idea where in the frame the camera will be focusing. In AF-C mode, a dancing array of red boxes appears around the focused area, highlighted in that color to indicate that the current focus point is only tentative and won't be locked in until you press the shutter release down all the way. Only one of the frantic boxes will actually be used to determine focus. Birds in flight—one of the most difficult of all autofocus targets—can often be grabbed using Automatic-area AF.

This mode's face-detection and tracking features merit a more detailed discussion of their own, which I'll provide in the next section.

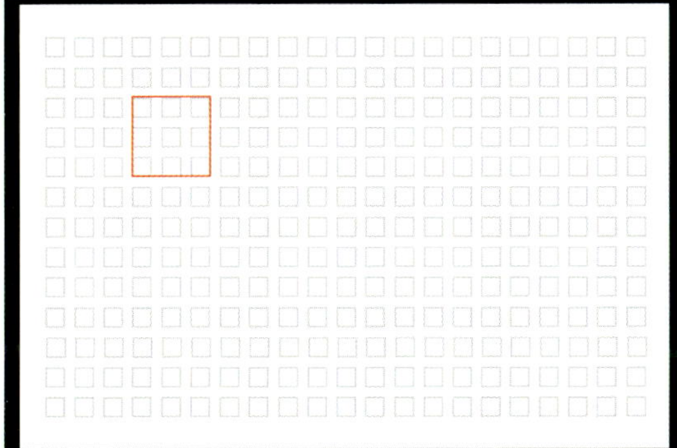

Figure 5.12 Wide-area AF zones can be moved around the frame. The Small-area version is shown here.

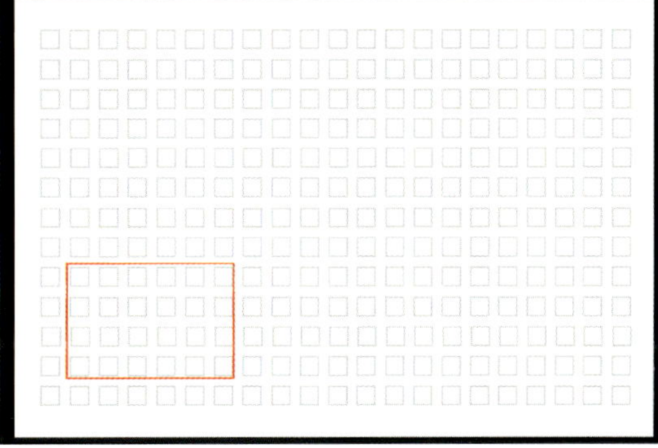

Figure 5.13 The Wide-area AF Large zones occupy a larger area of the frame and cannot be located as close to the edges as their Small counterparts.

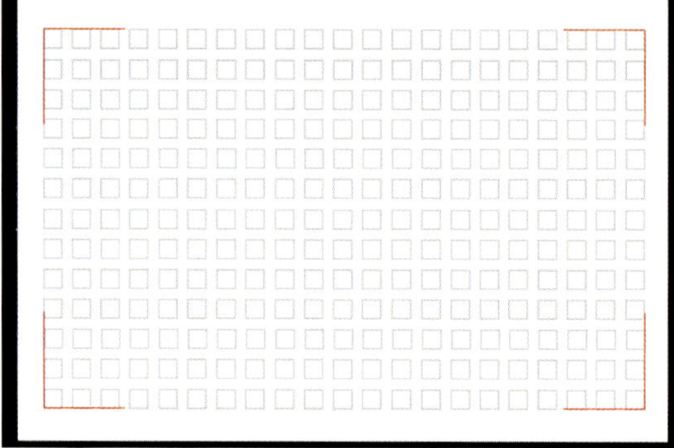

Figure 5.14 The red brackets show the area covered in Automatic-area AF.

REDUCING YOUR OPTIONS

If you find yourself using only certain AF-area modes, you can tell the Z5 to "hide" the modes you do not work with. Custom Setting a8: Limit AF-Area Mode Selection allows you to enable or disable any of the AF-area modes (except Single-point AF, which is mandatory). If you need more help activating this option, I'll explain it for you in Chapter 12.

Face/Eye Detection and Subject Tracking

The Auto-area AF feature has two great features that allow you to identify human targets and track any kind of moving subjects (birds-in-flight, people-in-flight, and others). *Face detection* allows the camera to locate potential portrait subjects when the visage of a human being appears in the frame. *Focus tracking with lock-on* directs the Z5 to follow the movement of a subject you specify and continue to focus on it as it roams around the frame. Note that you *must* be using Auto-area AF to use either of these two features. I'll explain face/eye detection first, and then detail subject tracking later.

Face/Eye Detection

Face and eye detection enable the Z5 to find, focus on, and track human faces or eyes and to detect and focus on animals. Use these modes for portraits and people pictures and for capturing images of your pets (at present only cats or dogs are detected with the most reliability). You'll get the best results when your subjects are facing the camera directly; the features become less accurate as the face turns away from the camera toward a profile view.

To activate face/eye detection, visit Custom Setting a4: Auto-area AF Face/Eye Detection. You'll find four choices:

- **Face and eye detection on.** The Z5 will look for both human faces and eyes and attempt to focus on the nearest eye. If the camera cannot positively identify an eye, it will switch to Face-detection mode automatically. This mode is the most versatile when your subjects are relatively close to the camera, as eyes will be relatively larger and easier to detect.

- **Face detection on.** The Z5 does not try to detect eyes, but instead looks only for human faces, and attempts to focus on the closest face. Use this mode for groups or when your subject is farther away from the camera.

- **Animal detection on.** The Z5 will try to detect animal faces and focus on them. I recommend turning this option off if no animals are present, as the feature sometimes "finds" the face of a dog or cat in unlikely places, such as shrubbery that happens to resemble a furry friend.

- **Off.** If no humans or animals are present, or you don't want them to receive special AF priority, you can disable face/eye detection using this option.

You can't directly select the focus zone yourself. Instead, a yellow border will be displayed on the LCD when the camera detects a face. You don't need to press the shutter release to activate this behavior—in this mode, the camera starts looking for faces immediately. Several faces may be detected, with a yellow border aligned with the selected face (usually, the face that is closest to the camera) or the selected eye (if eye detection is enabled). You have several options at your disposal:

- **Face or eye detected.** If at least one face or eye is found, a yellow border will appear around the detected feature.

- **Multiple faces/eyes.** If more than one face or eye is present, the yellow border will include one or two triangles indicating that you can use the left or right directional controls to move the highlighting to the next face or eye. Figure 5.15 shows what the screen looks like when an eye is detected (upper box) or just a face (lower box). **Note:** Both detection boxes cannot appear at once—only the eye *or* face frame will appear, depending on which the Z5 selects.

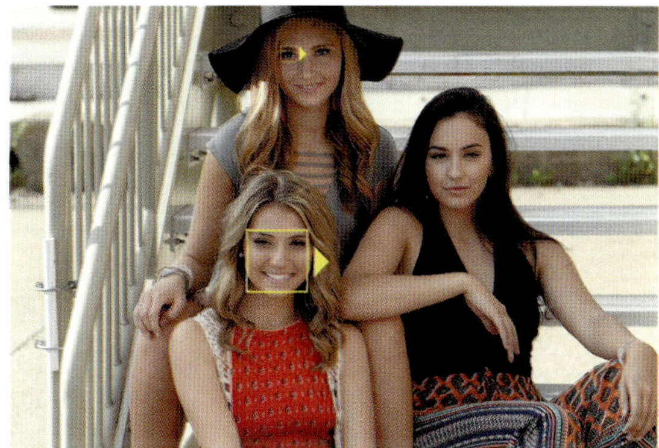

Figure 5.15 When an eye or face is detected, a yellow box appears around the eye (upper box) or face (lower box).

If faces/eyes are arranged at similar heights and the selected feature is in the middle, triangle "pointers" will appear at the left and right sides of the yellow border.

- **Select different face/eye.** Use the directional controls to switch to a different face or eye. If touch operation is enabled, you can tap a face with your finger and the Z5 will focus on that face (and take a picture immediately when you remove your finger from the screen if you've activated Touch Shutter).

- **Tracking.** If the subject with the highlighted face moves or you reframe the image, the camera will track and follow the selected face or eye.

- **Locking focus.** In AF-S mode, when you press down the shutter release halfway, the camera attempts to focus the face or eye. As sharp focus is achieved, the border turns green. If the camera is unable to focus, the border blinks red. Focus may also be lost if the subject turns away from the camera and is no longer detectable. In AF-C mode, the Z7 continues to focus on the selected face/eye until the shutter release is pressed down all the way to take the picture.

Subject Tracking

The useful Subject-tracking autofocus feature of Auto-area AF is one of those capabilities that can be confusing at first, but once you get the hang of it, it's remarkably easy to use. In fact, it's always available any time you're using Auto-area AF. Here's the quick introduction you need to subject tracking.

- **Choose refocus delay.** Navigate to Custom Setting a3: Focus Tracking with Lock-on. Choose the Blocked Shot AF Response value from 1 (Quick) to 5 (Delayed). This determines how quickly the camera refocuses when an intervening object passes in front of the subject you have chosen to track. With Quick, the Z5 will wait only a short moment, then refocus on the new object. With the maximum Delayed setting, the interrupting subject matter will be ignored for a period of time. You'll want to use a delay setting when shooting sports in which players or officials are likely to pass in front of the camera unexpectedly. A Quick setting will work well when shooting continuously, allowing the camera to refocus rapidly.

- **Ready, aim…** To select a subject for tracking, press the OK button at any time. A white border with directional arrows at its edges appears in the center of the frame. You can move the border around with the multi selector or sub-selector. Use that border to "aim" the camera until the subject you want to focus on and track is located within the border. (See Figure 5.16.) Because you can select at any time, if, say, you're shooting sports, you can wait until just before some action is going to begin, and then choose your subject.

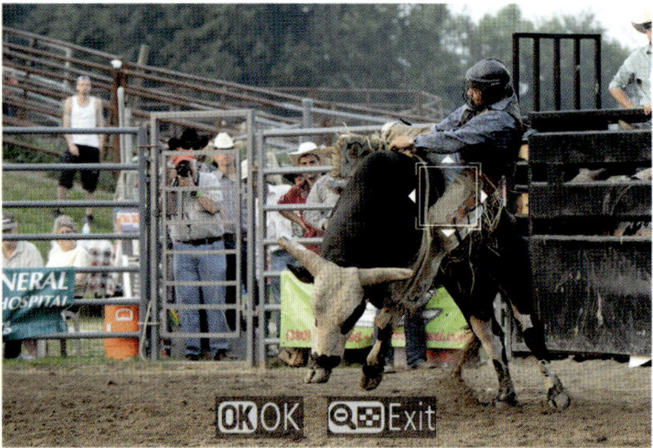

Figure 5.16 Press OK to produce a frame you can use to select an object to track.

- **Select your subject.** When you're ready, press the OK button (but *not* the sub-selector button) to activate tracking. The box will change from white to yellow. Press the center button again to de-select and re-select a different subject.

- **Touch options.** Note that if the touch screen is active, you have several options. Once you've enabled Touch Controls in the Setup menu, you can cycle among Touch AF (Off), Touch AF, and Touch Shutter/AF by tapping the touch icon at the left side of the monitor.

  - **Touch AF (only) is on.** You don't need to press the OK button. *Start* tracking by tapping your subject on the monitor. You'll bypass the white box completely. The yellow box will appear at the place you tap. If you've *already activated* tracking (with the touch screen or OK button), touching the monitor will move the yellow tracking box to the new subject.

  - **Touch shutter/AF is on.** Tap the screen, and the Z5 will *immediately* focus on that point and take a picture but will continue tracking at that point. This is a great feature. For example, if you unexpectedly see some action taking place, tap the touch screen to take a photo right away, and then continue to shoot (if you like) with the camera tracking the subject you just shot.

- **Reframe as desired.** Once the focus frame has turned yellow, it seemingly takes on a life of its own, and will "follow" your subject around on the LCD as you reframe your image. (In other words, the subject being tracked doesn't have to be in the center of the frame for the actual photo.) Best of all, if your subject moves, the Z5 will follow it as required.

- **Tracking continues.** The only glitches that may pop up might occur if your subject is small and difficult to track, or is too close in tonal value to its background, or if the subject approaches the camera or recedes sufficiently to change its relative size on the LCD significantly. The Z5 may also be unable to track subjects that leave the frame, are moving too fast, are too large/small, or too bright/dark. Because tracking uses subject distance, color, any patterns present, and brightness, it works best when used with subject matter that differs in colors/patterns, and brightness from its surroundings.

- **...Focus.** If you're not using the touch options, when you've activated tracking on your subject, press the shutter button halfway to activate the Z5's autofocus feature. In AF-S mode, the camera will lock focus, the focus frame will turn green, *and tracking will stop.* If you reframe the image, focus will be maintained. In AF-C mode, the focus frame will remain yellow and the camera will continue tracking and focusing until you press the shutter release down all the way to take the picture.

- **Or exit.** To cancel focus tracking, press the Zoom Out/Index button.

- **Take your picture.** Press the shutter release down all the way.

Store by Orientation

Some types of shooting call for different ways of choosing a focus point's orientation. For example, say you're shooting a sport like basketball that lends itself to both horizontal and vertical framing. You may rotate your camera constantly as the action unfolds but want the focus point to remain in the upper portion of your horizontal or vertical frame. That won't happen if you are shooting with a Z5 in its default mode. Your chosen focus point will stay fixed relative to the other points and "rotate" along with the camera, as shown at top in Figure 5.17.

The same focus point in the camera's array is used regardless of the Z5's orientation. If you've set your focus point for the basket or net when the camera is rotated in one direction vertically (that is, the top of the vertical frame), the focus point will encompass the right side of the frame when the camera is in the horizontal position, and evaluate the floor if you happen to rotate it vertically in the other direction.

With the Z5, however, you have another option, tucked away in Custom Setting a6: Store Points by Orientation. When enabled, the focus point does not shift as the camera is rotated, as shown in Figure 5.17. This feature allows *different* focus points to be selected for each of the three likely camera orientations (ignoring the possible, but less likely, upside-down horizontal position).

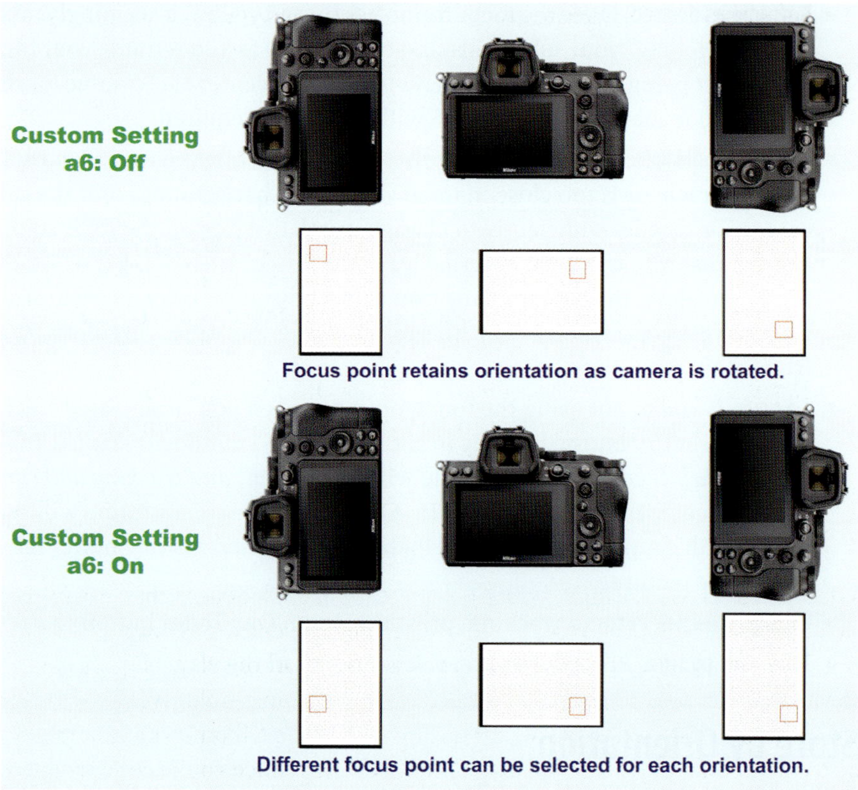

Figure 5.17 Store AF points by orientation—or not.

When Store Points by Orientation is activated, simply rotate the camera to any of the three configurations, and select the focus point you want. Repeat, if you like, for the other two. (It's best to do this during a lull in the action, although you can re-select points on the fly if you like.) Then, as you shoot, you'll notice the focus point shifting in the viewfinder as you rotate the camera. You don't need to keep the point in the same relative position in the frame (as I just described). You can select any focus point for any of the three orientations if, for example, you're shooting architecture and want to focus on a different position in the frame as you vary camera orientation.

Autofocus Activation... and More

The final considerations in using autofocus are the control or controls used to activate and lock autofocus, plus a few odds and ends. I'll cover them in ample detail in Chapter 12 under Custom Settings, which explains all the options, but here are some cross references if you feel you need some review. Descriptions of all of these can be found in Chapter 12.

- **Autofocus override.** After the Z5 has focused automatically, you can fine-tune focus using the focus ring on the lens while the shutter release is pressed halfway if you've set Custom Setting a13: Manual Focus Ring in AF Mode to Enable. To refocus using AF, lift your finger and press the shutter release down halfway once more.

- **Focus tracking with lock on.** As I mentioned, intervening subjects passing in front of your main area of interest can interfere with autofocus. Set a delay time before the camera refocuses using Custom Setting a3: Focus Tracking with Lock-On.
- **Limit AF-area mode selection.** As I mentioned earlier, you can limit the availability of AF-area modes using Custom Setting a8.
- **Focus point wrap-around.** Do you want the focus point to wrap around to the opposite side during manual selection? Use Custom Setting a9: Focus Point Wrap-Around.
- **Which controls activate/lock autofocus.** You can use a half-press of the shutter release or a press of the AF-ON button (or both), or another button. See the instructions for Custom Setting a7: AF Activation in Chapter 12 for your options.
- **Center/show focus point.** You can program the OK (multi selector center) button to either jump the active focus point to the center or to turn zoom on or off, using Custom Setting f3, as described in Chapter 12.

Manual Focus

I described the surprising revival of interest in manual focus at the beginning of this chapter. However, manual focus does require judgment and fast reflexes (if your subject is moving). On the one hand, autofocus does save time and allows us to capture subjects (particularly fast-moving sports) that are difficult to image sharply using manual focusing (unless you have training and know certain techniques). On the other hand, learning to apply the Nikon Z5's autofocus system most effectively also requires a bit of study and some practice. Then, once you're comfortable with autofocus, you'll know when it's appropriate to use the manual focus option, too. Your Z5 includes some useful features that help you focus manually—including magnification and *focus peaking*, a way of highlighting out-of-focus areas that may need correction just as "blinkies" show you what parts of the image are overexposed. I'll show you how to use these manual focus aids later in this chapter.

The important thing to remember is that focus isn't absolute. For example, some things that look in sharp focus at a given viewing size and distance might not be in focus at a larger size and/or closer distance. In addition, the goal of optimum focus isn't always to make things look sharp. Not all of an image will be or should be sharp. Controlling exactly what is sharp and what is not is part of your creative palette. Use of depth-of-field characteristics to throw part of an image out of focus while other parts are sharply focused is one of the most valuable tools available to a photographer. But selective focus works only when the desired areas of an image are in focus properly. For the digital photographer, correct focus can be one of the trickiest parts of the technical and creative process.

As I've noted several times, some subjects lend themselves to manual focus, especially close-up or *macro* photography, in which AF can be a creative hindrance. If you're photographing a flower, why let the camera decide which leaf or petal should be sharpest—particularly if you are using a relatively large aperture and selective focus as an effect? A mirrorless camera's live view is especially useful when focusing manually because you have extra tools at your disposal to focus precisely and quickly.

Here are the basic steps for quick and convenient setting of focus manually with the Z5:

- **Activate manual focus.** Switch to manual focus by sliding the switch on the lens to the M position, or by selecting Manual focus using the *i* menu, or by holding the Fn2 button and rotating the main command dial.

- **Aim at your subject and turn the control/focusing ring on the lens.** Turn the control/focusing ring until that appears to be in the sharpest possible focus. Note that while you can redefine the focus/control ring's function (as described in Chapter 12), in Manual focus mode it can *only* be used to adjust focus.

- **If you have difficulty focusing.** If you are unable to focus precisely, you have three options: zooming, magnification, and focus peaking. The first two give you a larger image to focus but have their own advantages and disadvantages. The third is a relatively new feature in the Nikon product line, gaining in popularity since more and more photographers are depending on Live View (with dSLRs) or the full-time live view provided by mirrorless cameras like the Z5.

  - **Zooming in optically.** If you are using a zoom lens (rather than a fixed focal length *prime* lens), you can zoom in on your subject using the longest available focal setting. Even if you plan to take a wide-angle photo, the reduced depth-of-field at a telephoto setting can make it easier to see the exact effect of slight changes in focus while zoomed in. With most lenses, when you zoom back out to take the picture, the center of interest will still be in sharp focus. However, some lenses (generally less expensive optics) can change focus as they zoom. The most blatant of these are called *varifocal* lenses. Sticklers refer to lenses that *don't* change focus as they zoom as "true" zoom or *parfocal* lenses. However, even a true zoom can change focus slightly when zooming.

  - **Magnification.** To magnify a portion of the image and enhance your ability to focus, press the Zoom In button located to lower right of the LCD monitor. As you press the button repeatedly, to enlarge the view to three different levels of magnification, a navigation window, seen at lower right in Figure 5.18, displays a yellow box at the approximate location within the overall frame of the magnified view. You can relocate the zoomed area using the multi selector or sub-selector joystick. Press the center button at any time to restore the zoom window to the center of the frame.

Figure 5.18 You can magnify the image to make manual focusing easier.

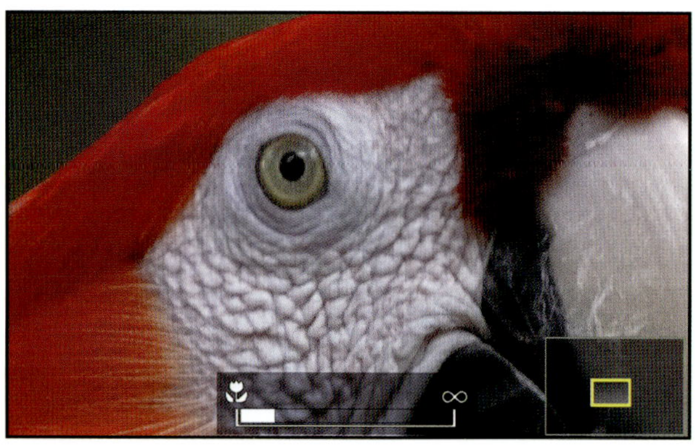

- **Focus peaking.** Activate focus peaking using the instructions for Custom Setting d9: Peaking Highlights in Chapter 12. Focus peaking provides a colored overlay around edges within your image that are sharply focused. As the color fades or becomes stronger, it is easier to determine when your subject is precisely focused. Choose Peak 1 (low sensitivity), Peak 2 (standard sensitivity), or Peak 3 (high sensitivity), depending on the contrast of your subject, as seen in Figure 5.19. The flowers shown tended to blend in with the foliage in the background, so I selected high sensitivity. The default peaking highlight color of red was fine in this case, but you can use Custom Setting d9 to change it to yellow, blue, or white. The alternate hue may be needed to provide a strong contrast between the peaking highlights and the color of your subject. Yellow might be the best choice to focus on, say, a red rose. Access the Peaking Color item of the Setup menu to adjust the color. To make the overlay even more visible, select High in the Peaking Level item; you can also turn peaking Off with this item, if desired.

- **Use the electronic rangefinder.** Position the focus point over the subject and rotate the focus ring until sharp focus is achieved using the electronic rangefinder feature. The focus point will change to green and the in-focus indicator at lower left in the display will change according to the symbols shown in Figure 5.20. Note that while the electronic rangefinder appears when in manual focus or manual focus override, it shows direction in which you should rotate the ring, with *most* lenses. Some lenses, especially those from third parties, rotate in the opposite direction, however.

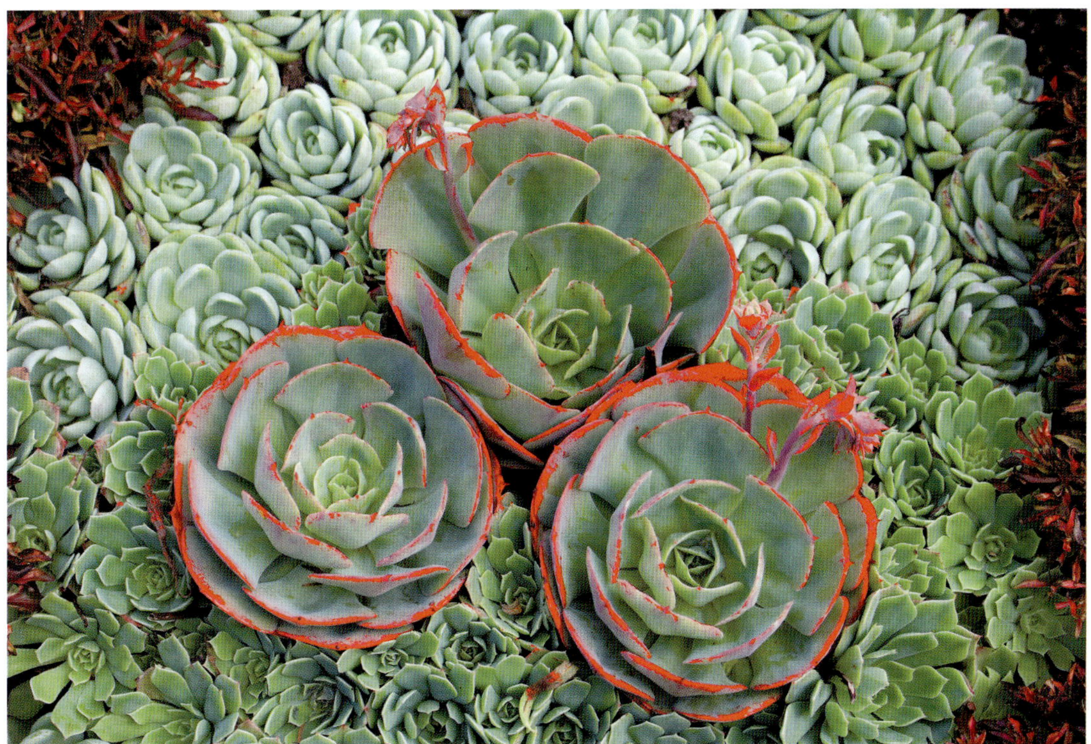

Figure 5.19 With Peaking Highlights activated, in-focus areas are highlighted in color.

Figure 5.20 The electronic rangefinder in the lower-left corner of the display shows manual focus status.

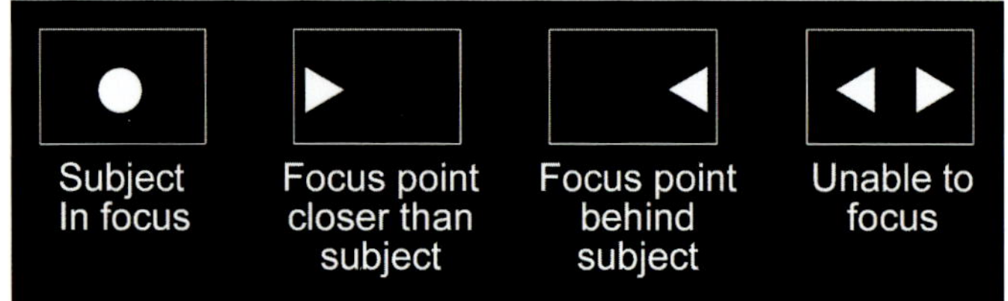

- **Preview depth-of-field.** Focusing is always done with the lens set to its largest f/stop (except in Manual exposure mode when Enable [the default] is specified for Custom Setting d7: Apply Settings to Live View). The maximum aperture provides the least depth-of-field, so focus snaps in and out more precisely. When the picture is captured, the Z5 closes down the iris to the "taking aperture," which is old-school terminology for the aperture used to take the picture (natch). If that f/stop is smaller than the maximum aperture, the depth-of-field in your finished image will be larger—but unknown to you without a preview. For critical applications, especially when you're using selective focus, you'll want to *see* the actual DOF on the live view screen.

  The Z5 doesn't have a Pv (Preview) button by default, but you can define one for, say, Fn1 or Fn2 in Custom Setting f2: Custom Controls. Then, when you press the defined Pv button, the lens will stop down to the aperture selected by you (in Manual mode) or by the camera (in Aperture-priority mode). (This doesn't work in Program or Shutter-priority mode, because the aperture isn't determined in either mode until you lock exposure or take a photo.) To open the aperture to maximum again, release the button.

Using the Focus/Control Ring

The focusing controls of the Nikon Z-series mirrorless cameras add some new wrinkles that can take some getting used to, whether you are a neophyte photographer or an old hand. One innovation is the substitution of a *control ring* to replace the familiar *focus ring* used on traditional lenses, while the second involves the Z-series' dependence on a technology called *focus-by-wire* to perform the actual focus adjustments.

When focusing manually, the control ring functions like a traditional focus ring in many ways. As you rotate the ring to the right, the plane of focus moves farther away, bringing more distant subjects into focus; after the focus plane reaches "infinity" further rotation has no effect. Rotate the ring to the left, however, and the camera focuses closer and closer until the minimum focus distance is reached. A helpful indicator bar, with the icon of a flower at left and an infinity symbol at right is displayed along the bottom of the screen. So far, manual focus with your Z5 is pretty much the same as with any Nikon camera you've used. A very few older Nikon lenses and some other camera vendors reverse the left/right directions, much to the consternation of those who switch platforms. If you have this problem, Custom Setting f5: Customize Command Dials has a Reverse Rotation option, as described in Chapter 12.

The cool new feature is that you can redefine the behavior of the control ring from its default of manual override of autofocus and fully manual focusing, with other customizable functions, including step-less aperture control, exposure compensation, and ISO sensitivity adjustment. The most popular of these options is probably the step-less (no-click) aperture setting for movie making, which allows changing the f/stop silently while capturing video. Some like the ability to add/subtract exposure compensation quickly, or the option to change ISO sensitivity on the fly with a single twist of the control ring. Just remember that when you're using an F-mount lens on the Z5 with the FTZ adapter, any control ring behaviors you've specified don't apply.

The second innovation comes from the Z5's focus-by-wire functions. Ordinarily, a lens has a mechanical linkage between the traditional focusing ring and the lens elements that move during focus adjustment. So, during manual focus, your rotation of the ring is translated into changes in focus. Motors built into the lens (or into the camera body with older AF lenses) take over to adjust the lens elements during autofocus, which is why the ring doesn't rotate when the camera is handling the focus chores. Focus override, which allows fine-tuning focus during the AF process, requires a special arrangement within the lens to allow the focus ring to assume control when the photographer wants to make adjustments without exiting to manual focus. Not all lenses include this capability, indicated by an A/M-M or MA-M switch on the side of the lens, and without it the focus ring can't be moved during AF without potentially damaging the mechanical components.

Thanks to focus-by-wire these shenanigans aren't necessary. With all Z-mount lenses, rotating the control ring (when it's set to function as a focus ring) delivers an electrical signal to the built-in motors. So, overriding the AF system is as simple as rotating the ring any time you want. That's cool enough all by itself. However, focus-by-wire enables the Z5 to adjust the "throw" of the lens during manual focus to match the speed with which you turn it.

In ancient times, it was common to require a *lot* of rotation of a focusing ring to focus from the minimum focus distance to infinity. The need to rotate, say, almost a full turn of the ring allowed for precise manual focus, which was a semi-great idea back in the day when autofocus didn't exist. However, when autofocus began to replace manual focus for the most part, lens designers began to produce lenses that required a reduced amount of throw to focus, so that each degree of rotation covered a larger portion of the focus distance from minimum to infinity. That led to faster focus, while making accurate manual focus more difficult.

Focus-by-wire, however, allows the Z5's AF operation to *adapt* to the rotational speed of the focus/control ring. Rotate rapidly, and the throw is relatively short—you may need to turn the ring only one-third of the way around to make a focus adjustment. Slow down your focusing motion, though, and each movement becomes more precise. You may have to rotate the ring all the way around to make the same adjustment that required only a one-third turn when done rapidly. You can easily see how this feature makes manual focus both more convenient and more precise.

Trap (Auto) Focus

This technique comes in handy when you know where the action is going to take place (such as at the finish line of a horse race), but you don't know exactly *when*. The solution is to prefocus on the point where the action will occur, and then tell your camera not to take the photo until something moves into the prefocus spot (see Figure 5.21). It's a good technique for sports action when you know that, say, a runner is going to pass by a certain position. You can also use trap focus for hand-held macro shots—set focus for a particular distance and then move the camera toward your subject. The shutter will trip automatically when your subject comes into focus.

Trap focus in Viewfinder mode isn't as difficult as you might think. The key is to decouple the focusing operation from the shutter release function. Just follow these steps:

1. **Confirm AF-ON button.** First, access Custom Setting f3 and make sure the definition for the AF-ON button is set to its default value, AF-ON, and not some other behavior. You want the AF-ON button to activate autofocus.

2. **Set Custom Setting a2 to Focus Priority.** The shutter will trip only when your subject is in focus when using AF-S.

3. **Set Custom Setting a7 to AF-ON Only.** The default setting for AF Activation is Shutter/AF-ON. With AF activation set to AF-ON Only, pressing the shutter release halfway down does *not* activate autofocus. That happens *only* when you press the AF-ON button.

4. **Set focus mode to AF-S.**

5. **Set your point selection mode to Single-point Area.**

6. **Make sure your lens is set to autofocus (either A or M/A).**

7. **Prefocus on the spot where the action will occur, or an equivalent distance.** Use the focus ring on your lens.

8. **Prefocus on the spot where the action will occur, or an equivalent distance.** I like to manually focus on that point to make sure it is the exact position I want to capture. For Figure 5.21, I focused on a plane between the third and fourth hurdles, which were located 30 feet apart (the standard for men's hurdle events). You can also press the AF-ON button to focus on that point, and then release the button. In either case, further AF activity will cease. The prefocused distance is the "trap" you've set for your pending subject.

9. **Reframe your picture, if necessary, so that nothing is at the prefocused distance.** If an object occupies that spot, the Z5 will take the photo immediately when you press the shutter release.

10. **Press and hold down the shutter release all the way.** The camera will not refocus, because you've disconnected the autofocus function from the shutter release.

11. **Trap sprung!** The picture will be taken when a subject moves into the prefocused area. Note that trap focus may not work well with some subjects, particularly when using small f/stops. Increased depth-of-field may cause the Z5 to take the photo when your subject has barely entered the trap and not yet perfectly in the preselected focus plane. Even so, trap focus is a very useful technique.

DANGER, WILL ROBINSON!

If you don't use trap focus often, or don't work with the AF-ON button as your primary autofocus start control regularly, don't make the mistake I did. One time I forgot that I had followed the steps above and used a different Nikon camera in the interim. The next time I picked up my Z5, it "refused" to autofocus—at least when I pressed the shutter release halfway. Much consternation followed until I remembered what I had done a few days earlier, pressed the AF-ON button, and found that the AF function was just fine. I had simply "turned off" the shutter release as an AF start control.

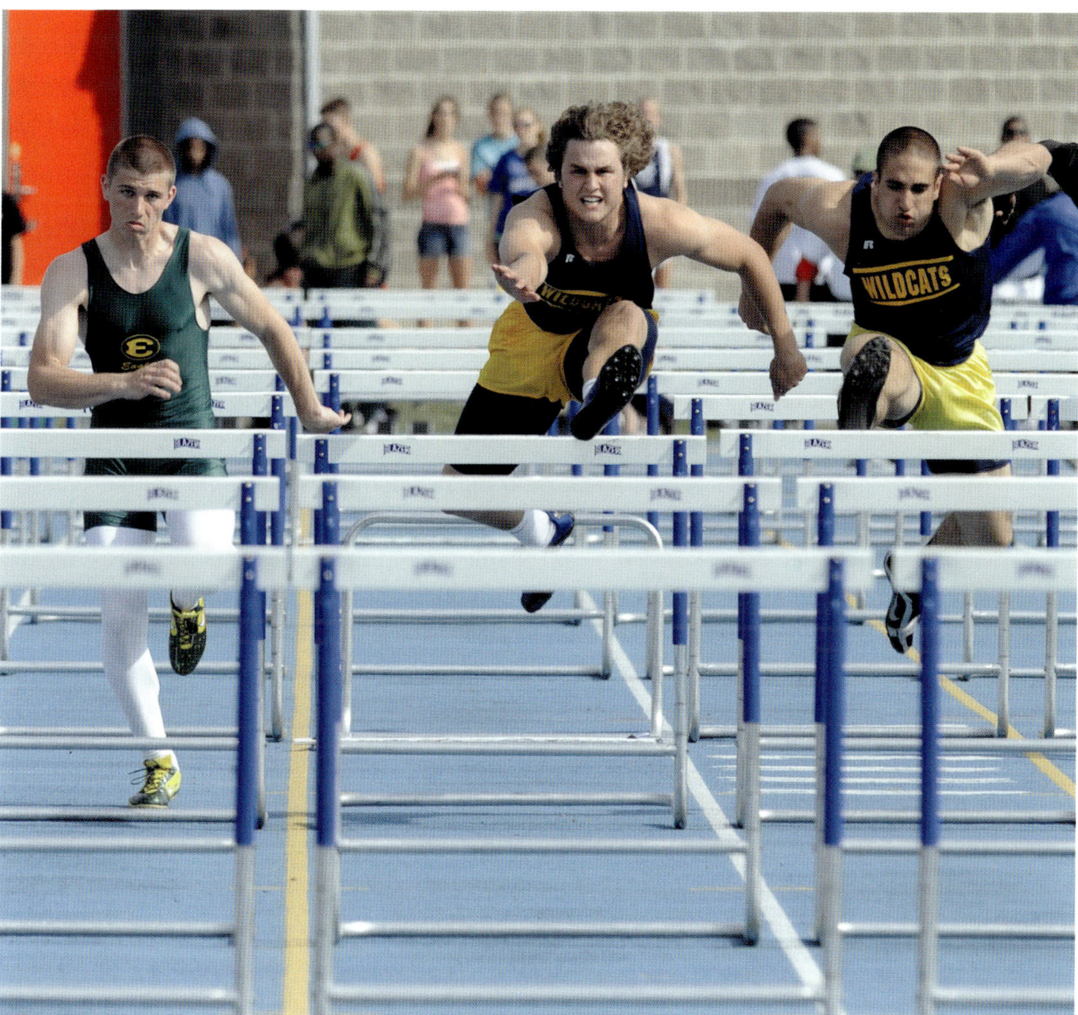

Figure 5.21 By prefocusing on a point between two of the hurdles, trap focus captured this athlete the instant he moved into the point of focus.

Back-Button Focus

Once you've been using your camera for a while, you'll invariably encounter the terms *back focus* and *back-button focus* and wonder if they are good things or bad things. Actually, they are *two different things,* and are often confused with each other. *Back focus* is a bad thing and occurs when a particular lens consistently autofocuses on a plane that's *behind* your desired subject. This malady may be found in some of your lenses, or all your optics may be free of the defect. The good news is that if the problem lies in a particular lens (rather than a camera misadjustment that applies to *all* your lenses), it can be fixed. I'll show you how to do that at the end of this chapter.

Back-button focus, on the other hand, is a tool you can use to separate two functions that are commonly locked together—exposure and autofocus—so that you can lock in exposure while allowing focus to be attained at a later point, or vice versa. It's a *good* thing, although using back-button focus effectively may require you to unlearn some habits and acquire new ways of coordinating the action of your fingers.

As you have learned, the default behavior of your Nikon Z5 is to set both exposure and focus (when AF is active) when you press the shutter release down halfway. When using AF-S mode, that's that: both exposure and focus are locked and will not change until you release the shutter button, or press it all the way down to take a picture and then release it for the next shot. In AF-C mode, exposure is locked and focus set when you press the shutter release halfway, but the Z5 will *continue to refocus* if your subject moves for as long as you hold down the shutter button halfway. Focus isn't locked until you press the button down all the way to take the picture.

What back-button focus does is *decouple* or separate the two actions. You can retain the exposure lock feature when the shutter is pressed halfway, but assign autofocus *start* and/or autofocus *lock* to a different button. So, in practice, you can press the shutter button halfway, locking exposure, and reframe the image if you like (perhaps you're photographing a backlit subject and want to lock in exposure on the foreground, and then reframe to include a very bright background as well).

But, in this same scenario, you *don't* want autofocus locked at the same time. Indeed, you may not want to start AF until you're good and ready, say, at a sports venue as you wait for a ballplayer to streak into view in your viewfinder, or when you're photographing a garden and expect a butterfly to alight somewhere nearby. With back-button focus, you can lock exposure on the spot where you expect the athlete or insect to be and activate AF at the moment your subject appears. The Z5 gives you a great deal of flexibility, both in the choice of which button to use for AF, and the behavior of that button. That's where the learning of new habits and mind-finger coordination comes in. You need to learn which back-button focus techniques work for you, and when to use them.

Back-button focus lets you avoid the need to switch from AF-S to AF-C when your subject begins moving unexpectedly. You retain complete control. It's great for sports photography when you want to activate autofocus precisely based on the action in front of you. It also works for static shots. You can press and release your designated focus button, and then take a series of shots using the same focus point. Focus will not change until you once again press your defined back button. (See Figure 5.22.)

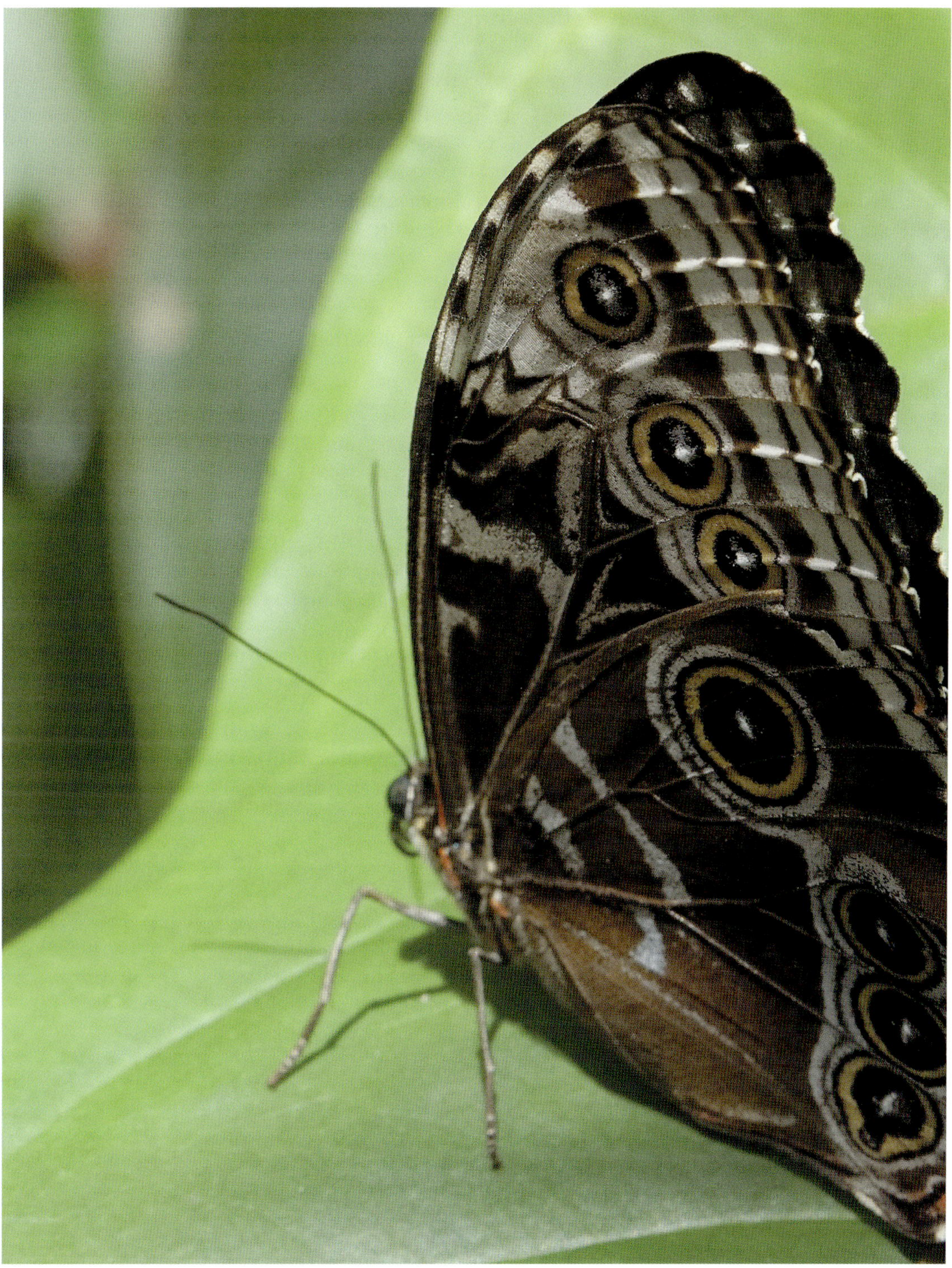

Figure 5.22 Lock your exposure for the garden by pressing the shutter release halfway; then activate autofocus when the butterfly decides where to land.

Want to focus on a spot without moving the focus point within your frame? Use back-button focus to zero in focus with the current focus area—no need to move it—then reframe. Focus will not change. Don't want to miss an important shot at a wedding on a photojournalism assignment? If you're set to *focus-priority* your camera may delay taking a picture until the focus is optimum; in *release-priority* there may still be a slight delay. With back-button focus you can focus first and wait until the decisive moment to press the shutter release and take your picture. The Z5 will respond immediately and not bother with focusing at all. Back-button focus can also save battery power. Constantly refocusing in AF-C mode can consume a lot of power.

Activating Back-Button Focus

Here's how to set up back-button focus on your Z5. Just follow these steps:

- **Assign exposure lock to shutter button.** That's the default behavior, so you should not need to make a change. However, double-check Custom Setting c1: Shutter Release Button AE-L to make sure that On (Half-Press) is enabled. In that mode, depressing the shutter button halfway always locks the exposure at the setting the camera has selected. (In Manual exposure mode, of course, exposure does not change until you adjust it yourself.)

- **Assign AF activation to AF-ON function only.** You'll find the key control for enabling back-button focus in Custom Setting a7: AF Activation. There, the options are Shutter/AF-ON or AF-ON only. With the former option, pressing the shutter release halfway *or* the AF-ON control will enable *both* autoexposure and autofocus. Select AF-ON only to decouple the two functions, so that AF activation starts *only* when you press your designated AF-ON button.

   Note that choosing AF-ON Only does not mean you must press the physical AF-ON button to activate autofocus. *Any* button that you assign the AF-ON behavior to will initiate autofocus. That button can be the actual AF-ON button, or another button, such as Fn1. In practice, you could assign AF-ON to the Fn1 button and a completely different function to the physical AF-ON button. Just remember which function belongs to which button.

- **Assign AF-ON function.** Use Custom Setting f2: Custom Controls (described in more detail in Chapter 12) and assign the AF-ON button to the control of your choice. As I've noted, most prefer to use the physical AF-ON button, and since that is its default function, you may need to make no change at all. But you can assign AF-ON to a different button if you like. In all cases, if you've followed these steps, the defined button is used to *initiate* autofocus. The shutter release button cannot be used to initiate autofocus.

Fine-Tuning the Focus of Your Lenses

Theoretically, at least, there should be no need at all to fine-tune the focus of native Z-mount lenses. With a traditional dSLR, the autofocus mechanism is a separate component located in the floor of the mirror box. That module can be slightly misaligned in relationship to the lens and the dSLR's optical manual focusing screen. AF fine-tune can correct for that error. The Z5, in contrast, calculates autofocus using the actual sensor image, and so should "see" any misalignment and correct for it automatically.

However, Nikon, in its wisdom, has included an AF fine-tune feature in the Z5. You can use it with both native Z-mount lenses as well as F-mount lenses attached using the FTZ adapter. In this section, I'll show you how to calibrate your lenses using the Z5's AF Fine-tune feature. The high resolution of the Z5 tends to make even slight focus errors visible, so AF Fine Tuning may be more useful than with cameras with fewer pixels, even given the camera's on-sensor PDAF pixels.

Why is the focus "off" for some lenses in the first place? There are lots of factors, including the age of the lens (an older lens may focus slightly differently), temperature effects on certain types of glass, humidity, and tolerances built into a lens's design that all add up to a slight misadjustment, even though the components themselves are, strictly speaking, within specs. A very slight variation in your lens's mount can cause focus to vary slightly. With any luck (if you can call it that) a lens that doesn't focus exactly right will at least be consistent. If a lens always focuses a bit behind the subject, the symptom is *back focus.* If it focuses in front of the subject, it's called *front focus.*

If it's the lens that's at fault, or if your camera consistently mis-focuses, you're almost always better off sending your lens or Z5 to Nikon to have them make it right. But that's not always possible or advised. Perhaps you need your lens recalibrated right now, or you purchased a gray market lens that Nikon isn't willing to fix. You may have a problem only with one or two lenses, while the rest focus with more accuracy. If you want to do the fine-tuning yourself, the first thing to do is determine whether your lens has a back-focus or front-focus problem.

For a quick-and-dirty diagnosis (*not* a calibration; you'll use a different target for that), lay down a piece of graph paper on a flat surface, and place an object on the line at the middle, which will represent the point of focus (we hope). Then, shoot the target at an angle using your lens's widest aperture and the autofocus mode you want to test. Mount the camera on a tripod so you can get accurate, repeatable results.

If your camera/lens combination doesn't suffer from front or back focus, the point of sharpest focus will be the center line of the chart, as you can see at top in Figure 5.23. If you do have a problem, one of the other lines will be sharply focused instead. Should you discover that your lens consistently front or back focuses, it needs to be recalibrated. Unfortunately, it's only possible to calibrate a lens for a single focusing distance. So, if you use a particular lens (such as a macro lens) for close focusing, calibrate for that. If you use a lens primarily for middle distances, calibrate for that. Close-to-middle distances are most likely to cause focus problems, anyway, because as you get closer to infinity, small changes in focus are less likely to have an effect.

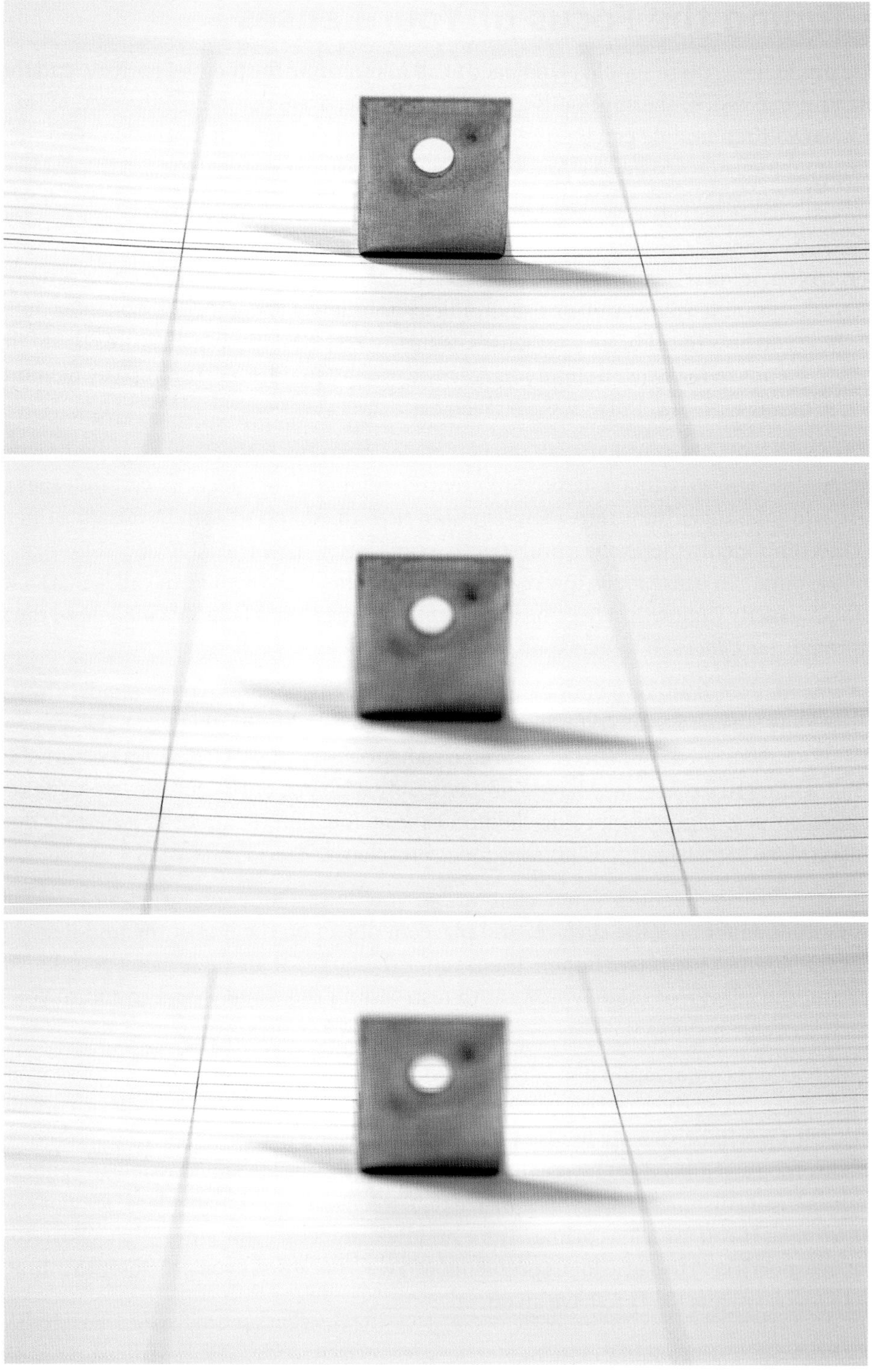

Figure 5.23 Correct focus (top), front focus (middle), and back focus (bottom).

Lens Tune-up Options

There are products available, such as Reikan FoCal ($89), a tool for both PCs and Macs that comes with software and a focusing target. Also available is the LensAlign MkII Focus Calibration system ($85). You can fine-tune your camera's focus manually using the instructions that follow.

To manually adjust your camera/lens AF setting, just follow these steps. The key tool you can use to fine-tune your lens is the AF Fine-Tune entry in the Setup menu, shown in Figure 5.24. You'll find the process easier to understand if you first run through this quick overview of the menu options:

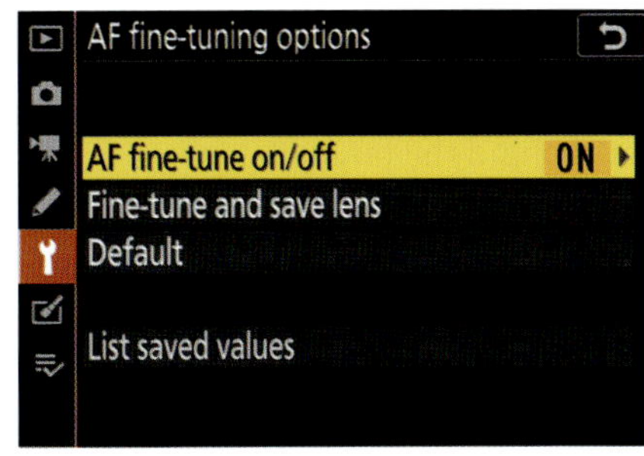

Figure 5.24 The AF Fine-Tune menu.

- **AF fine-tune (On/Off).** This option enables/disables autofocus fine-tuning for all the lenses you've defined using the menu entry. If you discover you don't care for the calibrations you make in certain situations (say, it works better for the lens you have mounted at middle distances, but is less successful at correcting close-up focus errors), you can deactivate the feature as you require. You should set this to On when you're doing the actual fine-tuning.

- **Fine-tune and save lens.** This setting lets you tune the autofocus calibration for the current Z-mount and CPU-chipped F-mount lenses (virtually all Nikon-brand autofocus lenses) mounted on the Z5. When you first fine-tune a lens, the default saved value will be 0 (zero). You can press the multi selector up/down buttons to choose a value between +20 and –20 for both wide-angle and telephoto positions of a zoom lens. Only a single +20 or –20 adjustment can be made for prime lenses.

  Positive numbers move the focal point farther from the camera and would be used if your lens consistently suffers from front-focus problems. Negative numbers move the focal point closer to the camera and would be used if your lens is plagued with consistent back focus. The value is relative and doesn't correlate to any particular distance or percentage.

- **Default.** This entry often confuses. It is a value that is applied to *every* lens mounted on the camera that doesn't already have a customized saved value associated with it. That is, if your Z5 has consistent front- or back-focus problems with *all* lenses, you can enter a value here, and the camera will apply the correction to each CPU lens you use. This default setting can be overridden by saved values you've stored for particular lenses. So, you can change the default focal plane for all lenses, and still further fine-tune specific lenses that need more autofocus correction. My recommendation is that if your camera and lenses are so out of whack that you need global correction and individual fine-tuning, you *really* ought to consider shipping the whole kit off to Nikon for proper calibration.

- **List saved values.** This screen shows you the saved fine-tuning values for all lenses. If the currently mounted lens has a stored value, it will be marked with a solid black box icon. You can delete lenses from this list by highlighting them and pressing the Trash button. You can also change the number or apply an alphanumeric name that can be used to identify a particular lens.

Evaluating Current Focus

The first step is to capture a baseline image that represents how the lens you want to fine-tune auto-focuses at a particular distance. You'll often see advice for photographing a test chart with millimeter markings from an angle, and the suggestion that you autofocus on a particular point on the chart. Supposedly, the markings that actually *are* in focus will help you recalibrate your lens. The problem with this approach is that the information you get from photographing a test chart at an angle doesn't actually tell you what to do to make a precise correction. So, your lens back focuses three millimeters behind the target area on the chart. So what? Does that mean you change the saved value by –3 clicks? Or –15 clicks? Angled targets are a "shortcut" that don't save you time.

Instead, you'll want to photograph a target that represents what you're actually trying to achieve: a plane of focus locked in by your lens that represents the actual plane of focus of your subject. For that, you'll need a flat target, mounted precisely perpendicular to the sensor plane of the camera. Then, you can take a photo, see if the plane of focus is correct, and if not, dial in a bit of fine-tuning in the AF Fine-Tuning menu, and shoot again. Lather, rinse, and repeat until the target is sharply focused.

You can use the focus target shown in Figure 5.25, or you can use a chart of your own, as long as it has contrasty areas that will be easily seen by the autofocus system, and without very small details that are likely to confuse the AF. Download your own copy of my chart from www.nikonguides.com/FocusChart.pdf (*the URL is case-sensitive*). Then print out a copy on the largest paper your printer can handle. (I don't recommend just displaying the file on your monitor and focusing on that; it's unlikely you'll have the monitor screen lined up perfectly perpendicular to the camera sensor.) Then, follow these steps:

1. **Position the camera.** Place your Nikon Z5 on a sturdy tripod with a remote release attached, positioned at roughly eye-level at a distance from a wall that represents the distance you want to test for. Keep in mind that autofocus problems can be different at varying distances and lens focal lengths, and that you can enter only *one* correction value for a particular lens. So, choose a distance (close-up or mid-range) and zoom setting with your shooting habits in mind.

2. **Set the autofocus mode.** Choose the autofocus mode (AF-C or AF-S) you want to test.

3. **Level the camera (in an ideal world).** If the wall happens to be perfectly perpendicular, you can use a bubble level, plumb bob, or other device of your choice to ensure that the camera is level to match. Many tripods and tripod heads have bubble levels built in. Avoid using the center column, if you can. When the camera is properly oriented, lock the legs and tripod head tightly.

4. **Level the camera (in the real world).** If your wall is not perfectly perpendicular, use this old trick. Tape a mirror to the wall, and then adjust the camera on the tripod so that when you look through the viewfinder at the mirror, you see directly into the reflection of the lens. Then, lock the tripod and remove the mirror.

5. **Mount the test chart.** Tape the test chart on the wall so it is centered in your camera's viewfinder. You should place the chart roughly 30X to 40X the focal length of the lens setting you'll be testing. For example, for a 100mm lens, place the chart 3,000mm from the camera (roughly 9.8 feet).

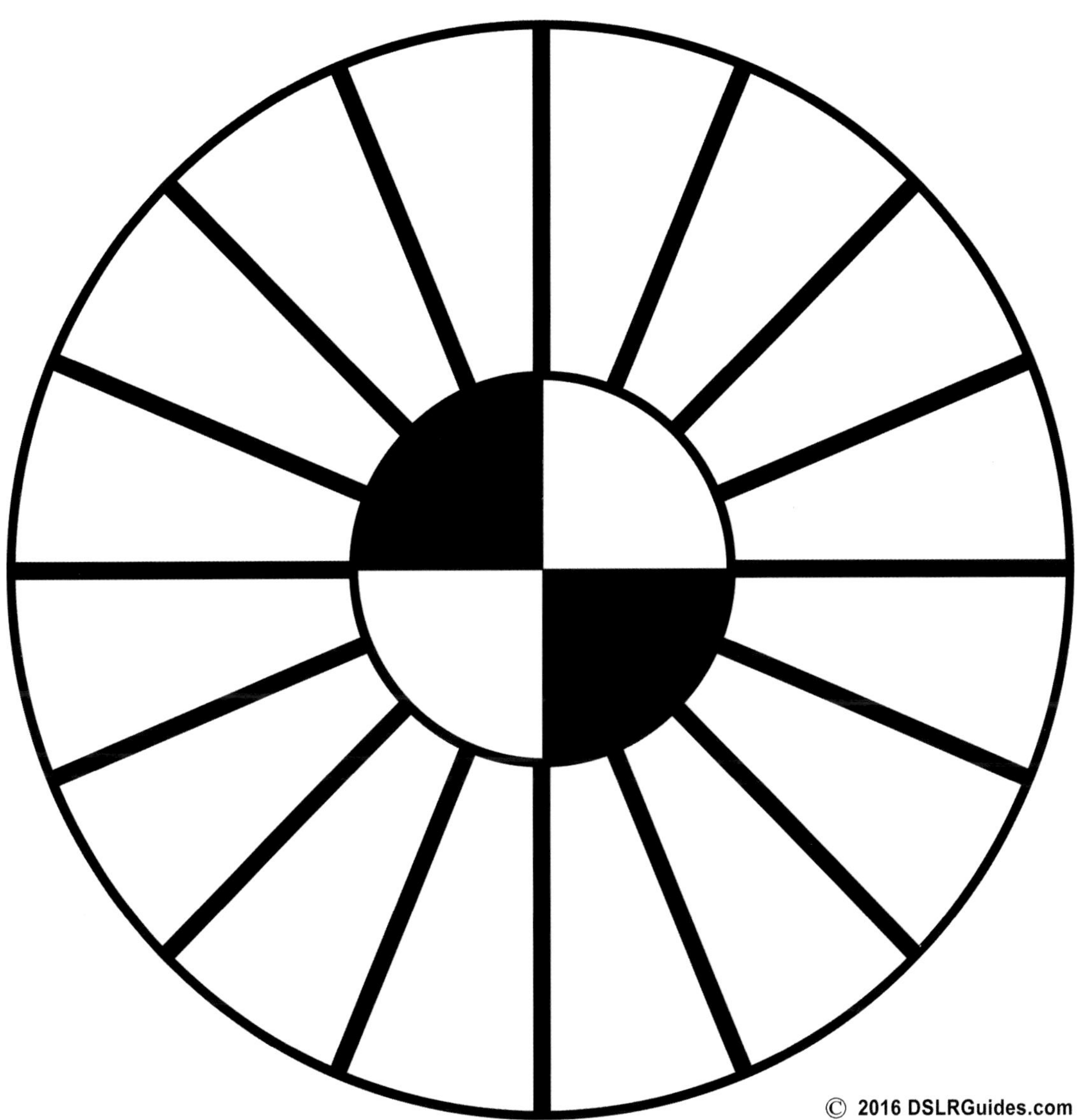

Figure 5.25 Use this focus test chart or create one of your own.

6. **Photograph the test chart using AF.** Allow the camera to autofocus, and take a test photo, using the remote release to avoid shaking or moving the camera.

7. **Make an adjustment and rephotograph.** Make a fine-tuning adjustment and photograph the target again. Follow the instructions in the next section. I've separated the fine-tuning adjustments from these steps because some people may want to just tweak the focus at a later time without going through all these evaluation steps. Follow steps 1 to 8 in the section that follows this one to make evaluation images at a range of corrections, say, –5 through +5.

8. **Evaluate the image.** If you have the camera connected to your computer with a USB cable and Camera Control Pro or other linkup software such as Nikon Transfer, or through a Wi-Fi connection, so much the better. You can view the image after it's transferred to your computer. Otherwise, *carefully* open the camera card door and slip the memory card out and copy the images to your computer.

9. **Evaluate focus.** Which image is sharpest? That's the setting you need to use for this lens. If your initial range doesn't provide the correction you need, repeat the steps between –20 and +20 until you find the best fine-tuning.

Changing the Fine-Tuning Setting

Adjust the fine-tuning for the lens you have mounted on the camera by following these steps:

1. **Mount lens.** If you haven't been running the test described previously, mount the Z-mount or F-mount CPU-equipped lens (with FTZ adapter) you want to fine-tune on the Nikon Z5. The camera will automatically recognize the lens you are using during the "calibration" process and display its name on the screen.

2. **Activate fine-tuning.** If you haven't already done so, choose AF Fine-Tune (On/Off) and turn it ON.

3. **Select Fine-Tune and Save Lens.** A screen similar to the one shown in Figure 5.26 will appear.

4. **Highlight Wide or Tele scales (Zoom lenses only).** If you're calibrating a zoom lens, dual scales will appear labeled Wide and Tele will be shown. Use the up/down controls to switch between the two scales. Prime (non-zoom lenses) will display only a single scale.

Figure 5.26 Change a saved value for a particular lens.

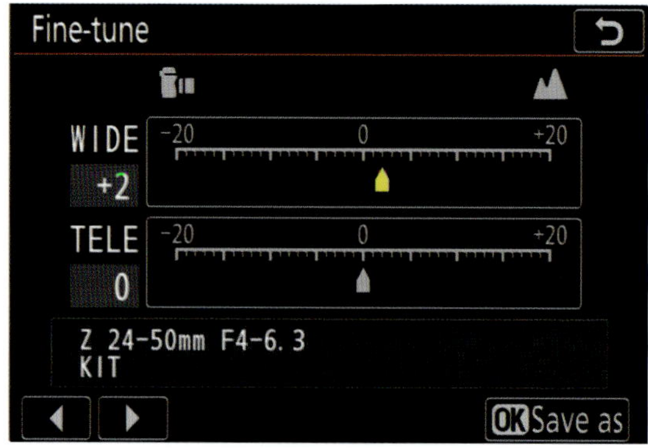

5. **Adjust focus.** Press the left/right directional controls to tell the Z5 to adjust the autofocus from +20 (move the focal point away from the camera to fix front-focus problems) to –20 values (move the focal point toward the camera to fix back focus). Make your change for both wide and tele scales if you're working with a zoom lens.

6. **Confirm adjustment.** Press OK when the value(s) you want are entered. You may have to run the test described above several times and use some trial and error to determine the correct adjustment.

7. **View saved values.** Choose List Saved Values to see the names of the lenses you've fine-tuned. (See Figure 5.27.) Highlight the lens you'd like to assign a number or alphanumeric name to and press the right directional button to produce the screen shown in Figure 5.28.

8. **Assign a label.** Choose a lens identifier, which can be a number or an alphanumeric name, using the standard Z5 text-entry screen. You can use a label of up to 22 characters. This identifier can be used to differentiate a particular lens from other lenses of the same type, if you own, say, some duplicate lenses. You can define fine-tuning parameters for up to 40 different lenses.

   That's not as far-fetched as you might think. Some organizations, such as newspapers, allow their photographers to use their favorite lenses exclusively, but they may need to share other specialized optics among several photographers. If you don't know which of the pooled AF-S Nikkor 600mm f/4G ED VR lenses you'll be using on any particular day, you can calibrate your camera separately for each of them.

9. **Confirm.** Press the Zoom In button to confirm and return to the Choose Lens Number screen.

10. **Exit.** Press MENU to exit.

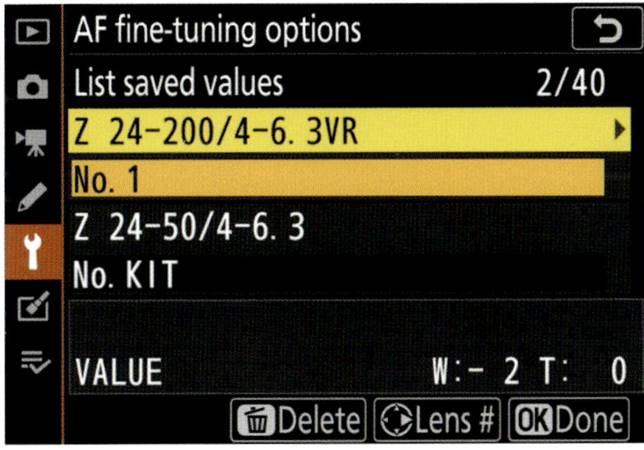

Figure 5.27 List the saved values you've stored.

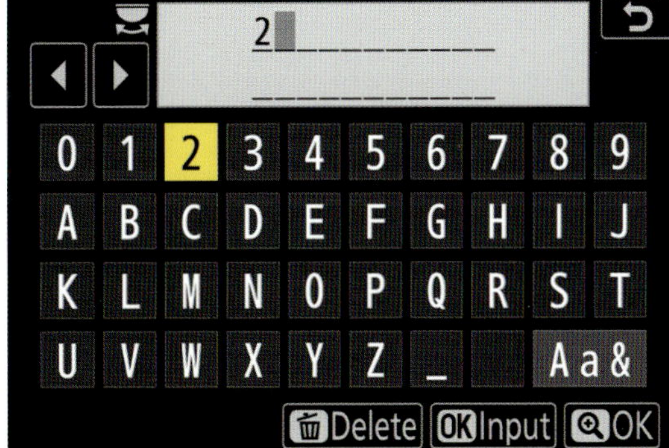

Figure 5.28 Assign a lens number, if necessary, to differentiate a particular lens from other lenses of the same type you may use.

Advanced Techniques 6

Your Z5 has more special features than a DVD box set. In designing its Z-series camera platform, Nikon drew on its expertise in providing leading-edge capabilities in the digital single-lens reflex realm and leveraged the advanced features possible with mirrorless technology. As a result, your Z5 has the kind of totally silent shooting that's not possible with conventional dSLRs and their clunky mechanical mirrors. You won't find in-body image stabilization in any Nikon dSLR, and cool features like focus-shift "stacking" are currently available only in high-end models like the Nikon D850. Other capabilities built into your Z5 are more common but have some special applications in a mirrorless model like the Z5. So, I've saved some of my favorite advanced techniques that the Z5 excels at for this chapter, which devotes a little extra space to some special features of the camera. This chapter covers special exposure options, including time-lapse photography and very long and very short exposures. You'll even find an introduction to using SnapBridge.

Continuous Shooting

Even a seasoned action photographer can miss the decisive instant during a football play when a crucial block is made, or a baseball superstar's bat shatters and pieces of cork fly out. Continuous shooting simplifies taking a series of pictures, either to ensure that one has more or less the exact moment you want to capture or to capture a sequence that is interesting as a collection of successive images, as seen in Figure 6.1. Your Nikon Z5 can capture up to 4.5 frames per second in Continuous H mode (only 2.5 fps in Silent Photography mode), and up to 4 fps in Continuous L mode.

I use continuous shooting *a lot*—and not just for sports. The upside is that I may be able to capture an image or a sequence that I could never grab in single-shot mode. The downside is that I end up with many shots to wade through to find the "keepers." I know that sounds like I am using my Nikon like a machine gun and hoping that I capture a worthwhile moment through sheer luck, but that's not really the case. Here are some types of scenes where the rapid-fire capabilities of the Z5 pay big dividends.

- **Action.** If you're shooting a fast-moving sport, continuous shooting is your only option. But it's important to remember that lightning-quick bursts don't replace good timing. A 90 mph fastball moves about 29 feet between frames when you're shooting at the Z5's maximum frame rate of 4.5 fps. A ball making contact with a bat is *still* likely to escape capture. Continuous shooting may provide its best advantages in capturing sequences, so that each shot tells part of the story.

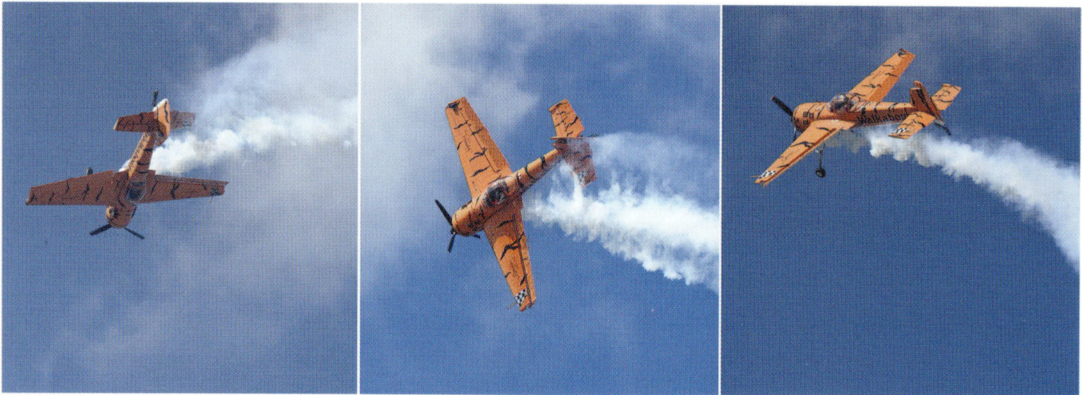

Figure 6.1 Continuous shooting allows you to capture an entire sequence of exciting moments as they unfold.

- **Bracketing.** I almost always set my camera to continuous shooting when bracketing. My goal is not to capture a bunch of different moments, each slightly different from the last, but, rather, to grab virtually the *same* moment, at different exposures (or, less frequently, with different white balance or Active D-Lighting settings). I can then choose which of the nearly identical shots has the exposure I prefer or can assemble some of them into a high dynamic range. The burst rate of the Z5 makes bracketing and hand-held HDR (high dynamic range) photography entirely practical. Software that combines such images does an excellent job of aligning images that are framed slightly differently when creating the final HDR version.

- **Ersatz vibration reduction.** I shoot three or four concerts a month, always hand-held, and always with VR turned on. I usually add a little simulated vibration reduction by shooting in continuous mode. While I have a fairly steady hand, I find that the *middle* exposures of a sequence are often noticeably sharper than those at the beginning, because my motions have "settled down" after initially depressing the shutter release button. My only caution for using this tool is to limit your shots during quiet passages, and avoid continuous shooting during acoustic concerts, if you are not using the electronic shutter. The rat-a-tat-tat of a Nikon Z5's mechanical shutter will earn you no friends. Activating the electronic shutter from the Photo Shooting menu is a better idea in such venues.

- **Variations on a theme.** Some subjects benefit from sequences more than others because some aspect changes between shots. Cavorting children, emoting concert performers (as described above), fashion models, or participants at weddings or other events all can look quite different within the span of a few seconds.

To use the Z5's continuous shooting modes use the *i* menu and navigate to Release Mode to select Continuous L or Continuous H. When you partially depress the shutter button, the viewfinder will display at the right side a number representing the maximum number of shots you can take at the current quality settings—the Shots Remaining indicator will show [r6] or some other value. That number will decrease as you take photos and they are stored in the Z5's buffer before being dumped onto the memory card. As the card catches up, the number will increase again.

Naturally, there are factors that can reduce both the number of continuous shots, as well as the frame rate. If you use slower memory cards or shoot RAW + JPEG, expect some performance penalties. Slow shutter speeds obviously reduce frame rates; you can't fire off 4.5 frames per second with a 1/4-second shutter speed, for example.

The frame rate you select will depend on the kind of shooting you want to do. For example, when shooting multiple exposures, if you're carefully planning and composing each individual exposure, you might not want to shoot continuously at all. But if your subject is moving, your double exposure might be more effective if you select a frame rate that matches the speed of motion of your target. Here are some guidelines:

- **4.0–4.5 fps.** High-Speed Continuous has a single top rate of 4.5 fps, but you can choose any setting between 1 and 4 fps for Low-Speed Continuous. A slightly slower rate can be useful for activities that aren't quite so fast moving. But, there's another benefit. If your frame rate is likely to be slowed by one of the factors I mentioned earlier, using a moderately slower frame rate can provide you with a constant shooting speed without the buffer filling.

- **1.0–3.0 fps.** You can set Low-Speed Continuous to use a relatively pokey frame rate, too. Use these rates when you just want to be able to take pictures quickly and aren't interested in filling up your memory card with mostly duplicated images. At 1 fps you can hold down the shutter release and fire away or ease up when you want to pause. At higher frame rates, by the time you've decided to stop shooting, you may have taken an extra three or four shots that you really don't want. Slow frame rates are good for bracketing, too. You'll find that slower frame rates also come in handy for subjects that are moving around in interesting ways (photographic models come to mind) but don't change their looks or poses quickly enough to merit a 4.5 fps burst.

- **Movie stills.** As I'll note in Chapter 14, you can take up to 50 single or continuous still photos in JPEG Fine * format using the dimensions of the movie frame (e.g., 1920 × 1080 pixels) while capturing video. Do that by enabling the shutter release button in Movie mode, if necessary, using Custom Setting f2: Custom Controls > Shutter-release button. (The default setting is Take Photos.) When the Photo/Movie switch is set to the Movie position, pressing the Release Mode button produces only two choices: Single frame or Continuous.

    - **Single-frame release mode.** You can take pictures without interrupting movie shooting; only one photo is taken each time the shutter release is pressed.

    - **Continuous mode.** The Z5 will capture images continuously for a period of up to three seconds while the shutter button is held down. The frames-per-second rate will depend on the frame rate you've selected for movie shooting. However, continuous capture works *only* when you are in Movie mode, but *not* actually capturing video. During video recording, only a single image will be captured even if the release mode is set to Continuous.

A Tiny Slice of Time

Exposures that seem impossibly brief can reveal a world we didn't know existed. Electronic flash freezes action by virtue of its extremely short duration—as brief as 1/50000th second or less. The Z5's optional external electronic flash unit can give you these ultra-quick glimpses of moving subjects. You can read more about using electronic flash to stop action in Chapter 9.

Of course, the Z5 is fully capable of immobilizing all but the fastest movement using only its shutter speeds, which range all the way up to 1/8000th second. Indeed, you'll rarely have need for such a brief shutter speed in ordinary shooting. (For the record, I don't believe I've *ever* used a shutter speed of 1/8000th second, except when testing a camera's ISO 25800 or higher setting outdoors in broad daylight.) But at more reasonable sensitivity settings, say, to use an aperture of f/1.8 at ISO 200 outdoors in bright sunlight, a shutter speed of 1/8000th second would more than do the job. You'd need a faster shutter speed only if you moved the ISO setting to a higher sensitivity (but why would you do that, outside of testing situations like mine?). Under less than full sunlight, even 1/4000th second is more than fast enough for any conditions you're likely to encounter.

Indeed, most sports action can be frozen at 1/2000th second or slower, as you can see in the image of a motocross leap in Figure 6.2; I caught the rider at the peak of his aerial arc, so 1/800th second was easily fast enough to freeze him in mid-stride.

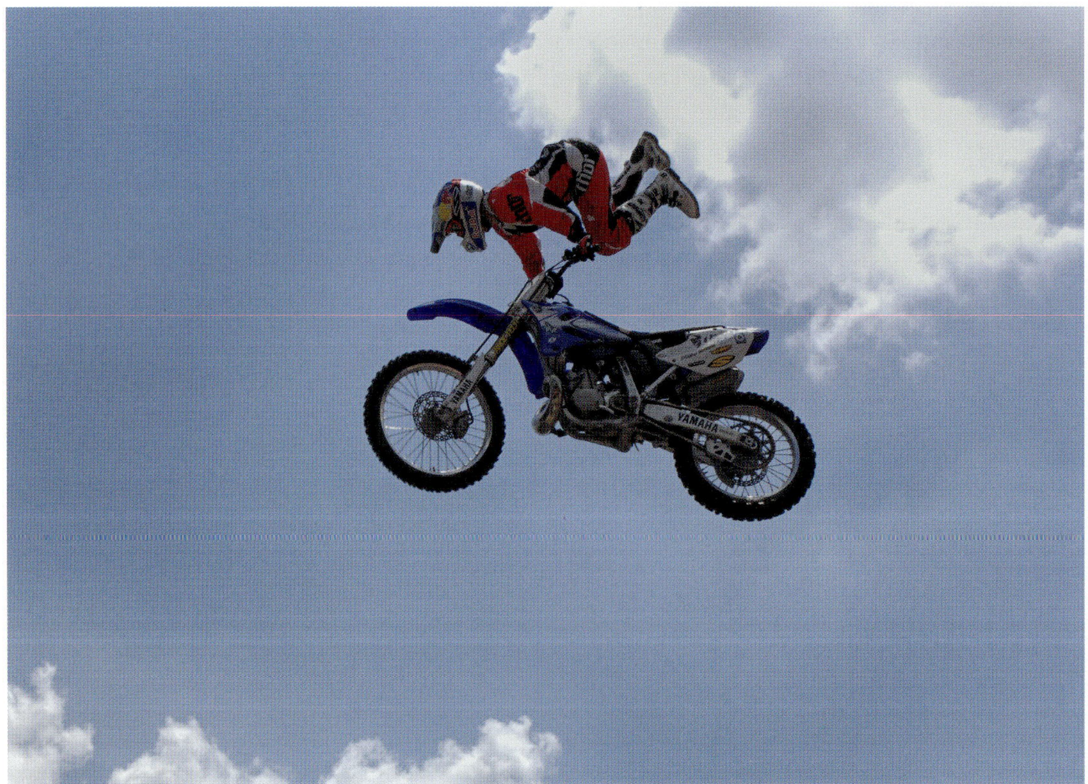

Figure 6.2 A shutter speed of 1/800th second was fast enough to stop this action.

Of course, in many sports a slower shutter speed is actually preferable—for example, to allow the wheels of a racing automobile or motorcycle, or the rotors on a helicopter to blur realistically, as shown in Figure 6.3. At top, a 1/1000th second shutter speed effectively stopped the rotors of the helicopter, making it look like a crash was impending. At bottom, I used a slower 1/200th second shutter speed to allow enough blur to make this a true action picture.

But if you want to do some exotic action-freezing photography without resorting to electronic flash, the Z5's top shutter speed is at your disposal. Here are two things to think about when exploring this type of high-speed photography:

- **You'll need a lot of light.** Very high shutter speeds cut extremely fine slices of time and sharply reduce the amount of illumination that reaches your sensor. To use 1/8000th second at an aperture of f/6.3, you'd need an ISO setting of 1600—even in full daylight. To use an f/stop smaller than f/6.3 or an ISO setting lower than 1600, you'd need *more* light than full daylight provides. (That's why electronic flash units work so well for high-speed photography when used as the sole illumination; they provide both the effect of a brief shutter speed and the high levels of illumination needed.)

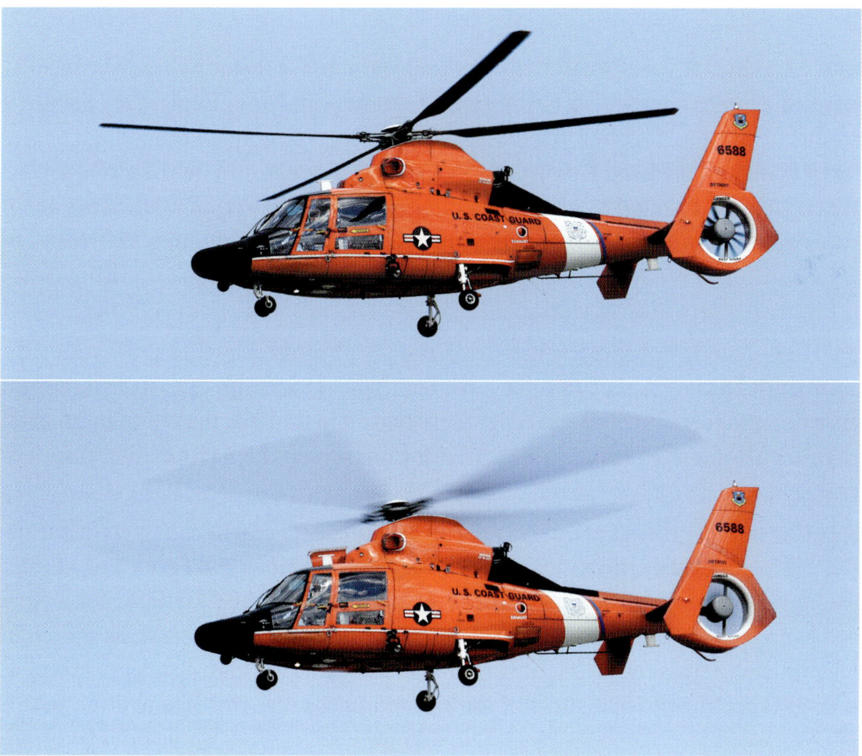

Figure 6.3 A little blur can be a good thing, as these shots of a helicopter at 1/1000th second (top) and 1/200th second (bottom) show.

- **High shutter speeds with electronic flash.** You might be tempted to use an electronic flash with a high shutter speed. Perhaps you want to stop some action in daylight with a brief shutter speed and use electronic flash only as supplemental illumination to fill in the shadows. Unfortunately, under ordinary conditions you can't use flash in subdued illumination with your Z5 at any shutter speed faster than 1/200th second. That's the fastest speed at which the camera's focal plane shutter is fully open. Shorter shutter speeds are achieved by releasing the rear curtain before the front curtain has reached the end of the frame, so the sensor is exposed by a moving slit (described in more detail in Chapter 9). The flash will expose only the small portion of the sensor exposed by the slit throughout its duration. (Check out "High-Speed Sync" in Chapter 9 if you want to see how you *can* use shutter speeds shorter than 1/200th, albeit at much-reduced effective flash power levels.)

Working with Short Exposures

You can have a lot of fun exploring the kinds of pictures you can take using very brief exposure times, whether you decide to take advantage of the action-stopping capabilities of your built-in or external electronic flash or work with the Nikon Z5's faster shutter speeds. Here are a few ideas to get you started:

- **Take revealing images.** Fast shutter speeds can help you reveal the real subject behind the façade, by freezing constant motion to capture an enlightening moment in time. Legendary fashion/portrait photographer Philippe Halsman used leaping photos of famous people, such as the Duke and Duchess of Windsor, Richard Nixon, and Salvador Dali to illuminate their real selves. Halsman said, *"When you ask a person to jump, his attention is mostly directed toward the act of jumping and the mask falls so that the real person appears."* Try some high-speed portraits of people you know in motion to see how they appear when concentrating on something other than the portrait. Figure 6.4 provides an example.

- **Create unreal images.** High-speed photography can also produce photographs that show your subjects in ways that are quite unreal. A motocross cyclist leaping over a ramp, but with all motion stopped so that the rider and machine look as if they were frozen in mid-air, make for an unusual picture. When we're accustomed to seeing subjects in motion, seeing them stopped in time can verge on the surreal.

- **Capture unseen perspectives.** Some things are *never* seen in real life, except when viewed in a stop-action photograph. MIT electronics professor Harold Edgerton's famous 1962 photo of a bullet passing through an apple was only a starting point. Freeze a hummingbird in flight for a view of wings that never seem to stop. Or, capture the splashes as liquid falls into a bowl, as shown in Figure 6.5. No electronic flash was required for this image. Instead, two high-intensity lamps at left and right and an ISO setting of 1600 allowed the camera to capture this image at 1/2000th second.

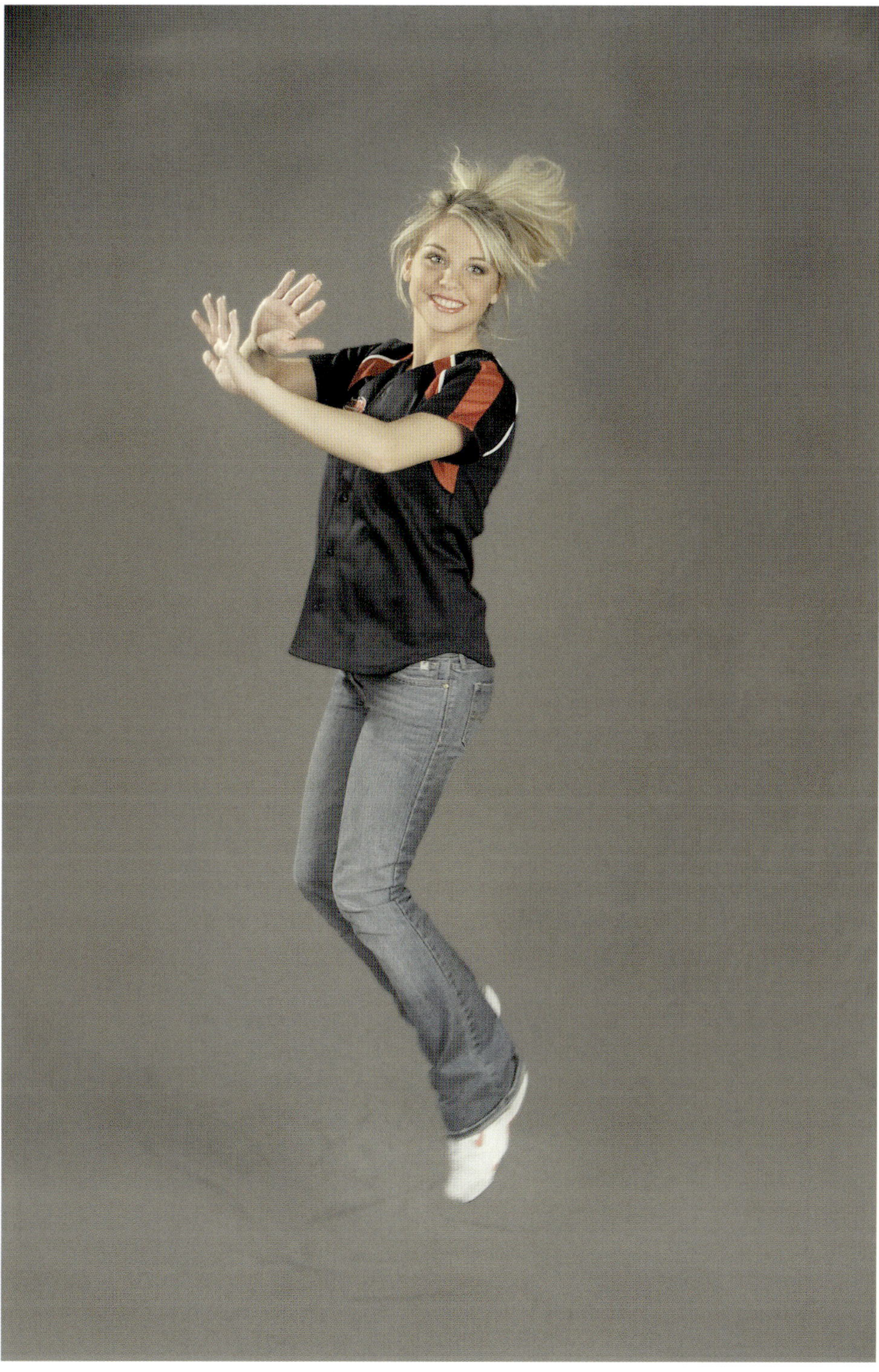

Figure 6.4 Shoot your subjects leaping and see what they look like when they're not preoccupied with posing.

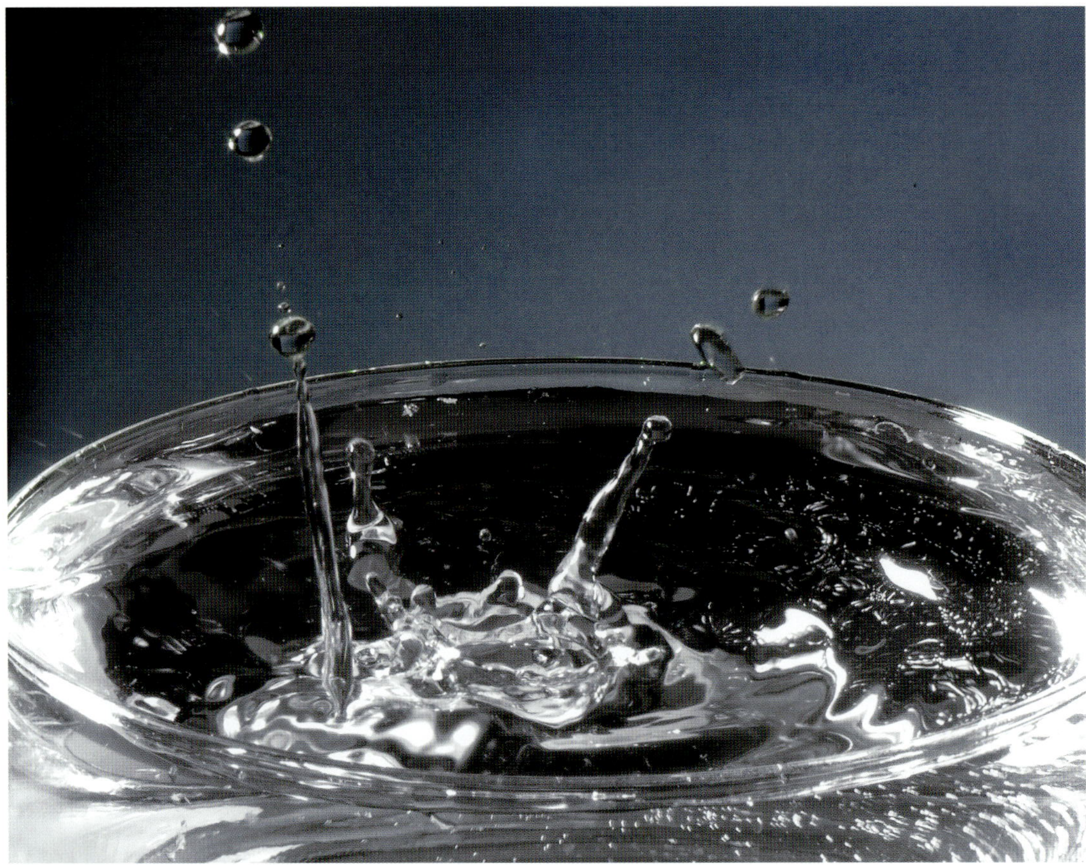

Figure 6.5 A large amount of artificial illumination and an ISO 1600 sensitivity setting allowed capturing this shot at 1/2000th second without use of an electronic flash.

- **Vanquish camera shake and gain new angles.** Here's an idea that's so obvious it isn't always explored to its fullest extent. A high enough shutter speed can free you from the tyranny of a tripod, and the somewhat limited anti-shake capabilities of image stabilization, making it easier to capture new angles, or to shoot quickly while moving around, especially with longer lenses. I tend to use a monopod or tripod frequently, and I end up missing some shots because of a reluctance to adjust my camera support to get a higher, lower, or different angle. If you have enough light and can use an f/stop wide enough to permit a high shutter speed, you'll find a new freedom to choose your shots. I have a favored Nikon AF-S 200-500mm f/5.6E ED VR lens that I use for sports and wildlife photography, almost invariably with a tripod, as I don't find the "reciprocal of the focal length" rule particularly helpful in most cases. I would *not* hand-hold this hefty lens at its 500mm setting with a 1/500th second shutter speed under most circumstances. However, at 1/2000th second or faster, it's entirely possible for a steady hand to use this lens without a tripod or monopod's extra support, and I've found that my whole approach to shooting animals and other elusive subjects changes in high-speed mode. Selective focus allows dramatically isolating my prey wide open at f/5.6, too. Of course, at such a high shutter speed, you may need to boost your ISO setting—even when shooting outdoors.

Long Exposures

Longer exposures are a doorway into another world, showing us how even familiar scenes can look much different when photographed over periods measured in seconds. At night, long exposures produce streaks of light from moving, illuminated subjects like automobiles or amusement park rides. Extra-long exposures of seemingly pitch-dark subjects can reveal interesting views using light levels barely bright enough to see by. At any time of day, including daytime (in which case you'll often need the help of neutral-density filters to make the long exposure practical), long exposures can cause moving objects to vanish entirely, because they don't remain stationary long enough to register in a photograph.

Three Ways to Take Long Exposures

There are actually three common types of lengthy exposures: *timed exposures*, *bulb exposures*, and *time exposures*. The Z5 offers all three. Because of the length of the exposure, all of the following techniques should be used with a tripod to hold the camera steady.

- **Timed exposures.** These are long exposures from 1 second to 30 seconds, measured by the camera itself. To take a picture in this range, simply use Manual or S modes and use the main command dial to set the shutter speed to the length of time you want, choosing from preset speeds of 1.0, 1.5, 2.0, 3.0, 4.0, 6.0, 8.0, 10.0, 15.0, 20.0, or 30.0 seconds (if you've specified 1/2-stop increments for exposure adjustments), or 1.0, 1.3, 1.6, 2.0, 2.5, 3.2, 4.0, 5.0, 6.0, 8.0, 10.0, 13.0, 15.0, 20.0, 25.0, and 30.0 seconds (if you're using 1/3-stop increments). The advantage of timed exposures is that the camera does all the calculating for you. There's no need for a stopwatch. If you review your image on the monitor and decide to try again with the exposure doubled or halved, you can dial in the correct exposure with precision. The disadvantage of timed exposures is that you can't take a photo for longer than 30 seconds.

- **Bulb exposures.** This type of exposure is so-called because in the olden days the photographer squeezed and held an air bulb attached to a tube that provided the force necessary to keep the shutter open. Traditionally, a bulb exposure is one that lasts as long as the shutter release button is pressed; when you release the button, the exposure ends. To make a bulb exposure with the Z5, set the camera on Manual mode and use the main command dial to select the first shutter speed immediately after 30 seconds—Bulb. Then, press the shutter or the button on a remote control (such as the MC-DC2) to start the exposure, hold it down, and then release it to close the shutter.

- **Time exposures.** On the Z5, this type of exposure is similar to Bulb, except you don't have to hold the shutter release down. Simply press the shutter release or your remote button to start the exposure and press a second time to stop the exposure. The setting is located just beyond Bulb when rotating the main command dial in Manual exposure mode and is labeled Time. I use this instead of Bulb most of the time, especially when using the MC-D2 release cable or making long exposures (where it would be tedious to stand there pressing a button during a Bulb exposure). You can start the exposure, go off for a few minutes, and come back to close the shutter (assuming your camera is still there). If you are *not* using a cable release, the advantage of using Bulb is you don't have to touch the camera twice; just press the button and release it when finished.

With shorter exposures it's possible for the vibration of manually opening and closing the shutter to register in the photo. For longer exposures, the period of vibration is relatively brief and not usually a problem. A typical time exposure I took in San Juan, Puerto Rico, is shown in Figure 6.6, left.

Note: If you choose Bulb or Time in Manual mode and then switch to Shutter-priority mode, the Bulb or Time setting will "stick," but the Z5 will *not* take a picture in either mode. Instead, an indicator on the display will flash, warning you to change to a usable setting. Nikon's reasoning is that you might not realize that Bulb or Time are no longer available, and wouldn't want the camera to choose some other setting on your behalf.

Working with Long Exposures

Because the Z5 produces such good images at longer exposures, and there are so many creative things you can do with long exposure techniques, you'll want to do some experimenting. Get yourself a tripod or another firm support and take some test shots with long exposure noise reduction both enabled and disabled (to see whether you prefer low noise or high detail) and get started. Here are some things to try:

- **Show total darkness in new ways.** Even on the darkest, moonless nights, there is enough starlight or glow from distant illumination sources to see by, and, if you use a long exposure, there is enough light to take a picture.

- **Blur waterfalls, etc.** You'll find that waterfalls and other sources of moving liquid produce a special type of long-exposure blur, because the water merges into a fantasy-like veil that looks different at varying exposure times, and with different waterfalls. Cascades with turbulent flow produce a rougher look at a given longer exposure than falls that flow smoothly, as you can see in Figure 6.6, right. Although blurred waterfalls have become almost a cliché, there are still plenty of variations for a creative photographer to explore.

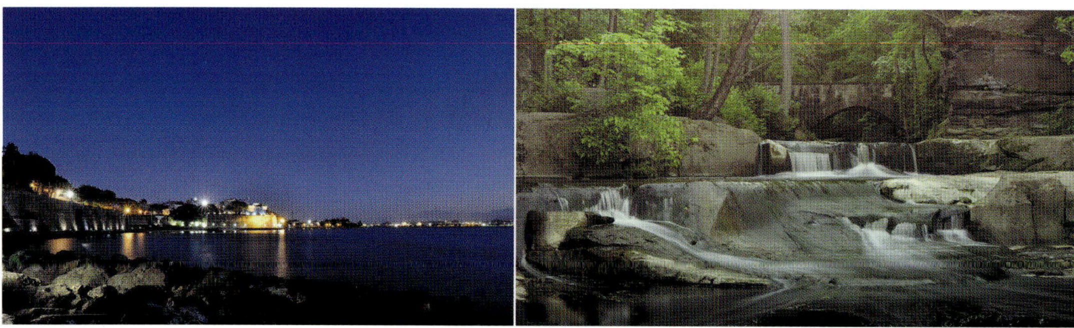

Figure 6.6 The Z5's time exposure setting can give you long time exposures, such as this 60-second shot of San Juan, Puerto Rico (left) or this cascade in Ohio (right).

- **Make people invisible.** One very cool thing about long exposures is that objects that move rapidly enough won't register at all in a photograph, while the subjects that remain stationary are portrayed in the normal way. That makes it easy to produce people-free landscape photos and architectural photos at night or, even, in full daylight if you use a neutral-density filter (or two) (or three) to allow an exposure of at least a few seconds. At ISO 100, f/22, and a pair of 8X (three-stop) neutral-density filters, you can use exposures of nearly two seconds; overcast days and/or even more neutral-density filtration would work even better if daylight people-vanishing is your goal. They'll have to be walking *very* briskly and across the field of view (rather than directly toward the camera) for this to work. At night, it's much easier to achieve this effect with the 20- to 30-second exposures that are possible, as you can see in Figure 6.7. At left, with an exposure of several seconds, the crowded street in Segovia, Spain, is fully populated. At right, with a 20-second exposure, the folks moving slowly (at left) show up as blurs; those standing still (at right) are portrayed normally; and the fast-moving walkers in the foreground are barely perceptible blurs.

- **Create streaks.** If you aren't shooting for total invisibility, long exposures with the camera on a tripod can produce some interesting streaky effects. Even a single 8X ND filter will let you shoot at f/22 and 1/6th second in daylight. Indoors, you shouldn't have a problem using long shutter speeds to get shots like the one shown in Figure 6.8.

- **Produce light trails.** At night, car headlights and taillights and other moving sources of illumination can generate interesting light trails, as shown in the image of the carnival ride in Figure 6.9. Your camera doesn't even need to be mounted on a tripod; hand-holding the Z5 for longer exposures adds movement and patterns to your streaky trails. If you're shooting fireworks with a tripod, a longer exposure may allow you to combine several bursts into one picture.

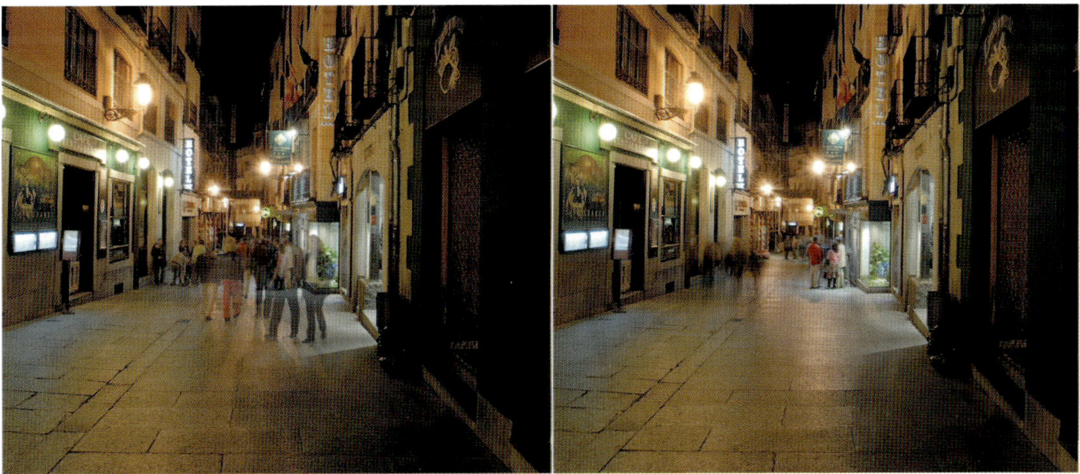

Figure 6.7 This European alleyway is thronged with people (left), but with the camera on a tripod, a 20-second exposure rendered most of the passersby almost invisible.

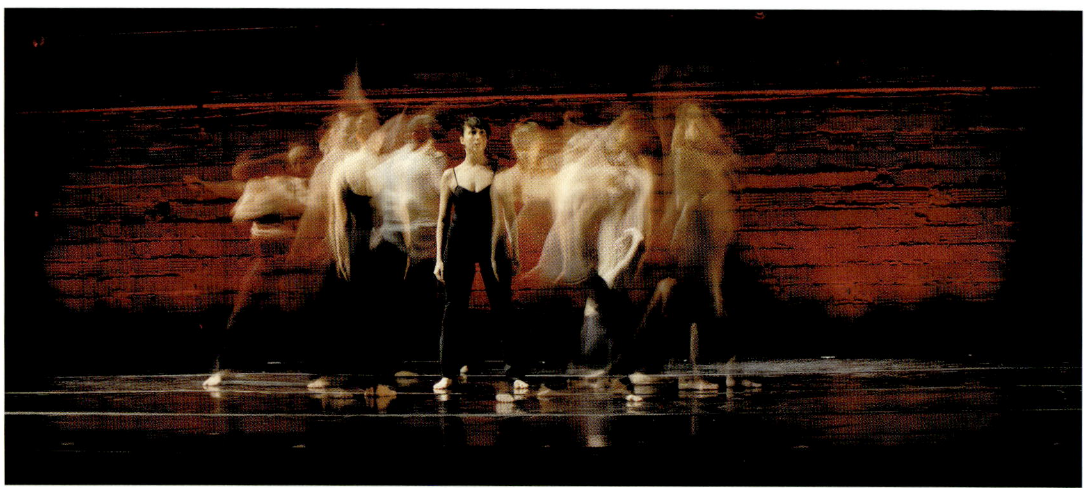

Figure 6.8 Long exposures can turn dancers into a swirling image.

Figure 6.9 The carnival ride's motion produces interesting light trails.

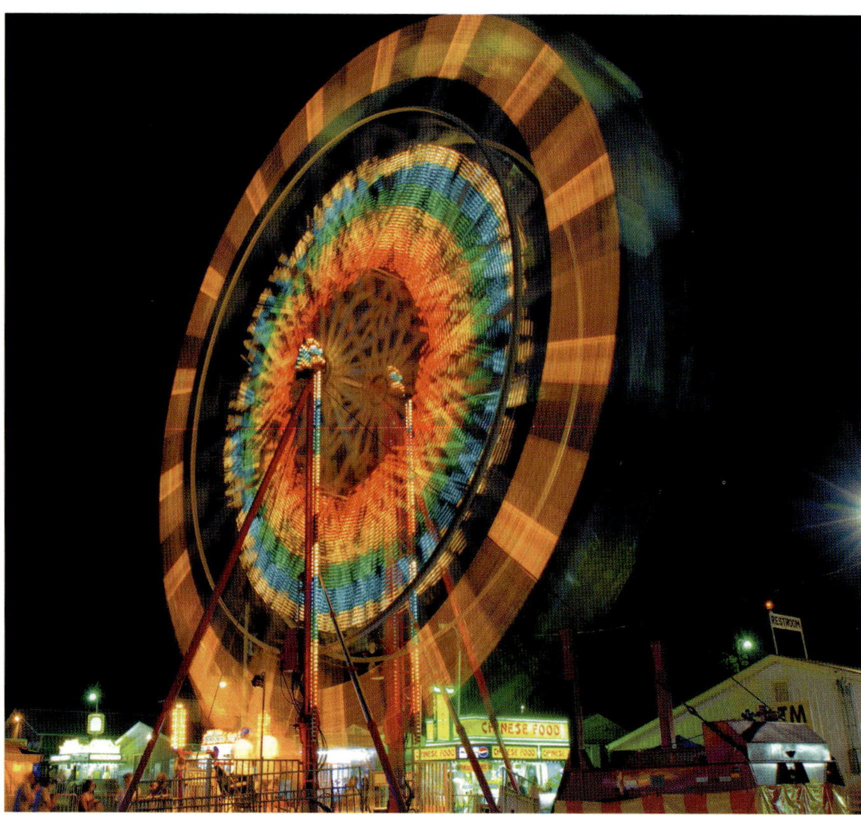

Delayed Exposures

Sometimes it's desirable to have a delay of some sort before a picture is actually taken. Perhaps you'd like to get in the picture yourself and would appreciate it if the camera waited 10 seconds after you press the shutter release to actually take the picture. Maybe you want to give a tripod-mounted camera time to settle down and damp any residual vibration after the release is pressed to improve sharpness for an exposure with a relatively slow shutter speed. It's possible you want to explore the world of time-lapse photography. The next sections present your delayed exposure options.

Self-Timer

The Z5 has a built-in self-timer with a user-selectable delay. Activate the timer by pressing the Release Mode button and rotating the main command dial to the self-timer icon. Press the shutter release button halfway to lock in focus on your subjects (if you're taking a group shot of yourself and several others, focus on an object at a similar distance and use focus lock). When you're ready to take the photo, continue pressing the shutter release the rest of the way. The lamp on the front of the camera will blink slowly for eight seconds (when using the 10-second timer) and the beeper will chirp (if you haven't disabled it in the Setup menu, as described in Chapter 13). During the final two seconds, the beeper sounds more rapidly, and the lamp remains on until the picture is taken. It's a good idea to close the viewfinder eyepiece shutter if you're not using live view or shooting in Manual exposure mode, to prevent light from the viewing window getting inside the camera and affecting the automatic exposure.

You can customize the settings of the self-timer. Your adjustments are "sticky" and remain in effect until you change them. Your options include:

- **Self-timer delay.** Choose 2, 5, 10, or 20 seconds, using Custom Setting c2. If I have the camera mounted on a tripod or other support and am too lazy to dig around for my wired remote, I can set a two-second delay that is sufficient to let the camera stop vibrating after I've pressed the shutter release. A longer delay time of 20 seconds is useful if you want to get into the picture and are not sure you can make it in 10 seconds.

- **Number of shots.** After the timer finishes counting down, the Z5 can take from 1 to 9 different shots. This is a godsend when shooting photos of groups, especially if you want to appear in the photo itself. You'll always want to shoot several pictures to ensure that everyone's eyes are open and there are smiling expressions on each face. Instead of racing back and forth between the camera to trigger the self-timer multiple times, you can select the number of shots taken after a single countdown. For small groups, I always take at least as many shots as there are people in the group—plus one. That gives everybody a chance to close their eyes.

- **Interval between shots.** If you've selected 2 to 9 as your number of shots to be snapped off, you can use this option to space out the different exposures. Your choices are 0.5, 1, 2, or 3 seconds. Use a short interval when you want to capture everyone saying "Cheese!" The 3-second option is helpful if you're using an external flash, as three seconds is generally long enough to allow the flash to recycle and have enough juice for the next photo.

Interval/Time-Lapse Photography

The Z5 is capable of both interval photography (for still pictures) and time-lapse video, both available from the Photo Shooting menu. The commands for both are described in Chapter 11. Who hasn't marveled at a time-lapse photograph of a flower opening, a series of shots of the moon marching across the sky, or one of those extreme time-lapse picture sets showing something that takes a very, very long time, such as a building under construction.

You probably won't be shooting such construction shots, unless you have a spare Z5 you don't need for a few months (or are willing to go through the rigmarole of figuring out how to set up your camera in precisely the same position using the same lens settings to shoot a series of pictures at intervals). However, other kinds of interval and time-lapse photography are entirely within reach. If you're willing to tether the camera to a computer (a laptop will do) using the USB cable, you can take time-lapse photos using the optional extra-cost Nikon Camera Control Pro.

For Figure 6.10, I pointed my camera out my office window in Florida, hoping to use Interval Timing Shooting to catch some manatees. I left the camera running for hours, capturing the three images shown in the figure. I've also used interval shooting for HDR images of sunsets. Typically, I aim the camera at the horizon and set it to shoot a three-shot bracket with a 3.0-stop increment. Then, I set the interval time to capture an image every 10 seconds.

- **Use AC power.** If you're shooting a long sequence of stills or a lengthy time-lapse movie, consider connecting your camera to an AC adapter, as leaving the Z5 on for long periods of time will rapidly deplete the battery. To minimize power drain, set Image Review to Off in the Playback menu, and enable Silent Photography in the Interval Timer Shooting entry.

- **Make sure you have enough storage space.** Unless your memory card has enough capacity to hold all the images you'll be taking, you might want to change to a higher compression rate or reduced resolution to maximize the image count.

- **Make a movie.** While stills shot at intervals are interesting, you can increase your fun factor by producing a time-lapse movie instead. You can also combine your interval shots into a motion picture using your favorite desktop movie-making software.

- **Protect your camera.** If your camera will be set up, make sure it's protected from weather, earthquakes, animals, young children, innocent bystanders, and theft.

- **Vary intervals.** Experiment with different time intervals. You don't want to take pictures too often or less often than necessary to capture the changes you hope to image.

Nikon Z5's built-in time-lapse photography feature allows you to take pictures for up to 999 intervals in bursts of as many as nine shots, with a delay of up to 23 hours and 59 minutes between shots/bursts, and an initial start-up time of as long as 23 hours and 59 minutes from the time you activate the feature. That means that if you want to photograph a rosebud opening and would like to photograph the flower once every two minutes over the next 16 hours, you can do that easily. If you like, you can delay the first photo taken by a couple hours, so you don't have to stand there by the Z5 waiting for the right moment.

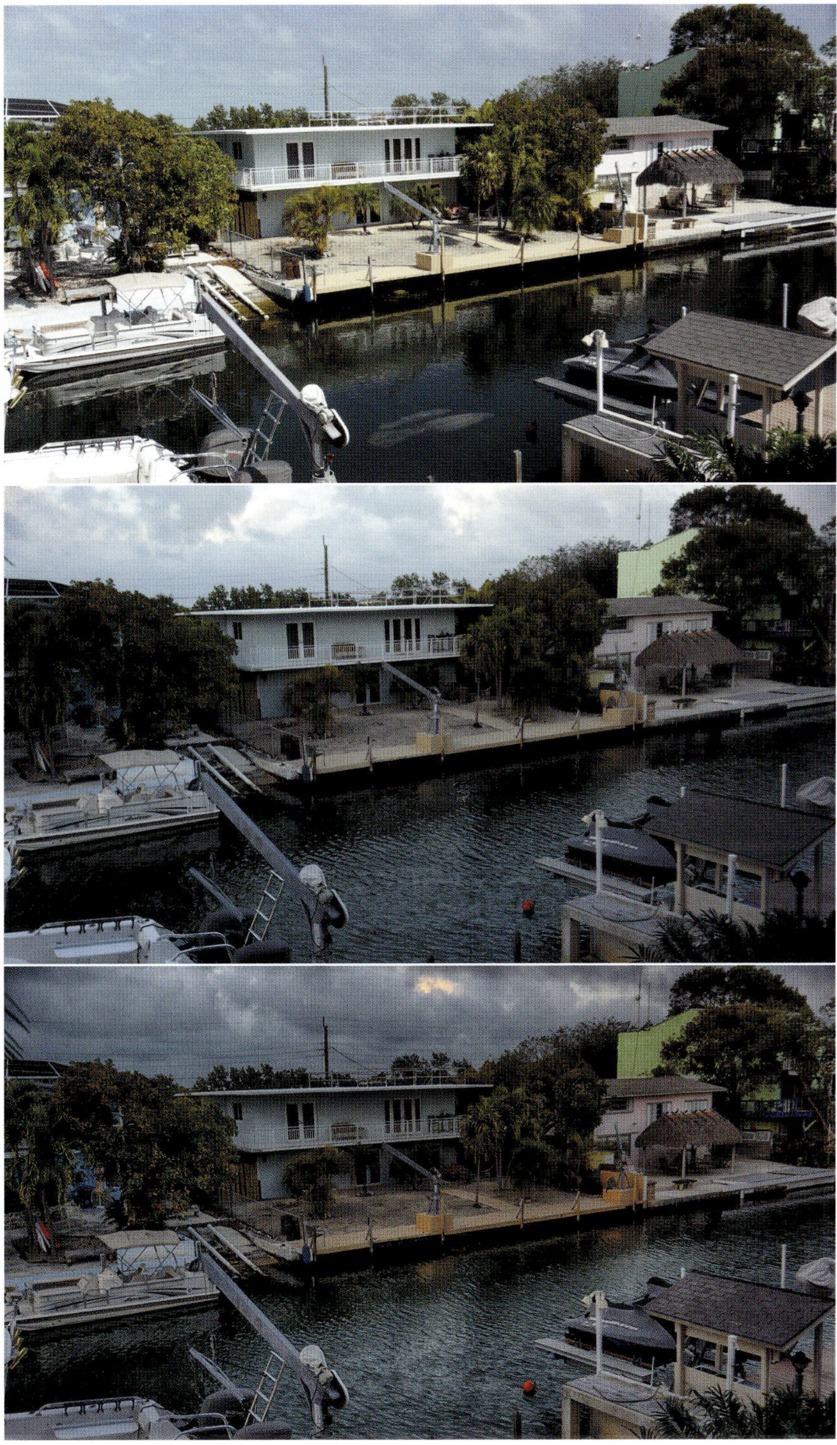

Figure 6.10 One of my time-lapse photos captured a mother manatee and her calf swimming by (top); the other exposures produced interesting variations on a static scene.

Movies Two Ways

Your Z5 allows you to capture time-lapse movies, rather than just a series of still pictures, in two ways. One is highly automated, while the other requires a little work on your part. I'll explain the differences between the two, and then show you how to use either of them.

- **Your camera does all the work.** If you use the Z5's Time-Lapse Movie option, which I'll describe shortly, the camera will take all the pictures using the interval and other parameters that you specify, and then combine them to produce a movie. You can watch the video as-is or use a video-editing program to combine it with other clips. The Time-Lapse movie entry is located in the Photo Shooting menu and is grayed out if the photo/movie selector switch is not set to the Movie position. I describe its parameters in Chapter 11, but the process basically works much like Interval Photography, which I will detail in the following sections.

- **Do it yourself.** You gain more flexibility and some options if you capture the individual frames using the Z5's Interval Timer, and then combine them in a video editor to produce a video. That allows you to have individual frames as stills—and at a higher resolution, too (up to the full 24 megapixels the Z5 offers)—as well as video (which is described in Chapter 11).

  In fact, you aren't limited to 1080p video, as you are when using the Time-Lapse Movie option. You can assemble the individual shots into a 4K movie, or even a faux 8K video (you'll need a high-end monitor to display any "8K" video you produce). Nikon calls the latter 8K Time-Lapse, which it is not, because the standard frame size for 8K video is 7680 × 4320, and the Z5's full-resolution frames measure 6016 × 4016 pixels.

Using Interval Photography

This next section will tell you everything you need to know to capture images using the Z5's built-in intervalometer—whether you intend to use the resulting still photos as such, or plan to combine them into a home-brewed time-lapse movie. To set up interval timer shooting, just follow these steps.

Before you start:

1. **Check your time.** The Z5 uses its internal clock to activate, so make sure the time has been set accurately in the Setup menu before you begin.

2. **Ignore release mode.** You don't need to set the camera for continuous shooting. The Z5 will take the specified number of shots at each interval regardless of release mode setting.

3. **Set up optional bracketing.** However, if you'd like to bracket exposures during interval shooting, set up bracketing prior to beginning. (You learned how to bracket in Chapter 4.) The Z5 will expose the requested number of bracketed images regardless of the number of shots per interval requested. Exposure, flash, ADL, and white balance bracketing can all be used.

4. **Position camera.** Mount the camera on a tripod or other secure support.

5. **Fully charge the battery.** You might want to connect the Z5 to the Nikon AC adapter power connector or use the USB Power option that I'll describe in Chapter 13 if you plan to shoot long sequences. Although the camera more or less goes to sleep between intervals, some power is drawn, and long sequences with bursts of shots can drain power even when you're not using the interval timer feature.

6. **Make sure the camera is protected** from the elements, accidents, and theft.

When you're ready to go, set up the Z5 for interval shooting:

1. **Access feature.** Choose Interval Timer Shooting from the Photo Shooting menu. (See Figure 6.11, left.)

2. **Specify a starting time.** Highlight Choose Start Day/Time and press the right directional button. A screen appears allowing you to choose either Now (to begin interval shooting immediately) or Choose Day/Time. To set a start time in the future, highlight Choose Day/Time, and press the right directional button. A screen appears that allows entering a Start Date, H (Hour), and M (Minute). You can set the current date, or up to seven days in the future. Hours are available in 24-hour format. Press OK when you've specified the start time. You'll be returned to the main screen shown in Figure 6.11, left.

3. **Set the interval between exposures.** Scroll down to the Interval entry and press the right directional button. In the screen that appears, you can use the left/right buttons to move among hours, minutes, and seconds, and use the up/down directional buttons to choose an interval from one second to 24 hours. Press the OK button when finished to move back to the main screen.

4. **Select the spacing and number of shots.** Highlight Intervals × Shots/Interval and press the right directional button. Use the left/right directional buttons to highlight the number of intervals (that is, how many times you want the camera activated) and the number of shots taken after each interval has elapsed (as many as nine images taken at each activation). The total number of shots to be exposed overall will be shown at far right once you've entered those two parameters. You can highlight each number column separately, so that to enter, say, 250 intervals, you can set the 100s, 10s, and 1s columns individually (rather than press the up button 250 times!). You can select up to 9,999 intervals, and 9 shots per interval for a maximum of 89,991 exposures with one interval shooting cycle. Press OK to return to the main screen. **Tip:** Your memory card won't hold 89,991 exposures at full resolution!

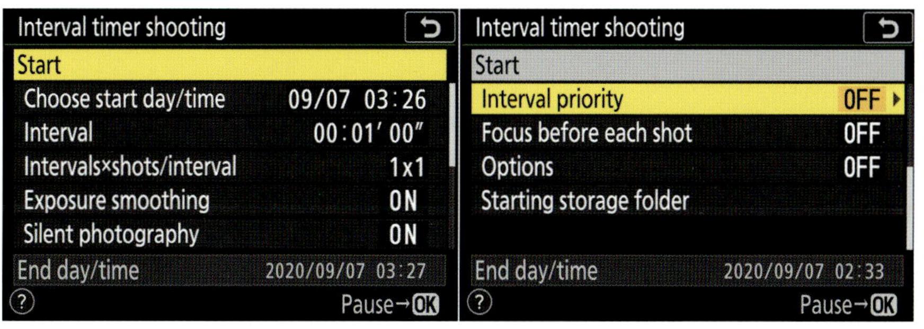

Figure 6.11 Interval timer shooting options.

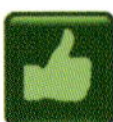

TIP The interval cannot be shorter than the shutter speed; for example, you cannot set one second as the interval if the images will be taken at two seconds or longer.

5. **Specify Exposure Smoothing.** You can turn this feature on or off. When activated, the Z5 will adjust the exposure of each shot to match that of the previous shot in P, S, or A mode. So, if you want the shutter speed to remain the same for each image (and don't care if the aperture is adjusted), use Shutter-priority mode. If you'd rather lock in your selected aperture (say, to keep the same depth-of-field), use Aperture-priority mode. Smoothing can also be used in Manual mode, but, of course, the Z5 won't vary either the shutter speed *or* aperture. You must have set ISO Sensitivity to Auto, to allow the camera to conform exposures by adjusting the ISO instead. Press OK to confirm.

6. **Activate Silent Photography (if desired).** You can choose On or Off for this parameter. When Silent Shooting is activated, the shutter will be silenced. This option comes in handy when you don't want your interval photography to disturb those who might be present, or you don't want them to know that you're shooting entirely.

7. **Set Interval Priority.** Scroll down the screen to reveal additional choices shown in Figure 6.11, right. Interval Priority can be set to On or Off. This parameter handles situations in which the shutter speed automatically selected in Program or Aperture-priority ends up being longer than the interval between shots. Perhaps you're shooting outdoors, and daylight has waned into night and a shutter speed of, say, 2 seconds is required even though your selected interval is one second.

   - **Interval Priority On:** The Z5 takes the picture at the specified interval anyway, even though the image may be taken at a shorter shutter speed and, therefore, underexposed. You can avoid the underexposure by activating Auto ISO Sensitivity, and selecting a minimum shutter speed that is shorter than the interval time. In that case, the Z5 will increase the ISO setting (if necessary) to produce the correct exposure using the automatically selected shutter speed.

   - **Interval Priority Off:** The chosen interval is lengthened to allow a correct exposure.

8. **Focus Before Each Shot.** Choose On to tell the Z5 to focus before each new exposure. Use this option if your subject is likely to move or, more commonly, a different subject is in the frame for some or all exposures. For example, if you were recording passersby on a busy street, some might be closer to the camera than others.

9. **Options.** Additional options available here:

   - **AE Bracketing.** You can set up exposure bracketing, including increment and number of shots that will be captured at each interval.

   - **Time-lapse Movie.** The Z5 will save the still photos captured in your interval sequence, *and also assemble a time-lapse movie.* You can choose the frame/size and frame rate (at both 4K and Full HD resolutions) and a destination card slot for your movie. Using this option avoids the need to shoot interval coverage and time-lapse movies separately and allows you to choose where to store the clip.

   - **Off.** Disables both options above.

10. **Starting Storage Folder.** Highlight New Folder and press the right directional button to tell the Z5 to create a new folder for each time-lapse sequence. This allows you to easily keep your sequences separate in their own folders. If you've chosen New Folder, you can also activate Reset File Numbering, which resets the numbering of each sequence to 0001 when a new folder is created. It's handy to have each sequence numbered separately.

11. **Activate shooting.** When all the parameters have been entered, scroll to the Start option at the top of the menu and press OK. If you've selected Now under Start Options, then interval shooting will begin immediately. If you chose a specific date/time instead, the appropriate delay will elapse before recording begins. Leave your camera turned on (and connected to an external power source if necessary). Once you activate interval shooting, immediately before the next shooting interval begins, the shutter speed display shows the number of intervals remaining and the aperture display shows the number of shots remaining in the current interval. Between intervals, you can view that information by pressing the shutter release button halfway; when you release the button, the data appears until the standby timer expires.

PAUSE OR CANCEL INTERVAL SHOOTING

While interval shooting is underway, you can review the images already taken using the Playback button. The monitor will clear automatically about four seconds before the next interval begins. Press the OK button between intervals (but not when images are still being recorded to the memory card) or choose the Interval Timer Shooting menu entry and select Pause. Interval shooting can also be paused by turning the camera on or off. To resume the Interval Timer Shooting menu again, press the multi selector left button, and choose Restart. You may also select Off to stop the shooting entirely.

Time-Lapse Movies

If you've mastered Interval Photography, shooting Time-Lapse movies to allow the Z5 to capture the individual frames and assemble them into a movie for you is a snap! The settings screen is similar to the one for interval shooting, with some additional options. The key entries include:

- **Start.** Unlike the similar Interval Timer found in the Photo Shooting menu, Time-Lapse Photography has no Start Options. Make your other settings, select Start, and time-lapse photography will begin automatically about three seconds later. Be sure to double-check your settings before triggering the camera.

- **Interval.** Select an interval between frames; use a longer value for slow-moving action, such as a flower bud unfolding. You might want to experiment and choose a time between shots of one minute or longer. Some blooms mature faster than others. Use a shorter value for movies, say, depicting humans moving around at a comical pace for a Charlie Chaplin–like effect. This parameter can be set from 1 second to 10 minutes.

- **Shooting time.** You can specify time-lapse movie duration. The longest movie you can create is a total of 7 hours, 59 minutes. That should be plenty for most applications. Andy Warhol's 1963 flick *Sleep* was only 5 hours, 20 minutes long!

- **Exposure Smoothing.** You can turn exposure smoothing on or off. When activated, the camera adjusts the exposure of each frame to match that of the previous frame in P, S, or A mode. That avoids sudden changes in exposure modes other than Manual exposure (which, of course, will remain at your manual settings throughout). Smoothing can also be used in Manual mode, but, of course, the Z5 won't vary either the shutter speed *or* aperture. You must have set ISO Sensitivity to Auto to allow the Z5 to compensate appropriately for changes in brightness. Press OK to confirm.

- **Silent photography.** Silences the shutter sound for unobtrusive or stealth video capture.

- **Image area.** You must scroll down to view this option, and those that follow. You can select FX-based movie format or DX-based movie format, which I'll explain in detail in Chapter 15. You can also turn Auto DX crop on or off, so the Z5 will recognize DX lenses and crop appropriately.

- **Frame size/frame rate.** Here you can select the frame size and frames per second setting for your time-lapse movie. You can choose from 4K, 3840 × 2160 30/15/24p; full HD, 1920 × 1060 60/50/30p (in both High Quality and Normal modes, also explained in Chapter 15); and standard HD, 1280 × 720 60/50p formats.

- **Interval priority.** This setting is similar to its intervalometer counterpart, as explained previously. It takes care of situations in which the shutter speed automatically selected in Program or Aperture-priority ends up being longer than the interval between shots. When enabled, the Z5 captures the movie frame at the specified interval, even though the image may be taken at a shorter shutter speed and underexposed.

  To compensate, activate Auto ISO Sensitivity, and select a minimum shutter speed that is shorter than the interval time. The Z5 will boost ISO to allow exposure at the correct interval. When disabled, the camera increases the interval you specified to allow correct exposure. However, with some subjects, the increased time may be visible in the finished movie as a jump or delay.

- **Focus before each shot.** Choose On to tell the Z5 to focus before each new exposure. Use this option if your subject is likely to move or, more commonly, a different subject is in the frame for some or all exposures. For example, if you were recording passersby on a busy street, some might be closer to the camera than others.

- **Destination.** Choose Slot 1 or Slot 2. Scroll down to see this last option in the list.

Star Trails

Star trails are another great application for both long exposures and interval shooting. You can shoot the night sky using long exposures with your Z5 mounted on a tripod. However, because of the rotation of the Earth, longer exposures will record the apparent motion of the celestial objects through the sky, producing a light trail. If you use a very, very long exposure, the light trail will record as continuous streaks, centered around the Polaris (the North Star) in the northern hemisphere and Sigma Octantis (which is, unfortunately, too dim to be easily seen with the naked eye) in the southern hemisphere.

Such long exposures can result in excessive noise and sensor overheating, so it's more common for photographers to take a series of individual exposures and combine them to produce a single star trail image. If you want your stars to appear as reasonably sharp points, you'll need to keep the exposure short enough that their movement in the sky isn't apparent. Fortunately, there's a simple formula you can use to calculate that exposure time, the "500 Rule." Divide 500 by the focal length of your lens to determine the longest exposure (in seconds) before stars start to produce a blurred trail. For example, with a 50mm lens, the longest exposure would be 10 seconds (500 divided by 50). Capturing the complete canopy of stars generally requires a wider viewing perspective. With the 16mm wide-angle setting, exposures could be as long as roughly 30 seconds.

For Figure 6.12, I set my camera to ISO 200, and used a basic exposure of 30 seconds at f/5.6. I selected an interval of 32 seconds and 170 total exposures, which totals about 90 minutes. Noise reduction was OFF! Then, I followed these steps, using Photoshop:

1. **Transfer files to a folder.** Select a folder on your computer and copy all your files to that location.
2. **In Photoshop:** Choose Files > Scripts > Load Files into Stack.
3. **Browse to folder.** Click the Browse button and navigate to the folder where your images are stored.
4. **Click OK.** Photoshop will create a file with one layer for each of your captured images.
5. **Select All layers.** Then click Layer Blending Options from the Layers palette and choose Lighten.
6. **Flatten image.** You'll want to flatten your image (the multi-layer file will be huge!). You'll end up with an impressive star trail image.

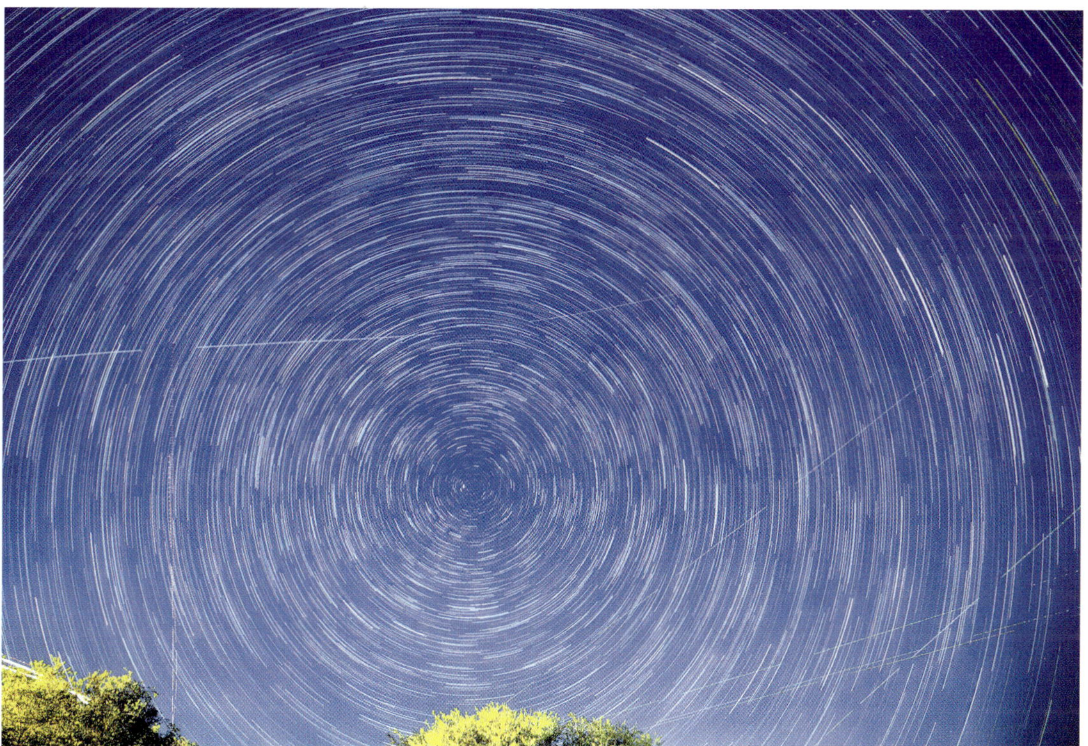

Figure 6.12 Capturing a star trail.

Multiple Exposures

Some of my very first images captured when I was a budding photographer at age 11 were double exposures. Some were unintentional, as my box camera, using 620-size film, could take several pictures on one frame if you forgot to wind it between shots. But my initial foray into special effects as a pre-teen were shots of my brother throwing a baseball to himself, serving as both pitcher and batter thanks to a multiple exposure.

The Z5's multiple exposure feature is remarkably flexible. It allows you to combine two to ten exposures into one image without the need for an image editor like Photoshop, and it can be an entertaining way to return to those thrilling days of yesteryear, when complex photos were created in the camera itself. In truth, prior to the digital age, multiple exposures were a cool, groovy, far-out, hep/hip, phat, sick, fabulous way of producing composite images. Today, it's more common to take the lazy way out, snap two or more pictures, and then assemble them in an image editor like Photoshop, or use the Z5's Image Overlay feature in the Retouch menu.

However, if you're willing to spend the time planning a multiple exposure (or are open to some happy accidents), there is a lot to recommend the multiple exposure capability that Nikon has bestowed on the Z5. For one thing, the camera is able to combine two to ten images using the RAW data from the sensor, producing photos that are blended together more smoothly than is likely for anyone who's not a Photoshop guru.

To take your own multiple exposures, just follow these steps (although it's probably a good idea to do a little planning and maybe even some sketching on paper first, if that's possible):

1. **Activate the feature.** Choose Multiple Exposure from the Photo Shooting menu. (See Figure 6.13.)

2. **Choose Multiple Exposure mode.** Select Multiple Exposure mode. A submenu appears with three choices:

   - **On (series).** The Multiple Exposure feature remains active even after you've taken a complete set of exposures for the number of shots you specified. Use this if you want to shoot several multiple exposures in a row. Remember to turn it off when you're done.

   - **On (single photo).** Once you've taken a single set of multiple exposures, the feature turns itself off.

   - **Off.** Use this option to cancel multiple exposures.

3. **Choose exposures per frame.** Select Number of Shots, choose a value from 2 to 10 with the multi selector up/down buttons, and press OK. (To capture Ana Popović, the world's best Serbian blues guitarist, for Figure 6.14, I used a three-shot multiple exposure.)

Figure 6.13 The Multiple Exposure menu.

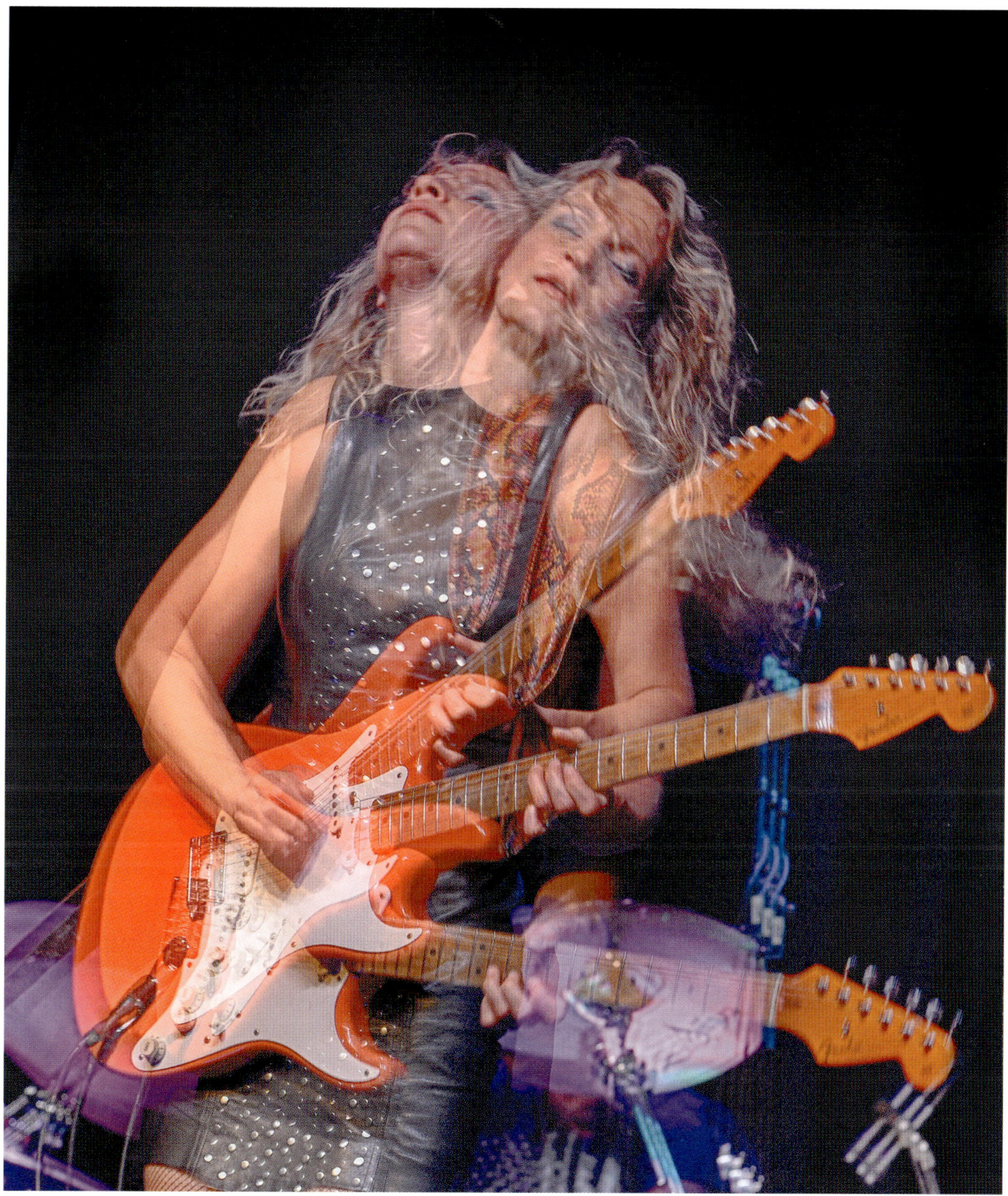

Figure 6.14 The Z5's Multiple Exposure capability allows combining images without an image editor.

4. **Specify ratio of exposure between frames.** Choose Overlay Mode and select Add, Average, Lighten, or Darken.

   - **Add.** Each new exposure is added to the previous shots, with each individual image fully exposed and overlaid on the others in the frame. Use when photographing a subject that is moving against a dark background, to track movement.

   - **Average.** The overall exposure is divided by the number of shots in the series, and each image is allocated that fraction of the overall exposure. Use this when shooting subjects with a great deal of overlap.

   - **Lighten.** The camera compares pixels in the same position in each exposure and uses only the brightest. This effect is similar to the Lighten blending mode in Photoshop, Lightroom, and other image-editing software. Use this to allow the lightest tones of each shot in the series to show through, such as multiple bursts in a fireworks show. The sky will remain dark, but the pyrotechnics will be captured perfectly. You may have to experiment with this setting until you become familiar with what it does to your images.

   - **Darken.** Similar to the Lighten blending mode, only just the darkest pixel is saved. You'd use this in situations that are the opposite of those typical of the Add selection. That is, if the background is light, and a darker subject is moving across that background, Darken would provide separate images.

5. **Confirm setting.** Press OK to set the ratio.

6. **Save Individual Images (NEF).** Ordinarily, the Z5 combines all the shots into a single exposure. However, you can ask the camera to save *all* the individual images in the series as RAW files by choosing On in the Save Individual Images (NEF) entry.

7. **Overlay Shooting.** This setting shouldn't be confused with Overlay mode, described above. If you select On, then each subsequent exposure is superimposed in the previous images on the LCD display as you shoot. That's particularly useful when you're capturing each image individually. For Figure 6.15, I shot two images of saxophonist Todd Cooper of the Alan Parsons Project individually, moving the camera slightly between shots to create a collage of sorts. It was easy to do in Live View mode using the overlay feature.

8. **Select First Exposure (NEF).** This is a great feature! You can select an existing RAW image on your memory card and use that as the background for your subsequent multiple exposures. As you capture the individual shots, they will be blended with the background image using the Overlay mode you've selected.

9. **Shoot your multiple exposure set.** Take the photo by pressing the shutter release button multiple times until all the exposures in the series have been taken. (In continuous shooting mode, the entire series will be shot in a single burst.) The blinking multiple exposure icon vanishes when the series is finished. **Reminder:** You'll need to deactivate the Multiple Exposure feature once you've finished taking a set in On (series) mode, as the setting remains even after the camera has been powered off.

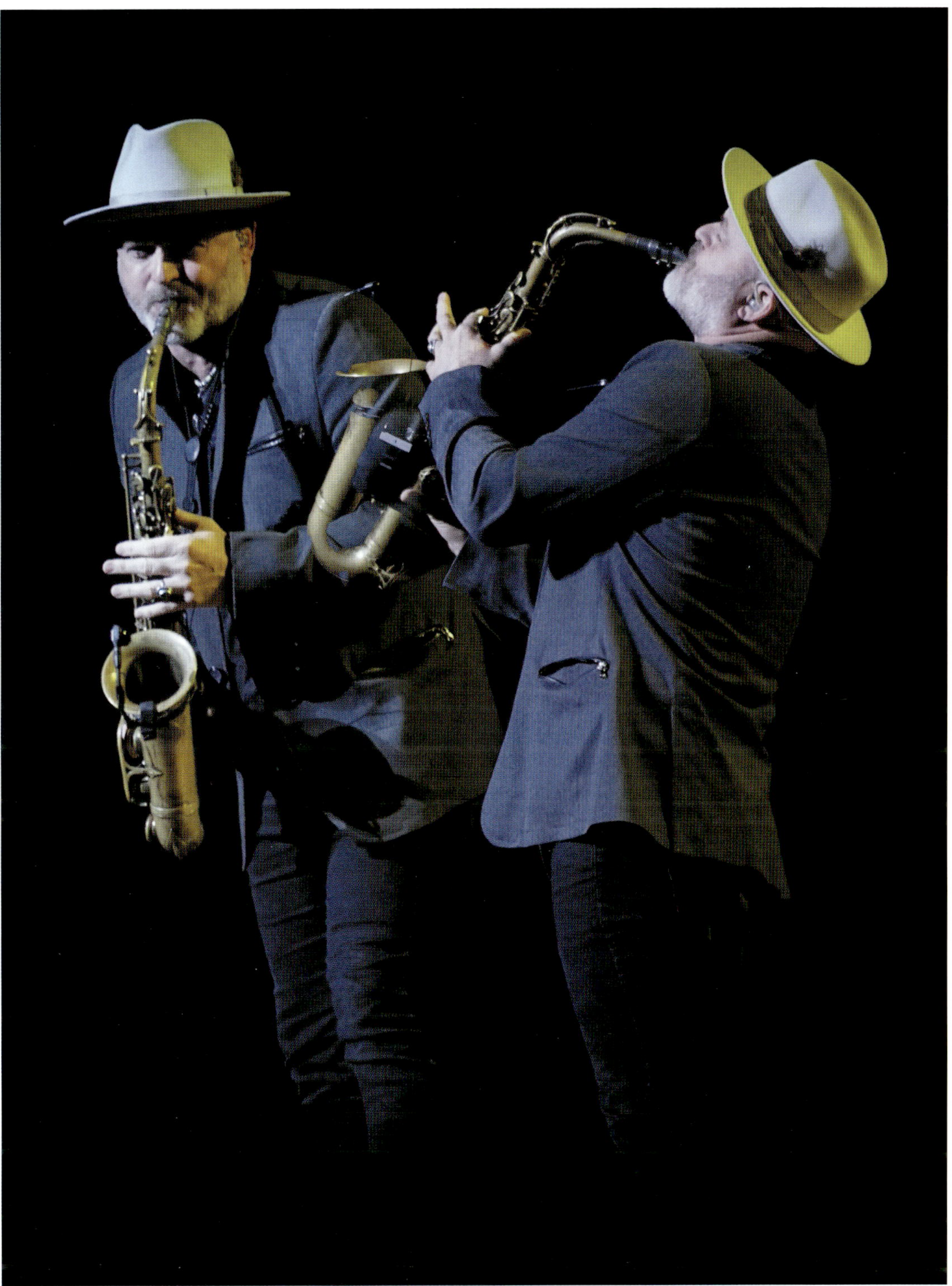

Figure 6.15 Overlay Shooting allows viewing superimposed images on the display for easier composition.

Keep in mind if you wait longer than 30 seconds between any two photos in the series, the sequence will terminate and combine the images taken so far. If you want a longer elapsed time between exposures, go to the Playback menu and make sure On has been specified for Image Review, and then extend the Standby Timer using Custom Setting c3: Power Off Delay to an appropriate maximum interval. The camera will grant you an additional 30 seconds beyond that. The Multiple Exposure feature will then use the monitor-off delay as its maximum interval between shots.

Geotagging with the Nikon GP-1a

A swarm of satellites in geosynchronous orbits above Earth became a big part of my life even before I purchased the Nikon Z5. I use the GPS features of my iPhone Xs Max and iPad Air and the GPS device in my car to track and plan my movements. When family members travel without me—most recently to Europe—I can use the Find my iPhone feature to see where they are roaming and vicariously accompany them with Google Maps' Street View features. And, since the introduction of the Nikon GP-1a accessory, GPS has become an integral part of my shooting regimen, too. Nikon has been de-emphasizing this gadget the last few years because it has become easy to transfer GPS information from your smartphone to your camera, but I prefer this standalone solution. It's easier to set up and doesn't require a link to an off-camera device.

The GP-1a unit makes it easy to tag your images with the same kind of longitude, latitude, altitude, and time stamp information that is supplied by the GPS unit you use in your car. (Don't have a GPS? Photographers who get lost in the boonies as easily as I do *must* have one of these!) The geotagging information is stored in the metadata space within your image files, and can be accessed by Nikon NX-i, or by online photo services such as mypicturetown.com and Flickr.

Geotagging can also be done by attaching geographic information to the photo after it's already been taken. This is often done with online sharing services, such as Flickr, which allow you to associate your uploaded photographs with a map, city, street address, or postal code. When properly geotagged and uploaded to sites like Flickr, users can browse through your photos using a map, finding pictures you've taken in a given area, or even searching through photos taken at the same location by other users. Of course, in this day and age it's probably wise not to include GPS information in photos of your home, especially if your photos can be viewed by an unrestricted audience.

Having this information available makes it easier to track where your pictures are taken. That can be essential, as I learned from a trip out west, where I found the red rocks, canyons, and arroyos of Nevada, Utah, Arizona, and Colorado all pretty much look alike to my untrained eye. I find the capability especially useful when I want to return to a spot I've photographed in the past and am not sure how to get there. I can enter the coordinates shown into my hand-held or auto GPS (or an app in my iPad or iPhone) and receive instructions on how to get there. That's handy if you're returning to a spot later in the same day, or months later.

Like all GPS units, the Nikon GP-1a obtains its data by triangulating signals from satellites orbiting Earth. It works with the Nikon Z5, as well as many other Nikon cameras. At about $312, it's not cheap, but those who need geotagging—especially for professional mapping or location applications—will find it to be a bargain.

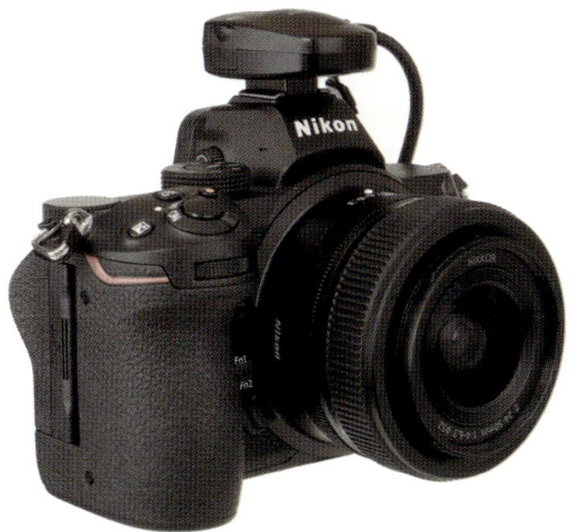

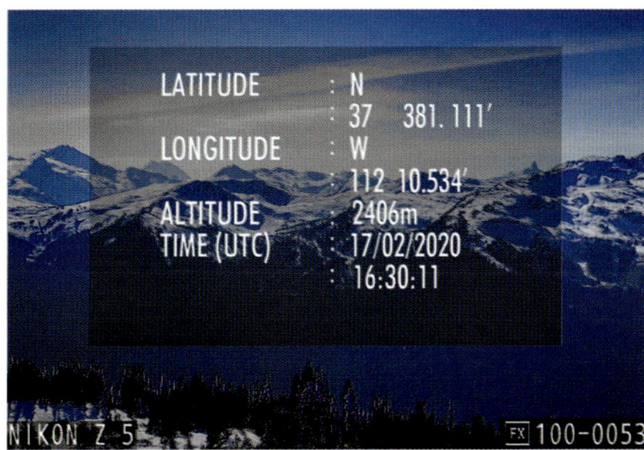

Figure 6.16 Nikon GP-1a geotagging unit (left). Captured GPS information can be displayed when you review the image (right).

The GP-1a (see Figure 6.16, left) slips onto the accessory shoe on top of the Nikon Z5. It connects to the remote/accessory port on the camera using the Nikon GP1-CA90 cable, which plugs into the connector marked CAMERA on the GP-1a.

EXTRA REMOTE

The GP-1a has a port labeled with a remote-control icon, so you can plug in the Nikon MC-DC2 remote release, and it will work just fine, even when the GPS accessory is attached.

A third connector connects the GP-1a to your computer using a USB cable. Nikon has released a utility for Windows and Mac operating systems that allows you to read GPS data from the GP-1a directly in your computer—no camera required. I tried the driver and discovered that the GP-1a couldn't "see" any satellites from inside my office (big surprise). I plan on trying it with my netbook outdoors, in a car, or in some other more satellite-accessible location. Once attached, the device is very easy to use. You need to activate the Nikon Z5's GPS capabilities in the GPS choice within the Setup menu's Location Data entry, as described in Chapter 13.

The first step is to allow the GP-1a to acquire signals from at least three satellites. If you've used a GPS in your car, you'll know that satellite acquisition works best outdoors under a clear sky and out of the "shadow" of tall buildings, and the Nikon unit is no exception. It takes about 40 to 60 seconds for the GP-1a to "connect." A red blinking LED means that GPS data is not being recorded; a green blinking LED signifies that the unit has acquired three satellites and is recording data. When the LED is solid green, the unit has connected to four or more satellites, and is recording data with optimum accuracy.

Next, set up the camera by selecting the GPS option found under Location Data in the Setup menu on the Nikon Z5.

There are four choices:

- **Download From Smart Device.** This setting allows you to download GPS/location data collected by your smart device, and then embed that information in the EXIF metadata within the image file. Choose Yes, and the data will be included *when you are not using a GPS device* while the two are connected for a period of up to two hours while the camera is powered up and the standby timer has not expired. If the GPS unit is connected, its location data *will be used instead* when both the GPS and smart device are in play.

- **Standby Timer.** Setting to Enable reduces battery drain by enabling turning off exposure meters while using the GP-1/1a after the time specified for the Standby Timer in Custom Setting c3: Power Off Delay (discussed in Chapter 12) has elapsed. When the meters turn off, the GP-1/1a becomes inactive and must reacquire at least three satellite signals before it can begin recording GPS data once more. Setting to Disable causes exposure meters to remain on while using the GP-1/1a, so that GPS data can be recorded at any time, despite increased battery drain.

- **Position.** This is an information display, rather than a selectable option. It appears when the GP-1/1a is connected and receiving satellite positioning data. It shows the latitude, longitude, altitude, and Coordinated Universal Time (UTC) values.

- **Set Clock From Satellite.** Choose Yes to allow the camera to update its internal clock from information provided by the GPS device when attached. Choosing No disables this updating feature. You might want to avoid updating the clock if you're traveling and want all the basic date/time information embedded in your image files to reflect the settings back home, rather than the date and time where your pictures are taken. Note that if the GPS device is active when shooting, the local date and time will be embedded in the GPS portion of the EXIF data.

Once the unit is up and running, you can view GPS information using photo information screens available on the color monitor (and described in Chapter 2). The GPS screen, which appears only when a photo has been taken using the GPS unit, looks something like Figure 6.16, right.

Focus Shift Shooting

If you are doing macro (close-up) photography of flowers or other small objects at short distances, the depth-of-field often will be extremely narrow. In some cases, it will be so narrow that it will be impossible to keep the entire subject in focus in one photograph. Although having part of the image out of focus can be a pleasing effect for a portrait of a person, it is likely to be a hindrance when you are trying to make an accurate photographic record of a flower, or small piece of precision equipment. One solution to this problem is focus stacking (which Nikon calls "Focus Shift Shooting"), a procedure that can be considered like HDR translated for the world of focus—taking multiple shots with different settings, and, using software as explained below, combining the best parts from each image in order to make a whole that is better than the sum of the parts. Focus stacking requires a non-moving object, so some subjects, such as flowers, are best photographed in a breezeless environment, such as indoors.

With the Z5's Focus Shift Shooting feature, the camera takes a series of pictures, adjusting the focus slightly between each image, refocusing from closest to your subject to the farthest point that needs to appear sharp. You end up with a series of up to 300 different images that can be combined using two simple Photoshop commands, which I will describe shortly.

You can visualize how focus stacking works if you examine Figure 6.17, which is cropped versions of three actual frames from one of my own focus shift series. All three used an exposure of 1/30th second at f/6.3 with my AF-S 24-120mm f/4G ED zoom at the 50mm setting. At top is the original exposure, with the lens focused on the nearest domino. The center image shows the 35th exposure in the series, in which the focus shift feature had adjusted focus on the last row of dominoes. In between were 33 intermediate-focus shots that I merged in Photoshop to produce the finished image at bottom. Here are the detailed steps you can take to use Focus Shift Shooting for your own deep-focus images:

1. **Set the camera firmly on a solid tripod.** A tripod or other equally firm support is absolutely essential for this procedure. You don't want the camera (or the subject) to move at all during the exposures.

2. **Attach a remote release, such as the MC-DC2.** You want to be able to trigger the camera without moving it. However, the procedure does pause for a short period of time once you activate it, perhaps giving your tripod/camera time to settle down even if you begin by poking the OK button with your finger.

3. **Attach a lens with an appropriate focus range.** Focus Shift Shooting uses the lens's built-in autofocus motor.

4. **Set the focus modes.** If shooting using the optical viewfinder, press the focus mode button and rotate the main dial to choose AF-S (single focus) and the sub-command dial to choose Single-Point AF.

5. **Set the quality of the images to JPEG FINE ∗.** Use the Photo Shooting menu to make this adjustment.

6. **Set the exposure, ISO, and white balance manually.** Use test shots if necessary, to determine the best values. This step in the Photo Shooting menu will help prevent visible variations from arising among the multiple shots that you'll be taking. You don't want the camera to change the ISO setting or white balance between shots.

   Note: Even though you'll be effectively increasing depth-of-field through focus stacking, you should still avoid the widest apertures of your lens, as they are rarely the sharpest f/stops. I always stop down at least 1.5 f/stops—using f/6.3 in the example. Shutter speed is not as important, because the camera is on a tripod, but I tend to avoid very slow speeds anyway. You can manually set a slightly higher ISO sensitivity, if needed, to obtain the shutter speed/aperture combination you want to use.

7. **Turn off image stabilization.** If your lens has VR and an on/off switch, slide the VR switch to Off.

8. **Set focus point to nearest object.** Use the directional buttons to position the red focus box on the subject nearest the camera lens.

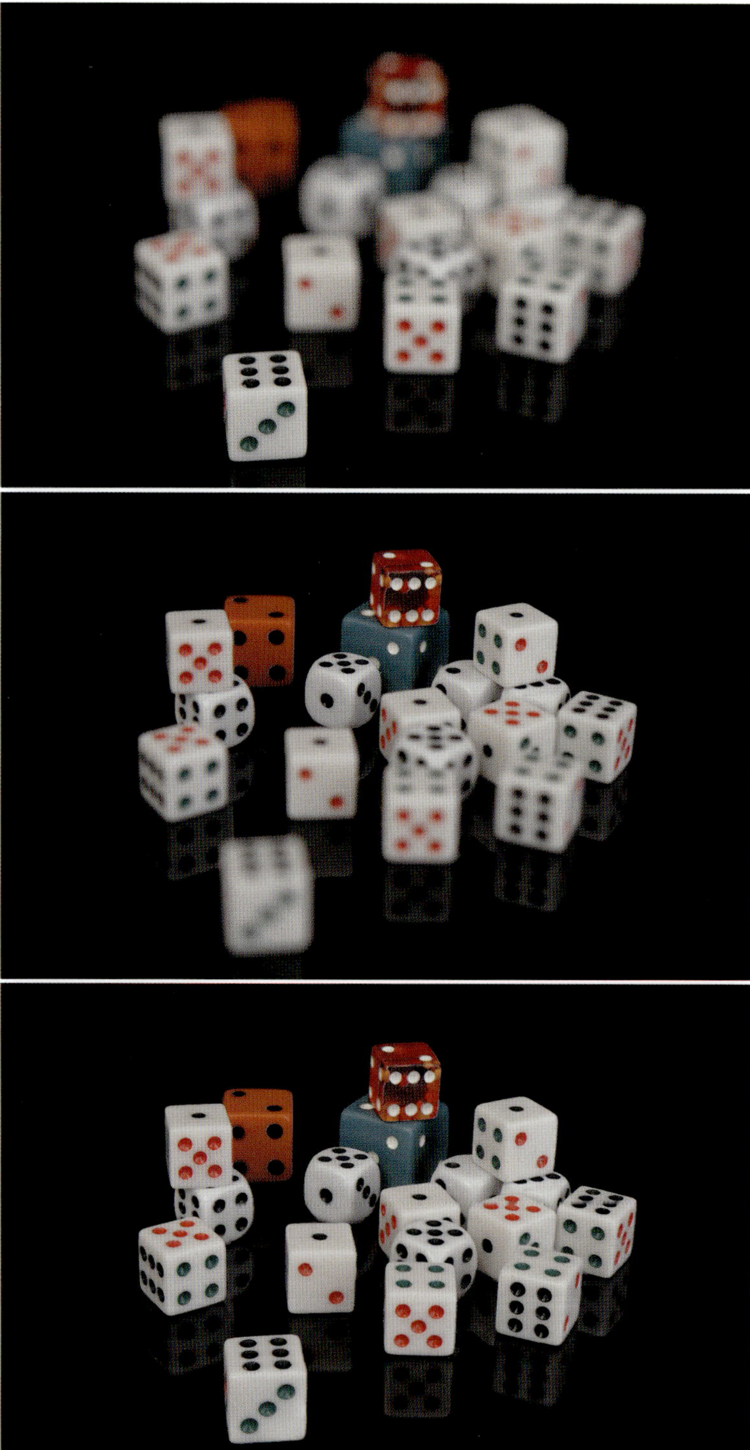

Figure 6.17 Closest focus (top), farthest focus (center), merged image (bottom).

9. Access the Focus Shift Shooting menu. You'll find it on the last page of the Photo Shooting menu and shown at left in Figure 6.18. Select an appropriate setting for each of the following six parameters, using my guidelines:

- **No. of Shots.** You can choose from 1 to 300 individually refocused shots. The number of images captured will depend on how finely you want to have the Z5 change focus between shots (and you'll combine this with the step width option described next). I rarely need more than 50 shots and used only 35 for the example shown earlier in Figure 6.17.

- **Focus Step Width.** You can specify values from 1 (a narrow slice per adjustment) and 10 (a much wider focus change). Nikon does not specify how much each increment changes the focus, for a very good reason: it *can't*. Depending on the focal length of your lens and your f/stop, the effective plane of apparent focus may vary from narrow, to very narrow, to super-narrow in macro shooting environments. (If you're confused, see "Circles of Confusion" in Chapter 5.)

  You may need some trial-and-error to choose the correct number of shots and focus step width. For example, with 50 shots and a wide focus step, the first 10 may encompass your entire subject and the last 40 may be wasted on completely out-of-focus images. It's often worthwhile to take a test shot, view a slide show of all your images, and decide whether to increase/decrease the number of shots and/or focus step width. (See Figure 6.18, right.)

- **Interval Until Next Shot.** You can select 00 seconds to 30 seconds. At 00 seconds, the Z5 will take all the photos consecutively at a rate of 3 frames per second in Single Shot or Continuous mode. (Don't use the self-timer release mode.) The 00-second setting works well when shooting by ambient light that doesn't change. However, you can use flash, too. Just specify an interval that is greater than the maximum recycle rate of your flash.

- **First-frame Exposure Lock.** Choose On and the camera will lock exposure at the settings calculated for the first shot. You'll use this most of the time, as you will get the best results if the illumination does not change between shots. Select Off to tell the Z5 to recalculate exposure for each frame. You might do that when shooting landscapes on a day with intermittent clouds. Your results may not be as good as if the lighting was kept consistent, however.

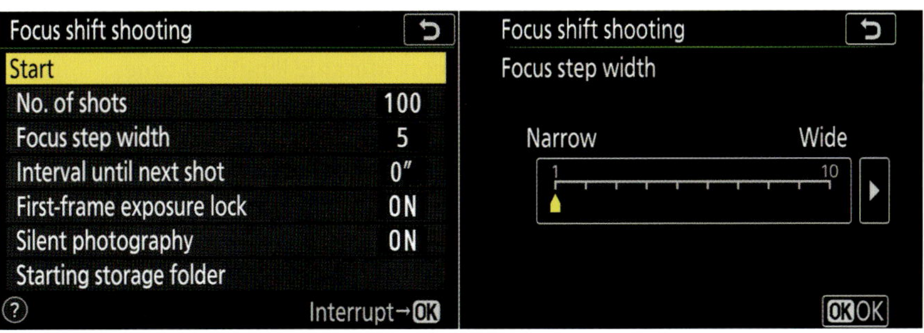

Figure 6.18 Focus Shift Shooting options.

- **Silent Photography.** You can capture your images (almost) silently using the electronic shutter if you activate this option. I prefer to hear the comforting click as my camera captures its sequence, but if you're in stealth or "do not disturb" modes, silent photography is available. Aperture adjustments may be the culprit if you've set First-Frame Exposure Lock to Off. Silent Photography disables use of the flash, long-exposure noise reduction, flicker reduction, exposure delay mode, and ISO settings from Hi 0.3 to Hi 1.0.

- **Starting Storage Folder.** Choose New Folder, and each time you shoot a sequence, the Z5 will create a fresh folder. I can't think of a reason you would not want to do that. Select Reset File Numbering, and the file numbering is reset each time a new folder is created, which makes it easier to differentiate between the first, last, and in-between images of your set.

10. **Capture images.** When all the parameters are locked in, highlight Start and press the OK button. The LCD monitor displays a "Preparing..." message and then commences the capture within a second or two. Note that Focus Shift is not "sticky." Once you've grabbed a sequence, the feature is turned off and you must Start again to repeat or change parameters and Start anew.

11. **Combine your images.** I'll describe the steps for that next.

The next step is to process the images you've taken in Photoshop. Transfer the images to your computer, and then follow these steps:

1. In Photoshop, select File > Scripts > Load Files into Stack. In the dialog box that then appears, navigate on your computer to find the files for the photographs you have taken, and highlight them all.

2. At the bottom of the next dialog box that appears, check the box that says, "Attempt to Automatically Align Source Images," then click OK. The images will load; it may take several minutes for the program to load the images and attempt to arrange them into layers that are aligned based on their content.

3. Once the program has finished processing the images, go to the Layers panel and select all the layers. You can do this by clicking on the top layer and then Shift-clicking on the bottom one.

4. While the layers are all selected, in Photoshop go to Edit > Auto-Blend Layers. In the dialog box that appears, select the two options, Stack Images and Seamless Tones and Colors, then click OK. The program will process the images, possibly for a considerable length of time.

5. If the procedure worked well, the result will be a single image made up of numerous layers that have been processed to produce a sharply focused rendering of your subject. If it did not work well, you may have to take additional images the next time, focusing very carefully on small slices of the subject as you move progressively farther away from the lens.

6. You'll want to flatten the final image before saving it. Given the 24MP resolution of the Z5, the stack of individual shots will easily be more than 2GB, which exceeds the maximum file size of some storage media and/or OS file systems.

Although this procedure can work very well in Photoshop, you also may want to try it with programs that were developed more specifically for focus stacking and related procedures, such as Helicon Focus (www.heliconsoft.com), PhotoAcute (www.photoacute.com), or CombineZM (https://combinezm.informer.com/).

Connecting to Your Smart Device or Computer

I can guarantee that soon after you finish a shooting session, you'll be overcome by the urge to share your still images or movies. For most of us, more than a few images are destined for display on Instagram, Twitter, or other social media platforms. Others will be cropped and tidied up in an image editor and printed for display or circulation in hard copy form. You may want to create a digital slide show or edit your video clips into a compelling movie. In all those cases, your first step will be to transfer your work to another device, whether it's a smartphone or tablet or your desktop/laptop computer.

Fortunately, you have lots of options. You can use a card reader or connect the camera to your computer using a USB cable to copy or move your images to your computer. Nikon's free software ViewNX-i can help you use Nikon Transfer 2 to copy files quickly. You can also connect your camera using the Z5's built-in Wi-Fi "hot spot" or Bluetooth LE (Low Energy) transceiver or use your home/office network's router. The camera itself can be controlled over those links so you can take pictures remotely.

AVOIDING THE I.T. RABBIT HOLE

Although the Z5 is an advanced enthusiast camera, it's unlikely that you'll be using the most advanced connection technology Nikon has to offer. For example, Nikon's optional, but very pricey (about $750), WT-7 transmitter has both wireless and Ethernet connections and can upload photos and movies to a computer, your smart device, or FTP server, plus control the Z5 remotely, or view/capture pictures (but *not* movies) wirelessly with a browser on your computer or smart device.

   All this is beyond the scope of this book, even if there were room for a 60-page chapter that deals with computer technology rather than photography. Instead, I'm going to provide you with an introduction to using basic SnapBridge and Wi-Fi/Bluetooth options that should get you up and running.

In a nutshell, your wireless connection options are these:

- **Camera to smart device using Bluetooth LE.** In this mode, you'll use SnapBridge and the Bluetooth capabilities built into both the smart device and the Z5.
- **Camera to smart device using the Z5's built-in Wi-Fi hot spot.** SnapBridge will link the two devices with your smart device logging in to the Wi-Fi access point built into the Z5.
- **Camera to computer using a wireless router.** Your camera will connect to your computer's access point supplied by your home/office router.
- **Camera to computer using the Z5's built-in Wi-Fi hot spot.** Your computer will connect to the Z5's built-in Wi-Fi access point directly, without need for an external network.

Once you're connected, you can perform a variety of functions, including controlling your camera using SnapBridge—when connected to a smart device, or Camera Control 2 (or other tethering software, such as Lightroom), when connected to a computer. I've found that most users end up working with SnapBridge-to-camera links most of the time, because they can do the following:

- **Auto uploads.** You can use SnapBridge to automatically upload JPEG images (but not RAW files) from your camera to your smart device.
- **Upload selected photos.** During image review, you can press the *i* button and choose Select to Send to Smart Device/Deselect to choose specific images to transfer to your smart device. You can also use the Select to Send to Smart Device entry in the Playback menu. Up to 1,000 photos can be marked for upload in one session.
- **Resize images.** Obviously, uploading full-resolution images to your smart device would be slow and use a lot of storage space on your device. SnapBridge defaults to low-resolution 2-megapixel images (which should be fine for smart device display or sharing on social media), and the app lets you specify a different upload size.
- **Add credits.** The app also lets you choose to embed comments and copyright information entered in the Setup menu (as described in Chapter 13) or entered using the SnapBridge app itself.
- **Multiple devices.** If you own multiple phones and tablets, you can pair the camera with as many as five different devices. However, the Z5 can connect to only one at a time. You can manually switch between devices using the connection options described shortly.
- **Remote control.** You can trigger the shutter using your smart device (as long as the camera is on), giving you wireless remote control without the need of purchasing an accessory.
- **Imprint photos.** You can overlay comments or the time the photo was taken.

Linking Camera to Smart Device

Connecting your Z5 to your smart device (phone or tablet) is generally done using the SnapBridge application on the device (although there are other apps that perform some of the same functions). As I noted earlier, the Z5's SnapBridge app supports *only* camera-to-smart-device communications. Your first step in using SnapBridge is to download and install the SnapBridge app onto your smart device from the Google Play store or the Apple iTunes store.

Make sure both Bluetooth and Wi-Fi are enabled on your smart device, and the Airplane mode in the Z5's Setup menu is set to Off. Then follow the steps that follow to link your camera and device using the camera's Setup menu. Your screens may vary depending on whether you are using an Android or iOS device, and whether Nikon has issued one of its frequent updates to SnapBridge since this book went to press. You may need to use your device's Settings menu to connect to the camera, which will appear as a connection option in the device's Bluetooth and Wi-Fi entries.

The steps for connecting your Z5 to your smart device using Bluetooth are similar on both iOS and Android devices. The individual screens shown may vary, but the steps will be more or less the same.

Here's how to connect using Bluetooth.

1. **On the camera: Navigate to Connect To Smart Device.** You'll find this entry in the Setup menu. As with all menu entries, and those that follow in this list, proceed by pressing the right directional arrow or pressing OK. The screen shown at top in Figure 6.19 appears.

2. **On the camera: Begin connection.** Highlight Start Pairing (Figure 6.19, center) and press the right button. A screen like the one in Figure 6.19, bottom is shown on the Z5 next. It contains the unique name of your camera, including its serial number.

3. **On the device: Open the SnapBridge app.** The screen shown at left in Figure 6.20 should appear. Tap the camera icon, if necessary, to produce it. Then tap the gear icon at the upper-right corner of that screen.

4. **On the device: Add Camera.** Tap Add Camera on the screen that appears at right in Figure 6.20.

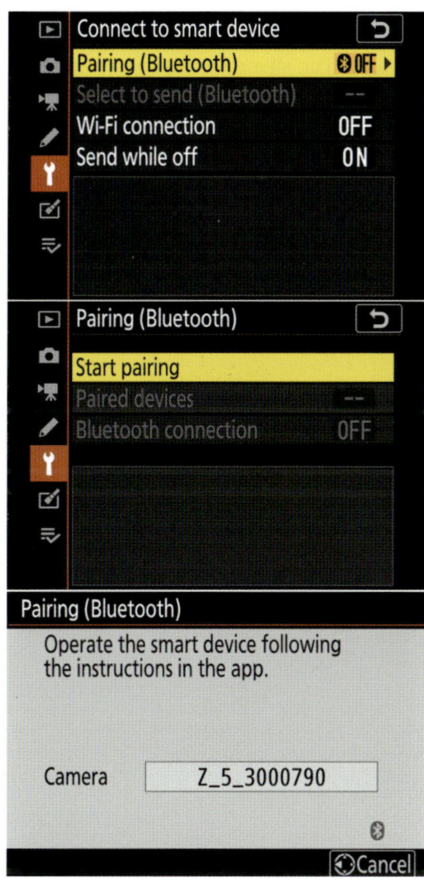

Figure 6.19 Connecting to a smart device with SnapBridge.

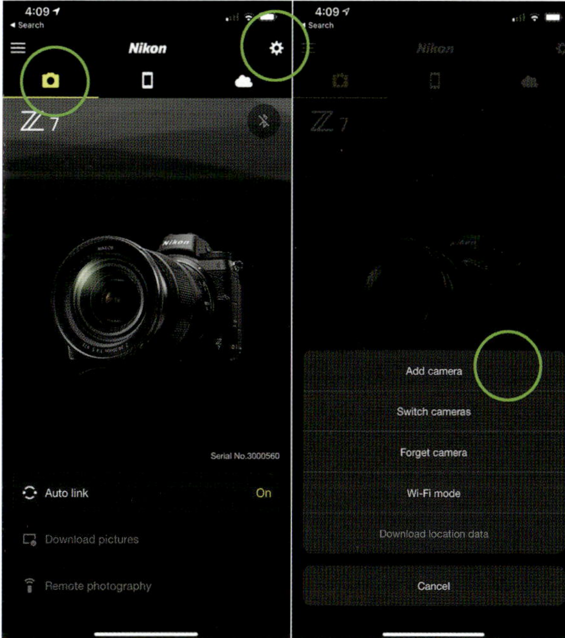

Figure 6.20 Add a camera.

5. **On the device: Select camera type.** The screen shown at left in Figure 6.21 appears. Tap the Mirrorless Camera icon.

6. **On the device: Choose connection type.** The screen shown at center left pops up. Tap Pairing (Bluetooth).

7. **On the device: Select camera.** The device will search for available camera connections and display informational screens while it searches. Tap Understood to dismiss them. Your Z5 should appear on the list of available connections (see Figure 6.21, center right). Tap your camera's name to continue.

8. **On the device: Connecting to camera.** The informational screen shown in Figure 6.21, far right appears as the connection to the camera is established.

9. **On the device: Select an accessory.** This screen (see Figure 6.22, far left) appears next on your smart device. Tap your camera's name.

10. **On the device: Connect Bluetooth.** The Bluetooth Pairing Request message appears on the device (see Figure 6.22, center left), along with an authorization code. The same code will appear on the Z5's LCD monitor. (See Figure 6.22 center.) If they match, press/tap OK on the camera and tap Pair on the device screen.

11. **On the device: Connection established/completed.** As final pairing takes place, the screens shown in Figure 6.22 center right and far right will be displayed. Tap OK to exit.

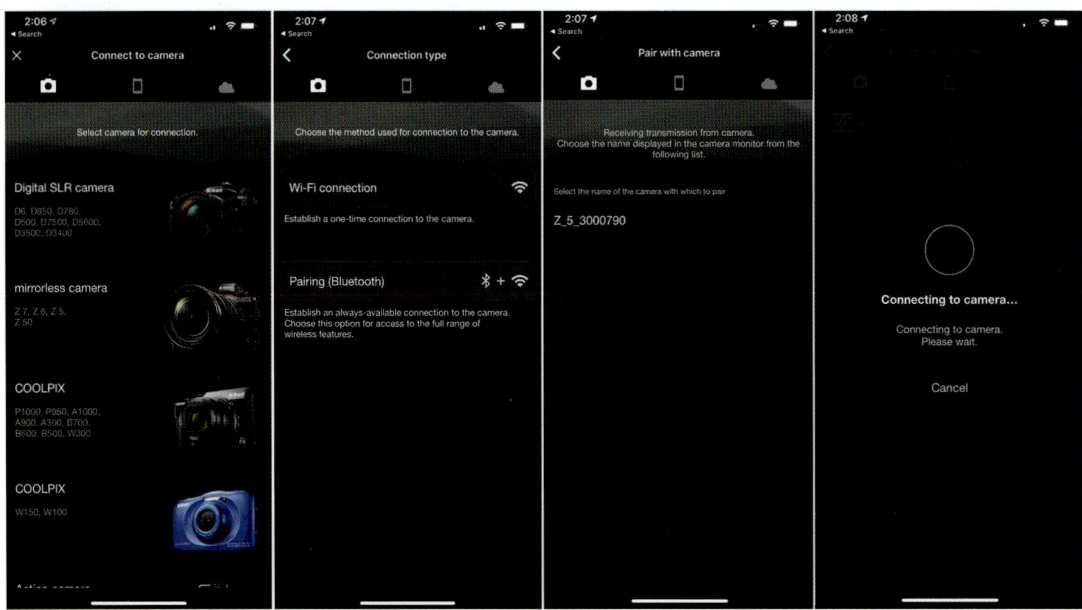

Figure 6.21 The Z5's connection screens lead you through linking your camera and smart device.

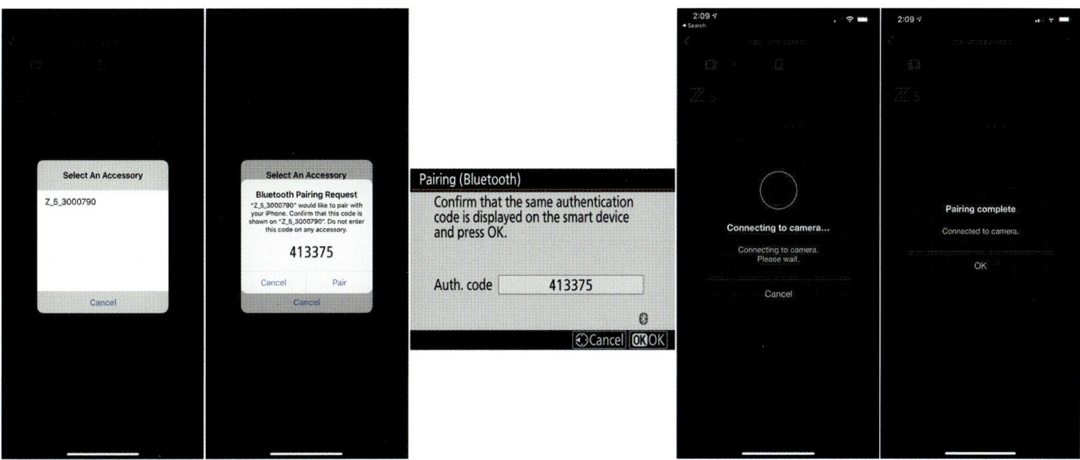

Figure 6.22 Making the final connection.

Using the SnapBridge App

When you first access the SnapBridge app, you'll be invited to register for Nikon Image Space and receive a Nikon ID. The app itself has a fairly simple interface, shown in Figure 6.23. You'll find menus at the top, with the main menu represented by three lines at upper left and a gear icon at upper right representing the Setup menu. Below them are icons representing a camera (left), smart device (center), and cloud (right).

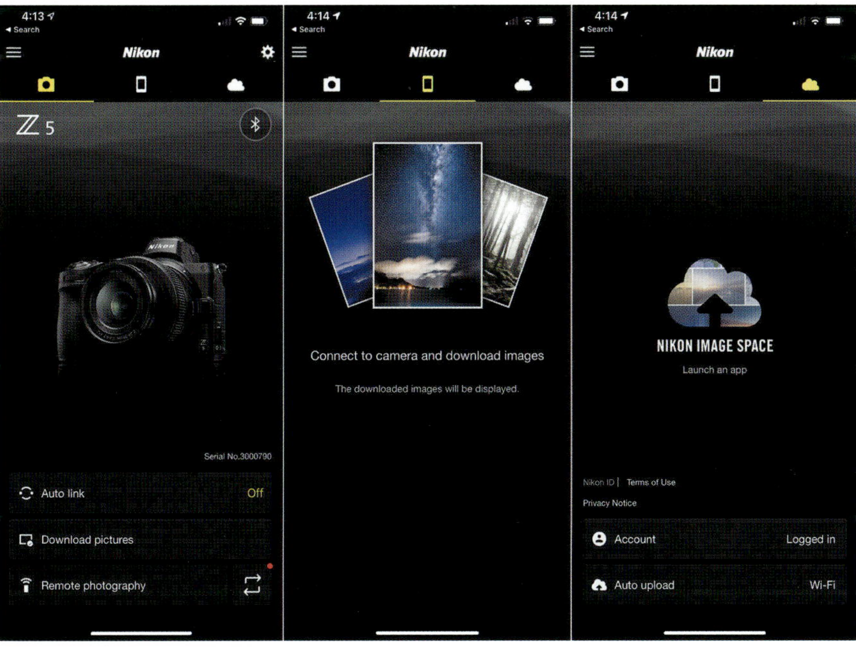

Figure 6.23 The Camera screen (left), Device screen (center), and Cloud/Nikon Image Space screen (right).

Camera Screen

The Camera screen, shown at left in Figure 6.23 includes indicators showing whether you're connected through Bluetooth or Wi-Fi, plus access to Auto Link Status, downloading pictures, and remote photography.

Main Menu

The items found in the main menu include (see Figure 6.24, left):

- **Location data accuracy.** SnapBridge can access your device's GPS information. Here you can select High, Medium, or Low accuracy, with the last using the least amount of power because the app reduces the frequency of its location checks.
- **Nickname.** This is the name of your smart device that will be displayed on connected cameras.
- **Show credits.** Enable to embed shooting information on comments in images uploaded to your device.
- **Add hashtag.** You can embed either #nikon or #snapbridge (or both) in the images you share on social media.
- **Nikon ID signup/edit profile.** Use this entry to sign up for a Nikon ID (used for Nikon Image Space and other purposes), or to edit the profile of an existing Nikon ID.
- **License agreement.** Displays a long list of disclaimers protecting Nikon from its customers.
- **Support.** Connects your smart device to a Nikon support site.

Figure 6.24 Main menu screen (left); Setup menu (right).

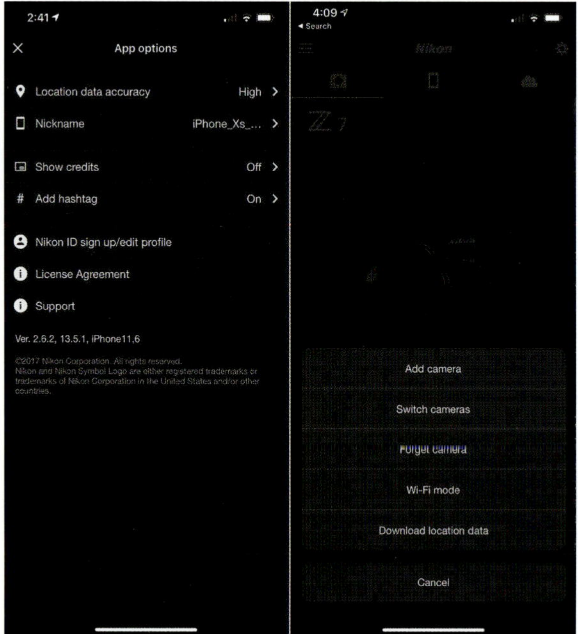

Setup Menu

The items found in the Setup menu include entries to allow you to add a new camera, switch to a different one (if you own multiple compatible Nikon cameras) or forget a connected camera. You might need the last entry if you're having problems with a connection and want to start over. Note that you'll also need to go to your device's own Settings menu to delete the device from its Bluetooth and Wi-Fi menus. You can also activate Wi-Fi mode or download location data from this screen. (See Figure 6.24, right.)

Auto Link

Enable this feature to allow your smart device to automatically link to your Z5. When active, the device can automatically download images as they are captured and synchronize location and clock information. Auto Link remains active even when your device is in "sleep" mode, so you may want to disable it to reduce battery drain. When Auto Link is active, you can set four additional parameters that the app will use as long as you've enabled the same parameters in the Z5's Setup menu, as explained in Chapter 13. (See Figure 6.25.)

- **Auto Link.** Connects the smart device to your camera automatically when both are powered up.
- **Auto Download.** If checked the smart device will automatically download as 2MP images if the Auto Select to Send option is enabled in the Connect to Smart Device entry of the Setup menu. Still photos taken during video capture are not sent automatically and must be transferred manually.

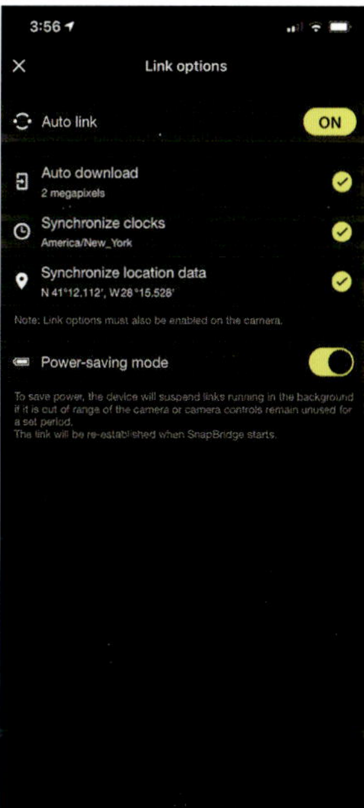

Figure 6.25 Auto Link settings.

- **Synchronize clocks.** If the Set Clock From Satellite option is set to Yes in the Location Data entry of the Setup menu, the smart device will supply the information to your camera when this is checked.
- **Synchronize Location Data.** Shared with the camera if location data is enabled on the Z5.
- **Power-saving mode.** When active the smart device will suspend any of the three links running in the background when the device is out of range of the camera, or the camera is idle. The links will be reestablished when SnapBridge is subsequently started on the device.

Download Pictures

You can initiate download of your photos from the camera to your smart device either using the Z5's commands, or this option within SnapBridge. When you access this choice, the Z5 will direct you to enable Wi-Fi, which is a much faster way of transferring images. The screens seen in Figure 6.26 (left and center left) appear. Tap Join in the first screen and wait while the connection is made.

A screen appears on the smart device with thumbnails of the available images on your memory card. Tap Select and then tap the lower-right corner of each image you want to transfer, as seen in Figure 6.26, center right. Then tap Download to initiate the transfer. The app will ask you if you want to transfer a compact 2-megapixel version, or the full 24MP camera JPEG. (See Figure 6.26, far right.)

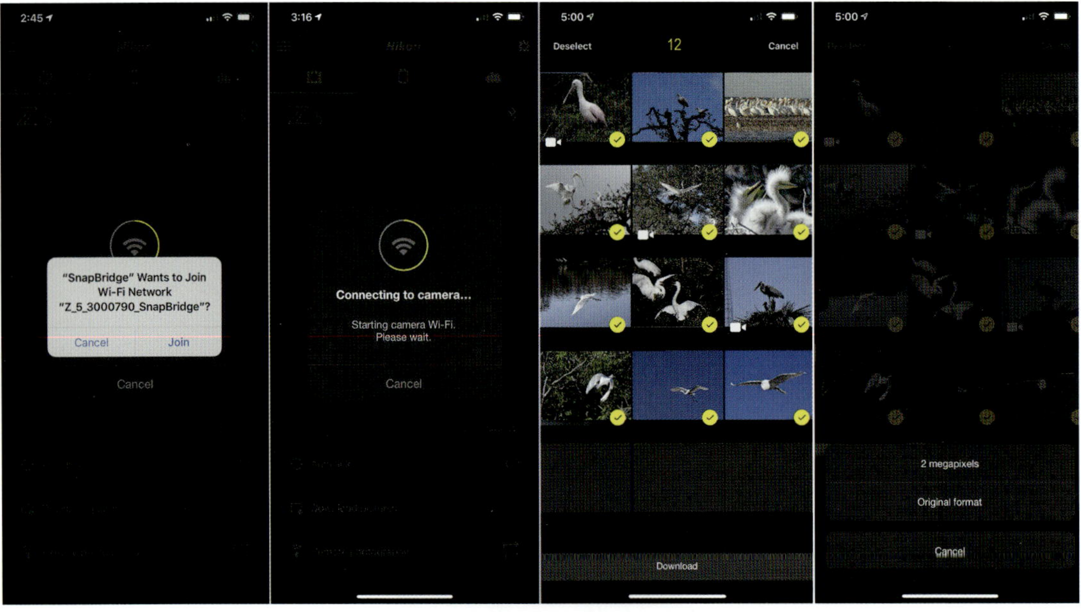

Figure 6.26 Switching to Wi-Fi (left and center left); selecting images to transfer (center right); choosing resolution (right).

Remote Photography

You can use the smart device to control the Z5 and take pictures remotely. The procedure is roughly the same whether the camera is currently connected using Bluetooth or Wi-Fi. If you're using Bluetooth, you'll be asked to switch to Wi-Fi mode, and the screens shown earlier at left and center left in Figure 6.26 appear. Once connected, you'll see the sensor image displayed on your smart device. (See Figure 6.27, left.)

At the top are still camera and movie camera icons. Tap either one to switch into that mode. A status line immediately below those icons show the current shooting mode, transfer image size, and battery status. You can tap the current shooting mode (S in the figure) to change to a different mode. Shooting settings including shutter speed, aperture, exposure compensation, ISO sensitivity, and white balance are arrayed along the bottom. Tap the appropriate icon to change that setting. (Exposure compensation is shown in the figure.) Tap anywhere in the frame to move the focus point to that location. A large circle representing the shutter button can be tapped to take a picture.

At lower right is a gear icon representing Setup for the remote photography function. Tap it and the screen shown at right in Figure 6.27 appears. Your options:

- **Download pictures.** Choose to transfer to the smart device either 2MP condensed versions of the pictures you take or their full-size versions (which will take considerably longer). RAW photos are always downloaded as JPEGs.

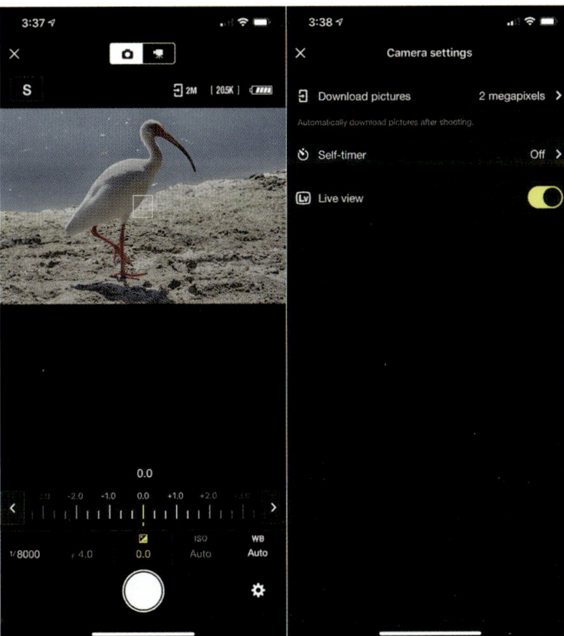

Figure 6.27 Shooting remotely.

- **Self-timer.** You can choose 3-, 5-, and 10-second self-timer delays before the smart device trips the shutter for you.

- **Live view.** Generally, you'll want to leave this option on, as it allows you to see the live view through your camera lens as you shoot remotely. If you turn it off, the view is not displayed, so you'll either be shooting blind or will need to be near your camera to view the monitor as you capture images. The only advantage to turning live view off is a slight improvement of battery life with the camera and smart phone's batteries.

Other Connection Options

In most cases, your Nikon Z5's Bluetooth and Wi-Fi capabilities, coupled with SnapBridge, will supply all the wireless connectivity you'll ever need. Some photographers, particularly those who shoot in a studio or at events, like to take the next step and shoot tethered, in which images captured by the camera show up almost instantaneously on a computer. Such transfers are most useful for quick edits, demonstrations, client previews, and evaluating images as they are taken. In most cases, *wireless* tethering is not especially practical, because the transfer takes too long.

Instead, photographers who need this capability generally use cables to link their cameras to the computer, and work with software specifically designed for tethering, such as Adobe Lightroom, Nikon Camera Control 2, Capture One Pro, or Helicon Remote.

If you need a wireless connection other than SnapBridge, you have several options. Nikon offers a free utility called the Wireless Transmitter Utility (see Figure 6.28), which Nikon says "allows users to connect the camera to networks via wired or wireless LANs. Wired connections are available with D6-, D5-, and D4-series cameras, the WT-7 and WT-4 wireless transmitters, and the UT-1 communications unit, wireless connections with cameras featuring built-in wireless LAN or with a WT-7, WT-6, WT-5, or WT-4 wireless transmitter." Ack!

Figure 6.28 Using the Wireless Transmitter Utility.

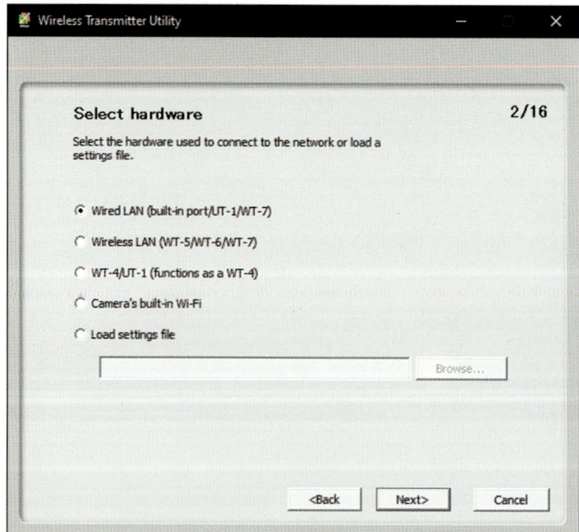

In (only slightly) less technical terms, it can use the Z5's built-in Wi-Fi to connect wirelessly to a computer in "Access Point Mode" with the camera serving as a wireless LAN access point. When connected in this way, the camera's Wi-Fi hot spot substitutes for an Internet connection (that is, the computer cannot communicate with the camera and the Internet simultaneously). As such, it's an option when working outdoors or in other locations that don't have a stand-alone router/wireless network.

As I noted earlier, I'm devoting all the available space in this book to photography topics and tips, rather than diverting pages to IT topics. That's because if you need these advanced capabilities you probably already know all about IP and MAC addresses, SSIDs, and other stuff and don't need an explanation from me.

Instead, I'm going to provide just an overview that will give you an idea of what's involved, and I'm not going to discuss the pricey WT-7 wireless transmitter at all, as most readers won't need a separate $750 component to connect to computers, FTP servers, or other devices over Ethernet or wireless networks.

For Access-Point Mode, to create a new host profile, visit the Connect to PC entry in the Setup menu, choose Network Options, then Direct Connection to PC and link to the Z5's access point, as summarized in Figure 6.29. As you build the profile, you'll be supplied with an authentication code by the utility when you pair the computer and camera.

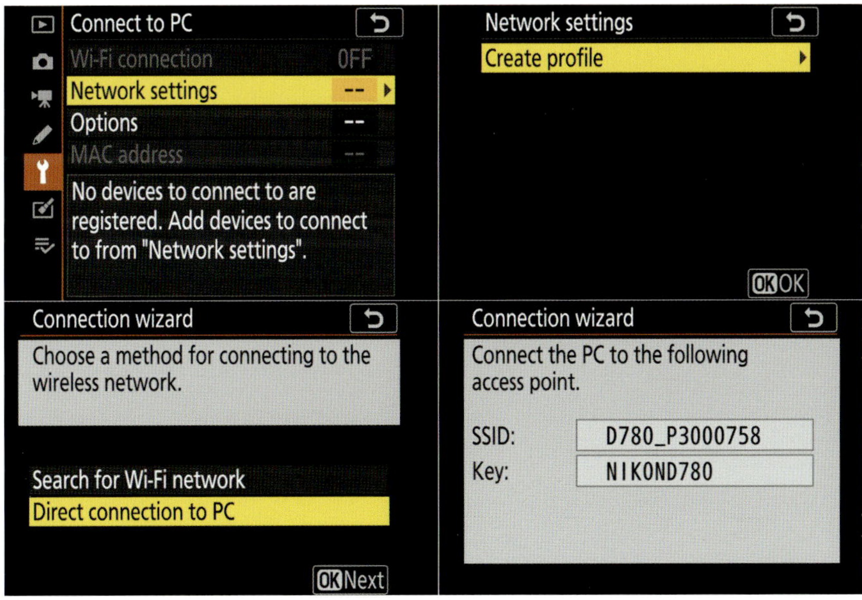

Figure 6.29
Connecting using Access-Point mode.

Infrastructure mode is also available, in which the camera connects to your computer on an existing business or home network through a wireless router. If you use this method, the computer can still connect to the Internet while communicating with your Z5. To use this option, you'll follow steps similar to Access-Point mode, but you will select Search for Wi-Fi network in the connection wizard. You can use the Z5's Direct Connection to PC option, and log on to an available network, as shown in Figure 6.30.

To connect without entering an SSID or encryption key, use Easy Connect. Press the Zoom In/QUAL button and OK and choose either Push-button WPS (For routers that have a WPS button), or PIN-entry WPS (for routers that require a PIN). You can usually get by with letting the router assign an IP address automatically.

Figure 6.30 Connect to your business/home network in Infrastructure mode.

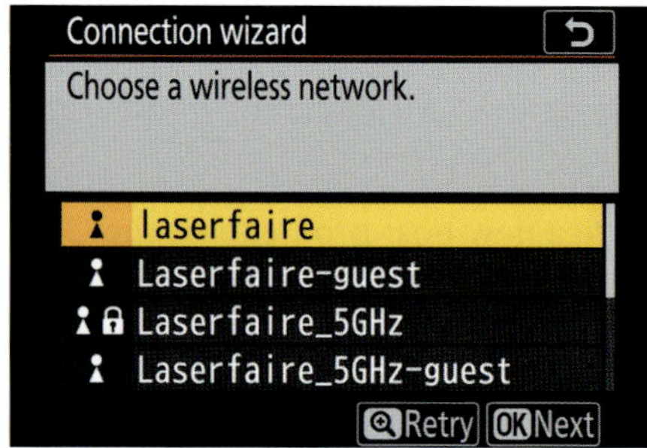

Focus on Lenses   7

It's not an overstatement to say that Nikon has built its reputation on its expertise in lenses. Founded in 1917 as Nippon Kogaku, K.K. (Japan Optical Company), the company specialized in optics for many years before it began producing cameras. In fact, all Canon cameras through mid-1947 used Nikkor lenses!

Of course, in the ensuing years Nikon has developed advanced camera technology, too, combining its proficiency in both arenas to produce the Z-series mirrorless cameras and superb S-series lenses. Photographers who started out using Nikon camera bodies and optics have tended to hang onto their lenses for many years, even as they upgraded to newer camera bodies with more features. Indeed, many of us have stuck with the Nikon brand at least partially because we were able to use our existing collection of lenses with our latest and greatest cameras. After all, an enthusiast's optics collection can easily have cost many times the price of the body itself.

Backward compatibility of lenses is a 60-year tradition for Nikon, which is what makes the Z5's innovative Z-mount so interesting and exciting. Nikon's SLR and dSLR product lines have always, with few exceptions, been able to work surprisingly well with virtually all Nikkor F-mount lenses dating back to the very first, introduced with the Nikon F itself in April 1959, and emblazoned *Nikkor-S Auto 1:2 f=5cm* (a 50mm f/2 lens). Since then, Nikon has sold more than 110 million F-mount lenses, and millions more are available from third parties like Tamron, Sigma, and Tokina. Nearly all are compatible with every Nikon single-lens reflex built since then, although those made before 1977 may need an inexpensive $35 modification to be used safely on bodies that debuted after that.

So, introducing the Z-mount for Nikon's full-frame and APS-C (DX) mirrorless cameras could have been a risky proposition, and perhaps not worth the possibility of current Nikon owners migrating to a different mirrorless platform, including current industry leader Sony and newcomer Canon. Fortunately, Nikon anticipated this possibility, and announced the Nikon Mount Adapter FTZ at the same time as the Z6 and Z7 cameras. Hundreds of F-mount Nikon lens models are compatible, from the AF-S Fisheye Nikkor 8-15mm f/3.5-4.5E ED zoom to the AF-S Nikkor 800mm f/5.6E FL ED VR super-telephoto, plus four Nikon teleconverter add-ons.

The availability of the FTZ adapter was essential to the success of Z-series cameras like the Z5 for these three reasons:

- **Dearth of native lenses.** The adapter compensates for the tiny number of native Z-mount lenses that were initially available for the Z-series cameras at introduction. Originally, only four lenses were announced along with the cameras: the Nikkor Z 24-70mm f/4 S, Nikkor Z 35mm f/1.8 S, Nikkor Z 50mm f/1.8 S, and Nikkor Z 58mm f/0.95 S Noct. Of course, in the years since, Nikon's Z-mount lens roster now includes a total of 16 different lenses and two tele-converters, with an additional eight more optics promised for the future as I write this.

  But the availability of the FTZ adapter at introduction meant that, right out of the gate, a huge selection of F-mount lenses were readily available for use with the Z-series cameras. Veteran Nikon owners were delighted to find our favorite F-mount lenses were compatible. My own 105mm f/1.4E ED lens (shown in Figure 7.1) is one of my favorite accessories for my Nikon mirrorless cameras.

- **Current owner loyalty.** Many current Nikon dSLR owners have been coveting the lighter weight, compact size, and other advantages of mirrorless cameras, and while there have been some defections, a large number of us have been waiting for an alternative from Nikon more suited to the enthusiast's needs than the ill-fated Nikon 1 line. Indeed, Nikon expects current Nikon dSLR fans to make up the bulk of purchases for the Z-series cameras. The FTZ adapter makes the adoption of any Z-mount camera much more seamless and less painful.

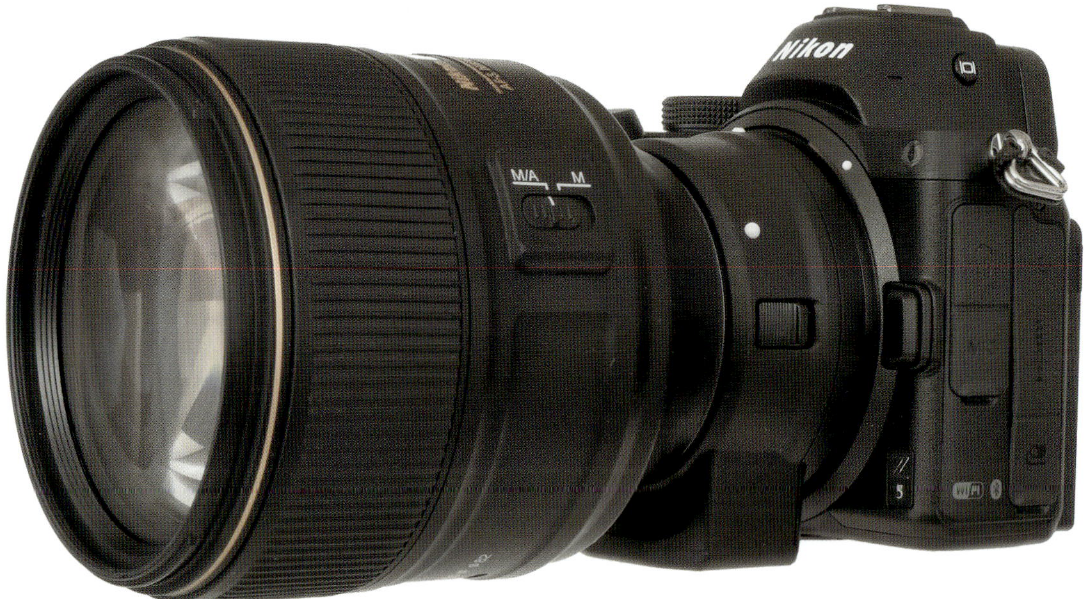

Figure 7.1 Nikon's excellent 105mm f/1.4E ED F-mount lens is a perfect match for the Z5.

■ **Technical innovations.** Nikon could have, perhaps, provided the Z-series cameras with a lens mount that would accept F-mount lenses without an adapter. However, that would have meant larger lenses, and the submitting to the technical restrictions imposed by the venerable 60-plus-year-old lens system. The F-mount, designed for film cameras, has a 44mm "throat" and a flange to focal plane (*registration*) distance of 46.5mm. These dimensions impose severe restrictions on lens design, including the maximum size of the largest aperture, and the angles at which photons can approach the sensor.

In contrast, the Z-mount's diameter is a generous 55mm, and the flange/registration distance a mere 16mm, the least of any competing camera from Nikon, Canon, Sony, Panasonic, Olympus, or Fujifilm. Nikon says it can use the mount's flexibility to design lenses that are both faster and optically superior. Indeed, the "S" moniker is said to *represent* Superior.

As a bonus, the reduced flange dimension means there is plenty of room between the sensor and the rear mount of many lenses designed for other camera platforms to be accommodated by additional adapters. Third-party manufacturers have already announced such add-ons to allow using certain Canon, Yashica/Contax, Leica, Minolta, Nikon, Pentax, and Olympus lenses in manual focus and exposure mode on the Z-series cameras. Although Nikon would prefer you purchase Nikkor lenses, it knows that the ability to use other optics on their cameras—even in manual focus mode—can allay some of the reservations of those considering a switch.

The current hybrid situation, in which there is a good but not comprehensive selection of Z-mount lenses for the Z5—but plentiful compatible lenses in the existing F-mount lineup—means that this chapter will be a hybrid, as well. For this book, at least, I'm going to embrace both Z-mount and F-mount products, so that I can explain the real-world options—especially to those who may be new to the Nikon world. After all, even if you did not own any Nikon lenses when you purchased your Z5, you probably will consider both types as you expand your optical horizons, because Z-mount and F-mount lenses work seamlessly with your camera. A vast number of affordable pre-owned F-mount lenses are available from sources like www.keh.com.

Later in this chapter, I'll have more details on how adapted F-mount lenses work with the Z5 and FTZ adapter. There are some differences, especially with older lenses, and with F-mount lenses that have vibration reduction built in. It's true that there is a mind-bending assortment of high-quality lenses available to enhance the capabilities of your camera. These lenses can give you a wider view, bring distant subjects closer, let you focus closer, shoot under lower light conditions, or provide a more detailed, sharper image for critical work. Other than the sensor itself, the lens you choose for your Z5 is the most important component in determining image quality and perspective of your images.

This chapter explains how to select the best lenses for the kinds of photography you want to do.

Sensor Sensibilities

Ever since Nikon introduced its first digital camera with a full-frame sensor (the Nikon D3, in August 2007), the debate over full-frame versus cropped-sensor DX cameras has been hot and heavy in the Nikon community. Full-frame cameras like the Z5 have a sensor that measures roughly 24 × 36mm, while APS-C (DX) cameras like the Nikon Z50 have a sensor that measures about 24 × 16mm. Each type of sensor has its own advantages. Full-frame sensors typically have larger pixels than their counterparts with equivalent resolution, and better low-light performance, while DX models offer extra telephoto "reach" thanks to their cropped sensors, which create an image from a smaller center portion of the image transmitted by the lens.

ARCHAIC NOMENCLATURE?

The common industry term for cameras with this smaller sensor is *APS-C*, which stands for Advanced Photo System—Classic. It refers to an ill-fated snapshot film format for cameras offered by Kodak and others from 1996 to about 2004. APS-C is one of many film-era terms that live on, including bulb exposure, rangefinder focus, and the designation "full frame" itself. You'll want to remember the APS-C designation when evaluating lenses from third-party vendors, as Nikon is the only company that uses the term *DX*.

Because many enthusiasts have been confused by the full-frame/crop debate, it's useful to look at exactly what the "crop factor" means. In addition to the term *crop factor*, you've probably also heard the term *lens multiplier*. In truth, both are misleading and inaccurate terms used to describe the same phenomenon: the fact that cameras like Nikon's high-end DX model, the D500, provide a field of view that's smaller and narrower than that produced by so-called FX (full-frame) cameras like the Z5 when fitted with the same lens.

Figure 7.2 quite clearly shows the phenomenon at work. The outer rectangle, marked 1X, shows the field of view you might expect with a 35mm lens mounted on a Z5 or another one of Nikon's FX cameras. The area marked 1.5X shows the field of view you'd get with that 35mm lens installed on a DX model like the Z50. It's easy to see from the illustration that the 1X rendition provides a wider, more expansive view, while the inner field of view is, in comparison, *cropped*.

The cropping effect is produced because the sensors of DX cameras, including the Z50, and the Nikon Z5/Z6/Z7 models in their crop modes, capture a smaller amount of area than full-frame sensors. As I mentioned earlier, all Nikon "full-frame" cameras have a sensor that's approximately the size of the standard 35mm film frame, 24mm × 36mm. Any DX sensor does *not* measure 24mm × 36mm; instead, it specs out at approximately 23.5mm × 15.7mm (in the case of the Z50). You can calculate the relative field of view by multiplying the actual focal length by 1.5.

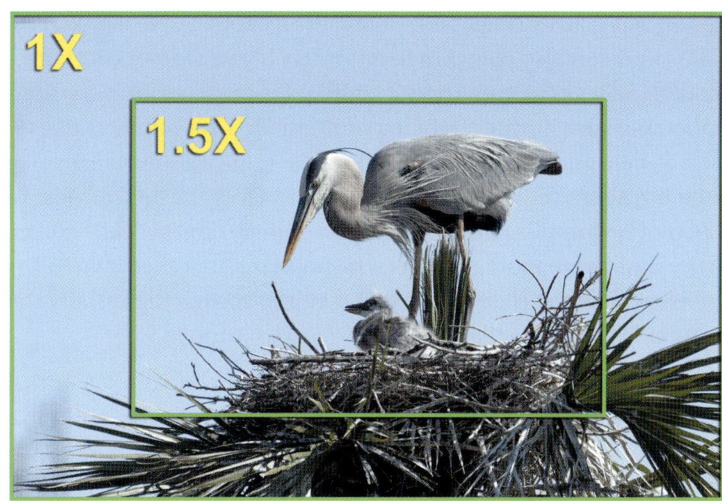

Figure 7.2 Nikon offers digital SLRs with full-frame (1X) crops, as well as DX (1.5X). The Z5 has other optional formats, too.

OTHER CROPS

The Z5 has additional optional crops, including 1:1 (which keeps the same vertical dimension, but snips off some of the image at either side), and 16:9, which is the same width as the full frame, but crops pixels at the top and bottom to mimic high-definition video proportions. DX mode is the only crop that preserves the 3:2 aspect ratio of the full-frame image. (See Figure 7.3.)

One advantage the Z5 has over its dSLR siblings is that it is able to completely fill the viewfinder and monitor frame with the image in DX crop mode. Non-mirrorless Nikon models mask off the unused area, so you're effectively forced to compose and view with a smaller preview. (They *can* fill the frame in live view mode, which mimics the Z5's full-time live view.)

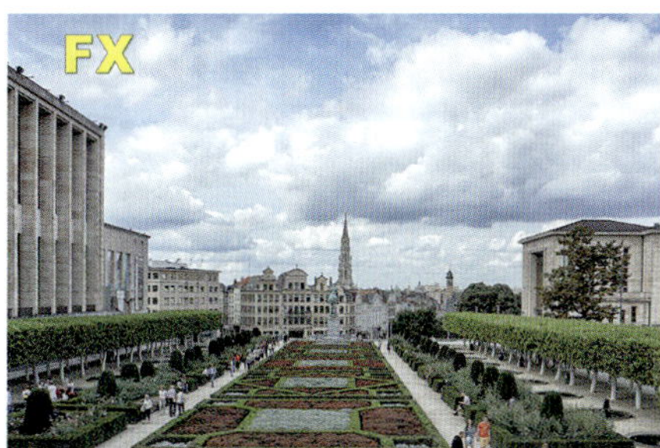

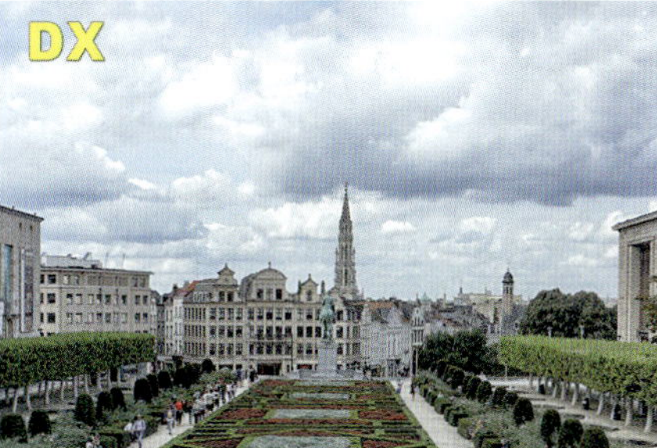

Figure 7.3 The Z5's full-frame field of view (top left); DX crop (top right); 16:9 crop (bottom left); and 1:1 crop (bottom right).

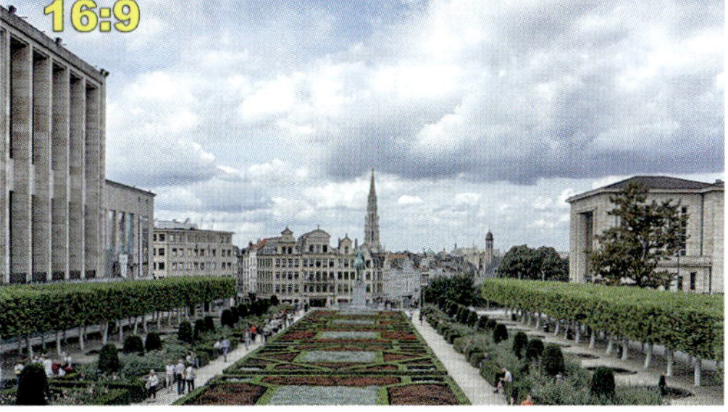

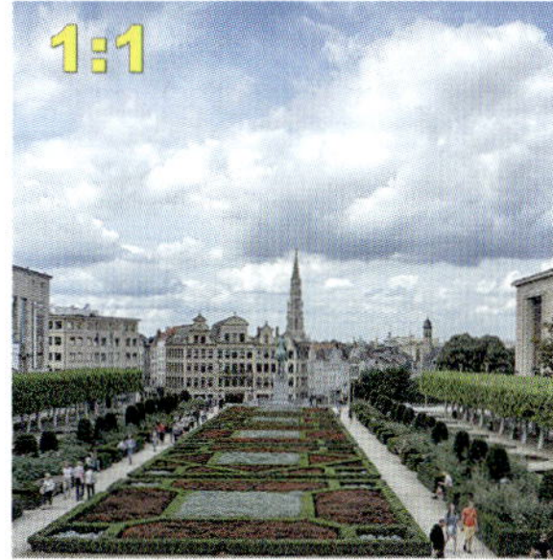

In the past, this translation was generally necessary only if you happened to use your full-frame camera accompanied by a DX model. It also comes in handy today if you are working with any lens using one of the Z5's crop modes and want to know how a familiar lens will perform. I strongly prefer *crop factor* over *lens multiplier,* because nothing is being multiplied; a 100mm lens doesn't "become" a 150mm lens—the depth-of-field and lens aperture remain the same, despite what you may have read elsewhere. (I'll explain more about these later in this chapter.) Only the field of view is cropped. But *crop factor* isn't much better, as it implies that the 24mm × 36mm frame is "full" and anything else is "less." I get e-mails all the time from photographers who point out that they own full-frame cameras with 33mm × 44mm sensors (like the Hasselblad X1D medium-format digital). By their reckoning, the "half-size" sensors found in cameras like the Nikon Z5 are "cropped."

If you work with both FX and DX cameras, or you use DX lenses on your Z5 (either F-mount or Z-mount versions), you might sometimes find it helpful to use the crop factor "multiplier" to translate a lens's real focal length into the full-frame equivalent, even though, as I said, nothing is being multiplied. Lenses designed for the DX format may or may not be usable for full-frame images on your Z5, so Nikon automatically switches to DX mode when it detects that a DX lens has been attached. If the camera is unable to discern that an APS-C lens has been mounted (although in my tests of a few Tamron and Sigma lenses it did a pretty good job), you can manually choose the DX crop in the Choose Image Area entry of the Photo Shooting menu.

An APS-C lens used *without* crop mode on an FX camera usually exhibits severe darkening, or *vignetting* in the corners of the image, because its image circle is generally smaller than the area of a full frame. Of course, the same lens at a longer focal length setting may produce an enlarged image coverage circle so that the lens is *almost* acceptable for full-frame use. Unfortunately, with the current firmware, the Z5 disables the Choose Image Area option when it thinks an APS-C/DX lens is mounted, so there is no way to experiment with any DX lenses you may already own.

The bad news for those who presently *do* own DX lenses is that the Z5's 24MP resolution is reduced to a paltry 10MP in DX. That means legacy DX lenses, while gaining the extra telephoto "reach" a crop format offers, comes at a steep cost in terms of resolution.

Choosing Native Z-mount Lenses

If you're new to FX photography or to the Nikon system, you're probably wondering which lenses from the vast array of available optics can be added to your growing collection (trust me, it will grow). You need to know which lenses are suitable and, most importantly, which lenses are fully compatible with your Nikon Z5. Nikon's current roster of Z-mount lenses is, of course, fully compatible. Here are some features common to most lenses using the Z5's native lens mount.

- **Nikon Z-mount bayonet.** Designed exclusively for attaching Z-series lenses to the Z50, Z7, Z6, Z5, and future models in the product line, the lens mount has 11 electrical *CPU contacts* that allow two-way communication with the camera. The data flow includes lens focal length, current and maximum f/stop, distance information supplied by the lens to the camera, autofocus functions, and aperture control.

Unlike Nikon F-mount lenses, the Nikon Z cameras do not have a physical aperture lever to change the f/stop from wide open (for viewing and focusing) to the aperture used to take the picture (in common photo parlance, the *taking aperture*). Your f/stop is set electronically by the camera based on its autoexposure calculation, or as specified by you (in A and M modes).

One byproduct of this system is that Z lenses need to have electrically compatible extension tubes and similar accessories; lower-cost manual alternatives have no way of physically setting the aperture.

- **Programmable control ring.** Your lens' focus ring is not just for focusing anymore! For that reason, Nikon has renamed this rotating band the *control ring*. When you're using manual focus mode, the control/focusing ring has one mandatory function: focus. You can always count on the control ring providing focus adjustment when you select M using the A/M switch on the lens, the Focus Mode entry in the Photo Shooting menu, or from the *i* menu. (Note that the switch takes precedence, regardless of what you've selected in the menus.)

  When either autofocus mode is active, the control ring can have one of four different behaviors, specified using Custom Setting f2: Custom Controls (Shooting):

  - **Focus (M/A).** The control ring can be used to fine-tune focus after autofocus has been achieved.

  - **Aperture.** You can use the control ring to set the aperture instead of one of the command dials.

  - **Exposure compensation.** If you add/subtract exposure using exposure compensation a lot, you'll love the optional ability to do this by rotating the control ring, rather than holding down the Exposure Compensation button while spinning either command dial.

  - **None.** The best use of this option is to prevent accidentally messing with the camera's autofocus setting. You won't be able to fine-tune focus, either on purpose or by mistake.

- **Stepping motor technology.** All the Z-series lenses with AF capabilities announced to date feature stepping motors for fast, quiet automatic focus. Fast is required for shooting sports or subjects that move unpredictably or rapidly, while quiet is desirable for both movie making (to avoid recording the sound of the AF motor in your video) and stealth shooting.

  A stepper motor is a brushless DC motor that divides one rotation into equal steps, allowing the camera to move quickly to one of those fixed steps without the need for electronic feedback or a sensor to confirm the amount of rotation. Nikon has been using stepper motors in its AF-P lenses for its dSLRs for several years (the "P" stands for the electronic pulse used to drive the motor). The technology allows changing focus mode (AF-S, AF-C, or M) without the need to flip a physical switch on the lens or camera body; you can do it within a menu.

- **Electromagnetic diaphragm mechanism.** Unlike conventional lenses, in which the blades of the lens diaphragm are operated by mechanical linkages, the aperture blades of Z-mount autofocus lenses are controlled by electronics ("focus-by-wire") for extra accuracy under demanding conditions like continuous shooting.

- **Special lens coatings.** Z-mount lenses can include what Nikon calls Super Integrated Coatings, and the S-line lenses have an additional Nano Crystal coating. Light is your friend when you're creating an image—except when unwanted photons (say, from illumination coming from backlighting or entering the lens diagonally) cause flare, glare, ghost images, or reduced contrast.

Vendors try to counter these effects by applying coatings to lenses, filters, and other optical devices. Often, multiple layers of anti-reflection coatings, such as those found in Nikon's Super Integrated Coatings, are needed to handle all the various wavelengths of light.

Nikon's additional Nano Crystal Coat's nanometer-sized (one millionth of a millimeter) particles work with *all* wavelengths of light and allow more of the desirable photons to pass unheeded. A complex lens with more than a dozen elements suffers only a 0.75 percent reduction in light, compared with a 15 percent loss with older coating technologies. The S-line lenses also benefit from rugged fluorine coatings on the front element that repels dust, dirt, water, and even grease, (making them easier to remove). The coatings have anti-reflective properties of their own.

- **Weather-sealed construction.** Moisture is unavoidable, especially when you must capture images in inclement weather. The Z5 itself has good weather sealing, and its lenses offer a significant amount of resistance to less-than-ideal shooting conditions (don't dunk your camera in water, however!).

- **Vibration reduction.** Nikon has added vibration reduction (VR) anti-shake capabilities to its DX Z-mount lenses to reduce blur from camera motion during exposures. That's useful because the Z50 does not have in-body image stabilization (IBIS) like the Z5, Z6, Z6 II, Z7, and Z7 II. Keep in mind S-series lenses designed for those cameras generally do *not* have VR (except, as I write this, the Nikkor Z 70-200mm f/2.8 S VR and Nikkor Z 24-200mm f4-6.3 VR zooms), so you will lose that facility when using those optics.

Better Lenses with Z-mount?

There's been a great deal of discussion about the advantages of Nikon's new Z-mount lenses. Much of it seems to assume that the larger 55mm diameter (and 52mm throat size) will make it possible to design lenses with faster maximum apertures, such as the 58mm f/0.95 Nikkor Noct. However, it's *not* simply that the larger opening lets in more light and they can now magically make lenses with larger f/stops. If that were true, there wouldn't already be lenses faster than f/1.4 for cameras with smaller "throats." An f/0.95 lens is available in Leica's 40.5mm mount, for example.

What the wider opening does is give lens designers more freedom in creating optics that are sharper, faster, and with fewer aberrations. For example, typical wide-angle lenses for dSLRs use a retrofocus design to move the optical center of the lens so the rear element does not protrude into the mirror chamber. To do that, the rear element must be very large in order to avoid vignetting and other forms of distortion. The Z-mount's 16mm registration distance and wider throat makes it easier to optimize the convergent and divergent elements without worrying about long exit pupil distances between the rear element and sensor plane.

Digital sensors, compared to film, have their particular challenges for lens designers, including the need for a less steep angle of incidence emerging from the rear element, because of the need to send photons down those deep "wells" in non-BSI sensors (like the sensor included in the Z5). Micro-lenses were the primary solution, especially when so many lenses designed for film (which is more tolerant of the angles) were in use. But, with the Z-mount's advantages we can expect much better lenses for our Z-series cameras.

Nikon Lens Overview

I'm dividing the rest of this chapter into three parts, generally arranged in order of relevance to new Z5 owners. First up, I'm going to list and describe all the native Z-mount lenses announced or available at the time this book was written. That section will help you decide which lenses to add as your collection of optics inevitably grows. For more detailed data, including up-to-date reviews and comparisons, you'll want to consult online resources like DPReview.com.

Next, for the benefit of those new to photography, I'm going to describe the different classes of lenses available, from the focal length ranges wide, normal, and telephoto to those with more specialized features, such as macro and perspective control lenses. If you're a veteran photographer, you can review or skim that section if you like; it's my attempt to address the needs of a broad range of enthusiasts in one book. Keep in mind that all of us were beginners at one point. I promise I didn't charge you extra for that section.

Finally, I'm going to introduce the variety of different F-mount lenses that many of you may already own or wish to use with your Z5. You can trust Nikon to expand its native Z-mount product line to include most or all those optics eventually, but until then, the large array of F-mount lenses remain an important resource for Nikon mirrorless camera owners.

Ingredients of Nikon's Alphanumeric Soup

Before we begin looking at the individual Z-mount lenses available, I want to address the cryptic letters and descriptors that Nikon applies to the names of its lenses, both Z-mount and F-mount. I've collected here an alphabetical list of lens terms you're most likely to encounter, either as part of the lens name or in reference to the lens's capabilities. Not all of these are used as parts of a lens's name, but you may come across some of these terms in discussions of Nikon optics:

- **AF, AF-D, AF-I, AF-P, AF-S.** In all cases, AF stands for *autofocus* when appended to the name of a Nikon F-mount lens. An extra letter is added to provide additional information. A plain old AF lens is an autofocus lens that uses a slot-drive motor in the camera body to provide autofocus functions. The D means that it's a D-type lens (described later in this listing); the I indicates that focus is through a motor inside the lens; and AF-P is used to designate lenses with that very quiet stepper motor that's especially useful for sound video applications. The most common Nikon focus designation for F-mount lenses is still AF-S, and the S means that a Silent Wave motor in the lens provides focusing. (Don't confuse a Nikon AF-S lens with the AF-S [Single-Servo Autofocus] mode.) Nikon has upgraded most of its older AF lenses in F-mount with AF-S (or AF-P) versions, but it's not safe to assume that *all* newer Nikkors are AF-S/AF-P, or even offer autofocus. For example, the PC-E Nikkor 24mm f/3.5D ED perspective control lens must be focused manually, and Nikon offers a surprising collection of other manual focus lenses to meet specialized needs.

- **AI, AI-S.** All Nikkor F-mount lenses produced after 1977 have either automatic aperture indexing (AI) or automatic indexing-shutter (AI-S) features that eliminate the previous requirement to manually align the aperture ring on the camera when mounting a lens. Within a few years, all Nikkors had this automatic aperture indexing feature (except for G-type lenses, which have no aperture ring at all), including Nikon's budget-priced Series E lenses, so the designation was dropped at the time the first autofocus (AF) lenses were introduced.

- **D.** Appended to the maximum f/stop of the lens (as in f/2.8D), a D-Series lens is able to send focus distance data to the camera, which uses the information for flash exposure calculation and metering.

- **DC.** The DC stands for defocus control, which allows managing the out-of-focus parts of an image to produce better-looking portraits and close-ups.

- **DX.** The DX lenses are designed for use with digital cameras using the APS-C-sized sensor having the 1.5X crop factor. The image circle they produce isn't large enough to fill up a full 35mm frame at all focal lengths, but they can be used on Nikon's full-frame dSLR models using the automatic/manual DX crop mode. DX lenses are available in both Z- and F-mounts.

- **E.** The E designation was used for Nikon's budget-priced E-Series optics, five prime and three zoom manual focus lenses built using aluminum or plastic parts rather than the preferred brass parts of that era, so they were considered less rugged. All are effectively AI-S lenses. They do have good image quality, which makes them a bargain for those who treat their lenses gently and don't need the latest autofocus features. They were available in 28mm f/2.8, 35mm f/2.5, 50mm f/1.8, 100mm f/2.8, and 135mm f/2.8 focal lengths, plus 36-72mm f/3.5, 75-150mm f/3.5, and 70-210mm f/4 zooms. (All these would be considered fairly "fast" today.)

  However, today the E designation is applied to lenses to represent those that stop down the lens to the "taking" aperture electronically. (During framing, focusing, exposure metering, and other pre-photo steps, the lens always remains at its maximum aperture unless you stop it down using a Preview—depth-of-field preview—button.) Non-E lenses use a lever (missing in mirrorless cameras) in the camera body that mates with a lever in the lens mount. Lenses with an E in their names, such as the 16-80mm f/2.8-4E ED VR optic, use an electronic mechanism instead.

- **ED (or LD/UD).** The ED (extra-low dispersion) designation indicates that some lens elements are made of a special hard and scratch-resistant glass that minimizes the divergence of the different colors of light as they pass through, thus reducing chromatic aberration (color "fringing") and other image defects. A gold band around the front of the lens indicates an optic with ED elements. You sometimes find LD (low dispersion) or UD (ultra-low dispersion) designations.

- **FX.** When Nikon introduced the Nikon D3 as its first full-frame camera, it coined the term "FX," representing the nominal 24mm × 36mm sensor format as a counterpart to "DX," which was used for its 16mm × 24mm APS-C-sized sensors. Although FX hasn't been officially applied to any Nikon lenses so far, expect to see the designation used more often to differentiate between lenses that are compatible with any Nikon digital SLR (FX) and those that operate only on DX-format cameras, or in DX mode when used on an FX camera.

- **G.** G-type lenses have no aperture ring, and you can use them at other than the maximum aperture only with electronic cameras like the Z5 that set the aperture automatically. Fortunately, this includes all Nikon F- and Z-mount digital cameras.

- **IF.** Nikon's *internal focusing* lenses change focus by shifting only small internal lens groups with no change required in the lens's physical length, unlike conventional double-helicoid focusing systems that move all lens groups toward the front or rear during focusing. IF lenses are more compact and lighter in weight, provide better balance, focus more closely, and can be focused more quickly.

- **IX.** These lenses were produced for Nikon's long-discontinued Pronea 6i and S APS film cameras. While the Pronea could use many standard Nikon lenses, IX lenses cannot be mounted on any Nikon digital SLR.

- **Micro.** Nikon uses the term *micro* to designate its close-up lenses. Most other vendors use *macro* instead.

- **N (Nano Crystal Coat).** Nano Crystal lens coating virtually eliminates internal lens element reflections across a wide range of wavelengths and is particularly effective in reducing ghost and flare peculiar to ultra-wide-angle lenses. Nano Crystal Coat employs multiple layers of Nikon's extra-low refractive index coating, which features ultra-fine crystallized particles of nano size (one nanometer equals one millionth of a millimeter).

- **NAI.** This is not an official Nikon term, but it is widely used to indicate that a manual focus lens is *Not-AI*, which means that it was manufactured before 1977, and therefore cannot be used safely on modern digital Nikon SLRs (other than the retro Df model) without modification.

- **NOCT (Nocturne).** Used originally to refer to the prized Nikkor AI-S Noct 58mm f/1.2, a "fast" (wide aperture) prime lens, with aspherical elements, capable of taking photographs in very low light. It's been revived to describe the 58mm f/0.95 Noct lens for Nikon's Z-series mirrorless cameras.

- **PC (Perspective Control).** A PC lens is capable of shifting the lens from side to side (and up/down) to provide a more realistic perspective when photographing architecture and other subjects that otherwise require tilting the camera so that the sensor plane is not parallel to the subject. Older Nikkor PC lenses offered shifting only, but more modern models, such as the PC-E Nikkor 24mm f/3.5D ED lens allow both shifting and tilting.

- **UV.** This term is applied to special (and expensive) lenses designed to pass ultraviolet light.

- **UW.** Lenses with this designation are designed for underwater photography with Nikonos camera bodies and cannot be used with Nikon digital SLRs.

- **VR.** Nikon has an expanding line of vibration reduction (VR) F-mount lenses, including several very affordable models in F-mount and, now, with its DX Z-mount lenses. These shift lens elements internally to counteract camera shake. The VR feature allows using a shutter speed up to 4.5 stops slower than would be possible without vibration reduction, according to Nikon.

Wide-to-Normal Zoom Lenses

Lenses are commonly categorized based on their focal length. *Rectilinear* lenses—that is, those that render straight lines without bending (as fisheye optics do)—are considered *ultra-wide-angle* if they have a focal length of about 12mm to 20mm. Those in the 20-35mm range are said to be *wide-angle* lenses. *Normal lenses* have a focal length roughly equivalent to the diagonal of the film or sensor, in millimeters, and so fall into the range of about 45mm to 60mm on a Z5. The boundaries between types of lenses is considered fuzzy, especially when describing zoom lenses that overlap focal lengths and types.

As I'll describe later in this chapter, lenses can also be classified either as *prime* (fixed focal length) or *zoom* (variable focal length) optics. I'm beginning the roster of native Z-mount lenses with the wide-to-normal zoom lenses first.

Nikkor Z 24-50mm f/4-6.3

This is one of two kit lenses available when the Z5 was introduced, the other being the Nikon Z 24-200mm f/4-6.3 zoom. If you already owned a Z-series camera and suitable optics, you might have purchased your Z5 as a body-only and passed on either of the available kit lenses. Even though I already owned the Z7, Z6, and Z50, I snapped up this lens, which was an irresistible bargain that offered something my other full-frame Z-mount lenses lacked: it's super compact. Best of all, it adds just $300 to the cost of the body alone (and is available separately for $400).

The retractable design of this 24-50mm lens mimics the popular "pancake" form factor that many favor in a walk-around lens, making it a great option for on-the-go travel photography. Retracted, it is less than three inches long. It's dust and moisture resistant, which can be especially useful when capturing images under less-than-ideal weather conditions (seasoned travelers know what I am talking about). The kit lens has a quiet stepping motor that offers quiet, accurate autofocus suitable for candid street photography and general shooting. Despite its low cost, it includes three aspherical elements and two low-dispersion elements for low distortion, excellent sharpness, and clarity.

Enthusiasts tend to dismiss kit lenses as cheap-o optics intended to keep the cost of entry-level cameras low. Even though this 24-50mm lens doesn't merit the "S" (superior?) nomenclature, it's an excellent basic lens that's worth having, even if only as a compact spare to use when you want to travel especially light.

Nikkor Z 14-30mm f/4 S

I love this lens! It was the first lens I got for my Z-series cameras beyond the initial three (50mm f/1.8, 35mm f/1.8, and 24-70mm f/4), because I needed something wider for architecture and landscape photography. It has a useful f/4 maximum aperture and, it too, extends from its most compact retracted form when zoomed. (See Figure 7.4, left and right.) Its MSRP is a stiff $1,300, but it's such a basic component I expect some Z5 owners to at least consider one, especially since no wider zoom is currently on Nikon's lens roadmap as I write this.

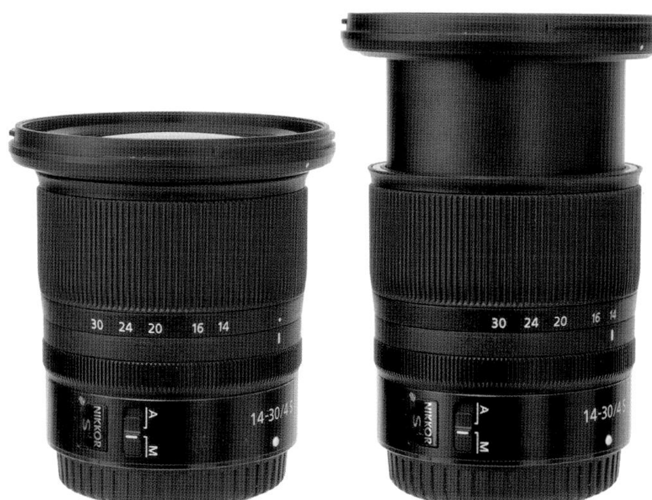

Figure 7.4 The Nikkor Z 14-30mm f/4 S retracted (left) and extended (right).

Keep in mind that if you also own a Z50, this lens operates as a 21-45mm wide-angle zoom, which gives you a little extra-wide perspective—and a much larger maximum aperture—than the 16-50mm kit lens available for that DX camera.

Nikkor Z 14-24mm f/2.8 S

Lens manufacturers frequently sell zooms with a given focal length range in tandems: an expensive f/2.8 version and a more affordable offering with an f/4 maximum aperture. If the 14-30mm lens described above is Nikon's full-frame Z-mount affordable ultra-wide/wide lens, this one—which has a slightly less ambitious 24mm maximum focal length—is the premium version. I hesitate to use the term "pro version" because both are S-series lenses and are incredibly sharp. This lens is priced at $2400.

The 14-24mm lens is quite a bit heavier than its 14-30mm counterpart, and about one-third longer, making it not your best choice as a walk-around lens if you don't need the fast f/2.8 maximum aperture. I expect it to be part of Nikon's Z-mount "magic trinity," along with the Nikkor Z 24-70mm f/2.8 S and Nikkor Z 70-200mm f/2.8 S, to supply full coverage of the focal lengths from 14mm to 200mm with no overlap.

Nikkor Z 24-70mm f/4 S

I was mildly surprised when Nikon unveiled this lens, with an f/4 maximum aperture, as its kit lens and sole zoom (at the time) for the original Z7 and Z6 cameras. One might have expected a lens in the popular 24-105mm or 24-120mm focal lengths that some pros might prefer for those original full-frame cameras. (The 24-105mm S-line lens—maximum aperture unspecified—did pop up on Nikon's lens map later.)

However, at the unveiling of the original Z-series cameras, Nikon had several challenging requirements to fulfill. In order to attract both existing Nikon dSLR owners and those currently using other platforms, the kit lens had to be exceptionally sharp. The kit lens also needed to be versatile, compact, and, most of all, affordable. As the 24-70mm focal length is also quite popular and considered versatile enough to use for everything from landscapes to portraits (despite its limited zoom range), Nikon selected this lens as its initial Z-mount zoom.

The lens is reasonably affordable at a little under $1,000 and compact enough to please those who turned to the Nikon mirrorless realm in search of reduced size and weight. This lens weighs less than 18 ounces and measures about 3 × 3.5 inches when collapsed. (See Figure 7.5, left.) In a brilliant stroke, Nikon designed the lens so that you don't need to press a button to retract it into its most compact configuration; just rotate the zoom ring past its widest 24mm setting, and you feel a brief resistance before the ring continues rotating while the lens retracts fully. However, it does get longer as you zoom, as you can see in Figure 7.5, right. This button-free retractable behavior has carried over to other zoom lenses introduced after launch.

This zoom, like all the Z-mount optics, is sufficiently sharp even wide open, and gets even better as you stop down. It focuses down to about 12 inches (for a reproduction ratio of 1:33) and has a minimum aperture of f/22 for a bit of extra depth-of-field if you need it.

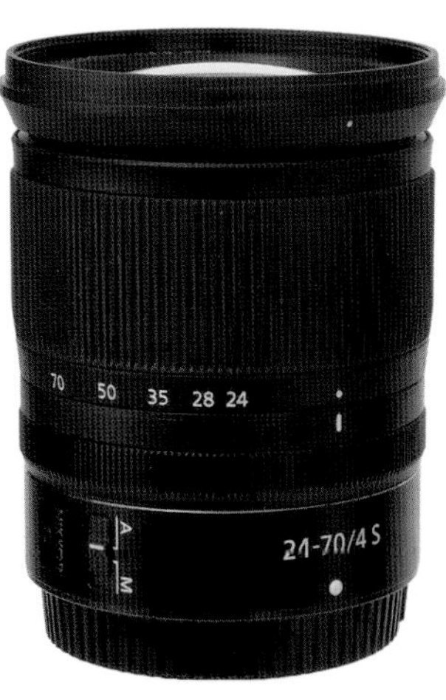
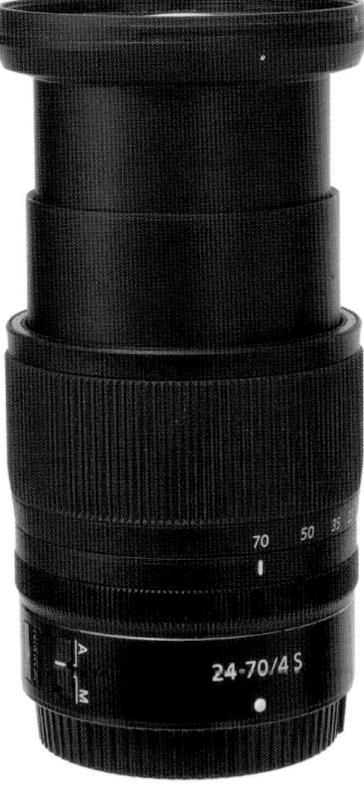

Figure 7.5 Relatively inexpensive, the 24-70mm lens (shown retracted and extended) is an impressive performer.

Nikkor Z 24-70mm f/2.8 S

Priced at more than double the tariff of the f/4 version, this $2,596 24-70mm f/2.8 lens should become the workhorse of professional photographers and enthusiasts who use this focal range a lot and value a large constant maximum aperture and superb sharpness for subjects ranging from landscapes to portraits. It features an innovative "multi-focus" system with *two* stepping motors for very fast, accurate, and quiet focus, making it ideal for movie shooting as well as stills.

Like other S-mount lenses, this one has three separate coatings on individual lens elements to suppress flare, ghosting, and reflections while optimizing contrast and color fidelity. The ARNEO coating minimizes ghost and flare effects from illumination reaching the lens surface in a vertical direction, even when the light source is contained within the frame. The Nano Crystal coating eliminates reflections inside the lens from visible light, reducing ghosting and flare from light entering the lens diagonally. Super Integrated multicoating improves color and contrast from internal reflections and is especially helpful in backlit situations and with lenses having a larger number of glass elements.

Another innovation is an organic LED (OLED) information panel on the top surface of the lens that displays aperture and focus distance, and depth-of field. A Lens Function button can be assigned custom behaviors and used in tandem with the control ring to make various exposure and other adjustments using controls on the lens itself. While the control ring is set, by default, to adjust manual focus, it can be redefined to control aperture or exposure compensation instead. This is a hefty lens, measuring 3.5 × 5 inches and tipping the scales at a tad more than 28 ounces.

Wide-Angle/Normal Prime Lenses

When the Nikon Z-series cameras were introduced, the company unveiled an array of high-quality "prime" (fixed focal length) lenses and rolled out zooms a little more slowly. Indeed, three of the first four lenses announced were fast wide-angle or normal prime lenses: 35mm and 50mm f/1.8 lenses, and the exotic 58mm f/0.95 Noct. Only one zoom, the 24-70mm f/4 lens described earlier, was available at launch.

Since then, the selection of both prime and zoom lenses has grown with Nikon promising roughly two dozen lenses available around the time this book is released. So, you'll have a broad selection of both prime and zoom lenses to choose from, with the wide-angle/normal primes covered in this section.

There are several considerations to ponder when choosing between prime and zoom lenses in any range. Here's a checklist of the most important factors, in addition to image quality and maximum aperture; those aspects take on additional meaning when comparing zooms versus primes.

- **Logistics.** As prime lenses offer just a single focal length, you'll need more of them to encompass the full range offered by a single zoom. More lenses mean additional slots in your camera bag, and extra weight to carry. Among the available, announced, and promised Z-mount lenses, you'll find 11 prime lenses and 13 zooms, all described in this chapter. Within Nikon's F-mount product line that you can use on your Z5 with an FTZ adapter, you can choose from a good selection of prime lenses in 28mm, 35mm, 50mm, 85mm, 105mm, 135mm, 200mm, and 300mm focal lengths, all of which are overlapped by a single zoom: the AF-S FX Nikkor 28-300mm f/3.5-5.6G ED VR lens. Even so, you might be willing to carry an extra prime lens or two in order to gain the speed or image quality that lens offers.

- **Image quality.** Prime lenses usually produce better image quality at their focal length than even the most sophisticated zoom lenses at the same magnification. Zoom lenses, with their shifting elements and f/stops that can vary from zoom position to zoom position, are, in general, more complex to design than fixed focal length lenses. That's not to say that the very best prime lenses can't be complicated as well. However, the exotic designs, aspheric elements, and low-dispersion glass can be applied to improving the quality of the lens, rather than wasting a lot of it on compensating for problems caused by the zoom process itself.

- **Maximum aperture.** Because of the same design constraints, zoom lenses usually have smaller maximum apertures than prime lenses, and the most affordable zooms have a lens opening that grows effectively smaller as you zoom in. The difference in lens speed verges on the ridiculous at some focal lengths. For example, the 24-50mm f/4-6.3 super-bargain kit lens Nikon offers for the Z5 gives you a 50mm f/6.3 lens when zoomed to its maximum focal length, while prime lenses in that focal length commonly have f/1.8 or faster maximum apertures. Indeed, the fastest f/2, f/1.8, f/1.2, and f/0.95 lenses are all primes, and if you require speed, a fixed focal length lens is what you should rely on.

- **Speed.** Using prime lenses takes time and slows you down. It takes a few seconds to remove your current lens and mount a new one, and the more often you need to do that, the more time is wasted. If you choose not to swap lenses, when using a fixed focal length lens, you'll still have to move closer or farther away from your subject to get the field of view you want. A zoom lens allows you to change magnifications and focal lengths with the twist of a ring and generally saves a great deal of time.

Let's move on to the prime lenses available in the wide-angle to normal range in Z-mount for the Z5.

Nikkor Z 20mm f/1.8 S

Super-sharp wide-angle prime lenses are a favorite of landscape photographers, and those doing street photography like wide-angle lenses that are fast enough to capture candid images at night or in murky surroundings. For about $1,050, this lens fills the bill for both types of photography, and other applications—such as interior and exterior architectural shots—as well.

It's a compact ultra-wide lens with two synchronized stepping motors to provide fast and accurate autofocus while remaining quiet enough for video or shooting stills in stealth mode. It has full-time manual focus override so you can fine-tune focus easily and uses Nikon's advanced lens coatings to suppress flare and ghosting under demanding conditions. Dust- and moisture-resistant (helpful for street shooting), it focuses a tad closer than eight inches, weighs about 18 ounces, and measures 3.33 × 4.27 inches.

Nikkor Z 24mm f/1.8 S

Like all the current non-zoom (prime) Z-mount autofocus lenses, this one has a maximum aperture of f/1.8. It makes an excellent lens for landscapes, architecture, and candid street photography when you have enough room to step back that the 20mm f/1.8 isn't needed. Its advanced optical system provides great sharpness even wide open, and it has both Nano Crystal and Super Integrated Coatings to minimize flare and ghosting for improved color fidelity and contrast.

It is priced at a little less than $1,000, which may seem a major investment for a camera that cost only $1,399 for the body alone, but those who need a fast moderately wide lens will prize its compactness and excellent image quality.

Nikkor Z 35mm f/1.8 S

Priced at a tad under $850, the Nikkor Z 35mm f/1.8 S lens is an exceptionally sharp basic wide-angle lens, suitable for landscapes, street photography, exterior architecture, and shooting interiors that aren't so cramped that they call for a wider lens. You can use it for photographing small groups, and it's especially valuable for available-light photography because of its fast f/1.8 maximum aperture.

It focuses down to 9.84 inches, not particularly close enough for true macro work with its 1:5.25 reproduction ratio (true macro lenses have a 1:2 or 1:1 or better reproduction ratio). Its minimum aperture is just f/16 if you're looking for a lens with extra depth-of-field. But this lens's nine-bladed rounded diaphragm produces pleasing bokeh wide open. (I explain bokeh later in this chapter.)

Overall, this lens (shown in Figure 7.6, left) is an excellent performer with two ED (extra-low-dispersion) and three aspherical elements with plenty of sharpness to match the Z5's resolution, so there's little need to consider an adapted F-mount 35mm lens, unless you already own one, or need the extra speed of Nikon's phenomenal 35mm f/1.4G optic, which costs almost exactly twice as much.

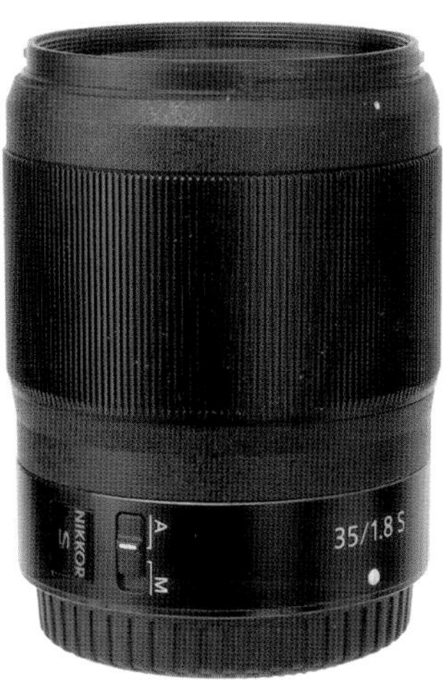
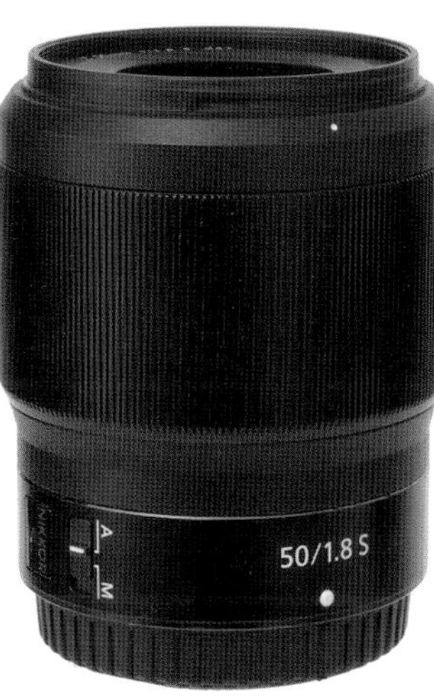

Figure 7.6 The Nikkor Z 35mm f/1.8 S is a fast wide-angle lens (left). The Nikkor Z 50mm f/1.8 S is an exceptionally sharp "normal" lens (right).

Nikkor Z 50mm f/1.8 S

In the dSLR world, 50mm f/1.8 "normal" lenses tend to be inexpensive "starter" prime lenses for those who need a lens faster than the typical zoom, but who can't afford pricier 50mm f/1.4 alternatives. This lens is inexpensive only in comparison with the other S-Line lenses, at $596, but for that price you get a super-sharp lens worthy of Nikon's "superior" classification. (See Figure 7.6, right.)

Lenses of this focal length lend themselves to general photography, and, with the automatic extension tubes for the Z-series that should be available in the near future, for macro work with subjects at distances closer than the 15.7 inches this lens can focus. You can also use it as a portrait lens with an f/1.8 maximum aperture that's excellent for selective focus three-quarter-length and head-and-shoulders portraits of individuals or twosomes. Its nine-blade aperture produces good bokeh. Even those new to photography will have heard the phrase "nifty 50" that is often applied to lenses of this focal length. Lodged between the realms of wide-angle and short telephoto focal lengths, a fast and sharp 50mm lens is an important tool for those looking for versatility at a (relatively) affordable price.

Nikkor Z 50mm f/1.2 S

This lens was introduced as this book was written and is, thankfully, a much more affordable alternative to the super-exotic 58mm f/0.95 S Noct discussed next. This lens is priced at $2100, which will save you enough from the $8,000 price tag on its glamorous f/0.95 sibling to allow you to buy several other lenses, or an extra Z-mount body. Because of its wide maximum aperture, it is a large-ish lens, a bit longer and wider than the 24-70mm f/2.8 S-series zoom and weighs 2.4 pounds. It should be the mainstream king of available-light shooting, great for indoor sports, portraiture, and any illustrative photography where selective focus is desirable. Its f/1.2 is "only" two-thirds of a stop less bright than the 58mm f/0.95 S Noct.

Nikkor Z 58mm f/0.95 S Noct

While I doubt that someone who relies on the Z5 as their primary camera will be seriously interested in this $8,000 lens, I concede that most of us who will never be able to afford one give it the same degree of interest we Hyundai drivers (like me) sinfully have toward Lamborghinis. Surprisingly, when this lens was finally released, a rather large number of well-heeled Z-series owners lined up to purchase one.

Yes, it is almost two full f/stops faster than a 50mm f/1.8 lens, meaning, on your average city street at night at ISO 1600 you could shoot wide open at 1/125th second instead of 1/30th second. Or, in full daylight and ISO 64 you'd need a shutter speed of 1/8000th second for your selective focus images at f/0.95. This lens is purported to be exceptionally sharp wide open, thanks to the Z-series cameras' wide "throat" that loosed many of the chains facing Nikon's lens designers.

Before you available-light photographers add this lens to your birthday "fantasy" list, keep in mind that it is a *manual focus* lens. Most folks buying such a lens would expect autofocus, at least, if not the ability to slice Julienne fries and run a few Android apps as a bonus.

Nikon claims exceptional performance, even wide open, using ultra-high refractive index aspherical (non-spherical) lens elements, and two (count 'em) different reflective coatings to combat glare: ARNEO (I'm still trying to find out what the acronym means) which reduces vertical incidental light and Nano Crystal coating to counter photons reaching the lens from a diagonal direction.

Its controls are as unconventional as its other design elements. In addition to the control ring found on other Z-mount lenses, it includes what Nikon calls a high-precision focus ring with "extreme accuracy and natural torque." On a manual focus lens with such a large maximum aperture and resulting shallow depth-of-field, you can bet that correct focus will be critical. It also includes a programmable Lens Fn button, and a novel LCD display (and accompanying DISP button) that can provide information on aperture, focal length, and depth-of-field.

Telephoto Lenses

Telephoto lenses also can have a dramatic effect on your photography, and Nikon is especially strong in the long-lens arena, with lots of choices in many focal lengths and zoom ranges. You should be able to find an affordable telephoto prime or tele-zoom to enhance your photography in several different ways. This section will outline your Z-mount options.

Nikkor 85mm f/1.8 S

If you shoot a great many portraits, you may want to invest in this lens, priced at around $800, especially for its great rendition of out-of-focus backgrounds (called "bokeh") and excellent image quality wide open. Unless you're shooting in tight spaces, you'll find it provides a pleasing perspective with human subjects, with minimal face "flattening" effect that longer effective focal lengths produce. It shares the same f/1.8 maximum aperture, special coatings, multiple autofocus drive motors, manual focus override, and programmable control ring found in the other Z-mount full-frame prime AF lenses.

As you can see from the listings so far, Nikon's early emphasis in its S-line lenses is in providing the best image quality it can in prime (non-zoom) lenses with reasonably fast maximum apertures. If your budget can afford to go with the flow, you won't be disappointed by any of these.

Nikkor Z 70-200mm f/2.8 S VR

This lens will end up being one of the most versatile optics in Nikon's Z-mount lineup. Even at $2,600, it's well worth the price because it can effectively replace three prime lenses while serving as a triple threat for portrait, sports, and event photography. It's sharp wide-open and the combination of in-body image stabilization and lens-based vibration reduction make it ideal for concert photography. (I routinely shoot performances like those illustrated in this book handheld at 1/180th second at f/2.8 or f/4 and am amazed at the results.

I also like it for portraits, both formal and candid, often going against conventional wisdom and zooming beyond 100-135mm for tight head-and-shoulders shots. The longer focal lengths (which many discourage because they tend to widen or flatten faces) afford great selective focus control and bokeh when shot wide open or at f/4.

As I'll explain later in this chapter, lens-based VR designed for cameras with IBIS is *not* overkill. When this lens (and other VR optics) is mounted on the Z5, the camera hands off image stabilization for pitch (tilting the lens up or down) and yaw (rotating from side to side) to the lens VR, because that system is better able to compensate for that type of movement.

This is another lens with the high-tech coatings and dual stepping motor multi-focus features described earlier. It also has the cool OLED information panel I mentioned in the description of the 24-70mm f/2.8 lens for display of aperture, focus distance, and depth-of field. It has two lens func-tion (L. Fn) buttons that can be assigned behaviors. Focusing down to 1.64 feet, while the 70-200mm f/2.8 Z-mount lens is a sturdy three pounds and measures 3.5 × 8.7 inches, it balances well. Its rotat-ing tripod collar can be removed to trim a bit of weight when you know you'll be shooting exclusively hand-held. (I advise using the lens tripod collar to mount your Z5 to a tripod when working with this lens to improve balance and avoid putting excess weight on the lens mount.)

Nikkor Z 24-200mm f4-6.3 VR

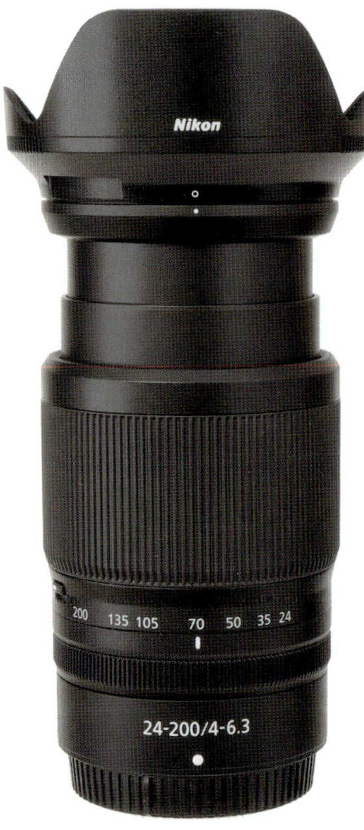

Figure 7.7 The affordable Nikkor Z 24-200mm f/4-6.3 VR zoom lens.

Nikon knew Z-series shooters on a budget would need a less pricey, less hefty zoom lens with a 200mm long end and would accept a slower maximum aperture to get one. However, the com-pany opted to expand the zoom range a bit to improve the ver-satility of its budget zoom option. This $900 lens (see Figure 7.7) is an all-in-one 8.3X zoom that extends from wide-angle to tele-photo focal lengths, with a variable maximum aperture of f/4 at 24mm to f/6.3 at the 200mm end of its range. It has enough "all-in-one" versatility to merit qualifying as one of the two kit lenses initially offered when the Z5 was unveiled. But don't confuse it as a budget version of the 70-200mm f/2.8 S-series optic. Here are some important considerations that can get lost in a crowded specifications list:

- **Not an S-series lens.** As you might expect from its modest price tag, this lens is not part of Nikon's S ("superior") lineup. How-ever, like all Z-mount lenses, it benefits from the freedom afforded lens designers by the new lens mount to use more advanced optical designs. The 24-200mm is plenty sharp.

- **Includes VR.** Note that this lens *does* include VR, which improves image stabilization along two of the five axes, an extra-important feature with longer lenses that tend to mag-nify camera motion because of their length and telephoto focal lengths.

- **It's not tiny.** While an affordable 70-200mm lens with, say, an f/4 maximum aperture would be significantly smaller than its f/2.8 counterpart, by extending this lens' focal length range to 24mm at the wide end Nikon necessarily produced a slightly larger product. However, this lens is still somewhat smaller than the 70-200mm f/2.8 optic, measuring 3.1 × 4.5 inches and weighing 20.2 ounces.

- **Closest focus.** It focuses down to 1.64 feet at 24mm and 2.3 feet at 200mm. With a minimum aperture of f/22–f/36 (depending on zoom setting), you can actually use this lens as a macro lens, assuming the camera/lens are mounted on a tripod and you don't mind the slight loss in image quality that diffraction effects produce at the smallest f/stops. (I'll explain diffraction in more detail in Chapter 11.)

I admit I find myself using this lens as a walk-around lens more than its upscale sibling, but I prefer the better bokeh the latter produces. The 24-200mm lens has a rounded seven-blade diaphragm, which offers pleasing out-of-focus highlights, but the 70-200mm optic's nine-blade design gives better results.

DX Lenses

I'm going to include brief descriptions of the APS-C (DX) lenses available for Z-mount cameras, simply for the sake of completeness. While each of them will work just fine on your Z5, the camera will automatically shift into DX crop mode (with no way to override) giving you reduced-resolution 10MP images with almost no offsetting advantages. These DX lenses are somewhat practical when mounted on higher-resolution cameras and, indeed, I have used my Nikkor Z 50-250mm DX on my Z7 from time to time to capture 18MP images with the full-frame equivalent of a 75-375mm lens. In general, though, you won't be using such lenses unless you also happen to own a Nikon Z50 or other APS-C Z-mount camera.

Nikkor Z 16-50mm DX f/3.5-6.3 VR

On an APS-C camera like the Z50, this $300 DX kit lens functions as the equivalent of a 24-75mm zoom, covering a modest wide-angle to portrait-length zoom range. On the Z5, it's a terribly slow (but compact!) lens that enforces a 10MP resolution penalty. On the plus side, it does include VR, focuses quickly, and provides decent image quality.

Nikkor Z 50-250mm DX f/4.5-6.3 VR

Like all DX lenses in Z-mount, this one has VR, not because it is a nice luxury, but because the initial Nikon APS-C camera, the Z50, didn't have in-body image stabilization *at all,* making lens VR an essential feature. Priced at $350, this lens makes little sense for Z5 owners, but you might have one if you also own an APS-C Z-series camera or upgraded to the Z5 from one.

Nikkor Z Teleconverter TC-1.4x/TC-2.0x

I've long used Nikon teleconverters for my F-mount lenses, generally the 1.4X and 1.7X versions with my Nikkor 200-500mm f/5.6 telephoto. I use these because they were *designed specifically for* the Nikon lenses they are compatible with and produce results that are superior to those of third-party lens/teleconverter manufacturers.

The good news is that Nikon introduced both 1.4x and 2.0x converters in Z-mount, each with excellent optical performance, and hefty price tags ($550 and $600, respectively). The bad news is that, as I write this, the converters are compatible only with the Nikkor Z 70-200mm f/2.8 VR S described above. It is expected they can also be used with the announced (but not yet available) 200-600mm and 100-400mm zooms (and other super zooms, including primes set for future announcements).

Both of these are designed for sports and wildlife photography and include fluorine coatings that harden the surface of the outermost lens elements to protect them when working in inclement conditions (even though converters are only directly exposed to the elements when changing lenses) and to simplify cleaning. With the TC-1.4x, you'll notice almost no loss of optical quality; the teleconverter uses the center portion of the host lens, effectively cropping out any optical defects at the edges of the frame. The image quality loss with the 2.0x converter isn't large.

The main cost is in maximum aperture—one or two f/stops. Your 70-200mm f/2.8 lens is transformed into a 105-280mm f/4 telephoto with the 1.4x converter, and the 2.0x converter gives you a 140-400mm f/5.6 super zoom. The light loss is a small price to pay for the versatility you gain.

Lenses to Come

The most current Nikon Z-mount lens map available as this book was written includes mysterious references to some lenses we can look forward to in the future. Nikon does not supply the aperture values or ranges for any of these lenses. They include an 18-140mm DX zoom that will be an extended-range walk-around lens for APS-C Z-series cameras. The rest appear to be full-frame optics. They include 28mm, 40mm, and a 60mm macro lens, all of them non-S-series lenses. The 28mm and 40mm are rumored to be compact "pancake" style lenses. There are two S-series zooms, a 24-105mm lens that I expect will have an f/4 maximum aperture, and a 100-400mm telephoto. As an S-series option, I expect the 100-400mm lens to have a constant maximum aperture, probably either f/2.8 (which would make it *very* expensive), or f/4. The 200-600mm lens will probably have an f/5.6 maximum aperture and, if we're lucky, be priced at around $1,500 or less.

Universal VR

As a Z5 owner, at this point you won't *necessarily* need to pay extra for purchasing lenses with *vibration reduction* (VR) built in, although some Z-mount lenses *do* include VR for reasons I'll explain shortly. But because the Z-series cameras include in-body image stabilization (IBIS), *every* lens you use—even adapted lenses and manual focus lenses—will have some form of VR available to counter camera movement as you shoot. After all, even the highest resolution lenses and sensors, like those found on the Z5, can do nothing to correct image sharpness lost due to movement. And while higher shutter speeds can eliminate most blur caused by *subject* movement, when it's the *camera* that's causing blur due to vibration, other approaches have to be taken. Your Z5 has improved technology that can help avoid blur caused by mechanical shutter movement and bounce, but when the entire camera and lens are vibrating, that's where *image stabilization* (IS) comes into play.

Image stabilization/vibration reduction can take many forms, and Nikon has expertise in all of them. *Electronic IS* is used in video cameras (and also available in the Z5 while shooting movies). It involves shifting pixels around from frame to frame so that pixels that are not moving remain in the same position, and portions of the image that *are* moving don't stray from their proper path. *Optical image stabilization*, which Nikon calls vibration reduction (VR), is built into many Nikon F-mount lenses, and a few Z-mount lenses as well, such as the 70-200mm f/2.8 and 24-200mm f/4-6.3 lenses discussed earlier. This type of vibration reduction involves lens elements that shift in response to camera movement, as detected by motion sensors included in the optics.

The final type of VR technology is called *in-body image stabilization* (IBIS) and is built-into the Z5. It adjusts the position of the sensor carriage itself along five different axes to counteract movement. The results can be spectacular, with up to a 5-stop improvement from in-body image stabilization technology. That is, a photograph taken at 1/30th second should have the same sharpness (at least in terms of resistance to camera shake) as one shot at 1/1000th second. In practical terms, you probably won't experience such a dramatic gain, however.

Of course, no amount of vibration reduction can eliminate blur from moving subjects, but you should find yourself less tied to a tripod when using longer lenses, or when working with wide-angle lenses under dim lighting conditions than in the past. If you're taking photos in venues where flash or tripods are forbidden, you'll find the Z5's image stabilization invaluable.

How It Works

As I mentioned, IBIS uses gyroscope-like motion sensors to detect camera motion. When such motion is sensed, the carriage holding the sensor is shifted a precise amount in the opposite direction. Movement can occur along one of five different axes, as shown in Figure 7.8:

- **X and Y axes.** These movements occur when the camera shifts in the x and y directions; that is, the camera moves from side to side or up and down within the plane of the sensor. Shifts in the x and y directions are likely to occur when shooting macro images hand-held but can take place any time. This motion is very easy for the IBIS to detect.

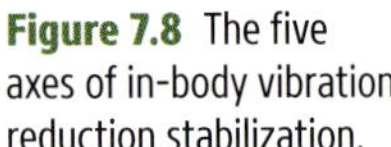

Figure 7.8 The five axes of in-body vibration reduction stabilization.

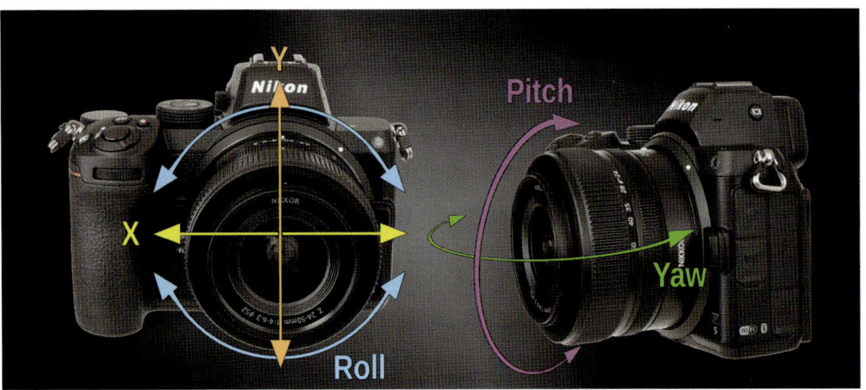

- **Roll.** This is the rotation of the camera along an axis passing through the center of the front of the lens, or an axis parallel to it. It's easiest to picture the rotational point as the center of the lens, but it may be located closer to your hand as you grip the camera body. Roll happens when you, say, align the horizon while shooting a landscape. There may be a tendency to continue to "correct" for the horizon as you shoot, producing vibration along the roll axis. Roll is especially noticeable in video clips because it's easy to see straight lines changing their orientation during a shot. This type of motion can also be easily handled by IBIS.

- **Pitch.** This type of movement happens when the camera shake is such that the lens is tilted up or down, often because the lens itself is a front-heavy telephoto lens. The magnification of the tele only serves to exaggerate the changes in pitch. Pitch movement tends to be less critical with wide-angle lenses. The Z5's in-body image stabilization is less adept at countering this type of movement. It's one case in which vibration reduction built into the lens potentially provides superior correction. That's what happens when you use either an F-mount or Z-mount lens that includes VR; the pitch (and roll) compensation is passed off to the lens itself.

- **Yaw.** Telephotos are also a major contributor to *yaw* vibrations, in which the camera pivots slightly as if you were shooting a panorama—even when you're *not*. VR built into Z-mount lenses (or any F-mount lenses attached with the FTZ adapter) provide higher degrees of correction.

Best of Both Worlds

While it's true that IBIS can do a great job correcting for camera shake along all five axes, VR built into the lens can potentially do a *better* job for some types of motion. In-body stabilization is best for countering movement in the x and y directions, and for compensating for roll; the cameras mechanism can detect side-to-side, up-and-down, and rotational movement of the sensor extremely well. IBIS is slightly less adept at detecting the motion of front-heavy telephoto lenses as they tilt up or down or rotate along a vertical axis. The magnification of the tele only serves to exaggerate the changes in pitch and yaw.

Fortunately, that's where vibration reduction built into lenses shines. If you are using a lens that does have VR—either a native Z-mount lens or one of the many F-mount lenses that include the feature—the Z5 uses the two technologies in tandem, allowing the lens to correct for pitch and yaw, while the in-body IS compensates for x, y, and roll movements. That makes a lot of sense, because in correcting for x, y, and roll, the camera is able to keep the sensor in the exact same plane to preserve precise focus and simply move the sensor carriage up, down, or slightly rotated to nullify the movement.

However, not all non-stabilized lenses benefit in identical ways from Nikon's stabilization technology. For best results, the system needs to know both focal length and focus distance to provide optimum stabilization. That's an advantage of VR: stabilization built into the lens always knows exactly what focal length setting and focus distance is being used. So, lenses that can communicate this information to the camera work best for "cooperative" mode. Focal length information is needed to correct for pitch and yaw, while x and y compensation need to know the focal distance. (Roll correction needs neither type of data and can do its thing just from what IBIS sees happening on the sensor.) However, when all the data is available, the full array of the camera's IS capabilities can be used to correct on all five axes.

Here's a quick summary of some things you should keep in mind:

- **Tripod use.** For best results, turn off vibration reduction when the camera is mounted on a tripod.

- **Vibration reduction doesn't stop action.** Please don't forget this! No type of stabilization is a panacea to replace the action-stopping capabilities of a faster shutter speed. If you need to use 1/1000th second to freeze a high jumper in mid-air, VR doesn't help you.

- **Stabilization might slow you down.** The process of adjusting the sensor to counter camera shake takes time, just as autofocus does, so you might find that VR adds to the lag between when you press the shutter and when the picture is taken. In a situation where you want to capture a fleeting instant that can happen suddenly, image stabilization might not be your best choice.

- **Give vibration reduction a helping hand.** When you simply do not want to carry a tripod all day and you'll be relying on the IBIS system, brace the camera or your elbows on something solid, like the roof of a car or a piece of furniture. Remember that an inexpensive monopod can be quite compact when not extended; many camera bags include straps that allow you to attach this accessory. Use a monopod for extra camera-shake compensation. Brace the accessory against a rock, a bridge abutment, or a fence and you might be able to get blur-free photos at surprisingly long shutter speeds. When you're heading out into the field to photograph wild animals or flowers and want to use longer exposures and think a tripod isn't practical, at least consider packing a monopod.

Using the FTZ Adapter

Nikon says that the $250 FTZ adapter (shown with the Nikkor 8-15mm f/3.5-4.5E fisheye zoom in Figure 7.9) is compatible with roughly 360 F-mount lenses. This includes more than 90 lenses that have full autofocus and autoexposure compatibility when using FX or DX AF-S type G/D/E, AF-P type G/E, AF-I type D, and AF-S/AF-I Teleconverters. As for other lenses:

- **AF, AF-D lenses.** You must focus these optics manually, but with AF-D lenses the electronic rangefinder will assist in determining correct focus, and Peaking Highlights (described in Chapters 5 and 12) works with either type. You can adjust the aperture electronically and use Aperture-priority autoexposure.

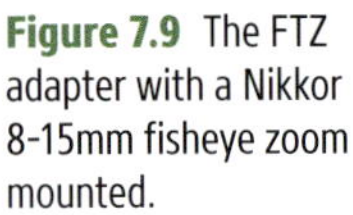
Figure 7.9 The FTZ adapter with a Nikkor 8-15mm fisheye zoom mounted.

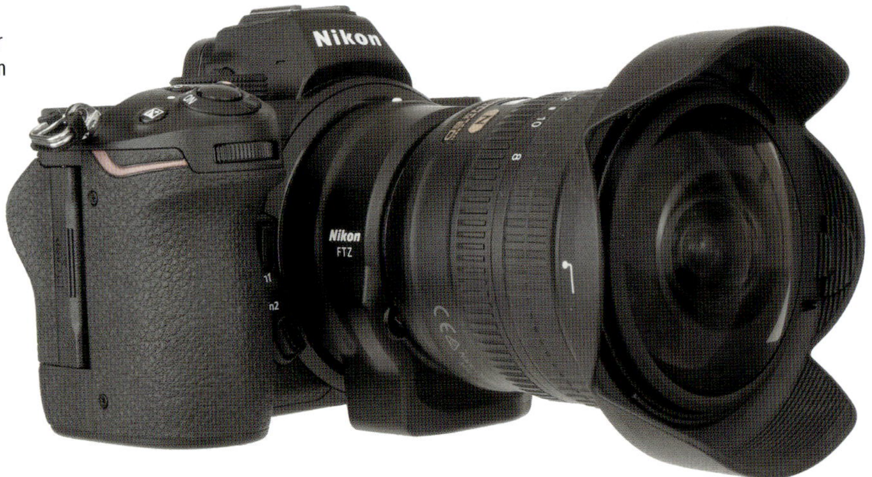

- **AI-P and all lenses with a CPU chip.** You get manual focus only (with Peaking Highlights) and Aperture-priority exposure.
- **AI, AI-S, and Series E lenses.** Manual focus and manual exposure only, but you can use the non-CPU Lens Data entry in the Setup menu to specify the maximum aperture and focal length of the lens, as described in Chapter 13. However, zoom focal length ranges are not supported. You may also be able to mount and use non-AI F-mount lenses (pre-1977) but may have mechanical interference problems.

As I noted earlier, DX lenses must be used in one of the Z5's crop modes if you want some assurance that the entire image area will be filled. Spotting DX lenses is easy: Nikon's versions all have the letters DX in their names.

The process is a bit more complicated when it comes to third-party manufacturers. Tamron uses the Di (Digitally integrated) designation for its lenses that are compatible with full-frame digital (and film) cameras and applies the Di II label to lenses suitable only for cropped-sensor models. With Sigma lenses, DG is used for lenses suitable for both FX and DX cameras, and DC indicates a DX-only model. Tokina seems to use the D (for FX) and DX (for DX) nomenclature. All three vendors have been making lenses for (full-frame) film cameras for many years, well before the digital/DX factor became a factor, so when purchasing one of their lenses you may not see a special designation, but, if the lens was introduced prior to about 2004, it's almost certainly a full-frame model.

That's the case with Nikon's older lenses, too, such as the Nikon AI, AI-S, or AI-P lenses, which are manual focus lenses produced starting in 1977 and effectively through the present day, because Nikon continues to offer a limited number of manual focus lenses for those who need them. All are full-frame models.

Nikon lenses produced prior to 1977 must have a minor conversion done to be used safely with most Nikon dSLRs and is recommended for Z5 owners as well, because of possible mechanical issues. John White at www.aiconversions.com will do the work for about $35 to allow these older lenses to be safely used on any Nikon digital camera.

Other Adapters

As I've noted, because of the Z5's 16mm flange distance, there is plenty of room for other adapters to allow using lenses from other manufacturers on your camera. Here are my recommendations.

- **Manual adapters.** You'll find inexpensive all-manual adapters for many different "foreign" camera mounts available. I like those offered by FotoDiox from Amazon and many other retailers and use them to attach Sony and Canon lenses to my Z-series cameras. I also use such manual adapters, priced at $15–$30 to attach *manual focus Nikon* lenses to my Z-series bodies. Indeed, when I am purchasing new manual-focus lenses I buy them in F-mount even if they are available in Z-mount versions. That allows me to use the same lenses on both types of Nikon cameras. Figure 7.10 shows one of the venerable Russian Helios 44-2 58mm f/2 manual focus lenses (a favorite creative lens because of its Lensbaby-like bokeh and distortion), mounted using a FotoDiox adapter.

- **Auto adapters.** A company called TechArt offers fully automatic adapters that let you use Sony mirrorless camera lenses and Canon EF lenses on your Z5 or other Z-series cameras. These (roughly) $250 adapters retain full autoexposure/autofocus features. Figure 7.11 shows a Canon EF 100-300mm zoom attached to my Z5. I've added a few Canon autofocus lenses to my kit because they are plentiful and cheap but produce sharp images. I also use some Sony E-mount lenses on my Z5 with a TechArt adapter for a different reason: I already own some very good lenses in focal length ranges Nikon doesn't yet support, such as the excellent Sony FE 24-105mm f/4 seen in Figure 7.12.

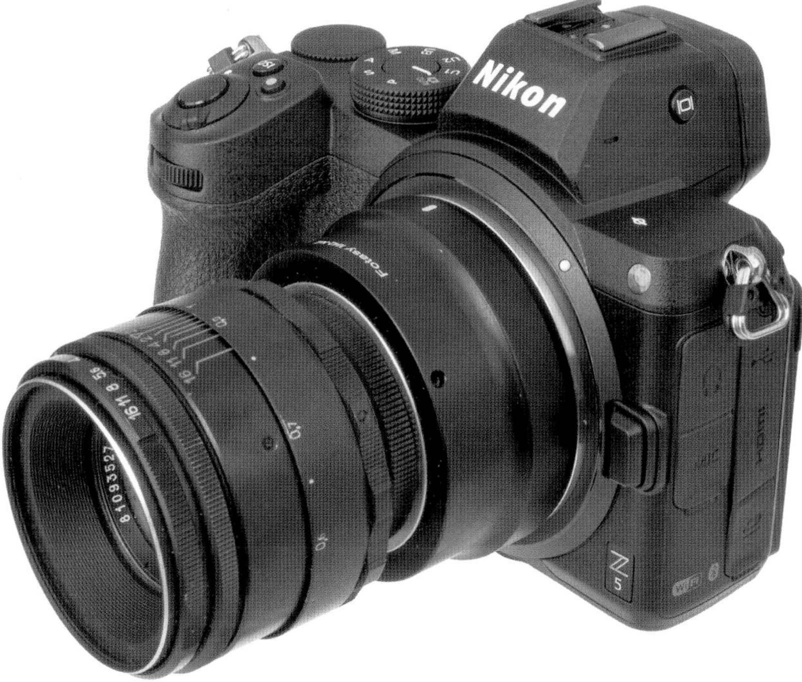

Figure 7.10 A Russian 58mm f/2 manual focus lens mounted on a FotoDiox adapter.

Figure 7.11 Canon EF 100-300mm f/4.5-5.6 lens with TechArt adapter.

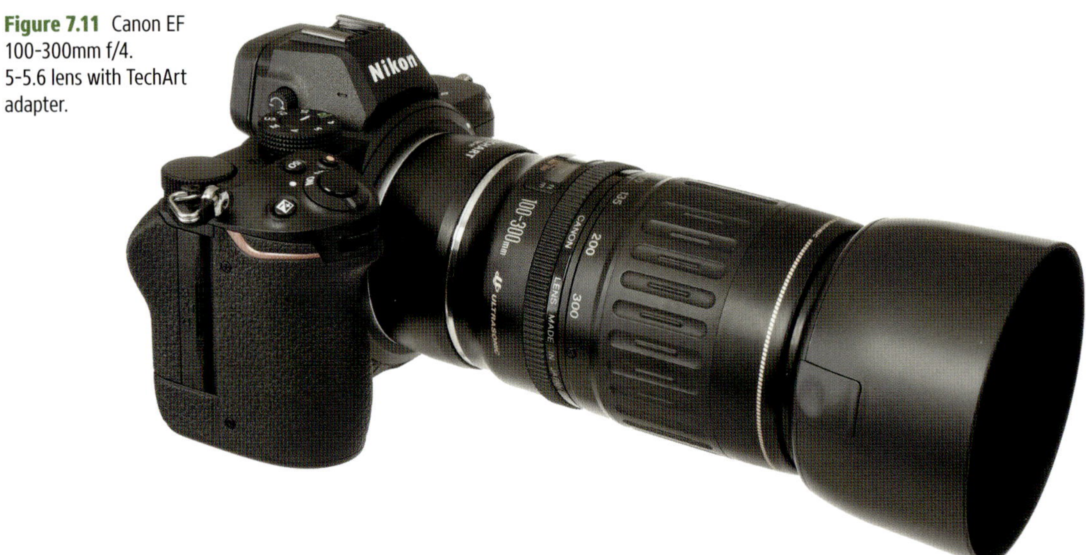

Figure 7.12 Sony FE 24-105mm f/4 lens mounted with a TechArt adapter.

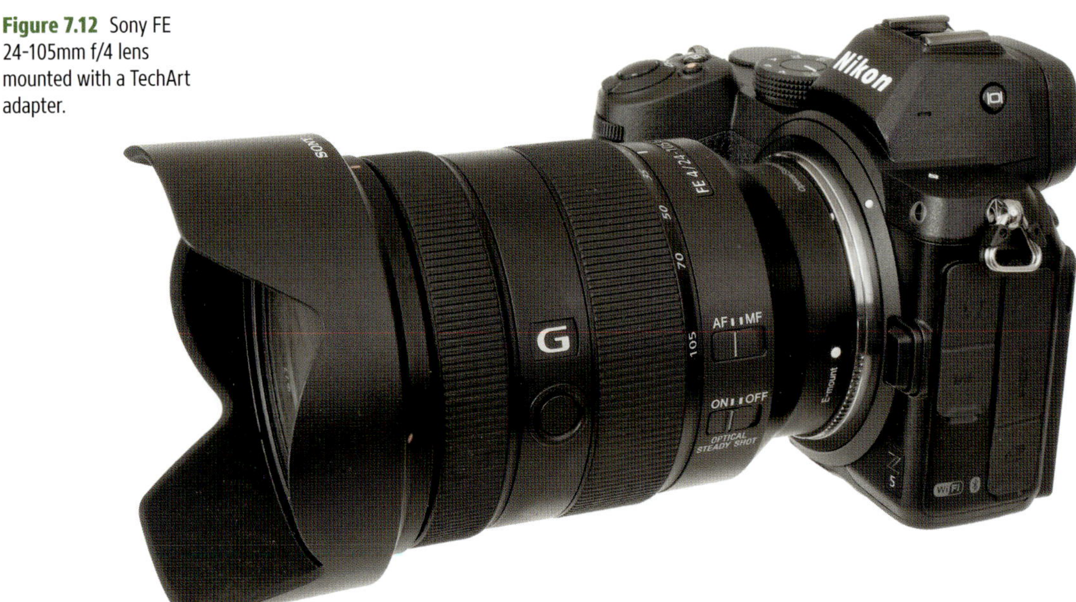

Categories of Lenses

Although I described the native Z-mount lenses earlier, I know that some new enthusiasts need a bit more general information on what lenses can do for them. Even old hands can use a refresher from time to time. So, in this section I'm going to provide an overview of the key aspects of lenses of various types.

Lenses can be categorized by their intended purpose—general photography, macro photography, and so forth—or by their focal length. The range of available focal lengths is usually divided into three main groups: wide angle, normal, and telephoto. Prime lenses fall neatly into one of these classifications. Zooms can overlap designations, with a significant number falling into the catch-all, wide-to-telephoto zoom range. This section provides more information about focal length ranges, and how they are used.

Any lens with a focal length of 12mm to 20mm is said to be an *ultra-wide-angle lens*; from about 20mm to 35mm is said to be a *wide-angle lens. Normal lenses* have a focal length roughly equivalent to the diagonal of the film or sensor, in millimeters, and so fall into the range of about 45mm to 60mm on a Z5. *Short telephoto lenses* start at about 70mm to 105mm, with anything from 135mm to 300mm qualifying as a conventional *telephoto.* For the Nikon Z5, anything from about 350mm to 400mm or longer can be considered a *super-telephoto.*

Using Wide-Angle and Wide-Zoom Lenses

To use wide-angle prime lenses and wide zooms, you need to understand how they affect your photography. Here's a quick summary of the things you need to know.

- **More depth-of-field.** Practically speaking, wide-angle lenses offer more depth-of-field at a particular subject distance and aperture. You'll find that helpful when you want to maximize sharpness of a large zone, but not very useful when you'd rather isolate your subject using selective focus (telephoto lenses are better for that).

- **Stepping back.** Wide-angle lenses have the effect of making it seem that you are standing farther from your subject than you really are. They're helpful when you don't want to back up or can't because there are impediments in your way.

- **Wider field of view.** While making your subject seem farther away, as implied above, a wide-angle lens also provides a larger field of view, including more of the subject in your photos.

- **More foreground.** As background objects retreat, more of the foreground is brought into view by a wide-angle lens. That gives you extra emphasis on the area that's closest to the camera. Photograph your home with a normal lens/normal zoom setting, and the front yard probably looks fairly conventional in your photo (that's why they're called "normal" lenses). Switch to a wider lens and you'll discover that your lawn now makes up much more of the photo. So, wide-angle lenses are great when you want to emphasize that lake in the foreground, but problematic when your intended subject is located farther in the distance.

- **Super-sized subjects.** The tendency of a wide-angle lens to emphasize objects in the foreground, while de-emphasizing objects in the background can lead to a kind of size distortion that may be more objectionable for some types of subjects than others. Shoot a bed of flowers up close with a wide angle, and you might like the distorted effect of the larger blossoms nearer the lens. Take a photo of a family member with the same lens from the same distance, and you're likely to get some complaints about that gigantic nose in the foreground.

- **Perspective distortion.** When you tilt the camera so the plane of the sensor is no longer perpendicular to the vertical plane of your subject, some parts of the subject are now closer to the sensor than they were before, while other parts are farther away. So, buildings, flagpoles, or NBA players appear to be falling backward. While this kind of apparent distortion (it's not caused by a defect in the lens) can happen with any lens, it's most apparent when a wide angle is used. The "falling-back" look is particularly troublesome with subjects that actually do get narrower toward the top, such as pyramids and the worst-case scenario Nova Scotia lighthouse seen in Figure 7.13.

- **Steady cam.** Hand-holding a wide-angle lens at slower shutter speeds, without vibration reduction, produces steadier results than with a telephoto lens. The reduced magnification of the wide-lens or wide-zoom setting doesn't emphasize camera shake like a telephoto lens does.

- **Interesting angles.** Many of the factors already listed combine to produce more interesting angles when shooting with wide-angle lenses. Raising or lowering a telephoto lens a few feet probably will have little effect on the appearance of the distant subjects you're shooting. The same change in elevation can produce a dramatic effect for the much-closer subjects typically captured with a wide-angle lens or wide-zoom setting.

Avoiding Potential Wide-Angle Problems

Wide-angle lenses have a few quirks that you'll want to keep in mind when shooting so you can avoid falling into some common traps. Here's a checklist of tips for avoiding common problems:

- **Symptom: converging lines.** Unless you want to use wildly diverging lines as a creative effect, it's a good idea to keep horizontal and vertical lines in landscapes, architecture, and other subjects carefully aligned with the sides, top, and bottom of the frame. That will help you avoid undesired perspective distortion. Sometimes it helps to shoot from a slightly elevated position, so you don't have to tilt the camera up or down.

- **Symptom: Excessive foreground.** The tendency of very wide-angle lenses to make foreground subjects appear large can be a problem with landscape and architectural photographs. Your landscape may have majestic mountains in the background, but most of your frame may be filled with the nearby terrain. Limited space forced me to use a wide-angle lens to capture Église Sainte-Marie in Nova Scotia, at 184 feet the tallest wooden building in North America. With my back at the edge of the roadway that passed in front of the structure, the edifice's parking lot occupied an excessive amount of space in my original uncropped shot (see Figure 7.14).

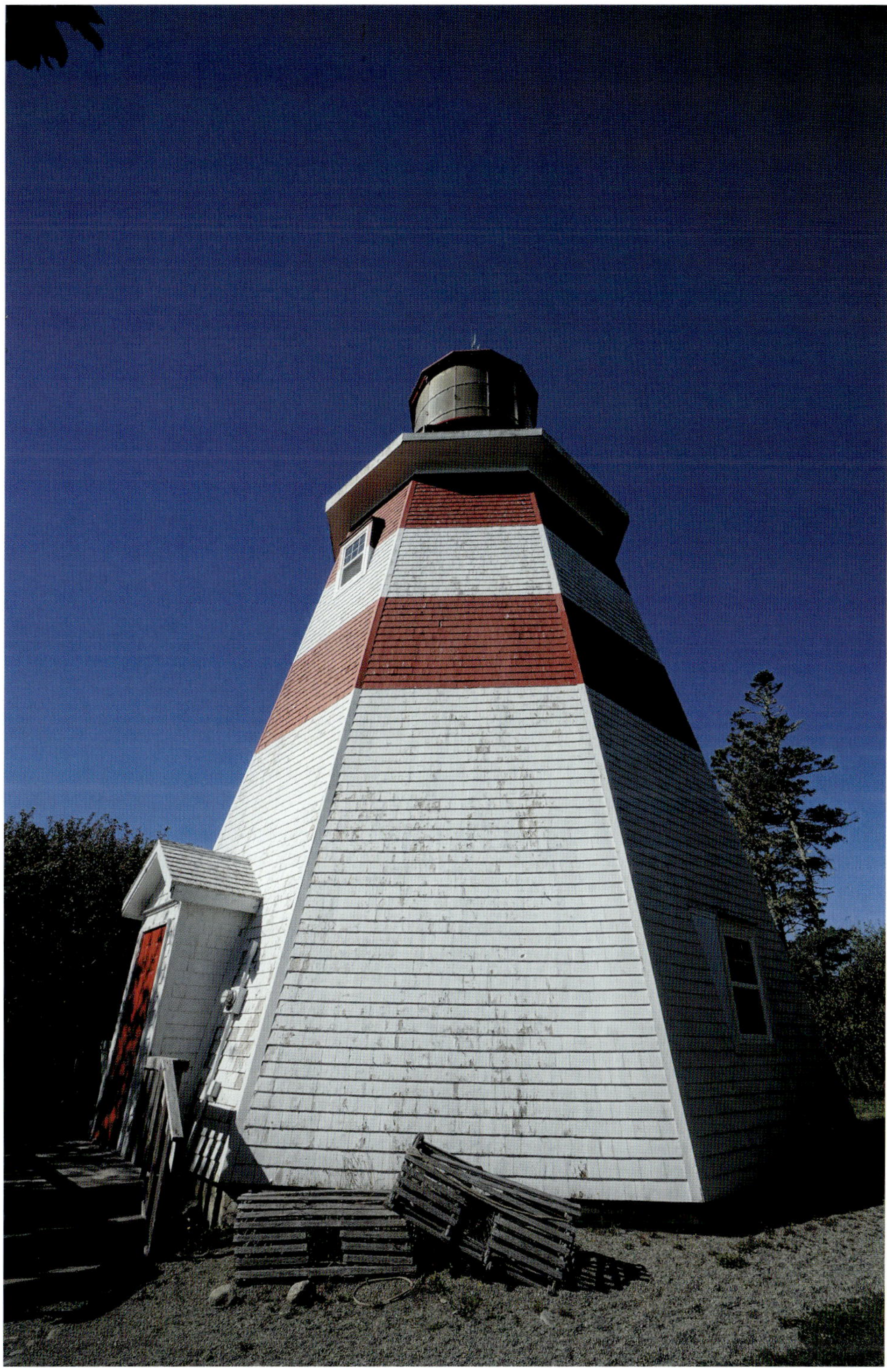

Figure 7.13 Tilting the camera back produces or accentuates this "falling-back" look in architectural photos.

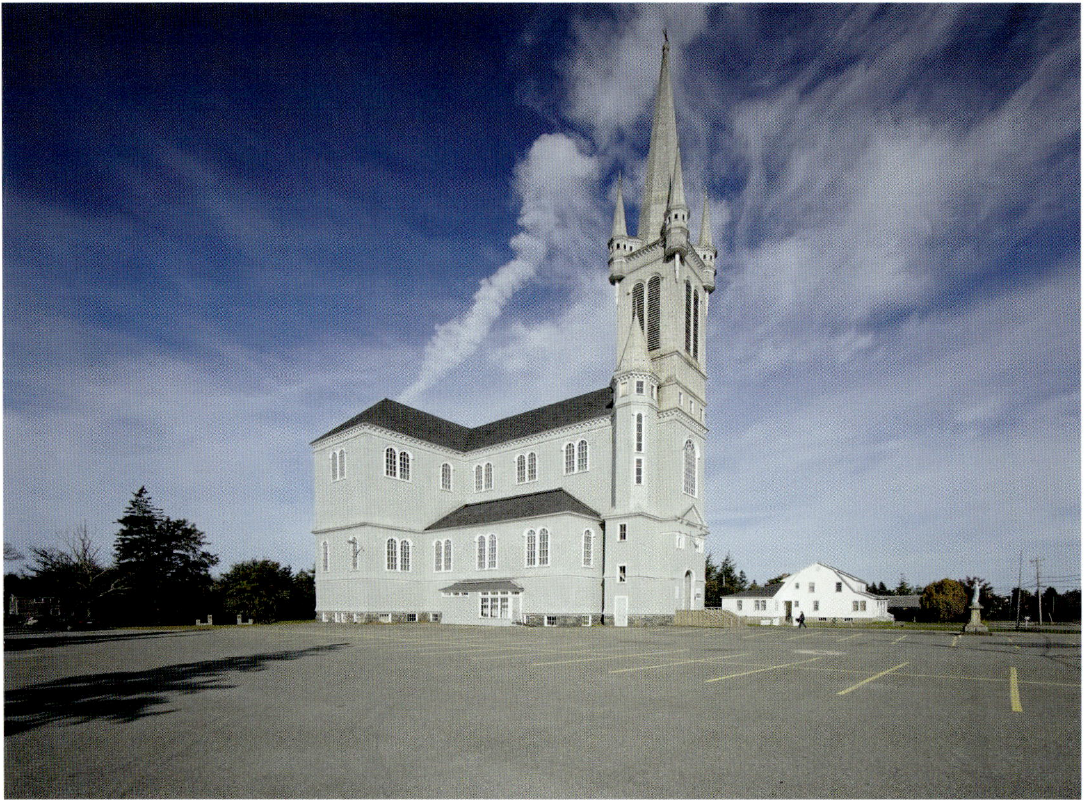

Figure 7.14 Wide-angle lenses can overemphasize the foreground in landscape and architectural shots.

- **Symptom: color fringes around objects.** Lenses are often plagued with fringes of color around backlit objects, produced by *chromatic aberration*, which is produced when all the colors of light don't focus in the same plane or same lateral position (that is, the colors are offset to one side). This phenomenon is more common in wide-angle lenses and in photos of subjects with contrasty edges. Some kinds of chromatic aberration can be reduced by stopping down the lens, while all sorts can be reduced by using lenses with low diffraction index glass (or ED elements, in Nikon nomenclature) and by incorporating elements that cancel the chromatic aberration of other glass in the lens.

- **Symptom: lines that bow outward.** Some wide-angle lenses cause straight lines to bow outward, with the strongest effect at the edges. In fisheye (or *curvilinear*) lenses, this defect is a feature. When distortion is not desired, you'll need to use a lens that has corrected barrel distortion. Manufacturers like Nikon do their best to minimize or eliminate it (producing a *rectilinear* lens), often using *aspherical* lens elements (which are not cross-sections of a sphere). You can also minimize barrel distortion simply by framing your photo with some extra space all around, so the edges where the defect is most obvious can be cropped out of the picture. Some image editors, including Photoshop and Photoshop Elements and Nikon Capture NX-D, have a lens distortion correction feature.

- **Symptom: dark corners and shadows in flash photos.** The Nikon Z5's optional external electronic flash are generally designed to provide even coverage for lenses as wide as 17mm. If you use a wider lens, you can expect darkening, or *vignetting*, in the corners of the frame.

Using Telephoto and Tele-Zoom Lenses

Here are the most important things you need to know. In the next section, I'll concentrate on telephoto considerations that can be problematic—and how to avoid those problems.

- **Selective focus.** Long lenses have reduced depth-of-field within the frame, allowing you to use selective focus to isolate your subject. You can open the lens up wide to create shallow depth-of-field or close it down a bit to allow more to be in focus. The flip side of the coin is that when you *want* to make a range of objects sharp, you'll need to use a smaller f/stop to get the depth-of-field you need. Like fire, the depth-of-field of a telephoto lens can be friend or foe. Figure 7.15 shows a photo of an old oil lamp shot with the Nikkor Z 85mm f/1.8 lens with a wide f/2.8 f/stop to de-emphasize the background.

- **Getting closer.** Telephoto lenses bring you closer to wildlife, sports action, and candid subjects. No one wants to get a reputation as a surreptitious or "sneaky" photographer (except for paparazzi), but when applied to candids in an open and honest way, a long lens can help you capture memorable moments while retaining enough distance to stay out of the way of events as they transpire.

- **Reduced foreground/increased compression.** Telephoto lenses have the opposite effect of wide angles: they reduce the importance of things in the foreground by squeezing everything together. This compression even makes distant objects appear to be closer to subjects in the foreground and middle ranges. You can use this effect as a creative tool to squeeze subjects together. You'll find the effect used all the time in TV shows, where the hero dashes toward the camera while racing between slow-moving automobiles, seemingly each just a foot or two apart.

- **Accentuates camera shakiness.** Telephoto focal lengths hit you with a double whammy in terms of camera/photographer shake. The lenses themselves are bulkier, more difficult to hold steady, and may even produce a barely perceptible see-saw rocking effect when you support them with one hand halfway down the lens barrel. Telephotos also magnify any camera shake. It's no wonder that vibration reduction is a popular feature when using longer focal lengths.

- **Interesting angles require creativity.** Telephoto lenses require more imagination in selecting interesting angles, because the "angle" you do get on your subjects is so narrow. Moving from side to side or a bit higher or lower can make a dramatic difference in a wide-angle shot but raising or lowering a telephoto lens a few feet probably will have little effect on the appearance of the distant subjects you're shooting.

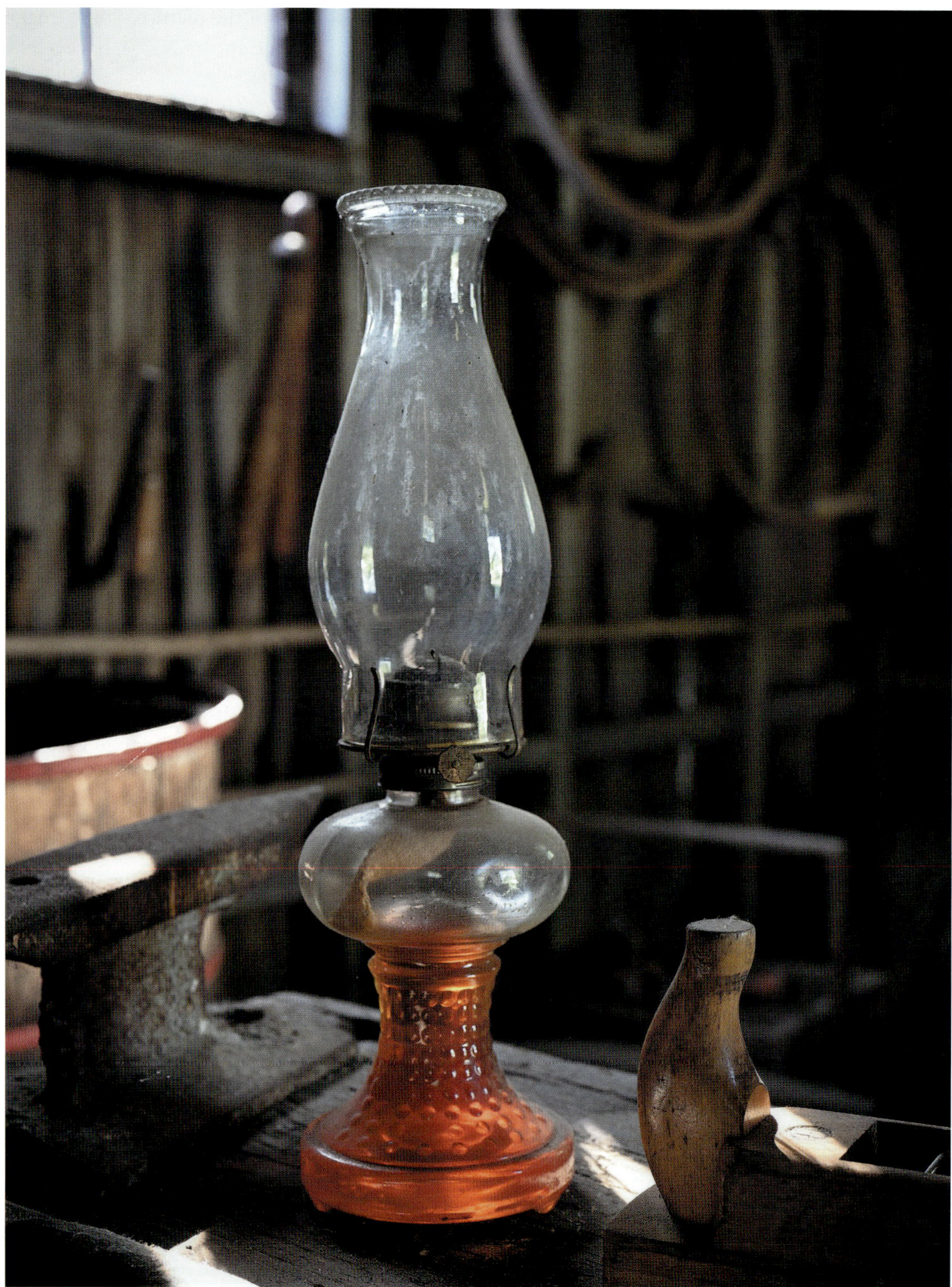

Figure 7.15 A wide f/stop helped isolate the lamp against its background.

Avoiding Telephoto Lens Problems

Many of the "problems" that telephoto lenses pose are really just challenges and are not that difficult to overcome. Here is a list of the seven most common picture maladies and suggested solutions.

- **Symptom: flat faces in portraits.** Head-and-shoulders portraits of humans tend to be more flattering when a focal length of 85mm to 105mm is used. Longer focal lengths compress the distance between features like noses and ears, making the face look wider and flat. A wide angle might make noses look huge and ears tiny when you fill the frame with a face. So, stick with 85mm to 105mm focal lengths, going longer only when you're forced to shoot from a greater distance, and wider only when shooting three-quarters/full-length portraits, or group shots.

- **Symptom: blur due to camera shake.** Use a higher shutter speed (boosting ISO if necessary), consider an image-stabilized lens, or mount your camera on a tripod, monopod, or brace it with some other support. Of those three solutions, only the first will reduce blur caused by *subject* motion; vibration reduction/image stabilization or tripod won't help you freeze a race car in mid-lap.

- **Symptom: color fringes.** Chromatic aberration is the most pernicious optical problem found in telephoto lenses. There are others, including spherical aberration, astigmatism, coma, curvature of field, and similarly scary-sounding phenomena. The best solution for any of these is to use a better lens that offers the proper degree of correction or stop down the lens to minimize the problem. But that's not always possible. Your second-best choice may be to correct the fringing in your favorite RAW-conversion tool or image editor. Photoshop's Lens Correction filter offers sliders that minimize both red/cyan and blue/yellow fringing.

- **Symptom: lines that curve inward.** Pincushion distortion is found in many telephoto lenses. You might find after a bit of testing that it is worse at certain focal lengths with your zoom lens. Like chromatic aberration, it can be partially corrected using tools like the correction tools built into Photoshop and Photoshop Elements, and the Distortion and Perspective tools in the Z5's Retouch menu (see Chapter 13). You can see an exaggerated example in Figure 7.16, especially at the edge; pincushion distortion isn't always this obvious.

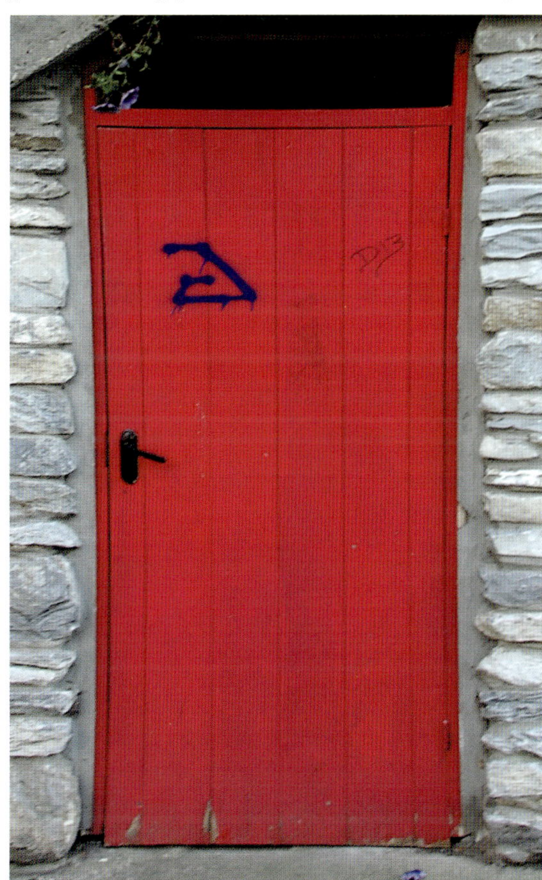

Figure 7.16 Pincushion distortion in telephoto lenses causes lines to bow inward from the edges.

- **Symptom: low contrast from haze or fog.** When you're photographing distant objects, a long lens shoots through a lot more atmosphere, which generally is muddied up with extra haze and fog. That dirt or moisture in the atmosphere can reduce contrast and mute colors. Some feel that a skylight or UV filter can help, but this practice is mostly a holdover from the film days. Digital sensors are not sensitive enough to UV light for a UV filter to have much effect. So, you should be prepared to boost contrast and color saturation in your Picture Controls menu or image editor if necessary.

- **Symptom: low contrast from flare.** Lenses are furnished with lens hoods for a good reason: to reduce flare from bright light sources at the periphery of the picture area, or completely outside it. Because telephoto lenses often create images that are lower in contrast in the first place, you'll want to be especially careful to use a lens hood to prevent further effects on your image (or shade the front of the lens with your hand).

- **Symptom: dark flash photos.** Edge-to-edge flash coverage isn't a problem with telephoto lenses as it is with wide angles. The shooting distance is. A long lens might make a subject that's 50 feet away look as if it's right next to you, but your camera's flash isn't fooled. You'll need extra power for distant flash shots. The Nikon SB-5000 and SB-910 Speedlights, for example, can automatically zoom coverage to illuminate the area captured by a 200mm telephoto lens, with three light distribution patterns (Standard, Center-weighted, and Even).

Telephotos and Bokeh

Bokeh describes the aesthetic qualities of the out-of-focus parts of an image and whether out-of-focus points of light—circles of confusion—are rendered as distracting fuzzy discs or smoothly fade into the background. *Boke* is a Japanese word for "blur," and the h was added to keep English speakers from rendering it monosyllabically to rhyme with *broke*. Although bokeh is visible in blurry portions of any image, it's of particular concern with telephoto lenses, which, thanks to the magic of reduced depth-of-field, produce more obviously out-of-focus areas.

Bokeh can vary from lens to lens, or even within a given lens depending on the f/stop in use. Bokeh becomes objectionable when the circles of confusion are evenly illuminated, making them stand out as distinct discs (see Figure 7.17, top), or, worse, when these circles are darker in the center, producing an ugly "doughnut" effect. A lens defect called spherical aberration may produce out-of-focus discs that are brighter on the edges and darker in the center, because the lens doesn't focus light passing through the edges of the lens exactly as it does light going through the center. (Mirror or *catadioptric* lenses also produce this effect.)

Other kinds of spherical aberration generate circles of confusion that are brightest in the center and fade out at the edges, producing a smooth blending effect, as you can see at bottom in Figure 7.17. Ironically, when no spherical aberration is present at all, the discs are a uniform shade, which, while better than the doughnut effect, is not as pleasing as the bright-center/dark-edge rendition. The shape of the disc also comes into play, with round smooth circles considered the best, and nonagonal or some other polygon (determined by the shape of the lens diaphragm) considered less desirable.

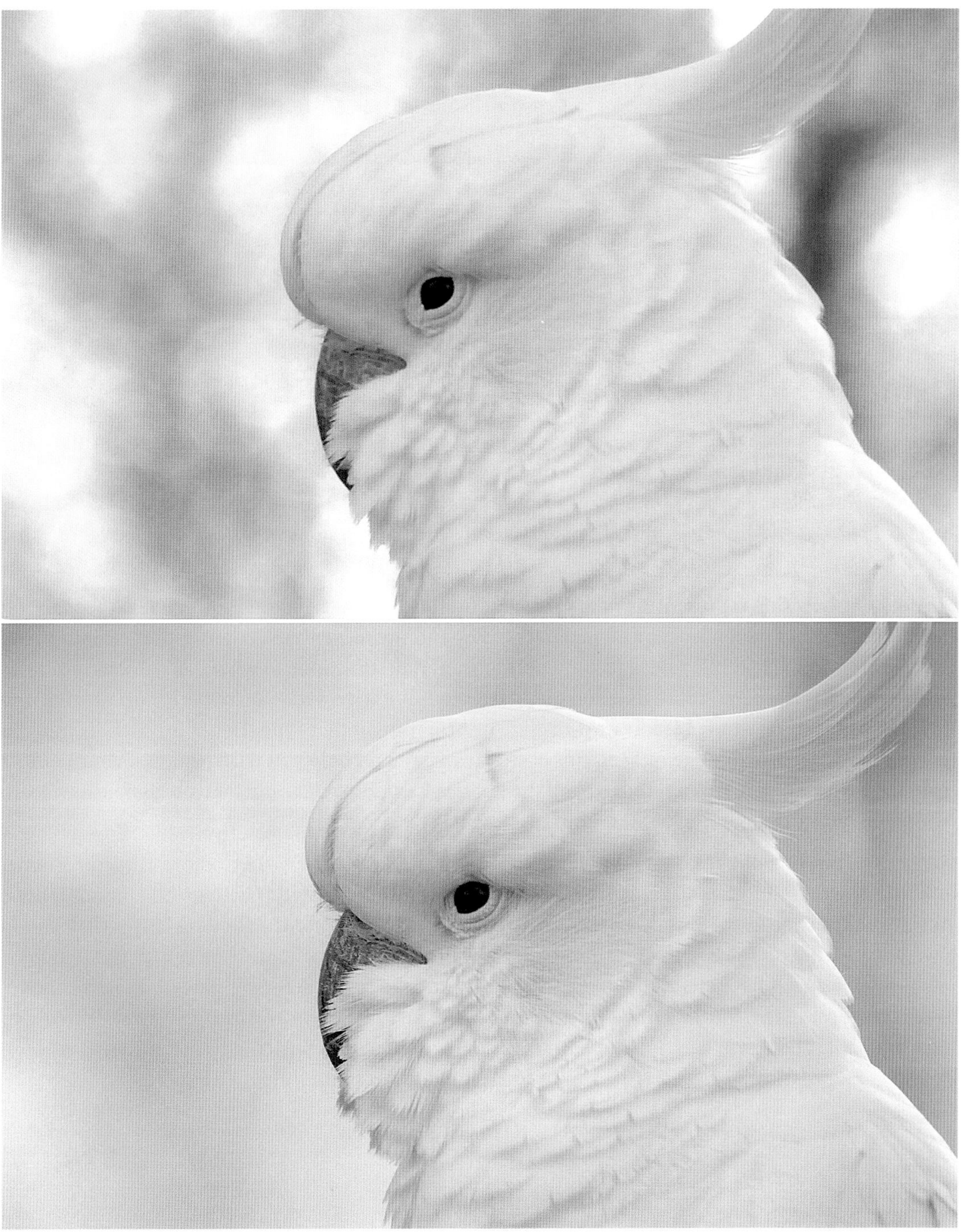

Figure 7.17 Bokeh is less pleasing when the discs are prominent (top), and less obtrusive when they blend into the background (bottom).

If you plan to use selective focus a lot, you should investigate the bokeh characteristics of a particular lens before you buy. Nikon user groups and forums will usually be full of comments and questions about bokeh, so the research is fairly easy.

BOKEH AND SPHERICAL ABBERATION

The characteristics of out-of-focus discs in your image are affected both by the number of blades in the aperture (rounder is better; sharp-sided polygons are worse), and the evenness of illumination of those discs. Highlights may be brighter on the edges and darker in the center because the lens doesn't focus light passing through the edges of the lens exactly as it does light going through the center. That's bad.

Using F-Mount Lenses

I explained working with the FTZ adapter to use F-mount lenses on your Z5 earlier in this book. While Nikon is continuing to expand its offerings of native Z-mount lenses, many veteran Nikon owners will continue to rely on F-mount lenses they already own, or may purchase such lenses specifically to use with their Z-series cameras because native versions may not be available for some time.

The following section represents my personal recommendations on Nikon F-mount lenses, based on the more than four dozen lenses I owned in the past and the more than 30 lenses that remain in my collection today. What follows are just my opinions, and descriptions of what has worked for me. If you want lens testing and more detailed qualitative/quantitative data, you're better off visiting one of the websites devoted to providing up-to-date information of that type. Here, my goal is simply to let you know the broad range of F-mount optics available and help you narrow down your choices from the vast array of lenses offered. Not all the lenses I mention will be currently available new from Nikon, but all can be readily found in mint used condition.

Generally, I'm not going to cover non-Nikon lenses. I expect it will be awhile before Tamron, Sigma, or Tokina begin to offer a full range of Z-mount lenses. As for adapted third-party F-mount lenses, your results may be hit-or-miss, as there were reports of incompatibilities among lenses that *should* have been usable on the Z5. In addition, I have always concentrated on Nikon optics in my books, primarily because I have stuck to Nikon products for most of my career. While Nikon lenses aren't always the best in their focal length/speed ranges, they are always near the top and have proved to be dependable and consistent. I'm not going to provide a lot of exact pricing information, as you can easily Google that, and prices have been trending upward for some time.

Macro Lenses

Some telephotos and telephoto zooms available for the Nikon Z5 have particularly close-focusing capabilities, making them *macro* lenses. Of course, the object is not necessarily to get close (get too close and you'll find it difficult to light your subject). What you're really looking for in a macro lens is to magnify the apparent size of the subject in the final image. Camera-to-subject distance is most important when you want to back up farther from your subject (say, to avoid spooking skittish insects or small animals). In that case, you'll want a macro lens with a longer focal length to allow that distance while retaining the desired magnification.

True macro lenses in Z-mount have been slow in arriving, but even though such optics are plentiful in the F-mount world, that doesn't mean you need to jump to one of those lenses (which I'll discuss shortly) immediately. I find that a set of automatic extension tubes available from third parties can convert one of your existing lenses into a workable macro lens. Figure 7.18 shows the Nikkor Z 50mm f/1.8 S lens mounted on a pair of FotoDiox Pro automatic extension tubes, which allow that lens to focus down to mere inches from your subject. The same tubes can be use with other Z-mount lenses to beef up their close-focusing capabilities.

In F-mount, however, Nikon also makes a range of full-frame lenses that are officially designated as macro optics. The most popular include:

- **AF-S Micro-Nikkor 60mm f/2.8G ED.** It also has ED lens elements for improved image quality. However, because it lacks an aperture ring, you can control the f/stop only when the lens is mounted directly on the camera or used with automatic extension tubes. Should you want to reverse a macro lens using a special adapter (the Nikon BR2-A ring) to improve image quality or mount it on a bellows, you're better off with a lens having an aperture ring. This $600 lens is an excellent choice if you want to capture 35mm slides and negatives using the Nikon ES-2 film digitizing adapter.

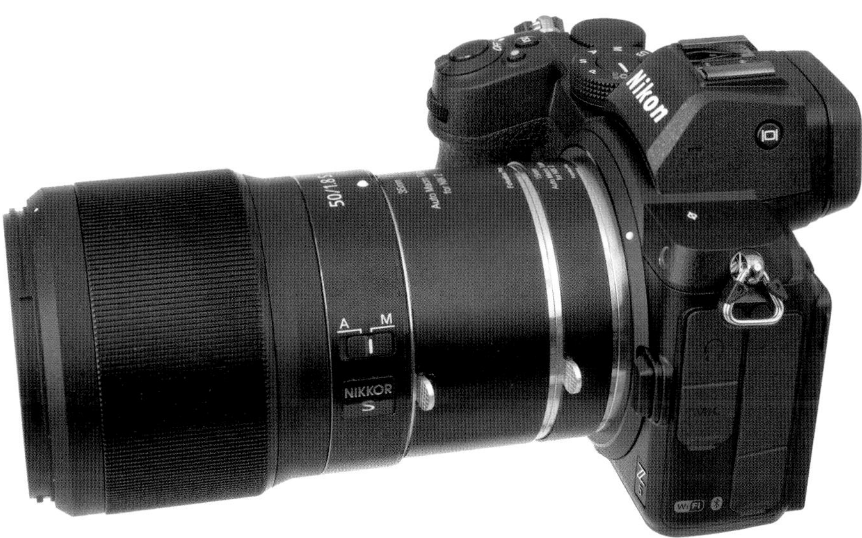

Figure 7.18 Extension tubes turn a 50mm lens into a macro optic.

- **AF-S VR Micro-Nikkor 105mm f/2.8G IF-ED.** While this $800 lens and the Z5 both offer VR, some 99 percent of the time, I shoot close-ups with my Z5 mounted on a tripod or, at the very least, on a monopod, so camera vibration is not much of a concern. Indeed, *subject* movement is a more serious problem, especially when shooting plant life outdoors on days plagued with even slight breezes. Because my outdoor subjects are likely to move while I am composing my photo, I find both VR and autofocus not very useful. I end up focusing manually most of the time, too. This lens provides a little extra camera-to-subject distance, so you'll find it very useful, but consider the older non-G, non-VR version, too, if you're in the market and don't mind losing vibration reduction features.

- **AF Micro-Nikkor 200mm f/4D IF-ED.** With a price tag of about $1,800, you'd probably want this lens only if you planned a great deal of close-up shooting at greater distances. It focuses down to 1.6 feet, and is manual focus only with the Z5, but provides enough magnification to allow interesting close-ups of subjects that are farther away. A specialized tool for specialized shooting.

- **PC Micro-Nikkor 85mm f/2.8D.** Priced about $2,000, this is a manual focus lens (on *any* camera; it doesn't offer autofocus features) that has both tilt and shift capabilities, so you can adjust the perspective of the subject as you shoot. The tilt feature lets you "tilt" the plane of focus, providing the illusion of greater depth-of-field, while the shift capabilities make it possible to shoot down on a subject from an angle and still maintain its correct proportions. If you need one of these for perspective control, you already know it; if you're still wondering how you'd use one, you probably have no need for these specialized capabilities. However, I have recently watched some very creative fashion and wedding photographers use this lens for portraits, applying the tilting features to throw parts of the image wildly out of focus to concentrate interest on faces, and so forth. None of these are likely pursuits of the average Nikon Z5 photographer, but I couldn't resist mentioning this interesting lens.

The F-Mount Magic Three

If you cruise the forums, you'll find the same three lenses mentioned over and over, often referred to as "The Trinity," "The Magic Three," or some other affectionate nickname. They are the three lenses you'll find in the kit of just about every serious Nikon photographer (including me). They're fast, expensive, heavier than you might expect, and provide such exquisite image quality that once you equip yourself with a member of the Trinity, you'll never be happy with anything else. One big advantage of these lenses is that they are all full-frame lenses, and so usable on both Nikon full-frame and DX cameras, and the hefty price you must pay for this collection won't be wasted.

Over the years, Nikon has gradually replaced the original members of the Magic Three with new lenses and upgraded the middle lens—the 24-70mm f/2.8—to VR status. The 24-70mm Z-mount kit lens is both less expensive and arguably sharper than its counterpart F-mount lens, so you should stick to that one, unless you already have an F-mount 24-70mm lens in your collection. (See Figure 7.19.)

Here are the Magic Three:

- **AF-S Nikkor 14-24mm f/2.8G ED.** I own this $1,750 lens, use it on the Z5, and its image quality is incredible, with very low barrel distortion (outward bowing at the edges) and very little of the chromatic aberrations common to lenses this wide. Because it has full-frame coverage, it's immune to obsolescence. It focuses down to 10.8 inches, allowing for some interesting close-up/wide-angle effects. The downside? The outward-curving front element precludes the use of most filters, although I haven't tried this lens with add-on Cokin-style filter holders, including one very expensive ($200) Lee Kit-SW150 Super Wide Filter Holder, which uses 150mm × 170mm and 150mm × 150mm filters. Usually, lack of filter compatibility isn't a fatal flaw for most users, as the use of polarizers, in particular, would be problematic at wider focal lengths. The polarizing effect would be highly variable because of this lens's extremely wide field of view.

- **AF-S Nikkor 24-70mm f/2.8E ED VR.** This $1,900 lens seems to provide even better image quality than any of its predecessors, especially when used wide open or in flare-inducing environments. (You can credit the new internal Nano Crystal Coat treatment for that improvement.) I recommend the Z-mount 24-70mm f/4 optic (and the 24-70mm f/2.8 Z-mount version) over this one, but if you already own one, it can be used on your mirrorless Nikon.

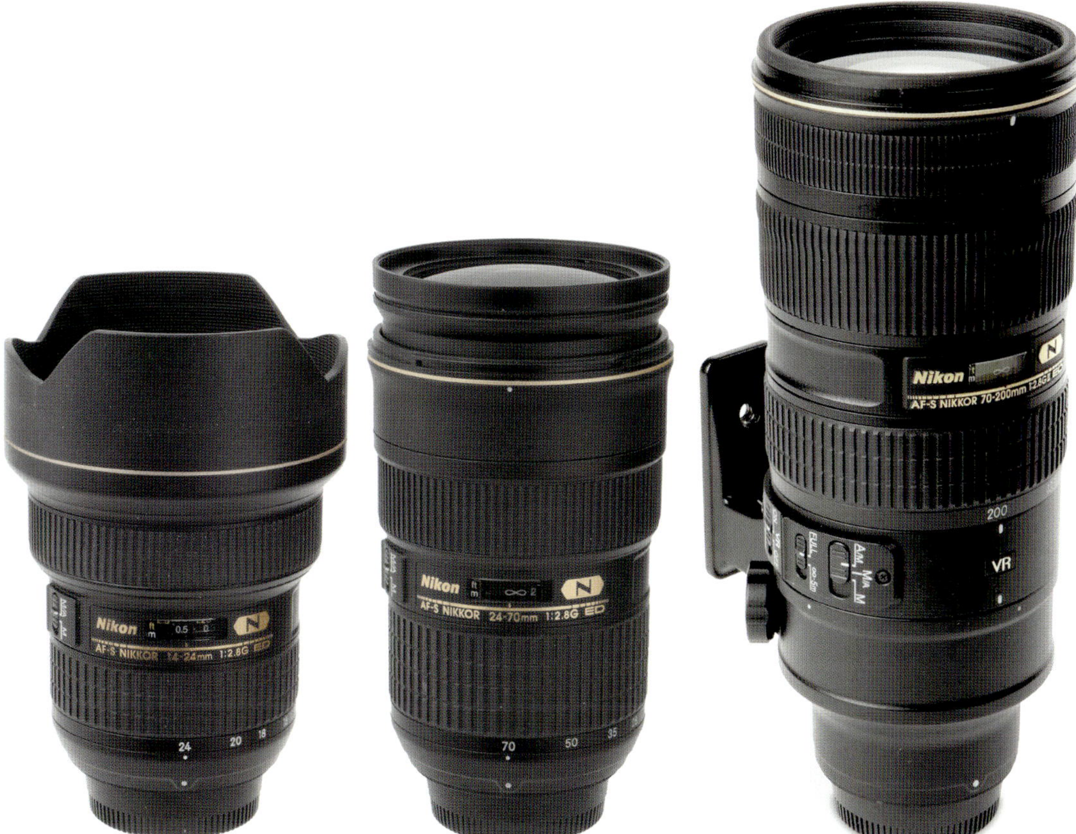

Figure 7.19 The reigning Magic Three.

- **AF-S Nikkor 70-200mm f/2.8E FL ED VR.** Not a lot to say about the latest version of this lens, introduced late in 2016 with a price tag of about $2,350. It replaces the AF-S Nikkor 70-200mm f/2.8G ED VR II, introduced in 2009, and which is still available at reduced prices from some retailers. The latest edition adds fluorite lens elements and improved VR, and exhibits less focus breathing than its predecessor, which is a worthy representative of the telephoto zoom range in this "ideal" trio of lenses. It does have better performance in the corners on full-frame cameras, but most of its other attributes remain the same.

  Nikon also offers an additional "affordable" replacement for its 70-200mm f/2.8 zoom. The Nikkor AF-S 70-200mm f/4G ED VR lens, priced at about $1,400, is a slower, lower-cost zoom with the same zoom range. It does focus down to 3.3 feet, but, unlike virtually all of Nikon's "pro" lenses, takes 67mm filters instead of the standard 77mm diameter filters. Plan to buy yourself a 67mm-77mm step-up ring.

Wide Angles

Among its FX lenses, Nikon has an interesting collection of wide-angle prime lenses and zooms, both old and new, that range in price from a few hundred dollars to around $2,000. Here's a list of some of the key lenses that are readily available. I'll describe the zooms and prime lenses separately.

- **17-35mm f/2.8D IF-ED.** This lens is still offered for about $2,000, and, unless you find a mint used copy, isn't even that affordable. It's an excellent lens, but the internal autofocus motor has been known to fail over time.

- **16-35mm f/4G ED VR AF-S.** A tiny bit slower with a constant f/4 maximum aperture, this $1,100 lens includes VR if you also use it for an F-mount Nikon, and the Z5 will automatically substitute its own IBIS. For hand-held shots, that means you won't miss f/2.8 at all. Instead of 1/60th second at f/2.8, you can shoot at 1/30th second at f/4 and expect the same sharpness.

- **18-35mm f/3.5-4.5G ED AF-S.** This is a $750 ultra-wide-angle zoom lens for those who don't want to spend the bucks for the 17-35mm and 16-35mm VR optics. It's small and light (at just under 14 ounces) and has three aspherical and two ED elements for great image quality.

Many photographers build a nice kit of lenses using only primes rather than zoom lenses. Most of these lenses are compact, light in weight, and fast, with an f/2.8 or better maximum aperture. Many of us grew up using only prime lenses—we're the folks you might have seen a few decades ago with two and three cameras around our neck, each outfitted with a different prime lens. We learned quickly how to use "sneaker zoom" to move in closer or to back up to change our field of view without swapping optics. Not all these lenses are ancient; Nikon has introduced an affordable 28mm f/1.8 lens, and two wide-angle f/1.4 lenses in 24mm and 35mm focal lengths are fairly recent additions.

- **20mm f/1.8G AF-S ED.** This is an $800 full-frame wide angle that works well on the Z5, giving you a large maximum aperture that provides a little more selective focus control despite the wide depth-of-field found in lenses of this focal length. In other words, you *can* throw your backgrounds and/or foregrounds out of focus if you shoot with this lens wide open.

- **24mm f/1.4G AF-S ED.** Oh, the howls of anguish and outrage could be heard world-wide, especially among photojournalists, when the predecessor of this lens, a 28mm f/1.4D AF optic, was discontinued without a replacement some years back. The old lens had a list price of about $2,000, and reportedly cost Nikon a lot more than that to make (which is why it was axed), and soon sold for up to $4,000 on the used market. This new, sharp, fast lens is a worthy successor, and a must-have for architectural photographers, photojournalists, and street shooters. Its roughly $2,000 price tag seems cheap compared to the prices commanded by the old 28mm f/1.4 lens.

- **24mm f/1.8G AF-S ED.** Introduced in September 2015, this lens gives you a mild wide-angle view and fast f/1.8 maximum aperture for a mere $750. It's a suitable substitute for the pricey f/1.4 version.

- **28mm f/1.8G AF-S ED.** If a maximum aperture of f/1.8 is fast enough for you, at $800, this lens is an amazing bargain at roughly one-third the price of its new 28mm f/1.4 cousin (described next) or the wider/faster 24mm f/1.4 optic listed above. It's got all the latest features, including the Nano Crystal lens coating found on most other recently introduced Nikkors for reduced flaring and ghost effects. Light in weight at 11 ounces, it focuses down to less than one foot. Unfortunately, unlike most of Nikon's "pro" lenses, it takes 67mm filters instead of 77mm filters. You may be able to find a very thin step-up ring that allows you to mount the larger filters without vignetting.

- **28mm f/1.4E AF-S ED.** Apparently, Nikon feels you can never have enough f/1.4 lenses in your lineup. Introduced in 2017, this lens commands a premium $2,000 price. It has nine diaphragm blades for smooth out-of-focus highlights (bokeh), and Nikon claims it has "stunning sharpness, edge-to-edge clarity, and virtually no distortion or aberrations."

- **35mm f/1.4G AF-S.** If you need a fast f/1.4 aperture and a slightly narrower field of view, this lens should fill the bill. It, too, takes 67mm filters, and is priced a few hundred dollars south of $2,000. Most photojournalists you know, and more than a few architectural photographers, probably own this lens.

- **35mm f/1.8G AF-S.** I recommend the current Nikon Z 35mm f/1.8 S lens over this one, but if you already own one, you can get by just fine with this F-mount version. Only one-half stop slower than the f/1.4 wide angle above, this lens costs about $525, and is a good performer as a fast wide-angle prime. It includes one aspheric and one ED element to provide excellent image quality and focuses down to about 10 inches. Its chief drawback is the odd-ball 58mm filter size; if you want to avoid buying yet another polarizer or neutral-density filter set, you'll need an adapter ring that doesn't cause vignetting with your current filters. Don't confuse this with the older, less-expensive 35mm f/1.8G AF-S DX Nikkor, which is not a full-frame lens.

Wide-to-Medium/Long Zooms

There aren't too many "do-everything" walk-around lenses for the Z5, other than the 24-70mm Z-mount lens, but this list offers some useful alternatives.

- **24-120mm f/4G ED AF-S VR.** I mentioned this lens earlier in the chapter as a basic walk-around optic. I really love the newest version of this lens. But caveat emptor! Nikon has offered *three* different lenses in this focal length range, and this latest model is the good one. Accept no substitute! The original 24-120mm f/3.5-5.6 AF-D lens was produced from 1996 through 2002 and was replaced in 2003 with a version having similar specs, but with an internal AF-S motor and vibration reduction. Neither lens was the sharpest optic in the drawer, but they were popular because of their useful focal length range. This latest version has a constant f/4 aperture, and produces much better image quality, with the VR making it an excellent walk-about lens for hand-held exposures. Priced in the $1,100 range, it's almost a bargain for what it does: giving you everything from moderate wide angle to short telephoto focal lengths.

  Last winter, when I moved my office to the Florida Keys temporarily to escape the brutal weather, I found myself unexpectedly needing to do some product photography on a seamless background. I was amazed to find that this lens functioned quite handily as a macro lens. It was even more versatile than I'd thought.

- **24-85mm f/3.5-4.5G AF-S ED VR.** Introduced in June 2012 with a current affordable $500 price tag and intended as a "cheap" full-frame lens for Nikon's new low-end FX cameras like the D610, this zoom works just fine on a Nikon Z5. It's shorter and lighter than the 24-120mm zoom.

- **28-300mm f/3.5-5.6G AF-S ED VR.** This is the closest thing Nikon offers to an "all-around" lens for F-mount and (adapted) Z-mount cameras. It's shy of two pounds at 28 ounces, fairly compact, and features the second edition of Nikon's vibration reduction technology. At a little less than $1,000, it's fairly affordable, too.

Telephoto and Normal Lenses

The "normal"-to-medium telephoto range is useful for photojournalism and street photography in situations where you have room to back up and don't want the apparent distortion that wider lenses can add when some elements are particularly close to the lens. Wide-angle and perspective distortion is just fine when you want to use it as a creative element, but if not, you'll want to consider one of these lenses. They're also good for portraits for the same reason: objects that are closer to the lens (such as human noses) aren't rendered disproportionately large, with more distant objects (ears) too small (which can be the case with wide-angle lenses). Humans look more natural when photographed with lenses in this range, as longer lenses (150mm and above) tend to "flatten" faces and make them appear wider. "Normal" is defined as focal lengths roughly equivalent to the diagonal of the image frame, which in the case of a full-frame camera is about 45mm (43.3mm precisely), and about 30mm on a DX camera like the Z5's stablemate the Z50.

Here are some normal-to-medium lenses:

- **50mm f/1.2 AI-S.** I'm including this older-design, manual focus lens because quite a mystique has developed around so-called "super-speed" optics, including the remarkable (and remarkably expensive) F-mount Nikon 58mm f/1.2 Noct (which can cost upward of $3,000 on the used market) and the upcoming Z-mount reboot with the $6,000 price tag. While both Nocts are sensational wide open, this one is merely good at f/1.2, but it's quite usable (and really sharpens up by f/2) and a *lot* more affordable at around $700. If you *must* have the fastest lens available, consider this one. Given the very shallow depth-of-field at wide apertures, you probably would want to focus this one manually, anyway. I own one and tend to use it more on my Nikon Df rather than with the Z5, because its true-retro design looks cool on the neo-retro Df.

- **50mm f/1.4G AF-S.** This is the replacement for the D-version of this lens. It's reasonably sharp, and costs more at around $450, but offers faster AF-S focusing. If you have a large collection of 52mm filters (which fit many old and new Nikon prime lenses), they won't fit on this lens without a step-down ring. It takes the larger 58mm variety.

- **58mm f/1.4G AF-S.** If you think that eight extra millimeters of focal length can't possibly make this lens worth an extra grand more than its 50mm f/1.4 cousin described above, you're missing the point. This one is, quite simply, one of the sharpest F-mount lenses Nikon offers, even wide open, besting its 24mm, 35mm, 50mm, and 85mm f/1.4 stablemates at maximum aperture. *That's* what you'll be paying roughly $1,700 for, and if you're a photojournalist or wedding photographer, you'll think it's worth it. Although it's an AF-S lens, autofocus is a bit on the slow side. I already own an old 58mm f/1.4 manual focus Nikkor, and the two lenses have nothing in common—including filter size. My 1960s-era 58mm takes Nikon's then-standard 52mm filters, and this one has a 72mm filter thread (not Nikon's 77mm "pro" size).

- **50mm f/1.8G AF-S.** Nikon updated the older D-version of this lens, adding an internal Silent Wave motor for faster focusing, deleting the useful aperture ring, and almost doubling the price to $220. This version makes sense for entry-level Nikon cameras, but it is suitable for the Z5 only if you need a fast 50mm lens and can't afford the tariff on the Z-mount version.

Medium-to-Long Telephoto

I tend to shoot either ultra-wide, with fisheyes or lenses (for landscapes, interiors, exteriors, street photography, and for perspective exaggeration), or use this medium-to-long telephoto focal length range (for portraits, sports, fashion, and isolating subjects using selective focus). Probably 80 percent of my images are made using lenses in one of those two categories. So, I tend to lump all the lenses in this group together in my mind. They all do about the same thing and, surprisingly, almost all equally well. Here are some brief descriptions of your choices:

- **70-300mm f/4-5.6G AF.** This is the low-end ($170), bargain lens in the group, which can be found for a couple hundred bucks. It's slow, lacks VR, but you can't beat the versatility it gives you at this price.

- **70-300mm f/4.5-5.6E AF-P ED VR.** New in 2017, and now priced at about $600, this lens replaces the older 70-300mm f/4.5-5.6G AF-S VR, which is still available for about $750. Either of these lenses are a better choice for most than the AF lens listed above, because they add AF-S focus and vibration reduction.

- **70-200mm f/2.8G ED AF-S VR II.** Anyone who can afford this lens will never regret their purchase.
- **80-400mm f/4.5-5.6G ED AF-S VR.** If you're looking for a telephoto zoom with a long focal length range, and have an extra $2,300 you don't need, Nikon may tempt you with this optically improved version, more road-hugging weight in its large frame (47 ounces), closer focusing, and flare-thwarting Super Nano Coat. Those in the prime of life willing to sling 5 pounds of Z5 and lens around their necks will find this to be a supremely versatile optic.

Medium Telephoto

One advantage of medium telephoto prime lenses is that they are all quite fast, with maximum apertures of f/1.4 to f/4, which makes them an excellent choice for portraits, sports, animals, and other subjects that don't call for a really long lens. Their large f/stops are great for selective focus and allow you to use faster shutter speeds for hand-held shooting.

- **85mm f/1.4G AF-S.** In its never-ending quest to upgrade its older AF lenses to AF-S, Nikon introduced this highly rated G version of the Cream Machine at $1,600. It's excellent, and offers a bit more autofocus speed.
- **105mm f/1.4E ED AF-S.** What a dream lens for the portrait shooter! I cut my teeth on a Nikkor 105mm f/2.5 manual focus lens many moons ago and used it for most of the portraits I shot until I purchased the 85mm f/1.4 and 70-200mm f/2.8 lenses. This lens ($2,200) should go to the top of any people-shooting photographer's wish list. It has superb sharpness wide open at f/1.4, great bokeh, and I find that its focal length is great for head-and-shoulders portraits when you want to defocus the background, or even part of your subject. (See Figure 7.20.) The tendency of this focal length to "flatten" faces isn't noticeable with the type of subjects I shoot. It could be a good lens for intimate street photography and some sports, too.
- **300mm f/4D AF-S IF-ED.** This lens isn't really a "medium" telephoto, but it is a prime lens, and I didn't want to toss it in with the more exotic lenses in the section that follows this one. I love this lens. Although I once shot sports professionally full-time, I only manage two or three events for each of my favorite sports these days (soccer, football, basketball, motor sports, hockey, volleyball, baseball, and track), and can't justify keeping the wonderful 300mm f/2.8 lens in my collection. This one is a more reasonably priced ($1,000–$1,500) alternative. It works fine with my Nikon teleconverters, so I can transform it into a 420mm f/5.6 (with the 1.4X converter) or 510mm f/6.3 (1.7X teleconverter) with ease. You'll probably use this lens mounted on a tripod or monopod most of the time, and, if so, you should be aware that the factory tripod mount flexes. I replaced mine with an improved mount from Kirk and get sharper images.
- **300mm f/4E AF-S PF ED VR.** We Nikon users are starting to get spoiled by the camera-freezing powers of vibration reduction, so the introduction of this replacement for the older 300mm f/4D lens was no surprise. Neither was the $2,000 price tag. VR makes this lens much more usable hand-held than its older sibling: you can often get shake-free images at 1/250th second or even slower, something generally not possible with the non-VR version.

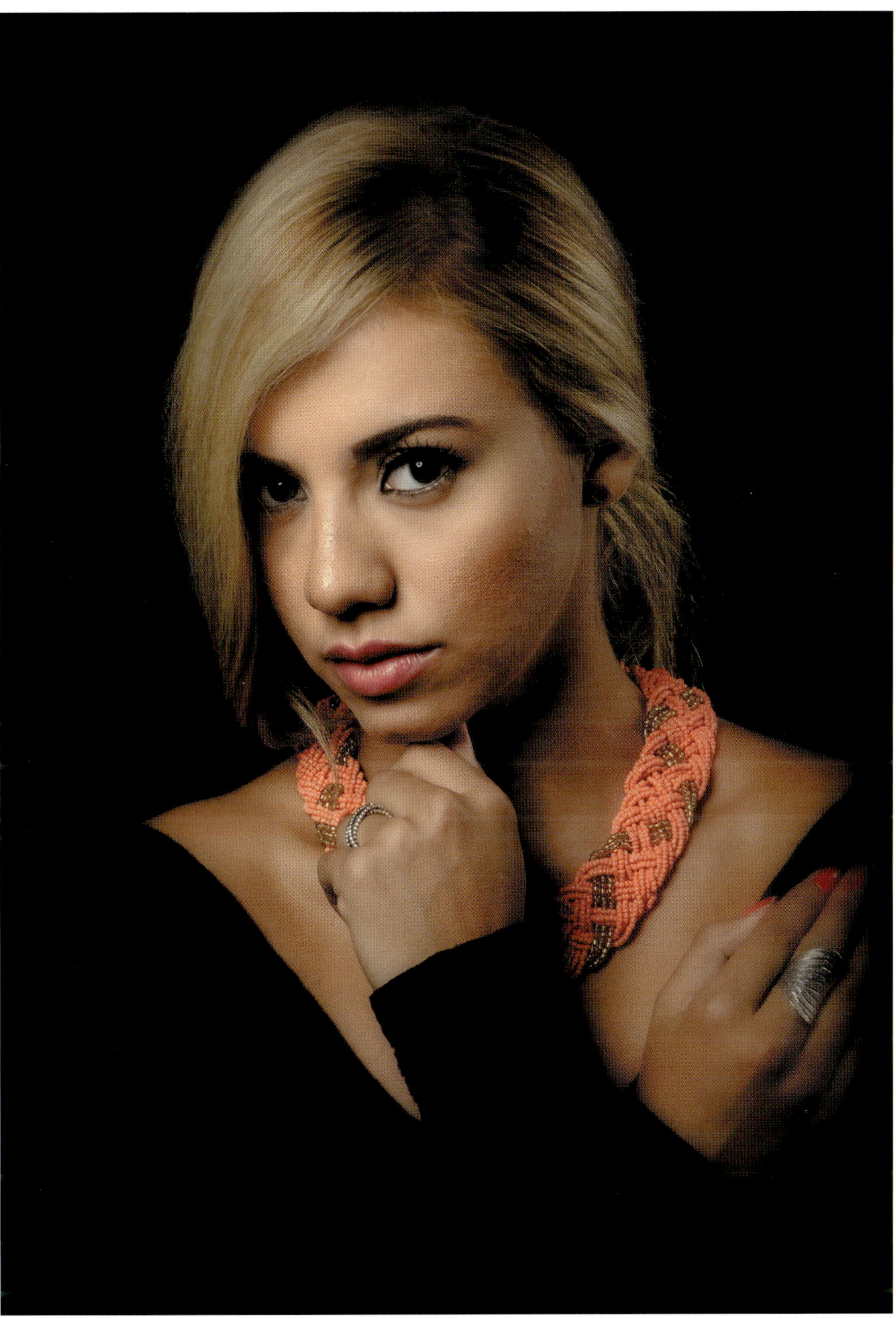

Figure 7.20 A lens with an f/1.4 maximum aperture is perfect for portrait photography.

Exotic Long Lenses

These are the lenses that most of us borrow, or lust after, and usually end up purchasing a car or a house with the funds instead. I see photographer friends hefting the 500mm f/4 or 600mm f/4 around sporting events all the time, and as I watch them huff and puff my envy evaporates. But if you're heavily involved in wildlife photography, sports, or double-naught spy activities, you can probably justify at least one of these. All are very fast, with constant maximum apertures of f/4 *or better,* feature the latest internal Silent Wave focus motors, and VR.

- **200-500mm f/5.6E ED AF-S VR.** Given a focal length range that tops out at 500mm, this is theoretically an "exotic" long lens. But its $1,400 price puts this super-zoom within the reach of the average Nikon-loving spendthrift. It's got vibration reduction (if you're also using it on an F-mount camera), focuses down to 7.2 feet, and has a constant maximum aperture that doesn't vary as you zoom from 200mm to 500mm. What's not to like? Well, its largest f/stop—f/5.6—is the main fly in the ointment, limiting sports shooters to daytime photography in many cases. Its best f/stops are f/8 and f/11, and even with VR you'd want to use shutter speeds of 1/2000th second or better (unless you're after some subject motion blur to represent movement). That translates into typical settings of 1/2000th second at f/11 and ISO 1000—in broad daylight. Wildlife photographers would probably want to use this lens mounted on a tripod, and low-light photography of any sort would call for higher ISO settings and/or a tripod. Even so, a 200-500mm zoom at this price is quite exciting and is a reasonable substitute for the 200-400mm lens described next.

- **200-400mm f/4G AF-S ED VR II.** This is an amazing lens, and one that a great many photographers who probably couldn't justify a copy end up mortgaging their houses to buy (at around $7,000). At least, that's what I glean from the forum postings by photographers who are agonizing over being forced to sell this lens to keep the wolf at bay. It's sharp, more than 14 inches long and seven pounds in heft, and one of the most versatile lenses in this group for wildlife and sports photographers. And, it's one of the few Nikon lenses that comes with its own "protective" filter, what Nikon calls a "dedicated protective glass" (which itself is furnished with a separate case). You can slip actual 52mm filters into a slot in the rear of the lens, though. The newest version, introduced in 2010, has the nano coating for reduced flare. This is another lens that almost demands a third-party replacement for the factory tripod collar. This lens is heavy enough that you'll be using it on a tripod or monopod most of the time.

- **200mm f/2G AF-S ED VR II / 300mm f/2.8G AF-S VR II IF-ED.** This pair of lenses is fast and primarily useful for sports photography under waning light conditions (both are a bit too short for wildlife in the wild). Priced in the $6,000 range, both are fast enough to be used with Nikon's 1.4X, 1.7X, or 2X teleconverters.

- **400mm f/2.8E AF-S FL ED VR / 500mm f/4E FL ED VR / 600mm f/4E FL AF-S ED VR / 800mm f/5.6E ED VR.** A set of these four lenses, all of the new E (electronic aperture control) type, will deduct more than $50,000 from your wallet, but they are the ultimate sports or wildlife lenses, or for capturing images of the Great Wall of China from the International Space Station. The 500mm and 600mm lenses were introduced in 2015, replacing earlier models with similar performance (and price tags).

Perspective Control/Special Lenses

My first perspective control lens was a 35mm f/3.5 PC-Nikkor that I still own. It was manual focus, manual exposure, manual aperture, shifted but didn't tilt, and I had to machine down part of the sliding mechanism so it wouldn't bump against the metering head of my Nikon film camera. In those days, PC lenses were used primarily for architectural photography and some product photography to allow keeping the focal plane of the camera parallel with a subject to avoid a tilted/distorted effect.

Things have changed! Today shift/tilt photography is so popular that Nikon and other vendors are building a faux perspective/focus control capability right into the camera as a "Miniature Effect" retouching aid. While lenses like Nikon's PC-E line are still useful for their original purpose—perspective control—I've seen some absolutely brilliant portrait and wedding photography that uses tilt/shift capabilities as a dreamy focus control. Wedding guru Parker Pfister comes to mind (although he's a Canon guy; don't hold it against him), but you can find this tool used everywhere you look. The lenses currently in the Nikon lineup are listed next, along with one additional "special" lens, an odd-ball fisheye that fit nowhere else in this chapter's discussions. A new 19mm PC-E lens is rumored but was not introduced at the time I wrote this book.

- **19mm f/4 PC-E ED.** The latest addition to the Nikon perspective control line is this $3,400 19mm ultra-wide-angle lens. When applied to architectural applications, the wider the shift/tilt lens the better, and this one beats the previous Nikkor 24mm champ, described next. It shifts plus or minus 12mm, tilts plus/minus 7.5 degrees, and has a minimum focus distance of less than 10 inches.

- **24mm f/3.5D PC-E ED.** Priced in the $2,200 range, this 24mm lens shifts plus or minus 11mm from side to side and plus or minus 8.5-degrees tilt. The mechanism rotates 90 degrees in two directions so you can apply the corrections/distortions from virtually any angle. It focuses down to about eight inches, so you can use its effects for close-ups and product/model photography. The big surprise for those who aren't old-timers is that this can be used as a *pre-set* lens. You set the f/stop you want to use on a ring and focus with the lens wide open. Then, when you're ready to shoot, press the aperture button and the lens stops down to the selected f/stop. However, Nikon has included an electronic auto aperture mechanism that can provide automatic stop-down with the Z5. The shifting/tilting mechanism precludes autofocus.

- **45mm f/2.8 PC-E ED Micro Nikkor.** With the same amount of shifting/tilting available, this $2,000-plus lens (and its 85mm counterpart, next) is classified as a macro lens, focusing down to about 10 inches and providing a half-life-size image on the sensor.

- **85mm f/2.8D PC-E Micro Nikkor.** This is the PC-E lens you'd want to use for your dreamy wedding portraits. Priced at about $2,000, it shifts and tilts the same amount as the other and focuses down to 1.3 feet.

- **16mm f/2.8D AF Fisheye-Nikkor.** Okay, I admit I'm the world's most avid fisheye user. I owned Nikon's exotic 7.5mm f/5.6 fisheye back in the days of film, and would have it today except that the lens required locking up the mirror and using an auxiliary viewfinder in a mode quite incompatible with any of Nikon's digital cameras. (Nikon later introduced fisheyes that didn't require mirror lock-up.) I still own Nikon's 16mm f/3.5 manual focus/pre-AI fisheye, as well as a Tokina 10-17mm fisheye zoom, a Sigma 15mm f/2.8 autofocus fisheye, and a Rokinon 12mm f/2.8 manual focus fisheye. This full-frame (non-circular image) autofocus model, which can be purchased for about $1,000, is probably the most practical of the bunch. It fills the FX frame with lines that exhibit a gloriously frightful amount of barrel distortion. When I travel overseas, I take along my two "main" lenses (17-35mm f/2.8 and 28-200G zoom) and a fisheye "fun" lens like this one.

- **8-15mm AF-S Fisheye-Nikkor f/3.5-4.5E ED.** This latest addition to my fisheye collection is an interesting zoom lens that allows you to go from a curved full-frame image to an eye-catching circular fisheye image with the touch of a zoom ring. It retails for about $1,250 new, but I picked up mine refurbished from Nikon for much, much less. As I was writing this book, I ventured out to photograph all 18 covered bridges in Ashtabula County, Ohio, including the one shown in Figure 7.21.

  I also purchased my 200-500mm f/5.6 as a Nikon refurb; both lenses came packaged and appearing exactly as new. I suspect the company sometimes unloads overstock at these bargain prices, so be sure to check out the Certified Refurbished pages that appear at the Nikon Store online (https://www.nikonusa.com/en/nikon-store/refurbished-cameras.page).

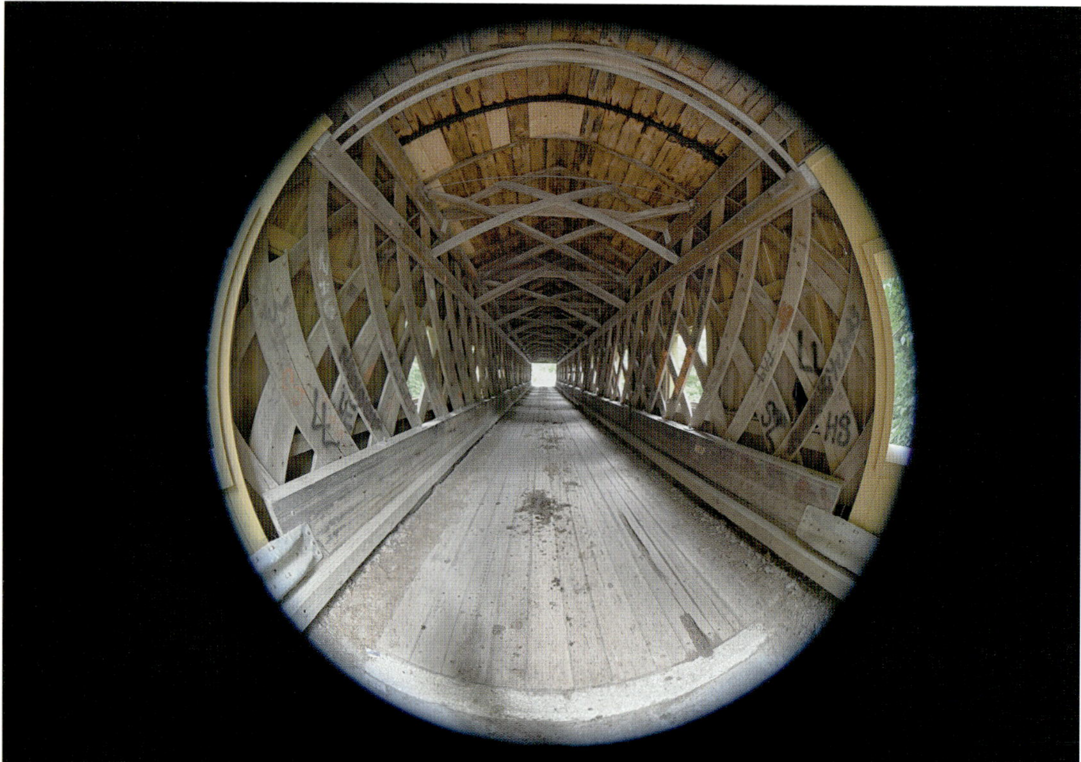

Figure 7.21 Fisheyes are great for shooting in tight spaces.

Mastering Light   8

The key tool we use to create and shape our images is light itself, in all its many forms and textures. Indeed, it's said that Sir John Herschel coined the term "photography" from the Greek words for "writing with light" in a paper read before the Royal Society in March 1839. Our dependence on the qualities of the light we use to produce our images is absolute. An adept photographer knows how to compensate for too much or too little illumination, how to soften harsh lighting to mask defects, or increase its contrast to evoke shape and detail. Sometimes, we must adjust our cameras for the apparent "color" of light, use a brief burst of it to freeze action, or filter it to reduce glare.

The many ways we can work with light deserve three full chapters in this book. This chapter introduces using *continuous* lighting (such as daylight, incandescent, LED, or fluorescent sources). I'll cover the brilliant snippets of light we call *electronic flash,* in Chapters 9 and 10.

Light That's Available

You'll often hear the term *available light,* meaning the ambient light at a scene, including whatever illumination is present outdoors during the day or at night, and that provided by lighting fixtures, windows, and other sources. In practice, available light includes any sort of illumination that's available, and can include supplementary lighting added by the photographer in the form of additional lamps, reflectors, or studio continuous light sources.

For our purposes, continuous lighting is exactly what you might think: uninterrupted illumination that is available all the time during a shooting session. Daylight, moonlight, and the artificial lighting encountered both indoors and outdoors count as continuous light sources (although all of them can be "interrupted" by passing clouds, solar eclipses, a blown fuse, or simply by switching a lamp off). Indoor continuous illumination includes both the lights that are there already (such as incandescent lamps or overhead fluorescent lights indoors) and fixtures you supply yourself, including photoflood lamps or reflectors used to bounce existing light onto your subject.

Electronic flash is notable because it can be much more intense than continuous lighting, lasts only a brief moment, and can be much more portable than supplementary incandescent sources. It's a light source you can carry with you and use anywhere. There are advantages and disadvantages to each type of illumination. Here's a quick checklist of pros and cons:

Continuous lighting differs from electronic flash, which illuminates our photographs only in brief bursts. Flash, or "strobe" light is notable because it can be much more intense than continuous lighting, lasts only a moment, and can be much more portable than supplementary incandescent sources. It's a light source you can carry with you and use anywhere. There are advantages and disadvantages to each type of illumination. Here's a quick checklist of pros and cons:

- **Lighting preview—Pro: continuous lighting.** With continuous lighting, thanks to the Z5's real-time sensor image through the viewfinder or LCD monitor, if you've opted to activate Custom Setting d7: Apply Settings to Live View, you'll always know exactly what kind of lighting effect you're going to get—including color balance—and, if multiple lights are used, how they will interact with each other. If the natural light present in a scene is perfect for the image you're trying to capture, you'll know immediately (see Figure 8.1).

- **Lighting preview—Con: electronic flash.** With flash, unless you have a modeling light built into the flash, the general effect you're going to see may be a mystery until you've built some experience, and you may need to review a shot, make some adjustments, and then reshoot to get the look you want. (In this sense, a digital camera's review capabilities replace the Polaroid test shots pro photographers relied on in decades past.) An image like the candle-lit scene in Figure 8.1 would have been difficult to achieve with an off-camera battery-powered flash unit, because it would be tricky to balance the illumination of the candles with the light from the flash. While the modeling light feature offered by some Nikon flash units can be helpful, it's not a true continuous modeling light.

- **Exposure calculation—Pro: continuous lighting.** Your Z5 has no problem calculating exposure for continuous lighting, because it remains constant and can be measured directly from the light reaching the sensor. The amount of light available just before the exposure will, in almost all cases, be the same amount of light present when the shutter is released. The Z5's Spot metering mode can be used to measure and compare the proportions of light in the highlights and shadows, so you can make an adjustment (such as using more or less fill light) if necessary. If you want the utmost precision, you can even use a hand-held light meter to measure the light yourself, and then set the shutter speed and aperture to match in Manual exposure mode.

- **Exposure calculation—Con: electronic flash.** Electronic flash illumination doesn't exist until the flash fires, and so can't be measured by the Z5's exposure sensor at the moment of exposure. Instead, the light must be measured by metering the intensity of a *pre-flash* triggered an instant *before* the main flash, as it is reflected back to the camera and through the lens. A less attractive alternative, available with higher-end Nikon flash units like the SB-5000 or SB-910, is to use a sensor built into the external flash itself and measure reflected light that bounces back, but which has not traveled through the lens. If you have a do-it-yourself bent, there are hand-held flash meters, too, including models that measure both flash and continuous light, so you need only one meter for both types of illumination.

- **Evenness of illumination—Pro/con: continuous lighting.** Of the continuous light sources, daylight, in particular, provides illumination that tends to fill an image completely, lighting up the foreground, background, and your subject almost equally. Shadows do come into play, of course, so you might need to use reflectors or fill in additional light sources to even out the illumination

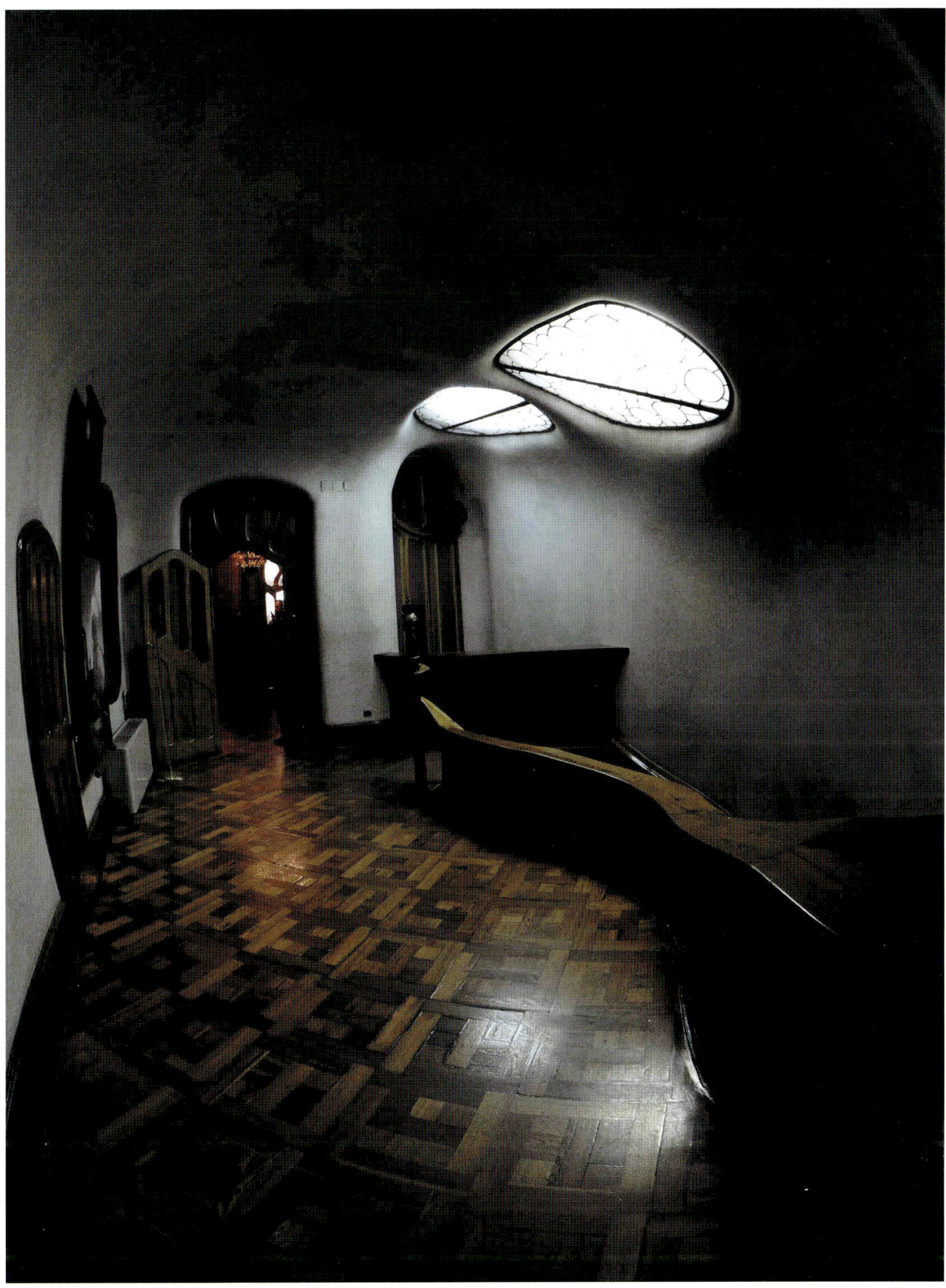

Figure 8.1 You always know how the lighting will look when using continuous illumination.

further. But, barring objects that block large sections of your image from daylight, the light is spread fairly evenly. Indoors, however, continuous lighting is commonly less evenly distributed. The average living room, for example, has hot spots near the lamps and overhead lights, and dark corners located farther from those light sources. But on the plus side, you can easily *see* this uneven illumination and compensate with additional lamps.

- **Evenness of illumination—Con: electronic flash.** Electronic flash units, like continuous light sources such as lamps that don't have the advantage of being located 93 million miles from the subject, suffer from the effects of their proximity. The *inverse square law*, first applied to both gravity and light by Sir Isaac Newton, dictates that as a light source's distance increases from the subject, the amount of light reaching the subject falls off proportionately to the square of the distance. In plain English, that means that a flash or lamp that's twelve feet away from a subject provides only one-quarter as much illumination as a source that's six feet away (rather than half as much). This translates into relatively shallow "depth-of-light." I'll discuss this aspect again in Chapter 9.

- **Action stopping—Pro: electronic flash.** When it comes to the ability to freeze moving objects in their tracks, the advantage goes to electronic flash. The brief duration of electronic flash serves as a very high "shutter speed" when the flash is the main or only source of illumination for the photo. Your Z5's shutter speed may be set for 1/200th second during a flash exposure, but if the flash illumination predominates, the *effective* exposure time will be the 1/1000th to 1/50000th second or less duration of the flash, as you can see in Figure 8.2, because the flash unit reduces the amount of light released by cutting short the duration of the flash. The only fly in the ointment is that, if the ambient light is strong enough, it may produce a secondary, "ghost" exposure, as I'll explain in Chapter 9.

- **Action stopping—Con: continuous lighting.** Action stopping with continuous light sources is completely dependent on the shutter speed you've dialed in on the camera. And the speeds available are dependent on the amount of light available and your ISO sensitivity setting. Outdoors in daylight, there will probably be enough sunlight to let you shoot at 1/2000th second and f/6.3 with a non-grainy sensitivity setting for your Z5 of ISO 400. That's a fairly useful combination of settings if you're not using a super-telephoto with a small maximum aperture. But inside, the reduced illumination quickly has you pushing your Z5 to its limits. For example, if you're shooting indoor sports, there probably won't be enough available light to allow you to use a 1/2000th second shutter speed (although I routinely shoot indoor basketball with my Z5 at ISO 1600 and 1/500th second at f/4). In many indoor sports situations, the lack of available light, and the Z5's increased visual noise at settings of ISO 6400 and above, you may find yourself limited to 1/500th second or slower.

- **Cost—Pro: continuous lighting.** Incandescent, fluorescent, or LED lamps are generally much less expensive than electronic flash units, which can easily cost several hundred dollars. I've used everything from desktop high-intensity lamps to reflector flood lights for continuous illumination at very little cost. There are lamps made especially for photographic purposes, too. Maintenance is economical, too: many incandescent or fluorescents use bulbs that cost only a few dollars, and LED lamps are not only much less costly to operate, they are virtually immortal.

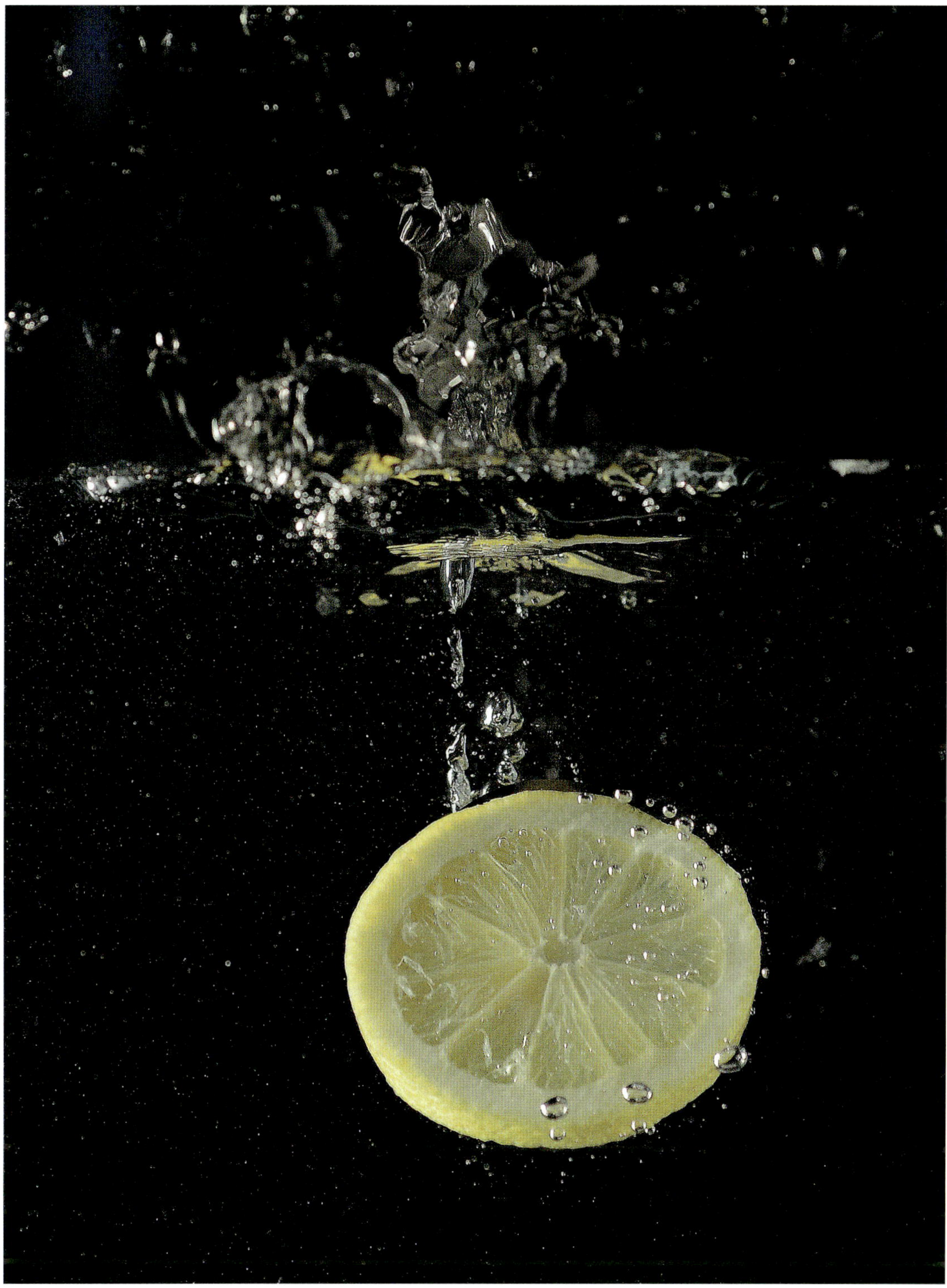

Figure 8.2 Electronic flash can freeze almost any action.

- **Cost—Con: electronic flash.** Electronic flash units aren't particularly cheap. The lowest-cost dedicated flash designed specifically for the Nikon dSLRs is about $150 (the SB-300), and it is probably not powerful enough for an advanced camera like the Z5. Such basic units are limited in features and intended for those with entry-level cameras like the Nikon D3500. Plan on spending some money to get the features that a sophisticated electronic flash offers.

- **Flexibility—Pro: electronic flash.** Electronic flash's action-freezing power allows you to work without a tripod in the studio (and elsewhere), adding flexibility and speed when choosing angles and positions. Flash units can be easily filtered, and, because the filtration is placed over the light source rather than the lens, you don't need to use high-quality filter material. For example, Roscoe or Lee lighting gels, which may be too flimsy to use in front of the lens, can be mounted or taped in front of your flash with ease.

- **Flexibility—Con: continuous lighting.** Because incandescent and fluorescent lamps are not as bright as electronic flash, the slower shutter speeds required (see "Action stopping," above) mean that you may have to use a tripod more often, especially when shooting portraits. The incandescent variety of continuous lighting gets hot, especially in the studio, and the side effects range from discomfort (for your human models) to disintegration (if you happen to be shooting perishable foods like ice cream). The heat also makes it more difficult to add filtration to incandescent sources. (It's no wonder that LED illumination is rapidly becoming the go-to continuous light source for photography.)

Continuous Lighting Basics

While continuous lighting and its effects are generally much easier to visualize and use than electronic flash, there are some factors you need to consider, particularly the color temperature of the light, how accurately a given form of illumination reproduces colors (we've all seen the ghastly looks human faces assume under mercury-vapor lamps outdoors), and other considerations.

One important aspect is color temperature. Of course, color temperature concerns aren't exclusive to continuous light sources, but the variations tend to be more extreme and less predictable than those of electronic flash, which output relatively consistent daylight-like illumination.

Living with Color Temperature

Nikon has been valiant in its efforts to help us tame the color balance monster. Some earlier Nikon pro cameras (the last one being the Nikon D2Xs) had a bindi-like white dot on their "foreheads," which measured ambient color temperature. Although this special sensor was abandoned by Nikon long before the Z5 was introduced, the technology lives on in the form of ExpoDisc filter/caps and their ilk (www.expoimaging.com), which allow the camera's built-in custom white balance measuring feature to evaluate the illumination that passes through the disc/cap/filter/Pringle's can lid, or whatever neutral-color substitute you employ. (A white or gray card also works.) To help us tangle with the many different types of non-incandescent/non-daylight sources, Nikon has provided the Z5 with seven different presets for fluorescents, sodium-vapor, and mercury-vapor illumination. If those aren't enough, you can select a specific color temperature, or capture and save up to six white balance settings for retrieval later.

In practical terms, color temperature is how "bluish" or how "reddish" the light appears to be to the digital camera's sensor. Indoor illumination is quite warm, comparatively, and appears reddish to the sensor. Daylight, in contrast, seems much bluer to the sensor. Our eyes (our brains, actually) are quite adaptable to these variations, so white objects don't appear to have an orange tinge when viewed indoors, nor do they seem excessively blue outdoors in full daylight. Yet, these color temperature variations are real, and the sensor is not fooled. To capture the most accurate colors, we need to take the color temperature into account in setting the color balance (or *white balance*) of the Z5—either automatically using the camera's smarts or manually using our own knowledge and experience. Table 8.1 provides a summary of what you need to know, and where you can look for explanations. You'll find a discussion of white balance bracketing in Chapter 4.

TABLE 8.1 White Balance Adjustment Options

TYPE OF ADJUSTMENT	OPTIONS	LOCATION	EXPLANATION
Color balance presets	Auto (three options); Incandescent; Fluorescent (seven options); Sunlight (three options, plus adjustment); Flash	Photo Shooting menu	Chapter 11
Choose color temperature	2,500K–10,000K	Photo Shooting menu	Chapter 11
Fine-tune color balance	Adjust white balance along blue/amber, magenta/green axes, or both	Photo Shooting menu	Chapter 11
Manual color balance	Capture white balance or use existing photo's white balance	Photo Shooting menu	Chapter 11
White balance bracketing/ Bracket order	2, 3, 5, 7, or 9 bracketed images using three increments	Custom Settings menu, BKT button/command dials	Chapter 4, Chapter 12

The only time you need to think in terms of actual color temperature is when you're making adjustments using the Choose Color Temp. setting in the White Balance entry within the Photo Shooting menu, which, as I'll describe in Chapter 11, allows you to dial in exact color temperatures, if known. You can also shift and bias color balance along the blue/amber and magenta/green axes, and bracket white balance.

In most cases, however, one of the three Auto settings in the Photo Shooting menu's White Balance entry—Keep White (Reduce Warm Colors), Normal, or Keep Warm Lighting Colors—will do a good job of calculating white balance for you. Auto can be used as your choice most of the time. Use the preset values ($Auto_0$, $Auto_1$, or $Auto_2$) or set a custom white balance that matches the current shooting conditions when you need to.

Remember that if you shoot RAW, you can specify the white balance of your image when you import it into Photoshop, Photoshop Elements, or another image editor using Capture NX-D, Adobe Camera Raw, or your preferred RAW converter. While color-balancing filters that fit on the front of the lens exist, they are primarily useful for film cameras, because film's color balance can't be tweaked as extensively as that of a sensor.

Color Rendering

Faithful color rendition goes beyond color temperature. So-called "white" light is produced by a spectrum of colors that, when added together, provide the neutral color needed for accuracy. Artificial light sources don't necessarily offer the same balanced spectrum found in sunlight. Some portions of the spectrum may be deficient or truncated or include gaps with certain wavelengths missing entirely. Astronomers use their knowledge of which elements absorb which colors of light to calculate the makeup of distant stars using spectrographs. In photography, the analysis of spectra is used to calculate the color rendering index, which measures how accurately colors are presented.

All artificial light sources have a color rendering index (CRI). That figure is calculated by rating eight different colors on a scale of 0 to 100, based on how natural the color looks compared to a perfect or "reference" light source at a particular color temperature. A CRI of 80-plus is considered acceptable; for critical applications like photography, a CRI higher than 93 is best. Incandescent and halogen bulbs typically have a CRI of 100 compared to a reference light source at the same color temperature. Standard LED lamps are rated at 83, although some can have CRIs as high as 98. Many types of fluorescent lights fall into the CRI 50 to 75 range.

Vendors, such as GE and Sylvania, may actually provide a figure known as the color rendering index on the packaging using a scale of 0 (some sodium-vapor lamps) to 100 (daylight and most incandescent lamps). Daylight fluorescents and deluxe cool white fluorescents suitable for photography might have a CRI of about 79 to 95, which is perfectly acceptable for most photographic applications. Less desirable are warm white fluorescents, which may have a CRI of 55. White deluxe mercury vapor lights are even less suitable with a CRI of 45, while low-pressure sodium lamps can vary from CRI 0 to 18. If you're using such a source not intended for photography, it may be worth your while to determine its color rendering index before you shoot. The figure is often supplied on the packaging of the light source.

White Balance Bracketing

As I explained in Chapter 4, with WB bracketing the Z5 takes a single shot, and then saves 2, 3, or 5 (your choice) JPEG copies, each with a different color balance. It's not necessary to capture multiple shots, as the camera uses the raw information retrieved from the sensor for the single exposure and then processes it to generate the multiple different versions. The bracketing adjustments are made only on the amber/blue axis (no bracketing in the magenta/green bias is possible), but you can select whether the bracketed shots are spread in the blue *or* amber directions (that is, each one bluer/less blue or yellower/less yellow) or balanced to provide both blue- and amber-oriented brackets.

Making these adjustments are the only times you're likely to be confused by a seeming contradiction in how color temperatures are named: warmer (more reddish) color temperatures (measured in degrees Kelvin) are the *lower* numbers, while cooler (bluer) color temperatures are *higher* numbers. It might not make sense to say that 3,400K is warmer than 6,000K, but that's the way it is. If it helps, think of a glowing red ember contrasted with a white-hot welder's torch, rather than fire and ice.

The confusion comes from physics. Scientists calculate color temperature from the light emitted by a mythical object called a black body radiator, which absorbs all the radiant energy that strikes it, and reflects none at all. Such a black body not only *absorbs* light perfectly, but it *emits* it perfectly when heated (and since nothing in the universe is perfect, that makes it mythical).

At a particular physical temperature, this imaginary object always emits light of the same wavelength or color. That makes it possible to define color temperature in terms of actual temperature in degrees on the Kelvin scale that scientists use. Incandescent light, for example, typically has a color temperature of 3,200K to 3,400K. Daylight might range from 5,500K to 6,000K. Each type of illumination we use for photography has its own color temperature range—with some cautions.

Daylight

Daylight is produced by the sun, and so is moonlight (which is just reflected sunlight). Daylight is present, of course, even when you can't see the sun. When sunlight is direct, it can be bright and harsh. If daylight is diffused by clouds, softened by bouncing off objects such as walls or your photo reflectors, or filtered by shade, it can be much dimmer, less contrasty, and more flattering for subjects such as people.

Daylight's color temperature can vary quite widely. It is highest in temperature (most blue) at noon when the sun is directly overhead, because the light is traveling through a minimum amount of the filtering layer we call the atmosphere. The color temperature at high noon may be 6,000K. At other times of day, the sun is lower in the sky and the particles in the air provide a filtering effect that warms the illumination to about 5,500K for most of the day. Starting an hour before dusk and for an hour after sunrise, the warm appearance of the sunlight is even visible to our eyes when the color temperature may dip to 5,000K–4,500K, as shown in Figure 8.3.

Because you'll be taking so many photos in daylight, you'll want to learn how to use or compensate for the brightness and contrast of sunlight, as well as how to deal with its color temperature. I'll provide some hints later in this chapter.

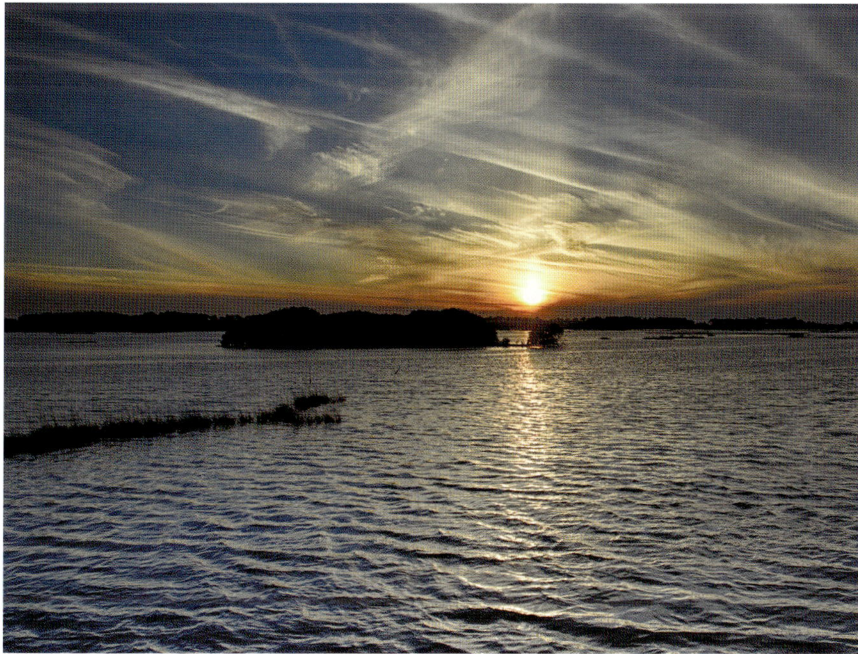

Figure 8.3 At dawn and dusk, the color temperature of daylight may dip as low as 4,500K.

Incandescent/Tungsten/Halogen Light

The term *incandescent* or *tungsten/halogen illumination* is usually applied to the direct descendents of Thomas Edison's original electric lamp. Such lights consist of a glass bulb that contains a vacuum, or is filled with a halogen gas, and contains a tungsten filament that is heated by an electrical current, producing photons and heat. Tungsten-halogen lamps are a variation on the basic light bulb, using a more rugged (and longer-lasting) filament that can be heated to a higher temperature, housed in a thicker glass or quartz envelope, and filled with iodine or bromine ("halogen") gases. The higher temperature allows tungsten-halogen (or quartz-halogen/quartz-iodine, depending on their construction) lamps to burn "hotter" and whiter. Although popular for automobile headlamps today, they've also been used for photographic illumination.

Although incandescent illumination isn't a perfect black body radiator, it's close enough that the color temperature of such lamps can be precisely calculated and used for photography without concerns about color variation (at least, until the very end of the lamp's life). As I noted earlier, the color rendering index of such lamps tends to be very high, so you need to account only for the color temperature.

Of course, old-style tungsten lamps are on the way out, at first replaced either by compact fluorescent lights (CFL) or newer, more energy-efficient (and expensive) tungsten and halogen lights, and, eventually by LED illumination. It appears that LED illumination is on track to supplant all of these for most applications in the near future. The other qualities of this type of lighting, such as contrast, are dependent on the distance of the lamp from the subject, type of reflectors used, and other factors that I'll explain later in this chapter.

Fluorescent Light/LEDs

Fluorescent light has some advantages in terms of illumination, but some disadvantages from a photographic standpoint. This type of lamp generates light through an electro-chemical reaction that emits most of its energy as visible light, rather than heat, which is why the bulbs don't get as hot. The type of light produced varies depending on the phosphor coatings and type of gas in the tube. So, the illumination fluorescent bulbs produce can vary widely in its characteristics.

That's not great news for photographers. Different types of lamps have different "color temperatures" that can't be precisely measured in degrees Kelvin, because the light isn't produced by heating. Worse, fluorescent lamps have a discontinuous spectrum of light that can have some colors missing entirely. A particular type of light source can lack certain shades of red or other colors (see Figure 8.4), which is why fluorescent lamps and other alternative technologies such as sodium-vapor illumination can produce strange hues, as in the figure, and ghastly looking human skin tones. Their spectra can lack the reddish tones we associate with healthy skin and emphasize the blues and greens popular in horror movies. As I mentioned earlier, their color rendering indexes are far from ideal.

Compact fluorescent lights (CFLs) are those spiraling bulbs that became popular as old-school tungsten bulbs were phased out. However, CFLs don't work in all fixtures and for all applications, such as dimmers (even if you purchase special "dimmable" CFLs), electronic timer or "dusk-to-dawn" light

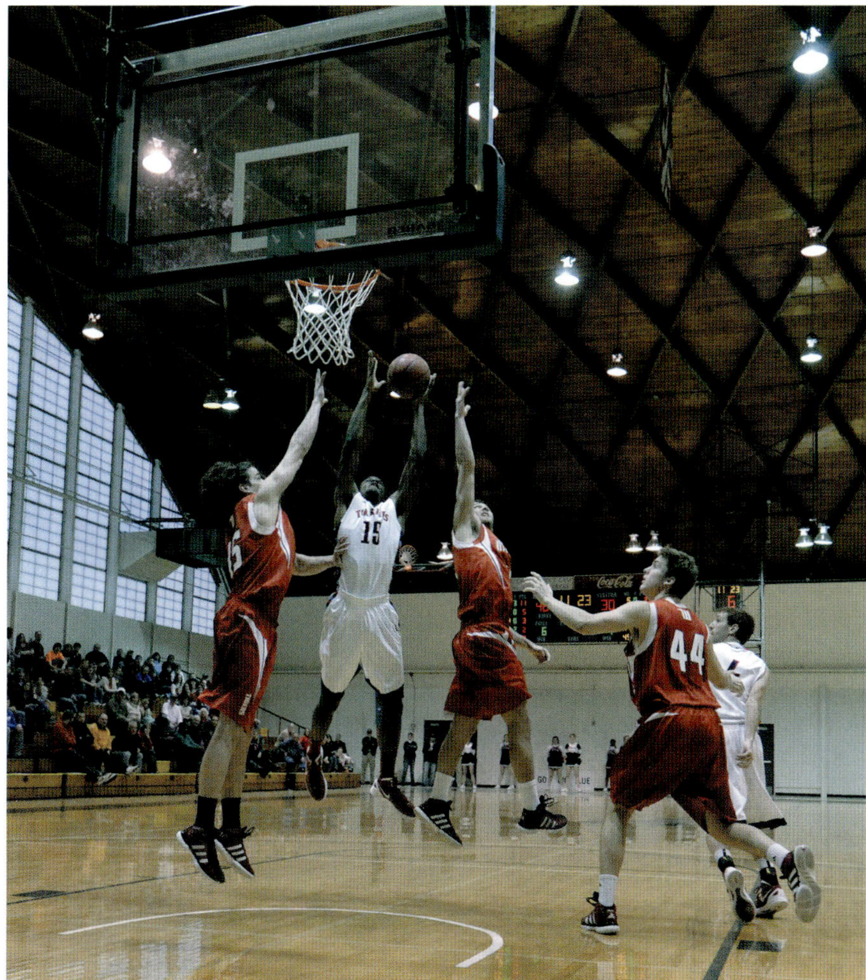

Figure 8.4 The uncorrected lighting in the gym added a distinct greenish cast to this image when exposed with a daylight white balance setting.

controllers, some illuminated wall switches, or with motion sensors. Only certain types of CFLs (cold cathode models) operate outside in cold weather; they emit IR signals that can confuse the remote control of your TV, air conditioner, etc.

Gaining in popularity are LED light sources, particularly for movies, in the form of compact units that clip onto the camera and provide a continuous beam of light to fill in shadows indoors or out, and/or to provide the main illumination when shooting video inside. Several vendors have introduced LED studio lights that are bright enough for general-purpose shooting. It's become obvious that LED illumination will soon become the most widely used continuous light source. They've already made dramatic inroads in the automotive industry for taillights, headlights, and interior illumination. Innovations like the Lume Panel Mini and Lume Cube (see Figure 8.5 left and right, respectively) will find broader use.

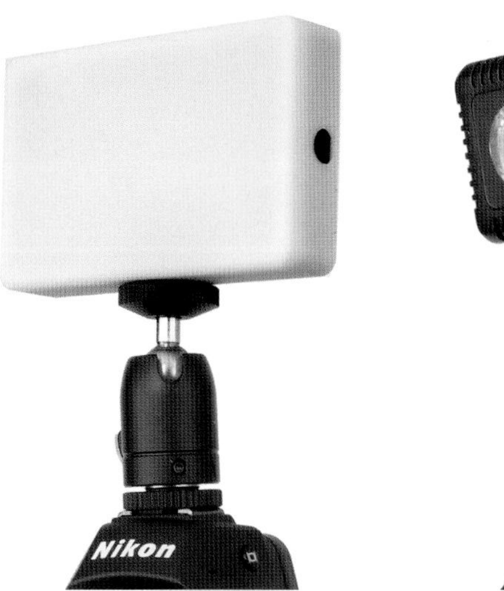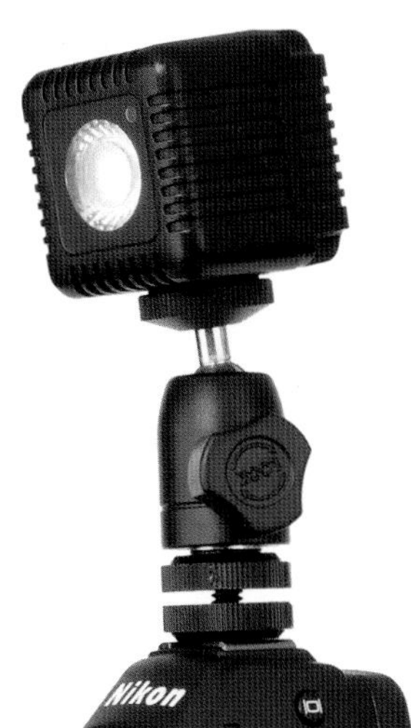

The credit-card size Panel Mini ($60) resides permanently in my camera bag as my fill light of choice. It's a half-inch thick, includes a soft plastic diffuser that provides an even light source, and can be adjusted from 1% to 100% brightness. Color temperature is adjustable from 3,200K to 5,600K, and it has a 96+ color rendering index. It runs for more than an hour on one charge. The Panel GO ($99) is similar but with double the light output. The panel's older sibling, the Lume Cube 2.0 ($90), is a brilliant variable-brightness LED lamp that can be triggered wirelessly using Bluetooth or its built-in optical sensor. It's waterproof down to 30 feet, so I often attach it to my Nikon 1 AW1 camera for underwater shooting.

Other Lighting Accessories

Once you start working with light, you'll find there are plenty of useful accessories that can help you. Here are some of the most popular that you might want to consider. These all work well with both continuous lighting, discussed in this chapter, as well as with electronic flash, which will be our focus in the chapter that follows this one.

Do-It-Yourself Lighting

The cool thing about continuous lighting is that anything that lights up can be used as a lighting tool for your Z5. Flashlights (for "painting with light" techniques), shop work lights, or even desktop high-intensity lamps, like the one seen in Figure 8.6, top, can be pressed into service at little or no cost (if you already happen to own something that will work). I used that desk lamp to shoot the image seen in Figure 8.6, bottom, simply because the lamp was bright enough to let me use a small f/stop to maximize depth-of-field, and it was really easy to see the lighting effect and move the lamp an inch or two to get different effects.

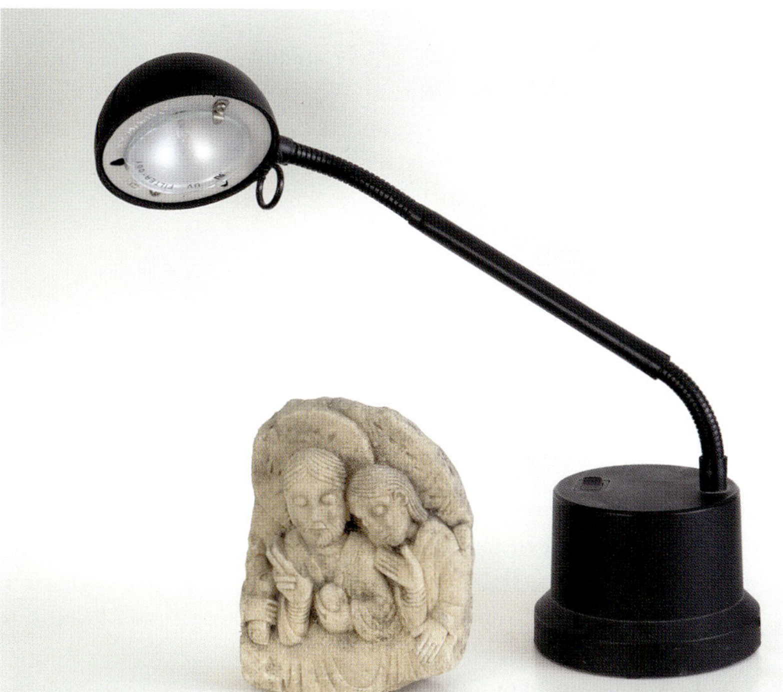

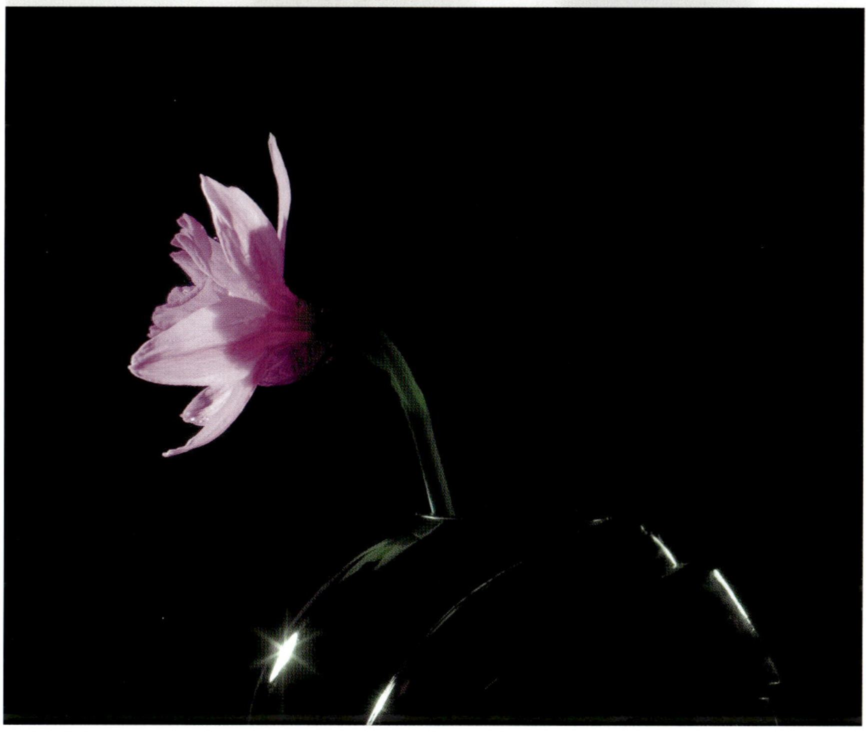

Figure 8.6 A desk lamp can be pressed into service as a light source for tabletop and macro photography.

Umbrellas

Umbrellas are just what you might think, a variation on those trusty shields-on-a-stick that protect us from the ravages of sun, rain, snow, or other elements of nature. Whether we know them as parasols (for the sun) or paraguas (for the water) on the Costa del Sol; as parapluies/ombrelles on the Riviera; or Sonnenschirme/Regenschirme (gotta love those Germans!); these inexpensive accessories are just as versatile for reflecting light as blocking it.

Indeed, you can use umbrellas in multiple roles:

- **Light reflector.** A silver umbrella can provide a softer, but not *too* soft light source, or a much softer source of illumination when a non-shiny white umbrella is used. The quality and quantity of the light that your Z5 sees can be further adjusted simply by moving the umbrella closer to your subject (for a softer illumination) or farther away (for more contrast).
- **Light diffuser.** A white umbrella diffuses and softens light, but a translucent white umbrella (of the "shoot-through" variety) can be reversed so that the illumination passes through the fabric and becomes even more soft and diffuse.
- **Light blocker.** Some umbrellas have a white or silver interior surface, and a black cover that prevents any light from leaking through the umbrella. Those models can be used to *block* light from other sources of illumination—even outdoors in daylight—to allow you to create subtle lighting effects.
- **Light colorizer.** Umbrellas may have a shiny golden, silver, or blue interior surface (as do many flat reflectors), and so can be used to add a rich warm tone, neutral sheen, or cold bluish cast to an image or shadows. You can use umbrella "colorizing" to create an effect or balance multiple light sources.
- **Soft box in an instant.** Many umbrellas can be fitted with a cover over their front that transforms them into a soft box. This conversion is more practical for use with electronic flash (covered in the next chapter) than for some kinds of continuous lighting, because of heat build-up. "Colder" forms of continuous lighting, such as fluorescent lights designed specially for photographic applications, can be used in soft box mode, however. Figure 8.7, left, shows both an umbrella and a soft box (described next).

Soft Boxes

Soft boxes are also handy for photographing shiny objects. They not only provide a soft light, but if the box itself happens to reflect in the subject (say you're photographing a chromium toaster), the box will provide an interesting highlight that's indistinct and not distracting.

You can buy soft boxes or make your own. Some lengths of friction-fit plastic pipe and a lot of muslin cut and sewed just so may be all that you need. Soft boxes are large square, rectangular (or round or octagonal) devices that may resemble an umbrella with a front cover and produce a similar lighting effect. They can extend from a few feet square to massive boxes that stand five or six feet tall—virtually a wall of light. With a light source or two inside a soft box, you have a very large, semi-directional light source that's very diffuse and very flattering for portraiture and other people photography.

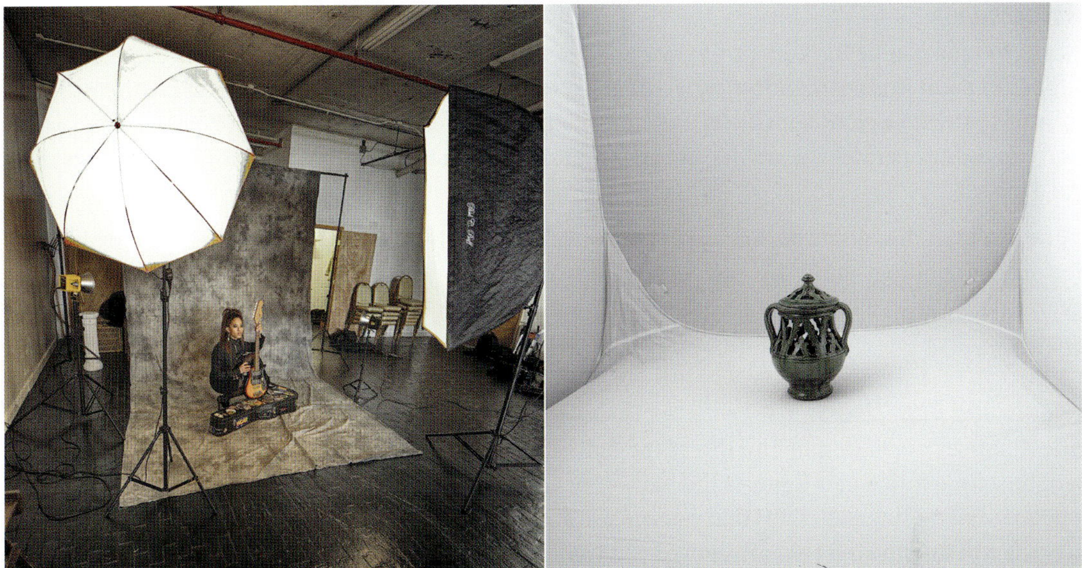

Figure 8.7 Umbrellas and soft boxes (left) can provide a soft, diffuse light source. Tents provide almost shadowless lighting for photographing shiny objects (right).

Tents

Tents, like the one seen at right in Figure 8.7, are useful for photographing shiny objects or any subject where you want to reduce the shadows and reflections to a minimum. The fabric of the tent is translucent, so you place the light sources around the sides or above, and a soft glow filters through to illuminate the image. You can still maintain subtle lighting effects by choosing to light up—or not light up—individual sides of the cube. The lens of the Z5 protrudes through a hole or slit in the tent, so you can photograph the shiniest subject without having you or your camera show up in the final picture.

Light Stands

Both electronic flash and incandescent lamps can benefit from light stands. These are lightweight, tripod-like devices (but without a swiveling or tilting head) that can be set on the floor, tabletops, or other elevated surfaces and positioned as needed. Light stands should be strong enough to support an external lighting unit, up to and including a relatively heavy flash with soft box or umbrella reflectors. You want the supports to be capable of raising the lights high enough to be effective. Look for light stands capable of extending six to seven feet high. The nine-foot units usually have larger, steadier bases, and extend high enough that you can use them as background supports. You'll be using these stands for a lifetime, so invest in good ones. I bought my light stands when I was in college, and I have been using them for decades.

Backgrounds

Backgrounds can be backdrops of cloth, sheets of muslin you've painted yourself using a sponge dipped in paint, rolls of seamless paper, or any other suitable surface your mind can dream up. Backgrounds provide a complementary and non-distracting area behind subjects (especially portraits) and can be lit separately to provide contrast and separation that outlines the subject, or which helps set a mood.

I like to use plain-colored backgrounds for portraits, and white or gray seamless paper backgrounds for product photography. You can usually construct these yourself from cheap materials and tape them up on the wall behind your subject or mount them on a pole stretched between a pair of light stands.

Snoots and Barn Doors

These fit over the flash unit and direct the light at your subject. Snoots are excellent for converting a light source into a hair light, while barn doors give you enough control over the illumination by opening and closing their flaps that you can use another flash as a background light, with the capability of feathering the light exactly where you want it on the background.

Electronic Flash with the Nikon Z5

9

The Nikon Z5 is compatible with a long list of Nikon SB-series Speedlights, dating back to the company's original professional-level flash unit, the SB-800, which was introduced in 2003. All Speedlights introduced since then use the Nikon Creative Lighting System (CLS), which allows efficient through-the-lens metering of flash exposures and wireless off-camera strobes for versatile multi-flash lighting. Although virtually everything else about the Z5 is new—from sensor to lens mount—it benefits from the availability of these mature, well-tested array of electronic flash options, including the latest SB-5000 unit, which can be triggered remotely through optical or radio links.

Some consider electronic flash a necessary evil, providing supplementary illumination that is often harsh or less natural looking, as well as difficult to use. However, what they are deriding is *bad* flash photography, as applied by photographers who don't understand how to use strobes properly or are too lazy to fully apply the creative versatility flash offers. They may feel that Speedlights are too expensive.

Fortunately, it's easy to become adept at using electronic flash, and fully featured Nikon units like the SB-500—which I'll describe later in this chapter—can cost as little as $250. Most settings can be adjusted using the menus built into your Z5, and even multi-flash shooting (covered in Chapter 10) can be mastered with only a few hours' practice.

Electronic flash has become the studio light source of choice for many pro photographers because it's more intense (and its intensity can be varied to order by the photographer using the strobe's power adjustment features) and freezes action. Flash frees you from the need for a tripod (unless you want to use one to lock down a composition), and has a snappy, consistent light quality that matches daylight. (While color balance changes as the flash duration shortens, some Nikon flash units can communicate to the camera the exact white balance provided for that shot.) And even pros will cede that an external flash mounted on the Nikon Z5 needn't be used in direct-flash mode, and has essential applications as an adjunct, particularly to fill in dark shadows or to serve as a wireless trigger for additional, off-camera strobes.

But electronic flash isn't as inherently easy to use as continuous lighting. As I noted in Chapter 8, electronic flash units do require a modest investment, don't show you exactly what the lighting effect will be (unless you use a second source or mode called a *modeling light* for a preview), and the exposure of electronic flash units is more difficult to calculate accurately.

This chapter and the next will show you how to manage all the creative and technical challenges, using optional external flash units. First, we'll look at the basics of working with flash, and then in Chapter 10, we'll explore the world of wireless flash photography.

Electronic Flash Basics

Electronic flash illumination is produced by photons generated by an electrical charge that is accumulated in a component called a *capacitor* and then directed through a glass tube containing xenon gas, which absorbs the energy and emits the burst of light. In automatic mode (which Nikon calls *iTTL*), the main flash is preceded by one or more mini-bursts that allow the Z5 to gauge how much light is bouncing back from your subject and background, and to communicate with other external flash units linked wirelessly. In practice, external strobes can be linked to the Z5 in several different ways:

- **Camera mounted/hardwired external dedicated flash.** Units offered by Nikon or other vendors that are compatible with Nikon's Creative Lighting System—CLS—can be clipped onto the accessory "hot" shoe on top of the camera or linked through a wired system such as the Nikon SC-28/SC-29 cables. I'll describe CLS later in this chapter.

- **Wireless dedicated flash.** A CLS-compatible unit can be triggered by signals produced by a pre-flash (before the main flash burst begins), which offers two-way communication between the camera and flash unit. The triggering flash can be a CLS-compatible flash unit in Master mode, or a wireless non-flashing accessory, such as the Nikon SU-800, which does nothing but "talk" to the external flashes. You'll find more on this mode in Chapter 10.

- **Wired, non-intelligent mode.** The Z5 does not have a dedicated old-style PC/X connector built in, but you can add one easily by sliding the Nikon AS-15 Sync Terminal adaptor into the hot shoe on top of the camera. The PC/X connector is a non-intelligent camera/flash link that sends just one piece of information, one way: it tells a connected flash to fire. There is no other exchange of information between the camera and flash. The PC/X connector can be used to link the Nikon Z5 with non-dedicated/non-CLS-friendly strobes, which can be studio flash units, manual non-CLS flash, flash units from other vendors that can use a PC cable, or even Nikon-brand Speedlights that you elect to connect to the Z5 in a non-CLS, "unintelligent" mode.

- **Radio/Infrared transmitter/receivers.** Another way to link flash units to the Z5 is through a radio transmitter/receiver system, using either a dedicated radio-compatible flash unit, such as the Nikon SB-5000 (see Figure 9.1, left), or an add-on wireless infrared or radio *transmitter*, like a PocketWizard, Radio Popper, a Paul C. Buff CyberSync trigger, or the Godox device shown in Figure 9.1, right. These are generally mounted on the accessory shoe of the Z5 and emit a signal when the Z5 sends a command to fire through the hot shoe. The simplest of these function as a wireless PC/X connector, with no other communication between the camera and flash (other than the instruction to fire). However, sophisticated units have their own built-in controls and can send additional commands to the receivers when connected to compatible flash units. I use one to adjust the power output of my Alien Bees studio flash from the camera, without the need to walk over to the flash itself.

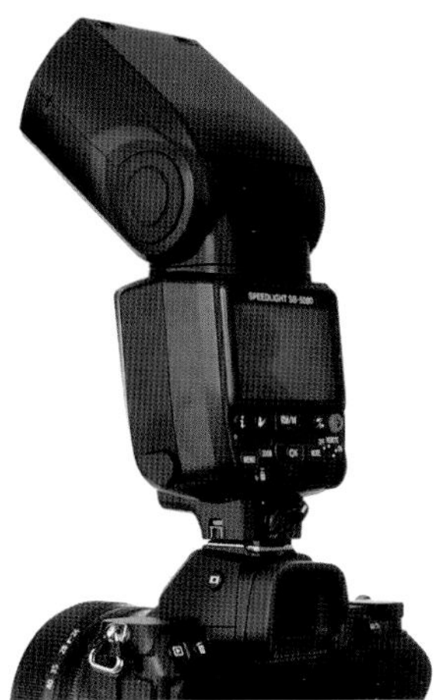
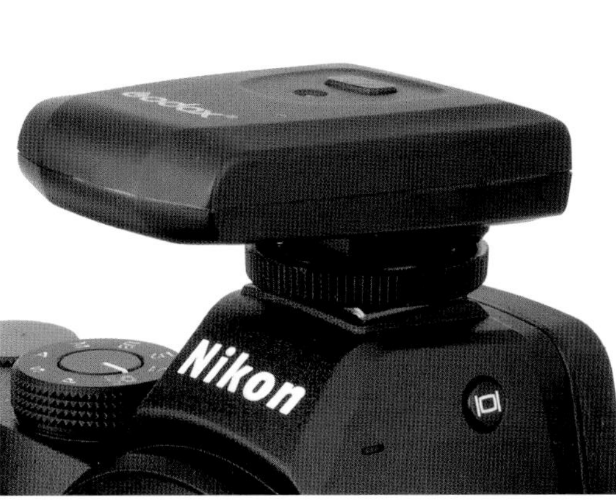

Figure 9.1 The Nikon SB-5000 offers radio control (left). Third-party add-ons also can use radio transmission to trigger electronic flash units (right).

- **Simple slave connection.** In the days before intelligent wireless communication, the most common way to trigger off-camera, non-wired flash units was through a *slave* unit. These can be small external triggers connected to the remote flash (or built into the flash itself) and set off when the slave's optical sensor detects a burst initiated by a flash connected to the camera. When it "sees" the main flash, the slave flash units are triggered quickly enough to contribute to the same exposure. The main problem with this type of connection—other than the lack of any intelligent communication between the camera and flash—is that the slave may be fooled by any pre-flashes that are emitted by the other strobes, and fire too soon. Modern slave triggers have a special "digital" mode that ignores the pre-flash and fires only from the main flash burst.

The Moment of Exposure

The Z5 has a vertically traveling shutter that consists of two curtains. Just before the flash fires, the front curtain opens and moves down to the opposite side of the frame, at which point the shutter is completely open. The flash can be triggered at this point (so-called *front-curtain sync*), making the flash exposure. Then, after a delay that can vary from 30 seconds to 1/200th second (or faster when *high-speed sync,* discussed later, is used), a rear curtain begins moving down the sensor plane, covering up the sensor again. If the flash is triggered just before the rear curtain starts to close, then *rear-curtain sync* is used. In both cases, though, a shutter speed of 1/200th second is the maximum that can be used to take a photo, unless you're using the high-speed 1/200th (Auto FP) sync setting.

Figure 9.2 illustrates how this works, with a fanciful illustration of a generic shutter (your Z5's shutter does *not* look like this). Both curtains are tightly closed at upper left. At upper right, the front curtain begins to move downward, starting to expose a narrow slit that reveals the sensor behind the shutter. At lower left, the front curtain moves downward farther until, as you can see at lower right in the figure, the sensor is fully exposed.

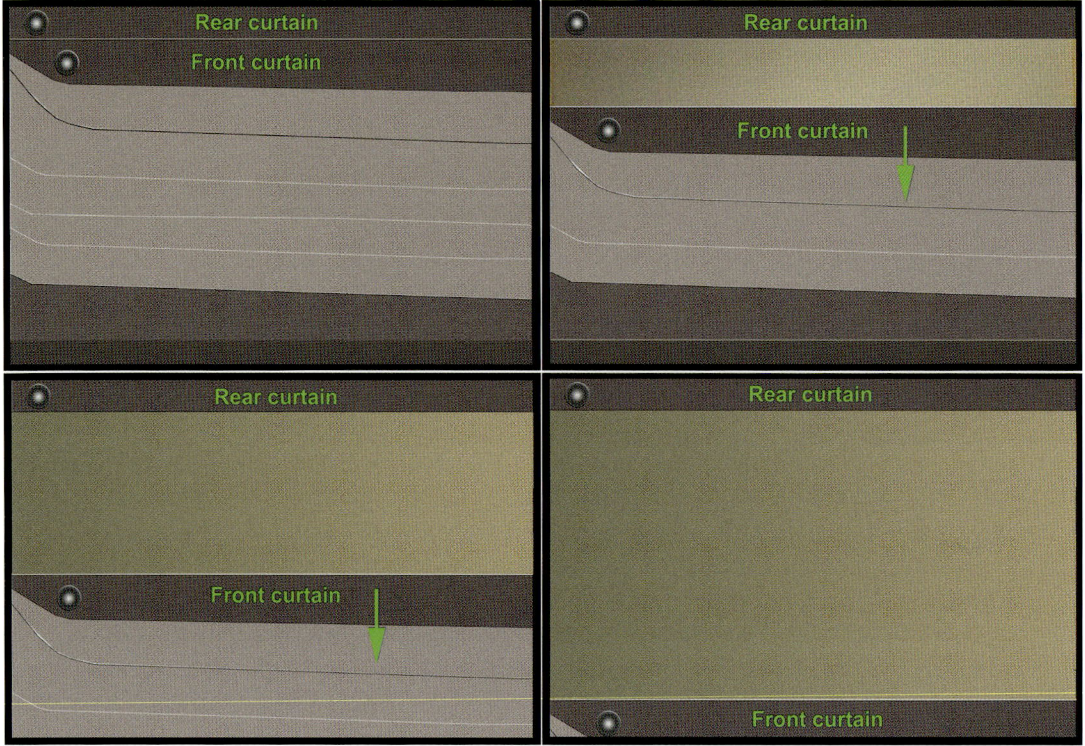

Figure 9.2 A focal plane shutter has two curtains, the lower, or front curtain, and an upper, rear curtain.

Here's a more detailed look at what transpires when you take a photo using electronic flash, all within a few milliseconds of time. The following list assumes you are using iTTL exposure mode.

1. **Flash sync mode.** After you've selected a shooting mode, choose the flash sync option available. You can access the Flash Mode entry in the Photo Shooting menu, press the *i* button, and navigate to the Flash Mode, which will be located third from the left in the top row (unless you've customized your *i* menu). If you change flash sync mode frequently, you can also define a button to summon the adjustment using Custom Setting f2: Custom Controls (described in Chapter 12). I'll explain your sync options shortly.

2. **Metering method.** Choose the metering method you want, from Matrix, Center-weighted, Spot, or Highlight-weighted metering.

3. **Activate flash.** Mount an external flash (or connect it with a cable) and turn it on. A ready light appears in the viewfinder and on the back of the dedicated flash when the unit is ready to take a picture (although the flash might not be *fully* charged when the indicator first appears).

4. **Check exposure.** Select a shutter speed when using Manual, Program, or Shutter-priority modes; select an aperture when using Aperture-priority and Manual exposure modes.

5. **Preview lighting.** If you want to preview the lighting effect, assign the Preview behavior to a button (Fn1 or Fn2 are the traditional choices). Press that button to produce a modeling flash burst.

6. **Lock flash setting (if desired).** Optionally, if the main subject is located significantly off-center, you can frame so the subject is centered, lock the flash at the exposure needed to illuminate that subject, and then reframe using the composition you want. Lock the flash level using the Flash Value (FV) Lock button you designate (many assign the Fn1 or Fn 2 button to this function, using Custom Settings f2). Press the FV lock button, and the flash will emit a monitor pre-flash to determine the correct flash level, and then the Z5 will lock the flash at that level until you press the FV lock button again to release it. FV lock icons appear in the display.

7. **Take photo.** Press the shutter release down all the way.

8. **Z5 receives distance data.** Z-mount lenses, as well as F-mount E-, D-, or G-series lenses attached using the FTZ adapter, now supply focus distance to the Z5.

9. **Pre-flash emitted.** The external flash sends out several pre-flash bursts. One series of bursts can be used to control additional wireless flash units in Commander mode, while another is used to determine exposure. The pre-flashes happen in such a brief period before the main flash that they are virtually undetectable.

10. **Exposure calculated.** The pre-flash bounces back and is measured at the sensor. It calculates brightness and contrast of the image to calculate exposure. If you're using Matrix metering (more on metering modes shortly), the Z5 evaluates the scene to determine whether the subject may be backlit (for fill flash), a subject requires extra ambient light exposure to balance the scene with the flash exposure, or classifies the scene in some other way. The camera-to-subject information as well as the degree of sharp focus of the subject matter is used to locate the subject within the frame. If you've selected Spot metering, only standard i-TTL (without balanced fill flash) is used. (See the sidebar i-TTL Flash Control.)

11. **Front curtain opens.** The exposure by ambient light begins when the physical shutter curtain is fully open.

12. **Flash fired.** At the correct triggering moment (depending on whether front or rear sync is used), the camera sends a signal to one or more flashes to start flash discharge. The flash is quenched as soon as the correct exposure has been achieved.

I-TTL FLASH CONTROL

CLS-compatible flash units include up to several Flash Control modes, depending on the model. (I'll explain them all later in this chapter.) With the one you'll use most often, TTL mode, the camera calculates and sets flash exposure (but applies any flash exposure compensation you dial in, as explained later). In Manual mode, you adjust the output level of the flash.

In TTL mode, the camera selects one of two variations:

- i-TTL balanced fill-flash. The Z5 analyzes the pre-flash reflection from all areas of the frame and adjusts the output to provide a balance between the main subject of your image and the background lighting.

- Standard i-TTL fill-flash. The brightness of the background is not considered in setting the flash output. This mode tends to emphasize the main subject, even if some background detail is lost. You can force the Z5 to select Standard i-TTL fill-flash by switching to Spot Metering mode. Use flash exposure compensation to adjust the main subject/background balance as required.

13. **Shutter closes.** The shutter closes and the live view from the sensor resumes. You're ready to take another picture. Remember to press the defined FV lock button (if used) again to release the flash exposure if your next shot will use a different composition.

14. **Exposure confirmed.** Ordinarily, the full charge in the flash may not be required. If the flash indicator in the viewfinder blinks for about three seconds after the exposure, that means that the entire flash charge was required, and it *could* mean that the full charge wasn't enough for a proper exposure. Be sure to review your image on the monitor to make sure it's not underexposed, and, if it is, make adjustments (such as increasing the ISO setting of the Z5) to remedy the situation.

UNIFIED FLASH CONTROL

Nikon electronic flash units have their own sets of controls, so Nikon has implemented a feature called *unified flash control,* which simply means that with compatible CLS flash, you can change duplicated settings on *either* the flash unit or camera (or remotely using the optional Camera Control 2 software) and the adjustments are automatically made on the other device. You don't have to worry about accidentally overriding your own settings. Currently, the flash units implementing unified flash control are the SB-300, SB-400, SB-500, and SB-5000.

A Tale of Two Exposures

Calculating the proper exposure for an electronic flash photograph is a bit more complicated than determining the settings for continuous light. The right exposure isn't simply a function of how far away your subject is (which the camera can figure out based on the autofocus distance that's locked in just prior to taking the picture). Various objects reflect more or less light at the same distance so, obviously, the camera needs to measure the amount of light reflected back and through the lens.

That measurement is complicated by two things: a picture taken using flash is actually *two separate exposures*: the exposure produced by the flash itself, and the exposure that results from the continuous, ambient light that is also illuminating your subject. If the Z5's calculations are correct, the plane in which your main subject resides will be properly exposed. However, anything more than slightly in *front of* or *behind* that plane will be overexposed or underexposed (respectively), thanks to the inverse square law I mentioned in Chapter 8. To recap, the intensity of the light is inversely proportional to the square of the distance. In practice, that means a light source that is 12 feet away from a subject provides only one-quarter as much illumination as the same source located 6 feet away. In f/stop terms, you need to open up two stops whenever the distance doubles. (See Figure 9.3.)

So, as you shoot, you need to consider "depth-of-light" (the range in which a subject is acceptably illuminated in front of and behind the plane used to calculate the exposure) in addition to depth-of-field. Fortunately, in many flash photography situations, the main subject is the closest thing to the camera, so there often won't be a problem with overexposed foreground objects.

Backgrounds, however, are another story. In daylight situations, balancing the flash and ambient illumination more or less takes care of itself automatically. Photographers generally let the daylight provide most of the exposure and use the flash only to fill in shadows.

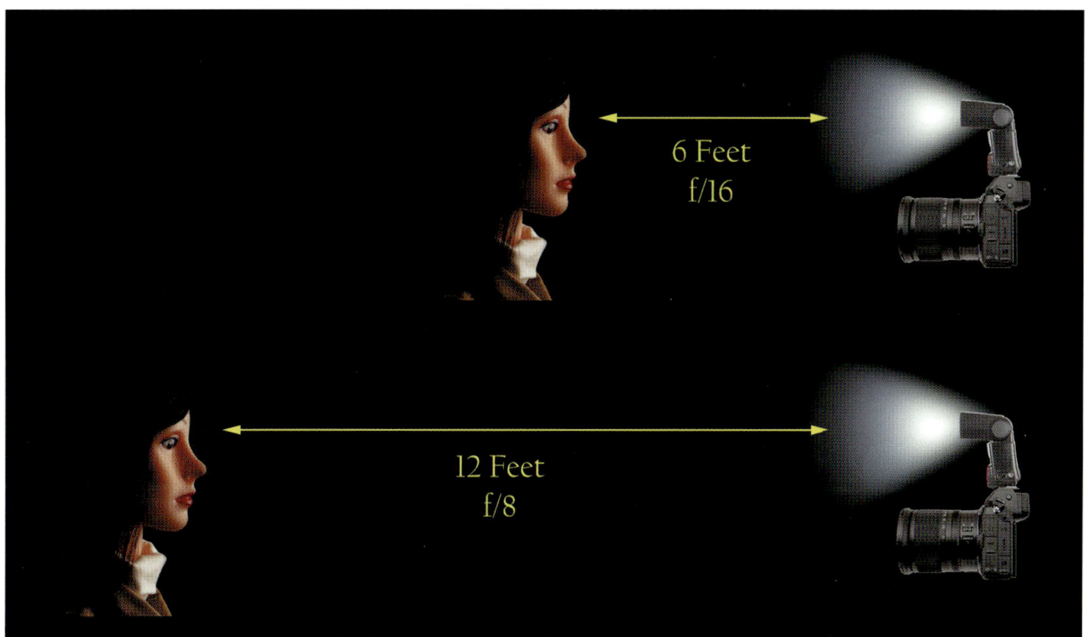

Figure 9.3 A light source that is twice as far away provides only one-quarter as much illumination.

However, if you're photographing indoors or at night, the background, not illuminated by the flash, will appear darker than the foreground subject. Fortunately, every flash picture consists of *two* exposures, the exposure produced by the flash, and a second exposure that results from the background illumination. For the flash exposure, the shutter speed is more-or-less irrelevant, as long as you're using a shutter speed slower than the synchronization speed of the camera—1/200th second in the case of the Nikon Z5. The f/stop selected, and the power output of the flash determine the exposure.

The ambient light exposure is more "normal," using both the shutter speed and aperture. Slower shutter speeds allow more ambient light to reach the sensor, and higher shutter speeds allow less. If you want to *minimize* the ambient portion of the exposure, use a higher shutter speed, up to 1/200th second when not using High-Speed Sync (discussed later in this chapter). To *maximize* the ambient exposure, use a slower shutter speed. The Z5 has a special Slow Sync shutter setting that automatically uses these slower speeds to balance flash/ambient exposures, but you can also use Custom Setting e2: Flash Shutter Speed to specify the slowest/fastest shutter speed used under normal conditions.

There are several complications involved in balancing flash and ambient light exposures. So-called "mixed" lighting is one of them. Your flash is balanced for daylight, while ambient light is often incandescent or some other "warm" illumination. This mixture is exaggerated in Figure 9.4, which shows the Plaza Mayor in Segovia, Spain, with the city's cathedral in the background lit by incandescent lamps, with the foreground illuminated by flash. The solution in this case would be to install an orange-tinted "warming" filter on the flash (many Nikon Speedlights include them) to balance the flash illumination with the incandescent background.

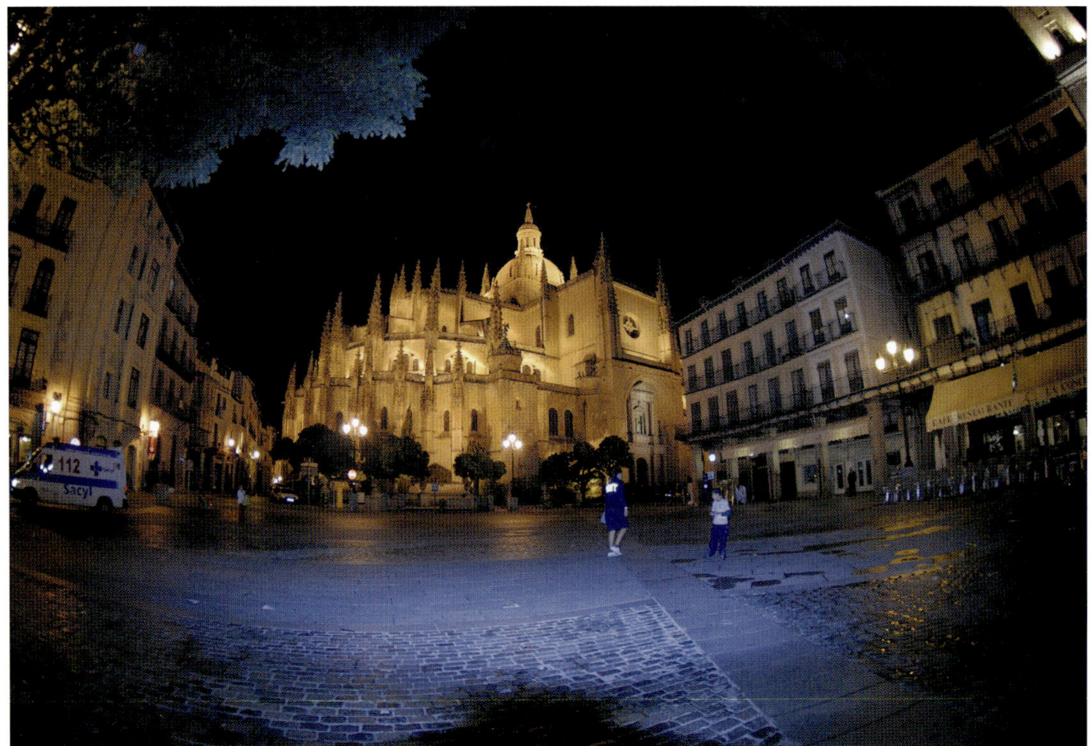

Figure 9.4 Electronic flash illuminated the foreground, and incandescent lighting illuminated the background in this mixed-lighting example.

The second problem that arises stems from the fact that while the flash exposure is concluded in an instant (typically 1/1000th to 1/50000th of a second), the ambient light continues for the entire time the shutter is open. So, you end up with *two* images produced by the *dual* exposures. If the subject is moving, the additional ambient light exposure produces a "ghost" image. The best way of handling that conundrum is to adjust the sync setting of the camera, and I'm going to explain how to do that shortly.

Measuring Exposure

By this time, you should be wondering how the Nikon Z5 measures the flash, as the flash burst isn't available for evaluation until it's triggered when you press the shutter release down all the way to take the picture. The solution is to fire the flash multiple times. The first pulse is a *monitor pre-flash* that can be analyzed, then followed virtually instantaneously by a series of pulses (if required) to communicate wirelessly with any optically triggered remote flash units. (You'll find more on advanced wireless lighting in Chapter 10.) Only then is the main flash triggered, which (when shooting in auto-flash mode) emits exactly the calculated intensity needed for a correct exposure. (All these pulses happen so quickly that they may appear to you to be a single burst.)

Because of the exposure calculations, the primary flash may be longer in duration for distant objects and shorter in duration for closer subjects, depending on the required intensity for exposure. This default through-the-lens evaluative flash exposure system is called i-TTL BL (for intelligent Through The Lens, Balanced Fill Flash) and can operate whenever you have attached a Nikon-dedicated flash unit to the Z5. There are additional modes that will be discussed later, and not all modes are available with every flash unit, but all the modes are listed in Table 9.1. These modes are set using your particular electronic flash's controls, as described in your unit's manual.

TABLE 9.1 Flash Modes

MODE	METERING MODES AVAILABLE	FUNCTION
TTL BL	Matrix, Center-weighted	Balanced Fill Flash.
Standard TTL	Spot	Only flash output used in exposure calculation.
TTL BL FP	Matrix, Center-weighted	Balanced Fill Flash, shutter speeds higher than 1/200th second available.
TTL FP	Spot	Flash and ambient illumination not balanced, shutter speeds higher than 1/200th second available.
AA (Auto Aperture)	N/A	Exposure measured by sensor on flash. Uses ISO and aperture information supplied by camera.
Automatic	N/A	Exposure measured by sensor on flash. Uses ISO and aperture information input to flash by user.
Manual	N/A	Exposure calculated by user.

The amount of light emitted by the flash is changed in an interesting way—interrupting the flash as the charge flows from the capacitor through the flash tube. When full power is required, either to supply the correct exposure in automatic modes or because you're using the flash in Manual mode at the full-power (1/1) setting, then all the energy in the capacitor flows through the flash tube. However, if less than full power is needed, the energy is stopped partway through the exposure by opening the circuit with a solid-state switch. In the olden days this was always done using a component called a *thyristor,* but today a component called an *insulated-gate bipolar transistor,* or IGBT, is more common.

Because the current is interrupted before the full power of the capacitor is used, the resulting burst becomes shorter as the power output is reduced. For example, with some Nikon flash units you might see a burst lasting about 1/1000th second at full power, but only a little longer than 1/10000th second at 1/16th power, or 1/40000th second at 1/128th power. (The SB-5000 adds a 1/256th power option, providing a 1/30800th second exposure.) This behavior is nifty when you want to freeze really fast action, such as falling water droplets—just use a lower power output level and/or work extremely close to your subject.

Because the full contents of the capacitor are not used with these partial flashes, the Speedlight is able to recycle more quickly, or even use the retained energy to fire multiple times in Repeating flash mode (described later in this chapter). The only downside is that shorter flash exposures tend to take on a bluish tinge as the duration decreases. That's because the burst starts out with a very cool color temperature and ends up much warmer at the end of the burst, averaging out to a hue that's pretty close to daylight in color balance. When you trim off the reddish end of the flash, your resulting image may be noticeably more blue. That's why the Flash color balance of the Z5 doesn't always produce a pleasing color rendition. You may have to fine-tune the white balance, as described in Chapter 11, or shoot RAW and correct in your image editor.

Those of you using studio flash units may be interested to know that your non-automatic strobes produce their varying power levels in a different way. With the typical studio flash, the capacitor is *always* fully discharged each time you take a picture and then recharged *to the level you specify* for the next shot. It happens very quickly because you're using AC power or a high-voltage battery pack instead of low-capacity alkaline or rechargeable cells.

If you set the flash for ½ power, the capacitor (or capacitors—studio flash may use several of them) is charged only halfway; at ¼ power it's only replenished to 25 percent of its capacity. Then, when you take the photo, the full contents of the capacitor are sent through the flash tube. That's why you need to "dump" your studio flash when you reduce the power output from a higher level. The capacitor retains the charge that was in there before and can't fire at the reduced capacity you want until the existing power is dumped and then replenished to the level you specify. Because of the way studio flash store and release their power, they can be designed to be more consistent at different power levels than your typical Nikon flash unit. Of course, wild color variations from flash units aren't a huge problem, but just something you should be aware of.

So, to summarize, with CLS-compatible flash units, your automatic exposure is calculated by measuring a pre-flash and determining an appropriate exposure from that. There are other exposure modes than i-TTL available from Nikon external flash units, and I'll get into them later in this chapter, but this section has described the process in a nutshell.

Guide Numbers

Guide numbers, usually abbreviated GN, were originally developed as a way of calculating exposure manually, but today are more useful as a measurement of the power of an electronic flash unit. A GN is usually given as a pair of numbers for both feet and meters that represent the range at ISO 100. For example, the Nikon SB-910 has a GN in i-TTL mode of 34/111 (meters/feet) at ISO 100 when using the coverage needed for a 35mm lens (the flash has a *zoom head* to spread/narrow the light for a range of focal lengths). To calculate the right exposure at that ISO setting, you'd divide the guide number by the distance to arrive at the appropriate f/stop.

Using the SB-5000 as an example, at ISO 100 with its GN of 113, if you wanted to shoot a subject at a distance of 10 feet, you'd use f/11.3 (or, f/11). At 5 feet, an f/stop of f/22 would be used. Some quick mental calculations with the GN will give you any particular electronic flash's range. Many years ago, Nikon offered a 45mm GN lens that could couple the f/stop setting of the lens with the focus distance. You specified the guide number of the flash using a scale on the lens itself, and as you focused closer or farther away the f/stop was reduced or increased to match. Today, guide numbers are most useful for comparing the power of various flash units, rather than actually calculating what exposure to use.

Choosing a Flash Sync Mode

In addition to the flash modes mentioned earlier, the Nikon Z5 has five *flash sync modes*, plus a sixth (High-Speed Sync, described later) that comes into play in some circumstances. The five main modes, plus Off (which disables the flash) are selected with the *i* menu or the Photo Shooting menu's Flash Mode entry. (See Figure 9.5 for the icons.) Those modes (which I've listed in logical order, so the explanation will make more sense, rather than the order in which they appear during the selection cycle) are as follows:

- **Fill flash/Front-curtain sync (available in Auto and PSAM modes).** This setting, available in all exposure modes, should be your default setting. In this mode the flash fires as soon as the front curtain opens completely. The shutter then remains open for the duration of the exposure, until the rear curtain closes. If the subject is moving and ambient light levels are high enough, the movement will cause that secondary "ghost" exposure that appears in front of the flash exposure.

- **Rear-curtain sync (available in PSAM modes).** With this setting, which can be used with Program, Shutter-priority, Aperture-priority, or Manual exposure modes, the front curtain opens completely and remains open for the duration of the exposure. Then, the flash is fired and the rear curtain closes. If the subject is moving and ambient light levels are high enough, the movement will cause a secondary "ghost" exposure that appears behind the flash exposure (trailing it). You'll find more on "ghost" exposures next.

  In Program and Aperture-priority modes, this setting tells the Z5 to combine rear-curtain sync with slow shutter speeds (just like slow sync, discussed below) to balance ambient light with flash illumination. (It's best to use a tripod to avoid blur at these slow shutter speeds.)

- **Red-eye reduction (available in Auto and PSAM modes).** In this PSAM-compatible mode, there is a one-second lag after pressing the shutter release before the picture is actually taken, during which the Z5 uses the attached flash unit's red-eye reduction feature, causing the subject's pupils to contract (assuming they are looking at the camera), and thus reducing potential red-eye effects. Don't use with moving subjects or when you can't abide the delay.

- **Slow sync (available in P or A modes).** This setting allows the Z5 in Program and Aperture-priority modes to use shutter speeds as slow as 30 seconds with the flash to help balance a background illuminated with ambient light with your main subject, which will be lit by the electronic flash. You'll want to use a tripod at slower shutter speeds, of course.

- **Slow-sync + Red-eye (available in Auto and PA modes).** This mode combines slow sync with the Z5's external flash red-eye reduction behavior when using Program or Aperture-priority modes.

- **Flash off (available in Auto and PSAM modes).** The flash does not fire, even if powered on.

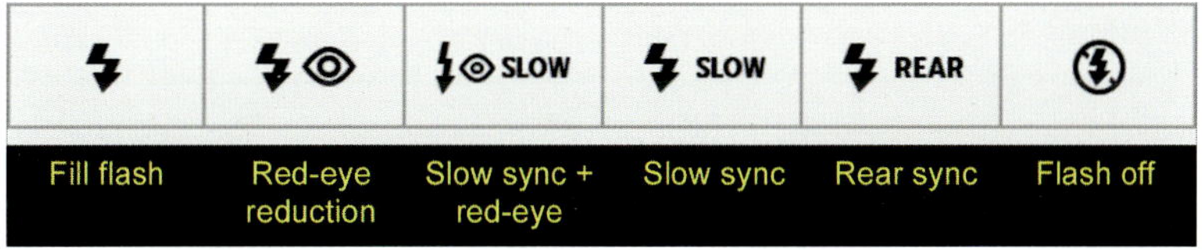

Figure 9.5 Icons for flash sync modes include fill flash/front-curtain sync, red-eye reduction, slow sync + red-eye, slow sync, rear-curtain sync, and flash off.

Ghost Images

The difference might not seem like much, but whether you use front-curtain sync (the default setting) or rear-curtain sync (an optional setting) can make a significant difference to your photograph *if the ambient light in your scene also contributes to the image.* At faster shutter speeds, particularly 1/200th second, there isn't much time for the ambient light to register, unless it is very bright. It's likely that the electronic flash will provide almost all the illumination, so front-curtain sync or rear-curtain sync isn't very important.

However, at slower shutter speeds, or with very bright ambient light levels, there is a significant difference, particularly if your subject is moving, or the camera isn't steady. In any of those situations, the ambient light will register as a second image accompanying the flash exposure, and if there is movement (camera or subject), that additional image will not be in the same place as the flash exposure. It will show as a ghost image and, if the movement is significant enough, as a blurred ghost image trailing in front of or behind your subject in the direction of the movement.

As I mentioned earlier, when you're using front-curtain sync, the flash goes off the instant the shutter opens, producing an image of the subject on the sensor. Then, the shutter remains open for an additional period (which can be from 30 seconds to 1/200th second). If your subject is moving, say, toward the right side of the frame, the ghost image produced by the ambient light will produce a blur on the right side of the original subject image. That makes it look as if your sharp (flash-produced) image is chasing the ghost (see Figure 9.6, top), which looks unnatural to those of us who grew up with lightning-fast Justice League–style superheroes (rather than modern dancers) who always left a ghost trail *behind them* (see Figure 9.6, bottom).

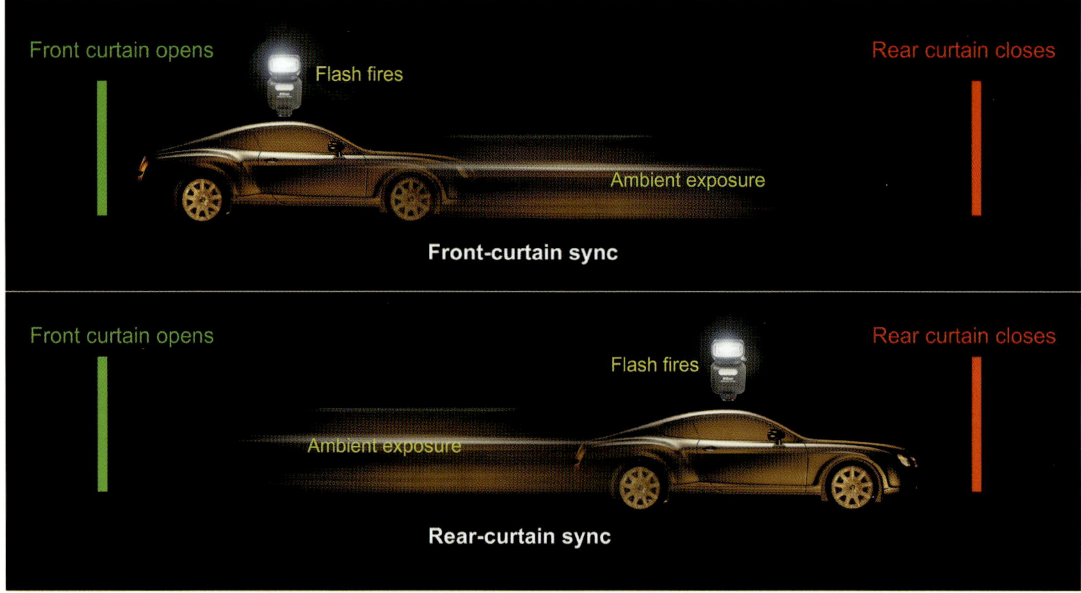

Figure 9.6 Front-curtain sync produces an image that trails in front of the flash exposure (top), while rear-curtain sync creates a more "natural-looking" trail behind the flash image (bottom).

So, Nikon provides rear-curtain sync to remedy the situation. In that mode, the shutter opens, as before. The shutter remains open for its designated duration, and the ghost image forms. If your subject moves from the left side of the frame to the right side, the ghost will move from left to right, too. *Then*, about 1.5 milliseconds before the rear shutter curtain closes, the flash is triggered, producing a nice, sharp flash image *ahead* of the ghost image.

Avoiding Sync Speed Problems

Using a shutter speed faster than 1/200th second can cause problems. Triggering the electronic flash only when the shutter is completely open makes a lot of sense if you think about what's going on. To obtain shutter speeds faster than 1/200th second, the Z5 exposes only part of the sensor at one time, by starting the second curtain on its journey before the first curtain has completely opened, as shown in Figure 9.7. That effectively provides a briefer exposure as a slit of the shutter passes over the surface of the sensor. If the flash were to fire during the time when the front and rear curtains partially obscured the sensor, only the slit that was actually open would be exposed.

You'd end up with only a narrow band, representing the portion of the sensor that was exposed when the picture is taken. For shutter speeds *faster* than 1/200th second, the rear curtain begins moving *before* the front curtain reaches the bottom of the frame. As a result, a moving slit, the distance between the front and rear curtains, exposes one portion of the sensor at a time as it moves from the top to the bottom. Figure 9.7 shows three views of our typical (but imaginary) focal plane shutter. At left is pictured the closed shutter; in the middle version you can see the front curtain has moved down about 1/4 of the distance from the top; and in the right-hand version, the rear curtain has started to "chase" the front curtain across the frame toward the bottom.

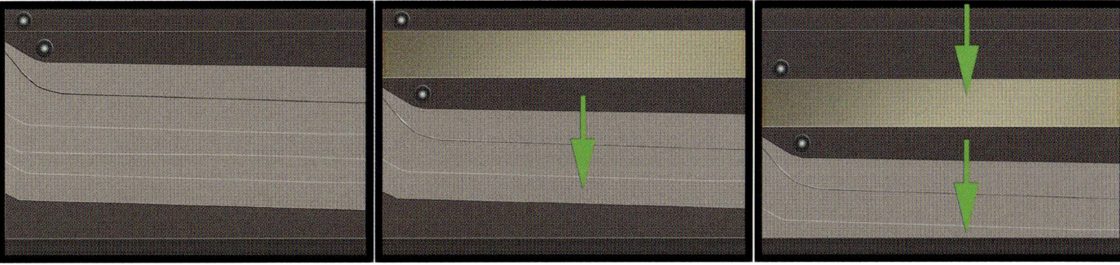

Figure 9.7 A closed shutter (left); partially open shutter as the front curtain begins to move downward (middle); only part of the sensor is exposed as the slit moves (right).

If the flash is triggered while this slit is moving, only the exposed portion of the sensor will receive any illumination. You end up with a photo like the one shown in Figure 9.8. Note that a band across the bottom of the image is black. That's a shadow of the rear shutter curtain, which had started to move when the flash was triggered. Sharp-eyed readers will wonder why the black band is at the *bottom* of the frame rather than at the top, where the rear curtain begins its journey. The answer is simple: your lens flips the image upside down and forms it on the sensor in a reversed position. You never notice that, because the camera is smart enough to show you the pixels that make up your photo in their proper orientation during picture review. But this image flip is why, if your sensor gets dirty and you detect a spot of dust in the upper half of a test photo, if cleaning manually, you need to look for the speck in the *bottom* half of the sensor.

I generally end up with sync-speed problems only when shooting in the studio, using studio flash units rather than my Nikon-dedicated Speedlights. That's because if you're using "smart" flash (like one of the Nikon Speedlights), the camera knows that a strobe is attached, and remedies any unintentional goof in shutter speed settings. If you happen to set the Z5's shutter to a faster speed in S or M mode, the camera will automatically adjust the shutter speed down to 1/200th second as soon as you turn on the flash (or prevent you from choosing a faster speed if the flash is already powered up). In A or P modes, where the Z5 selects the shutter speed, it will never choose a shutter speed higher than 1/200th second when using flash. In P mode, shutter speed is automatically set from 1/60th to 1/200th second when using flash.

But when using a non-dedicated flash, such as a studio unit plugged into an adapter mounted on the accessory shoe, the camera has no way of knowing that a flash is connected, so shutter speeds faster than 1/200th second can be set inadvertently. To avoid that problem with studio flash, I strongly recommend setting your camera to Manual exposure, and using the x200 shutter speed, which is

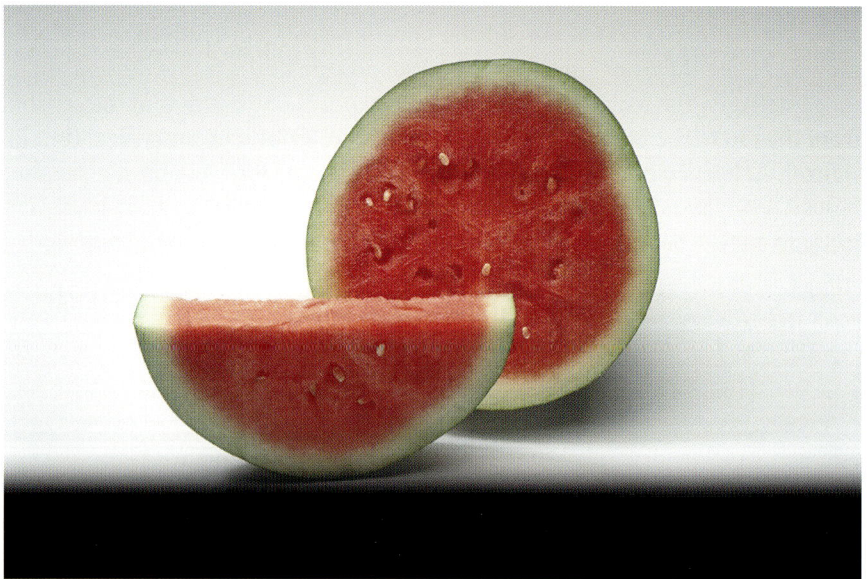

Figure 9.8 If a shutter speed faster than 1/200th second is used, you can end up photographing only a portion of the image.

located *past* the Bulb speed when rotating the main command dial all the way to the left. You won't have to worry as much about accidentally changing the shutter speed to an unusable setting; there is no speed *beyond* x200th second, and if you nudge the main command dial to the right, in Manual exposure mode, you'll get a Bulb or Time exposure, which will immediately become evident.

High-Speed Sync

Note that the Z5 can use a feature called *high-speed sync* that allows shutter speeds faster than 1/200th second with certain external-dedicated Nikon flash units. When using high-speed sync, the flash fires a continuous series of bursts at reduced power for the entire duration of the exposure, so that the illumination is able to expose the sensor as the slit moves. HS sync is set using the controls that adjust the compatible external flash. You don't need to make any special settings on the flash; the Z5 takes care of the details for you, as I'll describe in this section.

As I said earlier, triggering the electronic flash only when the shutter is completely open makes a lot of sense if you think about what's going on. To obtain shutter speeds faster than 1/200th second, the Z5 exposes only part of the sensor at one time, by starting the rear curtain on its journey before the front curtain has completely opened. That effectively provides a briefer exposure as a slit of the shutter passes over the surface of the sensor. If the flash were to fire during the time when the front and rear curtains partially obscured the sensor, only the area defined by the slit that was actually open would be exposed.

This technique is most useful outdoors when you need fill-in flash but find that 1/200th second is way too slow for the f/stop you want to use. For example, at ISO 200, an outdoors exposure is likely to be 1/200th second at, say, f/14, which is perfectly fine for an ambient/balanced fill-flash exposure if you don't mind the extreme depth-of-field offered by the small f/stop. But, what if you'd rather shoot at 1/1600th second at f/5.6? High-speed sync will let you do that, and you probably won't mind the reduced flash power, because you're looking for fill flash, anyway. This sync mode offers more flexibility than, say, dropping down to ISO 100.

High-speed sync is also useful when you want to use a larger f/stop to limit the amount of depth-of-field. Select a shutter speed higher than 1/200th second, and the faster-sync speed automatically reduces the effective light of the flash, without other intervention from you.

To use Auto FP sync with units like the Nikon SB-5000, SB-910/SB-900, SB-700, SB-500, SB-R200, and a few discontinued Speedlights like the SB-800 and SB-600, there is no setting to make on the flash itself. You need to use Custom Setting e1 to specify 1/200 s (Auto FP). When using P or A exposure modes, the shutter speed will be set to 1/200th second when a compatible external flash is attached. Higher shutter speeds than 1/200th second—all the way up to 1/8000th second—can then be used with full synchronization, at reduced flash output. There are also situations in which you might want to set flash sync speed to *less* than 1/200th second, say, because you *want* ambient light to produce secondary ghost images in your frame.

You can choose the following settings:

- **1/200 s (Auto FP).** This similar setting allows using the compatible external flash units with high-speed synchronization at 1/200th second or faster and activates auto FP sync when the camera selects a shutter speed of 1/200th second or faster in programmed and Aperture-priority modes. Other flash units will be used at speeds no faster than 1/200th second.

- **1/200 s.** At this default setting, only shutter speeds up to 1/200th second can be used with flash. **Note:** To lock in shutter speed at 1/200th second, rotate the main command dial in M or S modes to choose the x200 setting located after the 30 s (and Time and Bulb in Manual exposure) speeds. You'd use this when working with "dumb" studio flash units.

- **1/200 s–1/60 s.** You can also specify a specific shutter speed from the range of speeds 1/200th second to 1/60th second to be used as the synchronization speed for external flash units. Forcing a slower shutter speed produces a "slow-sync" effect. For example, when 1/60th second has been set as the maximum flash shutter speed, ambient light is more likely to contribute to the exposure. (See Figure 9.9.) That can help balance the flash exposure with available light falling on the background (use a tripod or VR to minimize ghost images). Or, that slow shutter speed can help generate ghost images when you intentionally want them to appear in your image, say, to create a feeling of motion.

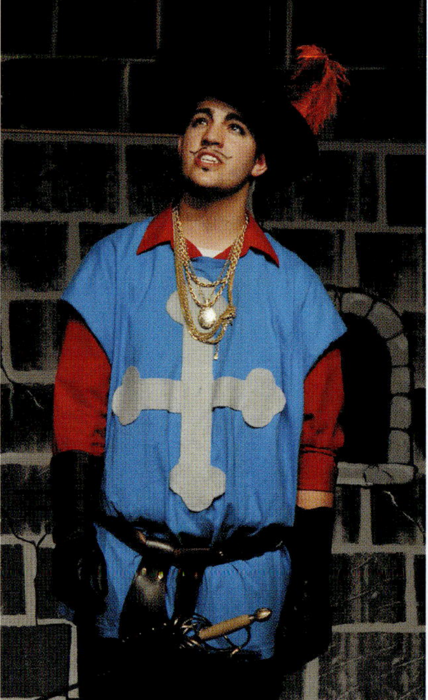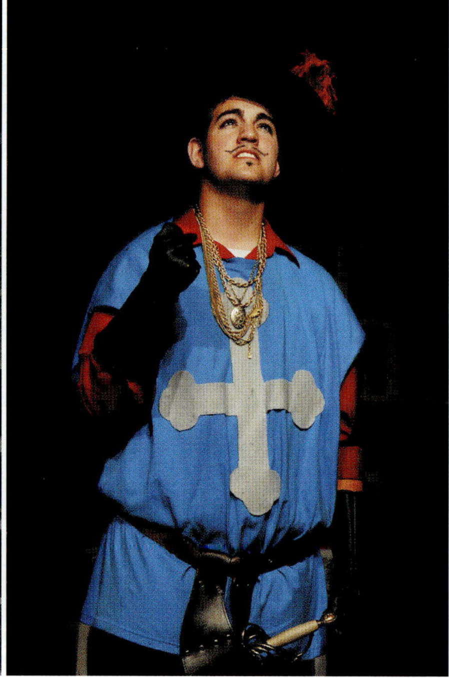

Figure 9.9 At 1/60th second, the ambient light behind the actor provided detail in the background (left). With a shutter speed of 1/200th second, the background is dark (right).

Using External Flash

In this section, we'll deal with the Nikon Creative Lighting System (CLS), which was introduced in July 2003, when the company unveiled the Speedlight SB-800, a flash unit compatible with early professional digital SLRs, such as the Nikon D2h/D2hs, and, within a few months, more affordable models like 2004's Nikon D70 and all subsequent dSLRs from the company. CLS has the following features, although not all of these are supported by every Nikon camera:

- **i-TTL.** Intelligent through-the-lens exposure control calculates exposure based on a monitor pre-flash that is fired a fraction of a second before the main burst, and then evaluated by the same RGB exposure sensor used for continuous light measurements. The system's intelligence allows sophisticated adjustments, such as balancing the flash exposure with the ambient light exposure, say, when you shoot in full daylight to fill in the shadows.

- **Advanced wireless lighting.** AWL is a system that uses the same pre-flash concept to communicate triggering and exposure information to external flash units that aren't physically linked to the camera and located within a reasonable distance (say, about 30 feet). You may be able to divide multiple flash units into up to three different "groups," and communicate with them using your choice of any of four "channels" (to avoid having your flash units triggered by the master flash of another Nikon photographer in the vicinity). I'll explain AWL in more detail in Chapter 10.

- **FV Lock.** A *flash value* locking system allows you to fix in place the current flash exposure so that you can, for example, measure flash exposure for a subject that is not in the center of the frame, and then reframe while using that value for subsequent exposures. You can define the Fn button to perform this function, as described in Chapter 12. When FV lock is activated, the Z5 meters only a center area measuring 8mm even if Matrix metering has been selected, when the flash is mounted in the hot shoe. In wireless modes, metering is done using the average of the entire frame.

- **Auto FP high-speed sync.** Focal plane HS sync allows synchronizing an external flash while using shutter speeds faster than 1/200th second. With a compatible flash and a camera like the Z5, shutter speeds up to 1/8000th second can be used, although only a part of the flash's illumination is used, and flash range is reduced (sometimes to as little as a few feet).

- **Focus assist.** Although the Z5 has focus assist illumination built-in, the CLS system also allows including wide-area AF-assist illumination to be built into the front of the flash unit, or into a flash connecting cable. Auxiliary focus assist illumination offers wider and/or more distant coverage.

- **Zoom coverage.** Some CLS-compatible flash units have a powered zoom head built in to allow changing the area covered by the flash to match the focal length of the lens in use, as communicated by the camera to the flash itself. Zooming can also be done manually.

- **Flash color information communication.** The exact color temperature of the light emitted by a CLS-compatible flash can vary, based on the duration of the flash burst. The flash is initially rather blue in color and becomes redder as the burst continues. The Speedlight is able to send information to the camera to allow adjusting white balance in AWB mode based on the true color information of the flash exposure.

If you want to temporarily disable a flash that's attached and powered up, a handy way to do this is to assign the Flash Disable/Enable function to the Fn1 or Fn2 buttons, using Custom Setting f2, as described in Chapter 12. Then, when you press the button, any external flash attached and powered up will not fire while the button is held down. This is useful if you want to temporarily disable the flash, say, to take a picture or two by available light, and then return to normal flash operation.

Using Flash Exposure Compensation

If the exposure produced by your flash isn't satisfactory, you can manually add or subtract exposure to the flash exposure calculated by the Z5. You can use the Flash Compensation entry in the Photo Shooting menu or assign Flash Mode/Flash Compensation to a button, such as Fn1, using Custom Setting f2: Custom Controls, as explained in Chapter 12. When assigned to a button, you can adjust Flash Mode by pressing the button and rotating the main command dial, and Flash Compensation by holding the button and rotating the sub-command dial. You can make adjustments from –3 EV to +1 EV in 1/3 EV increments.

As with ordinary exposure compensation, the adjustment you make remains in effect until you zero it out by pressing the Flash button and rotating the sub-command dial until 0 appears on the monochrome control panel and in the viewfinder. To view the current flash exposure compensation setting, press the Flash button. When compensation is being used, an icon will be shown in the display.

As also described in Chapter 12, you can use Custom Setting e3: Exposure Compensation for Flash to balance ambient light and flash exposure over the entire frame, or just take into account the background. The option specifies how the camera modifies the flash level when you apply exposure compensation. (The Z5 has separate ambient light exposure compensation and flash exposure compensation settings.) You can adjust one or the other, or both if you are using flash. This setting affects only *exposure compensation* (the ambient kind) when you are also using flash. It determines how ambient exposure compensation is applied when some of the illumination will also come from a flash unit.

- **Entire frame.** When you apply ambient exposure compensation (press the EV button on top of the camera to the right of the ISO button and rotate the main command dial), both ambient *and* flash exposure compensation are adjusted over the entire frame. That balances the exposure for the two elements.

- **Background only.** When this option is selected *only* ambient exposure compensation is changed when you apply it; flash exposure compensation is unaffected. So exposure compensation is applied only to the background areas of your image, which are typically illuminated by ambient light. Flash exposure compensation is not affected but can be set separately if you've assigned Flash Mode/Flash Exposure Compensation to a button using Custom Setting f2, as described earlier. If that's the case, just rotate the sub-command dial to adjust flash compensation.

EXPOSURE COMPENSATION COMBINES

An important thing to remember is that any ambient light and flash exposure compensation you specify *are combined*. So, if you select +2 EV using the Exposure Compensation button on the top of the camera (to the right of the ISO button), and then choose +2 flash exposure compensation, you end up with +4 EV added and, probably, an overexposed image.

Specifying Flash Shutter Speed

This is another way of specifying the shutter speed the Z5 will use when working with flash. Unlike Custom Setting e1: Flash Sync Speed described earlier, this setting determines the *slowest* shutter speed that is available for electronic flash synchronization when you're not using a "slow-sync" mode. When you want to avoid ghost images from a secondary exposure, you should use the highest shutter speed that will synchronize with your flash. This setting prevents programmed or Aperture-priority modes (which both select the shutter speed for you) from selecting a shutter speed that captures ambient light along with the flash.

With Custom Setting e2: Flash Shutter Speed, select a value from 30 s to 1/60 s, and the Z5 will avoid using speeds slower than the one you specify with electronic flash if you don't override that decision by deliberately choosing slow sync, slow rear-curtain sync, or red-eye reduction with slow sync. If you think you can hold the Z5 steady, a value of 1/30 s is a good compromise; if you have shaky hands, use 1/60 s or higher. Those with extraordinarily steady grips or who are using vibration reduction can try the 1/15 s setting. Remember that this setting only determines the slowest shutter speed that will be used, not the default shutter speed, which is set with Custom Setting e1.

Previewing Your Flash Effect

The Nikon Z5's compatible external units, including the SB-5000, SB-910, SB-700, and some earlier models, can simulate a modeling light, in the form of a set of repeated bursts of light that allow you to pre-visualize the effect the strobe will provide when fired for the main exposure. This modeling flash, turned on or off using Custom Setting e5, is not a perfect substitute for a real incandescent or fluorescent modeling lamp, as it lasts only for a short period of time and is not especially bright. However, it does assist in seeing how your subject will be illuminated, so you can spot any potential problems with shadows.

When this feature is activated, if you've assigned the Preview (depth-of-field) behavior to a custom button, pressing that control briefly triggers the modeling flash for your preview. Selecting Off disables the feature. You'll generally want to leave it On, except when you anticipate using the depth-of-field preview button for depth-of-field purposes (imagine that) and do *not* want the modeling flash to fire when the flash unit is charged and ready. Some external flash units, such as the SB-5000 and SB-910, have their own modeling flash buttons.

Flash Control

As I noted earlier, newer Nikon electronic flash units, such as the Nikon SB-5000, SB-500, SB-400, or SB-300 Speedlights are compatible with the unified flash control system, and can be adjusted by the Flash Control setting in the Photo Shooting menu. All other Nikon electronic flash units, including the SB-600, SB-700, SB-800, SB-900, and SB-910 must be adjusted using the controls *on the flash itself*. Not all of the options next can be accessed by every one of the Speedlights listed. For example, with the SB-400, you can only choose between TTL and Manual exposure, plus manual output levels. Unavailable options will be grayed out. To use the Flash Control menu entry, the flash must be mounted on the Z5's hot shoe, powered up, and not set in a Remote mode.

The exact options available from the Flash Control screen will vary, depending on the capabilities of the flash unit you are using. The initial screen may include some or all of the options shown in Figure 9.10, left. The Flash Control Mode screen for the SB-5000 is shown in Figure 9.10, right. I'll discuss each of the adjustments available, whether they are chosen from the Flash Control menu or using the flash unit's own controls, in the sections that follow. Consult your flash unit's manual for the exact procedures used to make the adjustments described.

Figure 9.10 Flash Control menu (left); setting flash modes (right).

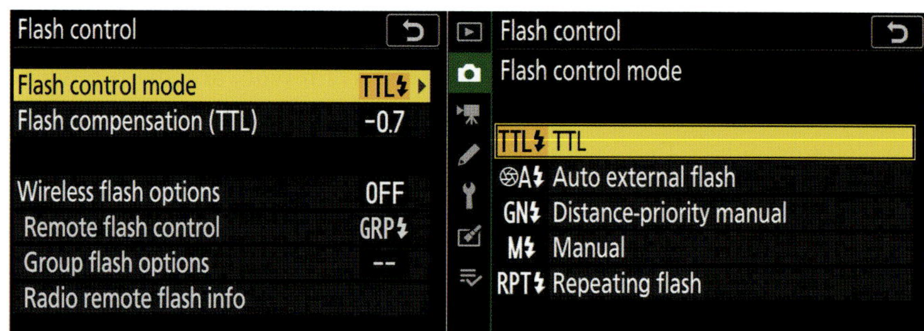

Working with Nikon Flash External Units

Nikon offers a wide range of external flash units that are compatible with CLS, ranging from the top-of-the-line SB-5000 to the entry-level SB-300, and will probably introduce more Speedlights during the life of this book. In addition, there are a number of older units that have been officially or unofficially discontinued, such as the SB-600, SB-400, SB-800, and SB-910/SB-900, which are still available, in both new and used condition. I'm going to concentrate on the most recent in the following sections.

Nikon SB-300

This entry-level Speedlight, at about $150, is the smallest and most basic of the Nikon series of Speedlights. The SB-300 has a limited, easy-to-use feature set suited for point-and-shoot photography and some slightly more advanced techniques. Do note however that it does not support wireless off-camera flash. The SB-300 has a moderate guide number of 18/59 at ISO 100. Its main advantage, then, is to provide some additional elevation of the flash above the camera to provide an improved coverage angle and less chance of red-eye effects. Its flash head tilts up to 120 degrees, with click stops at 120, 90, 75, and 60 degrees when the flash is pointed directly ahead. It has a zoom flash head. The SB-300 is lighter in weight at 3.4 ounces than the SB-400 it replaces and uses two AAA batteries.

Nikon SB-400

Recently discontinued, but still widely available new from many retailers, this entry-level Speedlight (see Figure 9.11) was, until the SB-300 was unveiled, the smallest and most basic of the series. The SB-400 has a limited, easy-to-use feature set suited for point-and-shoot photography and some slightly more advanced techniques. Do note however that, like the SB-300, it does not support wireless off-camera flash. The 4.5-ounce SB-400 has a moderate guide number of 21/69 at ISO 100 when the zooming head (which can be set to either 18mm or 27mm) is at the 18mm position. It tilts up to 90 degrees, allowing you to bounce the light off of a ceiling, but it cannot be rotated to the side.

Nikon SB-500

This Nikon flash unit ($250) has a guide number of 24/79 at ISO 100, a speedy recycle time of about 3.5 seconds, and runs on 2 AA batteries for up to 140 flashes. It includes a built-in LED video light with three output levels and can also be used for still photography as fill light, especially at the brightest setting. It's perfect for wireless mode (discussed in Chapter 10), with four wireless channels and two groups available in Commander mode. The SB-500's head tilts up to 90 degrees, with click-stops at 0, 60, 75, and 90. It rotates horizontally 180 degrees to the left and right, for flexible bounce-flash lighting. (See Figure 9.12.) If you need a zoom head to adjust flash output to better distribute light at various focal lengths, you're better off with the SB-700 even with its limited zoom range (described next); this unit lacks zooming capabilities.

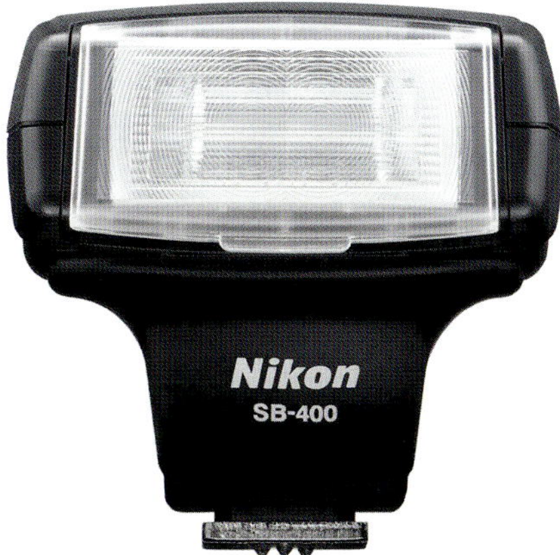

Figure 9.11 The Nikon SB-400 is an entry-level flash best suited for Nikon's entry-level dSLRs.

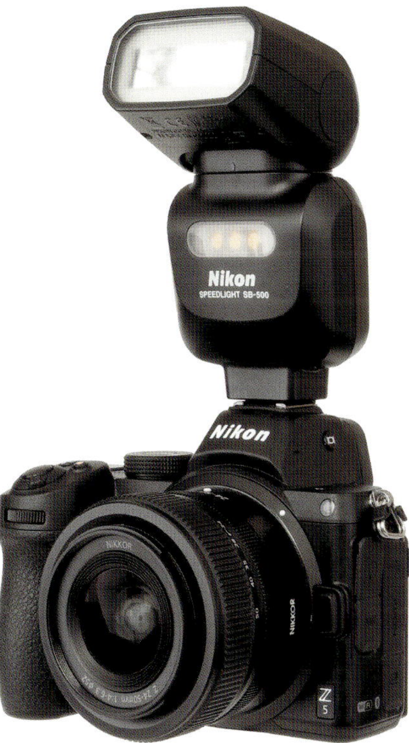

Figure 9.12 The Nikon SB-500.

Nikon SB-700

This affordable (about $330) unit has a guide number of 28/92 (meters/feet) at ISO 100 when set to the 35mm zoom position. It has many of the top-model SB-910's features, including zoomable flash coverage equal to the field of view of 24-120mm settings with a full-frame camera, and extra-wide 14mm coverage with a built-in diffuser panel. It has a built-in modeling flash feature, and a wireless Commander mode.

But the SB-700 lacks some important features found in the SB-910 and SB-5000. Depending on how you use your Speedlight, these differences may or may not be important to you. They include:

- **No repeating flash mode.** You can't shoot interesting stroboscopic effects with the SB-700 as you can with the SB-5000 or older SB-910/900 units.
- **No port for external power pack.** Using an external battery pack, like those available from Quantum and others, can be important for wedding and event photographers who want to fire off a bunch of shots quickly, while avoiding frequent changes of the AA batteries the SB-700 uses. An external pack has another benefit: more exposures before the Speedlight slows down to prevent overheating. External batteries don't generate heat inside the flash as internal batteries do.
- **No external PC/X sync socket.** This option, not found on the SB-700, is of limited use for those who want to attach an off-camera flash to the camera, which does have a PC/X contact.
- **Limited zoom range.** The SB-700's zoom head is limited to 24-120mm, plus 14mm with the diffuser panel. The ability to match the zoom head to the focal length you're using can match the coverage to the field of view, so the flash's output isn't wasted illuminating areas that aren't within the actual frame.

Nikon SB-R200

One oddball flash unit in the Nikon line is the SB-R200. This $180 unit is a specialized wireless-only flash that's especially useful for close-up photography and is often purchased in pairs for use with the Nikon R1 and R1C1 Wireless Close-Up Speedlight systems. Its output power is low at 10/33 (meters/feet) for ISO 100 as you might expect for a unit used to photograph subjects that are often inches from the camera. It has a fixed coverage angle of 78 degrees horizontal and 60 degrees vertical, but the flash head tilts down to 60 degrees and up to 45 degrees (with detents every 15 degrees in both directions). In this case, "up" and "down" has a different meaning, because the SB-R200 can be mounted on the SX-1 Attachment Ring mounted around the lens, so the pair of flash units are on the sides and tilted toward or away from the optical axis. It supports i-TTL, D-TTL, TTL (for film cameras), and Manual modes.

Nikon SB-910

The Nikon SB-910 was the flagship of the Nikon flash lineup until the SB-5000 model was unveiled. However, the SB-910 remains one of the most-used Nikon flash units (along with its predecessor, the SB-900), so I'll continue to include it in my coverage of Speedlights for the foreseeable future. It's still widely available new or used for about $400, and has a guide number of 34/111.5 (meters/

feet) when the "zooming" flash head (which can be set to adjust the coverage angle of the lens) is set to the 35mm position. It includes Commander mode, repeating flash, modeling light, and selectable power output, along with some extra capabilities.

The SB-910 was basically a slight reboot of the older SB-900, which gained a bad reputation for overheating and then shutting down after a relatively small number of consecutive exposures (as few as a dozen or so shots). The SB-910 also can overheat but features a different thermal protection system. Instead of disabling the flash as it begins warming up, the SB-910 increases the recycle time between flashes, giving the unit additional time to cool a bit before the next shot. While this "improvement" is not a real fix, it does encourage you to slow your shooting pace a bit to stretch out the number of flashes this Speedlight produces before it must be shut down for additional cooling.

Nikon estimates that you should be able to get 190 flashes from the SB-910 when using AA 2600 mAh rechargeable batteries, if firing the Speedlight at full output once every 30 seconds, with a minimum recycling time of 2.3 seconds (which gradually becomes longer as the flash heats up and the thermal protection kicks in). To get the maximum number of shots from your batteries, Nikon figures that AF-assist illumination, power zoom, and the LCD panel illumination are switched off.

There are some improvements, such as illuminated buttons and a restyled soft case, but, in general, the SB-910 is very similar to the SB-900 that we Nikon photographers have learned to know and fear. For example, you can angle the flash and rotate it to provide bounce flash. It includes additional, non-through-the-lens exposure modes, thanks to its built-in light sensor, and can "zoom" and diffuse its coverage angle to illuminate the field of view of lenses from 8mm to 200mm.

The SB-910/SB-900 also has its own powerful focus assist lamp to aid autofocus in dim lighting, and has reduced red-eye effects simply because the unit, even when attached to the Z5 and not used off-camera, is mounted in a higher position that tends to eliminate reflections from the eye back to the camera lens.

Nikon SB-5000

This $600 Speedlight is the flagship of the Nikon flash lineup. While it resembles the SB-910 and has a virtually identical guide number (34.5 meters, 113 feet), it more or less solves the overheating problem that plagued its top-line predecessors. A novel internal cooling system purportedly allows up to 90 consecutive shots, or 120 shots at five-second intervals without overheating. (Wedding photographers will love this.)

However, the big news is the addition of radio control to the optical triggering available with previous Nikon flash units that could be operated wirelessly. Radio control allows triggering the flash from a distance of nearly 100 feet—without requiring a line-of-sight connection. Best of all, you don't need to purchase two of these to use the SB-5000 wirelessly. Nikon already has a radio trigger in its product line, the WR-R10 wireless remote adapter that I have been using for years as a remote shutter release. As a trigger-only device, the WR-R10 has a longer range than the SU-800 commander used for optical wireless operation. The SB-5000 retains compatibility with Nikon's earlier optical wireless system, so your current flash units can be used with it in non-radio mode.

I power my SB-5000 (and all my other Speedlights) with Panasonic (formerly Sanyo) Eneloop AA nickel metal hydride batteries. These are a special type of rechargeable battery with a feature that's ideal for electronic flash use. The Eneloop cells, unlike conventional rechargeable batteries, don't self-discharge over relative short periods of time. Once charged, they can hold onto most of their juice for a year or more. That means you can stuff some of these into your Speedlight, along with a few spares in your camera bag, and not worry about whether the batteries have retained their power between uses. There's nothing worse than firing up your strobe after not using it for a month and discovering that the batteries are dead.

Note that the SB-5000 and many other Nikon flash units, like your camera, contains firmware that can be updated. The Custom Settings readouts on the flash itself will tell you what firmware version you currently have. If an update is required, you'll need to download the firmware module from the Nikon website. Load it onto a memory card, and then mount the flash on your Z5 and power it up. You'll find a fourth entry in the Firmware section of the Setup menu, marked S (for Speedlight or Strobe). The SB-910's firmware can be updated through the camera/flash connection just like the camera's own firmware.

Figure 9.13 shows the SB-5000 fastened to the optional Nikon SK-7 bracket and linked to a Nikon Z5 through the available SC-28 cable. There are a couple advantages to this configuration. First, the side-mounting moves the flash even farther from the axis of the lens, providing additional red-eye protection. You can still tilt the flash for bounce effects. I find this setup easier to hold, and not as awkward because you don't have a top-heavy flash unit mounted above the camera.

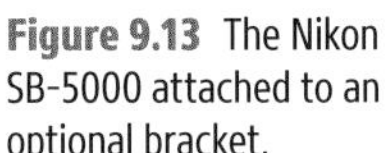

Figure 9.13 The Nikon SB-5000 attached to an optional bracket.

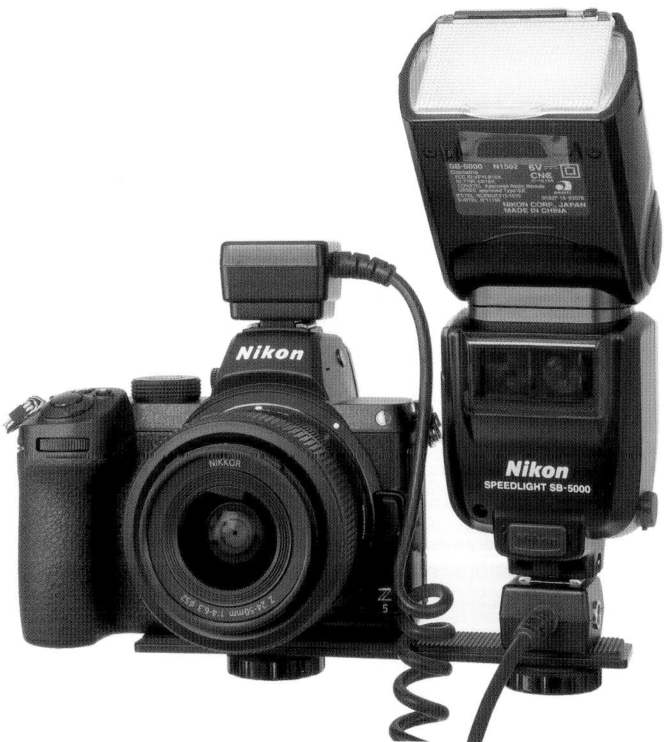

But, best of all, it's easy to uncouple the flash/SC-28 from the bracket and use both off-camera. There's no need to fuss with wireless modes, channels, groups, or other settings; the flash thinks that it's still connected directly to the Z5—which it is, of course. Another nine-foot cable, the SC-29, is available and has a built-in focus assist illuminator. I own both, but I like having the SC-29's focus-assist lamp on top of the camera, so that it is aimed at my subject should the Z5 need a bit of extra illumination for focusing. Although the SB-5000 has its own focus lamp, it may or may not be pointed at your subject when it comes time to use it.

Light Modifiers

The top-of-the-line Speedlights have a better array of included light-modifying tools than other Speedlights in the Nikon line. The standard pop-up white "card" slides out of the flash head. The card reflects a little fill illumination toward your subject when the flash is tilted to bounce off a ceiling or rotated and tilted to bounce off a wall or other surface. A wide-angle diffuser also slides out and rotates to cover the front of the flash and spread the light to cover lenses with focal lengths as wide as 12mm. The included diffuser dome (see Figure 9.14, center) provides softer illumination for direct flash, with the flash pointed at your subject, or something of a "bare bulb" effect when pointed upward. (The "bare bulb" concept dates back to film days when an electronic flash, flashbulb (!), or even an incandescent lamp was used without a reflector or shade to provide a flood of soft illumination that spread out in all directions from the source.)

Various filters are available for Nikon strobes to change the color of the light source. Two are included with the SB-910 and SB-5000, the SZ-2TN incandescent filter (shown in Figure 9.14, right) and the SZ-2FL fluorescent filter. The SJ-3 color filter set ($28) is 20 gelatin filters in eight different colors, including blue, yellow, red, and amber. The incandescent filter is most useful, because it changes the Speedlight's illumination to match typical indoor lamps, so you can use both to light a scene without

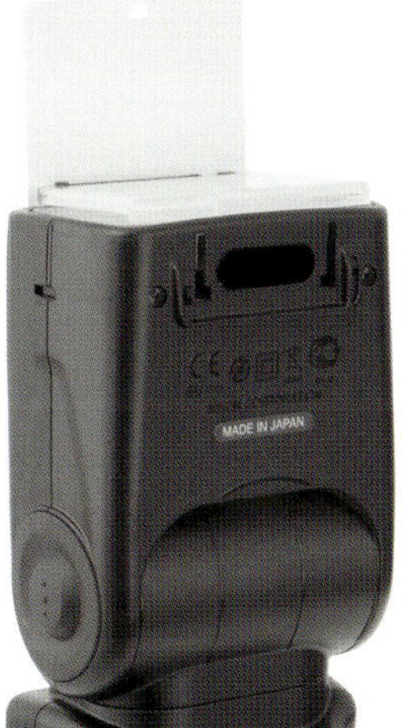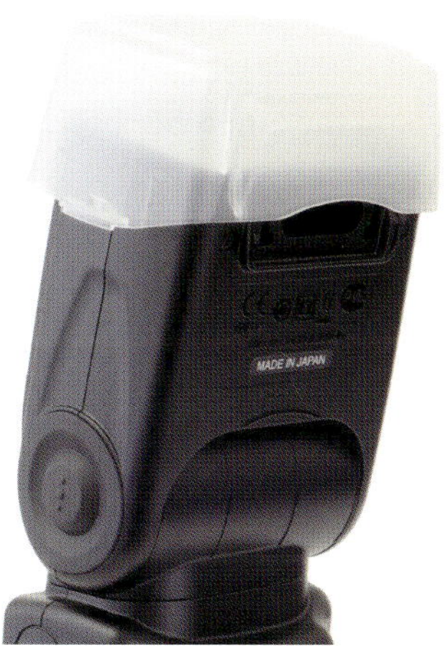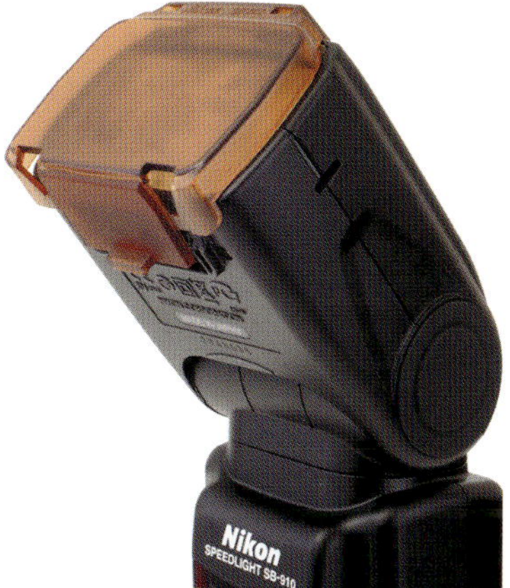

Figure 9.14 Left: The slide-out bounce card adds a kicker of light to fill in shadows or provide a catch light in the eyes of humans (or others). Center: The included diffuser dome produces a soft, flattering light. Right: The SZ-2TN incandescent filter warms the flash's illumination to match tungsten lighting.

encountering a nasty mixed-lighting situation. The nifty thing about the SZ-series filters is that they include a type of bar code that can be read by a sensor underneath the unit's flash head, so the strobe (and your Z5) "knows" that a particular filter has been fitted.

Other Accessories

The top-end flash units come with the AS-21 Speedlight Stand, which lets you give the strobe a broad "foot" that can rest on any flat surface when working in wireless mode. The stand has a tripod-type socket underneath, so you can also mount the flash on a tripod or light stand without needing to purchase a special adapter.

Not included are things like the WG-AS3 Water Guard, a $35 shield used when the flash is mounted on the Z5, to protect the hot shoe contact from moisture or (more likely) driving rain in sports photography situations. Well-heeled photographers who shoot weddings or events and don't already own a Quantum battery pack may be interested in the SD-9 High Performance Battery pack ($255), which holds up to eight AA batteries or the (now discontinued) SK-6 Power Bracket, which could be outfitted with four AA batteries and provides a side-mounted handle as well as an auxiliary power source.

Using Zoom Heads

External flash zoom heads can adjust themselves automatically to match lens focal lengths in use reported by the Z5 to the flash unit, or you can adjust the zoom head position manually if you want to use a setting that doesn't correspond to the automatic setting the flash will use. With older flash units, like the discontinued SB-600, automatic zoom adjustment wastes some of your flash's power, because the flash unit assumes that the focal length reported comes from a full-frame camera. Because of the 1.5X crop factor when the Z5 is used in DX mode, the flash coverage when the flash is set to a particular focal length will be wider than is required by the Z5's cropped image.

You can manually adjust the zoom position yourself, using positions built into the flash unit that more closely correspond to your Z5's field of view when using the SB-5000, SB-910, and SB-900 (which do not automatically take into account the difference between FX/full-frame and DX/APS-C coverage).

Flash Modes

I introduced flash modes (as well as *flash sync* modes) earlier in this chapter. External flash units have various flash modes included, which are available or not available with different camera models, including both the latest model dSLRs, some really ancient digital SLRs, and even more aged film cameras. A table showing most of the groups is included in the manuals for the external flash units, but the table is irrelevant for Z5 users (unless you happen to own an older digital or film SLR, as well). All you really need to know is that the Z5 is fully compatible with the Nikon SB-800 and all flashes introduced since that model debuted.

To change flash mode with the SB-5000, press the rotary multi selector right button to highlight the flash mode, then rotate the multi selector to choose the mode you want. Press the center OK button to confirm. With the SB-910 or SB-900, press the MODE button on the back-left edge, then release it and rotate the selector dial until the mode you want appears on the LCD. The TTL automatic flash modes available are described next. (The SB-700 has a sliding mode selector switch to the left of the Speedlight's LCD with positions for TTL, Manual, and GN settings. Those are the only modes available with that flash when you're using it as a Master. However, when the SB-700 is used as a remote flash triggered by a Master Commander flash, it can operate in Repeating mode.)

- **iTTL Automatic Balanced Fill Flash.** In both Matrix and Center-weighted camera exposure modes, the camera and flash balance the exposure so that the main subject and background are well-exposed. A TTL BL indicator appears on the LCD. However, if you switch to Spot metering, the flash switches to standard iTTL, described next.

- **Standard iTTL.** In this mode, activated when Spot metering is selected (or if you've fixed the flash exposure using FV Lock), the exposure is set for the main subject, and the background exposure is not taken into account. *Only* the flash exposure is measured and used to determine exposure. A TTL indicator appears on the LCD. In either iTTL Automatic Balanced Fill Flash or Standard iTTL modes, if the full power of the flash is used, the ready-light indicator on the flash and in the camera viewfinder will blink for three seconds. This is your cue that perhaps even the full power of the flash might not have been enough for proper exposure. If that's the case, an EV indicator will display the amount of underexposure (–0.3 to –3.0 EV) on the LCD while the ready-light indicator flashes.

- **AA: Auto Aperture flash.** An A indicator next to an icon representing a lens opening/aperture is shown on the LCD when this mode is selected. The SB-5000 or SB-910/SB-900 uses a built-in light sensor to measure the amount of flash illumination reflected back from the subject, and adjusts the output to produce an appropriate exposure based on the ISO, aperture, focal length, and flash compensation values set on the Z5. This setting on the flash can be used with the Z5 in Program or Aperture-priority modes. Like the A and GN modes described next, this option is a hold-over to provide compatibility with some older Nikon cameras, and not really useful for the Z5.

- **A: Non-TTL auto flash.** In this mode, the Speedlight's sensor measures the flash illumination reflected back from the subject and adjusts the output to provide an appropriate exposure, without the feedback about the aperture setting of the camera that's used with AA mode. This setting on the flash can be used when the Z5 is set to Aperture-priority or Manual modes. You can use this setting to manually "bracket" exposures, as adjusting the aperture value of the lens will produce more or less exposure; the flash has no idea what aperture you've changed to.

- **GN: Distance priority manual.** You enter a distance value, and the SB-5000 or SB-910/SB-900 adjusts light output based on distance, ISO, and aperture to produce the right exposure in either Aperture-priority or Manual exposure modes. You can choose this option from the Flash Control menu with the SB-5000. With the SB-910/SB-900, press the MODE button on the flash and rotate the selector dial until the GN indicator appears (the GN option appears only when the flash is pointed directly ahead, or is in the downward bounce position). Then press the OK button to confirm your choice. After that, you can specify a shooting distance by pressing the Function 2 button, and then rotating the selector dial until the distance you want is indicated on the LCD. Press the OK button to confirm. The SB-5000 or SB-910/SB-900 will indicate a recommended aperture, which you then set on the lens mounted on the Z5 in Manual exposure mode.

- **M: Manual flash.** The flash fires at a fixed output level. Press the MODE button and rotate the selector dial until M appears on the LCD panel. Press the OK button to confirm your choice. Choose the power output level you want, down to 1/256th power with the SB-5000 and 1/128th power with most other Nikon Speedlights. Calculate the correct f/stop to use, either by taking a few test photos with a flash meter or by the seat of your pants. Then, set the Z5 to Aperture-priority or Manual exposure and choose the f/stop you've decided on.
- **RPT: Repeating flash.** The flash fires repeatedly to produce a multiple flash strobing effect. To use this mode, set the Z5's exposure mode to Manual. Then set up the number of repeating flashes per frame, frequency, and flash output level, as described in Chapter 12.

Repeating Flash

Repeating flash is a function that can be used with external flashes like the SB-5000, SB-910, and SB-900. Check your manual for the exact buttons to press to make the following settings using Manual exposure mode:

1. **Set flash for RPT mode.** With the SB-5000, use the rotary multi selector right button (MODE button) to highlight mode, and then rotate the dial to select repeating flash. With the SB-910/SB-900, press the MODE button and rotate the selector dial until RPT is shown at upper left on the LCD. Then press the OK button to confirm.

2. **Choose Flash Output Level.** With these flash units, you must specify the power level of the flash. That level will determine the range of the number of flashes you can expect from the capacitor's charge. Use the flash mode controls on the SB-5000 to set output level. With the SB-910/SB-900, press the Function 2 button (on the SB-910) or the Function 1 button (on the SB-900) until the number of flashes is highlighted on the LCD (to the immediate right of the RPT indicator), and rotate the selector dial. Choose a power level from 1/8th to 1/128th power.

3. **Select number of shots.** Next, choose the number of shots in your series. With the SB-5000, use the Times setting to determine how many flashes to emit. With the SB-910, highlight the option by pressing the Function 3 button; it's the Function 2 button on the SB-900. The number of shots you can specify varies depending on the shutter speed and firing frequency (specified next).

4. **Choose frequency: how many shots per second.** This determines how quickly the series is taken. With the SB-5000, use the Hz setting. With the SB-910, highlight the option by pressing the Function 3 button; it's the Function 2 button on the SB-900.

The maximum number of shots in a series varies, depending on the shutter speed, output level, and frequency you select. The multiple flashes can be emitted only while the shutter is completely open, so a faster shutter speed limits the number of bursts that can be fired off at a given frequency. High output levels and high frequency settings both deplete the capacitor more quickly. So, the number of possible bursts will depend on the combination you choose. With the SB-910 or SB-5000, the maximum number of shots you can expect is about 90 (at 1/64th or 1/128th power), and frequencies of from 1 to 3 bursts per second. That's a large number of firings over a long period of time (30 seconds or more).

If you want very rapid bursts, expect fewer total flashes: the SB-5000 and SB-910 will give you 24 firings at 1/128th power and 20 to 100 firings per second. Still, that's quite a bit of flexibility if you think about it. You can get 24 bursts in just a bit more than one second at the 20Hz setting, or over five seconds at the 100Hz setting. I needed only four bursts to capture the plummeting lime seen in Figure 9.15. One thing you'll notice is that as moving objects slow or speed up, the distance between one "shot" in a series varies.

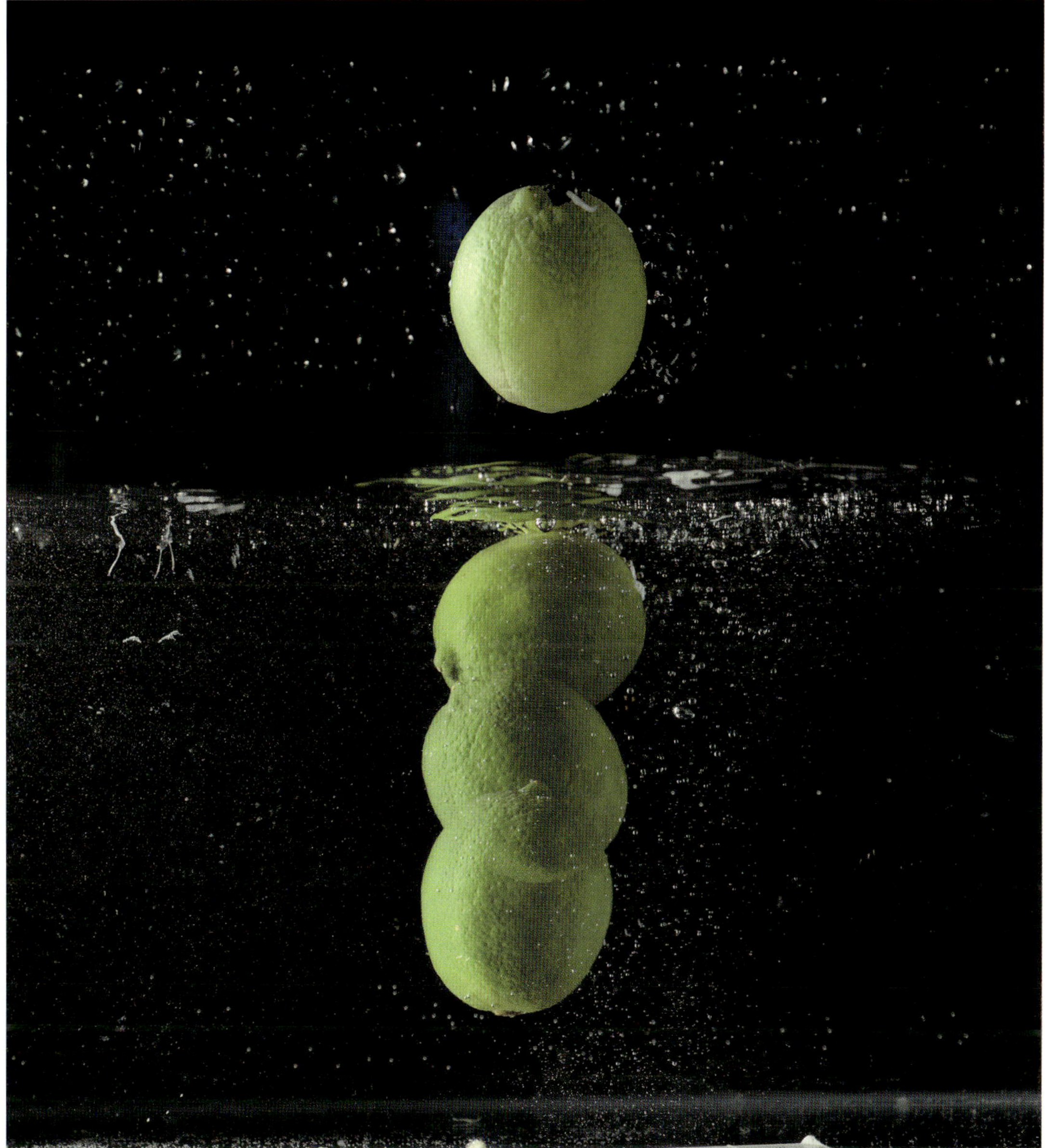

Figure 9.15 Capturing a lime as it plunges into a half-filled fish tank.

BURN OUT

When using repeating flash with the SB-910/SB-900, SB-700, SB-5000, or *any* large number of consecutive flashes in any mode (more than about 15 shots at full power), allow the flash to cool off (Nikon recommends a 10-minute time out) to avoid overheating the flash. The SB-5000 increases the recycling time to extend the useful period, while the SB-910/SB-900, SB-700, or SB-500 will signal you when it's time for a cooling-off period. The flash will actually disable itself, if necessary, to prevent damage.

As I mentioned in the last chapter, one of the chief objections to the use of electronic flash is the stark, flat look of direct/on-camera flash, as you can see in Figure 10.1. But as flash wizard Joe McNally, author of *The Hotshoe Diaries*, has proven, small flash units can produce amazingly creative images when used properly.

An on-camera flash is useful for fill light or as a master flash to trigger other units; the real key to effective flash photography is to get the flash off the camera, so its illumination can be used to paint your subject in interesting and subtle ways from a variety of angles.

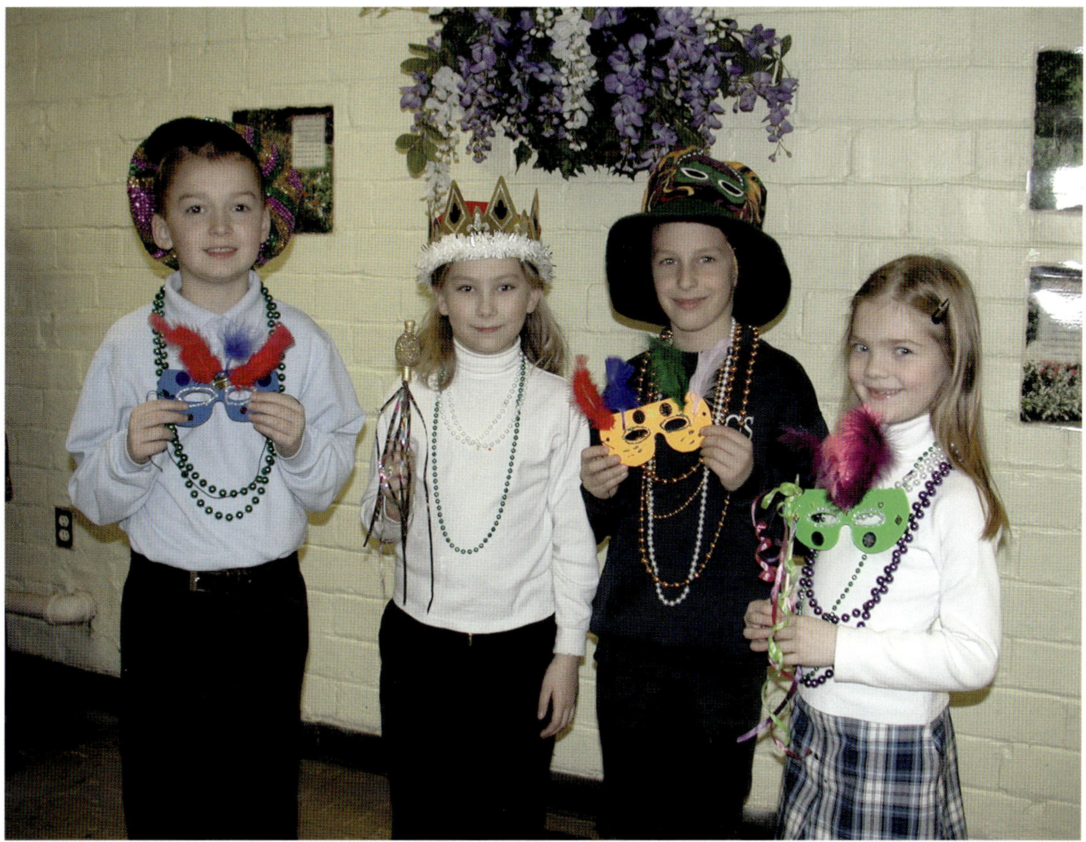

Figure 10.1 Direct flash is harsh and flat.

Of course, often, using a cable to liberate your external flash from the accessory shoe isn't enough. Nor is the use of just a single electronic flash always the best solution; two or more units can be combined in interesting ways to sculpt with light. What we have really needed is a way to trigger one—or more—flash units wirelessly, giving us the freedom to place the electronic flash anywhere in the scene and, if our budgets and time allow, to work in this mode with multiple flashes.

Nikon shooters have long had wireless flash capabilities, ever since the creation of the Nikon Creative Lighting System, described in Chapter 9. Like the i-TTL exposure system, the Advanced Wireless Lighting (AWL) system uses pre-flashes that fire before the main exposure to transmit triggering and exposure information to external flash units that aren't physically connected to the Z5. Depending on whether you're using the SB-5000 or one of the older flash units, you may be able to divide multiple flash units into as many as three different "groups" (six with the SB-5000) and communicate with them using your choice of any of up to four "channels" (to avoid interference from other Nikon photographers within range of your flash units who might be using the same channel).

It's not possible to cover every aspect of wireless flash in one chapter. There are too many permutations involved. For example, you can use external flash like the SB-700 or SB-5000, an SU-800 wireless trigger, or a PocketWizard-type device as the master. You may have one external "slave" flash or use several. It's possible to control all your wireless flash units as if they were one multi-headed flash, or you can allocate them into "groups" that can be managed individually. You may select one of four "channels" to communicate with your strobes. These are all aspects that you'll want to explore as you become used to working with the Z5's wireless capabilities.

What I hope to do in this chapter is provide the introduction to the basics so that you'll have the information you need to understand the step-by-step instructions for your Speedlight using the detailed manual supplied with the unit. Once you learn how to operate the Z5's wireless capabilities, you can then embark on your own exploration of the possibilities.

Elements of Wireless Flash

Here are some of the key concepts to electronic flash and wireless flash that I'll be describing in this chapter:

- **Master flash.** The *master* is the flash (or other device) that commands each of the additional flashes when using Commander mode.
- **Remote flashes.** For wireless operation, you need at least one flash unit not mounted on the camera, in addition to the master device (which can be another flash or a transmitter unit).
- **Channels.** Nikon's wireless flash system offers users the ability to determine on which of four possible channels the flash units can communicate.
- **Groups.** Nikon's wireless flash system lets you designate multiple flash units in separate groups (as many as three groups, or six groups with the SB-5000). You can then have flash units in one group fire at a different output level than flash units in another group. This lets you create different styles of lighting for portraits and other shots.

- **Lighting ratios.** You can control the power of multiple off-camera Speedlights assigned to each group, in order to adjust each unit's relative contribution to the image, for more dramatic portraits and other effects.

- **Control system.** The SB-5000, whether used alone or with other flashes, can use either the existing optical/infrared control system deployed with earlier Speedlights or the newer radio control offered with the SB-5000 flash or with the WR-R10 as a radio trigger.

Master Flash

The master flash is the commander that tells all the other units in a setup what to do, including when to fire, and at what intensity. It communicates with your Z5, and then, when the firing parameters are determined by the camera (or you, manually), passes along the information to the individual remote flash units. Your master can be one of the following:

- **An external flash with Commander capabilities.** Use a Nikon SB-5000, SB-910, SB-700, SB-500, or compatible earlier units to communicate with the remote Speedlights using optical or, with the SB-5000, radio control. When used as a master flash, the external strobe must be physically connected to the Z5. You can mount the flash on the camera's accessory hot shoe, or mount it on a cable, such as the SC-28 or SC-29, and then connect the other end of the cable to the Z5's accessory shoe. (See Figure 10.2.) The master flash can be set so that it does or does not contribute to the exposure, although, because it can be used off-camera, the latter mode offers more advantages.

- **The Nikon SU-800.** This device is an expensive non-flash (about $340) that does nothing but serve as an optical commander for CLS-compatible flash units (see Figure 10.3). It mounts on the hot

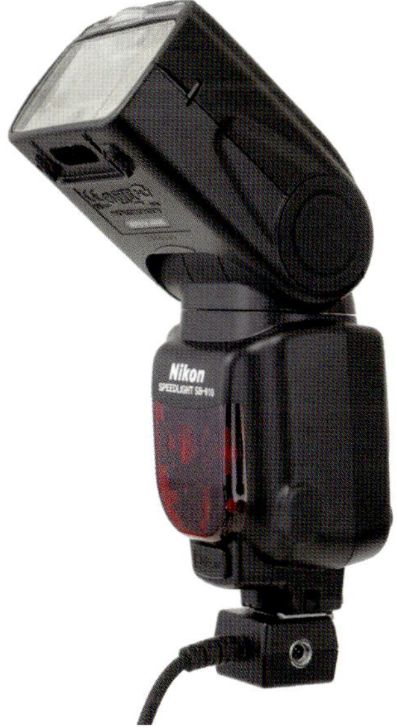

Figure 10.2 An external flash can be used as an off-camera master when connected to a cable that links it to the camera.

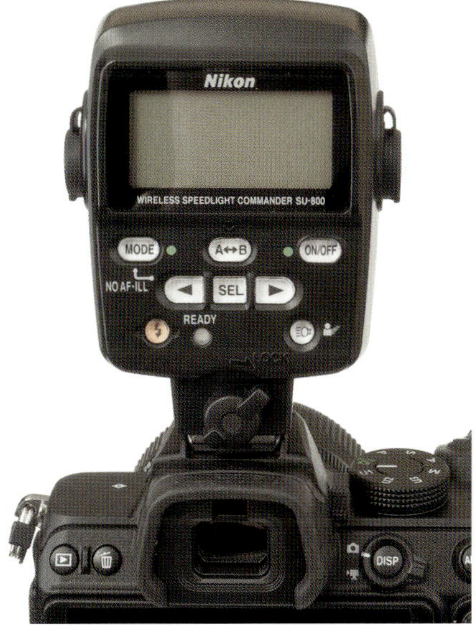

Figure 10.3 The Nikon SU-800 can serve as a master unit.

shoe of the camera and emits infrared signals (rather than monitor pre-flashes) to trigger the remote flash units. It otherwise functions exactly like a "real" master flash, communicating to groups of Speedlights over the same channels, and allowing i-TTL exposure control. It has two main uses. One application is as a commander for Nikon's wireless "macro" lights, the SB-R200 units. In that mode, it's ideal for any Nikon dSLR, as it serves as a trigger for models without a built-in flash, such as the Z5, Z7, D850, D810, D5, D4, D4s, D3, D3s, or D3x, and some earlier models. It's also a more convenient close-range substitute for an attached master because it emits no light to cast shadows.

I like to use my SU-800 for off-camera flash with no need to fuss with a cable connection or camera-mounted master flash unit. The Robert E. Lee re-enactor was standing in the shade, and the diffused light was not harsh (which is the most common reason for adding flash fill). However, the difference in illumination between him *and* the background was significant, making it impossible to set an exposure that would capture both him and the flag and tent behind him (Figure 10.4, left). I set the SB-500 to Manual exposure and 1/4 power, held it off to the left, and shot at 1/200th second and f/16 to get the photo at right. The SU-800's infrared control has an impressive 66-foot range under these conditions (that is, not under direct sunlight). It helped me enhance the image with the off-camera flash—which provided a nice catchlight in the General's eye—as the fill illumination.

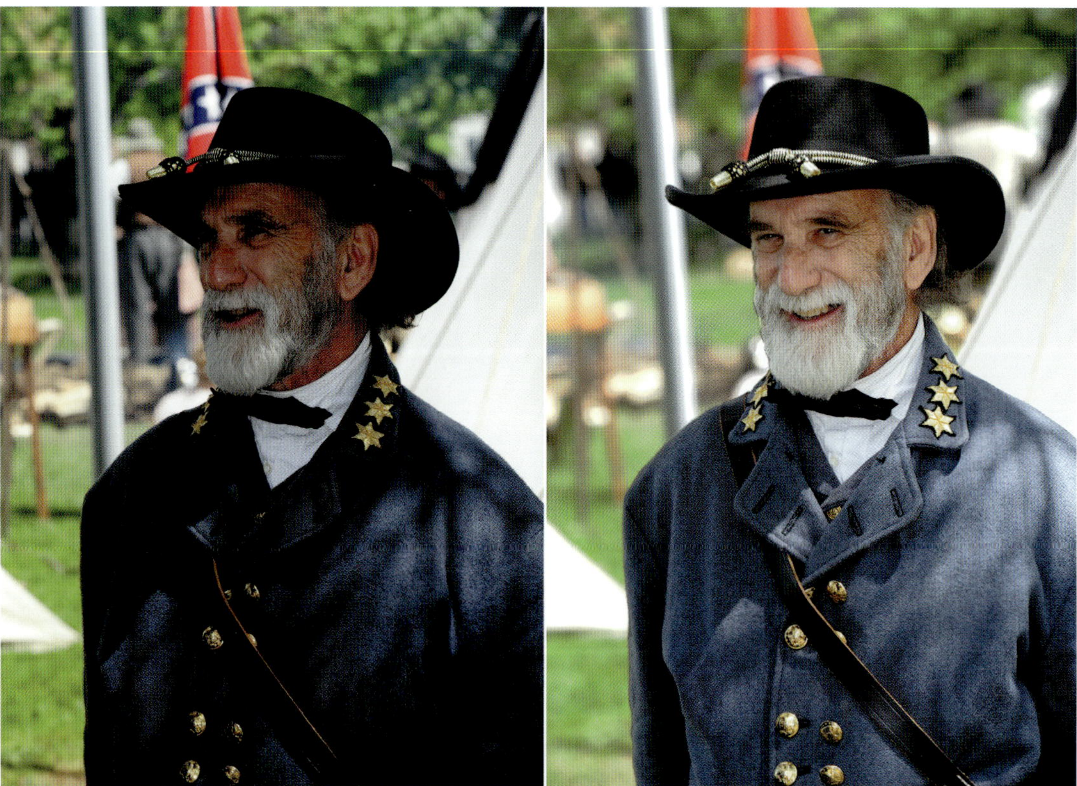

Figure 10.4 A flash can provide pleasing fill illumination outdoors in the shade.

- **Nikon WR-R10.** When working with the SB-5000 in radio control mode, this device, plugged into the remote control/accessory connector on the side of the camera, can serve as a master controller. Unless you purchased your unit very recently, you may need to send your unit in to Nikon for a firmware upgrade to Version 3.00 to allow flash control. The firmware upgrade cannot be performed by the user. To see if your unit requires an upgrade, attach it to the Z5, navigate to the Firmware Version entry in the Setup menu, and view the WR firmware notification.

- **Compatible third-party triggering devices.** These include models from PocketWizard and Radio Popper. The advantage of these devices is that, unlike the optical system used by Nikon's CLS products (limited to about 30 feet), third-party devices use radio control to extend your remote "reach" to as far as 1,500 feet or more. Their transmitters/receivers can work in concert with your own master flash, which controls the remote flashes normally when they're in range, with the radio control taking over when the transmitter senses that the remote flash isn't responding to the master's instructions.

THIRD-PARTY SOLUTIONS

I'm generally covering only Nikon-branded products in this book, because there are so many third-party devices that it's difficult to sort out all the options. However, there are two product lines I've had a lot of luck with—the PocketWizard transmitters and receivers (www.pocketwizard.com) and the X-series wireless devices available from Godox (www.godox.com). These devices attach to your camera (generally by mounting on the hot shoe) and connect to your flash to allow one or more flashes to communicate with the Z5.

PocketWizard makes several products specifically for Nikon cameras, including a transmitter, which locks onto the camera's accessory shoe (a shoe-mount flash can be mounted on top of the transmitter, if you wish). Your remote flash units can use PocketWizard transceivers.

The transmitter interprets the i-TTL data from the camera and converts it into a digital radio signal to command your remote flash units. Note that this radio control system is more versatile than the pulsed light pre-flashes and infrared communications the Speedlights and SU-800 use (respectively), working through walls and in bright daylight. The PocketWizard ControlTL system switches to high-speed sync mode automatically when you choose a fast shutter speed.

Cost-conscious shooters may also want to look into the Godox X-series wireless products, available in a variety of configurations. The advantage of the Godox system is that the company offers triggers, as well as both shoe mount and studio-style electronic flash units, all compatible with Nikon's CLS system.

The Godox XProN TTL wireless flash trigger ($69) can be mounted on the Z5's hot shoe and used to control Nikon SB-series Speedlights (with the flash connected to the Godox X1R-N receiver [$70]). No extra receiver is required for Godox's own shoe-mounted CLS-compatible flash units and studio flash.

Remote Flashes

To use the Advanced Wireless System, you'll want to work with at least one remote, or slave flash unit. You can use units that are compatible with CLS or, with the (now discontinued) SU-4 accessory, other Speedlights. The remote flash for optical control can be any unit compatible with the Creative Lighting System, including the current SB-5000 and SB-700, or simpatico discontinued models, such as the SB-910/SB-900, SB-800, or SB-600. (Of these, the SB-600 can't function as a master flash on its own.) You'll need to set the auxiliary Speedlights to remote mode. For radio control mode, at this writing only the SB-5000 is compatible as a remote. I expect additional remote flash units will be introduced by Nikon during the life of this book.

Channels

Channels are the discrete lines of communication used by the master flash to communicate with each of the remote units. The pilots, ham radio operators, or scanner listeners among you can think of the channels as individual communications frequencies.

If you're working alone, you'll seldom have to fuss with channels. Just remember that all the Speedlights you'll be triggering must be using the same channel, exactly like a CB radio or walkie-talkie. (Google these terms if you're younger than 40.) If every flash isn't set for the same channel, they will be unable to "talk" to each other, good buddy. I'll show you how to adjust channels shortly.

The channel ability is most important when you're working around other photographers who are also using the same Nikon CLS system. Each photographer sets his or her flash units to a different channel as to not accidentally trigger other users' strobes. (At big events with more than four photographers using Nikon flash, you may need to negotiate.)

Personally, I think it's unfortunate that Nikon was able to include only four channels when using optical control. Radio control is much more flexible; third parties with CLS-compatible systems offer many more channels. Godox, for example, provides 32 discrete channels and allows up to 99 different wireless ID settings, which makes signal interference highly unlikely no matter how many similar setups are in use simultaneously at a given venue. Radio control with the SB-5000 or WR-R10 offers just three channels (Ch5, Ch10, and Ch15), but the flash units are linked using pairing or a PIN code, which effectively increases the number of non-interfering connections. Don't worry about Canon or Sony photographers at the same event. Their wireless flash systems use different communication systems that won't interfere with yours.

It's always a good idea to double-check your flash units before you set them up to make sure they're all set to the same channel, and this should also be one of your first troubleshooting questions if a flash doesn't fire the first time you try to use it wirelessly.

Groups

Each flash unit can be assigned to one of three groups, labeled A, B, and C. (The SB-5000 has additional groups, D, E, and F.) All the flashes in a single group perform together as if they were one big flash, using the same output level and flash compensation values. That means you can control the relative intensity of flashes in each *group*, compared to the intensity of flashes assigned to a *different* group. A group needs at least one flash unit but can have more.

For example, you could assign one (or more) flash to Group A and use it as the main light in your setup. Group B could be used as the fill light and Group C designated as a hair or background light. The power output of each group could be set individually, so your main light(s) in Group A might be two or three times as intense as the light(s) in Group B (used for fill), while another power level could be set for the Group C auxiliary lights. You don't *have* to use all three groups, but it is an option.

But there's a lot more you can do if you've splurged and own two or more compatible external flash units. Some photographers own five or six Nikon Speedlights, including me, who has one of each model Nikon has offered, starting with the SB-800. As I mentioned, Nikon wireless photography lets you collect individual strobes into *groups* and control all the Speedlights within a given group together. You can operate as few as two strobes in two groups or three strobes in three groups, while controlling more units if desired. You can also have them fire at equal output settings versus using them at different power ratios. Setting each group's strobes to different power ratios gives you more control over lighting for portraiture and other uses.

This is one of the more powerful options of the Nikon wireless flash system. I prefer to keep my Speedlights set to different groups normally. I can always set the power ratio to 1:1 if I want to operate the flash units all at the same power. If I change my mind and need to make adjustments, I can just change the wireless flash controller and then be able to manipulate the different groups' output as desired.

Remember that with whatever equipment you are using, outdoors if you are using optical triggering, you must have a clear line-of-sight between the master flash or SU-800 unit and sensors on the front of the slave flash units. Indoors, this requirement isn't as critical because the pre-flash and IR signals bounce off walls and other surroundings. Radio control has a longer 98-foot (30 meter) range.

Lighting Ratios

Lighting ratios are the relative proportions of the illumination among the groups, as I just described. To get the most from the CLS system, you'll want to understand how ratios work. That's a topic that deserves a chapter of its own, but many Nikon Z5 owners will already be familiar with the concept. If not, there are plenty of good books and online tutorials available.

Using Ratios

When lighting a subject, you can use several electronic flash units, as shown in the highly simplified arrangement in Figure 10.5. In this case, the main flash is an external unit placed to the left of the subject, and slightly behind her. An additional flash mounted on the Z5's hot shoe provides less intense illumination to fill in the shadows. A third flash illuminates the background, providing separation between it and the subject. All three flashes are set to the same channel, and are assigned to different groups: A, B, and C.

That setup makes it possible to specify Manual flash mode, in which you control the intensity of the flash, instead of TTL mode, in which the Z5 interprets the light from the pre-flash and adjusts output automatically. In Manual mode you can specify a different intensity to each group, with, say, the main light (Group A) firing at full power, the fill light (Group B) at 1/4 power, and the background light (Group C) at one-eighth power. The most common way to balance lights set to different power outputs is to use ratios, which are easy to calculate by setting (or measuring, with an external light meter) the exposure of each light source alone. Once you have the light calculated for each source alone, you can figure the lighting ratio.

For example, suppose that the main light for the portrait setup in Figure 10.5 provides enough illumination that you would use an f/stop of f/11. The fill light you'll be adding is less intense, set to 1/4 power, and also located farther away from the subject (or is diffused, say, with an umbrella reflector).

Figure 10.5 Multiple electronic flash units can be set to different intensities.

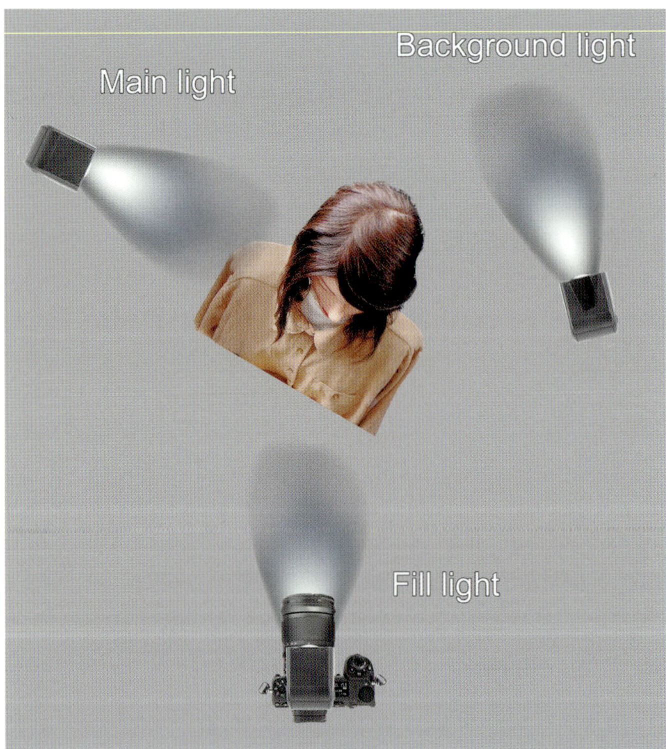

If the fill light produces an exposure, all by itself, of f/5.6, that translates into two f/stops' difference or, putting it another way, the main light source is four times as intense as the fill light. You can express this absolute relationship as the ratio 4:1. Because the main light is used to illuminate the highlight portion of your image, while the secondary light is used to fill in the dark, shadow areas left by the main light, this ratio tells us a lot about the lighting contrast for the scene.

In practice, only the lighting ratio produced by illumination falling on the main subject "counts." The light illuminating the background is just supplementary light and, in most cases, need not be taken into account in calculating the lighting ratio.

In practice, a 4:1 lighting ratio (or higher) is quite dramatic and can leave you with fairly dark shadows to contrast with your highlights. For portraiture, you probably will want to use 3:1 or 2:1 lighting ratios for a softer look that lets the shadows define the shape of your subject without cloaking parts in inky blackness.

If you use electronic flash equipped with a modeling light feature (or incandescent lighting), you will rarely need to calculate lighting ratios while you shoot. Instead, you'll base your lighting setups on how the subject looks, making your shadows lighter or darker depending on the effect you want. If you use electronic flash without a modeling light, or flash with modeling lights that aren't proportional to the light emitted by the flash, you can calculate lighting ratios. If you do need to know the lighting ratio, it's easy to figure by measuring the exposure separately for each light and multiplying the number of f/stops difference by two. A two-stop difference means a 4:1 lighting ratio; two-and-a-half stops difference adds up to a 5:1 lighting ratio; three stops is 6:1; and so forth. Figure 10.6 shows an example of 2:1, 3:1, 4:1, and 5:1 lighting ratios. I'll show you how to adjust the intensity of your Nikon Speedlights to achieve ratios shortly.

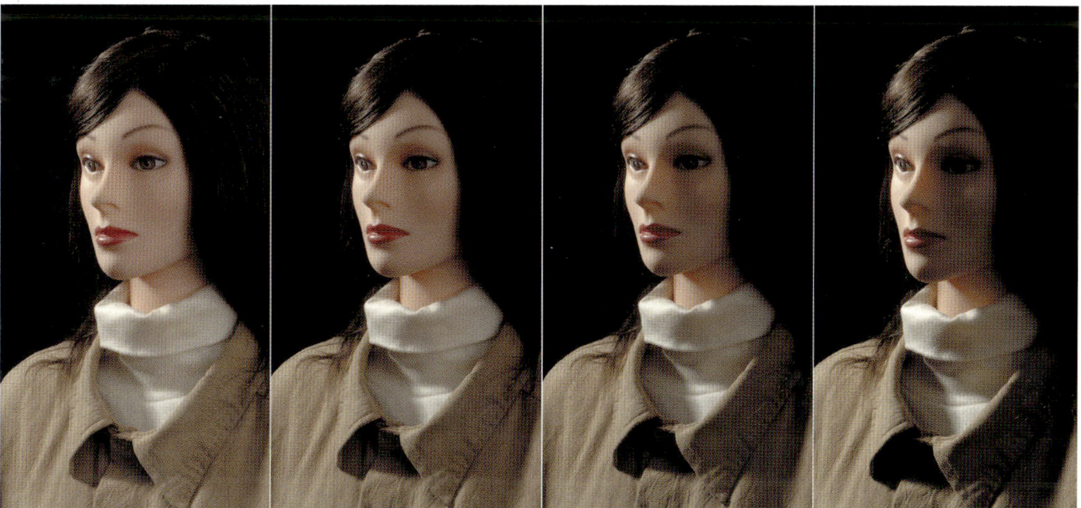

Figure 10.6 Left to right: Lighting ratios of 2:1, 3:1, 4:1, and 5:1.

Setting Your Master Flash

Nikon's wireless flash system gives you a number of advantages that include the ability to use directional lighting, which can help bring out detail or emphasize certain aspects of the picture area. It also lets you operate multiple strobes and establish lighting ratios, as described above, although most of us won't own more than two Nikon Speedlights. You can set up complicated portrait or location lighting setups. Since the top-of-the-line Nikon SB-5000 (and former champ SB-910) pump out a lot of light for a shoe-mount flash, a set of these units can give you near studio-quality lighting. Of course, the cost of these high-end Speedlights approaches that of some studio monolights—but the Nikon battery-powered units are more portable and don't require an external AC power source.

This chapter builds on the information in Chapter 9 and shows how to take advantage of the Z5's wireless capabilities. While it may seem complicated at first, it really isn't. Learning the Z5's controls takes a lot of effort, and once you get the hang of it, you'll be able to make changes quickly.

Since it's necessary to set up both the camera and the strobes for wireless operation, this guide will help you with both, starting with prepping the camera. To configure your camera for wireless flash, just follow these steps. (I'm going to condense them a bit, because many of these settings have been introduced in previous chapters.) I'm going to assume that you're using an external flash connected to the Z5 as a master strobe. I'll use the SB-5000 in the example that follows.

Setting Commander Mode for the SB-5000

If you're using an SB-5000 as your Master flash, setting it for Commander mode for automatic, through-the-lens (TTL) exposure calculation can be done using the Flash Control entry in the Photo Shooting menu. Just follow these steps:

1. Mount the SB-5000 flash on the Z5's accessory shoe and power it up. The Flash Control entry in the Photo Shooting menu is grayed out if a compatible flash unit (SB-500 or SB-5000) is not mounted and turned on.

2. Navigate to the Flash Control entry. As with all menu functions, you can press OK or press the right directional button to select this and the following entries.

3. The Flash Control screen will look like Figure 10.7, left. If you have not been using your flash as a wireless master, the Wireless Flash Options choice will be set to OFF.

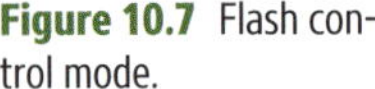

Figure 10.7 Flash control mode.

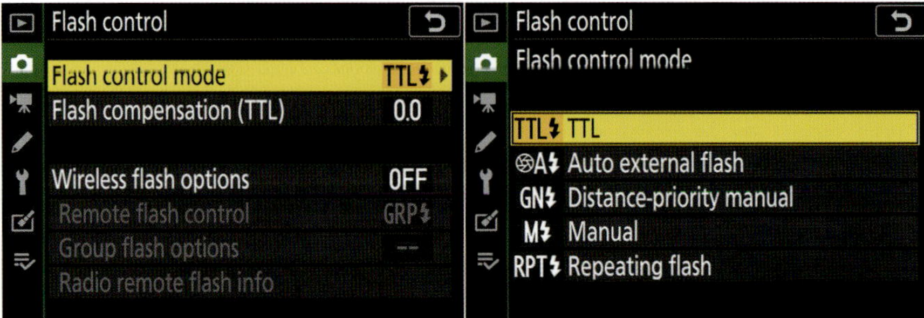

4. When wireless flash is disabled, you can access the Flash Control Mode entry and switch among TTL, Auto External Flash, Guide Number (Distance Priority Manual), Manual, and Repeating Flash. (See Figure 10.7, right.)

    - Set the TTL Flash Control Mode if you want the Z5 to calculate flash exposure for the main Commander flash and remote flash units.
    - Set the TTL Flash Control Mode to Manual if you want to set the output levels for your electronic flash yourself, rather than allow the Z5 to set the output automatically. (See "Lighting Ratios," above.)

5. In the Flash Control screen, select the Wireless Flash Options choice, shown at left in Figure 10.8.

6. In the next screen, shown at right in Figure 10.8, select Optical AWL.

7. Next, select Remote Flash Control, as seen in Figure 10.9, left.

8. Select Group Flash from the screen shown in Figure 10.9, right.

9. You will need to specify a group, mode, and output level. Select Group Flash Options, as seen at left in Figure 10.10. If you're working in TTL mode, the screen at right in the figure appears.

    - Master Flash sets the current flash as a Commander.
    - Group A, Group B, and Group C settings specify the mode of the individual groups. (Groups D and E are available in Radio control mode with the SB-5000.) Choose from TTL, AA, M, or --. If you select -- for any flash or Group, that flash or Group will not contribute to the exposure. (For example, you can set your Master Commander flash to -- and it will trigger other flashes wirelessly but will not emit a burst during the exposure.)

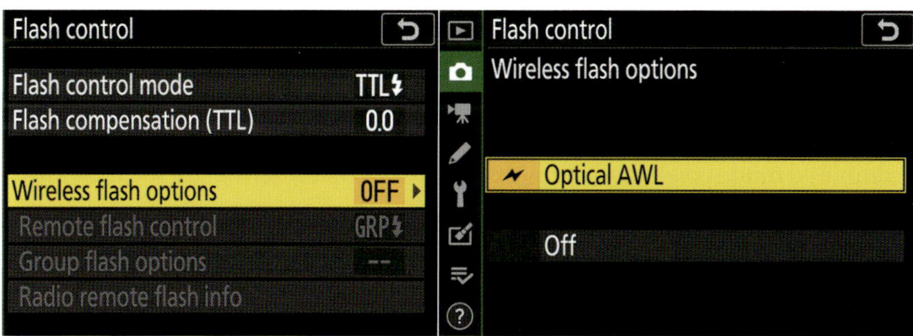

Figure 10.8 Activate Optical AWL.

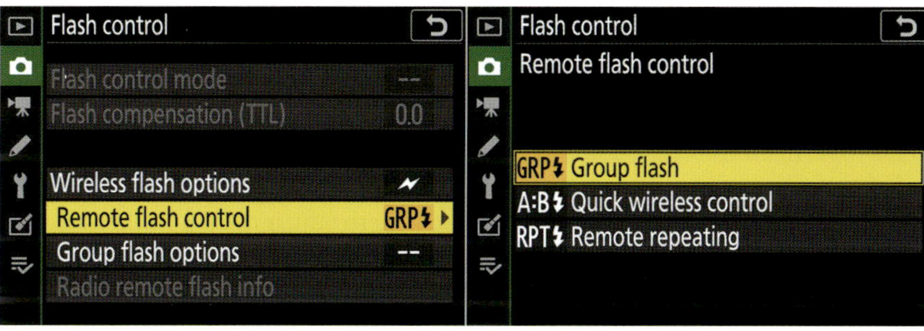

Figure 10.9 Specifying Group flash.

Figure 10.10 Setting group, mode, output level, and channel.

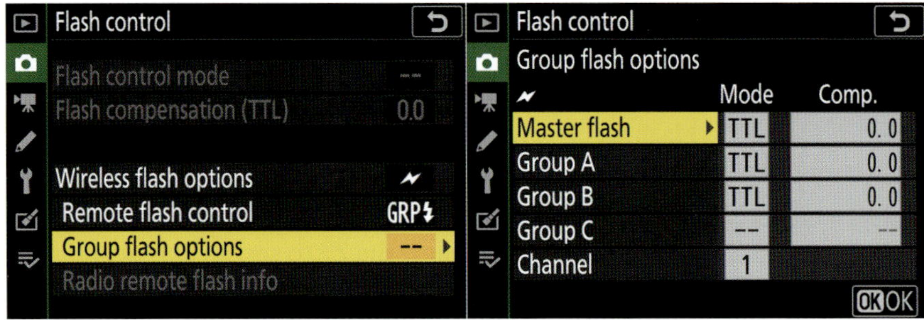

10. Comp. The term *Comp.* is misleading; it actually refers to output level. In the Comp. column you can specify flash exposure compensation (for TTL mode) or flash power level (for M mode).

11. Channel. Specify a Channel, selecting from available channels numbered 1–4. (Not all Nikon flashes can use all four channels.)

Wireless Flash Options

All adjustments of an SB-5000, SB-500, SB-400, or SB-300 mounted on the camera can be made using the Z5's menus. And, as I mentioned earlier, SB-910, SB-900, SB-800, SB-700, and SB-600 flash can be adjusted *only* using the controls on the flash units themselves. Under Wireless Flash Options, you can select three wireless modes:

- **Optical AWL.** Optical Advanced Wireless Lighting is the traditional wireless triggering method, available when using the SB-5000 or SB-500 flash units mounted on the camera. Radio AWL can be chosen when you have the WR-R10 unit attached to the camera's 10-pin connector and are using a radio-compatible off-camera flash, such as the SB-5000/SB-500.

- **Optical/Radio AWL.** This option combines both modes, allowing you to use a WR-R10 unit attached to the camera to trigger radio-compatible flashes, and an additional compatible flash unit mounted on the Z5 to trigger non-radio off-camera flash as a Commander using Optical AWL. When the combined mode is selected, Remote Flash Control (described in the list following this one) is set to Group Flash automatically.

  At this writing, the radio-controlled flash units must be SB-5000 Speedlights triggered either by another SB-5000, or by the WR-R10 transmitter mounted on the camera as a radio master. The camera-mounted optical master can be the SB-910/SB-900, SB-800, SB-700, SB-500, or SU-800 flash controller. If you're using the SB-500 as the optical Commander/master, you must choose this Optical/Radio AWL option. You do not need to specify this option with the other flash units listed; the combined mode is activated automatically.

- **Radio AWL.** Note that if you want to use the SB-5000 as a radio-controlled master flash, before attaching it to your camera, you should use the flash's controls to specify radio-controlled master flash mode, and choose group or remote repeating flash. Then, turn the flash off, attach the SB-5000 to the Z5, and power it up again. You will then be able to adjust the SB-5000 using the Z5's Flash Control menu, or with the controls on the flash itself.

Under the Remote Flash Control entry (shown earlier in Figure 10.9), these are your choices:

- **Group flash.** I described flash Groups earlier in this chapter. This entry allows you to specify separate flash control modes and flash levels for each group of remote units. When working with Optical AWL or Optical/Radio AWL, you can select the channel flashes used to communicate.
- **Quick wireless control.** This option is a fast way to specify flash ratios by adjusting the balance between Groups A and B, with the exposure being determined by TTL metering. That is, the camera determines the intensity of the flash units in Groups A and B, and you specify the ratio between them, with, say, Group A twice as powerful as Group B. Flash compensation for Groups A and B can also be set to add or subtract from the TTL-metered exposure.

  You can also set the output for any Group C flashes you use manually, perhaps to provide fill light. As with Group flash, if you're using Optical AWL or Optical/Radio AWL, you can select the channel used for communication.
- **Remote repeating.** This option is the multi-flash version of Repeating flash, which I explained at the end of Chapter 9. It is available only when using SB-5000 Speedlights. As with the single-flash version, you can choose flash output level, maximum number of flashes (Times), and Frequency (flashes per second). As with the previous two modes, if you're using Optical AWL or Optical/Radio AWL, you can select the channel used for communication.
- **Radio remote flash info.** If you are using radio control, this entry appears, and the flash units currently being managed are shown instead.

The next step is to set up each of your off-camera flashes as a remote. That's done using controls on the flash units themselves. I'll get to that after I've explained how to set Commander modes for some other Speedlights.

Setting Commander Modes for the SB-910 or SB-900

Setting Commander modes for the SB-910/SB-900 has been greatly simplified, compared to some previous Nikon Speedlights. If you'd rather use an attached flash as the master, just rotate the On/Off/Wireless mode switch to the Master position. Figure 10.11 shows the rear controls for the SB-700, SB-5000, SB-910, and SB-900.

You'll want to tell the SB-910/SB-900 which channel it is using to communicate with the other Speedlights. You'll need to do this separately for each of the SB-910/SB-900 units you are working with if you're using more than one. Here are the steps to follow. (I recommend doing several dry runs to see how setting up multiple flashes works before trying it "live.") The steps are almost identical between the SB-910 and SB-900 (shown at the bottom of Figure 10.11), differing primarily in the Function buttons used. In each case, the buttons numbered 1 through 3 are the first three buttons just south of the LCD panel starting from left to right.

1. **Set master flash to Commander mode.** On the master flash, rotate the power switch to the Master position, holding down the center lock release button of the switch so that it will move to the Master position. (This extra step is needed because Nikon knows you won't want to accidentally change from Master to Remote.)

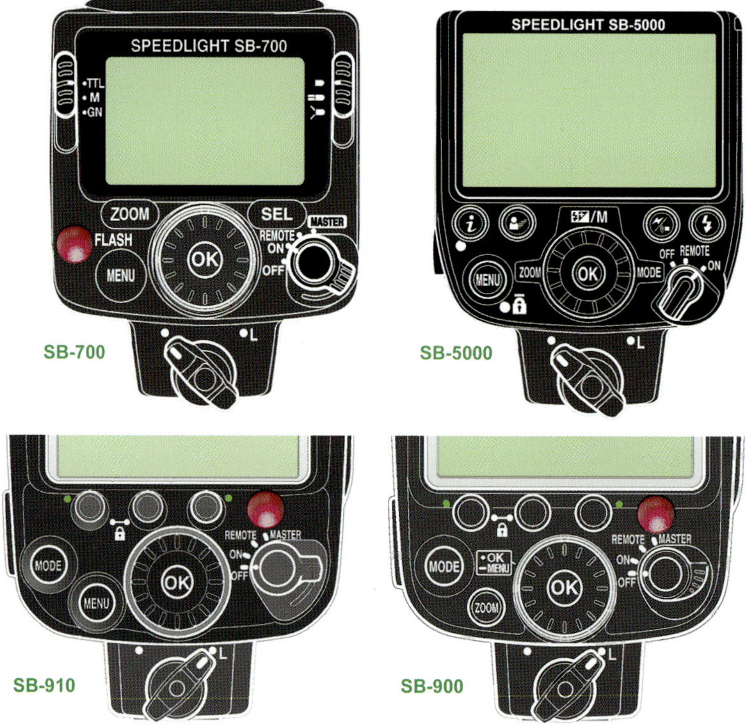

Figure 10.11 Location of the control buttons on the SB-700, SB-5000, SB-910, and SB-900 Speedlights.

2. **Access Mode.** Press the Function 2 button (Function 1 button on the SB-900) to highlight M on the LCD. (**Note:** M in this case stands for Master, not Manual.)

3. **Select Mode.** Press the MODE button and then spin the selector dial to choose the flash mode you want to use for that flash unit, from among TTL, A (Auto Aperture), M (Manual), or - -. Then, press OK.

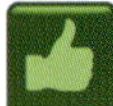 **TIP** Reminder: At the - - setting, the master flash is disabled; it will trigger the other units, but its flash won't contribute to the exposure—except if you're shooting very close to the subject using a high ISO setting. If an external flash is the master, try tilting or rotating the flash head away from your subject to minimize this spill-over effect.

4. **Set Flash Exposure Compensation.** Press the Function 3 button (Function 2 button on the SB-900) and rotate the selector dial to choose the flash compensation level (–3 to +3) or manual power level (1/1 to 1/128). The amount of EV correction appears at the right side of the display, opposite the master flash's mode indicator.

5. **Specify group.** Press the Function 2 button (Function 1 button on the SB-900) to move on to the Group Selection option. Press OK to choose Group A or rotate the selector dial to choose Group B or C, then press OK to confirm the group you've chosen.

6. **Set modes for group.** Once a group is highlighted, select the mode for that group. Press the MODE button and then spin the selector dial to choose the flash mode you want to use for that flash unit, from among TTL, A (Auto Aperture), M (Manual), or - -. Then, press OK.

7. **Set Flash Exposure Compensation for group.** Press the Function 3 button (Function 2 button on the SB-900) and rotate the selector dial to choose the flash compensation level for the current group as you did in Step 3. The amount of EV correction appears at the right side of the display, opposite the group's mode indicator.

8. **Repeat for other groups.** If you're using Group B and Group C, repeat steps 4 to 7 to set the mode and Flash Exposure Compensation for the additional groups.

9. **Specify channel.** Once the modes and compensation for all the groups have been set on the master flash, press the Function 3 button (Function 2 button on the SB-900) and rotate the selector dial to set a channel number that the master flash will use to control its groups.

10. **Set up remote flashes.** Now take each of the remote flash units and set the correct group and channel number you want to use for each of them. I'll describe this step later.

Setting Commander Modes for the SB-700

Setting Commander modes for the SB-700 is similar in concept to the settings for the SB-910 or SB-900. The controls for the SB-700 are shown at top left in Figure 10.11. If you want to use an attached SB-700 as the master flash, follow these steps:

1. **Set master flash to Commander mode.** On the master flash, rotate the power switch to the Master position, holding down the center lock release button of the switch so that it will move to the Master position.

2. **Choose mode.** There's a sliding switch on the left side of the SB-700. You can choose TTL, M (Manual), or GN modes.

3. **Set Flash Exposure Compensation.** Press the SEL button to select the master flash, then choose a flash compensation value/output level using the selector dial. Press OK to confirm.

4. **Specify group.** Press the SEL button to move on to the Group Selection option. Press OK to choose Group A or rotate the selector dial to choose Group B. (Group C is not available with the SB-700.) Set the flash exposure compensation value for each group using the selector dial. Then press OK to confirm.

5. **Specify channel.** Once the modes and compensation for all the groups have been set on the master flash, press the SEL button to highlight the Channel, then rotate the selector dial to set a channel number that the master flash will use to control its groups.

6. **Set up remote flashes.** Now take each of the remote flash units and set the correct group and channel number you want to use for each of them.

Setting Commander Modes for the SB-500

Setting Commander modes for the SB-500 is similar in concept to the settings for the SB-5000. If you want to use an attached SB-500 as the master flash, follow these steps:

1. **Mount the SB-500 on the Z5 and turn on the power.** Rotate the SB-500's power switch, located on the lower-right corner of the back of the unit, to the lightning bolt icon.

2. **On your Z5, navigate to the Flash Control entry.** Under the Flash Control entry, choose Commander mode. Select TTL flash mode in the center column, and any flash compensation in the third column (Comp.).

3. **Specify group.** In the Z5 menu, choose Group A or Group B. (Group C is not available with the SB-500.) Choose the exposure mode and flash exposure compensation value for each group using the entries in the second and third columns.

4. **Specify channel.** Once the modes and compensation for all the groups have been set on the master flash, choose a Channel. The mode indicator lamp (CMD) on the flash illuminates when settings are made on the Z5.

5. **Set up remote flashes.** Now take each of the remote flash units and set the correct group and channel number you want to use for each of them. I'll describe this step next.

Setting Remote Modes

Each of the external remote flash units must be set to Remote mode. With the SB-5000, that's as easy as rotating the On/Off switch to the Remote position. Then press the wireless setting button located at the 11 o'clock position above the switch and choose optical, direct remote, or radio control remote modes. (I'm covering only optical triggering here.)

Here's how to set up the Nikon SB-500, SB-700, SB-900, and SB-910 Speedlights as remote slave flash units. Note that you don't need to specify compensation/output level; that's handled by the master/commander flash. You just need to set the flash to Remote, then choose Group, Channel, and Zoom head function.

1. **Switch flash to remote mode.** With the SB-900/SB-910 or SB-700, rotate the power switch to the Remote position, holding down the center lock release button of the switch so that it will move to the Remote position. If you're using the SB-500, you'll set remote mode in Step 2.

2. **Select group.** With the SB-500, rotate the power switch to A or B to correspond with the remote flash group you selected for the master flash. With the SB-910, press the Function 2 button (Function 1 button on the SB-900) and choose Group A with the selector dial, and press OK. With the SB-700, press the SEL button to highlight the group, then press OK. Repeat for Group B or (with the SB-900/SB-910 only) Group C.

3. **Set channel.** With the SB-500, set the remote flash channel to Channel 3 (the only one available with that unit). With the SB-900/SB-910, press the Function 2 button to highlight the channel. If you're using the SB-700, press the SEL button until the channel is highlighted. Then, rotate the selector dial to choose the channel number. Make sure you choose the same channel number you set earlier on the master flash. Press OK to confirm.

4. **Choose zoom head position.** With the SB-910, press the Function 1 button (or the Zoom button on the SB-900 or SB-700) to highlight Zoom Head Position, and choose a zoom head setting with the selector dial. Press OK to confirm. With the SB-900 and SB-700 push the Zoom button multiple times to change zoom settings. The SB-500 does not have a zoom head.

5. **Repeat for each remote flash.** If you're using more than one remote/slave flash, repeat Steps 1 to 4 for each of the additional CLS-compatible units.

Radio Control

Radio control for all flashes used with Nikon dSLR and mirrorless cameras is still in its infancy. At the time I write this, only the expensive SB-5000 flash unit can be triggered by radio signals, and the only way to trigger an off-camera SB-5000 using radio control is with another SB-5000 or the Wireless Remote Controller WR-R10 or new WR-R11b. So, you'll end up spending at least $1,000 for a two-flash radio-controlled setup. Fortunately, Nikon allows you to mix optically and radio-controlled flash units. You do gain three extra groups (Groups D, E, and F, if you can afford flashes to populate them with), but only three groups (A, B, and C) can be used with Nikon's Quick Wireless Control setup. As always, I recommend consulting Nikon's 120-page guide to the SB-5000 if you want to sort out all the configurations and features of this complex flash. I can provide only an overview here, rather than a detailed how-to that explains all the available combinations.

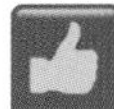

TIP As I mentioned earlier, a more affordable radio control system is available from vendors like Godox. You can purchase inexpensive receivers/transceivers (around $70) and some less pricey Godox flash units and retain TTL exposure calculation and control of the flash output levels right at the transmitter. Unfortunately, third-party solutions are updated more frequently than Nikon's own products (the SB-700, introduced in 2010, is still a current Nikon offering), so it's not practical to cover them in detail in a book like this. That's why I stick to describing Nikon's more stable product line almost exclusively.

The WR-R10 and WR-R11b plug into the remote/accessory port on the side of the Z5, as seen in Figure 10.12. You'll need to set the channel for this controller to the same channel used for your SB-5000, from Channel 5, 10, or 15. Then, you'll need to link the controller using the Wireless Remote (WR) Options entry in the Setup menu. You can connect using pairing (the most common, and easiest) or with a PIN, which is more secure and generally used only by professionals to avoid interference in environments in which there are multiple cameras being used with this same system.

Once you've set the channel on the WR-R10, press the MENU button on the SB-5000 (it's at lower left of the unit's back panel, as seen at upper right in Figure 10.11). Select CHANNEL and press the right button on the SB-5000's rotary multi selector to set the same channel as the WR-R10/WR-R11b. Then press the OK button on the SB-5000's multi selector.

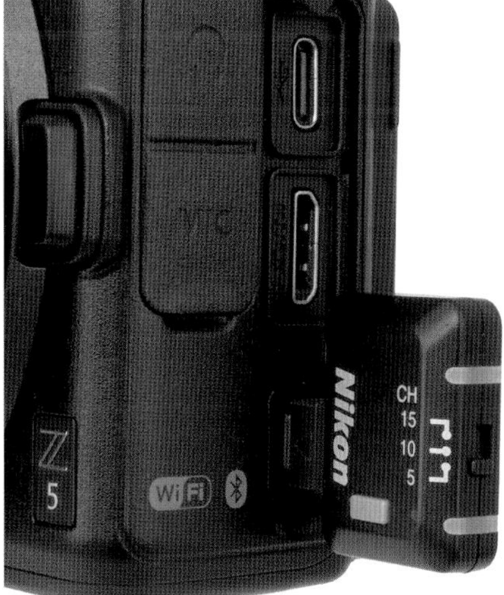

Figure 10.12 The controller plugs into the accessory port on the side of the Z5.

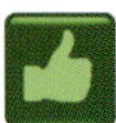 **NOTE** You *must* update a WR-R10's firmware to Version 3.0 to use radio control with your SB-5000. The update cannot be done by the user; you'll have to mail in your unit to Nikon's repair service, as I did.

From the SB-5000's MENU again, select Link Mode and choose either Pairing or PIN, to match the setting you specified in the Z5's Setup menu. Press the SB-5000's OK button to confirm. You can select PAIR > EXECUTE and press the SB-5000's OK button to commence pairing. Once the SB-5000 and controller have been paired, you won't have to do it again. However, you can pair with a second controller if you have multiple cameras or multiple controllers.

Concurrent use of optical control and radio control is tricky. You must use a Speedlight *other* than the SB-5000 (such as the SB-910) as an optical master flash mounted in the hot shoe and set to trigger optically controlled remote Speedlights in Groups A, B, C, and *also* have the controller attached to the camera so it can trigger additional radio-controlled SB-5000 flashes in Groups D, E, and F. It's unlikely that you'll have such a need (or even own the appropriate flash units). This mode could come in handy if you have a complex setup and need to control some flashes at a greater distance (which radio control provides, and optical control may not).

However, when using radio control, the distance between masters and remotes should be 98 feet or less. Up to 18 remote flash units can be used. Keep in mind that in radio control remote mode, the Z5's normal Standby Timer is disabled, over-riding any setting you've made in the camera. It's easy to run down your battery with extensive use, or if you forget to turn the flash or camera off.

Playback, Photo Shooting, and Movie Shooting Menus   11

Your Z5 has several convenient direct-access buttons (such as the ISO button on the top-right panel of the camera) and a customizable Information Edit screen that appears when you press the *i* button. However, many adjustments and settings require a trip to the Z5's extensive menu system, which has dozens of individual top-level entries and many additional options tucked away in sub-menus. But under that thicket of choices is the kind of versatility that makes the Nikon Z5 one of the most customizable, tweakable, and fine-tunable cameras Nikon has ever offered. If your camera doesn't behave in exactly the way you'd like, chances are you can make a small change in the menus that will tailor the Z5 to your needs.

However, just telling you what your options are and what they do doesn't really give you the information you need to use your camera to its fullest. What you really want to know is *why* you would want to choose a particular option, and *how* making a particular change will help improve your photographs in a given situation. That's a big job, and I'm going to devote three entire chapters to demystifying the Z5 menu choices for you.

This chapter will help you sort out the settings for the Playback, Photo Shooting, and Movie Shooting menus, which determine how the Z5 displays images on review, and how it uses many of its shooting features to capture photos and videos. The following chapters will focus on the Custom Settings menu (Chapter 12), and Setup, Retouch, and My Menu options (Chapter 13).

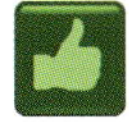 **TIP** While each entry in the Z5's menus will be summarized in Chapters 11, 12, and 13, some complex functions, such as flash and autofocus options, require longer explanations and step-by-step instructions. I included those descriptions in previous chapters and will not repeat that information.

As I've mentioned before, this book isn't intended to replace the Nikon manual available for your Z5, nor have I any interest in rehashing its contents. There is, however, some unavoidable duplication between the Nikon manual and the next three chapters, because, like the Nikon manual, I'm going to explain all the key menu choices and the options you may have in using them. You should find, though, that I will give you the information you really require in a much more helpful format, with plenty of detail on why you should make some settings that are particularly cryptic. Throughout, I'll indicate my personal setting preference for many of the entries.

I'm not going to waste a lot of space on some of the more obvious menu choices in these chapters. For example, you can probably figure out what the Format Card entry in the Setup menu does, and it has only two options: Yes and No. In this chapter, I'll devote no more than a sentence or two to the blatantly obvious settings and concentrate on the more confusing aspects of the Z5 setup, such as automatic exposure bracketing. I'll start with an overview of using the Z5's menus themselves.

Anatomy of the Nikon Z5's Menus

If you used any Nikon digital SLR before you purchased your Nikon Z5, you're probably already familiar with the basic menu system. The menus consist of a series of screens with entries, as shown in the illustration of the Playback menu (discussed next) in Figure 11.1. Navigating among the various menus is easy and follows a consistent set of rules:

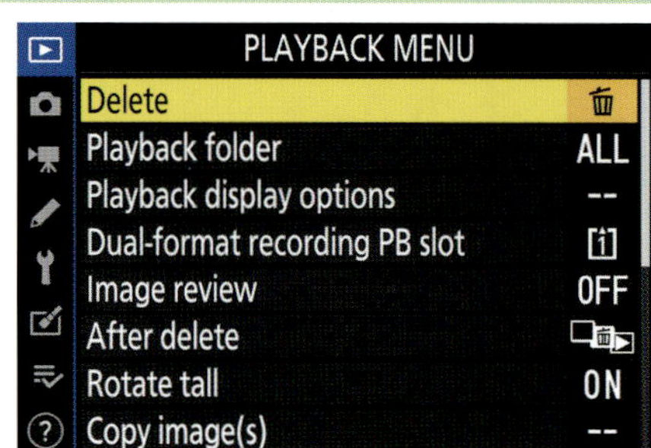

Figure 11.1 The multi selector's navigational buttons are used to move among the various menu entries shown here.

- **View menu.** Press the MENU button on the lower-right corner of the camera to display the main menu screens.

- **Navigate main menu headings.** Use the multi selector's left/right/up/down buttons to navigate among the menu entries to highlight your choice. Moving the highlighting to the left column lets you scroll up and down among the top-level menus. From the top in Figure 11.1, they are Playback, Photo Shooting, Movie Shooting, Custom Settings, Setup, Retouch, and My Menu, with Help access (when available) represented by a question mark at the bottom of the column.

- **Choose a top-level menu.** A highlighted top-level menu's icon will change from black-and-white to yellow highlighting. Use the multi selector's right button to move into the column containing that menu's choices. The selected top-level menu's icon will change from yellow to a color associated with that menu (blue for Playback, green for Photo Shooting, yellow-green for Movie Shooting, red for Custom Settings, orange for Setup, purple for Retouch, and gray for My Menu). The currently selected option will be highlighted in yellow, as shown in the figure. **Note:** You can also press the OK button of the multi selector to move into a top-level menu's entries, but it's usually simpler to just press the right button, because you'll be using the multi selector's directional buttons to navigate the menus anyway.

- **Select a menu entry.** Use the up/down buttons to scroll among the entries. If more than one screen full of choices is available, a scroll bar appears at the far right of the screen, with a position slider showing the relative position of the currently highlighted entry.

- **Choose options.** To work with a highlighted menu entry, press the OK button, the multi selector center button, or, more conveniently, just press the right button on the multi selector. Any additional screens of choices will appear. You can move among them using the same multi selector movements.

- **Confirm your choice.** You can activate a selection by pressing the OK button or, frequently, by pressing the right button on the multi selector once again. Some functions require scrolling to a Done menu choice or include an instruction to set a choice using some other button.

- **Exit menus.** Pressing the multi selector left button usually backs you out of the current screen and pressing the MENU button again usually does the same thing. You can exit the menu system at any time by tapping the shutter release button.

- **Returning to an entry.** The Nikon Z5 "remembers" the top-level menu and specific menu entry you were using (but not any submenus) the last time the menu system was accessed, so pressing the MENU button brings you back to where you left off. So, if you were working with an entry in the Custom Settings menu's Metering/Exposure section, then decided to take a photo, the next time you press the MENU button the Custom Settings menu and the Metering/Exposure entry will be highlighted, but not the specific submenu (b1 through b4) that you might have selected.

- **Accessing a frequently used entry.** If you use the same menu items over and over, you can create a My Menu listing of those entries. Or, if you'd rather have a rotating listing of the last 20 menu items you accessed, you can convert My Menu to a Recent Settings menu instead. I'll show you exactly how to do that in Chapter 13.

Playback Menu Options

The blue-coded Playback menu, shown in Figure 11.1, has 10 entries where you select options related to the display, review, transfer, and printing of the photos you've taken. The choices you'll find include the entries that follow. The last two entries, Slide Show and Rating, are not pictured in Figure 11.1, and do not appear until you scroll the listing on the screen to the bottom.

- Delete
- Playback Folder
- Playback Display Options
- Dual Format PB Slot
- Image Review
- After Delete
- Rotate Tall
- Copy Image(s)
- Slide Show
- Rating

Delete

Options: Selected, Select Date, All

My preference: N/A

Choose this menu entry and you'll be given three choices, shown in Figure 11.2, left: Selected (to choose individual images to delete); Select Date (to remove all photos taken on a particular day); or All (to remove all images in the folder currently selected for playback). (See Playback Folder entry, next.)

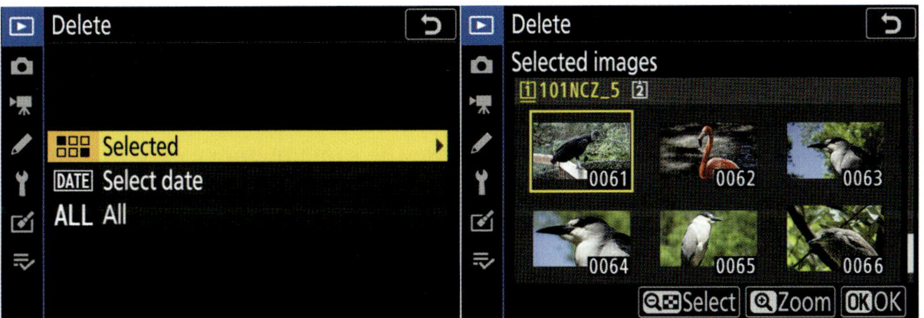

Figure 11.2 Choose selection method (left); Select individual images (right).

To select specific images or dates, follow these instructions:

1. **Choose Selected or Select Date.** Selection screens appear to allow you to choose which images to delete. To select by date, skip to Step 3.

2. **Mark individual selected images.** Scroll through the thumbnails of the images displayed using the multi selector's directional buttons. Hold down the Zoom In button to enlarge the highlighted thumbnail to full-screen view. Press the Zoom Out/Index button to mark a highlighted image for deletion, or to unmark one that has already been marked. A trash can icon is overlaid on the thumbnail when an image is marked for removal. (See Figure 11.2, right.) When finished marking, press OK to delete. Choose Yes from the Delete? screen that appears, or No to cancel.

3. **Select dates.** A list of dates on which pictures were taken appears. Press the right directional button to checkmark a date, or to unmark a date that has been selected. Once you've highlighted one or more dates, if you're sure you want to delete all those images, press OK, and give the Z5 the go-ahead to continue on the confirmation screen that pops up.

   If you want to double-check your images before removing them, press the Zoom Out/Index button to confirm your choices, and a scrollable screen of thumbnails displaying the images for the selected dates will be shown. You can press the Zoom In button to view a full-screen version of any highlighted image. When finished, press OK to return to the previous screen. Press OK again and choose Yes from the Delete All Images Taken on Selected Date screen, or No to cancel.

4. **Exit Delete menu.** To back out of the selection screens, press the MENU button.

Using this menu to delete images will have no effect on images that have been marked with an overlaid key icon when protected using the Protect option available from the *i* menu that appears when you press the *i* button during Playback. Keep in mind that deleting images in this way is slower than just wiping out the whole card with the Format command, so using Format is generally much faster than choosing Delete: All, and also is a safer way of returning your memory card to a fresh, blank state.

Playback Folder

Options: NCZ_5, All (default), Current

My preference: N/A

Your Nikon Z5 will create folders on your memory card to store the images that it creates. It assigns the first folder a number, like 100NCZ_5, and when that folder is filled, the camera automatically creates a new folder numbered one higher, such as 101NCZ_5. A folder is completely full when it contains 5,000 images, or a picture numbered 9999. If you use the same memory card in another camera, that camera will also create its own folder. Thus, you can end up with several folders on the same memory card, until you eventually reformat the card and folder creation starts anew.

This menu item allows you to choose which folders are accessed when displaying images using the Z5's Playback facility.

Your choices are as follows:

- **NCZ_5.** The camera will use only the folders on your memory card created by the Z5 and ignore those created by other cameras. Images in all the Z5's folders will be displayed. You can rename these folders using the Storage Folder > Rename entry in the Photo Shooting menu. Personally, I feel that the space between NCZ and 5 in the folder name is a waste of good ASCII, and will recommend some alternatives later in this chapter, using the Storage Folder entry of the Photo Shooting menu.

- **All (default).** All folders containing images that the Z5 can read will be accessed, regardless of which camera created them. You might want to use this setting if you swap memory cards among several cameras and want to be able to review all the photos (especially when considering reformatting the memory card). You will be able to view images even if they were created by a non-Nikon camera if those images conform to the Design Rule for Camera File system (DCF) specifications.

- **Current.** The Z5 will display only images in the current folder. For example, if you have been shooting heavily at an event and have already accumulated more than 5,000 shots in one folder (or an image has been stored that's numbered 9999) and the Z5 has created a new folder for the overflow, you'd use this setting to view only the most recent photos, which reside in the current folder. You can change the current folder to any other folder on your memory card using the Active Folder option in the Photo Shooting menu, described later in this chapter.

Playback Display Options

Options: Basic photo info: Focus Point; Additional Photo info: Exposure Info, Highlights, RGB Histogram, Shooting Data, Overview, None (Image only)

My preference: N/A

You'll recall from Chapter 3 that a great deal of information, available on multiple screens, can be cycled through by pressing the DISP button when reviewing images. This menu item helps you reduce/increase the clutter by specifying which information and screens will be available. To activate or deactivate an info option, scroll to that option and press the right multi selector button to add a checkmark to the box next to that item. Press the right button to unmark an item that has previously been checked. If no boxes are checked, only the default view—the image with basic information shown at the bottom of the frame—is displayed. Your additional info options include:

- **Focus Point.** Activate this option to display the active focus point(s) with red highlighting.

- **Exposure Info.** Shows only frame number and basic exposure information, including release mode, shutter speed, aperture, exposure compensation, and ISO sensitivity.

- **Highlights.** When enabled, overexposed highlight areas in your image will blink with a black border during picture review. That's your cue to consider using exposure compensation to reduce exposure, unless a minus EV setting will cause loss of shadow detail that you want to preserve. You can read more about correcting exposure in Chapter 4.

- **RGB Histogram.** Displays both luminance (brightness) and RGB histograms on a screen that can be displayed using the up/down multi selector buttons, as shown in Chapter 3. I explained the use of histograms in Chapter 4.

- **Shooting Data.** Activates the pages of shooting data shown in Chapter 3.
- **Overview.** Activates the overview screen shown in Chapter 3. You must scroll down the list to access this option.
- **None.** A screen with the image only and no photo information will be displayed.

Dual-Format Recording PB Slot

Options: Slot 1 (default), Slot 2

My preference: Slot 2

Your Z5 has two memory card slots, and an entry in the Photo Shooting menu, Role Played By Card in Slot 2 (discussed later in this chapter), allows you to define the function of the second slot. You can tell the Z5 to use the second slot for overflow once the Slot 1 card fills; copy each shot to both Slot 1 *and* Slot 2 for backup; or to save RAW images on Slot 1 and the JPEG versions on Slot 2.

This entry functions only when you are shooting in RAW+JPEG mode and have chosen RAW Slot 1—JPEG Slot 2 in the Role Played By Card in Slot 2 entry. It specifies which version of your dual-format images should be displayed during Playback. I prefer to have the JPEG images in Slot 2 shown, as they may be presented a tiny bit more quickly than the RAW (NEF) images.

Image Review

Options: On, On (Monitor only), Off (default)

My preference: N/A

There are certain shooting situations in which it's useful to have the picture you've just shot pop up on the monitor automatically for review. Perhaps you're fine-tuning exposure or autofocus and want to be able to see whether your most recent image is acceptable. Or, maybe you're the nervous type and just want confirmation that you actually took a picture. Image review has saved my bacon a few times when I accidentally made an inappropriate setting (such as specifying ISO 25600 when it really wasn't needed or desirable).

A lot of the time, however, it's a better idea to *not* automatically review your shots to conserve battery power (the LCD monitor and EVF are two of the major juice drains in the camera) or to speed up or simplify operations. For example, if you've just fired off a burst of eight shots during a football game, do you *really* need to have every frame display as the camera clears its buffer and stores the photos on your memory card? This menu operation allows you to choose which mode to use. You can elect to have the review image always appear, appear on the LCD monitor only, or never appear. Unfortunately, Nikon neglected to give us an On (Viewfinder Only) option for image review, but I'm going to give you several workarounds.

- **On.** Image review is automatic after every shot is taken, and your image will appear in the viewfinder or on the LCD monitor (depending on which you are using).
- **On (Monitor only).** Image review is displayed *only* on the rear-panel LCD monitor, and then only if you are *not* currently looking through the viewfinder; to see image review, move the camera away from your eye.

- **Off.** Images are displayed only when you press the Playback button. Nikon, in its wisdom, has made this the default setting.

> **QUENCH THAT MONITOR!**
>
> When I am shooting concerts and performances where the audience area is darkened, I don't want the LCD monitor lighting up after every shot and annoying people. Even so, I may want to review my images and would like them to appear immediately—just not on the monitor. There are several ways to activate that behavior.
>
> - If you select ON with this menu entry, if your Limit Monitor Mode Selection option (in the Setup menu, and described in Chapter 13) is set to activate Automatic Selection, as long as you keep your eye up to the viewfinder, the image preview will not appear on the monitor.
> - A better choice is to disable Automatic Selection and enable just Viewfinder Only or Monitor Only options. Then you can manually toggle between the viewfinder and monitor using the VF/Monitor button on the left side of the Z5's pentaprism. Your image review will appear *only* on the currently selected screen.
> - If you absolutely want to prevent having your image review appear on the monitor, visit the Limit Monitor Mode Selection entry and disable everything but Viewfinder Only.
> - A compromise is to use the Monitor Brightness entry in the Setup menu and set Manual Brightness to −5. This produces a very dark screen, which is unlikely to annoy those around you. It also makes it difficult to judge exposure from the monitor alone. (*That's what the histogram is for!*)

After Delete

Options: Show Next (default), Show Previous, Continue as Before
My preference: Show Next

When you've deleted an image, you probably will want to do one of three things: have the Z5 display the next picture (in the order shot); show the *previous* picture; or show either the next *or* previous picture, depending on which way you were scrolling during picture review. Your Z5 lets you select which action to take:

- **Show Next.** It's likely that you'll want to look at the picture taken after the one you just deleted, so Nikon makes this the default action.

- **Show Previous.** I use this setting a lot when shooting sports with a continuous shooting setting. After the sequence is taken, I press the Playback button to see the last picture in the series and sometimes discover that the whole sequence missed the boat. I sometimes go ahead and press the Trash button twice to delete the offending image, then continue moving backward to delete the five or six or eleven other pictures in the wasted sequence. You'll often find yourself with time on your hands at football games and feel the urge to delete a stinker series of shots to save time reviewing back at the computer (plus freeing up a little space on your card).

- **Continue as Before.** This setting makes a lot of sense: if you were scrolling backward or forward and deleting photos as you go, you might want to continue in the same direction weeding out bad shots. Use this setting to set your Nikon Z5 to behave that way.

Rotate Tall

Options: On (default), Off

My preference: Off

When you rotate the Z5 to photograph vertical subjects in portrait (tall), rather than landscape (wide) orientation, you probably don't want to view them tilted onto their sides later, either on the camera monitor and viewfinder or within your image viewing/editing application on your computer. The Z5 has a directional sensor built in that can detect whether the camera was rotated when the photo was taken and hide this information in the image file itself.

The orientation data is applied in two different ways. It can be used by the Z5 to automatically rotate images when they are displayed on the camera's monitor and viewfinder (when On is enabled), or you can ignore the data and let the images display in non-rotated fashion when Off is selected (so you have to rotate the camera to view them in their proper orientation). As mentioned earlier, your image-editing application can also use the embedded file data to automatically rotate images on your computer screen.

This menu choice deals only with whether the image should be rotated when displayed on the *camera LCD monitor* or *in the electronic viewfinder*. (If you de-activate this option, your image-editing software can still read the embedded rotation data and properly display your images.) When Rotate Tall is turned off, the Nikon Z5 does not rotate pictures taken in vertical orientation. The image is large on your display, but you must rotate the camera to view it upright.

When Rotate Tall is turned on, the Z5 rotates pictures taken in vertical orientation on the monitor screen so you don't have to turn the camera to view them comfortably. However, this orientation also means that the longest dimension of the image is shown using the shortest dimension of the monitor, so the picture is reduced in size (see Figure 11.3).

So, turn this feature On if you'd rather not turn your camera to view vertical shots in their natural orientation, and don't mind the smaller image. Turn the feature Off if, as I do, you'd rather see a larger image and are willing to rotate the camera to do so. Rotating the camera is no big deal, and worth the trouble in order to see the largest possible review image on the display.

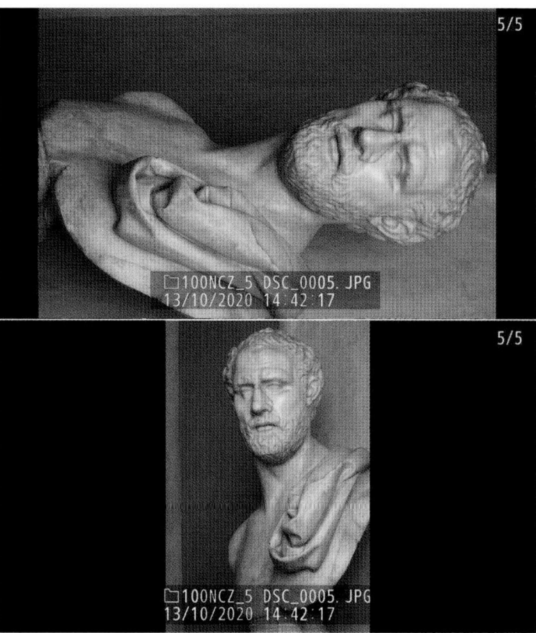

Figure 11.3 Rotate Tall: Off (top); Rotate Tall: On (bottom).

Copy Image(s)

Options: Select Source, Select Image(s), Select Destination Folder, Copy Image(s)

My preference: N/A

The ability to work with two memory cards simultaneously ranks as one of my favorite features in any Nikon camera that offers dual slots. One of the best uses for two cards is to make back-up images while traveling, or at any other time that your computer isn't easily accessible. Here are some examples of what I do:

- **Shoot to two cards simultaneously.** This gives you an instant backup in case pictures on your primary card become corrupt or erased. Ideally, your two cards should be equal in storage size.

- **Make a copy.** Use this Copy Image(s) facility to make a copy of images you shot on one card to your second card. Instead of shooting on two cards at once (which does slow down the Z5 a bit), use only one card when you take photos, then make a backup onto a second card at the end of the day. You can copy all or only some of the photos you've shot.

- **Make copies to distribute.** I bought a bunch of 8GB memory cards for $4 each, and find it's quick and easy to make multiple copies of photos, not for backup, but for distribution either on the spot, say, to provide models I've hired with some raw (not RAW) images or to send by snail mail to colleagues, friends, or family. Such small cards won't hold many 24MP images, but in many cases, that's enough space. No computer required!

- **Leave your laptop or external storage at home.** Since I've begun using Nikon cameras with dual memory card slots, I leave my hard disk/personal storage device with its built-in reader or my laptop at home more often. If I am going to be gone for only a day or two, it's easier to just make copies in the camera, and not bother with another external device.

To copy images from one card to another, just follow these steps (which are available only when two memory cards are present in the camera):

1. **Access copy menus.** Choose Copy Image(s) from the Playback menu. There are four choices that may be available to you: Select Source, Select Image(s), Select Destination Folder, and Copy Image(s)?. They are shown at upper left in Figure 11.4.

   - If you have images on only one card, all other choices will be grayed out, and the card containing images will be selected automatically.

   - If there are images on both cards already, you can choose Select Source to specify which card slot as the source to copy from.

   - If you have already marked some images previously, then all four choices will be available.

2. **Select Source.** If you have images on both cards and want to choose images from the non-default slot that is pre-selected, highlight Select Source and press the right button on the multi selector. Choose Slot 1 or Slot 2 and press the right button again to return to the previous menu.

Figure 11.4 These four screens allow you to select a source slot, specific images, destination folder, and initiate copying.

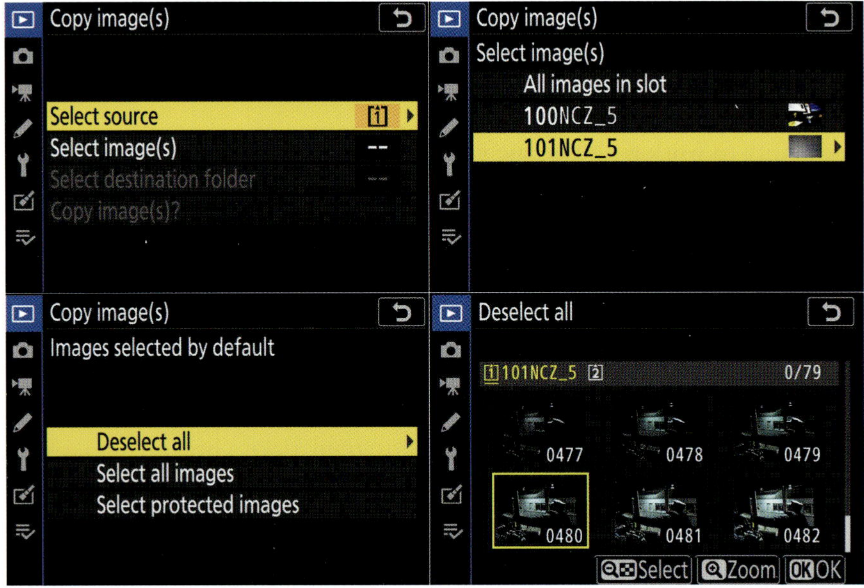

3. **Select images.** Highlight Select Image(s) and press the right button. The screen shown at upper right in Figure 11.4 appears. You can now choose from:

   - **All Images in Slot.** If you select this, all the images on the card will be selected and you'll be returned to the previous menu.

   - **Images in a folder in that slot.** If more than one folder resides on that card, all will be shown. Select a folder and press the right button, and the screen shown at lower left in Figure 11.4 appears. You can again choose Select All Images or Select Protected Images (which you have previously marked). The top choice in the list, Deselect All, automatically unselects previously selected images (if any) and takes you to the Deselect All/Select screen that allows you to highlight individual images and checkmark them with the OK button. (See Figure 11.4, lower right.)

4. **Select destination folder.** When finished selecting images, press OK to return to the Copy Image(s) screen. There, you can optionally choose Select Destination Folder and select a folder by number, or from a list of existing folders on the target card. If you do not specify a destination folder the Z5 will create one for you on the destination memory card.

5. **Start copying.** If you do not want to choose a specific destination, select Copy Image(s)?. You'll see a confirmation screen that displays the number of images that will be copied. Highlight Yes, press OK, and a progress screen with a green progress bar appears while the copying is underway. You'll see a Copy Complete message when the task is finished. Press OK, and then the MENU button twice to back out of the menus; or just tap the shutter release button.

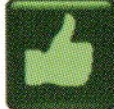

TIP The Copy command will ask for confirmation before overwriting images on the destination card that have the same name as the source images. You can choose Replace Existing Image, Replace All, Skip, or Cancel the rest of the copying operation.

Slide Show

Options: Start; Image Type: Still Images and Movies (default), Still Images Only, Movies Only, By Rating; Frame Interval: 2 (default), 3, 5, 10 seconds

My preference: N/A

This is the first of two entries on the second page of the Playback menu (and not shown in a figure). The Z5's Slide Show feature is a convenient way to review images in the current playback folder one after another, without the need to manually switch between them. Re-direct the output of your camera's video to an HDTV television, and you've got an instant camera-based large-screen audiovisual extravaganza. Your options include:

- **Start.** To activate a slide show, just choose Start from this entry in the Playback menu. During playback, you can press the OK button to pause the "slide show." When the show is paused, a menu pops up with choices to restart the show (by pressing the OK button again), change the interval between frames, or to exit the show entirely.

- **Image Type.** You can choose to display both still images and movies, still images only, movies only, or images with one to five Rating stars (or none at all). The Ratings feature means you can award a "star" value to images as you shoot, or at any later time, and then activate a slide show that displays *only* the images with a particular rating—or images with *several* ratings, say, *both* five-star and four-star photos. I'll explain Ratings in the next section. The default value is both stills and movies.

- **Frame Interval.** If you like, you can choose Frame Interval before commencing the show in order to select an interval of 2, 3, 5, or 10 seconds between "slides." The default value is 2 seconds.

As the images are displayed, press the up/down multi selector buttons to change the amount of information presented on the screen with each image. For example, you might want to review a set of images and the settings used to shoot them. During the show:

- **Change information.** At any time during the show, press the up/down directional buttons until the informational screen you want is overlaid on the images.

- **Manually change frames.** As the slide show progresses, you can press the left/right multi selector buttons to move back to a previous frame or jump ahead to the next one. The slide show will then proceed as before.

- **Pause.** Press the OK button. Highlight Restart and press OK again to resume.

- **Change playback volume (for movie images only).** Press the Zoom In button to increase volume or Zoom Out to decrease.

- **Exit to Playback menu.** Press the MENU button to exit the slide show and return to the Playback menu. Use this option when you want to change slide show parameters.

- **Exit to Playback mode.** Returns to previous playback mode (full frame or thumbnail).

- **Exit to Shooting mode.** Tap the shutter release button.

- **Restart/Adjust.** At the end of the slide show, as when you've paused it, you'll be offered the choice of restarting the sequence, changing the frame interval, or exiting the Slide Show feature completely.

Rating

Options: Zero to five stars

My preference: N/A

The Rating option allows applying a star rating from zero to five stars for individual images. I love this feature, and not because my work is so variable that my images customarily range in quality from zero-star stinkers to five-star exhibition-worthy shots. In practice, you can use the Rating system to categorize your photos any way you choose, using a variety of parameters.

Select this menu item and the image selection window will appear. You can use the left/right directional buttons or touch screen to scroll among your images to highlight one you want to rate. To view a highlighted image full frame, press and hold the Zoom In button. Rate a highlighted image using the up/down buttons to apply a rating from zero to five stars or tap the thumbnail on the monitor display one to five times. Press the down button to decrement stars, or to select the Trash icon to mark the picture for later deletion. Ratings cannot be applied to protected images. Press OK or tap Return to confirm and exit.

Images can also be rated during playback. When an image is shown on the screen as you review it, press the *i* button to show playback options (Rating, Select to Send to Smart Device/Deselect, Retouch, Choose Folder). Select Rating, and then use the controls to apply a rating as described above. Press OK or tap Return to confirm and exit.

I'm keen on the Rating feature because this capability is much more versatile than you might think. The stars don't have to relate to relative image quality. You can invent any other "code" you might like to apply. For example, if you like, one star can represent photos containing animals; two stars pictures with family members; three stars photos of landscapes; and so forth. Then, with the ratings applied, you can quickly access particular types of pictures.

Or, you could mark your photos to create five different slide shows (as described earlier) on a single memory card. On a lengthy European vacation, you could assign your best shots in Spain a single star; designate shots in France with two stars; those in Italy with three; Greece, four; and Germany, five stars. Then, choose By Rating as your Image Type for your Slide Show, and then activate a show using only images with a particular number of stars. Or, you could specify a show with, say, only one-star and three-star images to display a series of Spain and Italy photographs.

Photo Shooting Menu Options

The *i* menu allows you to make many of the most common adjustments, including image quality, image size, autofocus mode, white balance, AF mode, and flash settings, and can be customized to include other entries of your choice. You'll find some of these settings duplicated in the Photo Shooting menu (the first page of which is shown in Figure 11.5), along with options that you access second-most frequently when you're using your Nikon Z5, such as specifying noise reduction for long exposures or high ISO settings. You might make such adjustments as you begin a shooting session, or when you move from one type of subject to another. Nikon makes accessing these changes very easy.

This section explains the options of the Photo Shooting menu and how to use them. The options you'll find in these green-coded menus include:

- Reset Photo Shooting Menu
- Storage Folder
- File Naming
- Role Played by Card in Slot 2
- Choose Image Area
- Image Quality
- Image Size
- NEF (RAW) Recording
- ISO Sensitivity Settings
- White Balance
- Set Picture Control
- Manage Picture Control
- Color Space
- Active D-Lighting
- Long Exposure NR
- High ISO NR
- Vignette Control
- Diffraction Compensation
- Auto Distortion Control
- Flicker Reduction Shooting
- Metering
- Flash Control
- Flash Mode
- Flash Compensation
- Focus Mode
- AF-Area Mode
- Vibration Reduction
- Auto Bracketing
- Multiple Exposure
- HDR (High Dynamic Range)
- Interval Timer Shooting
- Time-lapse Movie
- Focus Shift Shooting
- Silent Photography

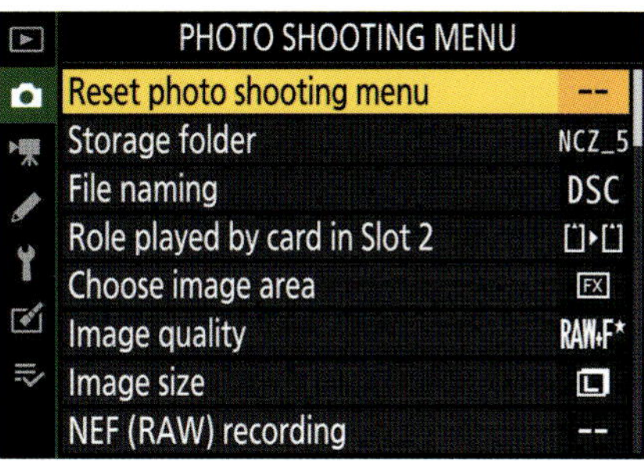

Figure 11.5 Common shooting settings can be changed in the Photo Shooting menu.

Reset Photo Shooting Menu

Options: Yes, No

My preference: N/A

The Nikon Z5 has, in effect, *four* different kinds of resets. This is one of them.

- **Photo Shooting menu reset.** Use this option to reset the values of the current Photo Shooting menu to the values shown in Table 11.1.
- **Movie Shooting menu reset.** The Movie Shooting menu has its own settings, which are reset separately, as described later in this chapter.
- **Custom Settings menu reset.** This option, which I'll describe in Chapter 12, is used to reset the Custom Settings entries. It has no effect on camera settings or Photo Shooting menu banks.
- **Setup menu reset.** This option resets all settings except for Language and Time Zone/Date to their default values. Use this option with caution, as it even erases copyright information and your user settings (described in Chapter 13). In that chapter I'll also show you how to save/load settings so you can retrieve settings you saved, even after you've used the Setup menu reset.

Table 11.1 shows the default values that are set using Reset Photo Shooting Menu. If you don't know what some of these settings are, I'll explain them later in this section.

TABLE 11.1 Default Photo Shooting Menu Values

FUNCTION	VALUE
Storage Folder	
Rename	NCZ_5
Select Folder by Number	100
File Naming	DSC
Role Played by Card in Slot 2	Overflow
Choose Image Area	FX (36 × 24)
Image Quality	JPEG normal
Image Size	Large
NEF (RAW) Recording	
NEF (RAW) Compression	Lossless compressed
NEF (RAW) Bit Depth	14 bit
ISO Sensitivity Settings	
ISO Sensitivity	
Auto	Auto
P,S,A,M	100
Auto ISO Sensitivity Control	On
Maximum Sensitivity	51200
Maximum Sensitivity Flash	Same as without flash
Minimum Shutter Speed	Auto
White Balance	$Auto_1$>Keep overall atmosphere
Fine Tuning	A−B:0, G−M:0
Choose Color Temp	5000K
Preset Manual	d-1
Set Picture Control	Auto
Color Space	sRGB
Active D-Lighting	Off
Long Exp. NR	Off
High ISO NR	Normal
Vignette Control	Normal
Diffraction Compensation	On
Auto Distortion Control	On
Flicker Reduction Shooting	Off
Metering	Matrix Metering
Flash Control	
Flash Control Mode	TTL
Wireless Flash Options	Off
Remote Flash Control	Group flash
Flash Mode	Fill flash
Flash Compensation	0.0
Focus Mode	Single AF
AF-Area Mode	Auto-area AF
Vibration Reduction	(Varies with lens)

FUNCTION	VALUE
Auto Bracketing	
Auto Bracketing Set	AE & flash
Number of Shots	0
Increment	1.0
Multiple Exposure	
Multiple Exposure Mode	Off
Number of Shots	2
Overlay Mode	Average
Keep All Exposures	On
Overlay Shooting	On
HDR (High Dynamic Range)	
HDR Mode	Off
Exposure Differential	Auto
Smoothing	Normal
Save Individual Images (NEF)	Off
Interval Timer Shooting	Off
Choose Start Day/Time	Now
Interval	1 min.
No. Intervals × Shots/Interval	0001x1
Exposure Smoothing	On
Silent Photography	On
Interval Priority	Off
Focus Before Each Shot	Off
Options	Off
Starting Storage Folder	
New Folder	No
Reset File Numbering	No
Time-Lapse Movie	Off
Interval	5 seconds
Shooting Time	25 minutes
Exposure Smoothing	On
Silent Photography	On
Choose Image Area	FX
Frame Size/Frame Rate	1920 × 1080; 60p
Interval Priority	Off
Focus Before Each Shot	Off
Destination	Slot 1
Focus Shift Shooting	
Number of Shots	100
Focus Step Width	5
Interval Until Next Shot	0
First-Frame Exposure Lock	On
Silent Photography	On
Starting Storage Folder	
New Folder	No
Reset File Numbering	No
Silent Photography	Off

Storage Folder

Options: Rename: NCZ_5 (default); Select Folder by Number: 100 (default); Select Folder from List
My preference: I use the Select Folder by Number option frequently to organize images by topic or time frame.

If you want to store images in a folder other than the one most recently created and selected by the Nikon Z5, you can switch among available folders on your memory card or create your own folder. Remember that any folders you create will be deleted when you reformat your memory card.

Why create your own folders? Perhaps you're traveling and have a high-capacity memory card and want to store the images for each day (or for each city that you visit) in a separate folder. Maybe you'd like to separate those wedding photos you snapped at the ceremony from those taken at the reception. As I mentioned earlier, the Nikon Z5 automatically creates a folder on a newly formatted memory card with a name like 100NCZ_5, and when it fills with 5,000 images (an increase from the limitation of 999 images in most previous Nikon cameras) or a picture numbered 9999, it will automatically create a new folder with a number incremented by one (such as 101NCZ_5).

Folders are always identified using a three-digit number, followed by a five-character folder name. Although the default characters are NCZ_5, you can specify a name of your choice. To create your own folder or select an existing folder:

1. **Access active folder entry.** Choose Storage Folder in the Photo Shooting menu and press the right multi selector button. The screen shown at left in Figure 11.6 appears.

2. **Choose function.** Three options are listed: Rename, Select Folder by Number, and Select Folder from List.

   - **Rename.** Highlight and select Rename and you'll be taken to a screen similar to the one shown at right in Figure 11.6, but with only five spaces to enter information for the naming scheme. Only numbers from 0 to 9, uppercase alpha characters, and an underline can be selected. Note that you can only change the name of your folder scheme—existing folders cannot be renamed. I like to name my folders using the scheme "NIKZ5." It does not provide any extra information beyond that of the default "NCZ_5," but it does make it very easy to differentiate between photos taken with my Z5, and those taken by another Z5 (most likely another photographer). See the section, "Entering Text on the Nikon Z5" for a primer on using the on-screen keyboard.

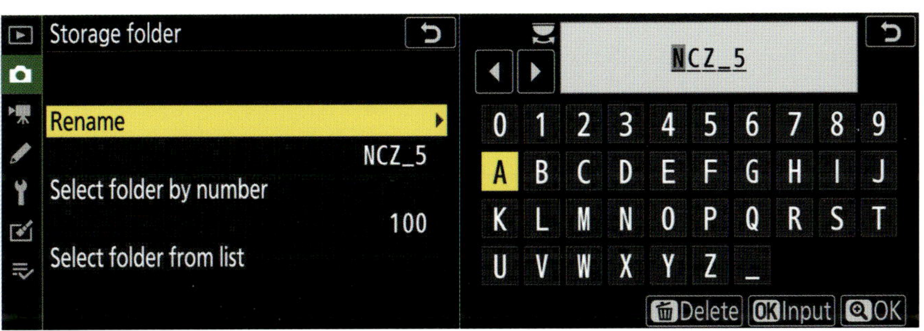

Figure 11.6 Change your folder naming scheme, create a new folder, or select an existing folder number.

- **Select Folder by Number.** If you've chosen this option, a screen appears with three digits representing the possible folder numbers from 100 to 999. (See Figure 11.7.) Use the left/right multi selector buttons to move between the digits, and the up/down buttons to increase or decrease the value of the digit. If a folder already exists with the number you dial in, an icon appears showing the folder is empty, partially full, or it has 5,000 images or a picture numbered 9999 (and can contain no more images).

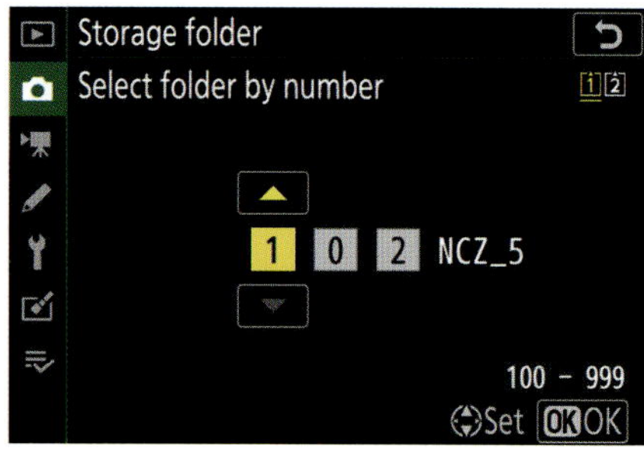

Figure 11.7 Select a folder by number.

Press OK to create the new folder and make it the active folder. You'd want to use this option to create a new folder *or* when you don't know whether a folder by a particular number already exists. If a folder with that number already resides on the memory card, you can use it (if it is not full); if it doesn't exist, you can create it.

- **Select Folder from List.** From among the available folders shown, scroll to the one that you want to become active for image storage and playback. This feature is handy when you want to display a slide show located in a particular folder. Use this option if you know that the folder you want to use already resides on the memory card. Press OK to confirm your choice and make the folder active.

3. **Exit menus.** Press the MENU button or tap the shutter release to exit.

Entering Text on the Nikon Z5

Your Z5 offers several opportunities to enter text, so you can change folder names, insert your name as "Artist," or provide copyright information. The Nikon Z5 uses a fairly standardized text-entry screen to name files, rename Picture Controls, create new folder names, and enter image comments and other text. You'll be using text entry with other functions that I'll describe later in this book. The screen looks like the one shown earlier in Figure 11.6, right, with some variations (for example, some functions have a less diverse character set, or offer more or fewer spaces for your entries). To enter text, just use the touch screen to "type" your characters or, alternatively, use the multi selector navigational buttons to scroll around within the array of alphanumerics. (I invariably use the touch screen for this, unless I am outdoors, wearing gloves, and really, really need to enter text.)

- **Highlight a character.** Use the touch screen or multi selector keys to scroll around within the array of characters.

- **Insert highlighted character.** Tap the character or press the multi selector OK button to insert the highlighted character. The cursor will move one place to the right to accept the next character.

- **Non-destructively move forward/backspace.** Use the main command dial to move the cursor within the line of characters you've entered. This allows you to skip ahead or backspace and replace a character without disturbing the others you've entered. Although it's a bit more difficult for the ham-handed, you can also tap the left/right triangles on the screen located to the immediate left of the text-entry area to move the cursor.

- **Erase a highlighted character.** To remove a character you've already input, move the cursor to highlight that character, and then press the Trash button or tap the trash can icon at the bottom of the screen.

- **Confirm your entry.** When you're finished entering text, press the Zoom In button to confirm your entry, then press the MENU button to return to the Photo Shooting menu, or twice (or just tap the shutter release) to exit the menu system entirely.

File Naming

Options: Choose three-letter prefix. Default: DSC
My preference: NZ5

The Nikon Z5, like other cameras in the Nikon product line, automatically applies a name like _ DSC0001.jpg or DSC_0001.nef to your image files as they are created. You can use this menu option to change the names applied to your photos, but only within certain strict limitations. In practice, you can change only three of the eight characters, the *DSC* portion of the filename. The other five are mandated either by the Design Rule for Camera File System (DCF) specification that all digital camera makers adhere to or to industry conventions.

DCF limits filenames created by conforming digital cameras to a maximum of eight characters, plus a three-character extension (such as .jpg, or .nef, or .wav in the case of audio files) that represents the format of the file. The eight-plus-three (usually called 8.3) length limitation dates back to an evil and frustrating computer operating system that we older photographers would like to forget (its initials are D.O.S.), but which, unhappily, lives on as the wraith of a file-naming convention.

Of the eight available characters, four are used to represent, in a general sense, the type of camera used to create the image. By convention, one of those characters is an underline, placed in the first position (as in _DSCxxxx.xxx) when the image uses the Adobe RGB color space (more on color spaces later), and in the fourth position (as in DSC_xxxx.xxx) for sRGB and RAW (NEF) files. That leaves just three characters for the manufacturer (and you) to use. Nikon, Sony, and some other vendors use DSC (which may or may not stand for Digital Still Camera, depending on who you ask), while Canon prefers IMG. The remaining four characters are used for numbers from 0000 to 9999, which is why your Z5 "rolls over" to DSC_0000 again when the 9999-number limitation is reached.

When you select File Naming in the Photo Shooting menu, you'll be shown the current settings for both sRGB (and RAW) and Adobe RGB. Press the right multi selector button, and you'll be taken to the (mostly) standard Nikon text-entry screen described above and allowed to change the DSC value to something else. In this version of the text-entry screen, however, only the numbers from 0 to 9 and characters A–Z are available; the filename cannot contain other characters. As always, press the Zoom In button to confirm your new setting.

Because the default DSC characters don't tell you much, don't hesitate to change them to something else. I use NZ5 for my Z5 and 850 for my Nikon D850. If you don't need to differentiate between different camera models, you can change the three characters to anything else that suits your purposes, including your initials (DDB_ or JFK_, for example), or even customize for particular shooting sessions (EUR_, GER_, FRA_, and JAP_ when taking vacation trips). You can also use the filename flexibility to partially overcome the 9999-numbering limitation. You could, for example, use the template Z51_ to represent the first 10,000 pictures you take with your Z5, and then Z52_ for the next 10,000, and Z53_ for the 10,000 after that.

That's assuming you don't rename your image files in your computer. In a way, filenaming verges on a moot consideration, because they apply *only* to the images as they exist in your camera. After (or during) transfer to your computer, you can change the names to anything you want, completely disregarding the 8.3 limitations (although it's a good idea to retain the default extensions). If you shot an image file named DSC_4832.jpg in your camera, you could change it to Paris_EiffelTower_32.jpg later. Indeed, virtually all photo transfer programs allow you to specify a template and rename your photos as they are moved or copied to your computer from your camera or memory card.

I usually don't go to that bother (I generally don't use transfer software; I just drag and drop images from my memory card to folders I have set up), but renaming can be useful for those willing to take the time to do it.

Role Played by Card in Slot 2

Options: Overflow (default), Backup, RAW Slot 1—JPEG Slot 2

My preference: Overflow for everyday shooting; Backup when traveling

This menu entry allows you to specify the function of the second memory card slot in the Nikon Z5, choosing to use the Slot 2 to accept overflow images when the primary card in Slot 1 fills up; create a backup of all the files stored on the primary card; or to split your RAW+JPEG files between primary and secondary slots. The Z5's Movie Shooting menu's Destination entry (discussed later in this chapter) offers a fourth option: you can select which slot is used to store your movie clips (and can therefore choose the largest memory card or fastest memory card for your movies). Here's how the secondary slot functions work:

Overflow

In this case, when the memory card in the primary slot fills up, the Z5 automatically switches over to the card in the Slot 2. The changeover happens quickly, and you're not even likely to notice, unless you have your eye on the "slot" indicators on the display. There are dozens of ways to use this capability:

- **"Limitless" Capacity.** My standard operating procedure is to put one Sony G-series 64GB or 128GB memory card in each slot. As a practical matter, that means I can shoot all day (or, sometimes all week) without changing memory cards, even if I am shooting landscapes and bracketing everything (either to optimize exposure, or, when the camera is mounted on a tripod, to capture files for later HDR processing). Or, I might be shooting sports/photojournalism, where the common practice is to change memory cards when your media is 80 percent full to eliminate the possibility of missing anything important due to a card change at an inopportune time. To be honest, I have yet to encounter a shoot (or even a single *trip*) in which I have filled up two 64GB or larger cards in a single session. But if you're using smaller cards and doing a lot of shooting, this capability can be a lifesaver.

- **Small/fast—with backup.** For some sports, if you are shooting continuously, you may want your fastest memory card in the primary slot to maximize write speed out of the camera's buffer, but the real speed demons in the memory card world can be expensive. So, instead of an affordable 64GB medium-speed card, you may put a (per gigabyte) more expensive 64GB high-speed card in the primary slot, and back it up with a slower (and cheaper) 16GB or 32GB card. You can capture images with the fastest card you've got, yet not have to worry about missing shots, because you have a backup card installed in Slot 2.

- **Put smaller cards to use.** If you don't think you'll need the overflow capacity, but still want to have it just in case, put a smaller card that you don't use much anymore in the secondary slot. If your large card that you didn't think would fill *does* come up short, you won't lose any shots. They'll be directed to that old 8GB card you put in the secondary slot for insurance. I sometimes do this when I am using several cameras and have a limited number of large cards at my disposal. For example, I often shoot with both my Nikon D6 and Z5 in the same session. I'll save the biggest cards for primary use, and use smaller cards in the Z5, knowing that any overflow shots will be stored on the small backup cards if necessary.

- **Stretch your budget.** After spending an arm and a leg for your Z5, you'd like to avoid replacing your old fast-but-limited-capacity 32GB SDHC memory cards for a little while. (Perhaps you're waiting for those new 256GB cards to come down in price.) With one 32GB card in each slot, you can double your shooting before it's time to swap cards.

Backup

In this case, each photograph you take is recorded on the memory cards in both the primary Slot 1 and secondary Slot 2. The write process takes slightly longer (so it may not be your best option when shooting sports), but it's otherwise a seamless way to create a backup copy of every image you take. If you're shooting RAW+JPEG, both files associated with each image are recorded on both slots. I absolutely love this feature, as I've mentioned before in this book. Here are some of my favorite applications:

- **Critical shots backed up instantly.** When I was a photojournalist, a lot of the images I took, particularly of spot news events, were literally once-in-a-lifetime shots that couldn't be duplicated under any circumstances. I also shot weddings, and while it was sometimes possible to restage a particular setup or pose, that was never a satisfactory option, even if done on the day of the nuptials. So, there was always a degree of trepidation until the film was processed or digital files backed up. With dual-slot backup capabilities, backup files can be made instantly, as you shoot. What a relief!

- **Great when there's No-Fi.** Many pros (and more than a few amateurs) rely on in-camera Wi-Fi connectivity (using the Z5's Wi-Fi capabilities, or other available accessories) to beam backups to a nearby laptop computer for safekeeping, or, at events, so that an assistant can process some images while photography continues. But, sometimes that's not possible, or, perhaps, you don't own the necessary equipment. Making a backup in your camera is a great alternative when wireless capabilities are unavailable or impractical. You can even shuttle the secondary slot card to an assistant at intervals while retaining the "main" copy of your images in the camera.

- **Leave your personal storage device or computer at home.** When I travel overseas, I like to pack light, with only a carry-on bag that holds my camera gear and some of my clothing, with the rest of my apparel relegated to the second tote that qualifies as a "personal" item. But I've always carried two card reader/personal storage devices or a laptop so I can make backup copies of my images while I travel. I've found that my dual-card Nikon cameras can easily replace the external backup options if I want to travel *extra* light on shorter trips. I can back up each image as it's shot automatically or shoot on one card (to allow faster capture) and make a duplicate with a card-to-card copy back in my hotel room in the evening. Or I can use the Z5's Copy Image(s) feature to make an extra copy of only the images I want.

- **Instant copy to share.** Want to give a traveling companion copies of all the images you shoot? Create a backup as you take the photos and hand over the copy on the spot. (Again, if you want to share only *some* of your pictures, you can use the Copy Image(s) feature instead.)

- **Segregate your images.** I've managed to accumulate a collection of 16GB and 32GB memory cards. I put these to work in travel photography applications on long trips. Each day I put a pair of these small capacity cards in my Z5, set the camera to Backup mode, and shoot the images for that day (or perhaps that day and the next). Each evening, I copy one of the cards to a small external hard disk drive attached to my MacBook Air, and store the original cards. I've got three copies of each day's shots and have them on separate memory cards for simple day-by-day organization.

RAW Slot 1—JPEG Slot 2

In this mode, when you're shooting RAW+JPEG, the NEF (RAW) files are saved to the card in the primary slot, and the JPEG files are saved to the card in the secondary slot. When you're using any other Quality setting (any JPEG option), the images are stored in the primary slot, until that card fills; then the photos overflow to the secondary slot. (This is effectively the same as the Backup option.) You'll find this mode useful under the following conditions:

- **Separate RAW and JPEG.** Perhaps you like to store your RAW and JPEG files in separate locations. This mode makes it easy to do that. Copy the card containing the RAW files to one destination on your computer, and the JPEG files from the other card to a second destination. The only complication is that the memory card in the primary slot is likely to fill up more quickly than the card with the smaller JPEG files in the secondary slot, so if you shoot to the capacity of the card in the primary slot, you'll need to replace it more often than you will the card with the JPEG files. Or, if you want the two cards to be mirror images of each other (but in different formats), you can swap them both out at the same time, with the secondary slot card only partially full.

- **Faster backup of RAW+JPEG.** If you shoot RAW+JPEG, using the Backup option means that you're saving *four* files each time you press the shutter release. That can slow you down in some situations if you're rapid-firing a sequence of images. Storing RAW files on one card and JPEG files on the other is a faster way of capturing a backup, because only two files are saved per click. If you have a problem with one of your JPEG files, you can easily produce a new JPEG from the RAW file. (Software options, such as the Nikon Capture NX-D, have a batch mode that simplifies creating JPEGs from NEFs *en masse,* in fact.) The reverse is not true, however. If your NEF file gets munged, your RAW information is lost forever, even though you still have the JPEG version. So, use this option carefully if your RAW files are especially important for a particular shooting session.

Choose Image Area

Options: FX (36 × 24) (default); DX (24 × 16); 1:1 (24 × 24); 16:9 (36 × 20)
My preference: FX (36 × 24)

Here you can specify how the Z5 uses the available image area:

- **Choose Image Area.** You can manually specify the image area to be used, which the Z5 will apply regardless of what type of lens is mounted on the camera. Use this option to force the image area issue (as when you're using a DX-format lens that the Z5 can't detect automatically), or to use a particular image area for all your shots in a session. Your choices include:
  - **FX format (36 × 24).** This is the full FX image-format area, roughly 36mm × 24mm, producing a 24MP image when Large is selected using the Image Size entry described shortly.
  - **DX format (24 × 16).** This fills the image frame with the image in the center 24mm × 16mm of the sensor, creating a 1.5X *crop factor*. (See Chapter 7 for more about the crop factor and lenses.) Your final image will be about 19.5MP.
  - **1:1 (24 × 24).** An image cropped to a square may be useful to emphasize a centered image, such as a close-up of a flower, when you want to direct the eye to the middle of the frame, rather than have it roam around within your image. The resulting 30MP photo still has outstanding resolution even though you're discarding pixels at left and right of the frame.
  - **16:9 (36 × 20).** This is a useful cropping that allows you to take still photos using the same 16:9 proportions as a high-definition movie frame. I like this crop when I'm producing storyboards for video productions, as my still image compositions will match the aspect ratio of the movies.

Image Quality

Options: NEF (RAW)+JPEG (Fine*, Fine, Normal*, Normal, Basic*, Basic), NEF (RAW), JPEG (Fine*, Fine, Normal*, Normal [default], Basic*, Basic)
My preference: NEF (RAW)+JPEG Fine* for everyday shooting; JPEG Fine* for sports

As I noted in Chapter 3, you can choose the image quality settings used by the Z5 to store its files. You can use this menu entry or opt for the quickest way by pressing the *i* button, selecting the Image Quality entry (by default the second from the left in the top row), and either rotating the command dial or pressing the OK button to select quality from a screen of choices.

You can choose NEF (RAW) only, NEF+ six different JPEG quality levels (Fine*, Fine, Normal*, Normal, Basic*, and Basic), or any of those six JPEG quality levels alone (with no NEF captured). When you elect to store only JPEG versions of the images you shoot, you can save memory card space as you bypass the larger RAW files. Or, you can save your photos as RAW files, which consume more than twice as much space on your memory card. Or, you can store both at once as you shoot.

Many photographers choose to save *both* JPEG and a RAW, so they'll have a JPEG version that might be usable as-is, as well as the original "digital negative" RAW file in case they want to do some processing of the image later. You'll end up with two different versions of the same file: one with a .jpg extension, and one with the .nef extension that signifies a Nikon RAW file.

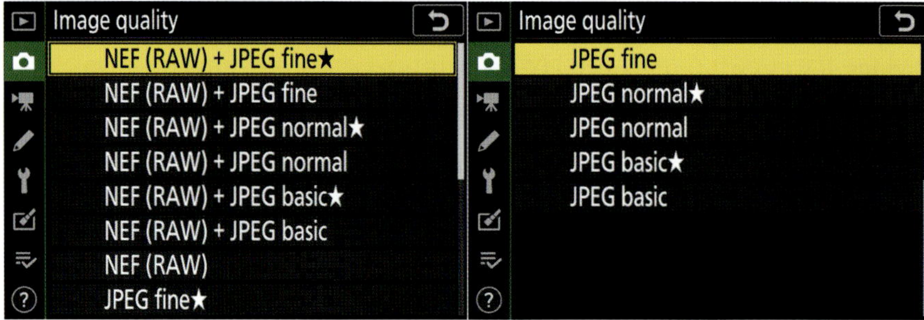

Figure 11.8 You can choose RAW, JPEG, or RAW+JPEG formats here.

To choose the combination you want using the menu system, access the Photo Shooting menu, scroll to Image Quality, and select it. Screens similar to the ones shown in Figure 11.8 (left and right) will appear. Scroll to highlight the setting you want, and either press OK or push the multi selector right button to confirm your selection.

In practice, you'll probably use the JPEG Fine* and RAW+JPEG Fine* (with the "extra quality" star) selections most often. Why so many choices, then? There are some limited advantages to using some of the higher compression and lower resolution options. Settings that are less than max allow stretching the capacity of your memory card so you can shoehorn quite a few more pictures onto a single memory card. That can come in useful when on vacation and you're running out of storage, or when you're shooting non-critical work that doesn't require 24 megapixels of resolution (such as photos taken for real estate listings, web page display, photo ID cards, or similar applications). Some photographers like to record RAW+JPEG Basic so they'll have a moderate-quality JPEG file for review only and no intention of using for editing purposes, while retaining access to the original full-resolution/uncompressed RAW file for serious editing.

For most work, using lower resolution and extra compression is false economy. You never know when you might need that extra bit of picture detail. Your best bet is to have enough memory cards to handle all the shooting you want to do until you have the chance to transfer your photos to your computer or a personal storage device.

Optimal Quality or Optimal Size?

Nikon has merged the JPEG-oriented "Optimal Quality" and "Optimum Size" options offered with previous cameras into the Image Quality entry. The difference:

- **Optimal Quality (marked with a star).** Choose this option if you want to maintain the best image quality possible at a particular JPEG setting and don't care if the file size varies. Because the Z5 will use only the minimum amount of compression required at each JPEG setting, file size will vary depending on scene content, and your buffer may hold fewer images during continuous shooting. If you're not shooting continuously, this setting will provide optimum image quality. Figure 11.9 shows a cropped portion of an image recorded with Optimal Quality (top) and one in which Size Priority was used to provide extra compression (bottom).

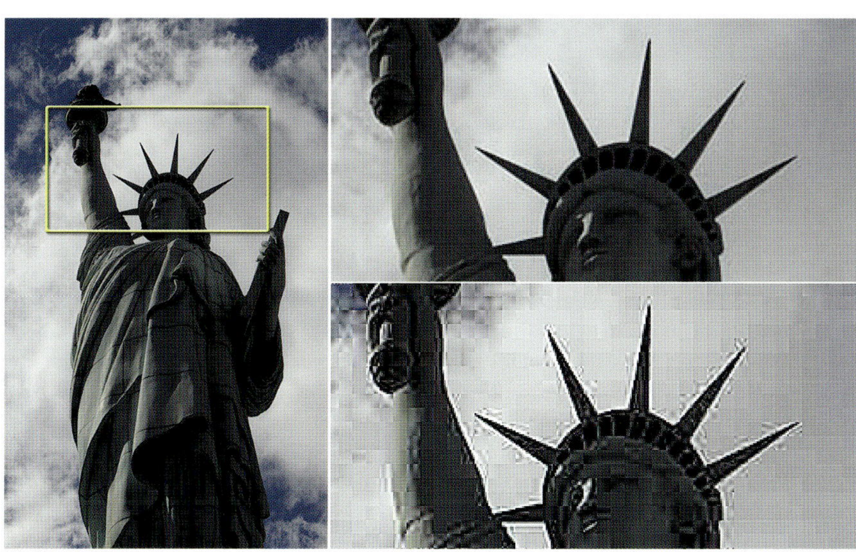

Figure 11.9 At low levels of JPEG compression, the image looks sharp even when you enlarge it enough to see the actual pixels (top); when using extreme JPEG compression (bottom), an image obviously loses quality.

- **Size Priority (no star).** When this option is selected, the Z5 will create files that are fairly uniformly sized JPEG images. Because some photos have content that is more easily compressible (for example, plain areas of sky can be squeezed down more than areas filled with detail), to maintain the standard file size the camera must apply more compression to some images, and less to others. As a result, there may be a barely noticeable loss of detail in the more heavily compressed images. The uniform file size also means that the Z5's buffer will hold the maximum number of shots during continuous shooting, allowing you to shoot longer sequences without the need to pause and wait for some images to be written to the memory card. In practice, you may find you can shoot continuously until the memory card fills.

JPEG vs. RAW

You'll sometimes be told that RAW files are the "unprocessed" image information your camera produces, before it's been modified. That's nonsense. RAW files are no more unprocessed than your camera film is after it's been through the chemicals to produce a negative or transparency. A lot can happen in the developer that can affect the quality of a film image—positively and negatively—and, similarly, your digital image undergoes a significant amount of processing before it is saved as a RAW file. Nikon even applies a name (EXPEED 6) to the digital image processing (DIP) chip used to perform this magic.

A RAW file is more similar to a film camera's processed negative. It contains all the information, captured in 12-bit or 14-bit channels per color (and stored in a 16-bit space), with no sharpening and no application of any special filters or other settings you might have specified when you took the picture. Those settings are *stored* with the RAW file so they can be applied when the image is converted to a form compatible with your favorite image editor. However, using RAW conversion software such as Adobe Camera Raw or Nikon Capture NX-D, you can override those settings and apply settings of your own. You can select essentially the same changes there that you might have specified in your camera's picture-taking options.

> ### HIDDEN JPEGS
>
> You may not be aware that your RAW file contains an embedded JPEG file, hidden inside in the JPEG Basic format. It's used to provide thumbnail previews of JPEG files, which is why you may notice an interesting phenomenon when loading a RAW image into a program like Nikon Capture NX or Adobe Lightroom. When the software first starts interpreting the RAW image, it may immediately display this hidden JPEG view which has, as you might expect, all the settings applied that you dialed into the camera. Then, as it finishes loading the RAW file, the application (Lightroom in particular) uses its own intelligence to fine-tune the image and display what it thinks is a decent version of the image, replacing the embedded JPEG. That's why you may see complaints that Lightroom or another program is behaving oddly: the initial embedded JPEG may look better than the final version, so it looks as if the application is degrading the image quality as the file loads. Of course, in all cases, once the RAW file is available, you can make your own changes to optimize it to your taste.
>
> There is a second use for these hidden JPEG files. If you shoot RAW without creating JPEG files and later decide you want a JPEG version, there are dozens of utility programs that will extract the embedded JPEG and save it as a separate file. (Google "JPEG extractor" to locate a freeware program that will perform this step for your Mac, PC, or other computer.)

RAW exists because sometimes we want to have access to all the information captured by the camera, before the camera's internal logic has processed it and converted the image to a standard file format. Even Compressed RAW doesn't save as much space as JPEG. What it does do is preserve all the information captured by your camera after it's been converted from analog to digital form.

So, why don't we always use RAW? Some photographers avoid using Nikon's RAW NEF files on the misguided conviction that they don't want to spend time in post-processing, forgetting that, if the camera settings you would have used for JPEG are correct, each RAW image's default attributes will use those settings and the RAW image will not need much manipulation. Post-processing in such cases is *optional*, and overwhelmingly helpful when an image needs to be fine-tuned.

Although some photographers do save *only* in RAW format, it's more common (and frequently more convenient) to use RAW plus one of the JPEG options, or, if you're confident about your settings, just shoot JPEG and eschew RAW altogether. In some situations, working with a RAW file can slow you down a little. RAW images take longer to store on the memory card, and must be converted from RAW to a format your image editor can handle, whether you elect to go with the default settings in force when the picture was taken, or make minor adjustments to the settings you specified in the camera.

As a result, those who depend on speedy access to images or who shoot large numbers of photos at once may prefer JPEG over RAW. Wedding photographers, for example, might expose several thousand photos during a bridal affair and offer hundreds to clients as electronic proofs for inclusion in an album. Wedding shooters take the time to make sure that their in-camera settings are correct, minimizing the need to post-process photos after the event. Given that their JPEGs are so good, there is little need to get bogged down shooting RAW.

Sports photographers also avoid RAW files. I recently photographed an air show that was an all-day affair, and, to make sure I didn't miss any peak moments as the aircraft flyovers, military sky-divers, and other action unfolded, I set my camera at the maximum rate and fired away. I managed to shoot

7,200 photos in a single day. I certainly didn't have any plans to do post-processing on very many of those shots, so carefully exposed and precisely focused JPEG images were my file format of choice that day.

JPEG was invented as a more compact file format that can store most of the information in a digital image, but in a much smaller size. JPEG predates most digital SLRs and was initially used to squeeze down files for transmission over slow dial-up connections. Even if you were using an early dSLR with 1.3MP files for news photography, you didn't want to send them back to the office over the telephone line communications that were common before high-speed Internet links became dominant.

But, as I noted, JPEG provides smaller files by compressing the information in a way that loses some image data. JPEG remains a viable alternative because it offers several different quality levels. At the highest quality Fine level, you might not be able to tell the difference between the original RAW file and the JPEG version.

In my case, I shoot virtually everything at RAW+JPEG Fine*. Most of the time, I'm not concerned about filling up my memory cards as I usually have my 128GB Sony G memory cards, and several more Sony G and Lexar 64GB cards with me. I also use a MacBook Air with an external 1TB hard drive. When shooting sports, I'll shift to JPEG Fine (with no RAW file) to squeeze a little extra speed out of my camera's continuous shooting mode, and to reduce the need to wade through eight-photo bursts taken in RAW format.

Image Size

Options: JPEG/TIFF: Large (default), Medium, Small; NEF (RAW): RAW L, RAW M, RAW S
My preference: Large

The next menu command in the Photo Shooting menu lets you select the resolution, or number of pixels captured in JPEG Format as you shoot with your Nikon Z5. (RAW formats are available only in Large size.) Your choices and the resolutions are shown in Table 11.2.

TABLE 11.2 Image Size Options

IMAGE AREA	SIZE	RESOLUTION	MEGAPIXELS
FX (36mm × 24mm)	Large	6016 × 4016	24.2MP
	Medium	4512 × 3008	13.6MP
	Small	3008 × 2008	6.0MP
DX (24mm × 16mm)	Large	3936 × 2624	10.3MP
	Medium	2944 × 1968	5.8MP
	Small	1968 × 1312	2.6MP
1:1 (24mm × 24mm)	Large	4016 × 4016	16.1MP
	Medium	3008 × 3008	9.0MP
	Small	2000 × 2000	4.0MP
16:9 (36mm × 20mm)	Large	6016 × 3384	20.4MP
	Medium	4512 × 2536	11.4MP
	Small	3008 × 1688	5.1MP

Select image sizes using this menu entry or by pressing the *i* button and accessing the Image Size option (located by default in the second row underneath the Image Quality setting). Rotate either command dial or press OK to select size from a screen.

NEF (RAW) Recording

Options: NEF (RAW) Compression: Lossless compressed (default), Compressed; NEF (RAW) Bit Depth: 12 bit, 14 bit (default)

My preference: Lossless compressed, 14 bit

When you've selected any NEF (RAW) setting for Image Quality, you can choose the type (amount) of compression applied to NEF (RAW) files as they are stored on your memory card, and whether the images are stored using 12-bit or 14-bit depth. The default values for type (Lossless compressed) and color depth (14 bit) work best for most situations, but there are times when you might want to use one of the other choices, as I'll explain later in this section. (Figure 11.10 shows the options available.)

Compression is a mathematical technique for reducing the size of a collection of information (such as an image; but other types of data or even programs can be compressed, too) in order to reduce the storage requirements and/or time required to transmit or transfer the information. Some compression algorithms arrange strings of bits that are most frequently used into a table, so that a binary number like, say, 1001011011100111 (16 digits long) doesn't have to be stored as two 8-bit bytes every time it appears in the image file. Instead, a smaller number that points to that position in the table can be used. The more times the pointer is used rather than the full number, the more space is saved in the file. Such a compression scheme can be used to reproduce exactly the original string of numbers, and so is called *lossless* compression.

Other types of compression are more aggressive and actually discard some of the information deemed to be redundant from a visual standpoint, so that, theoretically, you won't *notice* that details are missing, and the file can be made even more compact. The Nikon Z5's RAW storage routines can use this kind of size reduction, which is called *lossy* compression, to reduce file size by up to about half with very little effect on image quality. JPEG compression can be even more enthusiastic, resulting in images that are 15X smaller (or more) and which display noticeable loss of image quality.

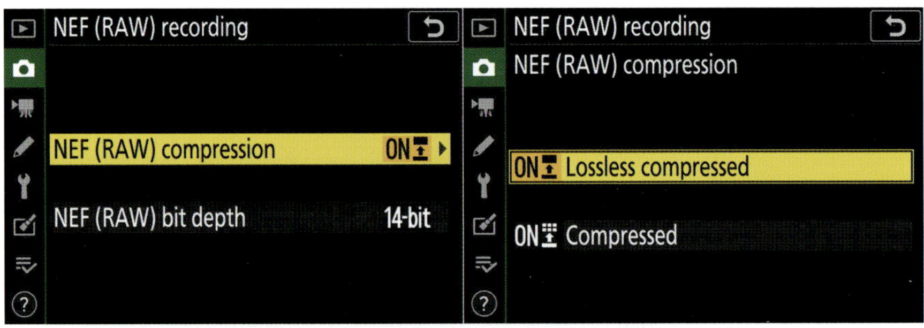

Figure 11.10 Your Image Quality choices occupy two screens.

Under Type in the NEF (RAW) Recording menu, you can select from:

- **Lossless compressed.** This is the default setting and uses what you might think of as reversible algorithms that discard no image information, so that the image can be compressed from 20 to 40 percent for a significantly smaller file size. The squeezed file can always be restored to its original size precisely, with no effect on image quality.

- **Compressed.** Use this setting if you want to store more images on your memory card and are willing to accept a tiny potential loss in image quality in the highlights, after significant editing. (I've never been able to detect any effect at all.) The Z5 can achieve from 40 to 55 percent compression with this option. It uses a two-step process, first grouping some very similar tonal values in the mid-tone and lighter areas of the image together, and then storing each group as a single value, followed by a lossless compression scheme that is applied to the dark tones, further reducing the file size. The process does a good job of preserving tones in shadow areas of an image, with only small losses in the midtone and lighter areas. The differences may show up only if you perform certain types of extensive post-processing on an image, such as heavy image sharpening or some types of tonal corrections.

The Bit Depth setting is another option that looks good on paper but, in the real world, is less useful than you might think. For most applications, the default value that produces 14-bit image files is probably your best choice, especially if you're exposing images that will be combined using HDR (high dynamic range) software later. In that case, you can definitely gain some extra exposure "headroom" using 14-bit processing. The 12-bit setting saves some space and speeds up processing but costs you a detectable amount of highlight detail.

As you may know, bit depth is a way of measuring the amount of color data that an image file can contain. What we call "24-bit color" actually consists of three channels of information—red, green, and blue—with one 8-bit bit assigned to each channel, so a 24-bit image contains three 8-bit channels (each with 256 different shades of red, green, or blue). A 24-bit color image can contain up to 16.8 million different colors (256 × 256 × 256; you do the math). Because each of the red, green, and blue channels always is stored using the same number of bits, it's become the custom to refer only to the channel bit depth to describe the amount of color information that can be collected.

So, when we're talking about 12-bit color, what we really mean are three 12-bit RGB channels, each capable of recording colors from 000000000000 to 111111111111 hues in a particular channel (in binary), or 4,096 colors per channel (decimal), and a total of 68,719,476,736 (68.7 billion) different hues. By comparison, 14-bit color offers 16,384 colors per channel and a total of 4,398,046,391,104 (4.4 trillion) colors.

The advantage of having such a humongous number of colors for an image that will, in the end, be boiled down to 16.8 million hues in Photoshop or another image editor is that, to simplify things a little, there is a better chance that the mere millions of colors you end up with have a better chance of being the *right* colors to accurately represent the image. For example, if there are subtle differences in the colors of a certain range of tones that represent only, say, 10 percent of a channel's colors, there would be only 26 colors to choose from in an 8-bit channel, but 410 colors in a 12-bit channel, and a whopping 1,638 colors in a 14-bit channel. The larger number of colors improves the odds of ending up with accurate hues.

It's not quite that simple, of course, because bit depth also improves the chances of having the right number of colors to choose from after the inevitable loss of some information due to noise and other factors. But in the real world, the difference between 26 colors and 410 colors is significant (which is why digital cameras always capture at least 12 bits per channel), and the difference between 12 bits and 14 bits (410 and 1,638 colors, respectively, in our example) is less significant. Because there is a penalty in terms of file size and the amount of time needed to process the image as it is recorded to your memory card, 14 bits per channel is not always your best option. Your two choices look like this:

- **12 bit.** Images are recorded at 12 bits per channel in the RAW file, and end up with 12 bits of information per channel that is translated during conversion for your image editor either into 12 bits within a 16-bits-per-channel space or interpreted down to 8 bits per channel.

- **14 bit.** This is the default bit depth for the Nikon Z5. At this setting, the Z5 grabs 16,384 colors per channel instead of 4,096, ending up as 14 bits in a 16-channel space or reduced to 256 colors by the RAW conversion software that translates the image for your image editor. You'll find that such 14-bit files end up almost one-third larger than 12-bit files. 14-bit images are great for HDR photography.

ISO Sensitivity Settings

Options: ISO sensitivity: 100 to 51200, plus Lo 1 to Lo 0.3 and Hi 0.3 to Hi 1; Auto ISO Sensitivity Control: On, Off; Maximum Sensitivity, Maximum Sensitivity with Flash, and Minimum Shutter Speed

My preference: Varies by subject type

This is the first entry on the second page of the Photo Shooting menu (see Figure 11.11). You can make direct ISO settings without resorting to this menu entry. Just press the ISO button, located just south of the shutter release, and then rotate the front control dial to switch between Auto ISO and fixed ISO settings, and the rear dial to select specific ISO values.

This menu entry has two parts, which give you more flexibility through its ISO Sensitivity and Auto ISO Sensitivity Control adjustments. The former is simply a screen that

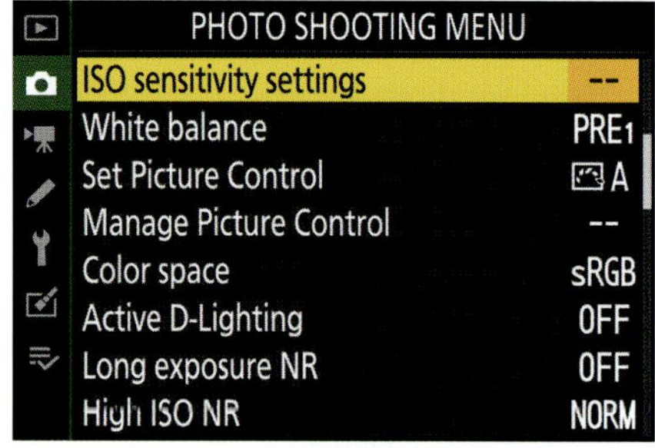

Figure 11.11 The second page of the Photo Shooting menu.

allows you to specify the ISO setting, just as you would by spinning the main command dial while holding down the ISO button on the top-right panel of the Z5. The available settings range from Lo 1 (ISO 50 equivalent) to ISO 100 through ISO 51200 up to Hi 1 (ISO 102,400 equivalent). The available settings are determined by the size of the increment you've specified in Custom Setting b1: 1/3-, 1/2-, or 1-step values. Use the ISO Sensitivity menu when you find it more convenient to set ISO using the color LCD monitor.

The Auto ISO Sensitivity Control menu entry lets you specify how and when the Z5 will adjust the ISO value for you automatically under certain conditions. This capability can be potentially useful, although experienced photographers tend to shy away from any feature that allows the camera to change basic settings like ISO that have been carefully selected. But you needn't fear Auto ISO. You can set some firm boundaries so the Z5 will use this adjustment in a fairly intelligent way.

When Auto ISO is activated, the camera can bump up the ISO sensitivity, if necessary, whenever an optimal exposure cannot be achieved at the current ISO setting. Of course, it can be disconcerting to think you're shooting at ISO 400 and then see a grainier ISO 6400 shot during LCD review. While the Z5 provides a flashing ISO-Auto alert in the display, the warning is easy to miss. Here are the important considerations to keep in mind when using the options available for this feature:

- **Off.** Set Auto ISO Sensitivity Control to Off, and the ISO setting will not budge from whatever value you have specified. Use this setting when you don't want any ISO surprises, or when ISO increases are not needed to counter slow shutter speeds. For example, if the Z5 is mounted on a tripod, you can safely use slower shutter speeds at a relatively low ISO setting, so there is no need for a speed bump. On the other hand, if you're hand-holding the camera and the Z5, set for Program (P) or Aperture-priority (A) mode, wants to use a shutter speed slower than, say, 1/30th second, it's probably a good idea to increase the ISO to avoid the effects of camera shake. If you're using a longer lens, a shutter speed of 1/125th second or higher might be the point where an ISO bump would be a good idea. In that case, you can turn the automatic ISO sensitivity control on, or remember to boost the ISO setting yourself.

- **Maximum sensitivity/Maximum sensitivity with flash.** Use these parameters to indicate the highest ISO setting you're comfortable having the Z5 set on its own. You can choose the max ISO setting the camera will use from ISO 200 up to ISO 102400, plus the "expanded" settings all the way up to Hi 1. Use a low number if you'd rather not take any photos at a high ISO without manually setting that value yourself. Dial in a higher ISO number if getting the photo at any sensitivity setting is more important than worrying about noise. When using the Maximum Sensitivity with Flash setting, you can specify Same As Without Flash, so the camera will perform similarly both with and without an optional flash.

  I've gotten surprisingly good results at ISO 25600; you should try it out yourself before ruling out this seemingly extreme ISO setting. Note that if you've selected an ISO setting that is *higher* than the Maximum Sensitivity you specify here, the Z5 will use the higher ISO value instead.

- **Minimum shutter speed.** This setting allows you to tell the Z5 how slow the shutter speed must be before the ISO boost kicks in, within the range of 30 seconds to 1/4000th second. The default value is Auto. When Auto is highlighted, press the right multi selector button, and a screen appears allowing you to fine-tune Auto to respond Slower or Faster.

If you set a value manually, 1/30th second is a good choice, because for most shooters in most situations, any shutter speed longer than 1/30th is to be avoided, unless you're using a tripod, monopod, or looking for a special effect. If you have steady hands, or the camera is partially braced against movement (say, you're using that monopod), a slower shutter speed, down to 1 full second, can be specified. Similarly, if you're working with a telephoto lens and find even a relatively brief shutter speed "dangerous," you can set a minimum shutter speed threshold of 1/250th second. When the shutter speed is faster than the minimum you enter, Auto ISO will not take effect.

Your Z5 is one smart camera in Auto ISO mode. For example, if you accidentally set a minimum shutter speed that is faster or slower than you've specified in Custom Setting e1: Flash Sync Speed or Custom Setting e2: Flash Shutter Speed, the camera will instead use a minimum shutter speed that is within the range set by e1 and e2. (You'll find more on these Custom Settings in Chapter 12.)

You'll recall that Program and Aperture-priority modes can adjust the camera's shutter speed. When Auto ISO is active, the camera will adjust the ISO setting *only* if the minimum shutter speed specified here would produce underexposure. In all other cases, the Z5 will simply adjust the shutter speed to produce an appropriate exposure and not touch the ISO setting.

In addition, the camera is clever enough to try to use faster shutter speeds with telephoto lenses (which are more subject to camera-motion blur). This feature works only with autofocus lenses; older manual focus lenses not equipped with a CPU chip (described in Chapter 7) are not compatible with this extra function.

White Balance

Options: Auto: $AUTO_0$ Keep White (default); $AUTO_1$ Keep Overall Atmosphere; $AUTO_2$ Keep Warm Lighting Colors; Presets: Natural Light Auto, Direct Sunlight, Cloudy, Shade, Incandescent, Fluorescent (seven types), Flash, Choose Color Temperature, Preset Manual

My preference: $AUTO_0$ (Keep White)

This setting lets you tweak the white balance setting the Z5 applies to JPEG images, and which it embeds in the RAW image for interpretation by your image editor when the NEF file is imported. Your camera has a bewildering array of white balance settings, including three Auto modes, and, in practice, all of them are, at best, a little bit wrong. However, many are close enough that you may not notice the difference; all the presets can be adjusted by you using white balance fine-tuning (as described in Chapter 8); and, when importing RAW files, you have even greater flexibility.

In addition to three varieties of full Auto white balance, this menu entry allows you to choose Natural Light Auto, Direct Sunlight, Cloudy, Shade, Incandescent, seven types of Fluorescent illumination, Flash, a specific color temperature of your choice, a preset value taken from an existing photograph, or a measurement you make. Some of the settings you make here can be duplicated using the Fn1 button on the front of the camera and main and sub-command dials, but the menus offer even more choices. Your white balance settings can have a significant impact on the color rendition of your images, as you can see in Figure 11.12, a shot of Clint Maedgen of the Preservation Hall Jazz Band.

The fastest way to change white balance settings is to use direct setting controls. Hold down the Fn1 button, then rotate the main command dial to choose one of the main settings. Your choices appear on the LCD monitor as you dial. When Auto, Fluorescent, K (Choose Color Temperature), or PRE (Preset Manual) are shown, you can also select a sub-option by holding down the Fn1 button and rotating the sub-command dial. You can also press the *i* button, select the White Balance icon (by default the first entry on the left of the second row), and rotate the main command dial and sub-command dial, as described above. I'll explain your options next.

This menu entry offers additional options, including fine-tuning presets and ability to capture and store custom preset color temperatures. Select the White Balance entry on the Photo Shooting menu, and you'll see an array of choices like those shown in Figure 11.13, left. (Three additional choices: Flash, K (Choose Color Temp.), and PRE Preset Manual are not visible until you scroll down to them.) If you choose Fluorescent, you'll be taken to another screen that presents seven different types of lamps, from sodium-vapor through warm-white fluorescent down to high-temperature mercury-vapor. If you know the exact type of non-incandescent lighting being used, you can select it, or settle on a likely compromise.

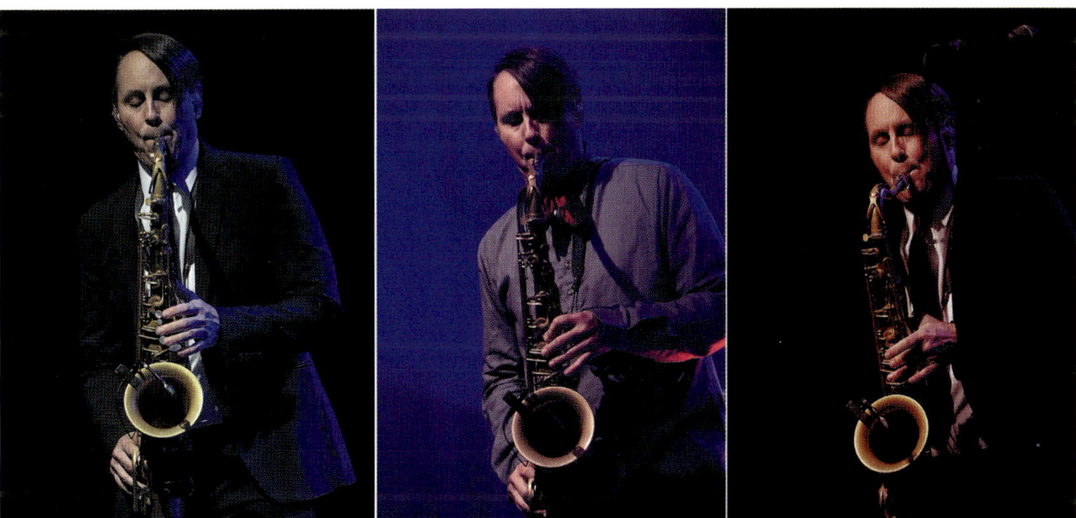

Figure 11.12 Adjusting color temperature can provide different results of the same subject at settings of 3,400K (left), 5,000K (middle), and 2,800K (right).

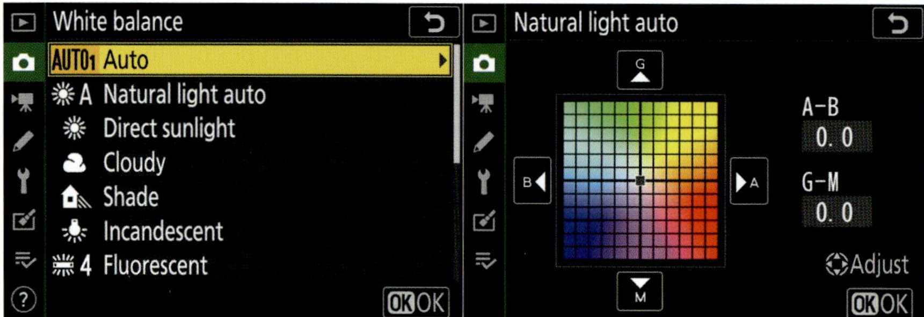

Figure 11.13 The White Balance menu has predefined values, plus the option of setting color temperature and presets you measure yourself (left). Specific white balance settings can be fine-tuned by changing their bias in the amber-blue, magenta-green directions—or along both axes simultaneously (right).

The Choose Color Temp. selection allows you to select from an array of color temperatures in degrees Kelvin (more on this in Chapter 8) from 2,500K to 10,000K, and then further fine-tune the color bias using the fine-tuning feature described below. Select Preset Manual to record or recall custom white balance settings suitable for environments with unusual lighting or mixed lighting, as described later in this section.

For all other settings, highlight the white balance option you want, then press the multi selector right button to view the fine-tuning screen shown in Figure 11.13, right. The screen shows a grid with two axes, an amber-blue axis extending left/right, and a green-magenta axis extending up and down the grid. By default, the grid's cursor is positioned in the middle, and a readout to the right of the grid shows the cursor's coordinates on the A-B axis (yes, I know the display has the end points reversed) and G-M axis at 0,0.

You can use the multi selector's up/down and right/left buttons to move the cursor to any coordinate in the grid, thereby biasing the white balance in the direction(s) you choose. The amber-blue axis makes the image warmer or colder (but not actually yellow or blue). Similarly, the green-magenta axis preserves all the colors in the original image but gives them a tinge biased toward green or magenta. Each increment equals about five mired units, but you should know that mired values aren't linear; five mireds at 2,500K produces a much stronger effect than five mireds at 6,000K. If you really want to fine-tune your color balance, you're better off experimenting and evaluating the results of a particular change.

When you've fine-tuned white balance, either using the Photo Shooting menu options or the defined WB button (Fn1 is the default), left/right triangles appear in the white balance section of the display to remind you that this tweaking has taken place.

Using Preset Manual White Balance

If automatic white balance or one of the predefined settings available aren't suitable, you can set a custom white balance using the Preset Manual menu option. You can apply the white balance from a scene, either by shooting a new picture on the spot and using the resulting white balance (Direct Measurement) or using an image you have already shot (Copy from Existing Photograph). You can use an existing preset or perform direct measurement from your current scene using a reference object (preferably a neutral gray or white object).

To use an existing white balance setting you've already stored, just follow these steps:

1. **Scroll to Preset Manual in the White Balance menu.** Press the right directional button. The screen shown in Figure 11.14 appears.

2. **Select preset.** Use the directional buttons to highlight the "slot" containing the value you stored earlier.

3. **Confirm.** Press OK to confirm and exit back to the Photo Shooting menu.

4. **Exit.** Press MENU to exit the Photo Shooting menu.

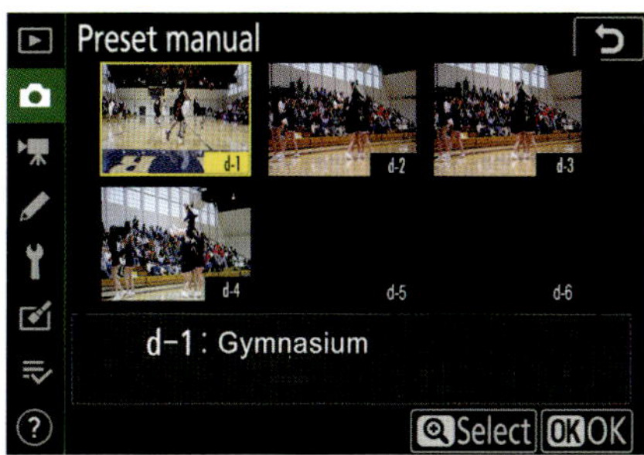

Figure 11.14 When you capture a scene's white balance, it will be stored in the selected slot.

You can also select an existing preset using the *i* menu:

1. **Press the *i* button.** Highlight the White Balance option at the left end of the bottom row.

2. **Select Preset.** Rotate the Command Dial until the Preset option (PRE) appears.

3. **Choose your preset.** Rotate the sub-command dial until the preset (numbered 1 to 6) appears.

4. **Exit.** Press the *i* button again to confirm and exit.

To capture a white balance setting, just follow these steps:

1. **Use gray or white reference.** Place the neutral reference, such as a white piece of paper or a gray card, under the lighting you want to measure. You can also use one of those white balance caps that fit on the front of your lens like a lens cap.

2. **Choose Preset Manual.** Press the *i* button, choose White Balance, and rotate the main command dial until Preset Manual (PRE) is selected.

3. **Select "slot."** Rotate the sub-command dial until the slot (d-1 to d-6) you want to use as your white balance register is shown. Press OK. The screen shown in Figure 11.15, top, appears.

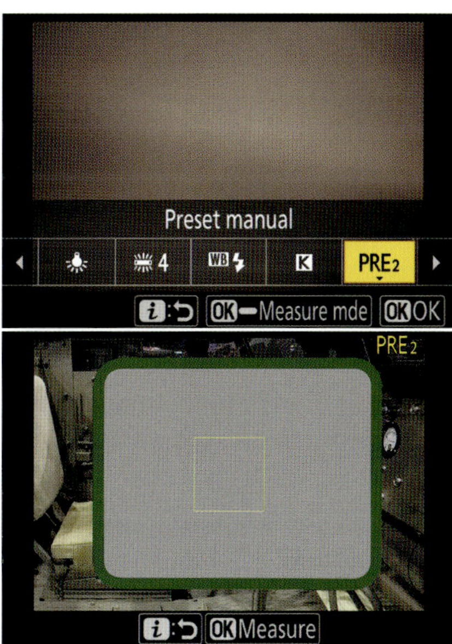

Figure 11.15 To define a new preset, highlight the PRE (top), and rotate the sub-command dial to choose a slot (d1 to d6). Then capture a neutral white or gray target (bottom).

4. **Activate Measure mode.** Press and hold the OK button until the screen shown at bottom in Figure 11.15 appears. In my illustration I've set up a gray card with a green border.

5. **Measure White Balance.** Tap the touch screen at the point where your gray or white reference appears or use the multi selector to move the target frame over that area. (Note that you can't relocate the frame if a flash is attached.) Then press OK again *or* press the shutter release down all the way.

6. **Success?** If the Z5 was able to capture the white balance information, a message Data Acquired appears. If it was unable to measure white balance, you'll be asked to try again. (Try using a different target if you fail on successive attempts.)

The preset value you've captured will remain in the slot until you replace that white balance with a new captured value. It can be summoned at any time (use the *i* button menu or Fn1) and when PRE is chosen with the main command dial, select your preset by rotating the sub-command dial until the desired white balance slot is displayed. You can also choose an existing image or protect a captured white balance from being over-written:

1. Choose Preset Manual from the White Balance menu.

2. A screen of thumbnails appears, showing the six "slots" numbered d-1 to d-6. Use the multi selector buttons to highlight one of the thumbnail slots and press the multi selector center button.

3. The next screen that appears (see Figure 11.16) has four options: Fine-tune, Edit Comment, Select Image, and Protect.

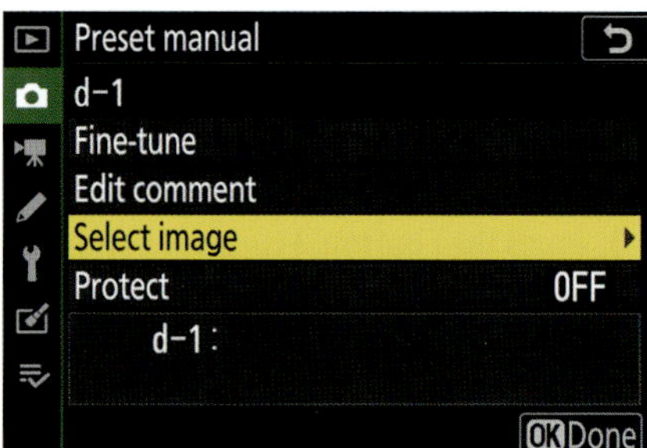

Figure 11.16 The Preset Manual screen lets you fine-tune preset white balance settings, label them with a comment, select an image to use as a white balance reference, and protect captured settings.

   - Choose Fine-tune to fine-tune the amber/blue/ magenta/green white balance of an image already stored in one of the four user slots.

   - Choose Edit Comment to add or change the comment applied to d-1 to d-6. The comment can be used as a label to better identify the white balance information in the slot, with terms like Gymnasium Daytime or Rumpus Room. (The standard Z5 text-editing screen shown earlier in this chapter appears.)

   - Choose Select Image to view the Z5's standard image-selection screen and highlight and choose the existing image you want to use. Press the Zoom In button to confirm your choice and copy the white balance of the selected image to the slot you selected in Step 2.

   - Choose Protect to lock the white balance setting currently stored in the selected slot. Use this to preserve a captured white balance setting.

4. Press OK to confirm your white balance setting.

> **A WHITE BALANCE LIBRARY**
>
> Consider dedicating a memory card to stow a selection of images taken under a variety of lighting conditions. If you want to "recycle" one of the color temperatures you've stored, insert the card and load one of those images into your choice of preset slots d-1 to d-6, as described above. Large memory cards are a bit pricey to make a dedicated memory card, but I have some old 16GB cards that I use for this.

Set Picture Control

Options: Original Picture Controls: Auto (default), Standard, Neutral, Vivid, Monochrome, Portrait, Landscape, Flat; Creative Picture Controls (01–20): Dream, Morning, Pop, Sunday, Somber, Dramatic, Silence, Bleached, Melancholic, Pure, Denim, Toy, Sepia, Blue, Red, Pink, Charcoal, Graphite, Binary, and Carbon

My preference: Standard: I can select other styles during RAW processing. Flat when extended dynamic range without HDR processing is needed.

Nikon has considerably expanded its Picture Control roster, adding 20 Creative Picture Controls that add special effects to your images as you shoot. The Picture Control styles allow you to choose your own sharpness (in three different ways, as I'll explain shortly), plus adjust contrast, color saturation, and hue settings applied to your images when using P, S, A, and M modes. The three types of Picture Controls available:

- **Original Picture Controls.** Your Z5 has seven predefined styles, which it calls Original Picture Controls: Standard, Neutral, Vivid, Monochrome, Portrait, Landscape, and Flat. There is also an Auto setting, which examines your image and applies one of these seven controls as appropriate. Flat is a relatively new option, with an extended, low-contrast dynamic range that lends itself to fine-tuning in an image editor. Movie shooters who plan to process their clips also love the versatility of the Flat setting, which allows preserving detail in highlights and shadows when correcting (or "grading") video in advanced movie-editing software.

  Note that each of the seven predefined styles has its own default settings for Sharpening (with four different sharpening modes), Contrast, Brightness, Saturation, and Hue. (Monochrome does not have Saturation or Hue settings.) For example, the default Sharpening is +4 for Vivid and Landscape; +3 for Standard and Monochrome; +2 for Neutral and Portrait; and +1 for Flat. The other settings available for the preset styles have their own defaults. Any changes you make are *edits* of the default values defined for that particular style.

- **Creative Picture Controls.** These are 20 new special effects styles, each assigned a number from 1 to 20. Nikon has given a fanciful name to each Creative Picture Control that more or less provides a hint to how the effect modifies your image. The available creative styles include Dream, Morning, Pop, Sunday, Somber, Dramatic, Silence, Bleached, Melancholic, Pure, Denim, Toy, Sepia, Blue, Red, Pink, Charcoal, Graphite, Binary, and Carbon. These 20 additional Creative Picture Controls offer the same parameter adjustments as Original Picture Controls, plus an Effect Level slider for specifying the *amount* of the special effects provided, on a scale from 0 to 100 in increments of 11 steps. You can edit the parameters of these Picture Controls, too. I'll explain Creative Picture Controls shortly.

■ **User Controls.** You can define up to nine Picture Controls of your own, numbered C-1 to C-9. Each User Control is based on one of the 27 predefined styles (any of the 7 Original or 20 Creative Controls). You'll use the Manage Picture Control entry (which follows this one).

While all the canned Original and Creative Picture Controls have their preset parameters, their most valuable trait is your ability to *edit* the settings of any of those 27 styles, so they better suit your taste. You can adjust the existing styles, in which case an asterisk appears next to their name in the menus or save your adjustments as a User Control. But wait, there's more! You can *copy* these styles to a memory card, edit them on your computer, and reload them into your camera at any time. So, effectively, you can have several sets of custom Picture Control styles available: those currently in your camera, as well as a virtually unlimited library of user-defined styles that you have stored on memory cards or create using Capture NX-D or ViewNX-i (a Windows program).

Moreover, Nikon insists that these styles have been standardized to the extent that if you re-use a style created for one camera (say, your Z5) and load it into a different compatible camera (such as a Nikon D850), you'll get substantially the same rendition. In a way, Picture Control styles are a bit like using a particular film. Do you want the look of Kodak Ektachrome or Fujifilm Velvia? (Even if you've never *used* these films, you've probably seen the results they produced.) Load the appropriate style created by you—or Google to find styles created by someone else.

As I've noted, using and fully managing Picture Control styles is accomplished using two different menu entries. This entry, Set Picture Control, has two functions: it allows you to *choose* an existing Original or Creative style and to *edit* any of those predefined styles that Nikon provides. The Photo Shooting menu entry that follows this one, Manage Picture Control, gives you the capability of creating and editing user-defined styles, using one of the canned Original or Creative Picture Controls as a foundation.

Choosing a Picture Control Style

To choose from one of the predefined Original or Creative styles or to select a user-defined style you've created (numbered C-1 to C-9), follow these steps:

1. Choose Set Picture Control from the Photo Shooting menu. The screen shown in Figure 11.17 appears. Remember that Picture Controls that have been modified from their standard settings have an asterisk next to their name.

2. Scroll down to the Picture Control you'd like to use. Initially, only the seven shown appear on the screen. As you scroll down, the final Original control, Flat, appears, followed by the Creative Controls, and, at the tail end of several screens, any User Controls you have created.

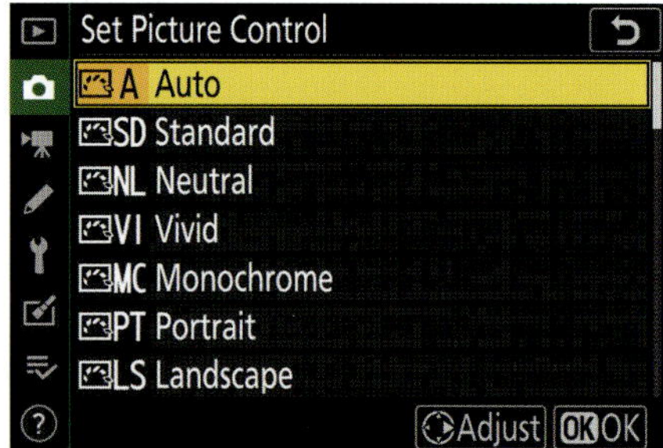

Figure 11.17 You can choose from Auto or the predefined Picture Controls shown here, as well as the Flat predefined control, the Creative Picture Controls, and the User Controls located farther down the scrolling list.

3. Press OK to activate the highlighted style. (Although you can usually select a menu item by pressing the multi selector right button, in this case, that button activates editing instead.)

4. Press the MENU button or tap the shutter release to exit the menu system.

Editing a Picture Control Style

You can change the parameters of any of Nikon's predefined Original Picture Controls (including Auto), Creative Picture Controls, or any of the (up to) nine user-defined styles you create. You are given the choice of using the quick-adjust/fine-tune facility to modify a Picture Control with a few sliders. You can edit these controls using this Set Picture Control entry in the Photo Shooting menu, and you can also edit them when you access a style from the *i* menu. To make quick adjustments to any Picture Control except the Monochrome style, follow these steps:

1. Choose Set Picture Control from the Photo Shooting menu.

2. Scroll down to the Picture Control you'd like to edit.

3. Press the multi selector right button to produce an adjustment screen similar to the one shown in Figure 11.18.

4. Use the Quick Sharp slider and the left/right directional buttons to change the three individual Sharpening adjustments (Sharpening, Mid-Range Sharpening, and Clarity) simultaneously. Alternatively, scroll down to each of those three adjustments and tweak Sharpening, Mid-Range Sharpening, or Clarity independently. (See the next section, "Super Sharpness," for an explanation of the latter parameter.)

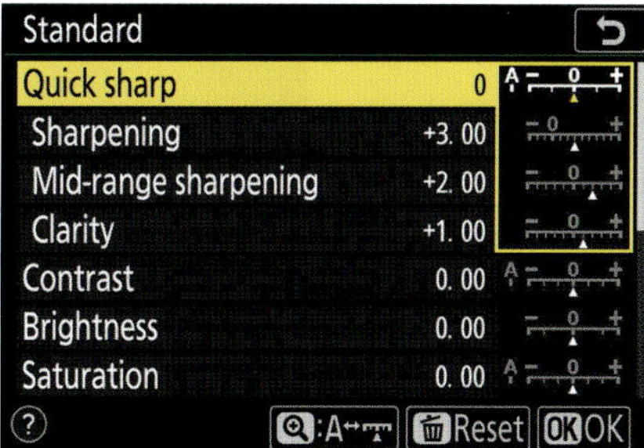

Figure 11.18 Sliders can be used to make quick adjustments to your Picture Control styles.

5. Next, scroll down to the Contrast, Brightness, Saturation, and Hue sliders with the multi selector up/down directional buttons, then use the left/right directional buttons to decrease or increase the effects. A gray triangle will appear under the original setting in the slider as you make a change. (Saturation and Hue cannot be adjusted for Monochrome.)

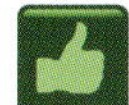

TIP You can adjust the Auto Picture Control, but each of your modifications are applied *on top of* the Auto adjustments. That is, in Auto Picture Control mode, the Z5 will automatically adjust, say, Contrast, and then apply any contrast adjustments you have specified, in the range Auto-2 to Auto+2.

6. Instead of making changes with the slider's scale, when you're working with the Contrast and Saturation adjustments, you can move the cursor to the far left and choose A (for Auto) and the Z5 will adjust these parameters automatically, depending on the type of scene it detects.

7. Press the Trash button to reset the values to their defaults.

8. Press OK when you're finished making adjustments.

> ## PICTURE CONTROLS WITH THE *i* MENU
>
> You can also perform the exact same functions just described using the *i* menu. Just press the *i* button, navigate to the Set Picture Control icon (located by default as the first icon on the left in the top row) and rotate the main command dial if all you want to do is select a Picture Control from a scrolling list. If you'd like to *edit* the control, press OK. The scrolling list appears as at left in Figure 11.19. When you've highlighted the control you want to edit, press the down button to produce a screen like the one seen in Figure 11.19, right. The column at the far right contains all the parameters listed in Steps 4 and 5 above, while the adjustment slider for the currently highlighted parameter appears at the bottom. Once you've made your edits, press OK to confirm and exit, or the *i* button to exit without making changes.

Figure 11.19 Picture Controls can be accessed and edited from the *i* menu.

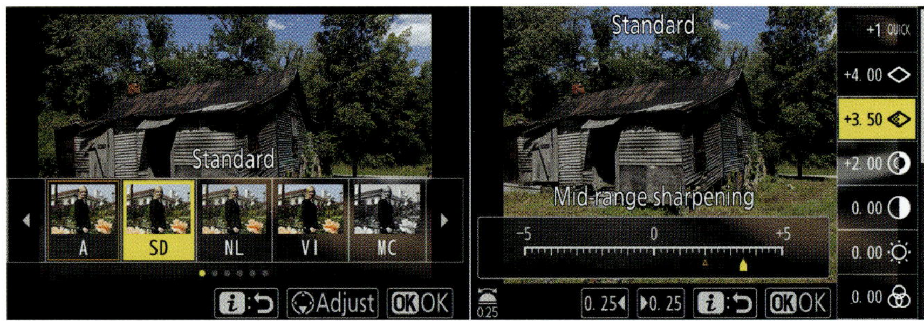

SUPER SHARPNESS

Amateur photographers like to be told that their pictures will be "clear and sharp," a simplification of picture quality that is likely to satisfy most of them. As an enthusiast, you know that many other factors also are part of image quality, including color, tonal range, and contrast. Indeed, sharpness itself is more complex than you might expect. Other parameters, such as Contrast, Brightness, Saturation, and Hue are virtually self-explanatory, because you've probably worked with them many times in Photoshop or another image editor.

When it comes to the adjustments you can make with the Z5 in terms of sharpness, there are three different parameters, and multiple ways of controlling them. The Z5's Picture Controls have separate sliders for all three, plus a fourth slider, Quick Sharp, which adjusts all of the three simultaneously. Here's a breakdown:

- **Sharpening.** This control affects the appearance of fine details and patterns, because it modifies the sharpness of the contours (edges) of your subjects. The lower the number, the softer those outlines will be; higher numbers produce more distinct details.

- **Mid-range sharpening.** Adjusts overall sharpness according to the fineness of patterns and lines in the mid-tones adjusted by the Sharpening and Clarity controls. In Movie mode, this parameter works only when Movie Quality has been set to High in the Movie Shooting menu.

- **Clarity.** This adjusts the overall sharpness of the image and the sharpness of thicker outlines without affecting brightness or dynamic range. Think of Clarity as a type of sharpening/enhancing effect applied to the mid-tones of an image. While sharpening generally adjusts only the contours of your subject matter, Clarity makes details sharper while maintaining the gradation of highlight and shadow areas. High values produce contrasty and vivid images with darkened colors and improved detail in the midtones. Low values reduce midtone detail and flatten colors. You might want to apply Clarity to make hazy or fog-clouded subjects look clearer without losing details, or when you want to soften hard-edge subjects. Your best bet is to play with the control to see how you like the results. The Z5 applies +1 Clarity by default to Standard, Vivid, Landscape, and Monochrome Picture Controls.

Editing the Monochrome Picture Control

Editing the Monochrome style is similar to customizing the other styles, except that the parameters differ slightly. Sharpening, Contrast, and Brightness are available, but, instead of Saturation and Hue, you can choose a filter effect (Yellow, Orange, Red, Green, or none) and a toning effect (black-and-white, plus seven levels of Sepia, Cyanotype, Red, Yellow, Green, Blue Green, Blue, Purple Blue, and Red Purple). (Keep in mind that once you've taken a JPEG photo using a Monochrome style, you can't convert the image back to full color.) To adjust Filters or Toning:

1. Choose Set Picture Control from the Photo Shooting menu.

2. Scroll down to the Monochrome Picture Control.

3. Press the multi selector right button to produce an adjustment screen similar to the one shown in Figure 11.20.

4. Set Sharpening, Contrast, and Brightness exactly as you would with the other Picture Controls.

5. Optionally, scroll down to Filter Effects or Toning (which appears after Filter Effects in the scrolling list and is shown at the bottom of the figure).

6. When Filter Effects is highlighted, you can choose Off, Yellow, Orange, Red, or Green. Press OK to finish or Trash to reset to the original values.

7. When Toning is highlighted, you can press the left/right directional buttons to choose a tone: Black/White, Sepia, Cyanotype, Red, Yellow, Green, Blue Green, Blue, Purple Blue, or Red Purple. Once you've selected a tone (other than Black/White), press the down button to move to the intensity control, then use the left/right buttons to set a toning strength from +1 to +7. Press OK to confirm, or Trash to reset.

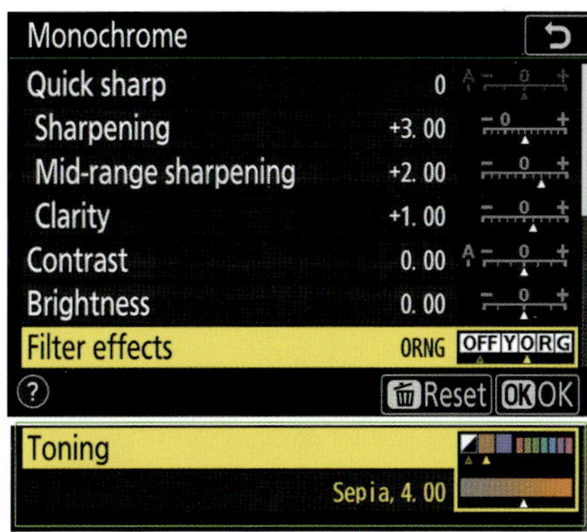

Figure 11.20 Editing Monochrome Picture Style parameters.

FILTERS VS. TONING

Although some of the color choices seem to overlap, you'll get very different looks when choosing between Filter Effects and Toning. Filter Effects add no color to the monochrome image. Instead, they reproduce the look of black-and-white film that has been shot through a color filter. That is, Yellow will make the sky darker and the clouds will stand out more, while Orange makes the sky even darker and sunsets more full of detail. The Red filter produces the darkest sky of all and darkens green objects, such as leaves. Human skin may appear lighter than normal. The Green filter has the opposite effect on leaves, making them appear lighter in tone. Figure 11.21 at left shows the same scene shot with no filter, then Yellow, Green, and Red filters.

The Sepia, Blue, Green, and other toning effects, on the other hand, all add a color cast to your monochrome image. Use these when you want an old-time look or a special effect, without bothering to recolor your shots in an image editor. Toning is shown at right in Figure 11.21.

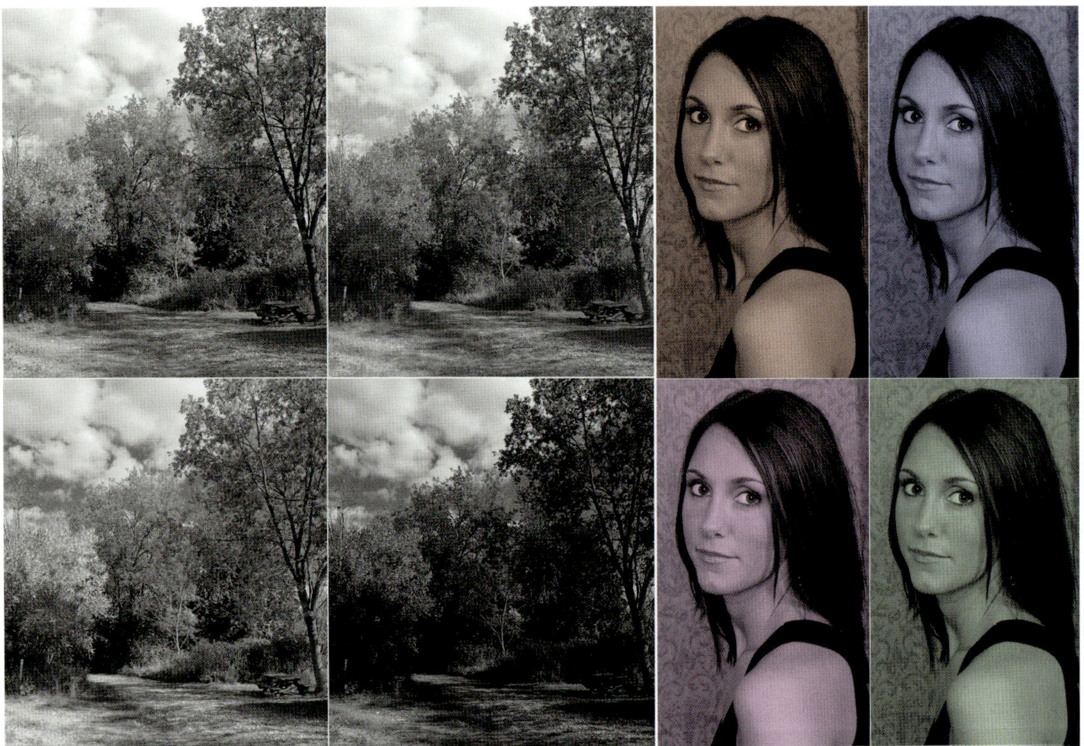

Figure 11.21 Left: Color filter effects: No filter (upper left); yellow filter (upper right); green filter (lower left); and red filter (lower right). Right: Toning effects: Sepia (upper left); Purple Blue (upper right); Red Purple (lower left); and Green (lower right).

Editing Creative Picture Controls

The Creative Picture Controls, located farther down the scrolling list after the predefined controls, have approximately the same adjustments found in the Original Picture Controls. However, you'll probably find adjusting them to be trickier, because it can be difficult to see how a particular parameter applies to a particular special effect. For example, you know that the Vivid original style emphasizes color saturation but what, exactly, goes into making, say, the Dream creative style? Simply looking at samples with a particular effect applied may not help, as you can see in Figure 11.22. The differences between many of the controls is subtle. Charcoal, Graphite, Binary, and Carbon may differ primarily in amount of contrast, for example.

Nikon provides some simplified descriptions, which may seem a little vague, like a New Age song title, forcing us poor users to evoke our own mental images with only fuzzy visual references. Nikon's summaries are along these lines (for what it's worth):

- **Dream.** Lightness, warmth, pale orange brightening darker areas with smooth edges and a soft appearance.
- **Morning.** Atmosphere of fresh morning air, dark areas brightened, with bluish tones with a sense of transparency. Refreshing image.
- **Pop.** Highest degree of saturation for more colorful tones and textures, even with brighter images.
- **Sunday.** Open atmosphere as if the image were captured on a Sunday afternoon. Increased contrast, blown highlights, for a stronger impression.

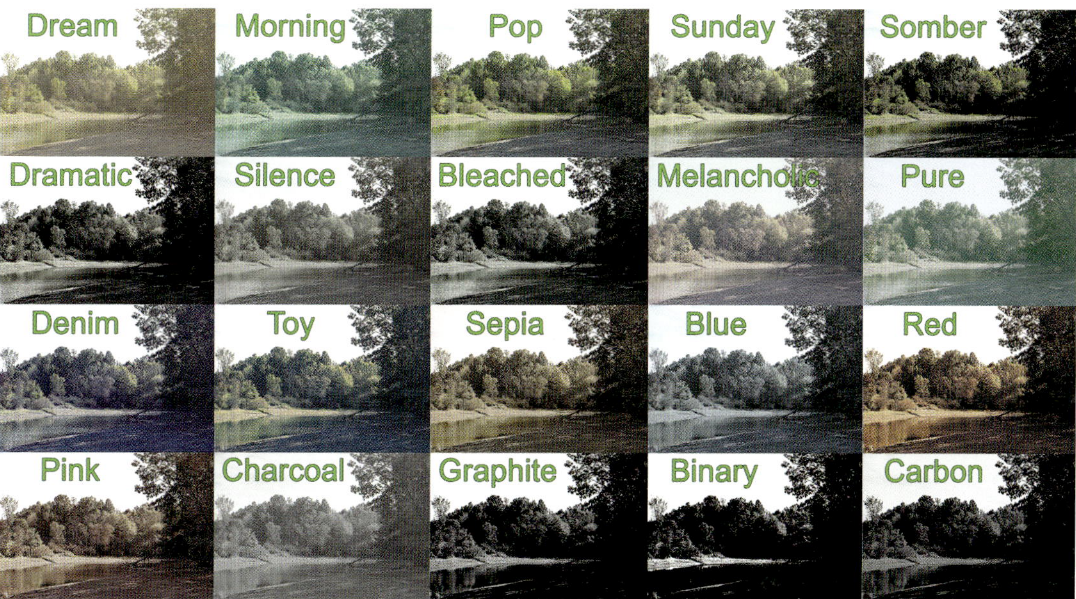

Figure 11.22 Creative Picture Controls.

- **Somber.** Melancholic, calm atmosphere, like after a rain, with increased saturation and suppressing brightness.

- **Dramatic.** Profound expression emphasizing light and shade, suitable for dramatic expression of light.

- **Silence.** Transient and lonely contemplative feeling; tranquil, soft images with reduced saturation.

- **Bleached.** Serious impression with greenish, low-saturation images and metallic feel. Minutely rendered details with tasteful silvery tone.

- **Melancholic.** Retro expression with slightly melancholic atmosphere, magenta tinged, restrained sharpness and saturation.

- **Pure.** Soft image, as if viewed through a veil, with soft bluish tone, tranquil ambience.

- **Denim.** Deep tone, strong blue shifted toward cyan, high saturation.

- **Toy.** Inspired by toy cameras, but deeper and calmer impression, with high saturation, blue shifted toward indigo.

- **Sepia.** First of the true "color-influenced" Creative Picture Controls, provides sepia images with faded colors, similar to a colorized monochrome picture.

- **Blue.** Yet more melancholy, this time with a quiet, bluish tone, similar to cyanotypes.

- **Red.** Retro images with heavy red tone.

- **Pink.** No relation to Alecia Beth Moore (P!nk), but still able to deliver a soft, gentle romantic tone with a pinkish atmosphere.

- **Charcoal.** Gentle, monochrome images resembling black-and-white drawings with minimal loss of detail in shadows and highlights, but softer edge sharpness.

- **Graphite.** Sharpened edges and lustrous blacks with crisp, accentuated contrast.

- **Binary.** Two-tone images for crisp black-and-white.

- **Carbon.** Stable, deep, dignified images with strong, black-based gradation.

As the names and descriptions of each of these 20 Creative Picture Controls don't adequately describe their effects, my recommendation is to evaluate each individually, and use the controls to tweak them to your preferences. The Dream style is shown in Figure 11.23 as an example. You can always adjust these styles and save them under a new name as a User Control, as I'll describe in the Manage Picture Control section that follows.

Figure 11.23 Adjusting Creative Picture Controls.

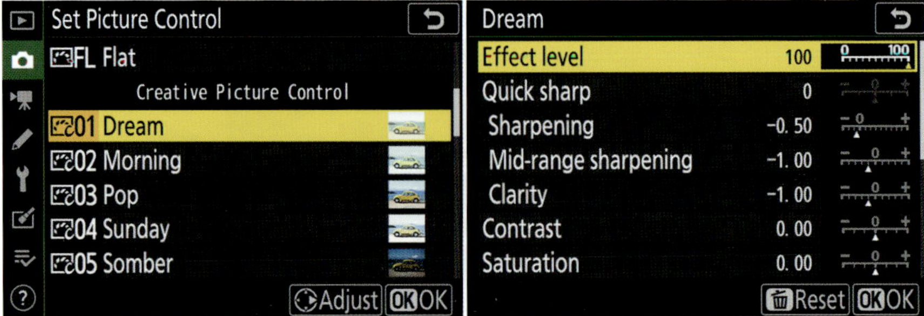

Manage Picture Control

Options: Save/Edit, Rename, Delete, Load/Save
My preference: N/A

The Manage Picture Control menu entry can be used to create new styles, edit existing styles, rename or delete them, and store/retrieve them from the memory card. Here are the basic functions of this menu item, which can be found on the Photo Shooting menu directly below the Set Picture Control entry:

- **Make a copy.** Choose Save/Edit (see Figure 11.24, left), select from the list of available Picture Controls, and press OK to store that style in one of the user-defined slots C-1 to C-9 (with slots C-1 to C-2 shown already occupied in Figure 11.24, right).

- **Save an edited copy.** Choose Save/Edit, select from the list of available Picture Controls, and then press the multi selector right button to edit the style, as described in the previous section. Press OK when finished editing, and then save the modified style in one of the user-defined slots C-1 to C-9.

- **Rename a style.** Choose Rename, select from the list of user-defined Picture Controls (you cannot rename the default styles), and then enter the text used as the new label for the style, using the standard Z5 text-entry screen shown earlier in this chapter in Figure 11.6. You may use up to 19 characters for the name.

- **Remove a style.** Select Delete, choose from the list of user-defined Picture Controls (you can't remove one of the default styles), press the multi selector right button, then highlight Yes in the screen that follows, and press OK to remove that Picture Control.

- **Store/retrieve style on card.** Choose Load/Save, then select Copy to Camera to locate a Picture Control on your memory card and copy it to the Z5, Delete from Card to select a Picture Control on your memory card and remove it, or Copy to Card to duplicate a style currently in your camera onto the memory card. This last option allows you to create and save on your Slot 1 card Picture Controls in excess of the nine that can be loaded into the camera at one time, for a maximum of 99 custom Picture Controls. Once you've copied a style to your memory card, you can modify the version in the camera, give it a new name, and, in effect, create a whole new Picture Control.

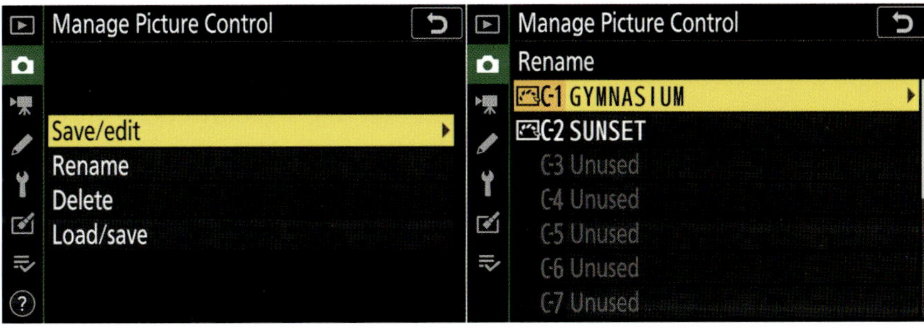

Figure 11.24 You can save, edit, rename, delete, or load and save Picture Controls (left). Picture Controls that you define can be stored in your Z5's settings (right).

Color Space

Options: sRGB (default), Adobe RGB

My preference: Adobe RGB

The Nikon Z5's Color Space option gives you two different color spaces (also called *color gamuts*), named Adobe RGB (because it was developed by Adobe Systems in 1998), and sRGB (supposedly because it is the *standard* RGB color space). These two color gamuts define a specific set of colors that can be applied to the images your Z5 captures.

You're probably surprised that the Nikon Z5 doesn't automatically capture *all* the colors we see. Unfortunately, that's impossible because of the limitations of the sensor and the filters used to capture the fundamental red, green, and blue colors, as well as that of the phosphors used to display those colors on the LEDs in your camera and computer monitors. Nor is it possible to *print* every color our eyes detect, because the inks or pigments used don't absorb and reflect colors perfectly.

On the other hand, the Z5 does capture quite a few more colors than we need. A basic 12-bit RAW image contains a possible 4.3 *billion* different hues (4,096 colors per red, green, or blue channel), which are condensed down to a mere 16.8 million possible colors when converted to a 24-bit (eight bits per channel) image. While 16.8 million colors may seem like a lot, it's a small subset of 4.3 billion captured, and an even smaller subset of all the possible colors we can see. A 14-bit RAW image has even more possible colors—16,384 per color channel, or 281 *trillion* hues.

The set of colors, or gamut, that can be reproduced or captured by a given device (scanner, digital camera, monitor, printer, or some other piece of equipment) is represented as a color space that exists within the larger full range of colors. That full range is represented by the odd-shaped splotch of color shown in Figure 11.25, as defined by scientists at an international organization back in 1931. The colors possible with Adobe RGB are represented by the black triangle in the figure, while the sRGB gamut is represented by the smaller white triangle. The location of the corners of each triangle represent the position of the primary red, green, and blue colors in the gamut.

A third color space, ProPhoto RGB, represented by the yellow triangle in the figure, has become more popular among professional photographers as more and more color printing labs support it. While you cannot *save* images using the ProPhoto gamut with your Z5, you can convert your photos to 16-bit ProPhoto format using Adobe Camera RAW when you import RAW photos into an image editor. ProPhoto encompasses virtually all the colors we can see (and some we can't), giving advanced photographers better tools to work with in processing their photos. It has richer reds, greens, and blues, although, as you can see from the figure, its green and blue primaries are imaginary (they extend outside the visible color gamut). Those with exacting standards need not use a commercial printing service if they want to explore ProPhoto RGB: many inkjet printers can handle cyans, magentas, and yellows that extend outside the Adobe RGB gamut.

Regardless of which triangle—or color space—is used by the Z5, you end up with some combination of 16.8 million different colors that can be used in your photograph. (No one image will contain all 16.8 million! To require that many, two-thirds of the pixels in a 24-megapixel image would have to be a different, distinct color!) But, as you can see from the figure, the colors available will be *different*.

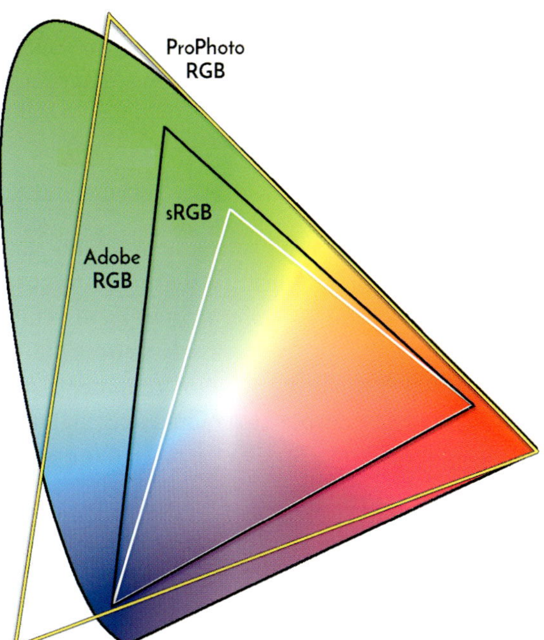

Figure 11.25 The outer curved figure shows all the colors we can see; the outlines show the boundaries of Adobe RGB (black triangle), sRGB (white triangle), and ProPhoto RGB (yellow triangle).

Adobe RGB, like ProPhoto RGB, is an expanded color space useful for commercial and professional printing, and it can reproduce a wider range of colors. It can also come in useful if an image is going to be extensively retouched, especially within an advanced image editor, like Adobe Photoshop, which has sophisticated color management capabilities that can be tailored to specific color spaces. As an advanced user, you don't need to automatically "upgrade" your Z5 to Adobe RGB, because images tend to look less saturated on your monitor and, it is likely, significantly different from what you will get if you output the photo to your personal inkjet. (You can *profile* your monitor for the Adobe RGB color space to improve your on-screen rendition using widely available color-calibrating hardware and software.)

While both Adobe RGB and sRGB can reproduce the exact same 16.8 million absolute colors, Adobe RGB spreads those colors over a larger portion of the visible spectrum, as you can see in the figure. Think of a box of crayons (the jumbo 16.8 million crayon variety). Some of the basic crayons from the original sRGB set have been removed and replaced with new hues not contained in the original box. Your "new" box contains colors that can't be reproduced by your computer monitor, but which work just fine with a commercial printing press. For example, Adobe RGB has more "crayons" available in the cyan-green portion of the box, compared to sRGB, which is unlikely to be an advantage unless your image's final destination are the cyan, magenta, yellow, and black inks of a printing press.

The other color space, sRGB, is recommended for images that will be output locally on the user's own printer, as this color space matches that of the typical inkjet printer fairly closely. You might prefer sRGB, which is the default for the Nikon Z5 and most other cameras, as it is well suited for the range of colors that can be displayed on a computer screen and viewed over the Internet. If you plan to take your image file to a retailer's kiosk for printing, sRGB is your best choice, because those automated output devices are calibrated for the sRGB color space that consumers use.

BEST OF BOTH WORLDS

If you plan to use RAW+JPEG for most of your photos, go ahead and set sRGB as your color space. You'll end up with JPEGs suitable for output on your own printer, but you can still extract an Adobe RGB version from the RAW file at any time. It's like shooting two different color spaces at once—sRGB and Adobe RGB—and getting the best of both worlds.

Of course, choosing the right color space doesn't solve the problems that result from having each device in the image chain manipulating or producing a slightly different set of colors. To that end, you'll need to investigate the wonderful world of *color management*, which uses hardware and software tools to match or *calibrate* all your devices, as closely as possible, so that what you see more closely resembles what you capture, what you see on your computer display, and what ends up on a printed hardcopy. Entire books have been devoted to color management, and most of what you need to know doesn't directly involve your Nikon Z5, so I won't detail the nuts and bolts here.

To manage your color, you'll need, at the bare minimum, some sort of calibration system for your computer display, so that your monitor can be adjusted to show a standardized set of colors that is repeatable over time. (What you see on the screen can vary as the monitor ages, or even when the room light changes.) I use the SpyderX monitor color correction system from Datacolor (www.datacolor.com) for my computer's 32-inch main display and two flanking 26-inch wide-screen auxiliary displays. The unit checks room light levels every five minutes and reminds me to recalibrate every week or two using a small sensor device, which attaches temporarily to the front of the screen and interprets test patches that the software displays during calibration. The rest of the time, the sensor sits in its stand, measuring the room illumination, and adjusting my monitors for higher or lower ambient light levels.

If you're willing to make a serious investment in equipment to help you produce the most accurate color and make prints, you'll want a more advanced system (up to $500) like the various other Spyder products from Datacolor or Colormunki from X-Rite https://www.xritephoto.com/colormunki/.

Active D-Lighting

Options: Auto, Extra High, High, Normal, Low, Off (default for most modes)

My preference: Off

Active D-Lighting is a feature that improves the rendition of detail in highlights and shadows when you're photographing high-contrast scenes. It's closely related to D-Lighting, which is a "non-active" internal retouching option available from the Z5's Retouch menu (and described in Chapter 13). Active D-Lighting, unlike the Retouch menu post-processing D-Lighting feature, applies its tonal improvements *while you are actually taking the photo.* That's good news and bad news. It means that, if you're taking photos in a contrasty environment, Active D-Lighting can automatically improve the apparent dynamic range of your image as you shoot, without additional effort on your part. However, you'll need to disable the feature once you leave the high-contrast lighting behind, and the process does take some time. You wouldn't want to use Active D-Lighting for continuous shooting of sports subjects, for example. There are many situations in which the selective application of D-Lighting using the Retouch menu is a better choice.

You have six choices: Auto, Extra High, High, Normal, Low, and Off (the default). You may need to experiment with the feature a little to discover how much D-Lighting you can apply to a high-contrast image before the shadows start to darken objectionably. Note that when this feature is activated, brightness and contrast Picture Control settings cannot be changed. Figure 11.26 shows a "before and after" example of Active D-Lighting applied to improve shadow detail. By the time the sample images shown have been half-toned and rendered to the printed page, the differences may be fairly subtle.

For best results, use your Z5's Matrix metering mode, so the Active D-Lighting feature can work with a full range of exposure information from multiple points in the image. Active D-Lighting works its magic by subtly *underexposing* your image so that details in the highlights (which would normally be overexposed and become featureless white pixels) are not lost. At the same time, it adjusts the values of pixels located in midtone and shadow areas, so they don't become too dark because of the underexposure. Highlight tones will be preserved, while shadows will eventually be allowed to go dark more readily. Bright beach or snow scenes, especially those with few shadows (think high noon, when the shadows are smaller) can benefit from using Active D-Lighting.

It's important to *always* keep in mind that Active D-Lighting not only adjusts the contrast automatically of your image, it modifies exposure for both existing light and flash as well, as I've noted. Exposure for both is reduced from about 1/3 stop (at the Low setting) to as much as 1 full stop less at the Extra High setting.

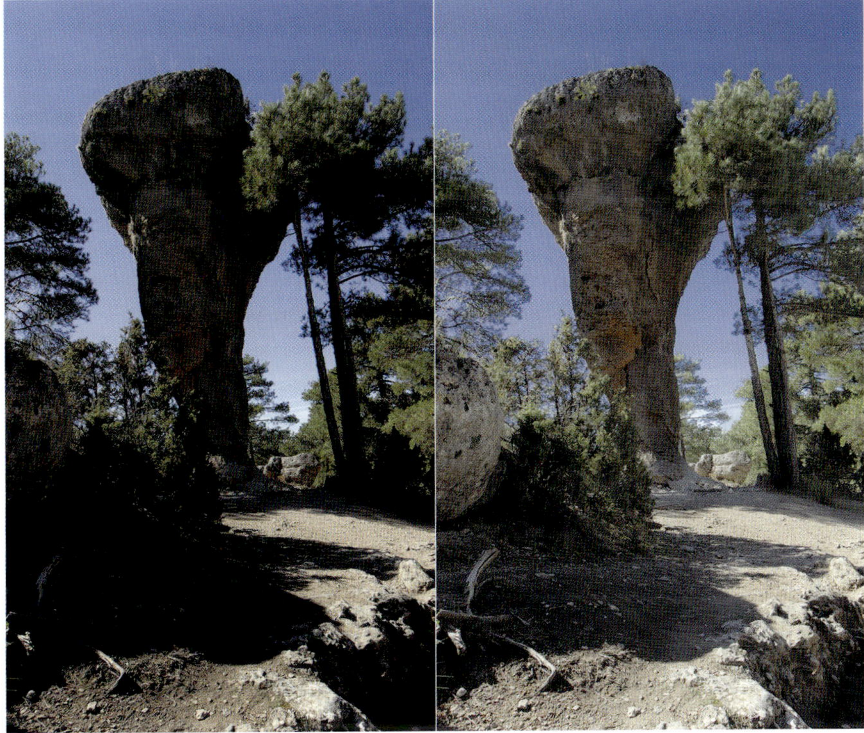

Figure 11.26 No D-Lighting (left); and high (right).

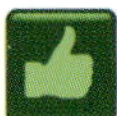

TIP In Manual exposure mode, Active D-Lighting does not adjust the exposure of your image; it simply shifts the center (zero) point of the analog exposure indicator in the display.

Nikon gives you a lot of flexibility in using Active D-Lighting. You can choose the setting yourself, or let the camera *vary* the amount of tweaking by using Active D-Lighting Bracketing. You'll find this is a useful feature, if used with caution.

Long Exposure NR

Options: Off (default), On

My preference: Off. I prefer to apply noise reduction when processing the RAW file.

Visual noise is that awful graininess caused by long exposures and high ISO settings, and which shows up as multicolored specks in images. This setting helps you manage the kind of noise caused by lengthy exposure times. In some ways, noise is like the excessive grain found in some high-speed photographic films. However, while photographic grain is sometimes used as a special effect, it's rarely desirable in a digital photograph. There are easier ways to add texture to your photos.

Some noise is created when you're using shutter speeds longer than eight seconds to create a longer exposure. Extended exposure times allow more photons to reach the sensor but increase the likelihood that some photosites will react randomly even though not struck by a particle of light. Moreover, as the sensor remains switched on for the longer exposure, it heats, and this heat can be mistakenly recorded as if it were a barrage of photons. This menu setting can be used to activate the Z5's long exposure noise-canceling operation performed by the EXPEED 6 digital signal processor.

- **Off.** This default setting disables long exposure noise reduction. Use it when you want the maximum amount of detail present in your photograph, even though higher noise levels will result. This setting also eliminates the extra time needed to take a picture caused by the noise reduction process. If you plan to use only lower ISO settings (thereby reducing the noise caused by ISO amplification), the noise levels produced by longer exposures may be acceptable. For example, you might be shooting a waterfall at ISO 100 with the camera mounted on a tripod, using a neutral-density filter and a long exposure to cause the water to blur. (Try exposures of 2 to 16 seconds, depending on the intensity of the light and how much blur you want.) (See Figure 11.27.) To maximize detail in the non-moving portions of your photos for the exposures that are one second or longer, you can switch off long exposure noise reduction.

- **On.** When exposures are longer than one second, the Nikon Z5 takes a second, blank exposure to compare that to the first image. Noise (pixels that are bright in a frame that *should* be completely black) in the "dark frame" image is subtracted from your original picture, and only the noise-corrected image is saved to your memory card. Because the noise-reduction process effectively doubles the time required to take a picture, you won't want to use this setting when you're rushed. Some noise can be removed later, using tools like the noise reduction features built into Adobe Camera Raw.

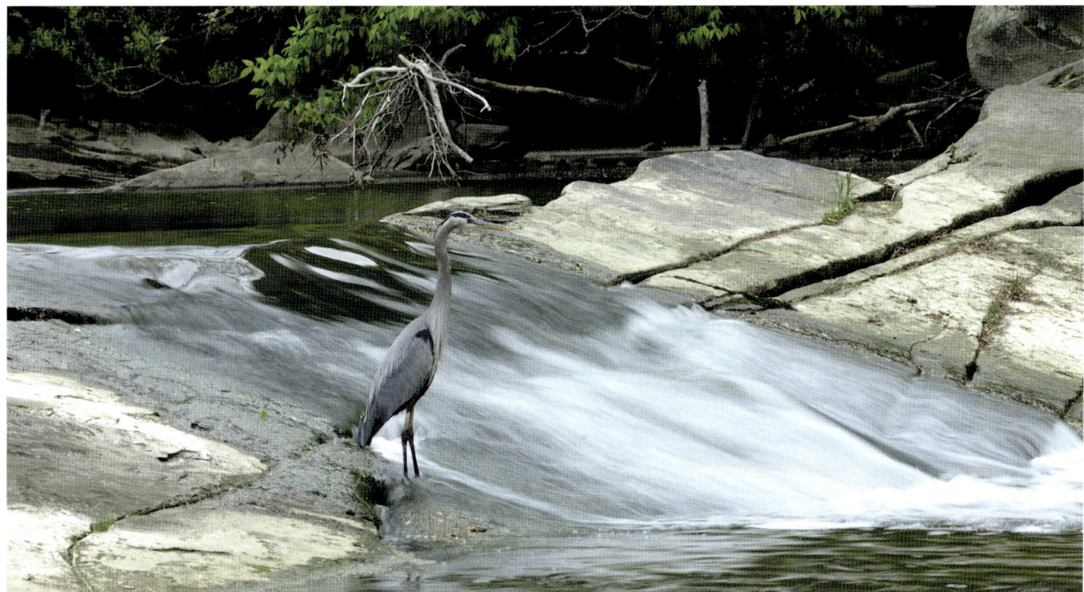

Figure 11.27 A long exposure with the camera mounted on a tripod produces this traditional moving-water photo.

High ISO NR

Options: High, Normal (default), Low, Off

My preference: Normal

Noise can also be caused by higher ISO sensitivity settings. The Nikon Z5 offers direct settings up to ISO 104400 and extended settings that go even higher, up to Hi 2 (the equivalent of ISO 102400). Although it costs you some detail, High ISO noise reduction, which can be set with this menu option, may be a good option in many cases. You can choose Off when you want to preserve detail at the cost of some noise graininess, and the Z5 will apply high ISO NR only at the highest settings. Or, you can select Low, Normal, and High noise reduction, which is applied when ISO sensitivity has been set to ISO 800 or higher.

The effects of high ISO noise are something like listening to a CD in your car, and then rolling down all the windows. You're adding sonic noise to the audio signal, and while increasing the CD player's volume may help a bit, you're still contending with an unfavorable signal-to-noise ratio that probably mutes tones (especially higher treble notes) that you really want to hear.

The same thing happens when the analog image signal is amplified: You're increasing the image information in the signal but boosting the background fuzziness at the same time. Tune in a very faint or distant AM radio station on your car stereo. Then turn up the volume. After a certain point, turning up the volume further no longer helps you hear better. There's a similar point of diminishing returns for digital sensor ISO increases and signal amplification as well.

As the captured information is amplified to produce higher ISO sensitivities, some random noise in the signal is amplified along with the photon information. Increasing the ISO setting of your camera raises the threshold of sensitivity so that fewer and fewer photons are needed to register as an exposed pixel. Yet, that also increases the chances of one of those phantom photons being counted among the real-life light particles, too.

Fortunately, the Nikon Z5's CMOS sensor and its EXPEED 6 digital-processing chip are optimized to produce the low noise levels, so ratings as high as ISO 12800 can be used routinely (although there will be some noise, of course), and even ISO 6400 can generate good results. I regularly shoot concerts at ISO 3200, and indoor sports at ISO 6400 with my Z5. I've even been impressed with results I get at ISO 25600 when High ISO NR is applied. Some kinds of subjects may not require this kind of noise cancellation, particularly with images that have a texture of their own that tends to hide or mask the noise.

Vignette Control

Options: High, Normal (default), Low, Off

My preference: Normal

This is the first entry on the next page of the Photo Shooting menu. (See Figure 11.28.) Some lenses may not be up to the challenge of covering the frame evenly, producing darkening in the corners of your images at certain focal lengths. If you consistently encounter vignetting, this option may help. You can choose from High, Normal, Low, and Off. It's difficult to quantify exactly how much corner-brightening each setting provides. Your best bet is to shoot some blank walls of a single color with lenses that seem to have this problem and try a few at each of the settings. Then select the value that best seems to counter vignetting with your particular lenses.

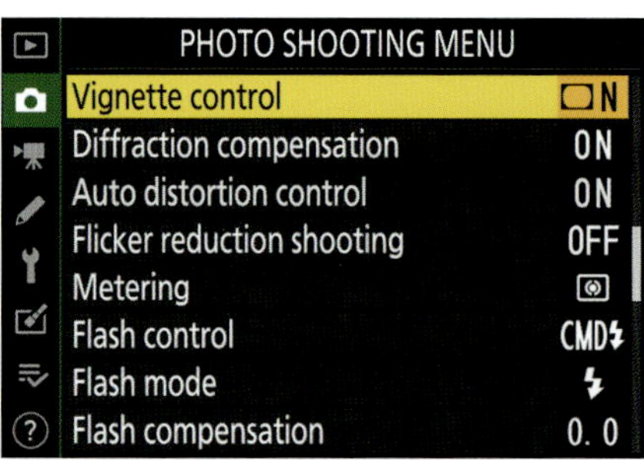

Figure 11.28 The next page of the Photo Shooting menu.

Diffraction Compensation

Options: On (default), Off

My preference: On

Diffraction is a phenomenon that reduces the sharpness of your image when working at smaller f/stops, especially f/22 or f/32 (if your lens has those apertures available). It can be especially acute with cameras, like the Z5, that have exceptionally high resolution. This feature attempts to counteract that effect and works well enough that I leave it enabled by default. Unfortunately, Nikon doesn't deign to tell you what diffraction actually is, or how much it affects your photographs.

Introductory photo courses hammer into budding photographers the idea that smaller f/stops increase sharpness by extending depth-of-field and optimizing the optical effects of particular lenses. In practice, while few lenses are their sharpest wide open, most achieve their maximum sharpness stopped down two or more f/stops; beyond that, diffraction kicks in, and can actually help *reduce* apparent sharpness, due to scattering and interference of individual photons as they pass through smaller lens openings. In effect, the edges of your lens aperture affects proportionately more photons as the f/stop grows smaller. The relative amount of space available to pass freely decreases, and the amount of edge surface that can collide with incoming light increases.

So, an f/stop of f/11 may produce a slight loss of overall sharpness compared to an opening of f/8 (although depth-of-field will increase); and f/16 will be less sharp than f/11. With the Z5, images are softened by an almost undetectable amount at every aperture—including wide open—but diffraction becomes more noticeable only at f/stops smaller than f/11. The difference is very slight.

Theoretically, this limit on sharpness should be independent of the resolution of the sensor, or the size of the sensor. The effects of diffraction *should* be the same at, say, f/11, regardless of what type of sensor is being used. However, in practice, smaller pixels do show the effects of diffraction more readily. The diffraction produces a multi-ringed pattern called an *airy disk* (it has nothing to do with air; the phenomenon was named after scientist George Airy), and when the peak area of this disk is large enough, compared to the pixel size of the sensor, or if two disks overlap, an effect may be visible in the image.

Typically, this happens at a particular f/stop with a particular pixel size, and that f/stop is said to be the diffraction limit for that camera/sensor. Point-and-shoot cameras, with their tiny sensors, may begin to show diffraction effects at f/5.6; a cropped-sensor camera at f/11; a lower-resolution full-frame camera (like the 20MP Nikon D5) at f/16; and a camera with *extremely* small pixels, like the Nikon Z5 at f/11.

Is the sharpness lost to diffraction more objectionable than the reduced *range* of sharpness produced by less depth-of-field at wider apertures? That's up to you. For example, most of the "product" shots in this book were taken with my old Nikon D4s at f/22 or f/32, even though that camera's small pixels also are prone to diffraction effects. Given the size the images are reproduced in these pages, I felt that the increased depth-of-field of the smaller apertures was worth the possible loss of sharpness from diffraction. In other words, even though more of my subjects were in focus, the overall sharpness of the sharpest parts of the image may be less.

The photons striking the edges of the diaphragm are disrupted from their paths and begin to interfere with those passing through the center of the lens. While this phenomenon takes place at all apertures, it is most pronounced at smaller f/stops, when the edges of the iris are proportionately larger compared to the entire lens opening.

The best analogy I can think of is a pond with two floating docks sticking out into the water, as shown in Figure 11.29. Throw a big rock in the pond, and the ripples pass between the docks relatively smoothly if the structures are relatively far apart (top). Move them closer together (bottom), and some ripples rebound off each dock to interfere with the incoming wavelets. In a lens, smaller apertures produce the same effect.

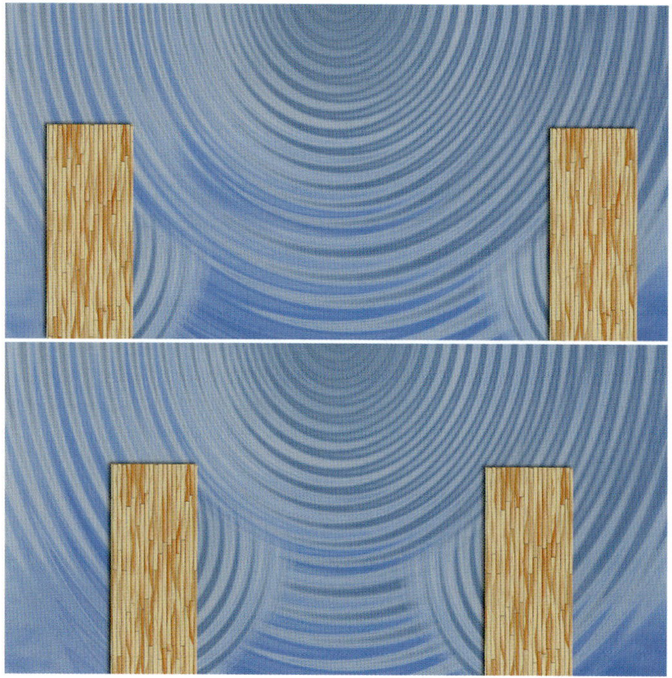

Other than the Diffraction Compensation algorithms Nikon has included in the Z5, there's no "cure" for diffraction-limited images, other than to use larger f/stops, or to apply some sharpening of the image in your editor (which is likely to be a losing cause). It is important, then, to be aware of the effects of diffraction on images captured with the Z5 and take them into account before choosing a small aperture.

Auto Distortion Control

Options: On (default), Off

My preference: On

As I explained in Chapter 7, wide-angle lenses are prone to barrel distortion, in which straight lines appear to bow outward, especially near the edges of the frame. Telephoto lenses often have the opposite problem: lines may bend inward, producing pincushion distortion. Both of these types of distortion can be easily corrected in your image editor, but your Z5's digital image processing chip has similar algorithms built in and can do the job for you. Your choices are easy: just select On or Off to enable or disable this feature. Note that with some lenses, On is chosen by default and this menu entry is grayed out and unavailable.

For the process to work, the lenses must be of a type that can communicate electronically with the camera to let the Z5 know what type of lens it is working with. All Z-mount lenses can supply the needed information, but if you're using a non-Z-mount lens with the FTX adapter, you should be working with a G- or D-type optic. The camera will warp the photo before saving it to your memory card, cropping a bit if necessary to exclude some areas of the image.

Flicker Reduction Shooting

Options: On, Off (default)

My preference: Use as needed

This option allows you to reduce or eliminate the banding, flickering, or alternate light/dark exposures that can appear when photographing under certain types of lighting, such as fluorescent or mercury-vapor sources. I find this effect quite vexing when shooting indoor sports such as basketball and volleyball in gymnasiums. During continuous shooting I often end up with frames that alternate between too dark and too light.

This flicker reduction feature uses the exposure meter to detect light flicker in the 100 and 120 Hz frequencies. When enabled, the camera delays shutter release timing a tiny bit to avoid the "dim" cycle of the light source and giving you a frame that's evenly lit and fully illuminated. If you're taking photos continuously (a common mode when capturing sports), the Z5 adjusts both the release timing and frame rate so you can capture each shot during the light source's maximum output. You may notice a slight shutter lag, and a reduction in frame rate, but both are trade-offs that pay back with more usable images under these conditions.

The feature may not work well for scenes with dark backgrounds, decorative or especially bright lighting, and is not effective when making Bulb or Time exposures, other shutter speeds slower than 1/100th second, and HDR, exposure delay mode, silent photography, and Continuous H (extended) burst shooting.

Metering

Options: Matrix (default), Center-weighted, Spot, Highlight-weighted metering

My preference: Matrix

This menu entry is a slower alternative to setting the metering mode than using the *i* menu. It exists primarily so you can assign this menu entry to a custom key using the Custom Setting f2: Custom Controls menu entry (explained in Chapter 12).

For example, if you tend to change metering mode frequently, even a visit to the *i* menu can be bothersome. Define, say, the Fn1 button to Metering, and each time you press that button you'll be able to rotate the command dial to flip among the four choices. Note that you can also define a button to immediately switch to a specific metering mode, so you can, for example, set Matrix metering as your default mode, then toggle to Spot metering while holding down the defined button.

I explained how to use each of these metering modes in Chapter 4 and won't repeat that information here.

Flash Control

Options: Flash control mode, Flash compensation (TTL), Wireless Flash options, Remote flash control, Group flash options, Radio remote flash info.

My preference: N/A

This entry is available only when the Nikon SB-5000, SB-500, SB-400, or SB-300 Speedlights are connected to the Z5 and powered up. I explained how to use the available options in Chapters 9 and 10 and will not duplicate that information here. All other Nikon electronic flash units, including the SB-600, SB-700, SB-800, SB-900, and SB-910 must be adjusted using the controls on the flash itself.

Before you howl "planned obsolescence!" you should know that *all* Nikon pro bodies that lacked a built-in flash have *always* required making most settings on the optional flash. The Z5's Flash Control feature is a relatively recent addition to the Nikon line, made possible by features built into the recent flash units cited, so you're actually gaining capability. If you connect any of the other Speedlights (I own all of them, and I tried), the Flash Control entry is grayed out.

Flash Mode

Options: Fill Flash (default), Red-eye Reduction, Rear-curtain sync, Flash Off

My preference: N/A

This setting specifies whether the Z5 uses Fill Flash, Red-eye Reduction, Rear-curtain sync, or disables the flash entirely. I explained when and why to use each of these in Chapter 9 and won't repeat that information here.

Flash Compensation

Options: +3.0 to –1.0 stops of exposure; Default: 0.0

My preference: N/A

As I explained in Chapter 9, you can use flash exposure compensation to adjust the flash output to balance the brightness of the main subject illuminated by the flash, compared to the background. Don't confuse this entry with Custom Setting e2: Exposure Compensation for Flash (described in Chapter 12), which tells the Z5 to apply flash exposure compensation to the background only, or to the entire frame. The two options work together to let you effectively balance your flash output between the two.

Focus Mode

Options: AF-S (default), AF-C, Manual Focus

My preference: N/A

This entry, the first on the next page of the Photo Shooting menu, is a slower alternative to using the *i* menu to switch from one focus mode to another, as explained in Chapter 5. (See Figure 11.30.) It can be assigned to a custom key if you need fast access to this setting.

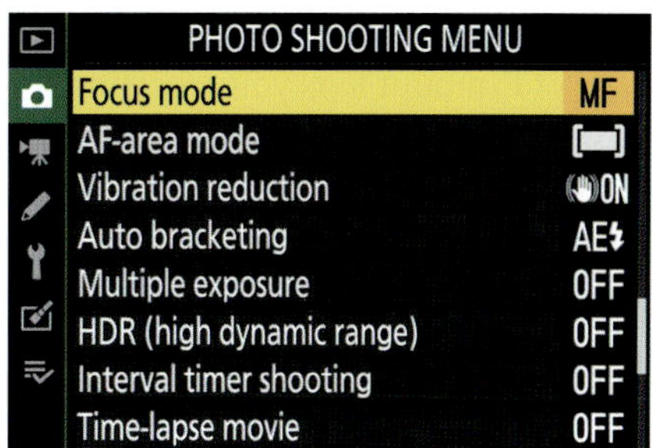

Figure 11.30 The next page of the Photo Shooting menu.

AF-Area Mode

Options: Pinpoint AF, Single-point AF (default), Dynamic-area AF, Wide-area AF (Small), Wide-area AF (Large), Auto-area AF

My preference: N/A

Like several entries discussed above, it duplicates its *i* menu counterpart, and can be assigned to a custom key for direct access. This menu entry is a slower alternative to using the *i* menu to switch from one focus mode to another, as explained in Chapter 5.

Vibration Reduction

Options: On (or Normal) (default), Spt (Sport), Off

My preference: N/A

Use this setting to enable vibration reduction. The options may vary depending on which lens you are using. When VR is enabled, an indicator appears at the left side of the viewfinder or LCD monitor. Use On (or Normal; the nomenclature varies depending on the lens) for subjects that are not moving to counter camera shake or photographer jitteriness. The Sport setting is recommended for fast and unpredictably moving subjects, especially if you're panning the camera to follow their movements. In that case, in Sport mode the Z5's vibration reduction ignores side-to-side movement and corrects only camera shake in other directions.

Use Off if the camera is locked down on a tripod. If you will be swiveling the camera on the tripod or using a monopod, then turning VR off is not required. If you use this setting frequently, you can assign the function to an *i* menu position using Custom Setting f1: Customize *i* menu. While the Z5 has on-sensor in-body image stabilization (as described earlier in Chapter 7), and some Z-mount lenses also have VR, you can also use F-mount lenses with the FTZ adapter, which themselves may include their own vibration reduction. When using an adapted lens without VR, use this menu entry to make VR adjustments for the camera. If the adapted lens does have VR, then the switches on the adapted lens overrides any setting you make here.

In that case, the adjustments you can make must be made using the lens switches and will vary by the type of F-mount lens you are using. If the adapted VR lens has Off, Normal, and Sport settings (the same as found in this menu entry) then VR adjustments can only be made using the lens switches. If the adapted lens has an Active setting, and you set the lens switch to Active, the Z5 uses the Normal VR setting instead.

Auto Bracketing

Options: Auto Bracketing Set (default: AE & Flash), Number of Shots (default: 0), Increment (default: 1.0)

My preference: N/A

This entry allows you to set up bracketing, a useful technique explained in detail in Chapter 4. I won't repeat the step-by-step instructions here. To recap, your options are as follows:

- **Auto Bracketing Set.** Autoexposure and Flash bracketing, Autoexposure Bracketing (only), Flash bracketing (only), White balance bracketing, Active D-Lighting bracketing.
- **Number of Shots.** Use the left/right directional buttons or the touch screen to specify the number of shots in your bracket set (or 0 to disable bracketing entirely). Up to nine can be selected, and you can choose whether to group them around overexposure or underexposure, as described in Chapter 4.
- **Increment.** From 0.3- (one-third stop) to 3.0-stop increments between bracketed exposures.

Multiple Exposure

Options: Multiple Exposure Mode: On (Series), On (Single Photo), Off; Number of Shots: 2 to 10; Overlay Mode: Add, Average, Lighten, Darken; Save Individual Images: On, Off, Select First Exposure (NEF)

My preference: Multiple Exposure Mode: On (Series); Number of Shots/Overlay Mode, varies

This option lets you combine from 2 to 10 exposures into one image without the need for an image editor such as Photoshop, and it can be an entertaining way to return to those thrilling days of yesteryear, when complex photos were created in the camera itself. In truth, prior to the digital age, multiple exposures were a cool, groovy, far-out, hep/hip, phat, sick, fabulous way of producing composite images. Today, it's more common to take the lazy way out, snap two or more pictures, and then assemble them in an image editor like Photoshop.

You can turn the Multiple Exposure feature off, direct the camera to continue taking multiple exposures until you turn it off (Series), or revert to non-multiple exposure mode after taking one picture (Single Photo). You can elect to keep all exposures, or discard all but the combined multiple exposure, and use a NEF (RAW) image on your memory card as the base photo on which subsequent pictures are overlaid. I provided a complete set of directions for using these multiple exposure features in Chapter 6, along with another example of the kind of results you can get.

You should keep in mind that some of Nikon's previous implementations of multiple exposure allowed you to choose between combining the exposures of each image to produce the final shot or dividing the exposures equally among the shots. The Z5 has additional options and calls the array of choices "Overlay Mode." Here's the difference:

- **Add.** In this mode, each new exposure is added to the previous shots. I use this when photographing a subject that is moving against a dark background. A series of renditions, each fully exposed, appears in the overlaid image to track the subject's movement. (See Figure 11.31, left.)
- **Average.** In this mode, the camera divides the overall exposure by the number of shots in the series and gives each shot that fraction of the overall exposure. That is, for a four-shot multiple series, the specified exposure for each is set at 1/4 of the total amount. I use this when shooting subjects with a great deal of overlap. (See Figure 11.31, right.)
- **Lighten.** The Z5 compares pixels in the same position in each exposure and uses only the brightest. This effect is similar to the Lighten blending mode in Photoshop, Lightroom, and other image-editing software.
- **Darken.** Similar to the Lighten blending mode, only just the darkest pixel is saved. You can use both Lighten and Darken overlay modes to create special effects like those you get in image editors.

The Z5 adds a useful feature, Save Individual Images (NEF), which, as you might expect, tells the camera to save the individual photos used to create the multiple exposure in separate RAW files. This capability can be useful in several ways. First, you may find that one specific frame of your multiple exposure might have made an excellent stand-alone image in its own right. When Save Individual Images is active, you can retrieve that frame and use it as you like. In addition, having all the shots of the multiple exposure available means you can use them to create your own multi-shot image in Photoshop or your favorite image editor. I do this most often when I discover that one frame doesn't

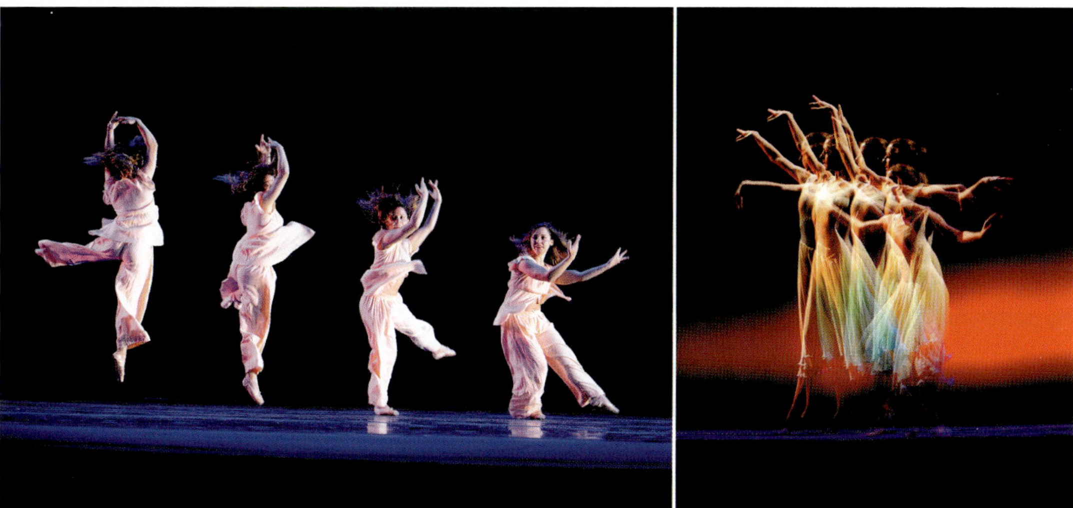

Figure 11.31 Multiple Exposures using Add (left) and Average (right) overlay modes.

"work" for a given multiple exposure image, but the others meld together well. I can create my own version manually, adjusting brightness, contrast, or other parameters as I go, to "fine-tune" what started out as an automated multiple exposure.

Also useful is the Select First Exposure (NEF) option. If you want to overlay all your subsequent multiple exposures on top of an existing image already on your memory card (say, a background that you'd like to merge with your sequence), you can choose this setting. You'll be taken to the Z5's standard image selection screen and offered the choice of any NEF image available on your card. This is a cool way of replacing boring one-color backgrounds with something more interesting.

HDR (High Dynamic Range)

Options: HDR mode: On (Series), On (Single Photo), Off (default); Exposure Differential: Auto (default), 1 EV, 2 EV, 3 EV; Smoothing: High, Normal, Low; Save individual Images (NEF)

My preference: HDR mode: On (Series); Exposure Differential: Auto

I was surprised at how well Nikon has solved the hand-held auto HDR problem, because there are two stumbling blocks that, at least theoretically, should lead to less-than-awesome results. First, when your camera can perform HDR for you on the fly, there is the tendency to put the feature to work under non-optimal conditions; specifically, impromptu hand-held situations. If you've done any traditional HDR, you know that the technique works best when the camera is mounted on a tripod, so that the bracketed exposures are virtually identical except for the exposure itself. Although all HDR software can correct for slight camera movement and align images that are slightly out of register, the results I've gotten have not been great. I expected hand-held HDR to be comparable. However, Nikon's implementation, especially in the Z5, does an excellent job.

The second theoretical weakness of the Z5's HDR feature is the limitation of combining just two shots to arrive at the final image. The best traditional HDR photos I've produced have involved at least three shots, and more frequently five or more, each separated by a stop of exposure. The Z5 takes two shots, total, and combines them. Despite these speed bumps, I've been pleased with my results. I outlined the steps in Chapter 4 and won't repeat them here.

Interval Timer Shooting

Options: Start; Start Options: Now, Choose Start Day and Start Time, Interval, No. of Intervals × Shots/Interval, Exposure Smoothing, On/Off, Silent Photography: On/Off, End Day/Time, Interval Priority: On/Off, Starting Storage Folder: New Folder, Reset File Numbering

My preference: N/A

The Nikon Z5's built-in time-lapse photography feature allows you to take pictures for up to 999 intervals in bursts of as many as nine shots, with a delay of up to 23 hours and 59 minutes between shots/bursts, and an initial start-up time of as long as 23 hours and 59 minutes from the time you activate the feature. That means that if you want to photograph a rosebud opening and would like to photograph the flower once every two minutes over the next 16 hours, you can do that easily. If you like, you can delay the first photo taken by a couple hours, so you don't have to stand there by

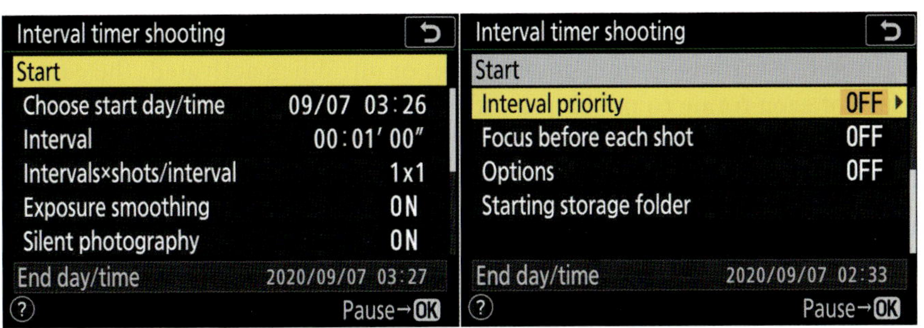

Figure 11.32 Interval timer shooting options.

the Z5 waiting for the right moment. The options are shown in Figure 11.32, and I explained how to use them in Chapter 6.

Or you might want to photograph a particular scene every hour for 24 hours to capture, say, a land-scape from sunrise to sunset to the following day's sunrise again. I will offer two practical tips right now, in case you want to run out and try interval timer shooting immediately: *use a tripod, and for best results over longer time periods, plan on connecting your Z5 to an external power source!*

> **4K/8K MOVIES?**
>
> One cool thing to do with interval timer captures is to assemble the individual shots into a video with 4K or faux 8K resolution using a video image editor. I explained this feature, too, in Chapter 6.

Time-Lapse Movie

Options: Start, Interval, Shooting Time, Exposure Smoothing, Silent Photography, Choose Image Area, Frame Size/Frame Rate, Interval Priority

My preference: None

As I said in Chapter 6, time-lapse movies correspond to interval timer shooting, described previously, but allow shooting video clips instead of still photographs (or a series of still photographs). The Z5 automatically creates a silent time-lapse movie at the frame resolution and rate you've selected in the Movie Shooting menu. Nikon recommends using a white balance other than Auto, and covering the eyepiece opening to prevent light from entering the viewfinder and affecting exposure. And, of course, you'll want to use a tripod and either a fully charged battery or optional AC adapter. While you can shoot 4K time-lapse video, the maximum length sequence you can capture is three minutes.

The options are very similar to those of interval timer shooting:

- **Start.** Unlike the similar Interval Timer found in the Photo Shooting menu, Time-Lapse Photography has no Start Options. Make your other settings, select Start, and time-lapse photography will begin about three seconds later.
- **Interval.** Select an interval between frames; use a longer value for slow-moving action (such as a flower bud unfolding), and a shorter value for movies, say, depicting humans moving around at a comical pace. You can select an interval from one second to 10 minutes.

- **Shooting Time.** You can specify time-lapse movie duration.

- **Exposure Smoothing.** You can turn exposure smoothing on or off. When activated, the camera adjusts the exposure of each frame to match that of the previous frame in P, S, or A mode. Smoothing can also be used in Manual mode, but, of course, the Z5 won't vary the shutter speed *or* aperture. You must have set ISO Sensitivity to Auto. Press OK to confirm.

- **Silent Photography.** Silences the shutter sound for unobtrusive or stealth video capture.

- **Choose Image Area.** Select FX-based movie format or DX-based movie format (see Chapter 15). You can also turn Auto DX crop on or off, so the Z5 will recognize DX lenses and crop appropriately.

- **Frame Size/Frame Rate.** Here you can select the frame size and frames per second setting for your time-lapse movie. You can choose from 3840 × 2160, 30/15/24p; 1920 × 1060, 60/50/30p (in both High Quality and Normal modes, also explained in Chapter 15); and 1280 × 720, 60/50p formats.

- **Interval Priority.** This setting is similar to its intervalometer counterpart, as explained previously. It takes care of situations in which the shutter speed automatically selected in Program or Aperture-priority ends up being longer than the interval between shots. When enabled, the Z5 captures the movie frame at the specified interval, even if a shorter shutter speed must be used, causing underexposure. You can activate Auto ISO Sensitivity and select a minimum shutter speed that is shorter than the interval time. When disabled, the camera increases the interval you specified to allow correct exposure.

Focus Shift Shooting

Options: Start, Number of Shots, Focus Step Width, Interval until Next Shot, First-Frame Exposure Lock, Silent Photography, Starting Storage Folder

My preference: N/A

This is one of two entries on the last page of the Photo Shooting menu (and not shown in a figure). Focus stacking is a great technique that allows combining a series of photos each taken using a different plane of focus, so that they can be combined in an image editor to produce a single image with greatly enhanced depth-of-field. Macro photographers (in particular) have long used focus stacking in their work. The Z7's Focus Shift Shooting feature greatly simplifies capture of the individual shots, which can include up to 300 different images. I covered this feature in detail in Chapter 6 and will not repeat that information here.

Silent Photography

Options: On, Off (default)

My preference: N/A

Because the Z5 has no mirror, one of the ker-plunks that punctuate dSLR picture taking is eliminated. However, the camera's mechanical shutter still produces its characteristic noise as it opens and closes for each shot. Silent Photography takes advantage of the Z5's electronic shutter by relying on that component alone to capture an image. In use, the camera "dumps" the current live view image from the sensor, then activates the sensor for the interval specified by the selected shutter speed. Because the physical shutter does not open or close, the process is entirely silent. In addition, the lack of shutter motion and mirror motion means that the camera vibrates less during the actual exposure. On and Off are your only options. When active, continuous shooting is reduced in speed, and flash, the camera's beeper, long exposure noise reduction, and electronic front-curtain shutter are disabled. You may notice distortion in moving objects, especially when panning because of the Z5's "rolling shutter." (I'll tell you more about rolling shutter effects in Chapter 15.) You may also see flicker, banding, or distortion under fluorescent, mercury-vapor, or sodium lamps.

Movie Shooting Menu

Some of the Movie Shooting menu's entries duplicate the entries in the Photo Shooting menu but apply specifically to video shooting. Others are unique to movie making. For entries that overlap those used for still photography, I'll simply refer to the relevant description earlier in this chapter. Many of the movie-related choices are discussed in more detail in Chapters 14 and 15 of this book.

- Reset Movie Shooting Menu
- File Naming
- Destination
- Choose Image Area
- Frame Size/Frame Rate
- Movie Quality
- Movie File Type
- ISO Sensitivity Settings
- White Balance
- Set Picture Control
- Manage Picture Control
- Active D-Lighting
- High ISO NR
- Vignette Control
- Diffraction Compensation
- Auto Distortion Control
- Flicker Reduction
- Metering
- Focus Mode
- AF-Area Mode
- Vibration Reduction
- Electronic VR
- Microphone Sensitivity
- Attenuator
- Frequency Response
- Wind Noise Reduction
- Headphone Volume
- Timecode

Reset Movie Shooting Menu

Options: Yes, No

My preference: N/A

Restores Movie Shooting menu options (only) to their default values (see Table 11.3). This is the first entry in the Movie Shooting menus (see Figure 11.33, left).

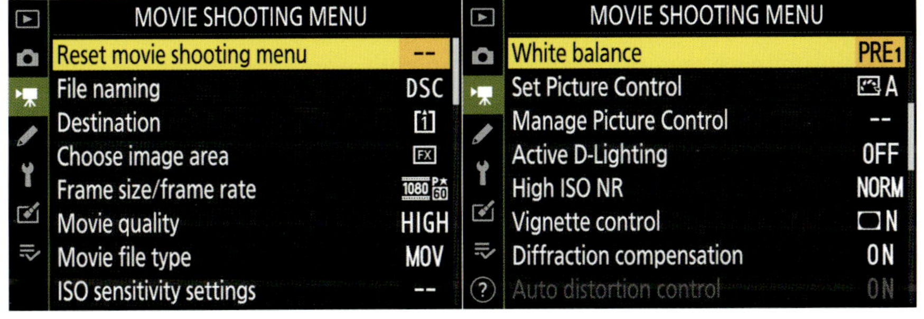

Figure 11.33 The first two Movie Shooting menus.

TABLE 11.3 Default Movie Menu Values

OPTION	DEFAULT	OPTION	DEFAULT
File Naming	DSC	Diffraction Compensation	On
Destination	Slot 1	Auto Distortion Control	On
Choose Image Area	FX	Flicker Reduction	Auto
Frame size/Frame rate	1920 × 1080, 60p	Metering	Matrix metering
Movie Quality	High quality	Focus Mode	Full-time AF
Movie File Type	Mov	AF-Area Mode	Auto-area AF
ISO Sensitivity Settings		Vibration Reduction	Same as photo settings
Maximum Sensitivity	25600	Electronic VR	Off
Auto ISO Control (Mode M)	On	Microphone Sensitivity	Auto
ISO Sensitivity (Mode M)	100	Attenuator	Disable
White Balance	Same as photo settings	Frequency Response	Wide range
Fine-tuning	A-B:0 G-M:0	Wind Noise Reduction	Off
Choose Color Temp.	5,000K	Headphone Volume	15
Preset Manual	d-1	Timecode	
Set Picture Control	Same as photo settings	Record timecodes	Off
Active D-Lighting	Off	Count-up method	Record run
High ISO NR	Normal	Drop frame	On
Vignette Control	Normal		

File Naming

Options: Three-character prefix; DSC is the default

My preference: None

You can specify substitutes for the DSC characters in filenames created for movie files, separately from the naming format you elect for still photos. The limitations and instructions are the same as for the File Naming entry in the Photo Shooting menu.

Destination

Options: Slot 1 (default), Slot 2

My preference: Slot with fastest memory card

Select the slot with the memory card you want to use to store your video files. You can select the XQD or SD slots. The selection screen helpfully displays the approximate length of the video that can be stored on the space remaining for each memory card. You'll generally want to select the slot containing your fastest memory card (as video capture requires a constant flow of data between camera and memory card) and usually your largest card with the most space available for your movies.

Choose Image Area

Options: FX (default), DX
My preference: FX

As you'll learn in Chapter 15, the movies the Z5 captures are cropped from the full sensor image to fit each movie frame into the 19:6 proportions of high-definition video. In full HD mode, the frame is cropped at top and bottom, but uses the full width of the sensor. In 4K UHD mode, a center portion of the frame is used, slightly smaller than the area covered by a DX (APS-C) frame, producing a 1.7X crop. This entry determines the image area used to crop the frame while in full HD movie shooting mode. It is independent of the Image Area setting you specify in the Photo Shooting menu. You have two options, FX and DX:

- **FX.** In this mode, the Z5's sensor area is cropped at top and bottom to fit the 19:6 aspect ratio of HD video, so the actual movie capture area measures 35.9mm × 20.2mm and is represented by the outer area in Figure 11.34. The FX-based movie format means that no "lens multiplier" is applied in full HD mode, and, say, a 100mm lens has its normal field of view. (I explained the "multiplier" misnomer in Chapter 7.)

- **DX.** When using the DX-based movie format to shoot full HD video, the image capture area measures a 23.5mm × 13.2mm portion of the sensor, represented by the yellow box in the figure. This smaller field of view produces a cropped, telephoto effect. Your 100mm lens has the effective field of view of a 150mm lens. Note that Electronic VR (discussed later in this chapter) crops the image a tiny bit more.

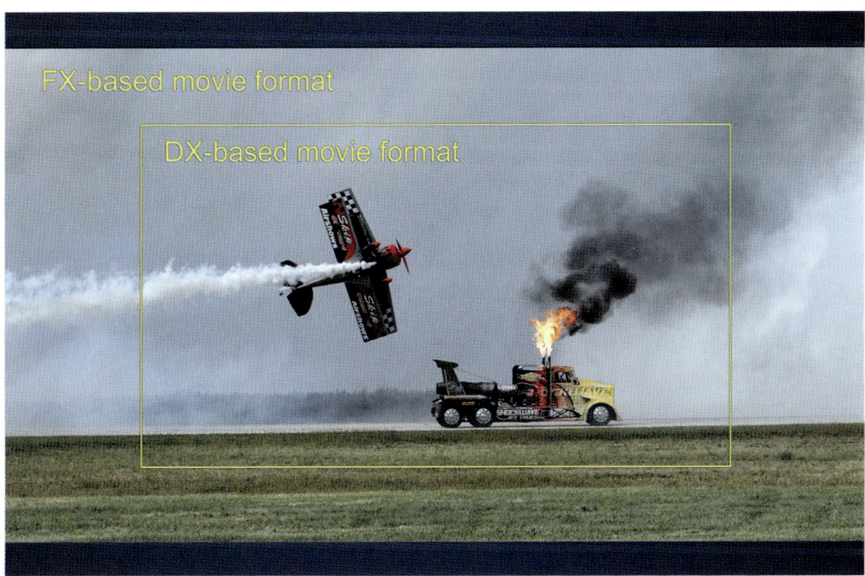

Figure 11.34 FX- and DX-based movie formats.

Frame Size/Frame Rate

Options: 4K Ultra High Definition: 3840 × 2160, 30/25p, 24p; Full HD: 1920 × 1080, 60/50p (default), 30/25p, 24p

My preference: Varies

Here you can select several different Ultra High Definition or Full High Definition video formats. Ultra HD is available at 3840 × 2160 in 30/25/24 frames per second and Full HD is available at 1920 × 1080 resolution at 60/50/30/25/24 frames per second. As I'll explain in Chapter 15, 50/25 fps are used for PAL video systems used overseas, while the others are compatible with the NTSC system used in the USA, Japan, and some other areas. Chapter 15 will provide more information on how to select the most appropriate frame size and transfer rate and explain your options for shooting silent slow-motion movies as well.

Movie Quality

Options: High Quality (default), Normal

My preference: High Quality when using a fast memory card

Select High Quality or Normal Quality. Your choice affects the sharpness/detail in your image and also the maximum bit rate that can be sustained and length of the movies you can record. You'll find more information on this parameter in Chapter 15.

Movie File Type

Options: MOV (default), MP4

My preference: MP4

The Z5 can use either MOV or MP4 movie formats. MP4 format is an industry standard for video. MOV, the default, is common on Macs. Most video editors can translate MP4 files into MOV and back again as long as the same codec was used for both. Your camera uses the standard H.264/MPEG-4 codec ("coder-decoder") using IPB (I-frame/P-frame/B-frame) Standard and Light. I prefer MP4, because it has better support for computers running operating systems other than MacOS. I'll explain file-type considerations in more detail in Chapter 15.

ISO Sensitivity Settings

Options: Maximum Sensitivity, Auto ISO control (Mode M), ISO Sensitivity (Mode M)

My preference: Varies by light levels

Similar to the ISO settings in the Photo Shooting menu, this version allows you to select a fixed ISO setting for Manual exposure mode, from ISO 100 to Hi 2. That allows you greater control over the ISO used. When shooting movies in P, A, and S exposure modes, Auto ISO sensitivity is always used.

However, if you want to use Auto ISO in Manual exposure mode, you can turn it on or off here, and specify the *maximum* ISO that will be selected automatically, from ISO 200 to Hi 2. **Note:** Using Auto ISO in Manual exposure mode effectively gives you autoexposure *even though you're shooting in Manual exposure mode.* I'll show you how to put this feature to work in Chapter 15.

White Balance

Options: Same as Photo Settings (default); Auto1, Incandescent, Fluorescent, Direct Sunlight, Flash, Cloudy, Shade, Choose Color Temperature, Preset Manual

My preference: Same as Photo Settings

Here you can select the white balance used to shoot movies; you can select from:

- **Same As Photo Settings.** The Z5 will use whatever white balance setting you've specified in the Photo Shooting menu and apply it to your videos.

- **Any of the other White Balance options.** The selection will apply *only* to video. If you're shooting still photographs in RAW format, you might not care about the white balance setting, as you can choose any color balance you want when the file is imported into your image editor. Movie clips, on the other hand, aren't so easy to adjust (think of them as moving JPEGs which, in a sense, they are), so you might want to set a specific white balance in this menu entry.

Set Picture Control

Options: Same as Photo Settings (default); Original Picture Controls: Auto, Standard, Neutral, Vivid, Monochrome, Portrait, Landscape, Flat; Creative Picture Controls (01–20): Dream, Morning, Pop, Sunday, Somber, Dramatic, Silence, Bleached, Melancholic, Pure, Denim, Toy, Sepia, Blue, Red, Pink, Charcoal, Graphite, Binary, and Carbon

My preference: Same as Photo Settings

You can specify Same as Photo Settings, or independently specify a Picture Control to be used only when shooting movies. The procedures for selecting and modifying a Picture Control in this menu entry is otherwise exactly the same as described earlier in this chapter. Check out the still photo discussion of Picture Controls for a complete explanation of this feature.

Manage Picture Control

Options: Save/Edit, Rename, Delete, Load/Save

My preference: N/A

This entry includes the Save/Edit, Rename, Delete, and Load/Save options that operate the same as the corresponding control in the Photo Shooting menu, described earlier in this chapter. To recap:

- **Make a copy.** Choose Save/Edit, select from the list of available Original or Creative Picture Controls, and press OK to store that style in one of the user-defined slots C-1 to C-9.

- **Save an edited copy.** Choose Save/Edit, select from the list of available Picture Controls, and then press the multi selector right button to edit the style, as described in the previous section. Press OK when finished editing, and then save the modified style in one of the user-defined slots C-1 to C-9.

- **Rename a style.** Choose Rename, select from the list of user-defined Picture Controls (you cannot rename the default styles), and then enter the text used as the new label for the style. You may use up to 19 characters for the name.

- **Remove a style.** Select Delete, choose from the list of user-defined Picture Controls (you can't remove one of the default styles), press the multi selector right button, then highlight Yes in the screen that follows, and press OK to remove that Picture Control.
- **Store/retrieve style on card.** Choose Load/Save, then select Copy to Camera to locate a Picture Control on your memory card and copy it to the Z5; Delete from Card to select a Picture Control on your memory card and remove it; or Copy to Card to duplicate a style currently in your camera onto the memory card.

Active D-Lighting

Options: Same as Photo Settings (default), Extra High, High, Normal, Low, Off (default)

My preference: Same as Photo Settings

Here you can specify Active D-Lighting used exclusively for movie shooting, or you can choose Same as Photo Settings (the default value) when your still and movie shooting is under similar conditions.

High ISO NR

Options: High, Normal (default), Low, Off

My preference: Normal

Movie shooting doesn't involve *long* exposures, so the Movie Shooting menu includes only a High ISO Noise Reduction entry. You can set it to High, Normal, Low, or Off. See the entry for this feature under the Photo Shooting menu, earlier in this chapter.

Vignette Control

Options: Same as Photo Settings; High, Normal (default), Low, Off

My preference: Normal

Set up this option using the same settings in the Photo Shooting menu or choose your own.

Diffraction Compensation

Options: On (default), Off

My preference: On

This entry works the same as its Photo Shooting menu counterpart.

Auto Distortion Control

Options: On (default), Off

My preference: On

This entry also works the same as its Photo Shooting menu counterpart. With some lenses, On is activated automatically and this setting is grayed out and unavailable.

Flicker Reduction

Options: Auto (default), 50Hz, 60Hz

My preference: Auto

This is the first entry on the next page of the Movie Shooting menu. (See Figure 11.35, left.) The flicker reduction parameters in movie shooting are slightly different from their still photography counterparts. Because movie capture is always continuous, and at 60/50/30/25/24 frames per second, the Z5 needs to know the frequency at which the light source is flickering. You can choose Auto to let the camera sense the frequency (this may be the best idea if you are unsure about the local power supply) or specify 50Hz or 60Hz as appropriate.

Alternatively, you can eschew this feature, shoot using Manual exposure, and select a shutter speed that may sync best with the light source's power (that is 1/125th, 1/60th, or 1/30th second for 60Hz and 1/50th or 1/25th second for 50Hz). I'll have additional caveats about choosing a shutter speed for movie making in Chapter 15.

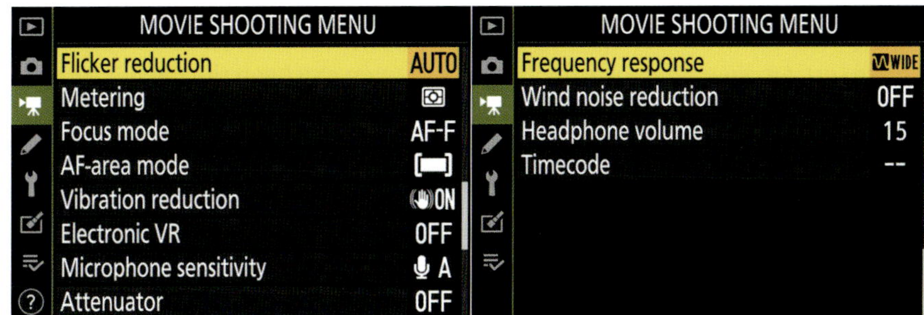

Figure 11.35 The next two pages of the Movie Shooting menu.

Metering

Options: Matrix metering (default), Center-weighted metering, Highlight-weighted metering

My preference: Matrix metering

Note that Spot metering is not available in movie mode, but this entry otherwise has exactly the same options as its counterpart in the Photo Shooting menu.

Focus Mode

Options: AF-S, AF-C, AF-F (full-time AF) (default), and MF

My preference: AF-F

For movie shooting, Nikon adds a full-time autofocus option (AF-F) to the AF-S, AF-C, and Manual focus modes used for still photography. You might consider it the *opposite* of AF-C: with AF-C, the Z5 starts focusing as soon as you press the shutter release halfway down, and continues until you press the release all the way down to take the picture. With AF-F, the camera starts focusing *immediately,* as soon as you rotate the still/movie switch next to the viewfinder to the Movie position. The Z5 then continues to adjust focus if you or your subject changes location, or you reframe the image.

Focus is locked when you press the shutter release halfway. You can then reframe or press the Movie button on top of the camera to begin capturing video using the focus setting you locked.

In effect, AF-F is full-time only prior to beginning capture. If you want the camera to refocus during capture, use AF-C instead.

AF-Area Mode

Options: Single-point AF, Wide-area AF (Small), Wide-area AF (Large), Auto-area AF (default)

My preference: Auto-area AF

The autofocus area modes available during video capture are similar to those used for still photography, as described in Chapter 5, except that Pinpoint AF and Dynamic Area AF are disabled.

Vibration Reduction

Options: Same as Photo Settings (default), On (Normal), Spt (Sport), Off

My preference: Same as Photo Settings

If you want to use the same settings specified for still photography, you can keep the default setting. However, if you exclusively shoot video with the camera mounted on a tripod, you can save time by disabling VR here, and activating it only when needed.

Electronic VR

Options: On, Off (default)

My preference: Off

Electronic VR is a type of anti-shake technology that has long been provided in pro and amateur camcorders. It's available only when shooting conventional 1080p, and *not* when shooting 1080p slow-mo or 2160p 4K video. In use, the camera reduces the frame size by about 10 percent when shooting in FX mode. It then examines successive frames looking for movement by comparing pixels that are in common between frames and noting when the pixels representing stationary objects appear to move. It then uses the extra border area outside the frame to counteract the motion by realigning the video frames so that pixels of parts of the image that don't move between frames (such as the background when you're shooting without any intentional panning movement) match. No trimming is necessary when shooting in DX mode, as the Z5 can use the area outside the crop to align the image.

If you're shooting with the Z5 mounted on a tripod, or connected to a gimbal, shoulder, hand-held, or other type of video camera stabilizer, you can safely turn this feature off. Disable electronic VR as well when you actually want a shaky, cinéma vérité look.

Microphone Sensitivity

Options: Auto Sensitivity (default), Manual Sensitivity, Microphone Off
My preference: Varies

This entry has three options that control your Z5's built-in microphone or any external microphone you attach. You can choose Auto Sensitivity; Manual Sensitivity, to set recording levels yourself (with a handy volume meter on screen showing the current ambient sound levels); or turn the microphone off entirely if you're planning to record silent video, use another sound recording source, or add sound in post-production.

Attenuator

Options: Enable, Disable (default)
My preference: Varies

When working in noisy environments, choose Enable to reduce the microphone gain and minimize audio distortion from background sounds.

Frequency Response

Options: Wide Range (default), Vocal Range
My preference: Varies

This is the first entry on the last page of the Movie Shooting menu (see Figure 11.35, right, shown earlier). Select from Wide Range frequency response to record a broad range of sounds, or Vocal Range to optimize audio recording for vocals. You'll find an entire section on recording sound in Chapter 15.

Wind Noise Reduction

Options: On, Off (default)
My preference: Varies

Wind blowing across your microphone can be distracting. This setting reduces wind noise (and may also affect other sounds, so use it carefully) for the built-in microphones *only*. Your external microphone, like the Nikon ME-1, may have its own wind noise reduction filter on/off switch.

Headphone Volume

Options: 15 (default); Values 0–30
My preference: N/A

Use this entry in Movie mode to adjust the volume of headphones you've plugged into the Z5's headphones jack.

Timecode

Options: Record Timecodes: On, On with HDMI Output, Off; Count-up Method: Record Run, Free Run; Timecode Origin: Reset, Enter Manually, Current Time; Drop Frame: On, Off

My preference: N/A

Advanced video shooters find SMPTE (Society of Motion Picture and Television Engineers)-compatible time codes embedded in the video files to be an invaluable reference during editing. To oversimplify a bit, the time system provides precise *hour:minute:second:frame* markers that allow identifying and synchronizing frames and audio. The time code system includes a provision for "dropping" frames to ensure that the fractional frame rate of captured video (remember that a 24 fps setting actually yields 23.976 frames per second while 30 fps capture gives you 29.97 actual "frames" per second) can be matched up with actual time spans.

As I noted in the introduction to this book, I won't be covering the most technical aspects of movie shooting in great detail (including detailed use of time codes, raw HDMI streaming, etc.). If you're at the stage where you're using time codes, you don't need a primer, anyway. However, the Time Code submenu does include the following options:

- **Record Timecodes.** Turn timecodes off or on. You can select On, or On with HDMI Output to append the time code to the HDMI video output, or Off to not use timecodes.

- **Count Up.** Choose Rec Run, in which the time code counts up only when you are actually capturing video, or Free Run (also known as Time of Day), which allows the time code to run up even between shooting clips. The latter is useful when you want to synchronize clips between multiple cameras that are shooting the same event. When using Free Run, even if the cameras record at different times, you'll be able to match the video that was captured at the exact same moment during editing. When Free Run is selected, the time code will always be recorded to the movie file (except for HFR clips).

- **Timecode Origin.** Normally, the Z5 uses the camera's internal clock to specify the hours:minutes:seconds, with frames set to :00 when you begin shooting. This entry allows you to manually enter any hour:minute:second:frame of your choice, or to Reset the start time to 00:00:00:00.

- **Drop Frame.** The 30 fps setting yields 29.97 actual frames per second, 60 fps gives you 59.95 frames per second, and 120 fps provides 119.9 fps, causing a discrepancy between the actual time and the time code that's recorded. Enable and the camera will skip some time code numbers in drop-frame mode at intervals to eliminate the discrepancy. When disabled (non-drop frame mode), you may notice a difference of several seconds per hour.

Unlike the Photo Shooting and Movie Shooting menu options, which you are likely to modify frequently as your picture-taking environment changes, Custom Settings are slightly more stable sets of preferences that let you tailor the behavior of your camera in a variety of different ways for longer-term use.

Some options are minor tweaks useful for specific shooting situations or make the camera more convenient to use. Perhaps you'd like to assign a frequently used feature to the Fn button or turn on the viewfinder grid display to make it easier to align vertical or horizontal shapes.

Best of all are the settings that improve the way the Z5 operates. Custom Setting b4, for example, provides a way to fine-tune the exposures your camera calculates for each of the metering modes: Matrix, Center-weighted, Spot, and Highlight-weighted. If you find that one or the other consistently over- or underexposes more than you like, it's easy to dial in a permanent correction. Should you feel that the Z5 is taking a few pictures that are out of focus, Custom Settings a1 and a2 can be used to tell it not to fire until optimum focus is achieved.

This chapter concentrates on explaining all the options of the Custom Settings menu and, most importantly, when and why you might want to use each setting.

Custom Settings Menu Layout

There are more than four dozen different Custom Settings, arranged in seven different categories, as shown in Figure 12.1: Autofocus, Metering/Exposure, Timers/AE Lock, Shooting/Display, Bracketing/Flash, Controls, and Movie. Some of those may seem to be an odd match. What does bracketing have to do with flash? Oh, wait! You can *bracket* flash (as well as non-flash) exposures. The category system does have an advantage. Once you're familiar with what settings are available within each category, you can select the Custom Settings menu, scroll down to the specific category you want, press the right button, and enter the Custom Settings system at that point, skipping the other entries.

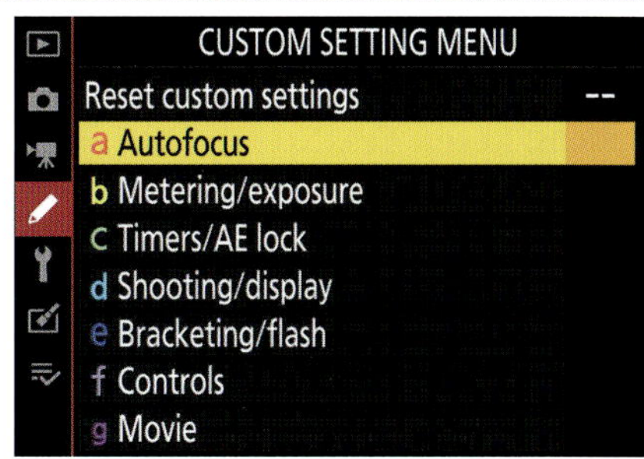

Figure 12.1 Entries are allocated among seven categories in the Custom Settings menu.

However, once you get past the main Custom Settings screen, the entries are one long scrolling list, so if you've guessed wrong about where you want to start, you can enter the list at any point and then scroll up or down until you find the entry you want. Or, press the left directional key to get back to the main screen, then move down to another entry point and re-enter. The Custom Settings menu items are all color- and letter-coded: **a** (red) for autofocus functions; **b** (yellow) for metering/exposure; **c** (green) for timers and AE lock features; **d** (light blue) for shooting/display functions; **e** (dark blue) for bracketing/flash; **f** (purple) for adjustments to the Z5's controls; and **g** (magenta) to adjust Movie mode functions.

For simplicity, in this book I have been consistently referring to the Custom Settings menu entries by their letter/names, so that you always know that when I mention Custom Setting a5, I am describing the fifth entry in the Autofocus menu: Focus Points Used. That terminology makes it easy to jump quickly to the specific entry. Note that for simplicity's sake, in the figures that illustrate each of the separate Custom Settings categories in this chapter, that category's entries are shown on as few screens as possible. In practice, as you scroll through the listings, the entries for a category may be spread over several different screens.

You can select a Custom Settings function as you do any menu entry, by pressing the multi selector right button, and navigating through the screen that appears with the up/down (and sometimes left/right) buttons. Confirming an option is usually done by pressing the OK button, pushing the multi selector right button, or sometimes by choosing Done when a series of related options have been chosen.

At the top level, you'll see these entries:

- Reset Custom Settings
- a. Autofocus
- b. Metering/Exposure
- c. Timers/AE Lock
- d. Shooting/Display
- e. Bracketing/Flash
- f. Controls
- g. Movie

Reset Custom Settings

Options: Reset: Yes, No

My preference: N/A

You can restore the settings of the Custom Settings banks to their default values. In Chapter 3, I provided a list of recommended Custom Settings menu bank settings for typical photo environments. Tables 12.1 to 12.7 show the default values as the Nikon Z5 comes from the factory, and after a reset. If you don't know what some of these settings are, I'll explain them later in this chapter. Be careful when changing any of your carefully tailored customized settings back to the defaults.

TABLE 12.1 Default Custom Settings Bank Values: Autofocus

FUNCTION	OPTION	DEFAULT
a1	AF-C priority selection	Release
a2	AF-S priority selection	Focus
a3	Focus tracking with lock-on	3
a4	Auto-area AF face detection/eye detection	On
a5	Focus points used	All
a6	Store points by orientation	No
a7	AF activation	Shutter/AF-ON
a8	Limit AF-area mode selection	All available
a9	Focus point wrap-around	No wrap
a10	Focus point options	
	Manual focus mode	On
	Dynamic-area AF assist	On
a11	Low-light AF	On
a12	Built-in AF-assist illuminator	On
a13	Manual focus ring in AF mode	Enable

TABLE 12.2 Default Custom Settings Bank Values: Metering/Exposure

FUNCTION	OPTION	DEFAULT
b1	EV steps for exposure cntrl.	1/3 step
b2	Easy exposure compensation	Off
b3	Center-weighted area	12mm
b4	Fine-tune optimal exposure	
	Matrix metering	0
	Center-weighted metering	0
	Spot metering	0
	Highlight-weighted metering	0

TABLE 12.3 Default Custom Settings Bank Values: Timers/AE Lock

FUNCTION	OPTION	DEFAULT
c1	Shutter release button AE-L	Off
c2	Self-timer	
	Self-timer delay	10 s
	Number of shots	1
	Interval between shots	0.5 s
c3	Power off delay	
	Playback	10 s
	Menus	1 min.
	Image review	4 s
	Standby timer	30 s

TABLE 12.4 Default Custom Settings Bank Values: Shooting/Display

FUNCTION	OPTION	DEFAULT
d1	CL mode shooting speed	3 fps
d2	Max. continuous release	100
d3	Sync release mode options	Sync
d4	Exposure delay mode	Off
d5	Shutter Type	Auto
d6	File number sequence	On
d7	Apply settings to live view	On
d8	Framing grid display	Off
d9	Peaking highlights	
	Peaking level	Off
	Peaking highlight color	Red
d10	View all in continuous mode	On

TABLE 12.5 Default Custom Settings Bank Values: Bracketing/Flash

FUNCTION	OPTION	DEFAULT
e1	Flash sync speed	1/200 s
e2	Flash shutter speed	1/60 s
e3	Exposure comp. for flash	Entire frame
e4	Auto Flash ISO sensitivity control	Subject and background
e5	Modeling flash	On
e6	Auto bracketing (Mode M)	Flash/speed
e7	Bracketing order	MTR>under>over

TABLE 12.6 Default Custom Settings Bank Values: Controls

FUNCTION	OPTION	DEFAULT
f1	Customize *i* menu	Set Picture Control; White balance; Image quality; Image size; Flash mode; Metering ; Wi-Fi connection; View memory card info; Release mode; Vibration Reduction; AF-area mode; Focus mode
f2	Custom Controls	
	Fn1	White balance
	Fn2	Focus/AF-area modes
	AF-ON	AF-ON
	Sub-selector	Focus point selection
	Sub-selector center	AE/AF lock
	Movie record	None
	Lens Fn	AE/AF lock
	Lens Fn2	AF-ON
	Lens control ring	Varies with lens

TABLE 12.6 Default Custom Settings Bank Values: Controls *(continued)*

FUNCTION	OPTION	DEFAULT
f3	OK button	
	Shooting mode	RESET/Select center focus point
	Playback mode	Zoom on/off
	Zoom on/off	1:1
f4	Shutter spd & aperture lock	
	Shutter speed lock	Off
	Aperture lock	Off
f5	Customize command dials	
	Reverse rotation direction	Exposure Compensation: Off
		Shutter speed/Aperture: Off
	Change main/sub	Exposure setting: Off
		Autofocus setting: Off
	Menus and Playback	Off
	Sub-dial frame advance	10 frames
f6	Release button to use dial	No
f7	Reverse indicators	-0+

TABLE 12.7 Default Custom Settings Bank Values: Movie

FUNCTION	OPTION	DEFAULT
g1	Customize *i* menu	Set Picture Control; White balance; Frame size and rate/Image quality; Microphone sensitivity; Choose image area; Metering; Wi-Fi connection; Destination; Electronic VR; Vibration reduction; AF-area mode; Focus mode
g2	Custom Controls	
	Fn1	White balance
	Fn2	Focus/AF-area modes
	AF-ON	AF-ON
	Sub-selector button	AE/AF lock
	Shutter release button	Take photos
	Lens control ring	Varies with lens
g3	OK button	Select center focus point
g4	AF speed	0
	When to apply	Always
g5	AF tracking sensitivity	4
g6	Highlight display	
	Display pattern	Off
	Highlight display enabled	248

a. Autofocus

The red-coded Autofocus options (see Figure 12.2) deal with some of the potentially most vexing settings available with the Nikon Z5. After all, incorrect focus is one of the most damaging picture killers of all the attributes in an image. You may be able to compensate for bad exposure, partially fix errant color balance, and perhaps even incorporate motion blur into an image as a creative element. But if focus is wrong, the photograph doesn't look right, and no amount of "I meant to do that!" pleas are likely to work. The Z5's autofocus options enable you to choose how and when focus is applied (using the AF-S or AF-C focus mode you selected on the camera body), the controls used to activate the feature, and the way focus points are selected from the available zones.

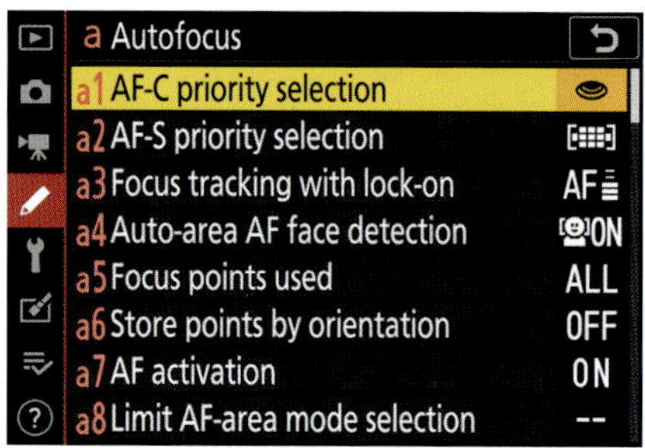

Figure 12.2 The Autofocus options menu.

a1 AF-C Priority Selection

Options: Release (default), Focus

My preference: Release

As you learned in Chapter 5, when not shooting movies, the Nikon Z5 has two primary autofocus modes, continuous-servo autofocus (AF-C) and single-servo autofocus (AF-S). (Movie mode adds a third: Full-time autofocus [AF-F].) This menu entry allows you to specify what takes precedence when you press the shutter release all the way down to take a picture: focus (called *focus-priority*) or the release button (called *release-priority*). You can choose from:

- **Release.** When this option is selected (the default), the shutter is activated when the release button is pushed down all the way, even if sharp focus has not yet been achieved. Because AF-C focuses and refocuses constantly when autofocus is active, you may find that an image is not quite in sharpest focus. Use this option when taking a picture is more important than absolute best focus, such as fast action or photojournalism applications. (You don't want to miss that record-setting home run, or the protestor's pie smashing into the Governor's face.) Using this setting doesn't mean that your image won't be sharply focused; it just means that you'll get a picture even if autofocusing isn't quite complete. If you've been poised with the shutter release pressed halfway, the Z5 probably has been tracking the focus of your image.

- **Focus.** The shutter is not activated until sharp focus is achieved. This is best for subjects that are not moving rapidly. AF-C will continue to track your subjects' movement, but the Z5 won't take a picture until focus is locked in. You might miss a few shots, but you will have fewer out-of-focus images.

a2 AF-S Priority Selection

Options: Release, Focus (default)

My preference: Focus

This is the counterpart setting for single-servo autofocus mode.

- **Release.** The shutter is activated when the button is depressed all the way, even if sharp focus is not quite achieved. Keep in mind that, unlike AF-C, the Z5 focuses only *once* when AF-S mode is used. So, if you've partially depressed the shutter release, paused, and then pressed the button down all the way, it's possible that the subject has moved, and release-priority will yield more out-of-focus shots than release-priority with AF-C.

- **Focus.** This default prevents the Z5 from taking a picture until focus is achieved and the in-focus indicator in the viewfinder glows steadily. If you're using single-servo autofocus mode, this is probably the best setting. Moving subjects really call for AF-C mode in most cases.

a3 Focus Tracking with Lock-on

Options: Blocked Shot AF Response: 5 (Delayed), 4, 3 (Normal) (default), 2, 1 (Quick)

My preference: Normal

Sometimes new subjects interject themselves in the frame temporarily. Perhaps you're shooting an architectural photo from across the street and a car passes in front of the camera. Or, at a football game, a referee dashes past just as a receiver is about to make a catch. This setting lets you specify how quickly the Z5 reacts to these transient interruptions that would cause relatively large changes in focus before refocusing on the "new" subject matter. Using the Blocked Shot AF Response slider shown in Figure 12.3, you can specify a long delay, so that the interloper is ignored, or a shorter delay, so that the Z5 immediately refocuses when a new subject moves into the frame.

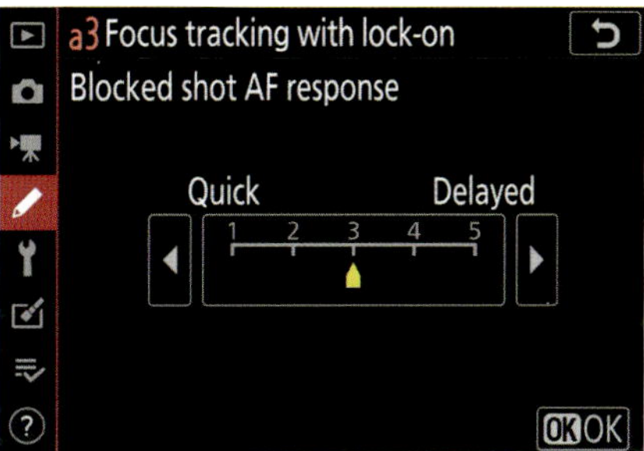

Figure 12.3 Options for Focus Tracking with Lock-On.

A setting of 5 (Delayed) causes the Z5 to ignore the intervening subject matter for a significant period of time. Use this setting when shooting subjects, such as sports, in which focus interruptions are likely to be frequent and significant. You can also choose a setting of 1 (Quick) which tells the Z5 to wait only a moment before refocusing. Very high continuous frame rates may work better when you allow refocusing to take place rapidly, without a lock-on delay. Intermediate settings from 2 to 4 provide different amounts of delay. The middle value, 3, offers an intermediate delay before the camera refocuses on the new subject. It's often the best choice when shooting sports in either of the continuous shooting modes, as the long delay can throw off autofocus accuracy at higher frames-per-second settings.

a4 Auto-Area AF Face/Eye Detection

Options: On (default), Off

My preference: On when shooting candid portraits or stage performances

The Z5's EXPEED 6 processor can analyze your image to find faces, allowing the camera to locate human subjects to autofocus on, and track them as they move. This is an incredibly powerful feature, especially for sports, stage performances, relentlessly moving children, and other action involving humans. I tend to use it for candid portraits and performances to speed up the autofocus process, and find it works best in single-shot mode or continuous frame rates in the 1–4.5 fps range. This menu entry allows you to turn face/eye-detection on or off.

a5 Focus Points Used

Options: All (default), 1/2 Every other point

My preference: Depends on subject

You can choose the number of focus points available when you manually select a zone using the multi selector up/down and left/right buttons or the sub-selector joystick. You have two choices:

- **All.** This is the default. Up to 273 points are available. The exact number used varies by the active AF-area mode.

- **1/2 Every Other Point.** The Z5 uses every other focus point/zone available for a given AF-area mode, for a total of 77 points (in an 11 × 7 array). (See Figure 12.4.) That's a reduction of greater than 2/3 of the available points/zones in each case. This can be the best choice for faster focus point selection when taking pictures of relatively large, evenly illuminated subject matter

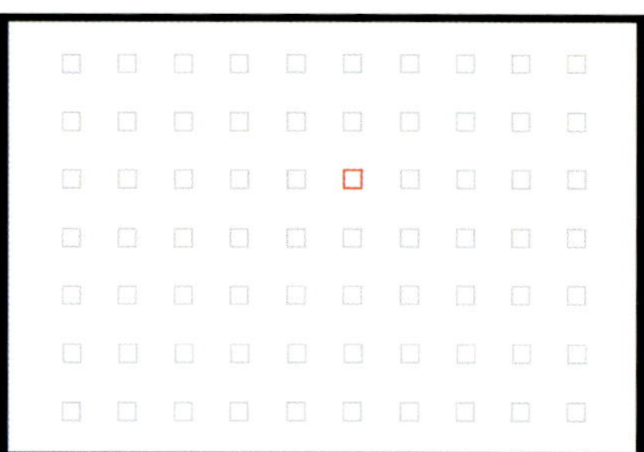

Figure 12.4 Every other focus point enabled.

such that choosing precise focus zones is not particularly beneficial. I often use Single Point AF and enable the Every Other Point option—the available focus areas are plenty and can be set quickly as action moves around the floor when photographing basketball games. The exceptions? When using Pinpoint AF or Wide-area AF (Large), the available focus points and nine AF zones remain exactly the same even though you have selected this option.

a6 Store Points by Orientation

Options: Yes, No (default)

My preference: Yes

Here you can choose whether separate focus points can be selected for landscape and portrait orientations of the camera, and whether you can select different AF-area modes in these orientations, as explained in detail in Chapter 5.

When you choose Off, the focus point will maintain the same relative position as you rotate the camera, and the AF-area mode will remain the same. Select On, and you can choose a different focus point when the camera is set to horizontal orientation, rotated 90 degrees clockwise from horizontal, or rotated 90 degrees counterclockwise from horizontal.

This is a very cool feature, and best visualized using Figure 5.17 supplied in Chapter 5 where Store Points by Orientation is explained in detail.

a7 AF Activation

Options: Shutter/AF-ON (default), AF-ON Only: Out-of-focus release, Enable (default), Disable

My preference: AF-ON Only for anyone proficient in back-button focus, described in Chapter 5

You can specify whether the camera focuses when the shutter release is pressed halfway or disable that behavior. You'd want to disable shutter release AF activation if you elect to use *back-button focus*. Your choices are as follows:

- **Shutter/AF-ON.** Pressing the shutter release halfway *or* a button you have defined for AF activation (as described under Custom Controls later in this chapter) always activates autofocus.

- **AF-ON Only.** Pressing the shutter release halfway does not activate autofocus. Instead, you can activate AF by pressing the button you've defined for that behavior using the Custom Controls commands described later, and in Chapter 5 under the back-button focus section.

  The Z5 allows additional fine-tuning of your AF-ON Only setting. When this option is highlighted, you can press the multi selector right button and choose from two Out-of-Focus Release options:

  - **Enable.** The Z5 can take photos when the shutter release is pressed all the way down, even if you have not pressed the AF-ON button and focus has therefore *not* taken place. You might find this useful to enable grab shots that take place without warning, and you want a photo even if it may not be in perfect focus. You still have the option of activating AF by pressing the AF-ON button before you press the shutter release all the way, but if you do not, the photo will still be captured.

  - **Disable.** You *must* activate AF by pressing the AF-ON button before using the shutter release to take a picture. It keeps the Z5 from taking a picture until after autofocus has been activated. This option applies only when focus-priority has been chosen for AF-C or AF-S and you are using an AF-area selection mode that allows the user to select the focus area or zones (in other words, all AF-area modes other than Auto-Area AF). This option will prevent you from accidentally taking out-of-focus pictures if you forget you are using AF-ON to activate autofocus and press the shutter release without remembering to initiate AF. This option is almost mandatory for new back-button focus users, at least until pressing the AF-ON button before shooting becomes a reflex.

a8 Limit AF-Area Mode Selection

Options: Pinpoint, Single-point AF, Dynamic-area AF, Wide-area AF (Small), Wide-area AF (Large), Auto-area AF (default is all available)

My preference: All available

AF-area modes are chosen by highlighting AF-area mode from the *i* menu and rotating either command dial. If there are certain area modes that you don't use, you can disable them using this menu item.

Single-point AF-area mode is always available and cannot be disabled. However, you can highlight any of the others and press the right directional button to remove the check box next to that mode's label to disable it. You can thus enable Single-point AF, plus any combination of Dynamic-area AF, both Wide-area AF options, or Auto-area AF. I explained this feature in Chapter 5.

a9 Focus Point Wrap-Around

Options: Wrap, No Wrap (default)

My preference: No Wrap

This is the first entry on the second page of the Autofocus menu (see Figure 12.5). This setting is purely a personal preference parameter. When you press the multi selector left/right and up/down buttons to choose a focus point, the Z5 can be told to stop when the selection reaches the edge of the 51-point array—or, it can continue, wrapping around to the opposite edge, like Pac-Man leaving the playing area on one side or top/bottom to re-emerge on the other. (I hope I'm not revealing my age, here.) Your choices are simple; decide which behavior you prefer:

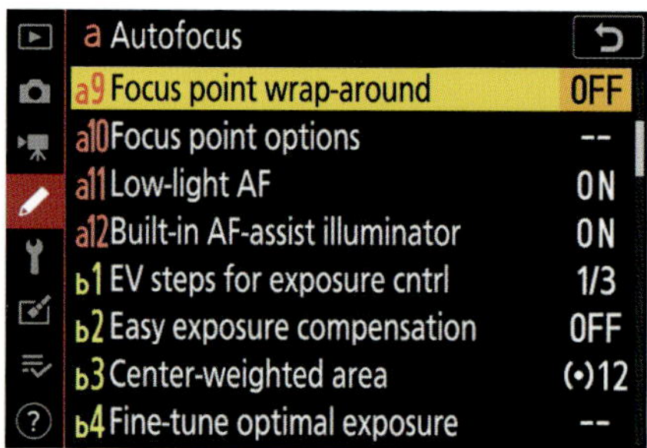

Figure 12.5 The next page of the Autofocus menu.

- **Wrap.** Pressing the left/right or up/down buttons when you've reached the edge of the focus point display wraps the selection to the opposite side, still moving in the same direction.
- **No Wrap.** The focus point selection stops at the edge of the focus zone array.

a10 Focus Point Options

Options: Manual Focus Mode: On (default), Off; Dynamic-area AF assist: On (default), Off

My preference: Manual Focus Mode: On; Dynamic-area AF assist: Off

How do you want the focus points displayed in the viewfinder?

Your choices for focus point options include:

- **Manual Focus mode.** When you're using manual focus instead of autofocus, the Z5 still monitors how well your image is in focus, using the active focus point. Here, you can choose how it is displayed.
  - **On.** Active point illumination is always shown when using manual focus. Select this option if you like to know what focus point is being used.
  - **Off.** Active point illumination is enabled during manual focus only during focus point selection as you move the point around the frame with the directional buttons or sub-selector.
- **Dynamic-area AF assist.** Select On to display both the focus point selected *and* the surrounding focus points when using Dynamic-area AF. Choose Off, and only the selected focus point is shown. When you're using Dynamic-area AF, you might want to choose On as a reminder that the cluster of points around the main focus point are active. However, once you become accustomed to using that AF-area mode, you can turn the display Off and slightly declutter your screen.

a11 Low-Light AF

Options: On (default), Off
My preference: Off

Low-light AF allows the Z5 to focus more accurately under dim illumination when using AF-S. The camera boosts AF response slightly by decreasing the refresh rate of the display. Normally the display refreshes 60 times per second (that is, 60Hz), and those rapid changes limit the ability of the AF system to read the embedded phase detection pixels in the sensor and calculate focus. By slowing down the refresh rate to 30Hz, the Z5 can focus more easily under low-light conditions. Even so, autofocus may be slower when this mode is activated, so the camera warns you by showing "Low-light" on the display. The feature is disabled when you've rotated the mode dial to the Auto position. I tend to leave this setting at Off, because under truly low-light conditions I prefer to switch to manual focus and fine-tune the focus plane myself. You'll find more detailed descriptions of Phase-detect AF and other autofocus aspects in Chapter 5.

a12 Built-in AF-Assist Illuminator

Options: On (default), Off
My preference: Off

There is an LED on the left front panel (as you hold the camera). It can illuminate to provide additional lighting to improve autofocus when using the AF-S focus mode. The illuminator is effective over a very narrow range (Nikon says 3'4" to 9'10") and its anemic burst of light can be obstructed by any lens hood you have mounted, or even a stray finger. I usually disable this feature, because I shoot so many photos at concerts and other events where the AF-assist light is distracting (or even forbidden—choreographers have told me dancers may orient their twirling moves on theater lights they perceive during a spin).

a13 Manual Focus Ring in AF Mode

Options: Enable (default), Disable

My preference: Enable

This setting is one you can ignore most of the time, and Nikon makes that especially easy: it doesn't appear on the menu at all unless you have one of the very few lenses that are compatible with it. At this writing, there are only six lenses in three different focal lengths capable of making this entry magically appear. They are the following AF-P optics that can be mounted on the Z5 using the FTZ adapter (I explained the difference between AF-P and AF-S lenses in Chapter 7.):

- AF-P Nikkor 10-20mm f/4.5-5.6G VR DX
- AF-P Nikkor 18-55mm f/3.5-5.6G DX (both VR and non-VR versions)
- AF-P Nikkor 70-300mm f/4.5-6.3G ED DX (both VR and non-VR versions)
- AF-P Nikkor 70-300mm f/4.5-5.6E ED VR

Note that all but the last are DX lenses. They'll work fine on the Z5; the camera will automatically switch to 19.5 MP DX "crop" mode. Those lenses and the lone full-frame lens (so far) allow using this entry to enable (or disable) the ability to fine-tune focus manually with the focus ring when the Z5 is set to an autofocus mode.

All other autofocus lenses compatible with the Z5 provide this ability automatically. When enabled, you can press the shutter release halfway down to autofocus (or press your AF-ON button), and then fine-tune focus by rotating the lens's focus ring. If at any time you want the Z5 to refocus automatically, release the shutter button or AF-ON button, and press again. You might want to disable this feature (when using an AF-P lens) to prevent accidentally straying from the Z5's autofocus adjustment. In most cases, however, it's a solution in search of a problem, and Nikon helpfully keeps this setting hidden.

b. Metering/Exposure

The yellow-coded Metering/Exposure Custom Settings (see Figure 12.5, shown earlier) let you define four different parameters that affect exposure metering in the Nikon Z5.

b1 EV Steps for Exposure Cntrl.

Options: 1/3 step (default), 1/2 step, 1 step

My preference: 1/3 step

This setting tells the Nikon Z5 the size of the "jumps" it should use when making exposure adjustments—either one-third or one-half stop. The increment you specify here applies to f/stops, shutter speeds, EV changes, and autoexposure bracketing. As with ISO sensitivity step value, you can select from 1/3 step (the default), 1/2 step, or 1 full-step increments.

Choose the 1/3-stop setting when you want the finest increments between shutter speeds and/or f/stops. For example, the Z5 will use shutter speeds such as 1/60th, 1/80th, 1/100th, 1/125th, and 1/160th second, and f/stops such as f/5.6, f/6.3, f/7.1, and f/8, giving you (and the autoexposure system) maximum flexibility.

With 1/2-stop increments, you will have larger and more noticeable changes between settings. The Z5 will apply shutter speeds such as 1/60th, 1/125th, 1/200th, and 1/500th second, and f/stops including f/5.6, f/6.7, f/8, f/9.5, and f/11. These coarser adjustments are useful when you want more dramatic changes between different exposures.

b2 Easy Exposure Compensation

Options: On (Auto Reset), On, Off (default)

My preference: Off

This setting potentially simplifies dialing in EV (exposure value compensation) adjustments by specifying whether the Exposure Compensation button must be pressed while adding or extracting EV compensation. Because of the possibility of confusion or error, I tend to leave this setting turned off, which is the default. Your choices are as follows:

- **On (Auto reset).** This setting allows you to add or subtract exposure by rotating the sub-command dial when in Program (P) or Shutter-priority (S) exposure modes, or by rotating the main command dial when using Aperture-priority (A) mode. Rotating either dial has no effect in Manual (M) exposure mode. (If you've reversed the behavior of the command dials using Custom Setting f8, the "opposite" command dial must be used to make the changes.) Any adjustments you've made are canceled when the camera is shut off, or the meter-off time expires and the Z5's exposure meters go back to sleep. That's a useful mode, because most of us have made an EV adjustment and then forgotten about it, only to expose a whole series of improperly exposed photos. You can still have "sticky" EV settings when Easy Exposure Compensation is turned on: just hold down the Exposure Compensation button when you make your changes. You can also increase the standby timer interval (using Custom Setting c3, described shortly) to a longer period so your adjustment will remain in force for a longer period of time.

- **On.** This setting brings the Easy Compensation mode into conformance with the Z5's behavior when the Exposure Compensation button is pressed: in either case, any EV modifications you make will remain until you countermand them. As I have mentioned several times, forgetting to "turn off" EV changes after you've moved on to a different shooting environment is a primary cause of over- and underexposure among those of us who are forgetful or who ignore the Z5's flashing EV warnings.

- **Off.** With this default setting, you must always press the Exposure Compensation button while rotating the main command dial to add or subtract exposure. Use this choice when you don't want any EV changes unless you deliberately make them by pressing the button.

b3 Center-Weighted Area

Options: 12mm (default), Average

My preference: 12mm

This setting changes the size of the Center-weighted exposure spot. Your choices include 12mm or full-frame average (which turns the metering mode from a center-weighted system to an old-fashioned averaging system). Check out Figure 4.6 in Chapter 4 to see the approximate area of the coverage. Note, if you're migrating from F-mount, some Nikon dSLRs allow you to change the size of the Center-weighted spot, but the Z5 gives you only the 12mm and full-screen averaging options. The spot is "fuzzy" anyway, and I've found changing the size really has very little effect most of the time.

b4 Fine-Tune Optimal Exposure

Options: Default (none), Plus or minus one stop in 1/6-stop increments for: Matrix metering, Center-weighted metering, Spot metering, Highlight-weighted metering

My preference: N/A

This setting is a powerful adjustment that allows you to dial in a specific amount of exposure compensation that will be applied, invisibly, to every photo you take using each of the four metering modes. No more can you complain, "My Z5 always underexposes by 1/3 stop!" If that is actually the case, and the phenomenon is consistent, you can use this custom menu adjustment to compensate.

Exposure compensation is usually a better idea (does your camera *really* underexpose that consistently?), but this setting does allow you to "recalibrate" your Z5 yourself. However, you have no indication that fine-tuning has been made, so you'll need to remember what you've done. After all, you someday might discover that your camera is consistently *over*exposing images by 1/3 stop, not realizing that your Custom Setting b4 adjustment is the culprit.

In practice, it's rare that the Nikon Z5 will *consistently* provide the wrong exposure in any of the four metering modes, especially Matrix metering, which can alter exposure dramatically based on the Z5's internal database of typical scenes. This feature may be most useful for Spot metering, if you always take a reading off the same type of subject, such as a human face or 18 percent gray card. Should you find that the gray card readings, for example, always differ from what you would prefer, go ahead and fine-tune optimal exposure for Spot metering, and use that to read your gray cards. To use this feature:

1. **Select fine-tuning.** Choose Custom Setting b4: Fine-tune Optimal Exposure from the Custom Settings menu.

2. **Consider yourself warned.** In the screen that appears, choose Yes after carefully reading the warning that Nikon insists on showing you every time this option is activated.

3. **Select metering mode to correct.** Choose Matrix, Center-weighted, Spot, or Highlight-weighted metering in the screen that follows by highlighting your choice and pressing the multi selector right button. (See Figure 12.6, left.)

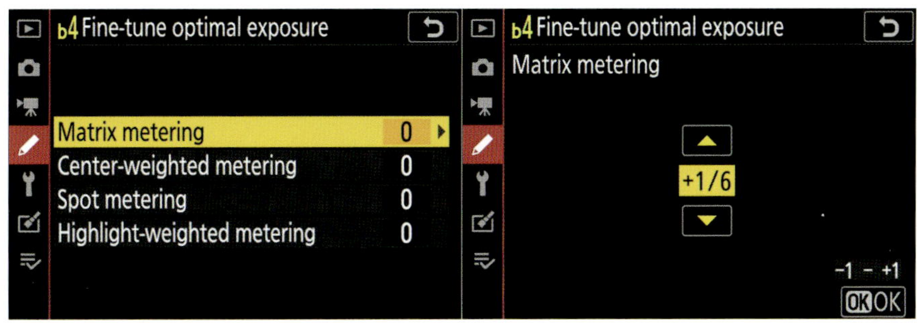

Figure 12.6 You can fine-tune any of four metering modes (left). Increments of 1/6 stop are available (right).

4. **Specify amount of correction.** Press the up/down buttons to dial in the exposure compensation you want to apply. You can specify compensation up to +/- one stop, in increments of 1/6 stop, half as large a change as conventional exposure compensation. Compensation of up to one full stop (plus or minus) can be entered. This is truly *fine-tuning.* (See Figure 12.6, right.)

5. **Confirm your change.** Press OK when finished. You can repeat the action to fine-tune the other exposure modes if necessary.

c. Timers/AE Lock

This category (see Figure 12.7) is a mixed bag of settings, covering how the shutter release and AE-L buttons interact (c1) and entries that adjust delay times (c2 and c3).

c1 Shutter-Release Button AE-L

Options: Off (default), On (half press), On (burst mode)

My preference: On when using back-button focus, as described in Chapter 5

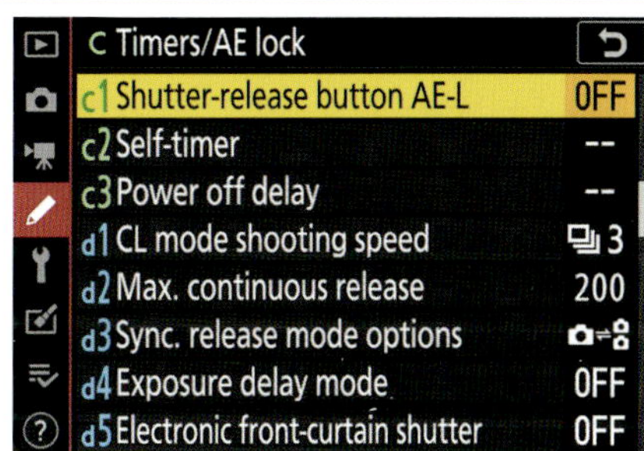

Figure 12.7 The Timers/AE Lock settings.

This is another of Nikon's easily confusing options for controlling how and when autofocus and exposure are activated and locked. The intent is to allow you to separate autofocus and autoexposure activation and locking.

- **Off.** Exposure is locked *only* when the defined AE-L/AF-L button is pressed. This is the default. The shutter release does not lock exposure.

- **On (half press).** Exposure locks when either the shutter release button is depressed *halfway,* or the designated AE-L/AF-L button is held down. If you always want exposure locked when the shutter release is pressed halfway, use this option. That makes the most sense when you are using back-button focus.

- **On (burst mode).** Exposure locks when the shutter release button is pressed down all the way. You'd do this during continuous shooting, when you press the shutter release and hold it down while your series of shots is captured. This option locks the exposure for the first image, ensuring that all the other images in the sequence are given the same exposure.

c2 Self-Timer

Options: Self-timer Delay (default: 10 sec.), Number of Shots (default: 1), Interval Between Shots (default: 0.5 sec.)

My preference: N/A

This setting lets you choose the length of the self-timer shutter release delay.

Your options include:

- **Self-timer delay.** The default value is 10 seconds. You can also choose 2, 5, or 20 seconds. If I have the camera mounted on a tripod or other support and am too lazy to attach the MC-DC2 cable release (I have three, one for each camera bag, so I *always* have one available), I can set a 2-second delay that is sufficient to let the camera stop vibrating after I've pressed the shutter release. I use a longer delay time if I am racing to get into the picture myself and am not sure I can make it in 10 seconds.

- **Number of shots.** After the timer finishes counting down, the Z5 can take from 1 to 9 different shots. This is a godsend when shooting photos of groups, especially if you want to appear in the photo itself. You'll always want to shoot several pictures to ensure that everyone's eyes are open and there are smiling expressions on each face. Instead of racing back and forth between the camera to trigger the self-timer multiple times, you can select the number of shots taken after a single countdown. For small groups, I always take at least as many shots as there are people in the group—plus one. That gives everybody a chance to close their eyes.

- **Interval between shots.** If you've selected 2 to 9 as your number of shots to be snapped off, you can use this option to space out the different exposures. Your choices are 0.5 seconds, 1, 2, or 3 seconds. Use a short interval when you want to capture everyone saying "Cheese!" The 3-second option is helpful if you're using flash, as 3 seconds is generally long enough to allow the flash to recycle and have enough juice for the next photo.

c3 Power Off Delay

Options: Separate settings for Playback, Menus, Image Review, Standby Timer

My preference: Varies

You can adjust the amount of time the display remains on when no other operations are being performed. If the EH-7P Charging AC adapter is attached, the displays will remain on for the maximum amount, about 10 minutes. With the Z5, you can specify separate values for Playback (the default is 10 seconds); Menus (the default is 1 minute); Image review (default 4 seconds); and Standby Timer (default 30 seconds). Choosing a brief duration for all or each of these can help preserve battery power. However, the Z5 will always override the review display when the shutter button is partially or fully depressed, so you'll never miss a shot because a previous image was on the screen.

Sports shooters and some others prefer a longer delay because they can keep their camera always "at the ready" with no delay to interfere with taking an action shot that unexpectedly presents itself. Extra battery consumption is just part of the price paid. For example, when I am shooting football, a standby timer of 20 seconds is plenty, because the players lining up for the snap is my signal to get ready to shoot. But for basketball or soccer, I typically set the standby timer for 30 minutes, because action is virtually continuous. My Z5 has plenty of power, and I carry two sets of spare batteries. I rarely shoot much more than 1,000 to 1,200 shots at any sports event, so that's often sufficient juice even with the standby timer set for 30 minutes or No Limit. The displays dim for a few seconds before the standby timer expires. Of course, if the standby timer has shut off, and the power switch remains in the On position, you can bring the camera back to life by tapping the shutter button.

d. Shooting/Display

This menu section (see Figure 12.8) offers a variety of mostly unrelated shooting and display options not found elsewhere, but which are not frequently changed, making them suitable for a Custom Settings entry. The figure shows only the first eight entries; you must scroll down to see the last three.

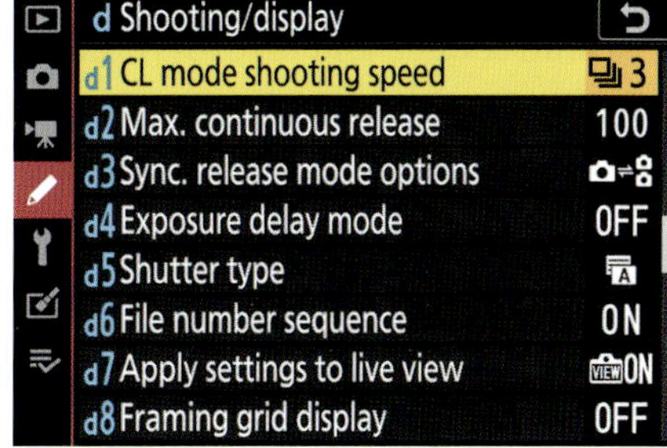

Figure 12.8 A mixed bag of entries is found in the Shooting/Display submenu.

d1 CL Mode Shooting Speed

Options: 1–4 fps (default: 3 fps)

My preference: Varies

You can specify the frames-per-second shooting rate for Continuous (Low) speed mode from 1 frame per second to 4 frames per second. Faster rates are better for sports action, such as the image shown in Figure 12.9.

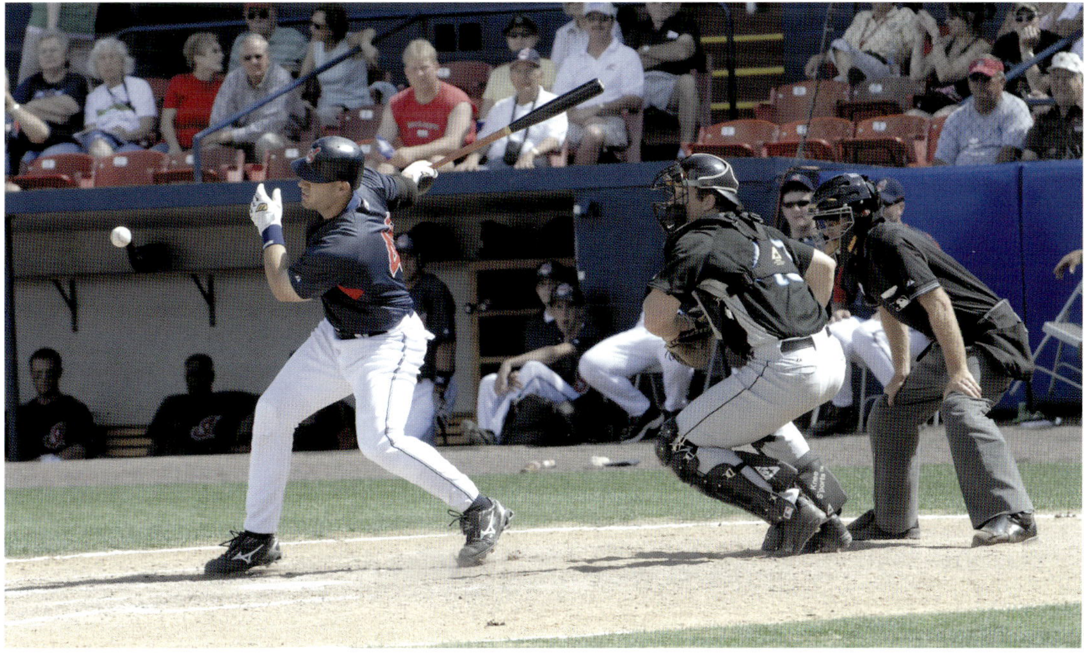

Figure 12.9 High frame rates can capture a critical moment when shooting sports action.

Choose one of these firing speed ranges for Continuous (Low) from among those available that is suitable for the kind of shooting environment you're in:

- **Normal continuous shooting.** I set my Z5 to the 1 fps rate most of the time, so that I can take multiple shots quickly without needing to press the shutter release repeatedly. A one-second rate isn't so fast that I end up taking a bunch of shots that I don't want, but it is fast enough that I can shoot a series.

- **Bracketing.** When I'm using bracketing, I generally have the Z5 set to shoot a bracketed set of three pictures: under, normal, and overexposure. With the camera set to 3 fps, I can press the shutter once and take all three bracketed shots, with basically the same framing, within about one second.

- **HDR bracketing.** On the other hand, if you're bracketing to combine individual images in an image editor to produce a high dynamic range photo, you'll want the exposures to be captured as quickly as possible. That will minimize any differences between the images, so they can be more easily aligned as they are merged.

- **Slower action sequences.** For some types of action, such as long-distance running, golf, swimming, or routine baseball plays, a rate of 2 fps might be sufficient. You can make this more reasonable speed available by defining it here as the continuous low-speed frame rate.

- **Faster action sequences.** You can specify higher frame rates, up to 4 fps when you want to grab more images in a brief burst. However, in most cases, you'll use Continuous High mode for this type of photography. Dialing in a slightly slower speed here makes it easy to switch back and forth just by changing the release mode dial from Continuous Low to Continuous High.

d2 Max. Continuous Release

Options: 1–100 shots; default 100

My preference: 100 shots

Use this setting to limit the number of consecutive shots that can be taken in one burst when using continuous shooting modes. Your choices are any value between 1 and 100. As your camera's buffer fills, continuous shooting will slow down and eventually pause while the Z5 dumps pictures to the memory card. (Use of the electronic shutter, described shortly, also reduces continuous frame advance rates.) If you find yourself waiting for the memory card to store images during continuous shooting, you might want to set a lower number, say, 30 images, so you don't have so many pictures stacked up that you're unable to continue with a subsequent shot.

Note: If you have your heart set on shooting endless sequences, you can do so. Just use any shutter speed of 1 second or slower in Shutter-priority or Manual exposure modes. The frame rate for such exposures will be so slow that it's effectively impossible to fill the Z5's buffer, and your camera will happily poke along capturing images for as long as you hold down the shutter release button. Whatever Maximum Continuous Release value you've set will be ignored.

d3 Sync. Release Mode Options

Options: Sync (default), No Sync

My preference: N/A

If you own multiple compatible Nikon cameras equipped with optional WR-1 or WR-R10 wireless remote controllers, you can configure them such that they all fire at the same time. One camera acts as a master that controls the shutter release of the additional cameras. Sports photographers love this capability, because they can install remote cameras, say, above a basketball rim, and then position themselves along the baseline to shoot action in the paint. One click of the master camera produces shots from both angles simultaneously. (This is basically how I cover basketball games, except for the part about having a second, remote-controlled camera mounted high above the rim.)

This is a rather esoteric feature, available only to those who own, say, two or more Nikon Z-series, D850, D500, or D5 cameras. Synchronized release is also available with some other models, including the D4 and D4s equipped with the optional WT-5 wireless transmitter. You can use this entry to activate or deactivate the feature, but it's probably a better idea to use Custom Setting f2 and assign Sync. Release Selection to a control, such as the Fn 1 button.

d4 Exposure Delay Mode

Options: 3, 2, 1, 0.5, 0.2 seconds, Off (default)

My preference: Off

This is a marginally useful feature (and mildly annoying if you forget to turn it off) that you can use to force the Nikon Z5 to snap a picture about 0.2, 0.5, 1, 2, or 3 seconds (your choice) after you've pressed the shutter release button all the way. It's useful when you are using shutter speeds of about 1/8th to 1/60th second hand-held and want to minimize the effects of the vibration that results when you depress the shutter button. It can also be used when the camera is mounted on a tripod, although the self-timer function, set to a two-second delay, is more useful in that scenario. When switched On, the camera will pause while you steady your steely grip on the camera, taking the picture about one second later. When turned Off, the picture is taken when the shutter release is pressed, as normal.

One interesting side-effect of this mode is that it separates the normally invisible pre-flash produced by any Z5's external flash that's connected with the delay. That can have an unwanted side-effect. For example, if you're shooting living subjects (human or animal), and set the delay for one second, your subject may be startled by the initial flash and close their eyes just before the main flash fires 1,000 milliseconds later. Longer delays can produce incorrect exposures if you happen to accidentally (or intentionally) reframe or pan during the interval between when the pre-flash fires (and the Z5 calculates exposure) and the moment when the shutter opens/flash fires to take the actual picture.

d5 Shutter Type

Options: Auto (default), Mechanical Shutter, Electronic Front-Curtain Shutter

My preference: Auto

Your Nikon Z5 has an electronic front-curtain shutter that can be used to commence an exposure without the need for the (potentially) vibration-causing physical shutter curtain. This setting allows you to specify whether the mechanical shutter or electronic shutter are always used (with several exceptions), or if the Z5 can choose the shutter type depending on shutter speed. The e-front curtain shutter would then be used at slow shutter speeds to reduce blur from camera shake induced by the mechanical shutter's movement.

Exceptions: If you've specified Silent Shooting in the Photo Shooting menu (see Chapter 11), the electronic front-curtain shutter is always used, regardless of the setting here. In addition, your electronic shutter is available only when you're using a shutter speed of 1/2000th second or slower, and an ISO setting of 25600 or lower. Finally, the Mechanical Shutter full-time option is not available with some lenses, such as the Z Nikkor 16-50mm DX f/3.5-6.3 and Z Nikkor 50-250mm DX f/4.5-6.3 kit lenses for APS-C cameras. Note that the mechanical shutter itself is fully available; you just can't mandate it—only Auto and Electronic Front-Curtain Shutter can be selected. Since the relevant lenses are DX models, this restriction should not affect most Z5 users.

In use, the Z5 "dumps" the current image display on the EVF or LCD monitor, then begins exposure. The camera's mechanical rear-curtain shutter terminates the exposure. So, while the electronic front-curtain shutter is quieter, this mode isn't totally silent. Its chief benefit is avoiding a tiny amount of vibration that can occur from "shutter bounce." (The mechanical front curtain isn't totally damped after it descends.) If you really want to avoid any possibility of shutter vibration, choose the 0.2-second setting in Custom Setting d4: Exposure Delay Mode, described above.

For true silent operation, use the Silent Photography setting in the Photo Shooting menu, described in Chapter 11. With Silent Photography you can use any shutter speed—but cannot use flash (or long exposure noise reduction). In addition, the camera's beep speaker is automatically turned off and your continuous-shooting frame rate will change. With the electronic front-curtain shutter, you *can* use flash, but have that 1/200th second top shutter speed limitation, and your beeper will sound if enabled. I explained front- and rear-curtain shutter components in more detail in Chapter 9.

d6 File Number Sequence

Options: On (default), Off, Reset

My preference: On

The Nikon Z5 will automatically apply a file number to each picture you take, using consecutive numbering for all your photos over a long period of time, spanning many different memory cards, starting over from scratch when you insert a new card or when you manually reset the numbers. Numbers are applied from 0001 to 9999, at which time the Z5 "rolls over" to 0001 again.

The camera keeps track of the last number used in its internal memory and, if File Number Sequence is turned On, will apply a number that's one higher, or a number that's one higher than the largest number in the current folder on the memory card inserted in the camera. You can also start over each time a new folder has been created on the memory card or reset the current counter back to 0001 at any time. Here's how it works:

- **On.** At this default setting, the Z5 will use the number stored in its internal memory any time a new folder is created, a new memory card is inserted, or an existing memory card is formatted. If the card is not blank and contains images, then the next number will be one greater than the highest number on the card *or* in internal memory (whichever is higher).

- **Off.** If you're using a blank/reformatted memory card, or a new folder is created, the next photo taken will be numbered 0001. File number sequences will be reset every time you use or format a card, or a new folder is created (which happens when an existing folder on the card contains 5,000 shots).

- **Reset.** The Z5 assigns a file number that's one larger than the largest file number in the current folder, unless the folder is empty, in which case numbering is reset to 0001. At this setting, new or reformatted memory cards will always have 0001 as the first file number.

HOW MANY SHOTS, REALLY?

The file numbers produced by the Z5 don't provide information about the actual number of times the camera's shutter has been tripped—called actuations. For that data, you'll need a third-party software solution, such as the free Opanda iExif (www.opanda.com) for Windows or the non-free ($39.95) GraphicConverter for Macintosh (www.lemkesoft.com). These utilities can be used to extract the true number of actuations from the Exif information embedded in a JPEG file.

d7 Apply Settings to Live View

Options: On (default), Off

My preference: On, except when using studio flash

This entry tells the Z5 to provide a preview in the EVF and LCD monitor displays that reflects how your current settings of white balance, Picture Controls, and exposure compensation will affect your image when the photo is actually taken. It's a good way to preview the "look" of your image as it is adjusted by your selected settings. In Manual exposure mode, you will even be able to preview how your *exposure* will change the image; the displays will actually lighten or darken to reflect exposure changes. Sounds like a good idea, right?

However, there are times when you don't want to see the effects of the settings you've made on the screen/EVF. For example, when you are using flash in Manual exposure mode, the camera has no way of knowing exactly how much light will be illuminating your scene. You'll especially want to change this setting to Off when working with "dumb" studio strobes connected using a hot-shoe adapter with an old-school PC/X connector. After all, that f/16 aperture may be ideal for a shot exposed by your studio strobes, but the Z5 will, when this entry is set to On, show you a preview based on the ambient light, rather than the flash. The result? Your viewfinder or LCD monitor image is very, very dim. You'll want to select Off so the camera will display the electronic image to viewable levels.

However, in all other cases, at the default On setting, display in the EVF or the LCD monitor reflects the *relative* effects of any white balance, Picture Control, or exposure compensation settings you've made. In that mode, this allows for a reasonable representation of what the photo will look like and enables you to evaluate whether the current settings will provide the effects you want.

The On option can be especially helpful when you're using any of the Picture Controls, because you can preview the exact rendition that the selected effect and its overrides will provide. It's also very useful when you're setting some exposure compensation, as you can visually determine how much lighter or darker each adjustment makes the image. And when you're trying to achieve correct color balance, it's useful to be able to preview the effect of your white balance setting.

If you'd like to preview the image *without* the effect of settings visible, you can set this feature to Off. Naturally, the display will no longer accurately depict what your photo will look like when it's taken. So, for most users, On is the most suitable option. Unfortunately, this setting has caused more than a few minutes of head-scratching among new users who switch to Manual exposure mode and find themselves with a completely black (or utterly white) screen. The black screen, especially, may fool you into thinking your camera has malfunctioned.

d8 Framing Grid Display

Options: On, Off (default)
My preference: Off

The Z5 can display a grid of lines overlaid on the viewfinder, offering some help when you want to align vertical or horizontal lines, particularly for architectural or scenic photography. Note that the intersections of these lines do *not* follow the Rule of Thirds convention, and so are less useful for composition, assuming you want to follow the Rule of Thirds guideline in the first place. If you happen to subscribe to the Rule of Quarters, you're all set. Your options for this grid display are On and Off (the default).

d9 Peaking Highlights

Options: Peaking Level: Off (default), Low, Standard, High; Peaking Highlight Color: Red (default), Yellow, Blue, White
My preference: N/A

This entry is the first on the last page of the Shooting/Display menu (see Figure 12.10). Focus peaking is a focusing aid available to provide colored highlights around the edges of objects as they come into sharp focus. You can choose from among red, yellow, blue, or white. If your subject has a predominant color, you should select a peaking color that contrasts. For example, you might want to use yellow as your peaking tone when photographing red roses. You can change the Peak Level (sensitivity) to low, standard, or high. I explained how to use focus peaking and showed you what it looks like in action in Chapter 5.

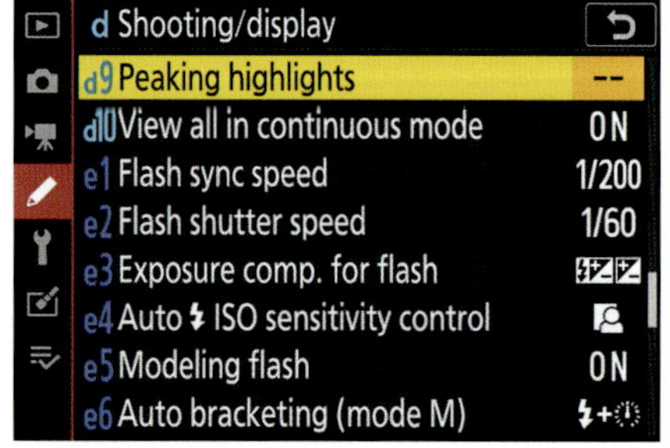

Figure 12.10 Last page of the Shooting/Display menu.

d10 View All in Continuous Mode

Options: On (default), Off

My preference: On

This setting lets you specify whether full-frame playback is used during burst shooting live view when shooting with Continuous Low, Continuous High, and Quiet Continuous. If you select Off, the monitor playback display and the monitor backlight are turned off during continuous exposures.

e. Bracketing/Flash

There are lots of useful settings in this submenu (see Figure 12.11) that deal with bracketing and electronic flash (hence the cleverly concocted name). I provided a thorough description of using bracketing in Chapter 4, and a complete rundown of flash options in Chapters 9 and 10. In this section, I'll offer a recap of the settings at your disposal.

e1 Flash Sync Speed

Options: 1/200 s (Auto FP), 1/200 s–1/60 s (default 1/200th s)

My preference: 1/200 s (Auto FP)

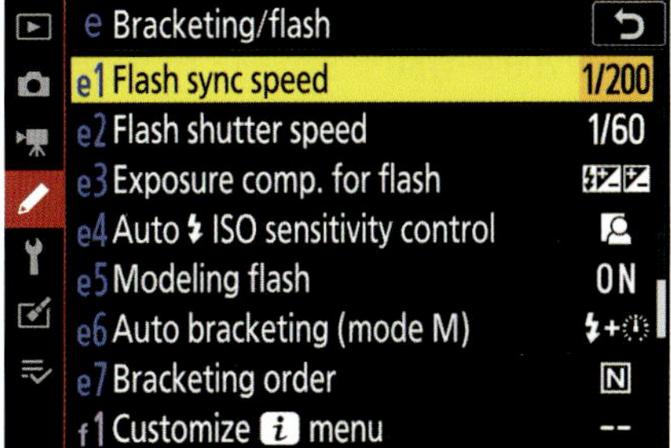

Figure 12.11 Bracketing and flash options are available in this menu.

As you learned in Chapter 9, the focal plane shutter in the Nikon Z5 must be fully open when the external flash fires; otherwise, you'll image one edge or the other of the vertically traveling shutter curtain in your photo. Ordinarily, the fastest shutter speed during which the shutter is completely open for an instant is 1/200th second. However, there are exceptions when you can use faster shutter speeds with certain flash units (such as the Nikon SB-5000, SB-910, SB-700, and SB-R200) for automatic FP (focal plane) synchronization. This is called *high-speed sync* (usually abbreviated HSS). The HSS feature allows you to use higher shutter speeds to supply fill flash, say, outdoors, where a shutter speed of 1/500th second might be needed to enable a wider aperture for reduced depth-of-field.

There are also situations in which you might want to set flash sync speed to *less* than 1/200th second, say, because you *want* ambient light to produce secondary ghost images in your frame. (I'll describe all these sync issues in Chapter 9.)

LOCKING FLASH SYNC

If you want to lock the shutter speed at the maximum sync speed you've specified, rotate the command dial to choose the *xnnn* setting located after the 30 s, Bulb, and Time speeds. If you've chosen 1/200 (Auto FP), that setting will display *x200*; If you've used the 1/200 s–1/60 s option, the lock speed, the setting will be locked at *x200* to *x60*.

To address your choice of flash sync speeds, you can choose from the following settings:

- **1/200 s (Auto FP).** At this setting, you may use individual shutter speeds up to 1/200th second with any Nikon flash. However, you can also use *faster* shutter speeds with flash units compatible with high-speed sync (such as those mentioned above). If one of those units is mounted and powered up:
    - **P or A mode:** The camera selects the shutter speed in both Program and Aperture-priority modes. With an HSS-compatible flash attached, the camera is free to select a shutter speed as fast as 1/8000th second.
    - **S or M mode:** In these modes, *you* select the shutter speed, and you can select one as fast as 1/8000th second in high-speed sync mode.
- **1/200 s–1/60 s.** You can specify a shutter speed from 1/200th second to 1/60th second to be used as the synchronization speed for flash units.

e2 Flash Shutter Speed

Options: 1/60th second (default) to 30 seconds

My preference: 1/60th second

This setting determines the *slowest* shutter speed that is available for electronic flash synchronization in the PASM exposure modes when you're not using a "slow sync" mode (described in Chapter 9). As you may know, when you're using flash, the flash itself typically provides virtually all of the illumination that makes the main exposure, and the shutter speed determines how much, if any, of the ambient light contributes to that second, non-flash exposure. Indeed, if the camera or subject is moving, you can end up with two distinct exposures in the same frame: the sharply defined flash exposure and a second, blurry "ghost" picture created by the ambient light.

If you *don't* want that second exposure, you should use the highest shutter speed that will synchronize with your flash. This setting prevents Program or Aperture-priority modes (which both select the shutter speed for you) from inadvertently selecting a "too slow" shutter speed. You can select a value from 30 s to 1/60 s, and the Z5 will *avoid* using speeds slower than the one you specify with electronic flash (unless you've selected slow sync, slow rear-curtain sync, or red-eye reduction with slow sync, as described in Chapter 9). The "slow-sync" modes do permit the ambient light to contribute to the exposure (say, to allow the background to register in night shots, or to use the ghost image as a special effect). For brighter backgrounds, you'll need to put the camera on a tripod or other support to avoid the blurry ghosts that can occur from camera shake, even if the subject is stationary.

If you are able to hold the Z5 steady, a value of 1/30 s is a good compromise; if you have shaky hands, use 1/60 s. Those with extraordinarily solid grips, a tripod, or a lens with vibration reduction can try the 1/15 s setting (or slower when using a tripod). Remember that this setting only determines the *slowest* shutter speed that will be chosen by the camera, not the default shutter speed.

e3 Exposure Compensation for Flash

Options: Entire Frame (default), Background Only

My preference: Background Only

Use this to specify how the camera modifies the flash level when you apply exposure compensation. Keep in mind that your Z5 has separate ambient light exposure compensation and flash exposure compensation settings. They enable you to adjust one or the other, or both if you are using flash. If you remember that, you'll know that this setting affects only *exposure compensation* (the ambient kind) when you are also using flash. It determines how ambient exposure compensation is applied when some of the illumination will also come from a flash unit:

- **Entire Frame.** When you apply ambient exposure compensation (press the EV button on top of the camera to the right of the ISO button and rotate the main command dial), both ambient *and* flash exposure compensation are adjusted over the entire frame. That balances the exposure for the two elements. While this works in many situations, you may find that with backgrounds and subject matter that differ widely in brightness, your results may be less than optimum.
- **Background Only.** When this option is selected *only* ambient exposure compensation is changed when you apply it; flash exposure compensation is unaffected. So, exposure compensation is applied only to the background areas of your image, which are typically illuminated by ambient light. Flash exposure compensation is not affected but can be set separately. I prefer to use this setting and control each type of exposure compensation myself.

e4 Auto Flash ISO Sensitivity Control

Options: Subject and Background (default), Subject Only

My preference: Subject and Background

This setting allows you to customize how Auto ISO sensitivity control makes its adjustments. If you choose Subject and Background, the Z5's exposure meters will take into account both your subject matter and the background and set the flash output for a level that is more likely to balance both. If you find a disparity between foreground and subject exposures, you can use Custom Setting e3 (above), select Background Only, and tweak exposure for foreground and background separately.

e5 Modeling Flash

Options: On (default), Off

My preference: On

The Nikon Z5, and certain compatible external flash units (like the SB-5000, SB-700, and SB-910/SB-900) have the capability of simulating a modeling lamp, which gives you the limited capability of previewing how your flash illumination is going to look in the finished photo. The modeling flash is not a perfect substitute for a real incandescent or fluorescent modeling lamp, but it does help you see how your subject is illuminated and spot any potential problems with shadows.

When this feature is activated, pressing the button you have defined as the Preview (depth-of-field) button on the Z5 briefly triggers the modeling flash for your preview. (You can define a Preview button using Custom Setting f2: Custom Controls, as described later in this chapter. The Z5, by default, does not have a depth-of-field preview control.)

Selecting Off disables the feature. You'll generally want to leave it On, except when you anticipate using the depth-of-field preview button for depth-of-field purposes (imagine that) and do *not* want the modeling flash to fire when the flash unit is charged and ready. Some external flash units, such as the SB-5000 and SB-910, have their own modeling flash buttons.

e6 Auto Bracketing (Mode M)

Options: Flash/Speed (default), Flash/Speed/Aperture, Flash/Aperture, Flash Only

My preference: Flash/speed

When you are using Manual exposure mode, the Z5 allows you to specify what exposure parameters—flash output, shutter speed, and aperture—are used to create the bracketed images. Here are your options and reasons to select each of them. Remember that these apply only when you are bracketing in Manual exposure mode.

- **Flash/Speed.** If you've selected AE Only in Auto Bracketing Set in the Photo Shooting menu, the camera will adjust only the shutter speed during bracketed exposures. If you selected AE & Flash, instead, the camera will also adjust the flash output level when flash is used. The aperture will remain the same, making this a good choice for HDR photos or other subjects where you want to keep the same amount of depth-of-field in successive shots.

- **Flash/Speed/Aperture.** The camera can use both shutter speed and aperture when AE Only is selected, plus flash output level if AE & Flash was selected and flash is used. This gives the Z5 the maximum amount of flexibility in choosing exposure parameter combinations. That's especially helpful when shooting bracket sequences of 7 or 9 shots (and/or with large increments, say, 3 stops, between shots). That's because such extreme adjustments in exposure may be difficult to achieve with only one or two parameters available—particularly when ambient light only is being bracketed. (The flash is able to adjust its output over a very wide range.)

- **Flash/Aperture.** The Z5 varies aperture only if AE Only is specified, or aperture and flash output if AE & Flash is selected in the Photo Shooting menu. Your selected shutter speed remains the same, so you would want to use this if retaining the same shutter speed is important (say, when shooting sports).

- **Flash Only.** The camera varies the flash output only when AE & Flash is active. No ambient light bracketing is done.

e7 Bracketing Order

Options: MTR > Under > Over (default), Under > MTR > Over

My preference: Under > MTR > Over, which orders frames by increasing exposure

Use this setting to define the sequence in which bracketing is carried out. Your choices are the default: MTR > Under > Over (metered exposure, followed by the version receiving less exposure, and finishing with the picture receiving the most exposure) and Under > MTR > Over, which orders the exposures from least exposed to most exposed (for both ambient and flash exposures). The same order is applied to white balance bracketing, too, but the values are Normal > More Yellow > More Blue and More Yellow > Normal > More Blue. (Nikon actually calls "yellow" by the term "amber," but I've found "yellow" easier to understand.)

This order works well if you are shooting at least three images in your sequence. If you set bracketing to just two exposures, the specified order is used, but one of the three is omitted. You'll find lots more about bracketing in Chapter 4. When doing ADL bracketing with the Z5, this setting has no effect.

f. Controls

You can modify the way various control buttons and dials perform when shooting still photos by using the options in this submenu. You can even modify the twelve adjustments that appear in the *i* menu. The seven Controls entries are shown in Figure 12.12. Note that you can also make some control adjustments for Movie mode, and I'll cover those in the section that follows this one.

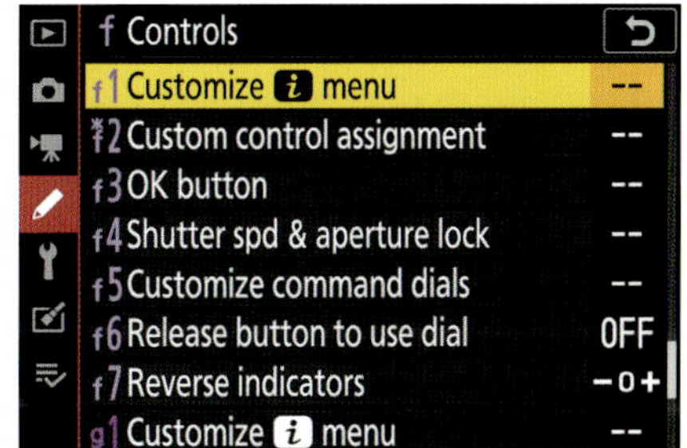

Figure 12.12 Modify the behavior of the Z5's controls with these menu options.

f1 Customize *i* Menu

Options: Allows defining functions available from the *i* menu. There are different functions that you can use to replace or add to those provided in the default version of the *i* menu.

My preference: Varies

If you've used previous Nikon cameras, you've probably noticed that the Z5 has fewer dedicated buttons than some of its stablemates. The D850, for example, has dedicated buttons for flash, image size/quality, metering mode, depth-of-field preview, bracketing, white balance, and focus modes, plus Help, Protect, and Picture Control functions. While two of these (white balance and focus modes) are assigned to the Z5's pair of function buttons (Fn1 and Fn2), others are available only from the traditional menus or the *i* menu.

The bad news is that the 12 default entries on the *i* menu may not be ones you use often. I don't use the Z5's wireless functions or Card Info feature very often. The rest of the time, those two functions are a waste of *i* menu real estate. The good news is that if you would rather have some other tools available in the *i* menu, there's a good chance you can replace your own "useless" *i* menu entries with those that are more to your liking. Your choices follow.

These 12 entries occupy the *i* menu by default. You can choose to keep these, move them, or replace them with other functions:

- Set Picture Control
- White Balance
- Image Quality
- Image Size
- Flash Mode
- Metering
- Wi-Fi Connection
- View Memory Card Info
- Release Mode
- Vibration Reduction
- AF-Area Mode
- Focus Mode

These definable functions are already available using other direct controls on the camera. Note that White Balance, Focus Mode, and AF-Area mode buttons duplicate functions already on the default *i* menu roster. That means you can replace a redundant *i* menu or dedicated button function with another of your choice.

- White Balance (Fn1)
- AF/MF Focus Mode (Fn2+command dial)
- AF-Area Mode (Fn2+sub-command dial)
- AF-ON (AF-ON button)
- Focus Point Selection (Sub-selector joystick)
- AE/AF Lock (Sub-selector button)

These three functions are available from dedicated buttons on the camera, and need not be assigned to the *i* menu or a different button (unless that's your preference):

- ISO Sensitivity
- Exposure Compensation
- Release Mode

These remaining functions are not by default available in the *i* menu or assigned to dedicated buttons. They are likely to be the best candidates to replace a function you don't use regularly:

- Choose Image Area
- Color Space
- Active D-Lighting
- Long Exposure NR
- High ISO NR
- Flash Compensation
- Auto Bracketing
- Multiple Exposure
- HDR
- Silent Photography
- Custom Control Assignment
- Exposure Delay Mode
- Electronic Front-Curtain Shutters
- Apply Settings to Live View
- Split-Screen Display Zoom
- Peaking Highlights
- Monitor/Viewfinder Brightness
- Bluetooth Connection

As noted earlier, I don't use the Wi-Fi Connection and Memory Card Info functions very often, so I replaced them with Flash Compensation and Multiple Exposure, respectively. It was easy to do:

1. Choose Custom Setting f1: Customize *i* menu. The two default functions I decided to replace are highlighted by the green box at upper left in Figure 12.13.

2. Highlight the Wi-Fi connection icon in the top row and press OK. From the screen that appears, scroll to Flash Compensation. Press OK to select and confirm. (See Figure 12.13, upper right.)

3. Next, highlight the Active D-Lighting icon in the bottom row and press OK.

4. Navigate to the Multiple Exposure function shown in Figure 12.13, lower left, and press OK.

5. You'll be returned to the Customize *i* menu screen, with your changes made in the menu, as shown in Figure 12.13, lower right. Note that I placed the Flash Compensation function right next to the default Flash function.

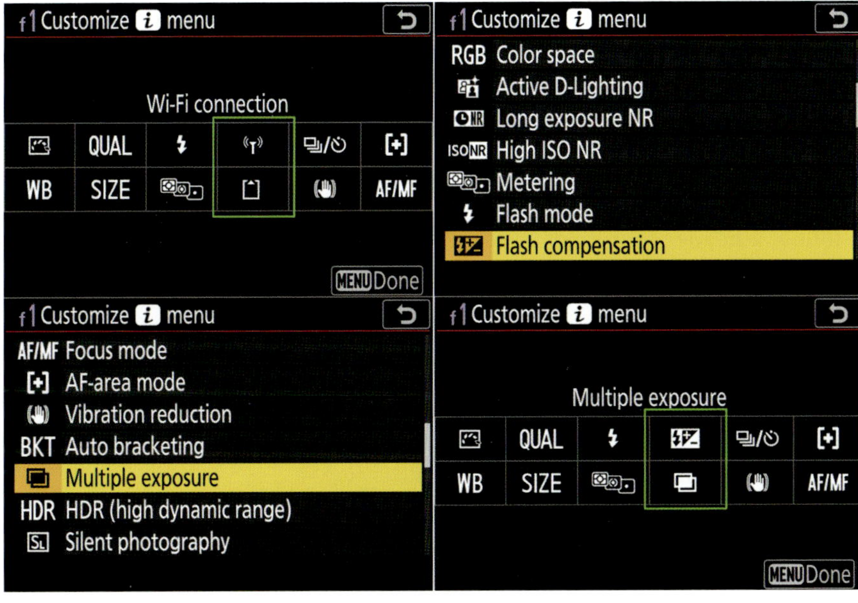

Figure 12.13 Two replaceable functions (upper left); adding Flash Compensation and Multiple Exposure (upper right and lower left); two new functions in place (lower right).

f2 Custom Controls

Options: Allows defining functions for nine separate controls

My preference: Varies

The programmable controls are Fn1, Fn2, AF-ON, Sub-selector joystick, Center button of sub-selector, Movie Record, Lens control ring, and two Lens Fn buttons. The Lens Fn1 and Fn2 buttons are found only on certain Nikon lenses, generally high-end longer lenses, including the 400, 500, 600, and 800mm G and E lenses, the 200-400mm f/4G VR II, 200mm f/2G, and 300mm f/2.8G VR II.

A total of 44 *different* actions can be programmed (plus None—no action), augmenting or *replacing* the button's original function. Always consider the side-effects of choosing your own non-standard control configuration. Your custom settings can be a boon, or if you don't remember the assignments

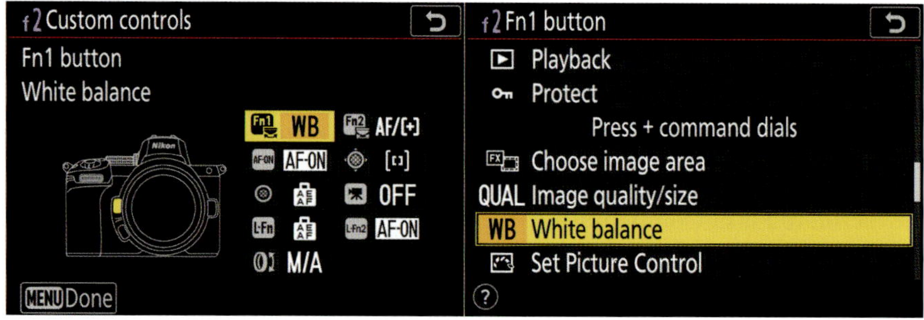

Figure 12.14 Highlight a control (left) and press OK to summon a list of possible definitions (right).

you've made as you work, a hindrance. To apply a definition, highlight the button name on the screen shown at left in Figure 12.14.

Then scroll through the list of available options, as shown at right in the figure. Some choices in the scrolling list are behaviors that require nothing more than a button press to activate. There are 22 of those in all. Nikon inserts a "Press" header at the start of the listing for those behaviors (AF-ON through Protect). For example, if a button is defined as Preview or Matrix Metering, you simply press and hold the button to activate the depth-of-field preview, or to switch from your current mode to Matrix Metering. When you release the defined button, the preview stops or the camera returns to your previous metering mode.

The other behaviors follow a header that reads "Press+ Command Dials." Those options include those listed from "Choose Image Area" to "Choose Non-CPU Lens Number." Behaviors that do use the command dials produce a screen that displays the options for that behavior, plus an icon prompt representing a main or sub-command dial (or both), as seen in Figure 12.15. In that example, you'd press and hold the defined button and rotate the main command dial to change the flash sync mode, and the sub-command dial to add/subtract flash exposure compensation.

When you've selected the behavior you want, press the OK button to confirm and return to the Custom Control Assignment menu. The possible behaviors make up a complex matrix, so I'm going to present your choices in Table 12.8.

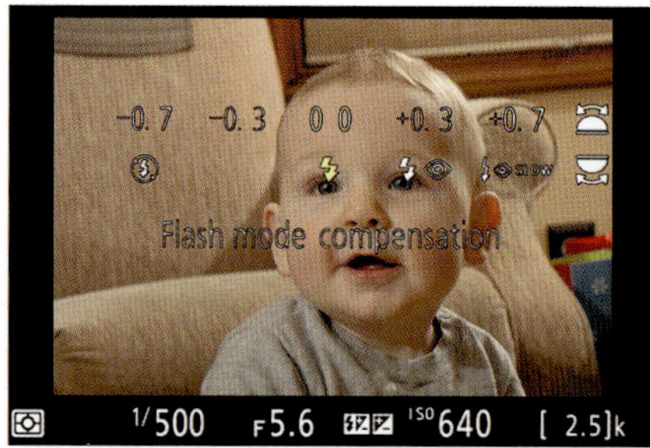

Figure 12.15 Some behaviors let you use the command dials for pairs of settings, such as flash mode and flash compensation.

TABLE 12.8 Buttons and Functions

BUTTONS	FN1	FN2	AF-ON	SUB-SELECTOR	SUB-SELECTOR CENTER	MOVIE RECORD	LENS FN	LENS FN2	LENS CONTROL RING
Default Value	White balance	Focus mode/AF-area mode	AF-ON	Focus point selection	AE/AF lock	None	AE/AF lock	AF-ON	Varies with lens
FUNCTIONS									
Reset center focus point			●		●				
AF-ON	●	●	●		●		●	●	
AF lock only	●	●	●		●		●	●	
AE lock (Hold)	●	●	●		●	●	●	●	
AE lock (Reset on release)	●	●	●		●	●	●	●	
AE lock only	●	●	●		●	●	●	●	
AE/AF lock	●	●	●		●	●	●	●	
Flash value lock	●	●			●	●	●	●	
Flash disable/enable	●	●			●	●	●	●	
Depth-of-field preview	●	●			●	●	●	●	
Matrix metering	●	●			●	●	●	●	
Center-weighted metering	●	●			●	●	●	●	
Spot metering	●	●			●		●	●	
Highlight-weighted metering	●	●			●		●	●	
Bracketing burst	●	●			●		●	●	
Sync. release selection	●	●			●	●	●	●	
Add NEF (RAW)	●	●			●	●	●	●	
Framing grid display	●	●			●	●	●	●	
Zoom on/off	●	●	●			●	●	●	
MY MENU	●	●				●	●	●	
Access top item in My Menu	●	●				●	●		
Playback	●	●				●	●		
Protect	●	●				●	●		
Choose image area	●	●			●	●	●		
Image quality/size	●	●				●			
White balance	●	●				●			
Set Picture Control	●	●				●			
Active D-Lighting	●	●				●			
Metering	●	●				●			
Flash mode/Compensation	●	●				●			
Focus/mode/AF-area mode	●	●				●			
Auto bracketing	●	●				●			

TABLE 12.8 Buttons and Functions *(continued)*

BUTTONS	FN1	FN2	AF-ON	SUB-SELECTOR	SUB-SELECTOR CENTER	MOVIE RECORD	LENS FN	LENS FN2	LENS CONTROL RING
Multiple exposure	■	■				■			
High Dynamic Range	■	■				■			
Exposure delay mode	■	■				■			
Shutter spd & aperture lock	■	■				■			
Peaking highlights	■	■							
Rating	■	■							
Choose non-CPU lens number	■				■	■			
Same as multi selector				■					
Focus point selection				■					
Focus (Manual/Auto)									■
Aperture									■
Exposure compensation									■
None	■	■	■		■	■	■	■	■

Assignment: Convenience

The definitions you assign to your controls are highly personal and should be implemented to reflect the features you will most need to have available at the press of a button or spin of a dial. Remember that once you re-assign a control from its default value, you must remember it in order to avoid becoming hopelessly confused. You'll no longer be able to loan your camera to another Z5 owner without risking confusing *them* as well.

But wait, there's more! The User Settings, represented by the U1, U2, and U3 positions on the mode dial, can each be populated with *their own* separate control settings. So, your Fn1 button might summon the White Balance menu when using U2, but Image Size when using U3 (if you so choose to set up the camera that way). While the Z5 offers, in effect, the ultimate in flexibility in assigning your controls, you may find that having separate control behaviors for, say, sports, landscapes, and movie shooting may not be manageable.

Even so, this section will offer some suggestions on assignments that have been useful to me, and which you might consider for your own control layout.

- **Quickly switch to an alternate focus mode or AF-area mode.** You might use Auto-area AF most of the time to let the Z5 select a focus point for you, yet quickly switch to Single Point mode while you hold down the defined button. You can then move the focus point around within the frame with the directional controls. The Focus mode/AF-area mode behavior allows you to press a defined button and then rotate the main dial to choose a focus mode with the main command dial, and the AF-area mode with the sub-command dial.

- **Switch metering modes.** If you use Matrix metering mode most of the time and want to be able to use Spot metering when appropriate, just assign a button to that function.
- **Disable/enable flash.** You can leave your external flash attached and powered up yet disable it quickly at the press of a defined button. That would allow you to intermingle photos taken by ambient light, and those in which flash illumination is added, on the fly.
- **Bracketing burst.** This option adds some versatility to exposure, flash, or ADL bracketing by telling the Z5 to take all the exposures in a bracketed set in one burst. You must have activated a bracketing program, as described in Chapter 4. Perhaps you've been shooting bracketed sequences in Single-shot mode (rather than continuous mode) and decide you want to capture an entire set at once. Define a key for the Bracketing Burst function and hold it down. Then, each time you press the shutter release an entire burst will be captured. If the release mode has already been set for a continuous mode or white balance bracketing has been selected, the Z5 will capture all the exposures in the set while the shutter release is held down.
- **Add a RAW image while shooting only JPEGs.** When the +RAW behavior is specified, pressing the defined key tells the Z5 to shoot an additional RAW image even if the current Image Quality setting is JPEG (only) while the button is held down. That will allow you to capture a NEF image if you think you might need one later, say, to adjust color balance for a picture taken under tricky illumination.
- **Activate the framing grid.** Even if you don't use the alignment grid often, you can define a key to produce it at the press of a button.
- **FAQs (Frequently Accessed Quickly).** Have a menu entry you need to access quickly—and often? The Fn2 button can be defined to jump to the top item in your My Menu list (as described in Chapter 13), which can be that most-used entry. Or, you can define the Fn2 button to produce the My Menu list, which you can populate with your own personal most-used items.
- **Choose Image Area.** If you're shooting in FX mode and decide you want to switch to one of the crop modes (perhaps you're shooting sports and need some extra "reach"), a defined button+command dial definition can invoke the image area of your choice. Note that you can enable/disable any of the crop modes (but not FX mode) so that rotating the command dial switches among as many or as few modes as you want. I enable only DX mode when shooting sports, so I can switch quickly from FX to DX and back again.
- **Other frequently used settings.** Other button+command dial definitions can let you switch exposure modes, change white balance, access multiple exposure options, or control HDR settings quickly, too.

f3 OK Button

Options: Shooting mode: RESET/Select Center Focus Point (default), Zoom On/Off, None; Playback mode: Thumbnail On/Off, View Histograms, Zoom On/Off (default), Choose Folder

My preference: Varies

There are two groups of options available here, one for use when the camera is in Shooting mode, and another when you're reviewing images in Playback mode. In Shooting mode:

- **RESET/Select center focus point.** This default setting lets you quickly select the center focus point in the viewfinder simply by pressing the multi selector center button.
- **Zoom on/off.** Use the OK button to zoom in on the area where the current focus point is located. (This would be especially useful for focusing manually.) Press a second time to return to full-frame view. Press the right button to select the zoom ratio, from Low Magnification (50 percent), 1:1 (100 percent), and High Magnification (200 percent).
- **None.** Nothing happens when the OK button is pressed. If you find yourself sloppily pressing the OK button in the heat of the moment while shooting, use this setting to deactivate it and avoid unwanted actions.

In Playback mode:

- **Thumbnail on/off.** This setting alternates between full-frame and thumbnail playback.
- **View histograms.** When selected, a larger histogram is displayed while the OK button is pressed.
- **Zoom on/off.** Use the OK button to toggle between full-frame or thumbnail playback (whichever is active) and playback zoom. You can choose Low Magnification, Medium Magnification, and High Magnification. This is the default behavior.
- **Choose folder.** This mode pops up the folder selection screen. You can highlight a folder and press the OK button again to view the images in that folder.

f4 Shutter Spd & Aperture Lock

Options: Shutter Speed Lock; Aperture Lock (default: Off for both)

My preference: Varies

There are times when you'll want to lock the shutter speed at a particular value when using Shutter-priority or Manual exposure modes and times when you want to lock down a particular f/stop when using Aperture-priority or Manual exposure modes. Use this entry to lock the shutter speed and/or aperture so it can't be changed. I use this most in the studio when I use Manual exposure and studio lights. Once I've set the exposure for a series of shots, I lock my Shutter Speed/Aperture Lock button and freeze the settings, so I don't have to worry about accidentally rotating a command dial.

If you think accessing this menu entry to lock shutter speed or aperture is needlessly complex, you're right. It makes a lot more sense to define a physical button to provide this function, as described earlier under f2: Custom Controls. I assigned the function to the Fn1 button. To lock the shutter speed and or aperture, I first set either or both to the value I want. Then, I press the Fn1 button and rotate the main command dial to lock/unlock shutter speed and the sub-command dial to lock/unlock aperture. An L symbol appears next to the locked setting on the top control panel and viewfinder/ LCD monitor displays.

Note that when the camera is set to Shutter-priority, you are able to enable/disable only the Shutter Speed Lock function. When set to Aperture-priority, only Aperture Lock is accessible. In Manual exposure mode, you can adjust either one, and in Program mode, neither can be locked.

f5 Customize Command Dials

Options: For Main and Sub-Command Dials: Reverse Rotation Direction, Change Main/Sub, Menus and Playback, Sub-dial Frame Advance

My preference: Varies

This menu entry can change the behavior of the command dials. Use the available tweaks to change the behavior of the dials to better suit your preferences, or if you're coming to the Nikon world from another vendor's product that uses a different operational scheme. Keep in mind that redefining basic controls in this way can prove confusing if someone other than yourself uses your camera, or if you find yourself working with other Nikon cameras that have retained the normal command dial behavior. The reason that the dials are set for their default directions is to match the direction of rotation of the aperture ring/sub-command dial (when changing the aperture). Turning any of the three to the left decreases exposure, while rotating to the right increases exposure. Your options include:

- **Reverse rotation direction.** This option allows you to reverse the rotation direction for Exposure Compensation and Shutter Speed/Aperture selection. You can reverse the direction for either or both. By default, rotating the main command dial counterclockwise causes shutter speeds to become shorter in Manual and Shutter-priority modes; rotating the sub-command dial counterclockwise selects larger f/stops. If you want to reverse the directional orientation of the dials (so you'll need to rotate the main command dial clockwise to specify shorter shutter speeds, etc.), put a checkmark in the box next to Shutter Speed/Aperture. To reverse direction for Exposure Compensation, put a checkmark in that box. Uncheck the boxes to return to the original Z5 scheme of things.
- **Change main/sub.** This option doesn't reverse directions: it swaps the functions of the two dials. You can swap the behaviors of the dials for Exposure Setting, Autofocus Setting, or both.
  - **Exposure setting.** Choose On, and the main dial will set the aperture in Manual and Aperture-priority modes, and the sub-command dial will adjust the shutter speed in Manual and Shutter-priority modes. (The opposite of the default assignments for these dials.) You can also choose ON (Mode A) and the main command dial will be used to set aperture in Aperture-priority mode *only*. In Manual exposure mode, main command and sub-command dials keep their default shutter speed/aperture assignments (respectively).
  - **Autofocus setting.** This option works in conjunction with any button you've assigned the Focus mode/AF-area mode function using Custom Setting f2. If you specify On, the focus mode can be selected with the sub-command dial and AF-area mode with the main command dial.

- **Menus and playback.** You can change the orientation of the command dials when navigating menus and playback options, too. By default, the main command dial is used to select an image during full-frame playback; move the cursor left or right during thumbnail viewing, and move the menu highlighting up or down. The sub-command dial is used to display additional photo information in full-frame playback, to move the cursor up and down, and to move back and forth between menus and submenus. (Note that you can also use the multi selector directional buttons for these functions.) When set to On or On (Image Review Excluded), the functions assigned to the dials are reversed.

- **Sub-dial frame advance.** If you've turned the Menus and Playback option to On, you can set the sub-command dial so that while reviewing images in full-frame mode, the Z5 skips ahead either 10 or 50 frames, or allows you to select a folder.

f6 Release Button to Use Dial

Options: Yes, No (default)

My preference: Yes

Normally, any button used in conjunction with a command dial, such as the Exposure Compensation or ISO buttons, must be held down while the command dial or sub-command dial is rotated. Choose Yes for this option if you want to be able to press the button and release it, and then rotate the command dial. You can continue to make adjustments until the button is pressed again, the shutter release button is pressed halfway, or the standby timer elapses. This option can also be applied to these functions assigned to buttons using Custom Setting f2 or g2 (Custom Controls):

- Choose Image Area
- Image Quality/Size
- White Balance
- Set Picture Control
- Active D-Lighting
- Metering
- Flash mode/Compensation
- Focus mode/AF-area mode

- Auto Bracketing
- Multiple Exposure
- HDR (High Dynamic Range)
- Exposure Delay Mode
- Shutter Spd & Aperture Lock
- Peaking Highlights
- Choose non-CPU Lens Number
- Microphone Sensitivity

Chose No to return to the Z5's default behavior, which requires that the button be held down while the adjustment is made. I like to use the Yes option and avoid having to remember to hold down a button while I make my changes.

f7 Reverse Indicators

Options: Direction of exposure indicators: -0+ (default), +0-

My preference: -0+

You can change the exposure indicators on the display so that the negative values are shown at the left (-0+) and positive values to the right, or the reverse (+0-). You might want to reverse indicators to match a "foreign" camera system you're coming to the Nikon world from, or, if you use the aperture ring on lenses that have them, to match what happens when the ring is rotated. (Older Nikon lenses have the smallest aperture on the ring to the left, and the largest to the right, so rotating the aperture ring to the right increases exposure; to the left decreases exposure.) The current directional orientation is relatively new, so you might also prefer to reverse the indicators if you're a veteran user of older cameras (Nikon D3s and before) and are disoriented by the change. My oldest camera still in frequent use is a Nikon D3200, and it uses the current scheme, so I've gone with the flow.

g. Movie

This submenu has only six settings, shown in Figure 12.16. Here you can set separately for movie shooting some of the button assignments available for still shooting. You'll find more about movie shooting in Chapters 14 and 15.

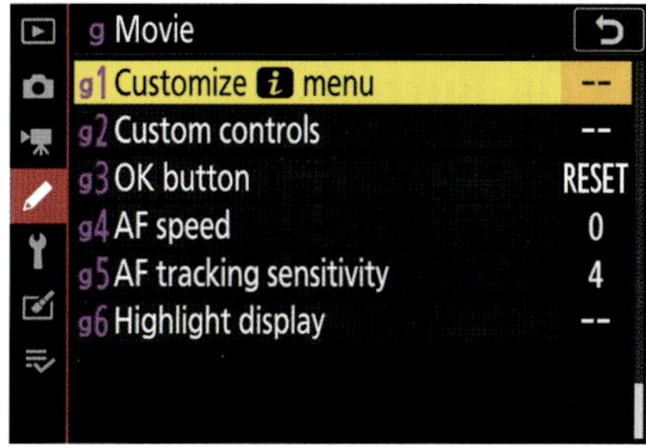

Figure 12.16 The Movie Shooting menu.

g1 Customize *i* Menu

Options: Allows defining functions available from the *i* menu. There are 22 different functions that you can use to replace or add to those provided in the default version of the *i* menu that's active in Movie mode.

My preference: Varies

When in Movie mode, the *i* button summons its own version of the *i* menu, with a slightly different collection of settings. The defaults are Set Picture Control, White Balance, Frame Size and Rate/Image Quality, Microphone Sensitivity, Choose Image Area, Metering, Wi-Fi Connection, Destination, Electronic VR, Vibration Reduction, AF-area mode, and Focus Mode. Your choices include the following (options that already are assigned to buttons are noted):

- Choose Image Area
- Frame Size and Rate/Image Quality
- Exposure Compensation (EV button)
- ISO Sensitivity (ISO button)
- White Balance (Fn1)
- Set Picture Control
- Active D-Lighting
- Metering Mode
- AF/MF Focus Mode (Fn2+command dial)
- AF-Area Mode (Fn2+sub-command dial)
- Vibration Reduction
- Electronic VR
- Microphone Sensitivity
- Attenuator
- Frequency Response
- Wind Noise Reduction
- Headphone Volume
- Peaking Highlights
- Highlight Display
- Monitor/Viewfinder Brightness
- Bluetooth Connection
- Wi-Fi Connection

g2 Custom Controls

Options: Definitions for Fn1, Fn2, AF-ON, Sub-selector Button, Shutter Release Button, Lens Control Ring

My preference: N/A

You can define the action that any of these controls perform when pressed in Movie mode. Keep in mind that these settings are used only when capturing video and that the buttons not listed retain their still photography functions; in Live View, the behaviors you've defined for still photography all apply (see Table 12.9).

g3 OK Button

Options: Allows defining functions for Select Center Focus Point (default), Zoom On/Off, Record Movies, or None

My preference: Varies

In Movie mode you can redefine the OK button to Select Center Focus Point, Zoom On/Off, or Record Movies, or None.

g4 AF Speed

Options: Autofocusing speed (+/−5), When to Apply: Always, Only While Recording

My preference: Varies

The speed with which the Z5 autofocuses takes on a different significance when you're shooting movies, because any AF changes are recorded within the movie itself. You may want focus to change slowly as a scene unfolds and people or objects move within the frame, or the frame itself is recomposed. Or, during action sequences, you might prefer to have AF keep pace with subject and camera changes and focus rapidly. This entry lets you speed up or slow down focus speed in Movie mode, using a slider moved via the touch screen or directional buttons. The When to Apply option can be set to Always (in which case the camera's autofocus will refocus constantly at the speed you select) or Only While Recording (so the focus speed is changed only when you're actually capturing video). When using AF-F (full-time autofocus) you might prefer normal focusing speed (which is equivalent to +5—as fast as possible) as you compose your shot, and then have the camera switch automatically to a preferred slower speed once you start recording. (See Figure 12.17.)

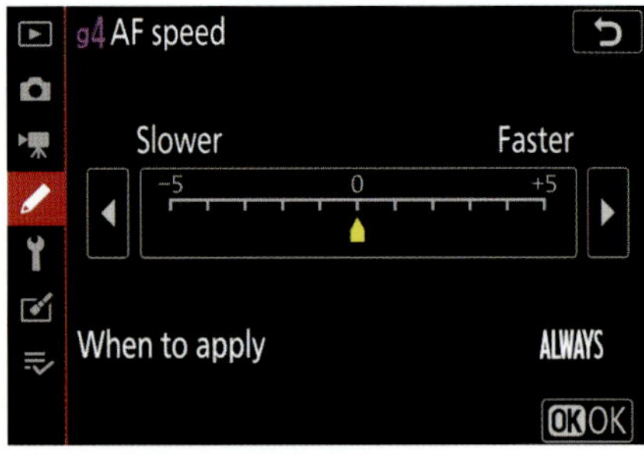

Figure 12.17 Setting AF Speed.

TABLE 12.9 Movie Functions

BUTTONS	FN1	FN2	AF-ON	SUB-SELECTOR BUTTON	SHUTTER RELEASE	LENS CONTROL RING
Default Value	White Balance	Focus/AF-area modes	AF-ON	AE/AF Lock	Take photos	Focus (Manual/Automatic)
FUNCTIONS						
Power aperture (open)	✓					
Power aperture (close)		✓				
Exposure compensation +	✓					
Exposure compensation -		✓				
Framing grid display	✓	✓		✓		
Protect	✓	✓				
Select Center Focus Point			✓	✓		
AF-ON			✓			
AF lock only			✓	✓		
AE lock (hold)			✓	✓		
AE lock only			✓	✓		
AE/AF lock			✓	✓		
Zoom on/off			✓			
Take photos					✓	
Record movies			✓	✓	✓	
Choose image area	✓	✓		✓		
White Balance	✓	✓				
Set Picture Control	✓	✓				
Active D-Lighting	✓	✓				
Metering Mode	✓	✓				
Focus Mode/AF-area Mode	✓	✓				
Microphone sensitivity	✓	✓				
Peaking highlights	✓	✓				
Rating	✓	✓				
Focus (Manual/Autofocus)						✓
Power aperture						✓
Exposure compensation						✓
None	✓	✓	✓	✓		✓

g5 AF Tracking Sensitivity

Options: 7 (low) to 1 (high)

My preference: Varies

This is roughly the movie equivalent of Custom Setting a3: Focus Tracking with Lock-on for still photography. It specifies how quickly the Z5's AF system responds when the subject either exits the frame or something else intervenes—the referee at a football game is the classic example.

A setting of 7 (Low) causes the Z5 to ignore the intervening subject matter for a significant period of time. Use this setting when shooting subjects, such as sports, in which focus interruptions are likely to be frequent and significant. You can also choose a setting of 1 (High) which tells the Z5 to wait only a moment before refocusing. The middle value, 4, the default, offers an intermediate delay before the camera refocuses on the new subject.

g6 Highlight Display

Options: Display Pattern: Pattern 1 (forward diagonal lines), Pattern 2 (back-leaning diagonal lines), Off (default); Highlight Display Threshold: 255, 248 (default), 235, 224, 213, 202, 191, 180

My preference: 235

Video has its own version of the still photography's Highlights display ("blinkies"), commonly known as Zebra display, because it uses contrasting stripes to represent blown highlights. It warns you when the brightest areas of your image may be overexposed when capturing video—but does so *before* you begin capture. Instead of solid flashing indicators, the camera displays one of two striped "zebra" patterns in the affected areas. The zebra stripes jump out at you and make it easy to identify exactly which highlights may be overexposed. You can then adjust exposure or lighting to bring the highlights under control. You can assign Highlight Display to one of the *i* menu spots or a defined key using Custom Settings g1 or g2, respectively.

This menu entry allows you to specify how bright a highlight must be to trigger the zebra effect, using one of eight different brightness levels from 255 (100% white) to 180 (a relatively light gray). Your choice will depend on how important highlights are.

So, exactly how bright *is* too bright? A value of 255 indicates pure white, so any Zebra pattern visible when using this setting indicates that your image is extremely overexposed. Any details in the highlights are gone and cannot be retrieved. Settings from 213 to 235 can be used to make sure facial tones are not overexposed. As a general rule of thumb, Caucasian skin generally falls in the 235 range, with darker skin tones registering as low as 213, and very fair skin or lighter areas of your subject edging closer to 248. Once you've decided the approximate range of tones that you want to make sure do *not* blow out, you can set the camera's Zebra pattern sensitivity appropriately and receive the flashing striped warning on the LCD of your camera. (See Figure 12.18.) The pattern does not appear in your final image, of course—it's just an aid to keep you from blowing it, so to speak.

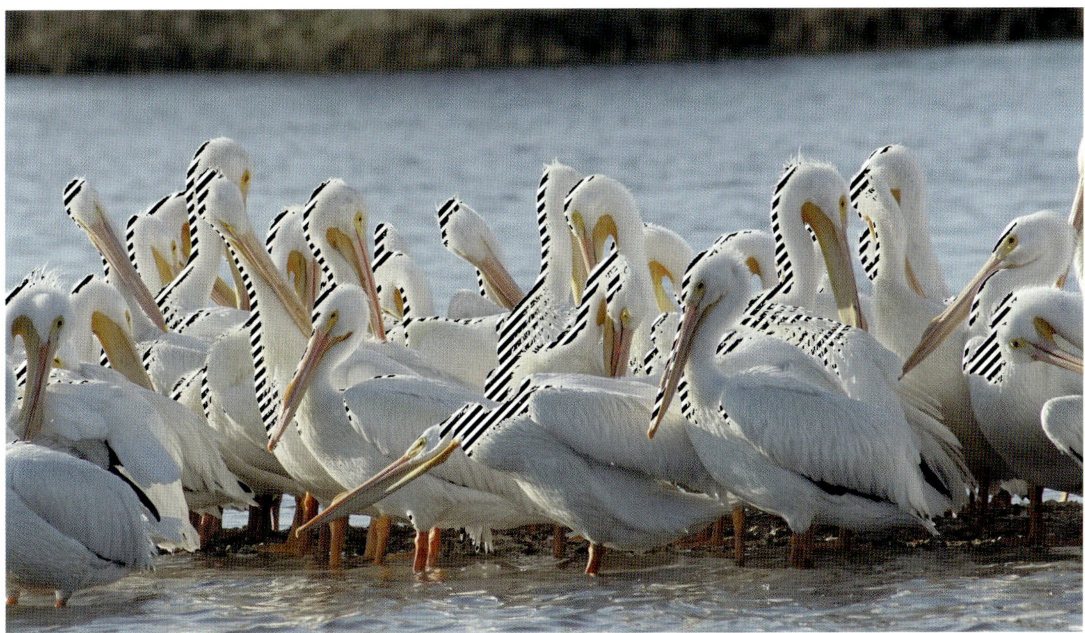

Figure 12.18 The flashing stripes show an area is overexposed.

Zebra patterns are a much more useful tool than "blinkies," because you are given an alert *before* you take the picture and can actually specify exactly how bright *too bright* is. The feature is not new: it has long been used in video equipment, dating back before the digital age. Veteran videographers will note that Nikon uses a section of the 0–255 brightness value scale, rather than the traditional IRE measure of a video signal level, in which numbers from 70 to 100/100+ are used. The Zebra feature has been a staple of professional video shooting for a long time, as you might guess from the moniker assigned to the unit used to specify brightness: IRE, a measure of video signal level, which stands for *Institute of Radio Engineers.*

The Setup Menu, Retouch Menu, and My Menu

13

We're not done covering the Nikon Z5's options yet. There are three more menus to deal with. These include the Setup menu (which deals with adjustments that are generally outside the actual shooting experience, such as formatting a memory card, adjusting the time, or checking your battery); the Retouch menu (which enables you to fine-tune the appearance of images by trimming, adding filter effects, or removing red-eye); and the My Menu system, which can help you set up a customized menu that contains only the entries you want, or your most recently accessed entries.

Setup Menu Options

There is a long list of entries in the orange-brown coded Setup menu. The first page of entries is shown in Figure 13.1. All the Setup menu options let you make additional adjustments on how your camera *behaves* before or during your shooting session, as differentiated from the Photo Shooting menu, which adjusts how the pictures are actually taken. Your choices include:

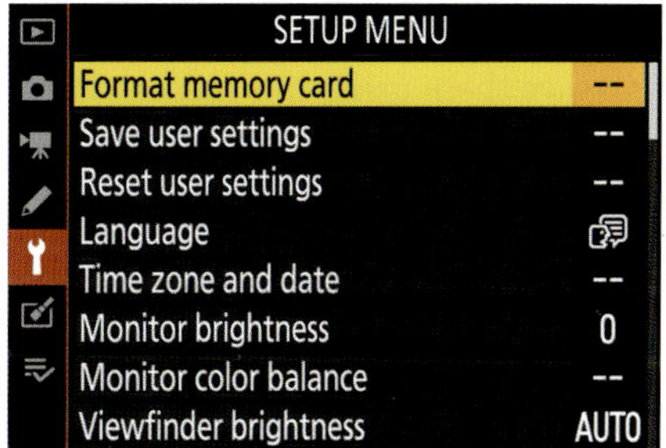

Figure 13.1 The Setup menu allows you to adjust how the Z5 behaves.

- Format Memory Card
- Save User Settings
- Reset User Settings
- Language
- Time Zone and Date
- Monitor Brightness
- Monitor Color Balance
- Viewfinder Brightness
- Viewfinder Color Balance
- Limit Monitor Mode Selection
- Information Display
- AF Fine-Tuning Options
- Non-CPU Lens Data

- Clean Image Sensor
- Image Dust Off Reference Photo
- Pixel Mapping
- Image Comment
- Copyright Information
- Beep Options
- Touch Controls
- HDMI
- Location Data
- Wireless Remote (WR) Options
- Assign remote (WR) Fn Button
- Airplane mode

- Connect to Smart Device
- Connect to PC
- Conformity Marking
- Battery Info
- USB Power Delivery
- Energy Saving
- Slot Empty Release Lock
- Save/Load Menu Settings
- Reset All Settings
- Firmware Version

Format Memory Card

Options: Yes, No

My preference: N/A

I recommend using this menu entry to reformat your memory card after each shoot. Although you can move files from the memory card to your computer, creating a blank card, or delete files using the Playback menu's Delete feature, both of those options can leave behind stray files (such as those that have been marked as Hidden or Protected). Format removes those files completely and beyond retrieval (unless you use a special utility program) and establishes a spanking-new fresh file system on the card. All the file allocation table (FAT or exFAT) pointers (which tell the camera and your computer's operating system where all the images reside) are reset, efficiently pointing where they are supposed to on a blank card.

Save User Settings

Options: Save to U1, Save to U2, Save to U3

My preference: N/A

User settings are groups of camera shooting settings that the Z5 stores in one of three memory "slots," labeled U1, U2, and U3. Set up your camera with the settings you want to be able to recall and save them using this menu entry. Then rotate the mode dial to the U1, U2, or U3 position when you want to access them.

Available settings include:

- Shutter speed in S and M modes
- Aperture in A and M modes
- Flexible Program settings in P mode
- Exposure and flash compensation
- Metering, Autofocus, and AF-area modes

- Flash mode
- Focus point
- Bracketing settings
- Most adjustments in Photo Shooting, Movie Shooting, and Custom Settings menus, except for those listed next

The settings you *cannot* save include:

Photo Shooting Menu:

- Storage Folder
- Choose Image Area
- Manage Picture Control
- Multiple Exposure
- Interval Timer Shooting
- Time-lapse movie
- Focus-shift shooting

Movie Shooting Menu:

- Choose Image Area
- Manage Picture Control

Follow these steps to store your settings:

1. **Choose mode.** Rotate the mode dial to the shooting mode you'd like to store, such as P, A, S, or M.

2. **Adjust settings.** Enter the settings you want to store on the camera, using the camera controls, Photo Shooting, and Custom Settings menus. (Setup menu entries cannot be saved.)

3. **Select Save User Settings.** Navigate to this entry in the Setup menu.

4. **Choose memory register.** Choose Save to U1, Save to U2, or Save to U3 and press the right directional button.

5. **Save.** Choose Save Setting on the confirmation screen or Cancel to abort.

Reset User Settings

Options: Reset U1, Reset U2, Reset U3

My preference: N/A

You can return the settings stored in the U1, U2, or U3 registers to their factory default values using this menu entry. Simply select the entry, choose Reset U1, Reset U2, or Reset U3, and press the right directional button. Press OK to confirm.

Language

Options: In the Americas: English, Spanish, French, Portuguese

My preference: English, of course, but steadily improving in Spanish

Nikon's thrown us a curveball in the language option department. Instead of the couple dozen languages offered in most other Nikon cameras, Z5 bodies sold in North and South America offer only the official languages on those continents. The change was either done "for user convenience" (which is rarely true) or to prevent gray market imports from one area of the world to another.

If you'd like to see your menus and prompts in German, Japanese, or some other language, you'll need to buy a camera built for Europe or Asia, respectively. One potential (but theoretical) fix might be to install the firmware updates available from Nikon websites in, say, Germany or Japan, but it would be wise to check with Nikon first to make sure that's even possible and/or won't munge your camera.

This change won't impact a large number of us, but for expats who want to use their native tongue, it's an inconvenience, at best.

Time Zone and Date

Options: Time Zone, Date and Time, Date Format, Daylight Saving Time (default: Off)
My preference: N/A

Use this menu entry to adjust the Z5's internal clock. Your options include:

- **Time zone.** A small map will pop up on the setting screen and you can choose your local time zone. I sometimes forget to change the time zone when I travel (especially when going to Europe), so my pictures are all time-stamped incorrectly. I like to use the time stamp to recall exactly when a photo was taken, so keeping this setting correct is important.
- **Date and time.** Use this setting to enter the exact year, month, day, hour, minute, and second.
- **Date format.** Choose from Y/M/D (year/month/day), M/D/Y (month/day/year), or D/M/Y (day/month/year) formats.
- **Daylight saving time.** Use this to turn daylight saving time On or Off. Because the date on which DST goes into effect each year has been changed from time to time, if you turn this feature on you may need to monitor your camera to make sure DST has been implemented correctly.

Monitor Brightness

Options: −5 to +5 (default: 0)
My preference: N/A

Choose this menu option and a screen appears allowing you to specify brightness (see Figure 13.2). Use the multi selector up/down keys to adjust the brightness to a comfortable viewing level. Under the lighting conditions that exist when you make this adjustment, you should be able to see all 10 swatches from black to white. If the two left-end swatches blend together, the brightness has been set too low. If the two whitest swatches on the right end of the strip blend together, the brightness is too high. Brighter settings use more battery power but can allow you to view an image on the monitor outdoors in bright sunlight. When you have

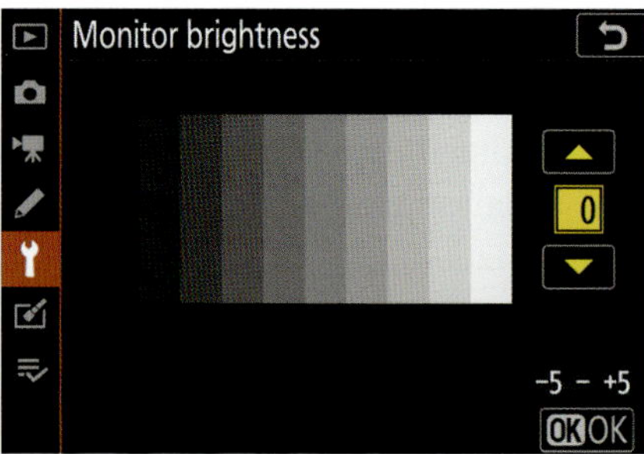

Figure 13.2 Choose to adjust brightness.

the brightness you want, press OK to lock it in and return to the menu. Although the Z5 has a great viewfinder, you'll still find yourself using the monitor for both preview and review functions. I often tilt the LCD upward when shooting from low perspectives, so I don't have to crouch or kneel, or tilt it forward when I am holding the camera overhead, for a periscope view.

Monitor Color Balance

Options: Adjust color balance

My preference: N/A

This entry allows you to adjust the color balance of the LCD monitor using an image residing on your memory card. An adjustment screen, like the one shown in Figure 13.3, appears. The large thumbnail image at upper left will be the last photograph taken, or, if you are using Playback mode, the last photograph viewed. You can also press the Zoom Out button (located next to the lower-right corner of the monitor) to select an image on your memory card from a thumbnail list.

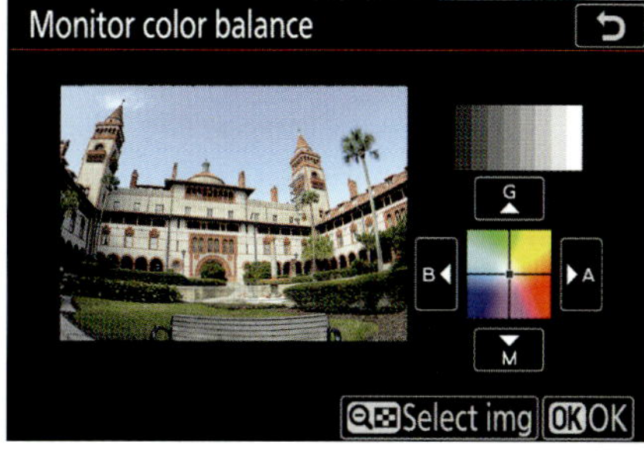

Figure 13.3 Fine-tune monitor color balance.

Use the multi selector directional buttons to bias the monitor hue along the blue/amber (left/right buttons) and/or green/magenta (up/down buttons) axes. The grayscale tone strip above helps you judge the neutrality of your selected balance settings. Press OK to confirm your adjustment. Note that changing the monitor color balance has *no* effect on the color balance of the photos you take.

Viewfinder Brightness

Options: Auto (default); Manual: –5 to +5

My preference: N/A

You can also adjust the brightness for the electronic viewfinder. Unlike the monitor brightness adjustment, the Viewfinder option includes an Auto setting that will modify brightness based on ambient light conditions. In Manual mode, while peering through the viewfinder at the grayscale patches, you can brighten/darken the display using the same plus/minus 5 range. Use the multi selector up/down keys to adjust the brightness to a comfortable viewing level. When you have the brightness you want, press OK to lock it in and return to the menu.

Viewfinder Color Balance

Options: Adjust color balance

My preference: N/A

This is the first entry in the next page of the Setup menu. (See Figure 13.4.) Viewfinder color balance is adjusted using the same procedure described above for Monitor Color Balance, while looking through the viewfinder window.

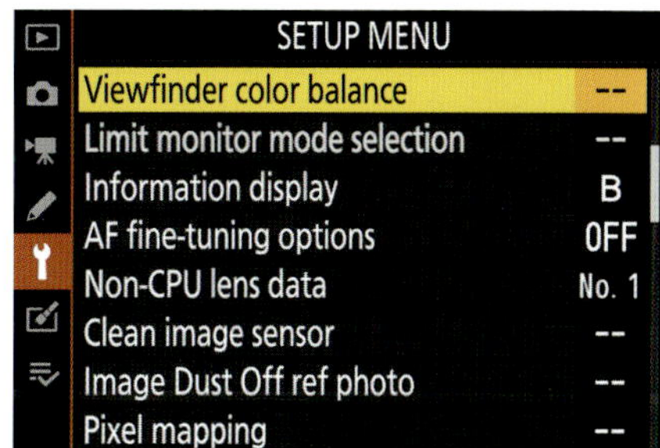

Figure 13.4 The second page of the Setup menu.

Limit Monitor Mode Selection

Options: Enable/Disable: Automatic Display Switch, Viewfinder Only, Monitor Only, Prioritize Viewfinder; Default: Enable All

My preference: Enable All

One of my favorite Z5 features is the ability to use the electronic viewfinder for tasks that, on a digital SLR, require looking at the LCD monitor. For example, I can keep the camera up to my eye and make menu adjustments and review images I've shot in Playback mode—even under the brightest daylight conditions.

This menu item lets you choose which monitor viewing modes are available when you press the monitor mode button (located on the left side of the Z5's "pentaprism" hump). Pressing the button repeatedly cycles among the options you've enabled. At least one *must* be enabled (you cannot disable all of them). Your options are as follows:

- **Automatic Display Switch.** The active display always switches from the monitor to the viewfinder when you place your eye up to the viewfinder (or when anything else comes in proximity to the sensor located above the viewfinder window). When you remove your eye from the EVF, the display switches to the LCD monitor. This is often the most convenient mode. However, you may encounter unwanted switching if something other than your eye comes within roughly two inches of the sensor. For example, if you've swiveled the monitor and are using the touch screen, a finger may switch the display.

- **Viewfinder Only.** The monitor is disabled, and the viewfinder is used exclusively for shooting, navigating menus, or image playback. This is my preferred mode in dark venues—especially concerts—where an illuminated LCD can distract or annoy others. I can access most camera features with the menus and viewfinder, so, for example, I don't need to fumble with my fingers to locate the ISO or Exposure Compensation direct access buttons. I also use Viewfinder Only outdoors when the monitor washes out or is difficult to view.

- **Monitor Only.** The viewfinder is disabled, and display is directed to the LCD monitor only. This is my choice when I'm composing and shooting using the monitor—say for macro photography or other scenes shot with the camera at waist level or lower or mounted on a tripod. I don't want the eye sensor to switch to the EVF as I work, so I switch to the Monitor Only setting.

- **Prioritize Viewfinder.** With this option, when you're shooting pictures, the display is directed to the viewfinder exclusively; it turns on when you move your eye to the EVF and turns off when you remove your eye. That saves more than a little power, especially if there are intervals when you are not taking photos at all, but don't want to turn off the Z5. (The sensor and the electronic viewfinder or sensor can always be active when the camera is powered up, in contrast to digital SLRs that are, effectively, in a low-power mode until you start using the exposure meters, autofocus mechanism, or LCD monitor.)

  When you're reviewing images in Playback mode, while capturing movies, or when menus are displayed, the monitor *will* turn on when you remove your eye from the viewfinder.

Information Display

Options: Manual: Dark on Light (B) (default), Light on Dark (W)

My preference: Light on Dark

This menu entry refers to the shooting information screen that appears as you cycle through the various displays by pressing the DISP button. You can set this display to dark lettering on a light background (which you may prefer in dim locations) or light lettering on a dark background (which is often the best choice for viewing the monitor in daylight). I prefer the light-on-dark color scheme; if ambient light is really bright, I use the viewfinder instead of the monitor anyway.

AF Fine-Tuning Options

Options: AF Fine-Tune On/Off (default: Off), Fine-tune and Save Lens, Default, List Saved Values

My preference: N/A

Troubled by lenses that don't focus exactly where they should, producing back-focus or front-focus problems? No need to send your lens and/or camera into Nikon for servicing. The Nikon Z5 allows you to fine-tune focus for up to 40 different lenses and adjust focus for both wide and telephoto ends of the zoom range for zoom lenses. Best of all, it works perfectly with both Z-mount and F-mount lenses (using the FTZ adapter).

You'll probably never need to use this feature, but if you do, it's priceless. To fine-tune your lenses, first perform some tests to see just how much fine-tuning is required. The only problem I've run into is that with some lenses, particularly short focal length lenses, using large negative values (0 to –20) to move the focal point closer to the camera sometimes results in being unable to focus to infinity. If you run into that, you may be better off sending the lens to Nikon so they can recalibrate the focus for you.

This menu option has four choices, shown in Figure 13.5:

- **AF Fine Tune (On/Off).** Enable/disable application of your AF fine-tuning changes.
- **Fine-tune and Save Lens.** View or enter an adjustment for the lens currently mounted on your camera.
- **Default.** Set the default value to be applied to lenses that haven't been recalibrated. You'd use this if your Z5 has a certain amount of front- or back-focus problems with all lenses. Use with caution, as it affects every CPU lens that you use.
- **List Saved Values.** View, label, and delete tuning values you've saved.

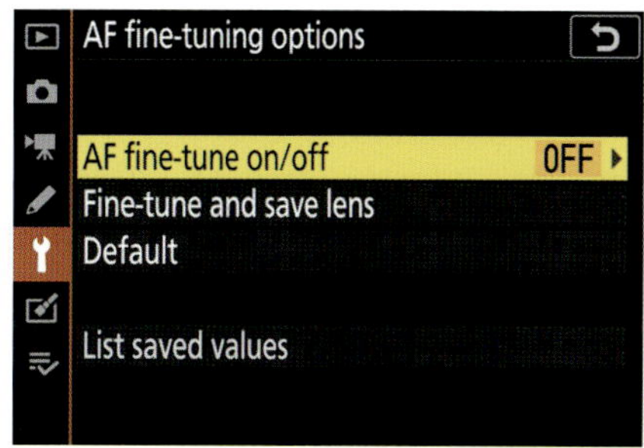

Figure 13.5 The autofocus of lenses can be adjusted here.

Because the adjustments made with the AF Fine-Tune setting are potentially so dangerous to your focusing health, I'm not even going to provide an overview in this chapter. (Knowing just enough to hurt yourself can be a real possibility.) Instead, you'll find a thorough discussion of using this feature in Chapter 5.

Non-CPU Lens Data

Options: Lens Number, Focal Length (mm), Maximum Aperture
My preference: N/A

This is an odd entry, as it contributes absolutely nothing to the operation of your camera, other than enabling it to embed the focal length and maximum aperture available of some older manual focus lenses in the EXIF data embedded in your image file.

One of the best accessories for the Z5 is the FTZ adapter, which makes it easy to mount Nikon F-mount lenses to the Z5. It gives you four types of functionality in PSAM modes:

- **AF-S, AF-P, and AF-I lenses, plus AF-S/AF-I teleconverters.** These retain all their features, including autofocus and autoexposure.

- **AF and AF-D lenses.** You must focus these optics manually, but with AF-D lenses the electronic rangefinder will assist in determining correct focus. Peaking Highlights (described in Chapter 12) works with either type. You can adjust the aperture electronically and use Aperture-priority autoexposure.

- **AI-P and all lenses with a CPU chip.** You get manual focus only (with Peaking Highlights) and Aperture-priority exposure.

- **AI, AI-S, and Series-E lenses.** These lenses offer manual focus and manual exposure only, but you can still use this menu entry to specify the maximum aperture and focal length of the lens (zoom focal length ranges are not supported). That information will be included in the EXIF metadata but *not* the actual aperture used to take the photo. You may also be able to mount and use non-AI F-mount lenses (pre-1977) but may have mechanical interference problems.

For AI, AI-S, and Series-E lenses, you'll need to specify lens focal length data and maximum aperture. The Nikon Z5 allows defining up to 20 different lenses, and you can choose any of them with a quick trip to this menu entry (or to the equivalent menu item in My Menu, described later in this chapter), or using a button defined for this feature, as described for Custom Setting f2 in Chapter 12.

To enter this information, follow these steps using the screen shown in Figure 13.6. Note that you can configure the lens's information even if the lens is not mounted on the Z5.

1. Choose Non-CPU lens data from the Setup menu.

2. Highlight Lens Number and press the multi selector left/right buttons to choose a number. If you are defining several lenses, I recommend numbering them in order of increasing focal length, or, if you prefer, in order of frequency of use.

3. Scroll down to Focal Length (mm) and use the multi selector left/right buttons to choose a focal length between 6mm and 4000mm.

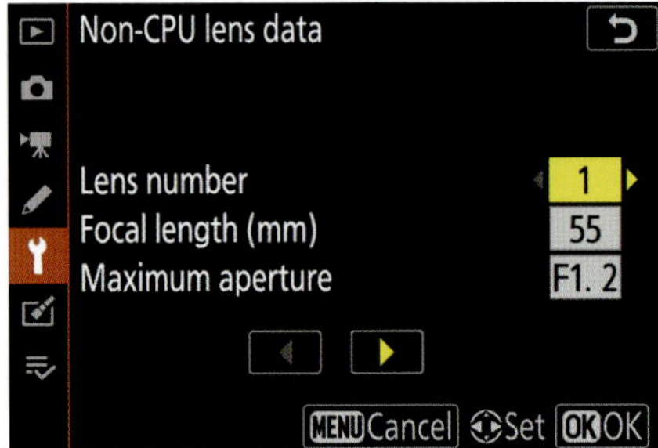

Figure 13.6 You can enter focal length and maximum aperture of up to 20 manual focus lenses.

4. Scroll down to Maximum Aperture and use the multi selector left/right buttons to choose a maximum f/stop between f/1.2 and f/22.

5. Choose Done. You can now select the lens number using a button you define for the function.

Clean Image Sensor

Options: Clean Now; Automatic Cleaning: Clean at Shutdown, Cleaning Off

My preference: Automatic Cleaning (Clean at Shutdown)

This entry gives you some control over the Nikon Z5's automatic sensor cleaning feature, which removes dust through a vibration cycle that shakes the sensor until dust, presumably, falls off. If you happen to take a picture and notice an artifact in an area that contains little detail (such as the sky or a blank wall), you can access this menu choice, place the camera with its base downward, and choose Clean Now. A Cleaning Sensor message now appears, and the dust you noticed has probably been shaken off.

You can also tell the Z5 when you'd like it to perform automatic cleaning without specific instructions from you. Select from:

- **Clean Now.** Triggers the dust-shaking cycle immediately. For best results, remove the lens and point the camera downward so the dust can fall outside the camera body.
- **Automatic Cleaning: Clean at shutdown.** This removes any dust that may have accumulated since the camera has been turned on, say, from dust infiltration while changing lenses.
- **Automatic Cleaning: Cleaning Off.** No automatic dust removal will be performed. Use this to preserve battery power, or if you prefer to use automatic dust removal only when you explicitly want to apply it.

Image Dust Off Ref Photo

Options: Start, Clean Sensor and Then Start

My preference: N/A

This menu choice lets you "take a picture" of any dust or other particles that may be adhering to your sensor. The Z5 will then append information about the location of this dust to your photos, so that the Image Dust Off option in Capture NX-D can be used to mask the dust in the NEF image.

To use this feature, select Image Dust Off Ref Photo, choose either Start or Clean Sensor and Then Start, and then press OK. If directed to do so, the camera will first perform a self-cleaning operation by applying ultrasonic vibration to the top layer of the sensor. I recommend doing this—you might as well capture your reference photo with a sensor that is as clean as possible.

Then, a screen will appear asking you to take a photo of a bright featureless white object 10cm (about four inches) from the lens. Nikon recommends using a lens with a focal length of at least 50mm. If you're using a zoom lens, zoom to the longest focal length. Note that the dust-off information can be applied to *all* your images, not just those taken with the lens used to capture the reference photo.

Point the Z5 at a solid-white card and press the shutter release. If the reference object is too dark or light, you may be asked to try again with a different object. An image with the extension .ndf will be created and can be used by Nikon Capture NX-D as a reference photo if the "dust-off" picture is placed in the same folder as an image to be processed for dust removal.

Pixel Mapping

Options: Start

My preference: N/A

Even with the most sophisticated manufacturing techniques and quality control measures, producing a sensor with absolutely no defects among 24 million individual photosites is quite a challenge. Sometimes a pixel "dies" and becomes permanently dark or, worse, becomes stuck or "hot" so that it will shine through brightly in areas that should be dark or even black. Pixel mapping provides your Z5 with a way to detect those defective pixels and automatically map them, so they no longer contribute to your images. Instead, information from surrounding pixels will be used to determine how that photosite appears in your image.

If you notice what appears to be a bad pixel, compare several different shots to see if it appears in the same place. Keep in mind that some "bad" pixels can be caused by overheating and will return to normal once your camera has been powered down for a short period. If you need to permanently correct for a bad pixel, just follow these steps:

1. Place a lens cap over your lens and the supplied eyepiece cap (or some other light blocker) over the viewfinder eyepiece.
2. Select Pixel Mapping from the Setup menu. This entry may not be available if the camera already overheated or your battery is not fully charged.
3. Press the right directional button and choose Start.
4. The control panel will display a buSY message.
5. When the operation is complete, turn off the camera.

Image Comment

Options: Attach Comment, Input Comment

My preference: N/A

This is the first entry on the next page of the Setup menu. (See Figure 13.7.) The Image Comment is your opportunity to add a copyright notice, personal information about yourself (including contact info), or even a description of where the image was taken (e.g., Browns Super Bowl 2021), although text entry with the Nikon Z5 is a bit too clumsy (even when using the touch screen) for doing a lot of individual annotation of your photos. (But you still might want to change the comment each time, say, you change cities

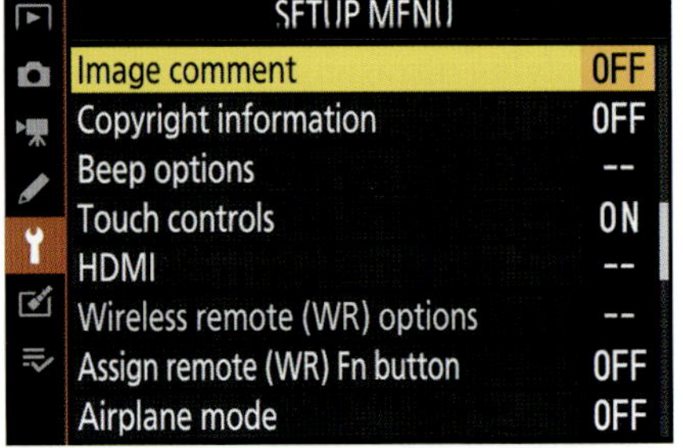

Figure 13.7 The third page of the Setup menu.

during your travels.) The embedded comments can be read by many software programs, including Nikon ViewNX-i or Capture NX-D.

The standard text-entry screen described in Chapter 2 can be used to enter your comment, with up to 36 characters available. For the copyright symbol, embed a lowercase "c" within opening and closing parentheses: (c). You can input the comment, turn attachment of the comment On or Off using the Attach Comment entry, and select Done when you're finished working with comments. If your fingers are too fat for typing on the touch screen or you find typing with a cursor too tedious, you can enter your comment in Nikon Capture NX-D and upload it to the camera through a USB cable.

Copyright Information

Options: Attach Copyright Information, Artist, Copyright

My preference: N/A

This is an expansion of the Image Comment capability, allowing you to specify the name of the "artist" (photographer), and enter copyright information. Use the standard Nikon text-entry screen described earlier. Highlight the Attach Copyright Information option and press the right multi selector button to mark/unmark it to control whether your copyright data is embedded in each photo as taken. The touch screen comes in useful for this input, as well.

Beep Options

Options: Beep On, Beep Off (default), Volume, Pitch

My preference: Beep Off

The Nikon Z5's internal beeper provides a (usually) superfluous chirp to signify various functions, such as the countdown of your camera's self-timer, the termination of time-lapse recording, or autofocus confirmation in AF-S mode (unless you've selected release-priority in Custom Setting a2). You can (and probably should) switch it off if you want to avoid the beep because it's annoying, impolite, distracting (at a concert or museum), or undesired for any other reason. Note that the beeper is automatically squelched if you've activated Silent Photography in the Photo Shooting menu. Choose this menu entry, and select one of the following:

- **Beep On/Off.** Enable or disable the beeper.
- **Volume.** Select values of 1 (soft) through 3 (loud). A quarter-note icon appears in the monochrome control panel and the shooting information display.
- **Pitch.** Select High for a high-pitched beep, or Low for a deeper tone.

Touch Controls

Options: Enable (default), Disable touch controls, Full-frame playback flicks
My preference: N/A

This entry allows you to specify whether LCD monitor touch controls are enabled or disabled, and whether to use left/right or right/left flicks to advance to the next image during full-frame playback. I described touch controls in Chapter 2.

HDMI

Options: Output Resolution (default: Auto); Advanced: Output Range, External Recording Control
My preference: N/A

This entry deals with the Nikon Z5's High-Definition Multimedia Interface (HDMI) video connection. The port allows you to play back your camera's images on HDTV or HD monitors using a type-C cable, such as the HDMI cable HC-E1, which Nikon does not provide to you, but which is readily available from third parties. I use HDMI playback for slide shows. I also captured most of the screenshot images in this book using the HDMI output and a video frame grabber. Before you link up, you'll want to choose from the following options:

- **Output Resolution.** Select Auto and the camera will sense the correct output resolution to use. Auto will be applied (even if you select another resolution) when the HDMI port is used to display the camera's image during movie capture, and movie playback. That limitation can be a problem; the camera may not be able to detect the required resolution in Auto mode. My BlackMagic Intensity Shuttle, for example, requires using the 1080i setting. It displays output from my Z5 at that setting in still mode, but when I change to movie mode the camera switches to Auto and the HDMI output is no longer available.

  If you want to use a different resolution under other circumstances (say, when you're viewing still images), you can choose Auto, plus specific formats including 480p (640 × 480 progressive scan); 576p (720 × 576 progressive scan); 720p (1280 × 720 progressive scan); 1080p (1920 × 1080 progressive scan); or 1080i (1920 × 1080 interlaced scan). A 4K output option 2160p (3840 × 2160 progressive scan) is also available and should be used only with a 4K-compatible device.

  Note: HDMI output is disabled when your movie resolution/frame rate is 1920 × 1080 120/100p, or when operating the camera using SnapBridge or Camera Control 2.

- **Advanced.** This cryptic entry leads you to a screen where you can select more parameters:

  - **Output Range.** Choose Auto (the default, and the best choice under most circumstances); Limited Range; or Full Range. In most cases, the camera will be able to determine the output range of your HDMI device. If not, Limited Range uses settings of 16 to 235, clipping off the darkest (0–16) and brightest (235–255) portions of the image. Use Limited Range if you're plagued with reduced detail in the shadows of your image. Full Range may be your choice if shadows are washed out or excessively bright. It accepts video signals with the full range from 0 to 255.

- **External Recording Control.** When enabled, this option allows you to use the camera controls to stop and start recording when connected to an external recorder (favored by serious videographers). The recorder must support the Atomos Open Protocol, used by the popular Atomos Shogun, Sumo, and Ninja recorders. When active, an STBY (Standby) or REC (Recording) icon appears on the monitor. To keep the camera display and HDMI output from timing out, choose Custom Setting c3: Power Off Delay and set Standby Timer to Unlimited.

Location Data

Options: Standby Timer (default: Enable), Position, Set Clock from Satellite (default: Yes)

My preference: N/A

This menu entry has options for using GPS information. You can supply the Z5 with location information from your smartphone or tablet using the SnapBridge app installed on your device. You can also clip the Nikon GP-1/GP1a Global Positioning System (GPS) accessory onto your camera's accessory shoe and plug it into the remote/device port. It has four options, none of which turn GPS features on or off, despite the misleading "Enable" and "Disable" nomenclature (what you're enabling and disabling is the automatic exposure meter turn-off):

- **Standby Timer.** This setting is useful when you have an external GPS receiver connected to the camera. Choose Enable to reduce battery drain by turning off exposure meters while using the GP-1/1a after the time specified in Custom Setting c3: Power off Delay: Standby Timer has elapsed. When the meters turn off, the GP-1/1a becomes inactive and must reacquire at least three satellite signals before it can begin recording GPS data once more. Setting to Disable causes exposure meters to remain on, so that GPS data can be recorded at any time, despite increased battery drain.

- **Position.** This is an information display, rather than a selectable option. It appears when the GP-1/1a is connected and receiving satellite positioning data. It shows the latitude, longitude, altitude, and Coordinated Universal Time (UTC) values. (See Figure 13.8.)

- **Set Clock From Satellite.** Choose Yes to allow the camera to update its internal clock from information provided by the GPS device when attached. No disables this updating feature. You might want to avoid updating the clock if you're traveling and want all the basic date/time information embedded in your image files to reflect the settings back home, rather than the date and time where your pictures are taken. Note that if the GPS device is active when shooting, the local date and time will be embedded in the GPS portion of the EXIF data.

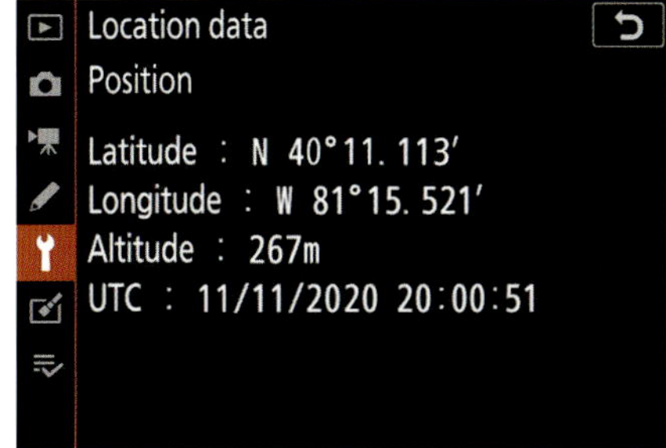

Figure 13.8 Position data is displayed when a GPS device is active and linked to satellites.

Wireless Remote (WR) Options

Options: LED lamp: On (default), Off; Link mode: Pairing (default), PIN
My preference: N/A

This option, which is grayed out unless the WR-R10 transmitter is plugged into the remote/accessory port on the Z5, allows you to make several settings for the Nikon WR-10 radio remote control. The system consists of the WR-T10 transmitter, shown at bottom in Figure 13.9, and the WR-R10 receiver, which is attached to the camera (see Figure 13.9, top). The set, which allows triggering cameras and compatible electronic flash units (such as the SB-5000), has a practical range of about 66 feet, and costs about $200. (If you use one WR-R10 receiver as an intermediate master and a second on the camera, range extends to 164 feet.) A single transmitter can be used to control multiple cameras that have a receiver installed.

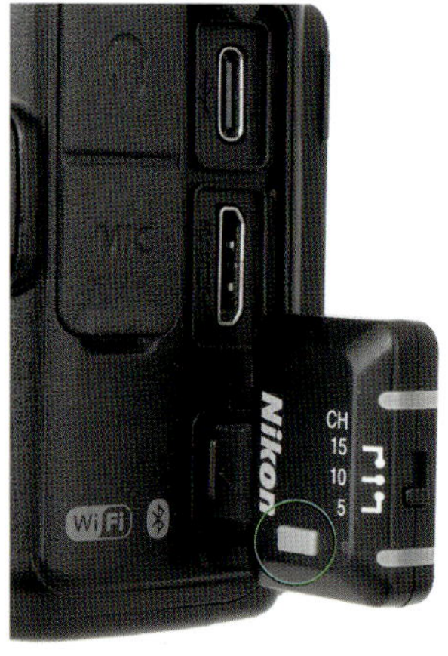

The system is also compatible with the WR-1, a sophisticated transceiver with a much longer (roughly 400 foot) range, 15 channels, and additional features such as more sophisticated camera group control (to fire multiple cameras simultaneously). It also costs a great deal more, at around $650.

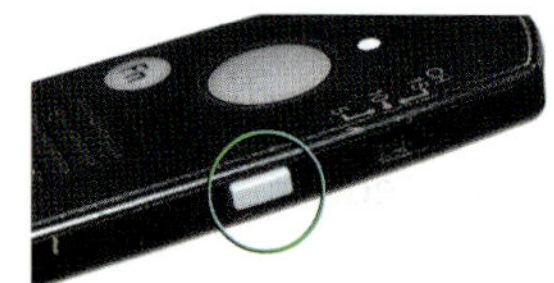

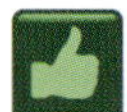 **TIP** While useful as a remote control, my favorite feature of the WR-10 radio control system is the ability to use the transmitter's function button to activate some other feature on the camera, such as autoexposure/autofocus lock. I'll explain those options in the next section.

Figure 13.9 Press the Pairing buttons on the WR-R10 receiver and WR-T10 transmitter simultaneously.

To use the WR-R10, insert the receiver into the remote/accessory port. Make sure the transmitter and receiver are using the same channel (15, 10, or 5), and then pair them by pressing the gray pairing buttons indicated by green circles in Figure 13.9, simultaneously. The LEDs on top of the receiver will alternate red and green to show that pairing has taken place; thereafter, the receiver's green LED will flash to indicate there is a connection.

This menu entry has two options, which most Z5 owners may never need to use:

- **LED lamp.** You can enable or disable this lamp. I sometimes turn the blinking lamp off when I am working in dark environments and don't want to distract others around me—or make them aware that I am taking stealth photos with a remote control. Disabling the LEDs also saves power, but you'll have no operational feedback when they're off.

- **Link mode.** You can choose whether the transmitter and receiver are linked using pairing (the usual procedure) or through a PIN, which is possible when working with the Nikon SB-5000 flash (or any radio-controlled flash Nikon may introduce after this book is written). If you're using the WR-1 transceiver, you must use pairing as the link mode.

Assign Remote (WR) Fn Button

Options: Preview, FV Lock, AE/AF Lock, AE Lock Only, AE Lock (Reset on Release), AF Lock Only, AF-ON, Flash Enable/Disable, +RAW, None (default)

My preference: AF-ON

Radio remote control is cool, but I *really* like the WR-10 system's ability to trigger any of nine different features on the camera, using the transmitter's Fn button. I most often use the button to start autofocus on the Z5 using the AF-ON behavior. You might love the ability to tell the camera to add an NEF (RAW) picture to the JPEG image you've specified for that one picture, then switch back to JPEG only mode.

Select Assign Remote (WR) Fn button, and then choose from: Preview, FV Lock, AE/AF Lock, AE Lock Only, AE Lock (Reset on release), AF Lock Only, AF-ON, Flash Enable/Disable, +RAW, or None.

Airplane Mode

Options: Enable, Disable (default)

My preference: Enable

Like the Airplane Mode on your smartphone or tablet, this option turns off the Z5's Wi-Fi and Bluetooth capabilities. I enable the feature any time I am not planning to use Bluetooth, Wi-Fi, or GPS, because it saves a lot of power.

Connect to Smart Device

Options: Pairing, Select to Send (Bluetooth), Wi-Fi Connection, Send While Off

My preference: N/A

This is the first entry on the next page of the Setup menu (see Figure 13.10). Use this entry to set up your Snap-Bridge or Wi-Fi connection to your smartphone, tablet, or computer. Wi-Fi, Bluetooth, and your Z5's other connectivity options were covered in detail in Chapter 6, and the instructions for setting up your smart device won't be repeated here.

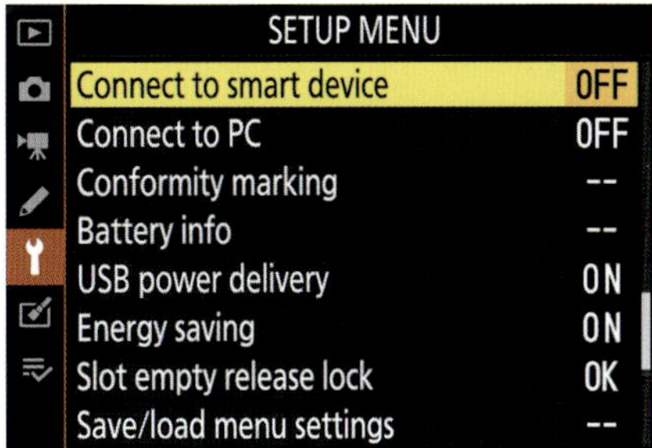

Figure 13.10 The next page of the Setup menu.

Connect to PC

Options: On, Off (default)

My preference: N/A

You can instruct your Z5 to automatically upload new still photos (but not movies) to your smart device or computer when the camera and device are linked. If they are not connected, the Z5 will mark a maximum of 1,000 photos and upload them the next time a wireless connection is made. As I noted in Chapter 6, the Nikon Network Guide contains detailed information on using this advanced feature.

Conformity Marking

Options: Display only. No selections.

My preference: N/A

This entry does nothing but display the various international standards with which the Z5 complies. It's included here because Nikon can easily update the listing during a firmware upgrade. The alternative might be to print new labels (like the one with the serial number of the camera located behind the tilting LCD monitor on the Z5) each time a change is made.

Battery Info

Options: None. This screen is purely informational.

My preference: N/A

When invoked, you can see the following information:

- **Charge.** The current battery level, shown as a percentage from 100 to 0 percent.
- **No. of shots.** This shows the number of actuations with the current battery since it was last recharged. This number can be larger than the number of photos taken, because other functions, such as white balance presetting, can cause the shutter to be tripped.
- **Battery Age.** Eventually, a battery will no longer accept a charge as well as it did when it was new and must be replaced. This indicator shows when a battery is considered new (0); has begun to degrade slightly (1,2,3); or has reached the end of its charging life and is ready for replacement (4). Batteries charged at temperatures lower than 41 degrees F may display an impaired charging life temporarily, but return to their true "health" when recharged above 68 degrees F.

USB Power Delivery

Options: Enable, Disable

My preference: N/A

Allows you to specify whether power supplied to the Z5 by external sources through the USB Type-C port can be used to power the camera, thereby limiting the drain on the camera's battery. A USB Power Delivery icon appears at the left side of the shooting display when the camera is being powered from an external source. A battery must be installed in the camera even if external power is being used to operate it.

Your options are as follows:

- **Enable.** The Z5 can be operated through a power source connected via the USB port. Power will be drawn *only* while the camera is on, except if a Bluetooth upload is in progress or the camera is storing an image on a memory card when the camera is turned off.
- **Disable.** When power is supplied to the USB port, charging of the battery will take place, but the camera cannot be operated using the external source's juice.

Energy Saving

Options: Enable, Disable

My preference: N/A

This is an additional power-saving option that turns off the shooting display roughly 15 seconds before the Standby Timer you set using Custom Setting c3: Power Off Delay. This setting is overridden if your Standby Timer has been set for No Limit or a delay of less than 30 seconds. It also does not take effect if the Z5 is connected to another device using the HDMI port, when attached to an AC adapter or power from the USP Type-C port, or if the camera is connected to a computer and exchanging data.

When enabled, energy is saved and your battery life extended, but the display refresh rate may be reduced. Disable this setting, and battery life will not be extended. The display screen may still dim a few seconds before the standby timer expires.

Slot Empty Release Lock

Options: Release Locked, Enable Release (default)

My preference: Release Locked

This option gives you the ability to snap off "pictures" without a memory card installed—or to lock the camera shutter release if that is the case. It is sometimes called play mode, because you can experiment with your camera's features or even hand your Z5 to a friend to let them fool around, without any danger of pictures actually being taken.

Back in our film days, we'd sometimes finish a roll, rewind the film back into its cassette surreptitiously, and then hand the camera to a child to take a few pictures—without actually wasting any film. It's hard to waste digital film, but "shoot without card" mode is still appreciated by some, especially camera vendors who want to be able to demo a camera at a store or trade show, but don't want to have to equip each and every demonstrator model with a memory card. Choose Enable Release to activate "play" mode or Release Locked to disable it.

The pictures you actually "take" are displayed on the LCD monitor with the legend "Demo" superimposed on the screen, and they are, of course, not saved. Note that if you are using the optional Camera Control Pro 2 software to record photos from a USB-tethered Z5 directly to a computer, no memory card is required to unlock the shutter even if Release Locked has been selected.

Save/Load Menu Settings

Options: Save Menu Settings, Load Menu Settings
My preference: N/A

You can store many camera settings to your memory card in a file named NCSETxxx, and then reload them later using this menu item. This is a good way to archive your favorite camera settings for the Playback menu, all Photo/Movie Shooting menus, Custom Settings menu, the Setup menu settings, and all My Menu items. You can restore your settings if you've messed them up or save multiple sets of settings to multiple memory cards. If you own more than one Z5, this is a handy way to share settings between them. You can save only one group of settings at a time to a particular card (always in the Primary slot); the default NCSETUPK cannot be changed. Well, it *can* be changed in your computer, but if you do, the Z5 will not be able to find it on the memory card. If you want to save multiple settings, simply use multiple memory cards. This might be a good use for all those 256MB SD cards you have left over from your point-and-shoot snapshooting days.

Note that storing/restoration is an all-or-nothing proposition. When you select Save Settings, all your current settings are stored on the memory card; choose Load Settings, and the camera's current settings are replaced with the values stored on the memory card. The following settings are saved:

- **Playback.** Playback display options; Image review; After delete; After burst, show; Rotate tall.
- **Photo Shooting menu.** File naming, Choose image area, Image quality, Image size, NEF (RAW) recording, ISO sensitivity settings, White balance, Set Picture Control (Custom controls are saved as Auto), Color space, Active D-Lighting, Long exposure NR, High ISO NR, Vignette control, Diffraction compensation, Auto distortion control, Flicker reduction shooting, Metering, Flash control, Flash mode, Flash compensation, Focus mode, AF-area mode, Vibration reduction, Auto bracketing, Silent photography.
- **Movie Shooting.** File naming, Choose image area, Frame size/frame rate, Movie Quality, Movie file type, ISO sensitivity settings, White Balance, Set Picture Control (Custom controls saved as Auto), Active D-Lighting, Vignette control, Diffraction compensation, Auto distortion control, Flicker reduction, Metering, Focus mode, AF-area mode, Vibration reduction, Electronic VR, Microphone sensitivity, Attenuator, Frequency Response, Wind noise reduction, Headphone volume, Timecode (except Timecode origin).
- **Custom Settings menu.** All Custom Settings except d3.
- **Setup menu.** Language, Time zone and date (except Date and Time), Information display, Non-CPU lens data, Clean image sensor, Image comment, Copyright information, Beep options, Touch controls, HDMI, Location Data (except Position), Wireless Remote Options, Assign Remote Fn button, Slot empty release lock.
- **My Menu/Recent Settings.** All My Menu entries, All recent settings, Active tab.

Reset All Settings

Options: Reset, Do Not Reset
My preference: N/A

This entry and the next are the sole residents of the last page of the Setup menu, and not shown in a separate figure. This one resets all settings, including Copyright Information, and other user-generated settings, except Language and Time Zone and Date. You should save your current settings to a memory card before using this entry, just to be safe. This command requires use of a confirmation screen to make sure you don't remove your settings accidentally. After the reset, you'll be instructed to turn the camera off. The next time the Z5 is powered up, the default settings will be in place.

Firmware Version

Options: Display only. No selections.
My preference: N/A

You can see the current firmware release in use in the menu listing.

Retouch Menu

The Retouch menu contains the post-processing options you can apply to your images after you've taken a photo. When reviewing an image, press the *i* button, and select Retouch from the menu that pops up to jump directly to this menu and begin processing that image.

- NEF (RAW) Processing
- Trim
- Resize
- D-Lighting
- Red-Eye Correction
- Straighten

- Distortion Control
- Perspective Control
- Monochrome
- Image Overlay
- Trim Movie
- Side-by-Side Comparison (Available from *i* menu in Playback mode only)

The Retouch menu (see Figure 13.11) is most useful when you want to create a modified copy of an image on the spot, for immediate printing or e-mailing without first importing into your computer for more extensive editing. You can also use it to create a JPEG version of an image in the camera when you are shooting RAW-only photos. You can retouch images that have already been processed by the Retouch menu, except for copies created with the Image Overlay and Trim Movie > Choose start/end point options. You may notice some quality loss when applying more than one retouch option.

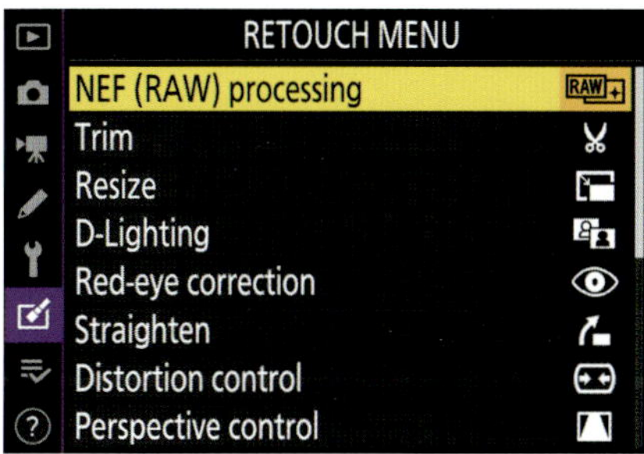

Figure 13.11 The Retouch menu allows simple in-camera editing.

Important exceptions: Note that Image Overlay can *only* be accessed from this menu; it is not available from the *i* menu during image playback. Conversely, Side-by-Side Comparison is *not* available from the Retouch menu; you must invoke it during Playback by pressing the *i* button and choosing it from the *i* menu.

To create a retouched copy of an image:

1. Select an image. For most of the retouching options, you have two ways of selecting an image:
   - **When accessing during Playback.** Press the *i* button, choose Retouch from the screen that pops up, press the right directional button, and then select the retouching option you want to use from the Retouch menu.
   - **When entering using the MENU button.** Navigate to the Retouch menu and select the option you want to use. You'll be presented either with the standard Z5 image selection thumbnails, or options you can select before selecting an image to process. I'll note your options with each entry that follows.

2. **Choose image retouching option.** From the Retouch menu, select the option you want from those available and press the multi selector right button. The Nikon Z5's standard image selection screen appears. Scroll among the images as usual with the left/right multi selector buttons, press the Zoom In button to examine a highlighted image more closely, and press OK to choose that image.

   Note: If you elect to work on an image that has been captured in dual NEF+JPEG format, *only* the NEF (RAW) image will be retouched. If you have an image on your memory card that was recorded by a different model camera, the Z5 may not be able to display or retouch the image.

3. **Manipulate image.** Work with the options available from that particular Retouch menu feature and press OK to create the modified copy, or Playback to cancel your changes. Keep in mind that if the delay for Menus that you've specified in Custom Setting c3: Power Off Delay expires, the Z5 will exit the menu screen and any unsaved changes canceled. You may want to select a longer power off delay for Menus.

4. **View copy.** A retouched JPEG image will be the same size and quality as the original, except for copies created using the NEF (RAW) Processing, Trim, and Resize options. Resized or Cropped copies created from NEF and TIFF images are always saved as JPEG Fine images. During review, retouched copies are overlaid with a paint brush icon in their upper-left corner.

DOUBLE DUTY

Once you've retouched an image using one of the Retouch menu's entries, you can apply most of the remaining options to the manipulated copy (except for those produced by Trim Movie). Any that are not available will be grayed out. That said, it's probably not a good idea to retouch a retouched copy, as you'll lose some image quality each time.

NEF (RAW) Processing

Options: Select Image(s) individual, by date, or by folder; Choose destination; Image Quality (Fine*, Fine, Normal*, Normal, Basic*, or Basic), Image Size (Large, Medium, or Small), White Balance, Exposure Compensation, Set Picture Control, High ISO Noise Reduction, Color Space, Vignette Control, Active D-Lighting, and Diffraction Compensation

My preference: N/A

Use this tool to create a JPEG version of any image saved in a RAW version. You can select from among several parameters to "process" your new JPEG copy right in the camera.

1. **Choose a RAW image.** There are two ways to select an image: from the NEF (RAW Processing) entry in the Retouch menu, and by highlighting an NEF image during Playback and then pressing the *i* button. Choose one method and follow either Step 2a or Step 2b.

2a. **From the Retouch menu.** A selection screen appears, offering three choices. Once you've made your selections, you'll be taken to the NEF processing screen shown in Figure 13.12.

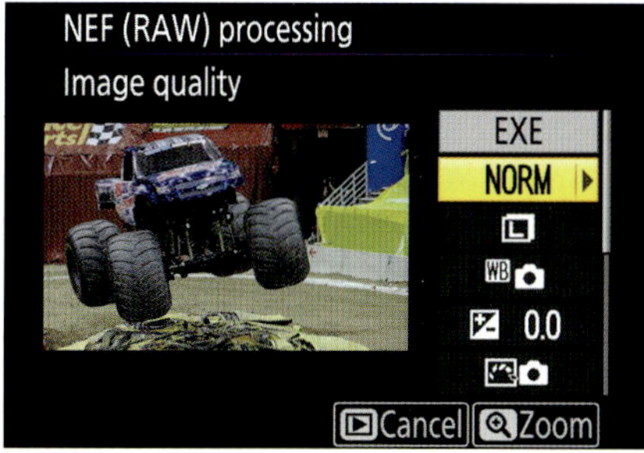

   - **Select Images.** The standard Z5 image selection thumbnail screen showing *only* NEF files appears. Navigate among them. Press and hold the Zoom In button to temporarily enlarge a thumbnail to full screen. Press the Zoom Out/Index button to select a highlighted image. When you're done selecting, press OK to confirm.

Figure 13.12 Adjust the parameters and then save your JPEG copy from a RAW original file.

   - **Select Date.** All NEF images taken on a certain date will be selected and processed.

   - **Select All Images.** All NEF images on your memory card will be selected and processed.

2b. **During Playback.** Select an NEF (RAW) image during playback. Press the *i* button and choose Retouch. You'll be whisked immediately to the NEF (RAW) Processing entry of the Retouch menu (as shown earlier in Figure 13.11). Press the right directional button to proceed to the processing screen (Figure 13.12), and only the single image you were reviewing will be processed.

3. In the NEF (RAW) processing screen you can use the multi selector up/down keys to select from ten different attributes of the RAW image information to apply to the JPEG copies made of your selected image(s). Choose Image Quality (Fine, Normal, or Basic, plus * versions of each), Image Size (Large, Medium, or Small), White Balance, Exposure Compensation, Set Picture Control, High ISO Noise Reduction, Color Space, Vignette Control, D-Lighting, and Diffraction Compensation.

4. Press the Zoom In button to magnify the image temporarily while the button is held down.

5. Press the Playback button if you change your mind, to exit from the processing screen.

6. When all parameters are set, highlight EXE (for Execute) and press OK. The Z5 will create a JPEG file for each of the selected images with the settings you've specified, and show an Image Saved message on the monitor when finished.

Trim

Options: Various sizes

My preference: N/A

This option creates copies in specific sizes based on the final size you select, chosen from among 1:1, 3:2, 4:3, 5:4, 16:9, 4:5, 3:4, 2:3, and 9:16 aspect ratios (proportions). You can use this feature to create smaller versions of a picture for e-mailing without the need to first transfer the image to your own computer. If you're traveling, create your smaller copy here, insert the memory card in a card reader at an Internet café, your library's public computers, or some other computer, and e-mail the reduced-size version. Just follow these steps:

1. **Select your photo.** Choose Trim from the Retouch menu. You'll be shown the standard Nikon Z5 image selection screen. Scroll among the photos using the multi selector left/right buttons and press OK when the image you want to trim is highlighted. While selecting, you can temporarily enlarge the highlighted image by pressing the Zoom In button.

2. **Choose your aspect ratio.** Rotate the main command dial to change from 3:2, 4:3, 5:4 (and their inverses), plus 1:1, and 16:9 aspect ratios. These proportions happen to correspond to the proportions of common print sizes, including the two most popular sizes: 4 × 6 inches (3:2) and 8 × 10 inches (5:4).

3. **Crop in on your photo.** Press the Zoom In button to crop in on your picture. The pixel dimensions of the cropped image at the selected proportions will be displayed in the upper-left corner (see Figure 13.13) as you zoom. The trim sizes vary depending on the Image Size and Aspect Ratio selected. The current framed size is outlined in yellow.

4. **Move cropped area within the image.** Use the multi selector left/right and up/down buttons to relocate the yellow cropping border within the frame.

5. **Save the cropped image.** Press OK to save a copy of the image using the current crop and size or press the Playback button to exit without creating a copy. Copies created from JPEG Fine, Normal, or Standard have the same Image Quality setting as the original; copies made from RAW files or any RAW+JPEG setting will use JPEG Fine compression. Note that you may not be able to zoom in on a cropped image during Playback once it has been saved.

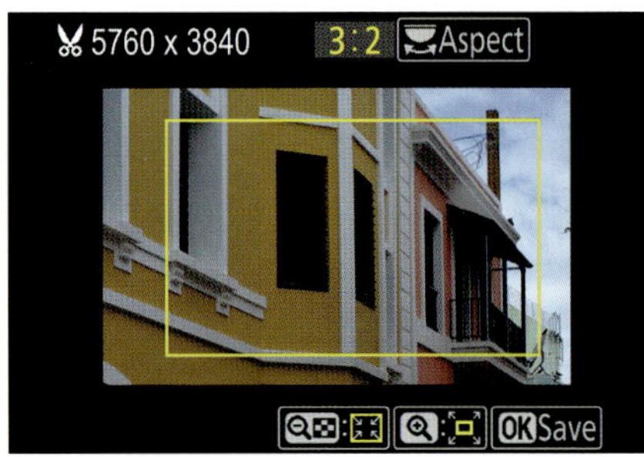

Figure 13.13 The Trim feature of the Retouch menu allows in-camera cropping.

Resize

Options: Select Image, Choose Destination, Choose Size

My preference: N/A

This option creates smaller copies of the selected images. It can be applied while viewing a single image in full-size mode (just press the *i* button while viewing a photo) or accessed from the Retouch menu (especially useful if you'd like to select and resize multiple images). You might want smaller images to post on a website or send by e-mail.

1. **Select image.** If accessing from the Retouch menu, you can choose to select multiple images; if you are reviewing an image during Playback and access using the *i* menu, only the image you were viewing will be processed.

2. **Choose destination.** Select Slot 1 or Slot 2.

3. **Choose size.** Next, select the size for the finished copy, from 2304 × 1536 (3.5MB), 1920 × 1280 (2.5MB), 1280 × 856 (1.1MB), or 960 × 640 (0.6 megabytes).

4. **Confirm.** Press OK to create your copy. Note that, as with Trim, you may not be able to zoom in on a resized image during Playback once it has been saved.

D-Lighting

Options: High, Normal, Low

My preference: N/A

This option brightens the shadows of pictures that have already been taken. Once you've selected your photo for modification, you'll be shown side-by-side images with the unaltered version on the left, and your adjusted version on the right. Press the multi selector's left/right buttons to choose from High, Normal, or Low corrections. (See Figure 13.14.) Press the Zoom In button to magnify the image. When you're happy with the corrected image on the right, compared to the original on the left, press OK to save the copy to your memory card.

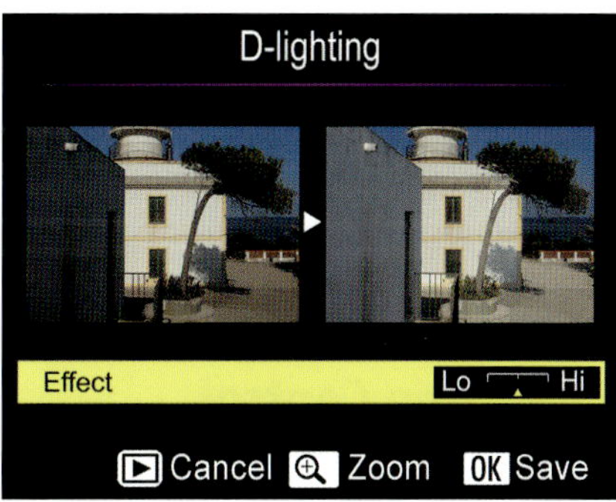

Figure 13.14 An image with dark shadows can be improved with post-shot D-Lighting.

Red-Eye Correction

Options: No setting. Use function as required.

My preference: N/A

This Retouch menu tool can be used to attempt to remove the residual red-eye look that remains after applying the Nikon Z5's other remedies, such as the red-eye reduction feature of your external flash. (You can use the red-eye tools found in most image editors, as well.)

Your Nikon Z5 has a marginally effective red-eye reduction flash mode. Unfortunately, your camera is unable, on its own, to totally *eliminate* the red-eye effects that occur when an electronic flash (or, rarely, illumination from other sources) bounces off the retinas of the eye and into the camera lens. Animals seem to suffer from yellow or green glowing pupils, instead; the effect is equally undesirable. The effect is worst under low-light conditions (exactly when you might be using a flash) as the pupils expand to allow more light to reach the retinas. The best you can hope for is to *reduce* or minimize the red-eye effect.

The best way to truly eliminate red-eye is to raise the external flash up off the camera so its illumination approaches the eye from an angle that won't reflect directly back to the retina and into the lens. If your image still displays red-eye effects, you can use the Retouch menu to make a copy with red-eye reduced further. First, select a picture that was taken with flash (non-flash pictures won't be available for selection). After you've selected the picture to process, press OK. The image will be displayed on the monitor. You can magnify the image with the Zoom In button, scroll around the zoomed image with the multi selector buttons, and zoom out with the Zoom Out button. While zoomed, you can cancel the zoom by pressing the OK button.

When you are finished examining the image, press OK again. The Z5 will look for red-eye, and, if detected, create a copy that has been processed to reduce the effect. If no red-eye is found, a copy is not created.

Straighten

Options: Rotation

My preference: N/A

Use this to create a corrected copy of a crooked image, rotated by up to five degrees, in increments of one-quarter of a degree. Use the right directional button to rotate clockwise, and the left directional button to rotate counterclockwise. The amount of your correction will be visible on the display. Press OK to make a corrected copy, or the Playback button to exit without saving a copy. Note that you will lose some picture information during this process, as the Z5 must trim the edges of the rotated image to produce the rectangular final image.

Distortion Control

Options: Auto, Manual

My preference: N/A

This option produces a copy with reduced barrel distortion (a bowing out effect) or pincushion distortion (an inward-bending effect), both of these forms of *peripheral distortion* are most noticeable at the edges of a photo. You can select Auto to let the Z5 make this correction or use Manual to make the fix yourself visually. Use the right directional button to reduce barrel distortion (bowing outward of lines at the edges) and the left directional button to reduce pincushion distortion (which produces lines bowing inward). In both cases, some of the edges of the photo will be cropped out of your image. Press OK to make a corrected copy, or the Playback button to exit without saving a copy. Note that Auto cannot be used with images exposed using the Auto Distortion Control feature described earlier in this chapter.

Perspective Control

Options: Adjust tilt

My preference: N/A

This option lets you adjust the perspective of an image, reducing the falling-back effect produced when the camera is tilted to take in the top of a tall subject, such as a building (see Figure 13.15). Use the multi selector buttons to "tilt" the image in various directions and visually correct the distortion.

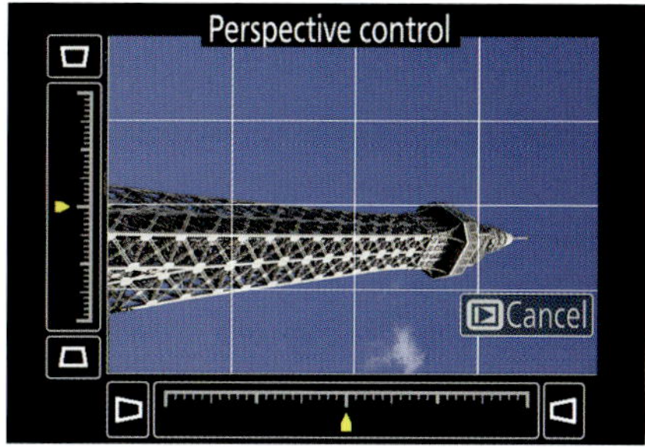

Figure 13.15 Perspective Control lets you fix "falling-back" distortion when photographing tall subjects.

Monochrome

Options: Black-and-white, Sepia, Cyanotype

My preference: N/A

This Retouch choice allows you to produce a copy of the selected photo as a black-and-white image, sepia-toned image, or cyanotype (blue-and-white). You can fine-tune the color saturation of the previewed Sepia or Cyanotype version by pressing the multi selector up button to increase color richness, and the down button to decrease saturation. When satisfied, press OK to create the monochrome duplicate, which will be assigned its own filename. Cancel by pressing the Playback button.

Image Overlay

Options: Combine two RAW photos, Add, Lighten, Darken

My preference: N/A

This feature, and the next two, are on the last page of the Retouch menu (not shown in a figure). It allows you to combine two RAW photos (only NEF files can be used) in a composite image that Nikon claims is better than a "double exposure" created in an image-editing application, because the overlays are made using RAW data. To produce this composite image, follow these steps:

1. Choose Image Overlay. Select Add, Lighten, or Darken, and then press the right directional button. A screen will be displayed, with the Image 1 box highlighted.

2. Press OK and the Nikon Z5's image-selection screen appears. Choose the first image for the overlay and press OK. You can press and hold the Zoom In button to view the thumbnail as a full-frame image. Note that only Large NEF (RAW) files with the same image area and bit depth can be selected. Small and Medium NEF (RAW) images are not available, nor can you combine FX/DX or 12-bit/14-bit images.

3. Press the multi selector right button to highlight the Image 2 box and press OK to produce the image selection screen. Choose the second image for the overlay.

4. By highlighting either the Image 1 or Image 2 boxes and pressing the multi selector up/down buttons, you can adjust the "gain," or how much of the final image will be "exposed" from the selected picture. You can choose from X0.5 (half-exposure) to X2.0 (twice the exposure) for each image. The default value is 1.0 for each, so that each image will contribute equally to the final exposure.

5. Use the multi selector right button to highlight the Preview box and view the combined picture. (See Figure 13.16.) Press the Zoom In button to enlarge the view.

6. When you're ready to store your composite copy, press the multi selector down button when the Preview box is highlighted to select Save, and press OK. The combined image is stored in JPEG * format on the memory card and displayed full frame for your review.

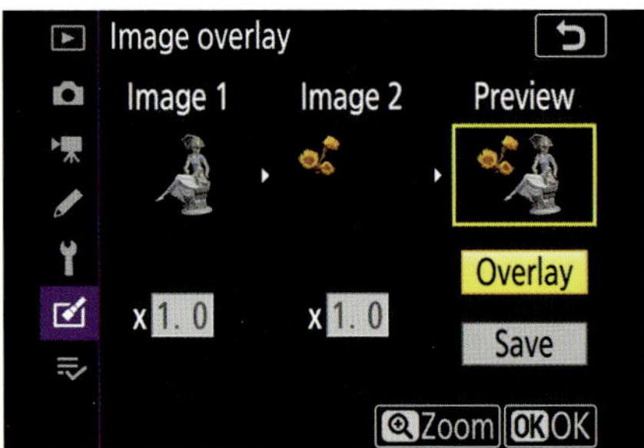

Figure 13.16 Overlay two RAW images to produce a "double exposure."

Trim Movie

Options: Choose Start/End Point, Save Selected Frame
My preference: N/A

You can do limited editing of movies in the camera (actually, just modest trimming), choosing a start point, end point, and also storing a selected frame as a still image. I'll show you how to edit movies using this capability in Chapter 14.

Side-by-Side Comparison

Options: Examine pair of images
My preference: N/A

Use this option to compare a retouched photo side-by-side with the original from which it was derived. It is available *only* when one or more retouched images exist on your memory card to compare. Don't look for Side-by-Side Comparison in the Retouch menu. It doesn't appear there. You can invoke this option only by viewing an image during Playback and pressing the *i* button and choosing Retouch from the menu that pops up.

To use Side-by-Side Comparison:

1. Press the Playback button and review images in full-frame mode until you encounter either a source image that has been retouched *or* the retouched copy of that image that you want to compare. A retouched copy will have the retouching icon displayed in the upper-left corner. It doesn't matter which you choose, but you must select either an original image that has been retouched or a retouched copy of it. Then, press the *i* button, highlight Retouch, press the right directional button, and then scroll down to Side-By-Side comparison in the Retouch menu that appears.

2. The original and retouched image will appear next to each other, with the retouching options you've used shown as a label above the images. Note that the source image will *not* be displayed if the retouched copy was generated from an image that was marked as Protected, or which has been deleted.

3. Highlight the original or the copy with the multi selector left/right buttons and press the Zoom In button to magnify the image to examine it more closely.

4. If you have created more than one copy of an original image, select the retouched version shown, and press the multi selector up/down buttons to view the other retouched copies. The up/down buttons will also let you view the other image used to create an Image Overlay copy.

5. When done comparing, press the Playback button to exit.

Using My Menu

The last menu in the Z5's main menu screen has two versions: Recent Settings and My Menu. The default mode is Recent Settings, which simply shows an ever-changing roster of the 20 menu items you used most recently. You'll probably find it more useful to activate the My Menu option instead, which contains only those menu items that you deposit there extracted from the Playback, Photo Shooting, Movie Shooting, Custom Settings, Setup, and Retouch menus, based on your own decisions on which you use most. Remember that the Z5 always returns to the last menu and menu entry accessed when you press the MENU button. So, you can set up My Menu (see Figure 13.17) to include just the items accessed most frequently, and (as long as you haven't used another menu) jump to those items instantly by pressing the MENU button.

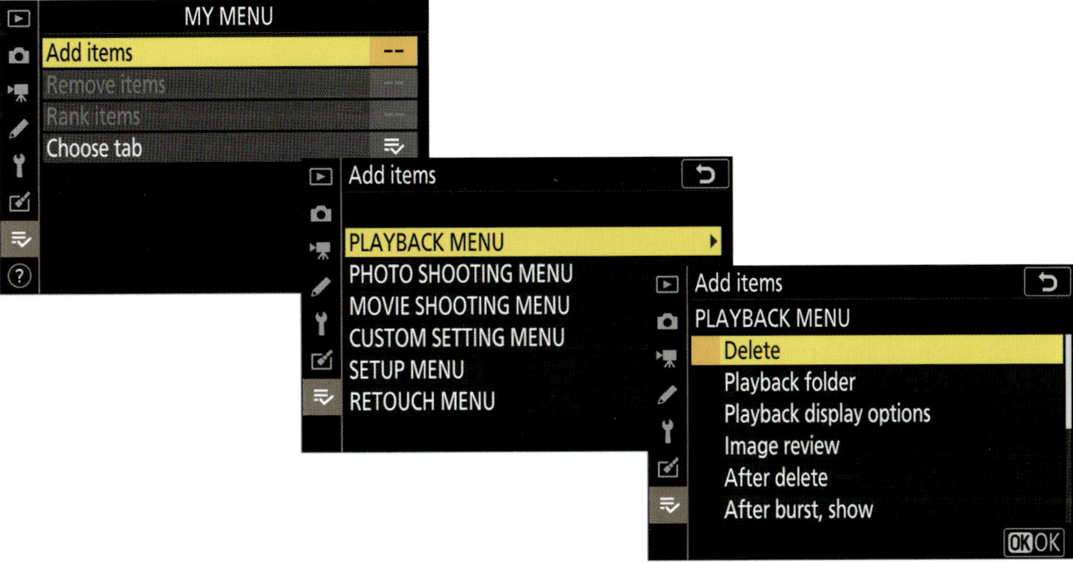

Figure 13.17 You can include your favorite menu items in the fast-access My Menu.

Switching back and forth is easy. The My Menu and Recent Settings menus each has a menu choice called Choose Tab. Highlight that entry and press the right multi selector button to view a screen that allows you to activate either the My Menu or Recent Settings menu. Press OK to confirm.

I tend to include frequently used functions that aren't available using direct access buttons in My Menu. For example, I include High ISO NR, Long Exp. NR, and Battery Info there, because I may want to turn noise reduction on or off, or check the status of my battery during shooting. I *don't* include ISO or WB changes in My Menu, even though they are available in the menu system, because I can quickly change those values by pressing their dedicated buttons (the ISO and Fn1 buttons, respectively) and rotating the main and sub-command dials.

You can add or subtract entries on My Menu at any time, and re-order (or rank) the entries so the ones you access most often are shown at the top of the list. Here's all you need to know to work with My Menu. To add entries to My Menu:

1. Select My Menu and choose Add Items.
2. A list of the available menus will appear (Playback, Photo Shooting, Movie Shooting, Custom Settings, Setup, and Retouch menus). Highlight one and press the multi selector's right button.
3. Within the selected menu, choose the menu item you want to add and press OK.
4. The label Choose Position appears at the top of the My Menu screen. Use the up/down buttons to select a rank among the entries and press OK to confirm and add the new item.
5. Repeat steps 1–4 if you want to add more entries to My Menu.

To reorder the menu listings:

1. Within the My Menu screen, choose Rank Items.
2. Use the up/down buttons to select the item to be moved and press OK.
3. Use the up/down buttons to relocate the selected item and press OK.
4. Repeat steps 2–3 to move additional entries.

To remove entries from the list, you can simply press the Trash button while an item is highlighted in the My Menu screen. To remove multiple items, follow these steps:

1. Within the My Menu screen, choose Remove Items.
2. A list with check boxes next to the menu items appears. Scroll down to an item you want to remove and press the multi selector right button to mark its box. If you change your mind, highlight the item and press the right button again to unmark the box.
3. When finished, highlight Done and press the OK button.
4. Press OK to confirm the deletion.

Capturing Video with the Z5

14

Shooting movies is as easy as flipping a switch—the Photo mode/Movie mode switch located to the right of the viewfinder. If you're looking for no-fuss, casual video, after you've selected Movie mode, just rotate the mode dial to the green Auto position and press the red Movie button located on top of the Z5, just southwest of the shutter release button. Capture will start; press the Movie button again to stop recording. That's all there is to grabbing good video clips.

But if you want to go beyond "good" to "excellent," you'll want to read this chapter and the next one, which will introduce you to the full range of the Z5's sophisticated movie-making capabilities. While I listed and briefly described all the options in the camera's Movie Shooting menu in Chapter 11, there's a great deal more to learn and put into practice.

Quick Start Checklist

The following is a list of things to keep in mind as you improve your movie-making skills and take your video work to the next level. Some of these items are recaps of information you learned about still photo shooting; others are of special concern for movie-making. Even if you decide to just skim through this chapter for now and come back for more after you've explored movie-making, you should at least read this section before you begin your epic documentary or feature production.

- **Stills, too.** You can take a cropped high-resolution still photograph, even while you're shooting a movie clip, by pressing the shutter release button all the way down. You won't miss a still shot because you're shooting video, nor will your video be interrupted. The still image is cropped to the 16:9 movie aspect ratio and saved in the same resolution as your movie frame size, using the JPEG * quality setting. That gives you a 1920 × 1080 (2MP) image in HD mode and a 3840 × 2160 (8MP) image in UHD (4K) mode.

    If you've chosen a Continuous release mode *only one photograph* will be taken each time you press the shutter release button during movie capture. Up to 50 different shots can be captured while shooting one movie.

- **No flash.** While you can shoot still photos while capturing video, you cannot use flash when the selector switch is set to the Movie position.

- **Exposure compensation.** When shooting movies, exposure compensation is available in plus/minus 3 EV steps in 1/3 EV increments. (Remember that still photos offer plus/minus 5 EV steps.)

- **Size matters.** Individual movie files can be up to 4GB in size (this will vary according to the resolution you select), and no more than 29 minutes, 59 seconds in length. A single movie may consist of as many as eight separate files, each 4GB in size. The actual number of files and their length varies depending on the frame size and frame rate you've selected. The speed and capacity of your memory card may provide additional restrictions on size or length.

- **Use the right card.** You'll want to use a fast card if possible. If you insist on using a slower card the recording may stop after a minute or two, given that full HD can require a transfer rate of 28 Mbps; 56 Mbps in High Quality format; and 144Mbps when shooting 4K video. In any case, choose a memory card with at least 32GB capacity. While some older cards are available in 16GB sizes, they are likely to be too slow for the High Quality setting.

  I've standardized on 64GB Sony Series SF-G memory cards when I'm shooting movies; one of these cards will hold at least three to six hours of video, and have the world's fastest transfer rates (at least, as I write this) of 300MB/second read and 299MB/second write speeds. However, in any case, the camera cannot shoot a continuous movie scene for more than about 29 minutes. You can start shooting the next clip right away, though, missing only about 30 seconds of the action. Of course, that assumes there's enough space on your memory card and adequate battery power.

- **Carry extra cards.** You're probably used to shooting still photographs. It's easy to estimate how much of your memory card's capacity you've already consumed, and how much is left, based on the shots remaining indicator on the Z5's LCD monitor and viewfinder displays. Video usage is a bit of a different animal. While the camera does show how much space you have remaining for a clip as you shoot, it's often difficult to make the connection to the remaining capacity of your memory card. It's necessary to make a trip to the Movie Shooting menu to see exactly how much space you have left. So, the best practice is to carry along many more cards than you think you need. I stuff two 64GB cards in my camera bag—enough for 6 hours of video each—but always carry along five 32GB cards as backup.

- **Add an external mic.** For the best sound quality, and to avoid picking up the sound of the autofocus or zoom motor, get an external stereo mic. I'll have more advice about capturing sound and describe specific types of microphones in Chapter 15.

- **Minimize zooming.** While it's great to be able to use the zoom for filling the frame with a distant subject, think twice before zooming. Unless you are using an external mic, the sound of the zoom ring rotating will be picked up and it will be audible when you play a movie. Any more than the occasional minor zoom will be very distracting to friends who watch your videos. And digital zoom will degrade image quality. Don't use the digital zoom if quality is more important than recording a specific subject such as a famous movie star far from a distance.

- **Use a fully charged battery.** A fresh battery will allow about 85 minutes of capture at normal (non-winter) temperatures, but that can be shorter if there are many focus adjustments. Individual clips can be no longer than about 29 minutes, however.

- **Keep it cool.** Video quality can suffer terribly when the imaging sensor gets hot so keep the camera in a cool place. When shooting on hot days especially, the sensor can get hot quicker than usual; when there's a risk of overheating, the camera will stop recording and it will shut down about five seconds later. Give it time to cool down before using it again.

- **Just press the Movie button.** You don't have to hold it down. Press it again when you're done to stop recording.

Lean, Mean, Movie Machine

The Z5 is an awesome video camera, one of the best ever offered by the company that introduced the first movie-making capabilities in an interchangeable-lens still camera—the Nikon D90—in 2008. And how far we've come since then! The D90 captured monaural movies using manual focus at a fixed 24 frames per second for up to five whole minutes at 1280 × 720p (standard HD) resolution. If you dropped down to coarse 640 × 424 and 320 × 216 frame sizes, you could shoot a clip as long as 20 minutes.

Your Z5, on the other hand, is packed with features that owners of many dedicated video camcorders only dreamed about a few years ago. I'll explain all the features in detail later in this chapter and the next, but you should check out this list if you want an overview:

- **Full HD capture.** You can record full high-definition video with 1920 × 1080 resolution at 60, 30, 25, and 24 progressive scan frame rates using the full sensor. If you want some extra telephoto "reach" from video captured using only the DX (APS-C/Super 35) area of the sensor, you can select those rates. I'll explain frame rates and other parameters later in this chapter.

- **4K video capture.** Ultra High Definition (UHD) video capture (3840 × 2160 resolution) is available at 30, 25, and 24 progressive scan rates, using a 1.7X crop factor.

- **Zebra stripe highlight display.** Highlights overexposed (by a factor you can specify) can be shown with a zebra-stripe overlay. I showed you how to set the parameters for this option in Chapter 12.

- **Phase detection AF.** Fast, continuous autofocus is essential for capturing smooth movie clips, so the Z5 uses its PDAF pixels in both 4K and HD video modes.

- **Focus Peaking for Manual Focus.** In-focus objects can be indicated by color outlines in the display. You can find more information on this, and an illustration, in Chapter 12.

- **IBIS and Electronic VR.** Shoot SteadyCam hand-held shots without SteadyCam hardware, thanks to the Z5's in-body image stabilization (which shifts the sensor itself to compensate for motion) and an extra electronic VR mode that shifts the *image pixels* around to reduce blur from camera motion. I'll explain how electronic VR operates in more detail later in this chapter.

- **Easy AF point placement.** Use the touch screen or the sub-selector joystick to locate the active focus point accurately during capture.

- **Output to an external video recorder.** The Z5 is perfect for use with an external monitor, like the affordable Atomos Ninja V ($600). It can output "clean" video through the HDMI port (more on that later) so you store your clips on an external device while previewing and viewing your movies on a large, bright screen.

- **Timecode.** Your video can include embedded timecodes, which are numeric codes that can be used to synchronize, log, and identify media. I introduced the Timecode option in Chapter 11.

- **Customization.** You can select separate settings for still photo and movie shooting modes, in the Photo Shooting and Movie Shooting menus, allowing you to customize the operation of your Z5 for each mode.

Capturing Video

In the Movie Shooting menus (see Figure 14.1), you can make the following choices, also described in Chapter 11, along with a description of the various options each entry offers. I won't repeat that information here. Many of these entries are like those for still photography in the Photo Shooting menu.

- **File Naming.** I recommend using a different substitution in Movie mode for the default DSC characters in filenames created for movie files. I use NZ5 for still photos and MOV for video files. The limitations and instructions are the same as for the File Naming entry in the Photo Shooting menu, as described in Chapter 11.

- **Destination.** Select Slot 1 or Slot 2 as the storage card for your video. Generally, you'll want to use the slot that contains the fastest memory card.

- **Choose Image Area.** This entry determines image area used when shooting movies.

  - **Choose Image Area.** This provides two variations: FX and DX, which allow you to capture full HD movies using what Nikon calls "FX-based movie format" and "DX-based movie format." The latter carves a 16:9 (HDTV) proportioned area from the full-frame view, as shown within the yellow box at top in Figure 14.2. Within the video arena, DX/APS-C movies are usually referred to as *APS-C/Super 35,* the latter being a common term for that video cropped format. Fortunately, the Z5 doesn't use a mask to mark off the cropped area. Instead, it helpfully enlarges the captured portion to fill the frame, as seen at bottom right in the figure. The normal FX-format view is shown at bottom left. Note that 4K UHD movies are always cropped, using a 1.7X crop factor.

Figure 14.1 Movie Shooting menu.

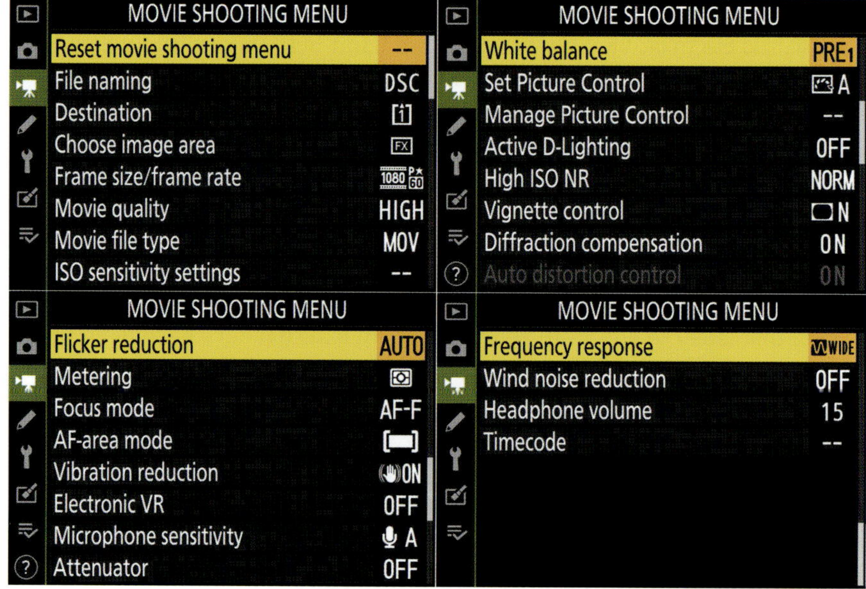

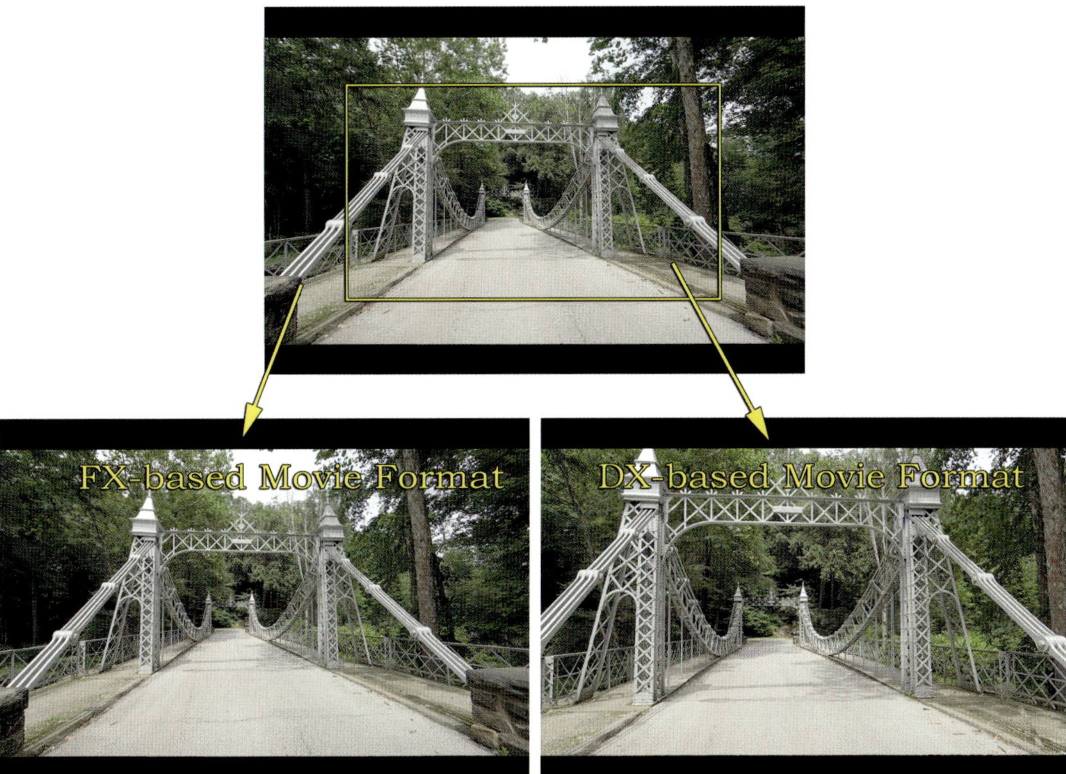

Figure 14.2 FX-based and DX-based movie formats.

USING DX LENSES

If you use the FTZ adapter to mount a lens that the camera recognizes as a DX/APS-C lens, the Z5 will switch to DX-based movie format automatically (without the need to specify FX or DX with the Choose Image Area entry, which is grayed out, in any case). As in still photo mode, you cannot force the camera to use the DX lens as if it were a full-frame optic. Remember that the Z5 may or may not detect APS-C (DX) lenses from third-party manufacturers.

When Electronic VR is selected, the Z5 provides a slight additional crop (to allow adjusting the frame to compensate for camera movement).

- **Frame Size/Frame Rate.** Here you can select any of 10 different video formats for conventional movies, plus three additional settings for slow-motion video. The conventional settings provide 4K video at 3840 × 2160 resolution at 30/25/24 frames per second, using the 1.7X crop, and Full HD at 1920 × 1080 resolution at 60/50/30/25/24 frames per second. As I explained earlier, 50/25 fps are used for PAL video systems overseas, while the other frame rates are compatible with the NTSC system used in the USA, Japan, and some other areas.

WHAT FRAME RATE: 24 FPS OR 30/60/120 FPS?

Even intermediate movie shooters can be confused by the choice between 24 fps and 30/60/120 fps, especially since those are only nominal figures (with the Z5, the 24 fps setting yields 23.976 frames per second; 30 fps gives you 29.97 actual "frames" per second; 60 fps yields 59.94). The difference lies in the two "worlds" of motion images, film and video. The standard frame rate for motion picture film is 24 fps, while the video rate, at least in the United States, Japan, and other places using the NTSC standard, is 30 fps (60 interlaced *fields* per second). Most computer video-editing software can handle either type and convert between them. The choice between 24 fps and 30 fps is determined by what you plan to do with your video. Your camera can also shoot at 25/50 fps for use with PAL systems, which don't use NTSC standards.

The short explanation is that, for technical reasons I won't go into here, shooting at 24 fps gives your movie a "film" look, excellent for showing fine detail. (I'll have more to say about that later in this chapter.)

However, if your clip has moving subjects, or you pan the camera, 24 fps can produce a jerky effect called "judder." A 30/60 fps rate produces a home-video look that some feel is less desirable, but which is smoother and less jittery when displayed on an electronic monitor. I suggest you try both and use the frame rate that best suits your tastes and video-editing software.

- **Movie Quality.** Select High Quality or Normal Quality. Your choice affects the sharpness/detail in your image and the maximum bit rate that can be sustained and length of the movies you can record. If you have fast memory cards and will be displaying your video at larger sizes, you'll want to use High Quality, which is my preference. Note that 4K video can *only* be captured using the High Quality setting; the Movie Quality entry is grayed out when you've specified UHD capture. It's usually possible to convert a video into a lower-resolution version in a movie-editing program.

- **Movie File Type.** As I described in Chapter 11, you can choose MOV or MP4 file types. MOV is the preferred file type for Macintosh devices (but is also compatible with Windows), while MP4 is a more widely adopted standard compatible with Macs and PCs. Movie-editing software can convert back and forth between either.

- **ISO Sensitivity Settings (for Movies).** Like the ISO settings in the Photo Shooting menu, as explained in Chapter 11, this version allows you to select a fixed ISO setting for Manual exposure mode, from ISO 100 to ISO 104400, plus Hi 0.3, 0.7, Hi 1, and Hi 2. That allows you greater control over the ISO used. When shooting movies in P, A, or S exposure modes, Auto ISO sensitivity is always used. However, if you want to use Auto ISO in Manual exposure mode, you can turn it on or off here, and specify the *maximum* ISO that will be selected automatically, from ISO 100 to Hi 2.0.

- **White Balance.** Here you can select the white balance used to shoot movies. You can choose:
  - **Same As Photo Settings.** The Z5 will use whatever white balance setting you've specified in the Photo Shooting menu.
  - **Any of the other white balance options.** The selection will apply *only* to video. The white balance of movie clips isn't easy to adjust, so you will usually want to set a specific white balance in this menu entry or opt for Auto white balance. I usually keep this setting the same as selected for still photos.

- **Set Picture Control.** You can specify Same as Photo Settings, or independently specify a Picture Control to be used only when shooting movies. The procedures for selecting and modifying a Picture Control in this menu entry is otherwise the same as described in Chapter 11.

  However, of special note here is the Flat Picture Control (available in both still and movie modes), which produces a dull, washed-out rendition. Why would you want that? Flat captures a wider dynamic range than other Picture Control modes, including Standard, giving you a better "raw" video image to fine-tune in your video-editing software, using your program's video color grading functions. Grading is used to adjust contrast, color, saturation, detail, black level, and white point, and is especially powerful when used with relatively flat images, like those produced by the Flat Picture Control.

- **Manage Picture Control.** This entry includes the Save/Edit, Rename, Delete, and Load/Save options that operate the same as the corresponding control in the Photo Shooting menu, described in Chapter 11. You can make a copy of a Picture Control, save an edited copy, rename, or remove a style, or retrieve a Picture Control from a memory card.

- **Active D-Lighting.** You can choose Same as Photo Settings, Extra High, High, Normal, Low, or Off.

- **High ISO NR.** Movie shooting doesn't involve *long* exposures, so the Movie Shooting menu includes only a High ISO Noise Reduction entry. You can set it to High, Normal, Low, or Off. See the entry for this feature under Photo Shooting menu, earlier in Chapter 11.

- **Vignette Control/Diffraction Compensation/Auto Distortion Control.** These three all operate the same as for still photo shooting and were described in Chapter 11.

- **Flicker Reduction.** Choose Auto, or select either 50Hz or 60Hz, as described in Chapter 11.

- **Metering.** Only Matrix, Center-weighted, and Highlight-weighted metering, as described in Chapter 4, are available. Spot metering is not available in Movie mode.

- **Focus Mode.** In addition to AF-S, AF-C, and Manual focus, Full-time AF (AF-F) is available in Movie mode. Unlike AF-S or AF-C, the AF-F autofocus mode doesn't need to be activated by pressing the shutter release or AF-ON button; AF-F functions as its name suggests: it is active at all times when you're in Movie mode. While power consumption is greater, there is less of a lag in achieving sharp focus once you begin video capture.

- **AF-Area Mode.** Only Single-Point AF, Wide-Area AF (Small), Wide-Area AF (Large), and Auto-Area AF are available. Pinpoint AF is not available in Movie mode.

- **Vibration Reduction.** This menu entry controls the Z5's built-in body image stabilization. You can choose Same as Photo Settings, On (Normal), Sport, or Off.

- **Electronic VR.** As I said earlier in this chapter and in Chapter 11, this electronic form of image stabilization does not shift the sensor's carrier mechanism, as IBIS does. Instead, the electronic version crops the video frame slightly, and shifts the entire frame up, down, left, right, or diagonally enough to counter some camera movement in the x and y directions. A "waving hand" indicator appears at the right side of the display when Electronic VR is active. Maximum sensitivity for movie shooting is fixed at ISO 25600. Keep in mind that, because of the cropping, the angle of view is reduced slightly, producing a slight focal length "multiplier" effect.

- **Microphone Sensitivity.** This entry has three options that control your Z5's built-in microphone or any external microphone you attach. You can choose Auto Sensitivity, Manual Sensitivity to set recording levels yourself (with a handy volume meter on screen showing the current ambient sound levels), or turn the microphone off entirely if you're planning to record silent video, use another sound recording source, or add sound in post-production. (See Figure 14.3.)

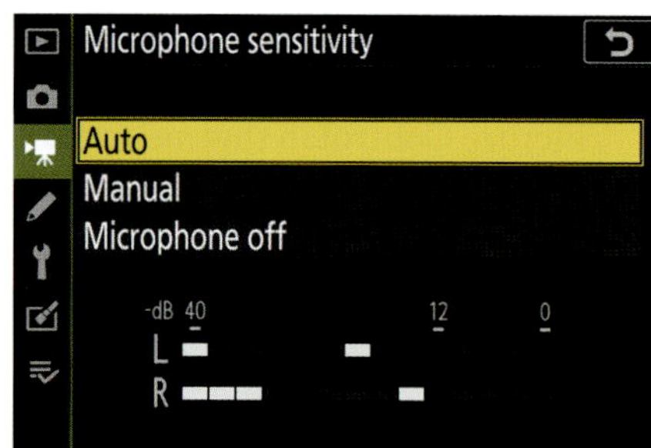

Figure 14.3 Microphone sensitivity can be set manually, using the Z5's audio meter as a reference.

- **Attenuator.** Enable this feature to minimize audio distortion from background sounds when capturing video in loud environments.

- **Frequency Response.** Select from Wide Range frequency response to record a broad range of sounds, or Vocal Range to optimize audio recording for vocals. You'll find an entire section on recording sound in Chapter 15.

- **Wind Noise Reduction.** Wind blowing across your microphone can be distracting. This setting reduces wind noise (and may also affect other sounds; so, use it carefully) for the built-in microphones *only*. Your external microphone, like the Nikon ME-1, may have its own wind noise reduction filter on/off switch.

- **Headphone Volume.** You can set a volume from 1 to 30; the default is 15.

- **Timecode.** As I've noted in several places in this book, including Chapter 11, advanced video editing and other software-oriented topics, such as Photoshop, are generally beyond the scope of this book. In any case, using timecodes is a fairly advanced procedure, and those who use them don't need instruction from me.

However, the ability to embed timecodes in video is a new and highly useful feature for Nikon interchangeable-lens cameras. As I said in Chapter 11, where all the timecode options are described, they provide precise *hour:minute:second:frame* markers that allow identifying and synchronizing frames and audio. The time code system includes a provision for "dropping" frames to ensure that the fractional frame rate of captured video (remember that a 24 fps setting actually yields 23.976 frames per second while 30 fps capture gives you 29.97 actual "frames" per second) can be matched up with actual time spans.

Shooting Your Movie

By this time, you're ready to capture some video. To shoot your movies, follow these steps:

1. **Plug in the microphone.** If you want to use an external monaural or stereo microphone with a 3.5mm stereo mini plug, attach it to the microphone jack on the left side of the camera.

2. **Choose an exposure mode.** Select Program, Shutter-priority, Aperture-priority, or Manual exposure. The Z5 uses Matrix metering based on readings from the sensor itself to determine exposure.

3. **Adjust exposure.** The adjustments you can make depend on the exposure mode you select.
   - **Program/Shutter-priority.** Adjust only exposure compensation by pressing the EV button on top of the camera and rotating the main command dial. The screen image will brighten and darken as you make adjustments. Shutter speed and ISO sensitivity are selected for you by the Z5.
   - **Aperture-priority.** You can change the f/stop by rotating the sub-command dial and adjust exposure compensation with the EV button and the main command dial. Shutter speed and ISO sensitivity are selected for you by the Z5.
   - **Manual exposure.** The main command dial changes the shutter speed (from 1/25th to 1/4000th second), and the sub-command dial adjusts the aperture. Press the ISO button and rotate the main command dial to change the ISO sensitivity.

4. **Enable movie recording.** Activate movie recording by rotating the Photo/Movie switch to the Movie position.

5. **Choose a focus and AF-area mode.** Select from autofocus or manual focus with the *i* menu or Fn2 button. Then choose AF-S or AF-F. Select an AF-area mode.

6. **Set audio level.** Use the Microphone Sensitivity entry in the Movie Shooting menu to specify audio recording level, using Auto Sensitivity to allow the Z5 to set the volume, or Manual Sensitivity to adjust using an audio meter (seen at the bottom of Figure 14.3). You can also turn off audio to record a silent movie, say, if you plan to add a voice-over track, music, or other audio in post-production using your video-editing software.

7. **Start/Stop recording.** Press the red-dotted movie recording button to lock in focus and begin capture. Press again to stop recording. The LCD monitor display as you're capturing video looks like Figure 14.4. The viewfinder display has the same information, arranged slightly differently, and not overlaid on the image area. You can press the DISP button to increase or decrease the amount of information overlaid on the screen during movie recording.

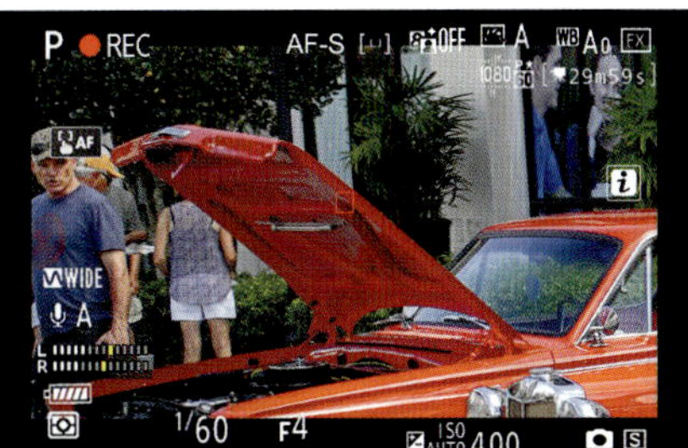

Figure 14.4 The LCD monitor display during movie capture.

8. **No flash.** You can't use electronic flash during movie recording, but you *can* use the built-in LED movie light on the Nikon SB-500 unit.

Using the *i* Button

The *i* button, which is so useful in Photo mode, also offers real-time adjustment of parameters and controls while you capture your video. These are not only important for fine-tuning your movies as you capture them but allow for some special tools that veteran videographers will know and love, but which may be new to still photographers. Here's a description of the useful options that pop up when you press the *i* button. (See Figure 14.5.) Many of these are also available in the Movie Shooting menu, as explained in Chapter 11. I'll point out which settings are those you might want to use during actual capture. As I described in Chapter 12, there is a Custom Setting g1: Customize *i* menu entry that allows you to swap out and change Movie mode *i* menu items.

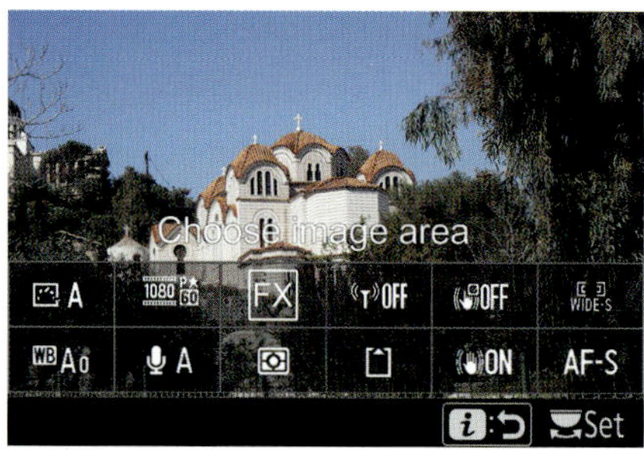

Figure 14.5 *i* button options.

- **Picture Control.** You can use any of the Picture Controls described in Chapter 11 in Movie mode and specify them here.

- **Frame Size/Rate and Image Quality.** Select your frame size/rate here and choose High or Normal quality.

- **Choose Image Area.** You can select the image area for movie mode, as described earlier in this chapter.

- **Wi-Fi Connection.** Control your wireless connection here (or, if you prefer, substitute a function you find more useful).

- **Electronic VR.** Turn it on or off.

- **AF-Area Mode.** Choose from among the available modes.

- **White Balance.** Set your white balance for movie shooting here.

- **Microphone Sensitivity.** It's useful to be able to use the *i* menu while shooting video to adjust the sensitivity of your microphone on the fly. As this adjustment controls both the built-in and optional external stereo microphones, you might find yourself needing to make your mic more sensitive or less sensitive as the ambient sound conditions change. For example, if you were capturing a clip with only background sound (no vocals) and someone started using a jackhammer a block away, you might want to reduce microphone sensitivity to minimize the clamor.

- **Metering Mode.** Select Matrix, Center-weighted, or Highlight-weighted. Remember that Spot is not available when shooting movies.

- **Destination.** Use this option to change your destination card slot on the fly.

- **Vibration Reduction.** You can turn in-body image stabilization on and off.

- **Focus Mode.** Choose AF-S, AF-C, AF-F, or Manual focus.

Stop That!

You might think that setting your Z5 to a faster shutter speed will help give you sharper video frames. But the choice of a shutter speed for movie making is a bit more complicated than that. First, you can't select the shutter speed at all for your movies when you're using Auto, P, S, or A exposure modes. You can select a shutter speed only if you switch to Manual exposure. Here's how it works:

- **Program and Shutter-priority modes.** The Z5 selects the shutter speed (such as 1/30th second) and ISO sensitivity appropriate for your lighting conditions. Your only exposure adjustment option is to press the EV button and add/subtract exposure compensation. As you might guess, P and S modes are not the best choices for those who want to shoot creatively.

- **Aperture-priority mode.** This is the mode to use when you want to put selective focus to work by choosing an aperture that will provide more, or less, depth-of-field. In A mode, you can select any f/stop available with your lens, and the Z5 will choose a shutter speed and ISO setting to suit. Generally, if you choose a large aperture, the camera will lower the ISO sensitivity as much as it can, to allow sticking with a shutter speed of 1/30th second. It will then select shorter shutter speeds, if necessary, under very bright illumination. My Z5 has jumped up to 1/200th second outdoors under bright daylight when I try to shoot at f/1.8 or f/1.4. In A mode, you can still add or subtract exposure compensation.

- **Manual exposure mode.** In this mode, you have control of aperture, shutter speed (from 1/25th second all the way up to 1/8000th second), and ISO—even if your settings result in video that is completely washed out, or entirely black. Because video capture is in the range of 24 to 60 frames per second, you can't select a shutter speed that is longer than the frame interval. That is, if your video mode is 1920 × 1080 at 30 fps, you can't choose a shutter speed longer than 1/30th second.

SEMI-MANUAL EXPOSURE?

The ISO Sensitivity Settings entry in the Movie Shooting menu allows you to enable a feature called Auto ISO Control (Mode M). When activated, the Z5 will attempt to adjust the ISO setting to provide the correct exposure based on the current shutter speed, aperture, and exposure compensation values you've specified. That means you can select a suitable shutter speed (subject to the recommendations described next), and an f/stop, and the Z5 will effectively provide you with autoexposure in Manual exposure mode.

So, how do you select an appropriate shutter speed? As you might guess, it's almost always best to leave the shutter speed at 1/30th second and allow the overall exposure to be adjusted by varying the aperture and/or ISO sensitivity. We don't normally stare at a video frame for longer than 1/30th or 1/24th second, so while the shakiness of the *camera* can be disruptive (and often corrected by VR), if there is a bit of blur in our *subjects* from movement, we tend not to notice. Each frame flashes by in the blink of an eye, so to speak, so a shutter speed of 1/30th second works a lot better in video than it does when shooting stills.

Higher shutter speeds introduce problems of their own. If you shoot a video frame using a shutter speed of 1/200th second, the actual moment in time that's captured represents only about 12 percent of the 1/30th second of elapsed time in that frame. Yet, when played back, that frame occupies the full 1/30th of a second, with 88 percent of that time filled by stretching the original image to fill it. The result is often a choppy/jumpy image, and one that may appear to be *too* sharp.

The reason for that is more social imprinting than scientific: we've all grown up accustomed to seeing the look of Hollywood productions that, by convention, were shot using a shutter speed that's half the reciprocal of the frame rate (that is, 1/48th second for a 24 fps movie). Movie cameras use a rotary shutter (achieving that 1/48th second exposure by using a 180-degree shutter "angle"), but the effect on our visual expectations is the same. For the most "film-like" appearance, use 24 fps and 1/60th second shutter speed.

Faster shutter speeds do have some specialized uses for motion analysis, especially where individual frames are studied. The rest of the time, 1/30th or 1/60th of a second will suffice. If the reason you needed a higher shutter speed was to obtain the correct exposure, use a slower ISO setting, or a neutral-density filter to cut down on the amount of light passing through the lens.

A good rule of thumb when shooting progressive video (as opposed to interlaced video, which is not offered by the Z5) is to use 1/60th second or slower when shooting at 24 fps; 1/60th second or slower at 30 fps; and 1/126th second or slower at 60 fps.

Viewing Your Movies

Once you've finished recording your movies, they are available for review. Film clips show up during picture review, the same as still photos, but they are differentiated by a movie camera icon overlay and "Play" prompt. Press the multi selector center button to start playback. During playback, you can perform the following functions:

- **Pause.** Press the multi selector down button to pause the clip during playback. Press the multi selector center button to resume playback.

- **Rewind/Advance.** Press the left/right multi selector buttons to rewind or advance (respectively). Press once for 2X speed, twice for 8X speed, or three times for 16X speed. Hold down the left/right buttons to move to the end or beginning of the clip.

- **Start Slo-Mo playback.** Press the down button while the movie is paused to play back in slow motion.

- **Skip 10 seconds.** Rotate the main command dial to skip ahead or back in 10-second increments.

- **Skip to index.** Rotate the sub-command dial to skip to the next or previous index marker. If there are no indices saved, the command dial moves to the last or first frame of the clip. Movies with indices are indicated by a "paddle" icon at the top of the screen during playback.

- **Change volume.** Press the Zoom In and Zoom Out buttons to increase/decrease volume.

- **Trim movie/Save frame.** Press the *i* button and follow the steps in the next section.

- **Exit Playback.** Press the multi selector up button or the Playback button to exit playback.

- **Return to shooting mode.** Press the Movie button to return to Shooting mode.

- **View menus.** Press the MENU button to interrupt playback to access menus.

Trimming Your Movies

In-camera editing is limited to trimming the beginning or end from a clip, and the clip must be at least two seconds long. For more advanced editing, you'll need an application capable of editing AVI movie clips. Google "AVI Editor" to locate any of the hundreds of free video editors available, or use a commercial product like Corel Video Studio, Adobe Premiere Elements, or Pinnacle Studio. These will let you combine several clips into one movie, add titles, special effects, and transitions between scenes.

In-camera editing/trimming can be done from the Retouch menu, or during Playback. The procedure is the same. To do in-camera editing/trimming, follow these steps:

1. **Start movie clip.** Use the Playback button to start image review and press the multi selector center button to start playback when you see a clip you want to edit. It will begin playing. Then follow the instructions beginning with Step 2.

   Or, you can access the Edit Movie choice in the Retouch menu when you see the clip on the screen that you want to edit.

2. **Activate edit.** To remove video from the beginning of a clip, view the movie until you reach the first frame you want to keep, and then press the down button to pause. The movie progress bar at the bottom left of the screen will show the current position in the movie. You can move back and forth frame by frame while the video is paused by pressing the left/right buttons or rotating the main or sub-command dials.

3. **Trim move.** To trim video from the end of a clip, watch the movie until you reach the last frame you want to keep and then press the down button to pause. You can jump to the next saved index point in the clip by rotating the main command dial.

4. **Select start/end point.** When the video is paused, press the *i* button to show the movie edit options, and select Choose Start/End Point (see Figure 14.6). You'll be asked whether the current frame should be the start or end point. Highlight your choice and press OK again.

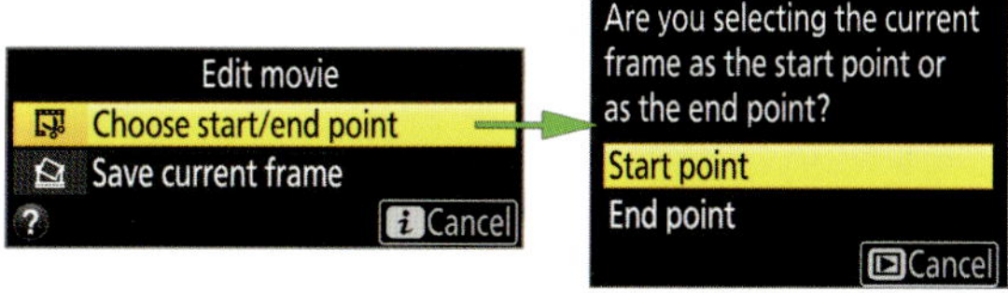

Figure 14.6 Choose editing options from this menu.

5. **Resume playback.** Press the multi selector center button to start or resume playback. (See Figure 14.7 for the viewfinder display; the LCD monitor display is similar.) You can use the Pause, Rewind, Advance, and Single frame controls plus the main command dial (to jump to the next saved index point) as described previously to move around within your clip. Note that your trimmed movie must be at least two seconds long.

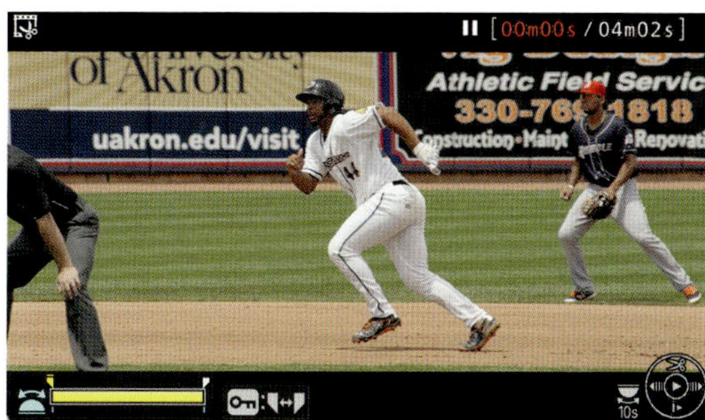

Figure 14.7 Edit your movie.

6. **Confirm trim.** A Proceed? prompt appears. Choose Yes or No and press OK.

7. **Save movie.** You have four choices when saving the trimmed movie:

   - **Save As New File.** The trimmed clip will be stored as a new file, and the original movie preserved.
   - **Overwrite Existing File.** The trimmed clip replaces the original movie on your memory card. Use this option with caution, as you'll be unable to restore your unedited clip.
   - **Cancel.** Return to the editing mode.
   - **Preview.** View the trimmed version. You can then save as a new file, overwrite, or cancel.

   You'll see a Saving Movie message and a green progress bar as the Z5 stores the trimmed clip to your memory card. Storage takes some time, and you don't want to interrupt it to avoid losing your saved clip. So, make sure your camera has a fully charged battery before you start to edit a clip.

Saving a Frame

You can store any frame from one of your movies as a JPEG still, using the resolution of the current video format. Just follow these steps:

1. Pause your movie at the frame you want to save by pressing the down directional button.
2. Press the *i* button and choose Save Selected Frame.
3. Your frame will be stored on the memory card.

Tips for Shooting Better Video

Once upon a time, the ability to shoot video with a digital still camera was one of those "gee whiz" gimmicks camera makers seemed to include just to have a reason to get you to buy a new camera. That hasn't been true for many years now, as the video quality of many digital still cameras has gotten quite good. Indeed, feature films have been shot entirely or in part using Nikon dSLRs, and the Showtime television series *Dexter* included many scenes captured with a Nikon D800. The Z5 really ups the ante by incorporating video capabilities that have been enhanced or simply not available with previous Nikon still cameras.

But producing good-quality video is more complicated than just buying good equipment. There are techniques that make for gripping storytelling and a visual language the average person is very accustomed to seeing, but also unaware of. After all, by comparison we're used to watching the best productions that television, video, and motion pictures can offer. Whether it's fair or not, our efforts are compared to what we're used to seeing produced by experts. While this book can't make you a professional videographer, there is some advice I can give you that will help you improve your results with the camera.

There are many different things to consider when planning a video shoot, and when possible, a shooting script and storyboard can help you produce a higher-quality video.

Using an External Recorder

If you're truly becoming an advanced videographer, you'll probably be working with the Z5's ability to output "clean" non-compressed HDMI video to an external monitor or video recorder, including the Atomos Shogun lineup, which includes versions that are quite affordable, at least in terms of professional video gear. You can choose models both with and without an external LCD monitor, and capture to solid-state drives (SSD), a laptop's internal or connected hard drive, or other media. Such equipment allows very high transfer rates and is certainly your best choice if you're shooting 4K video.

Probably the best of the lot for Nikon Z5 owners is the Atomos Ninja V, an extremely portable unit with a 5.2-inch screen and a $600 price tag that's currently the lowest for this type of device. Its size is a definite plus—if you're shooting video with a smaller, lightweight camera, you're going to need an equally compact recorder/monitor, such as the roughly 13-ounce Ninja V. Add a battery, HDMI cable, and a 2.5-inch solid-state drive, and you're ready to go.

The Ninja V has HDMI input and output jacks on its left edge, which you can see in Figure 15.1. The latter allows you to daisy-chain an even larger monitor or other device. A power button, headphone jack, microphone/audio input, and remote jack reside on the other edge. The touch screen enables you to view your video and access the monitor/recorder's menus and controls, which is convenient (except outdoors in cold weather when you're wearing gloves and might wish you had a few buttons to press instead). The only other "defect" of the unit is the noise produced by its fan; even when you're using an external microphone with your Z5, the fan noise may be picked up in a quiet room.

By the time this book is published, I'm hoping Nikon will offer a Filmmaker's kit similar to the one developed for the Nikon Z6. The Z6 version is an attractive bundle that includes the camera with Nikkor S 24-70mm f/4 S lens, plus the FTZ adapter, the Atomos Ninja V, a Rode VideoMic Pro+ microphone, Moza Air 2 three-axis hand-held gimbal, a coiled HDMI cable, and extra battery, at a savings of roughly $650 over buying these components separately. Nikon throws in a 12-month Vimeo Pro membership and an online course in how to make music videos, hosted by Chris Hersman, a Nikon Ambassador. The features of the Z5 are just as good for video shooting (at least when it comes to full HD movies), so it's a reasonable bet that Nikon will offer a Filmmaker's Kit for your camera, too.

Why use an external monitor/recorder like the Ninja V, when your Z5 has its own nifty monitor and can store quite a lot of video on its cards? From a monitor standpoint, an external unit's screen is larger, easier to see, and offers more flexibility in positioning. The Z5's screen tilts up or down; mounted on a ballhead like the one in the figure, you can adjust an external screen to any angle, including reversing it to point in the same direction as the lens, so vloggers can monitor themselves as they record or stream their video blog.

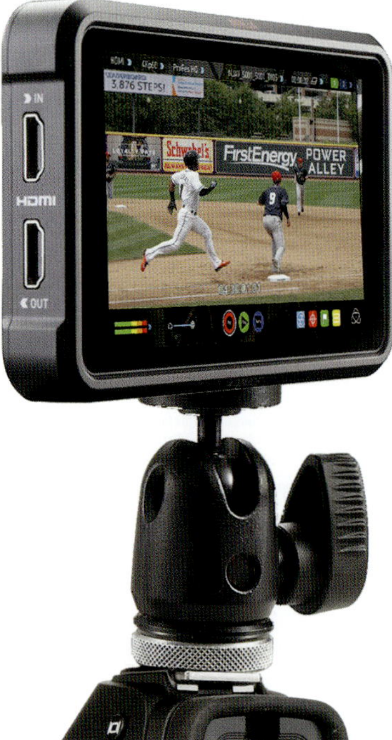

Figure 15.1 The Atomos Ninja V monitor/recorder.

But the best value may come from the recording capabilities of such a device. Internal video is saved to your memory card in the standard H.264/MPEG-4 Part 10 format as a MOV or MP4 file, which compresses that stream of images as much as 50X. That video has only 8 bits of information: good, but somewhat limited in the dynamic range that can be included. Depending on your scene, you may lose some detail in the highlights or shadows.

> **TECH ALERT**
>
> Unless you're venturing into professional videography, you probably aren't obsessed with all those numbers in the previous paragraph. However, if you're terminally curious, the important things to keep in mind are:
>
> - **Transfer bit rate.** This is the speed the Z5 outputs its video to your memory card or external recorder. High transfer rates (such as 144 megabits per second) require fast memory cards; an external recorder should be able to suck up video as quickly as your camera can deliver it.
> - **Encoding.** Although the "clean" video output to the HDMI port is not compressed, it is *encoded* using a procedure called *chroma subsampling,* which does reduce the amount of information that needs to be transferred. Chroma subsampling takes advantage of the fact that human beings don't detect changes in color (chroma) as easily as they do for brightness (luma). The designation 4:2:2 simply indicates that the full amount of brightness information is passed along ("4") while the two chroma values are sampled at half that rate ("2:2"). Subsampling in this way reduces the bandwidth of the otherwise uncompressed video signal by as much as one-third with no visual difference.

Fortunately, the Z5 can also simultaneously direct its movie output through the HDMI port in "clean" video to recorders like the Ninja V, where it is stored on a removable SSD (solid-state drive). When capture is completed, the SSD is connected to a computer using a USB cable.

The HDMI port on the Z5 accepts an HDMI mini-C cable. Nikon offers the HC-E1, but I prefer to purchase less-pricey third-party cables, which I buy in convenient lengths of 3 feet, 6 feet, 10 feet, or longer. The cable can be connected to the monitor, recorder, or other device of your choice. (Some of the screenshots in this book were output to a Blackmagic Intensity shuttle that allowed capturing stills of the Z5's menus, live view, and video.) Here's a recap of the information originally presented in Chapter 13, listing what you need to know to output to the HDMI port using the Setup menu options.

- **Output Resolution.** Select Auto and the camera will sense the correct output resolution to use. Auto will be applied (even if you select another resolution) when the HDMI port is used to display the camera's image during movie live view, movie capture, and movie playback. I have found Auto will not work reliably with some devices, like my Intensity Shuttle, which works best when I use 1080i. If you're having difficulties, you can manually set the Z5 to one of the available output resolutions individually until you find the best setting. (See Figure 15.2.)

  If you want to use a different resolution, specific formats include 480p (640 × 480 progressive scan); 576p (720 × 576 progressive scan); 720p (1280 × 720 progressive scan); 1080p (1920 × 1080 progressive scan); or 1080i (1920 × 1080 interlaced scan). A 4K output option 2160p (3840 × 1260 progressive scan) is also available and should be used only with a 4K-compatible device.

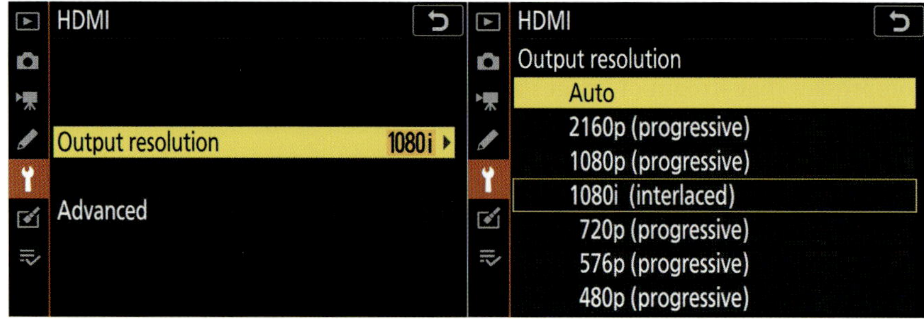

Figure 15.2 Choose output resolution.

- **Advanced.** This cryptic entry leads you to a screen where you can select more parameters:

  - **Output Range.** Choose Auto (the default, and the best choice under most circumstances; it works fine with my Intensity Shuttle); Limited Range; or Full Range. The Z5 is usually able to determine the output range of your HDMI device. If not, Limited Range uses settings of 16 to 235, clipping off the darkest (0–16) and brightest (235–255) portions of the image. Use Limited Range if you're plagued with reduced detail in the shadows of your image. Full Range may be your choice if shadows are washed out or excessively bright. It accepts video signals with the full range from 0 to 255. (See Figure 15.3.)

  - **External Recording Control.** When enabled, this option allows you to use the camera controls to stop and start recording when connected to an external recorder (favored by serious videographers). The recorder must support the Atomos Open Protocol, used by the popular Atomos Shogun and Ninja recorders. When active, a STBY (Standby) or REC (Recording) icon appears on the live view monitor. This control is not available when shooting 4K or Slow-Mo video.

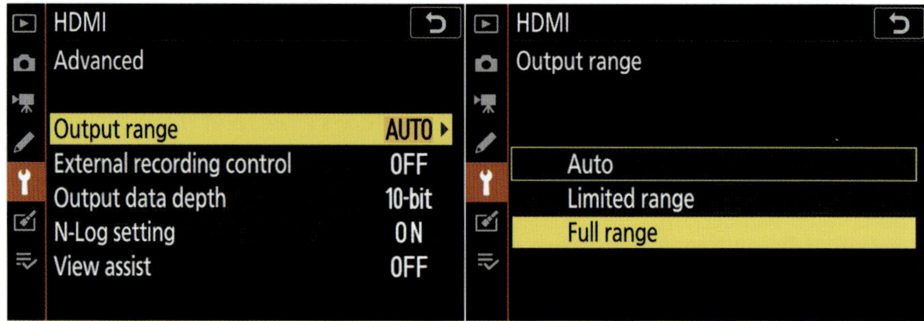

Figure 15.3 Select an output range.

Refocusing on Focus

Although I explained the Z5's autofocus and manual focus options in Chapter 5, there are some special considerations for focus when capturing video. The availability of usable AF when capturing movies, thanks to the Z5's on-sensor PDAF, is extremely important. The camera now more quickly and reliably is able to gauge subject distance, tracking, and refocusing on subjects; you really don't want inaccurate focus in video clips, where inconsistent focus is quite obvious when the movie is viewed.

Your three autofocus modes work extremely well. AF-S focuses once and is useful for non-moving subjects; AF-C only refocuses while you're holding down the shutter release or AF-On button. That's particularly useful when you want to retain focus on a particular subject but refocus at your command as needed when the subject moves. AF-F (Full-time AF) is available if you need the Z5 to refocus constantly as you capture. Use Custom Setting g4: AF Speed to control whether the camera refocuses quickly to follow a moving subject or refocuses more slowly to switch from one subject to another. Custom Setting g5: AF Tracking Sensitivity can enable/disable the Z5's ability to switch quickly when a different subject intervenes between the camera and the original subject. Both these fine-tuning behaviors can be used creatively to concentrate/deconcentrate attention on a particular subject or area of the frame.

Manual focus, with help from Focus Peaking (which is not available when using the Zebra feature), is an option, particularly for those who want to "pull" or "push" focus, a creative technique for redirecting the viewer's attention from one subject to another, located in the foreground or background. The only complications are that the Z5's electronic focus isn't particularly linear, so a certain degree of rotation of the focus/control ring doesn't result in the same amount of adjustment of the focus; in addition, experienced videographers may not like that the Nikon focus ring operates in the opposite direction of many/most other systems. While you can reverse the rotational direction of dials, you can't do that with the focus/control ring. Since focusing is "by-wire" rather than mechanical, I believe Nikon could have added this option if it wanted to, and did in the Nikon Z7 II and Z6 II.

Lens Craft

I covered the use of lenses with the Z5 in more detail in Chapter 7, but a discussion of why lens selection is important when shooting movies may be useful at this point. In the video world, not all lenses are created equal. The two most important considerations are depth-of-field, or the beneficial lack thereof, and zooming. I'll address each of these separately.

Depth-of-Field and Video

Have you wondered why professional videographers have gone nuts over still cameras that can also shoot video? The producers of *Saturday Night Live* could afford to have their director of photography use the niftiest, most-expensive high-resolution video cameras to shoot the opening sequences of the program. Instead, they opted for digital SLR cameras. One thing that makes digital still cameras so attractive for video is that they have relatively large sensors, which provides improved low-light performance and results in the oddly attractive reduced depth-of-field, compared with many professional video cameras.

But wait! you say. No matter what size sensor is used to capture a video frame, isn't the number of pixels in that frame the same? That's true—the final resolution of a full HD 1080p video image is exactly 1920 × 1080 pixels. For standard HD (720p) the resolution is 1280 × 720 pixels (which the Z5 does not offer), and for ultra HD/4K (2160p), the resolution is 3820 × 2160 pixels. The final resolution, at least for the most common 1080p resolution, is the same, whether you're capturing that frame with a point-and-shoot camera, a professional video camera, or a digital SLR like the Nikon Z5. But that's only the *final* resolution. The number of pixels used to *originally* capture each video frame varies by sensor size.

For example, your Z5 does *not* use only its central 1920 × 1080 pixels to capture a full HD video frame. If it did that, you'd have to contend with a huge "crop" factor. That doesn't happen with full HD! (See Chapter 7 for a longer discussion of the effects of the so-called "crop" factor.) The Z5 applies a crop (1.7X) only to 4K video, as I'll explain shortly.

Instead, in full HD mode, when the Z5 is set for *FX-based movie format* (which I'll illustrate later in this chapter), it captures a video frame using an area that stretches across the full width of the sensor,

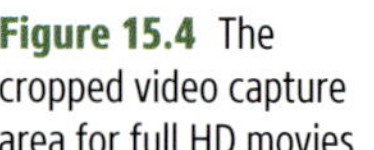

Figure 15.4 The cropped video capture area for full HD movies.

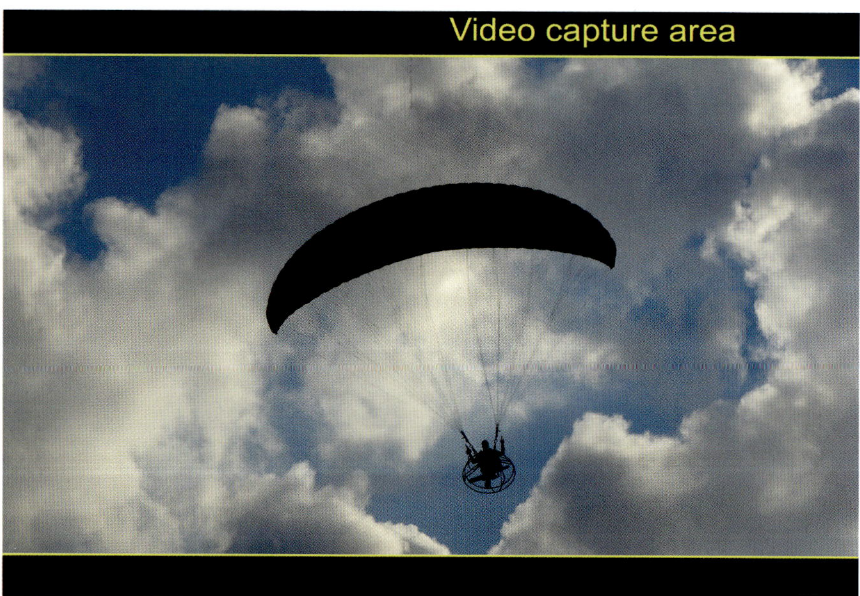

using the *proportions* of a 16:9 area of its sensor. The pixels within that area are then sub-sampled using only *some* of the available photosites to reduce the captured frame to the final 1920 × 1080 video resolution. Your wide-angle and telephoto lenses retain roughly their same fields of view, and you can frame and compose your video through the viewfinder normally, with only the top and bottom of the frame cropped off to account for the wider video aspect ratio. (See Figure 15.4.)

As you learned in Chapter 7, a larger sensor calls for the use of longer focal lengths to produce the same field of view, so, in effect, a larger sensor like the full-frame FX sensor used in the Z5 has reduced depth-of-field. And *that's* what makes cameras like the Z5 attractive from a creative standpoint. Less depth-of-field means greater control over the range of what's in focus. Your Z5, with its larger sensor, has a distinct advantage over even DX models like the D850, is miles ahead of consumer camcorders in this regard, and even does a better job than many professional video cameras. (Some professional video cameras do use large sensors.) Figure 15.5 compares some typical sensor sizes.

The picture changes, so to speak, when the Z5 is capturing 4K video. The camera uses only a central area of the frame, a bit smaller than the DX-based movie format area shown in Figure 15.5, producing an effective 1.7X crop. When you're shooting 4K video, your 24-50mm kit lens has an effective equivalent focal range of about 41-85mm instead. You'll need to keep that in mind, especially when you're looking for an ultra-wide-angle perspective for your video. That heavy 1.7X crop makes it difficult to get a true wide-angle perspective when shooting 4K with the Z5. Nikon's most affordable wide-angle Z-mount zoom, the Nikkor Z 14-30mm f/4 S yields the equivalent of about 24mm at its widest zoom setting and becomes a 50mm normal lens at its maximum focal length. Using that smaller area of the sensor produces video that is noticeably more grainy than the Z5's full HD movies captured using the full width of the sensor.

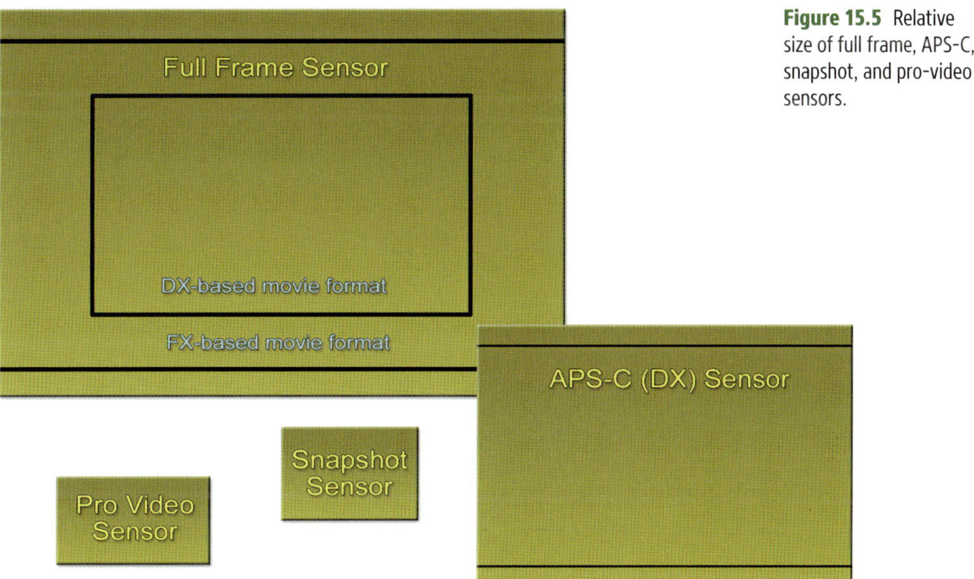

Figure 15.5 Relative size of full frame, APS-C, snapshot, and pro-video sensors.

Zooming and Video

When shooting still photos, a zoom is a zoom is a zoom. The key considerations for a zoom lens used only for still photography are the maximum aperture available at each focal length ("How *fast* is this lens?), the zoom range ("How far can I zoom in or out?"), and its sharpness at any given f/stop ("Do I lose sharpness when I shoot wide open?").

When shooting video, the priorities may change, and there are two additional parameters to consider. The first two I listed, lens speed and zoom range, have roughly the same importance in both still and video photography. Zoom range gains a bit of importance in videography, because you can always/usually move closer to shoot a still photograph, but when you're zooming during a shot most of us don't have that option (or the funds to buy/rent a dolly to smoothly move the camera during capture). But, oddly enough, overall sharpness may have slightly less importance under certain conditions when shooting video. That's because the image changes in some way many times per second (24/30/60 times per second with the Z5), so any given frame doesn't hang around long enough for our eyes to pick out every single detail. You want a sharp image, of course, but your standards don't need to be quite as high when shooting video.

Here are the remaining considerations:

- **Zoom lens maximum aperture.** The speed of the lens matters in several ways. A zoom with a relatively large maximum aperture lets you shoot in lower light levels, and a big f/stop allows you to minimize depth-of-field for selective focus. Keep in mind that the maximum aperture may change during zooming. A lens that offers an f/3.5 maximum aperture at its widest focal length may provide only f/5.6 worth of light at the telephoto position.

- **Zoom range.** Use of zoom during actual capture should not be an everyday thing unless you're shooting a kung-fu movie. However, there are effective uses for a zoom shot, particularly if it's a "long" one from extreme wide angle to extreme close-up (or vice versa). Most of the time, you'll use the zoom range to adjust the perspective of the camera *between* shots, and a longer zoom range can mean less trotting back and forth to adjust the field of view. Zoom range also comes into play when you're working with selective focus (longer focal lengths have less depth-of-field) or want to expand or compress the apparent distance between foreground and background subjects. A longer range gives you more flexibility.

- **Linearity.** Interchangeable lenses may have some drawbacks, as many photographers who have been using the video features of their interchangeable-lens digital cameras have discovered. That's because, unless a lens is optimized for video shooting, zooming with a particular lens may not necessarily be linear. Rotating the zoom collar manually at a constant speed doesn't always produce a smooth zoom. There may be "jumps" as the elements of the lens shift around during the zoom. Keep that in mind if you plan to zoom during a shot and are using a lens that has proved, from experience, to provide a non-linear zoom. (Unfortunately, there's no easy way to tell ahead of time whether you own a lens that is well-suited for zooming during a shot.)

Keeping Things Stable and on the Level

Camera shake's enough of a problem with still photography, but it becomes even more of a nuisance when you're shooting video. The image-stabilization feature found in many Nikon lenses (and some third-party optics) can help minimize this. That's why Nikon's VR-capable zoom lenses (described in Chapter 7) make an excellent choice for video shooting if you're planning on going for the hand-held cinema verité look.

The Z5 also has an *electronic VR* option, which I've described several times in this book. It's available only in 1080p mode (other resolutions, including 1920 × 1080 slow-motion and 4K are disabled). To recap, electronic vibration reduction reduces the frame size by about 10 percent (in FX mode only; in DX mode the camera has the pixels outside the APS-C frame to play with) and uses the extra image area to realign the frames to counteract any camera motion.

Just realize that while hand-held camera shots—even image stabilized—may be perfect if you're shooting a documentary or video that intentionally mimics traditional home movie making, in other contexts it can be disconcerting or annoying. And even VR can't work miracles. It's the camera movement itself that is distracting—not necessarily any blur in your subject matter.

If you want your video to look professional, putting the Z5 on a tripod will give you smoother, steadier video clips to work with. It will be easier to intercut shots taken from different angles (or even at different times) if everything was shot on a tripod. Cutting from a tripod shot to a hand-held shot, or even from one hand-held shot to another one that has noticeably more (or less) camera movement can call attention to what otherwise might have been a smooth cut or transition.

Remember that telephoto lenses and telephoto zoom focal lengths magnify any camera shake, even with VR, so when you're using a longer focal length, that tripod becomes an even better idea. Tripods are essential if you want to pan from side to side during a shot, dolly in and out, or track from side to side (say, you want to shoot with the camera in your kid's coaster wagon). A tripod and (for panning) a fluid head built especially for smooth video movements can add a lot of production value to your movies.

ROLL ON, SHUTTER

Another side-effect to watch out for occurs when panning or capturing moving subjects, caused by the Z5's *rolling shutter.* Because the camera captures all the horizontal lines one at a time, the last line in a frame is captured a fraction of a second later (about 15 ms) after the first line. So, if the subject or camera is moving from side to side, a vertical subject will appear to lean backward, causing what is termed a "Jell-O effect." There's no way to eliminate this defect, but you should be aware of it when shooting. You may be able to minimize capturing moving subjects or edit offending clips out of your finished video.

Shooting Script

A shooting script is nothing more than a coordinated plan that covers both audio and video and provides order and structure for your video when you're in planned, storytelling mode. A detailed script will cover what types of shots you're going after, what dialogue you're going to use, audio effects, transitions, and graphics. A good script needn't constrain you: as the director you are free to make changes on the spot during actual capture. But, before you change the route to your final destination, it's good to know where you were headed, and how you originally planned to get there.

When putting together your shooting script, plan for lots and lots of different shots, even if you don't think you'll need them. Only amateurish videos consist of a bunch of long, tedious shots. You'll want to vary the pace of your production by cutting among lots of different views, angles, and perspectives, so jot down your ideas for these variations when you put together your script.

If you're shooting a documentary rather than telling a story that's already been completely mapped out, the idea of using a shooting script needs to be applied more flexibly. Documentary filmmakers often have no shooting script at all. They go out, do their interviews, capture video of people, places, and events as they find them, and allow the structure of the story to take shape as they learn more about the subject of their documentary. In such cases, the movie is typically "created" during editing, as bits and pieces are assembled into the finished piece.

Storyboards

A storyboard makes a great adjunct to a detailed shooting script. It is a series of panels providing visuals of what each scene should look like. While the ones produced by Hollywood are generally of very high quality, there's nothing that says drawing skills are important for this step. Stick figures work just fine if that's the best you can do. The storyboard just helps you visualize locations, placement of actors/actresses, props, and furniture, and helps everyone involved get an idea of what you're trying to show. It also helps show how you want to frame or compose a shot. You can even shoot a series of still photos and transform them into a "storyboard" if you want, such as in Figure 15.6.

Storytelling in Video

Today's audience is used to fast-paced, short-scene storytelling. To produce interesting video for such viewers, it's important to view video storytelling as a kind of shorthand code for the more leisurely efforts print media offers. Audio and video should always be advancing the story. While it's okay to let the camera linger from time to time, it should only be for a compelling reason and only briefly. Above all, look for movement in your scene as you shoot. You're not taking still photographs!

It only takes a second or two for an establishing shot to impart the necessary information. For example, many of the scenes for a video documenting a model being photographed in a rock 'n' roll music setting might be close-ups and talking heads, but an establishing shot showing the studio where the video was captured helps set the scene.

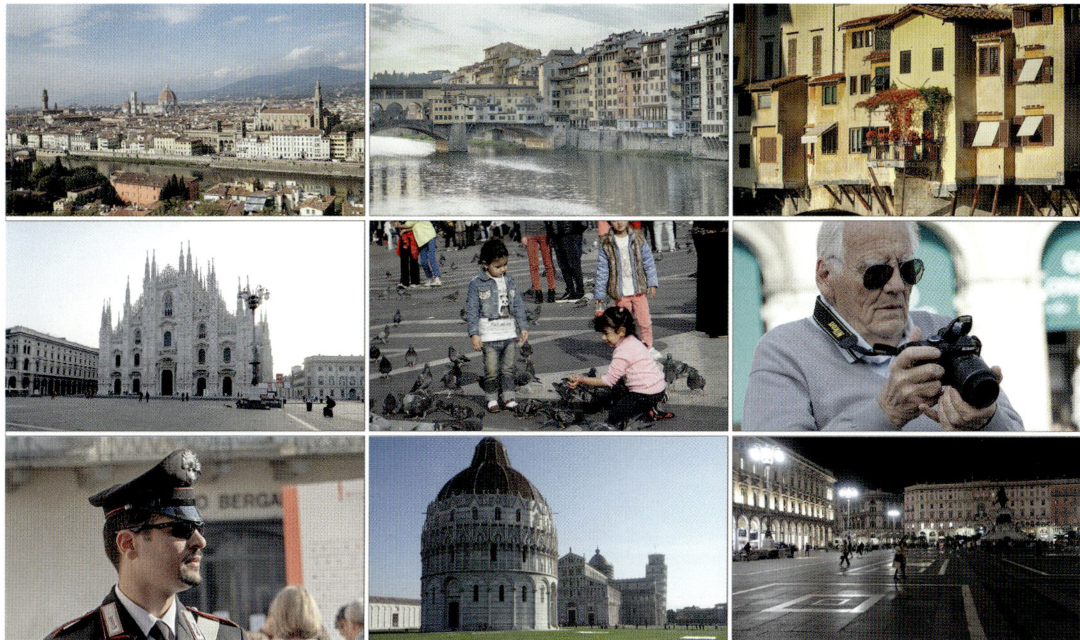

Figure 15.6 A storyboard is a series of simple sketches or photos to help visualize a segment of video.

Provide variety too. If you put your shooting script together correctly, you'll be changing camera angles and perspectives often and never leave a static scene on the screen for a long period of time. (You can record a static scene for a reasonably long period and then edit in other shots that cut away and back to the longer scene with close-ups that show each person talking.)

When editing, keep transitions basic! I can't stress this one enough. Watch a television program or movie. The action "jumps" from one scene or person to the next. Fancy transitions that involve exotic "wipes," dissolves, or cross fades take too long for the average viewer and make your video ponderous.

Composition

In movie shooting, several factors restrict your composition, and impose requirements you just don't always have in still photography (although other rules of good composition do apply). Here are some of the key differences to keep in mind when composing movie frames:

- **Horizontal compositions only.** Some subjects, such as basketball players and tall buildings, just lend themselves to vertical compositions. But movies are shown in horizontal format only. So, if you're interviewing a local basketball star, you can end up with a worst-case situation like the one shown in Figure 15.7. If you want to show how tall your subject is, it's often impractical to move back far enough to show him full-length. You really can't capture a vertical composition. Tricks like getting down on the floor and shooting up at your subject can exaggerate the perspective but aren't a perfect solution.

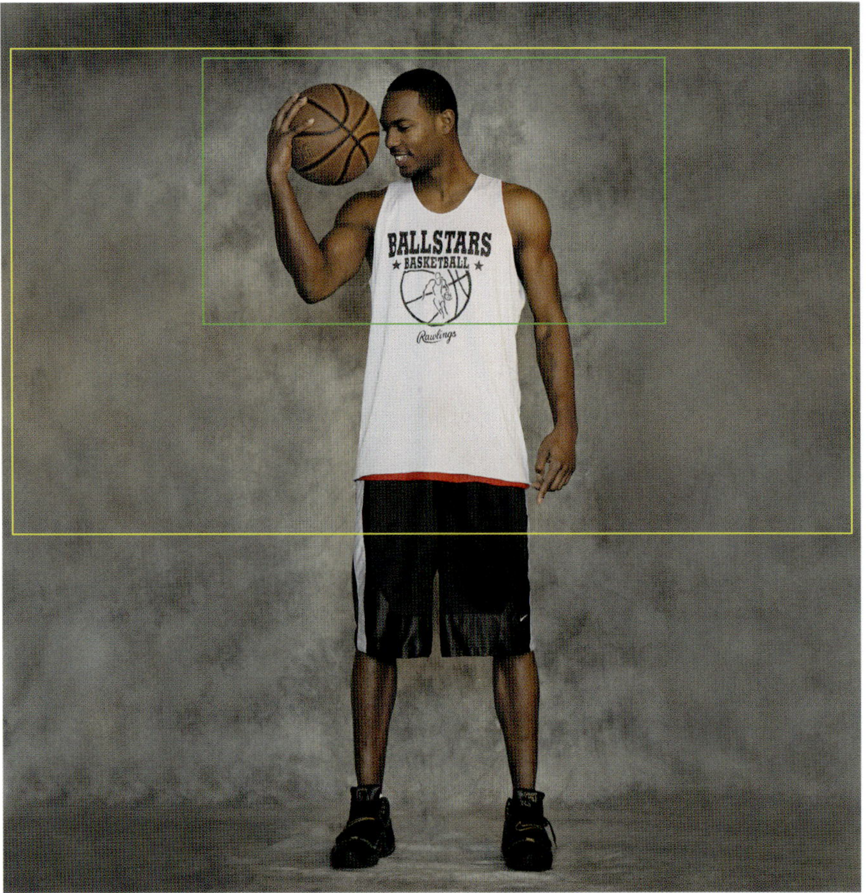

- **Wasted space at the sides.** Moving in to frame the basketball player as outlined by the yellow box in Figure 15.7 means that you're still forced to leave a lot of empty space on either side. (Of course, you can fill that space with other people and/or interesting stuff, but that defeats your intent of concentrating on your main subject.) So, when faced with some types of subjects in a horizontal frame, you can be creative, or move in *really* tight. For example, if I was willing to give up the "height" aspect of my composition, I could have framed the shot as shown by the green box in the figure and wasted less of the image area at either side.

- **Seamless (or seamed) transitions.** Unless you're telling a picture story with a photo essay, still pictures often stand alone. But with movies, each of your compositions must relate to the shot that preceded it, and the one that follows. It can be jarring to jump from a long shot to a tight close-up unless the director—you—is very creative. Another common error is the "jump cut" in which successive shots vary only slightly in camera angle, making it appear that the main subject has "jumped" from one place to another. (Although everyone from French New Wave director Jean-Luc Goddard to Guy Ritchie—Madonna's ex—have used jump cuts effectively in their films.) The rule of thumb is to vary the camera angle by at least 30 degrees between shots to make it appear to be seamless. Unless you prefer that your images flaunt convention and appear to be "seamy."

- **The time dimension.** Unlike still photography, with motion pictures there's a lot more emphasis on using a series of images to build on each other to tell a story. Static shots where the camera is mounted on a tripod and everything is shot from the same distance are a recipe for dull videos. Watch a television program sometime and notice how often camera shots change distances and directions. Viewers are used to this variety and have come to expect it. Professional video productions are often done with multiple cameras shooting from different angles and positions. But many professional productions are shot with just one camera and careful planning, and you can do just fine with your Z5.

Here's a look at the different types of commonly used compositional tools:

- **Establishing shot.** Much as it sounds, this type of composition, as shown in Figure 15.8, upper left, establishes the scene and tells the viewer where the action is taking place. Let's say you're shooting a video of your offspring's move to college; the establishing shot could be a wide shot of the campus with a sign welcoming you to the school in the foreground. Another example would be for a child's birthday party; the establishing shot could be the front of the house decorated with birthday signs and streamers or a shot of the dining room table decked out with party favors and a candle-covered birthday cake. In the example, I wanted to show the studio where the video was shot.

- **Medium shot.** This shot is composed from about waist to head room (some space above the subject's head). It's useful for providing variety from a series of close-ups and makes for a useful first look at a speaker. A medium shot is used to bring the viewer into a scene without shocking them. It can be used to introduce a character and provide context via their surroundings. (See Figure 15.8, upper right.)

- **Close-up.** The close-up, usually described as "from shirt pocket to head room," provides a good composition for someone talking directly to the camera. Although it's common to have your talking head centered in the shot, that's not a requirement. In Figure 15.8, center left, the subject was offset to the right. This would allow other images, especially graphics or titles, to be superimposed in the frame in a "real" (professional) production. But the compositional technique can be used with Z5 videos, too, even if special effects are not going to be added. A close-up generally shows the full face with a little head room at the top and down to the shoulders at the bottom of the frame.

- **Extreme close-up.** When I went through broadcast training, this shot was described as the "big talking face" shot and we were actively discouraged from employing it. Styles and tastes change over the years and now the big talking face is much more commonly used (maybe people are better looking these days?) and so this view may be appropriate. Just remember, the Z5 is capable of shooting in high-definition video and you may be playing the video on a high-def TV; be careful that you use this composition on a face that can stand up to high definition. (See Figure 15.8, center right.) An extreme close-up is a very tight shot that cuts off everything above the top of the head and below the chin (or even closer!). Be careful using this shot since many of us look better from a distance!

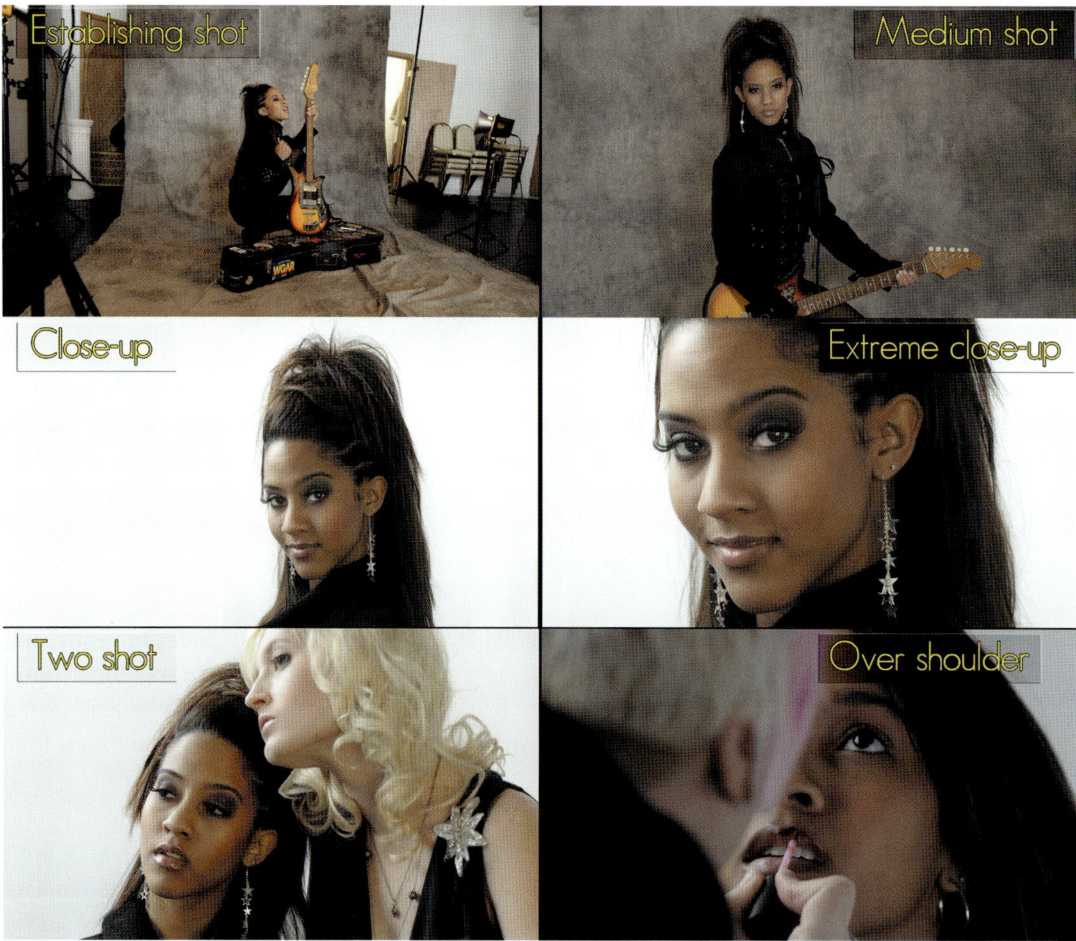

Figure 15.8 Use a full range of shot types.

- **"Two" shot.** A "two shot" shows a pair of subjects in one frame. They can be side by side or one in the foreground and one in the background. (See Figure 15.8, lower left.) This does not have to be a head-to-ground composition. Subjects can be standing or seated. A "three shot" is the same principle except that three people are in the frame. This version can be framed at various distances such as medium or close-up.

- **Over shoulder shot.** Long a composition of interview programs, the "over-shoulder shot" uses the rear of one person's head and shoulder to serve as a frame for the other person. This puts the viewer's perspective as that of the person facing away from the camera. (See Figure 15.8, lower right.) An "over-shoulder" shot is a popular shot for interview programs. It helps make the viewers feel like they're the one asking the questions.

Lighting for Video

Much like in still photography, how you handle light pretty much can make or break your videography. Lighting for video can be more complicated than lighting for still photography, since both subject and camera movement are often part of the process.

Lighting for video presents several concerns. First off, you want enough illumination to create a useable video. Beyond that, you want to use light to help tell your story or increase drama. Let's take a better look at both.

Illumination

You can significantly improve the quality of your video by increasing the light falling in the scene. This is true indoors or out, by the way. While it may seem like sunlight is more than enough, it depends on how much contrast you're dealing with. If your subject is in shadow (which can help them from squinting) or wearing a ball cap, a video light can help make them look a lot better.

Lighting choices for amateur videographers are a lot better these days than they were a decade or two ago. An inexpensive incandescent video light, which will easily fit in a camera bag, can be found for $15 or $20. You can even get a good-quality LED video light for less than $100. Work lights sold at many home improvement stores can also serve as video lights since you can set the camera's white balance to correct for any color casts. You'll need to mount these lights on a tripod or other support, or, perhaps, to a bracket that fastens to the tripod socket on the bottom of the camera.

Much of the challenge depends upon whether you're just trying to add some fill-light on your subject versus trying to boost the light on an entire scene. A small video light will do just fine for the former; it won't handle the latter. Fortunately, the versatility of the Z5 comes in quite handy here. Since the camera shoots video in Auto ISO mode, it can compensate for lower lighting levels and still produce a decent image. For best results though, better lighting is necessary.

Creative Lighting

While ramping up the light intensity will produce better technical quality in your video, it won't necessarily improve the artistic quality of it. Whether we're outdoors or indoors, we're used to seeing light come from above. Videographers need to consider how they position their lights to provide even illumination while up high enough to angle shadows down low and out of sight of the camera.

When lighting for video, there are several factors to consider. One is the quality of the light. It can either be hard (direct) light or soft (diffused) light. Hard light is good for showing detail but can also be very harsh and unforgiving. "Softening" the light, but diffusing it somehow, can reduce the intensity of the light but make for a kinder, gentler light as well.

While mixing light sources isn't always a good idea, one approach is to combine window light with supplemental lighting. Position your subject with the window to one side and bring in either a supplemental light or a reflector to the other side for reasonably even lighting.

Lighting Styles

Some lighting styles are more heavily used than others. Some forms are used for special effects, while others are designed to be invisible. At its most basic, lighting just illuminates the scene, but when used properly it can also create drama. Let's look at some types of lighting styles:

- **Three-point lighting.** This is a basic lighting setup for one person. A main light illuminates the strong side of a person's face, while a fill light lights up the other side. A third light is then positioned above and behind the subject to light the back of the head and shoulders. (See Figure 15.9, left.)

- **Flat lighting.** Use this type of lighting to provide illumination and nothing more. It calls for a variety of lights and diffusers set to raise the light level in a space enough for good video reproduction, but not to create a mood or emphasize a scene or individual. With flat lighting, you're trying to create even lighting levels throughout the video space and minimize any shadows. Generally, the lights are placed up high and angled downward (or possibly pointed straight up to bounce off a white ceiling). (See Figure 15.9, right.)

- **"Ghoul lighting."** This is the style of lighting used for old horror movies. The idea is to position the light down low, pointed upward. It's such an unnatural style of lighting that it makes its targets seem weird and "ghoulish."

- **Outdoor lighting.** While shooting outdoors may seem easier because the sun provides more light, it also presents its own problems. As a rule of thumb, keep the sun behind you when you're shooting video outdoors, except when shooting faces (anything from a medium shot and closer) since the viewer won't want to see a squinting subject. When shooting another human this way, put the sun behind her and use a video light to balance light levels between the foreground and background. If the sun is simply too bright, position the subject in the shade and use the video light for your main illumination. Using reflectors (white board panels or aluminum foil–covered cardboard panels are cheap options) can also help balance light effectively.

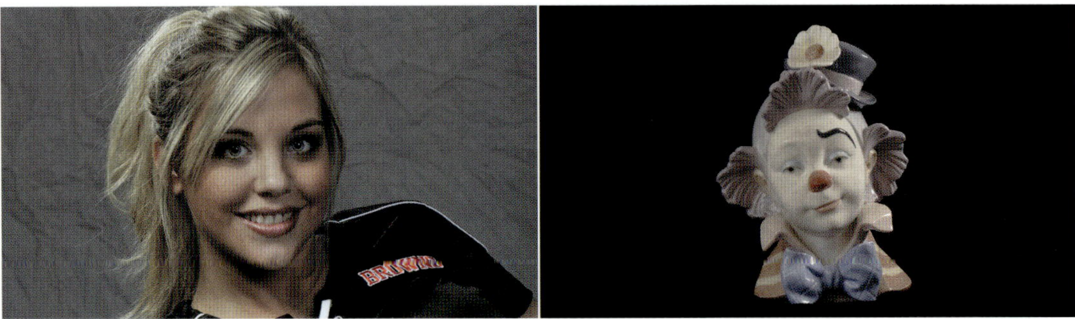

Figure 15.9 With three-point lighting (left), two lights are placed in front and to the side of the subject and another light is directed on the background to provide separation. Flat lighting (right) was bounced off a white ceiling and walls to fill in shadows as much as possible. It is a flexible lighting approach since the subject can change positions without needing a change in light direction.

Audio

When it comes to making a successful video, audio quality is one of those things that separates the professionals from the amateurs. We're used to watching top-quality productions on television and in the movies, yet the average person has no idea how much effort goes in to producing what seems to be "natural" sound. Much of the sound you hear in such productions is recorded on carefully controlled sound stages and "sweetened" with a variety of sound effects and other recordings of "natural" sound. Google "Foley artist" some time and you'll discover this part of a production is, indeed, a rich and complex art form.

Tips for Better Audio

Since recording high-quality audio is such a challenge, it's a good idea to do everything possible to maximize recording quality. Here are some ideas for improving the quality of the audio your camera records:

- **Get the camera and its microphone close to the speaker.** The farther the microphone is from the audio source, the less effective it will be in picking up that sound. While having to position the camera and its built-in microphone closer to the subject affects your lens choices and lens perspective options, it will make the most of your audio source. Of course, if you're using a very wide-angle lens, getting too close to your subject can have unflattering results, so don't take this advice too far. It's important to think carefully about what sounds you want to capture. If you're shooting video of an acoustic combo that's not using a PA system, you'll want the microphone close to them, but not so close that, say, only the lead singer or instrumentalist is picked up, while the players at either side fade off into the background.

- **Use an external microphone.** You'll recall the description of the camera's external microphone port in Chapter 2. As noted, this port accepts a stereo mini-plug from a standard external microphone, allowing you to achieve considerably higher audio quality for your movies than is possible with the camera's built-in microphones (which are disabled when an external mic is plugged in). An external microphone reduces the amount of camera-induced noise that is picked up and recorded on your audio track. (The action of the lens as it focuses can be audible when the built-in microphones are active.)

  The external microphone port can provide plug-in power for microphones that can take their power from this sort of outlet rather than from a battery in the microphone. Nikon provides optional compatible microphones such as the ME-1 ($135) (see Figure 15.10) or the wireless ME-W1 ($199); you also may find suitable microphones from companies such as Shure and Audio-Technica. If you are on a quest for superior audio quality, you can even obtain a portable mixer that can plug into this jack, such as the affordable Rolls MX124 (around $150) (www.rolls.com), letting you use multiple high-quality microphones (up to four) to record your soundtrack.

Figure 15.10 Nikon
ME-1 external stereo
microphone.

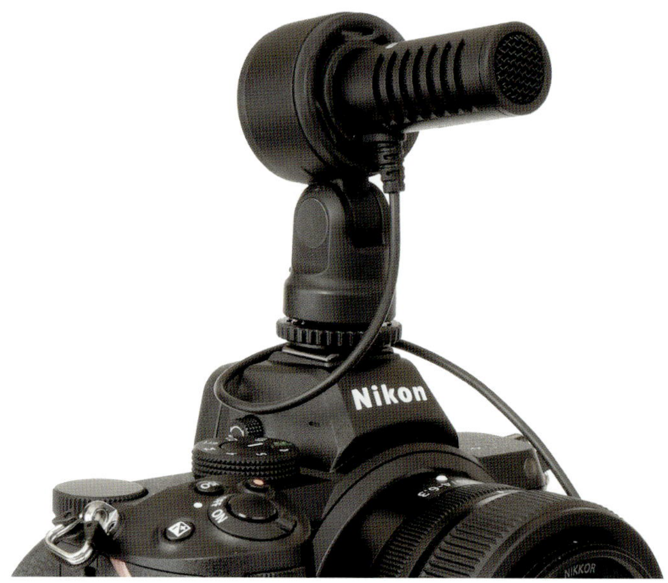

One advantage that a sound-mixing device like the BeachTek DXA-Micro Pro 2 ($150) offers over the stock Z5 is that it adds an additional headphone output jack to your camera, so you can monitor the sound actually being captured by the recorder (you can also listen to your soundtrack through the headphones during playback, which is *way* better than using the Z5's built-in speaker). The adapter has two balanced XLR microphone inputs and can also accept line input (from another audio source) and provides cool features like AGC (automatic gain control), built-in limiting, and VU meters you can use to monitor sound input.

- **Hide the microphone.** Combine the first few tips by using an external mic, and getting it as close to your subject as possible. If you're capturing a single person, you can always use a lapel microphone (described in the next section). But if you want a single mic to capture sound from multiple sources, your best bet may be to hide it somewhere in the shot. Put it behind a vase, using duct tape to fasten the microphone, and fix the mic cable out of sight (if you're not using a wireless microphone).

- **Turn off any sound makers you can.** Little things like fans and air handling units aren't obvious to the human ear but will be picked up by the microphone. Turn off any machinery or devices that you can plus make sure cell phones are set to silent mode. Also, do what you can to minimize sounds such as wind, radio, television, or people talking in the background.

- **Make sure to record some "natural" sound.** If you're shooting video at an event of some kind, make sure you get some background sound that you can add to your audio as desired in post-production.

- **Consider recording audio separately.** Lip-syncing is probably beyond most of the people you're going to be shooting, but there's nothing that says you can't record narration separately and add it later. It's relatively easy if you learn how to use simple software video-editing programs like iMovie (for the Macintosh) or Windows Movie Maker (for Windows PCs). Any time the speaker is off-camera, you can work with separately recorded narration rather than recording the speaker on-camera. This can produce much cleaner sound.

External Microphones

The single-most important thing you can do to improve your audio quality is to use an external microphone. The Z5's internal stereo microphones mounted on the front of the camera will do a decent job but have some significant drawbacks, partially spelled out in the previous section:

- **Camera noise.** There are plenty of noise sources emanating from the camera, including your own breathing and rustling around as the camera shifts in your hand. Manual zooming is bound to affect your sound, and your fingers will fall directly in front of the built-in mics as you change focal lengths. An external microphone isolates the sound recording from camera noise.

- **Distance.** Anytime your Z5 is located more than 6 to 8 feet from your subjects or sound source, the audio will suffer. An external unit allows you to place the mic right next to your subject.

- **Improved quality.** Obviously, Nikon wasn't able to install a super-expensive, super-high-quality microphone, even on a $2,000 camera. Not all owners of the Z5 would be willing to pay the premium, especially if they didn't plan to shoot much video themselves. An external microphone will almost always be of better quality.

- **Directionality.** The Z5's internal microphone generally records only sounds directly in front of it. An external microphone can be either of the directional type or omnidirectional, depending on whether you want to "shotgun" your sound or record more ambient sound.

You can choose from several different types of microphones, each of which has its own advantages and disadvantages. If you're serious about movie making with your Z5, you might want to own more than one. Common configurations include:

- **Shotgun microphones.** These can be mounted directly on your Z5, although, if the mic uses an accessory shoe mount, you'll need the optional adapter to convert the camera's shoe to a standard hot shoe. I prefer to use a bracket, which further isolates the microphone from any camera noise. One thing to keep in mind is that while the shotgun mic will generally ignore any sound coming from *behind* it, it will pick up any sound it is pointed at, even *behind* your subject. You may be capturing video and audio of someone you're interviewing in a restaurant, and not realize you're picking up the lunchtime conversation of the diners seated in the table behind your subject. Outdoors, you may record your speaker, as well as the traffic on a busy street or freeway in the background.

- **Lapel microphones.** Also called *lavalieres*, these microphones attach to the subject's clothing and pick up their voice with the best quality. You'll need a long enough cord or a wireless mic. These are especially good for video interviews, so whether you're producing a documentary or grilling relatives for a family history, you'll want one of these.

- **Hand-held microphones.** If you're capturing a singer crooning a tune or want your subject to mimic famed faux newscaster Wally Ballou, a hand-held mic may be your best choice. They serve much the same purpose as a lapel microphone, and they're more intrusive—but that may be the point. A hand-held microphone can make a great prop for your fake newscast! The speaker can talk right into the microphone, point it at another person, or use it to record ambient sound. If your narrator is not going to appear on-camera, one of these can be an inexpensive way to improve sound.

- **Wired and wireless external microphones.** This option is the most expensive, but you get a receiver and a transmitter (both battery-powered, so you'll need to make sure you have enough batteries). The transmitter is connected to the microphone, and the receiver is connected to your Z5. In addition to being less klutzy and enabling you to avoid having wires on view in your scene, wireless mics, such as the Nikon MW-W1, let you record sounds that are physically located some distance from your camera. Of course, you need to keep in mind the range of your device and be aware of possible signal interference from other electronic components in the vicinity.

WIND-NOISE REDUCTION

Always use the wind screen provided with an external microphone to reduce the effect of noise produced by even light breezes blowing over the microphone. Many mics, such as the Nikon ME-1, include a low-cut filter to further reduce wind noise. However, these can also affect other sounds. You can disable the low-cut filters for the ME-1 by changing a switch on the back from L-cut (low cutoff) to Flat. Other external mics also have their own low-cut filter switch.

Special Features

The Z5 also has two audio frequency ranges (Wide and Vocal Range) and an Attenuator, described in Chapter 11, so you can tailor your microphone capture to your subject matter (for ambient sound or voice recording). Audio levels can be adjusted while recording, and the camera's internal microphones have improved wind noise reduction.

Troubleshooting and Prevention   16

One of the nice things about modern electronic cameras like the Nikon Z5 is that they have fewer mechanical moving parts to fail, so they are less likely to "wear out." No film transport mechanism, no wind lever or motor drive. You don't even have to worry about complicated mechanical linkages from camera to lens to physically stop down the lens aperture. Instead, tiny, reliable motors are built into each autofocus lens (and you lose the use of only *that* lens should something fail). Of course, the camera also has a moving shutter (if you're not using the electronic shutter), and that can fail, but the mechanical shutter is built rugged enough that you can expect it to last several hundred thousand shutter cycles or more. Unless you're shooting sports in continuous mode day in and day out, the shutter on your Z5 is likely to last as long as you expect to use the camera.

The only other things on the camera that move are switches, dials, buttons, and the doors that open to allow you to remove and insert the memory card. Unless you're extraordinarily clumsy or unlucky and manage to damage one of the memory card slots there's not a lot that can go wrong mechanically with your Nikon Z5.

On the other hand, one of the chief drawbacks of modern electronic cameras is that they are modern *electronic* cameras. Your Z5 is fully dependent on batteries; without them, the camera can't be used. There are numerous other electrical and electronic connections in the camera (many connected to those mechanical switches and dials), and components like the color LCD monitor that can potentially fail or suffer damage. The camera also relies on its "operating system," or *firmware*, which can be plagued by bugs that cause unexpected behavior. Luckily, electronic components are generally more reliable and trouble-free, especially when compared to their mechanical counterparts from the pre-electronic film camera days.

Of course, film cameras of the last 10 to 20 years had almost as many electronic features as digital cameras, but, believe it or not, there were whole generations of film cameras that had *no* electronics or batteries. I still own a dozen Nikon F/F2 cameras that don't even have a built-in light meter!

Digital cameras have problems unique to their breed, too; the most troublesome being the need to clean the sensor of dust and grime periodically. This chapter will show you how to diagnose problems, fix some common ills, and, importantly, learn how to avoid them in the future.

Upgrading Your Firmware

The camera relies on its "operating system," or *firmware*, which should be updated in a reasonable fashion as new releases become available. The firmware in your Nikon Z5 handles everything from menu display (including fonts, colors, and the actual entries themselves), what languages are available, and even support for specific devices and features. Upgrading the firmware to a new version makes it possible to add or fine-tune features while fixing some of the bugs that sneak in.

Firmware upgrades are used most frequently to fix bugs in the software, and much less frequently to add or enhance features. The exact changes made to the firmware are generally spelled out in the firmware release announcement. You can examine the remedies provided and decide if a given firmware patch is important to you. If not, you can usually safely wait a while before going through the bother of upgrading your firmware—at least long enough for the early adopters (such as those who haunt the Digital Photography Review forums at www.dpreview.com) to report whether the bug fixes have introduced new bugs of their own. Each new firmware release incorporates the changes from previous releases, so if you skip a minor upgrade you should have no problems.

WHEN TO UPGRADE YOUR FIRMWARE

I *always* recommend waiting at least two weeks after a firmware upgrade is announced before changing the software in your camera. This is often in direct contradiction to the online Nikon "gurus" who breathlessly announce each new firmware release on their web pages, usually with links to where you can download the latest software. *Don't do it!* Yet. Nikon has, in the past, introduced firmware upgrades that were buggy and added problems of their own. If you own a camera affected by a new round of firmware upgrades, I urge you to wait and let a few million over-eager fellow users "beta test" this upgrade for you. Within a few weeks, any problems (if any develop) will surface and you'll know whether the update is safe. Your camera is working fine right now, so why take the chance?

How It Works

If you're computer savvy, you might wonder how your Nikon Z5 is able to overwrite its own operating system—that is, how can the existing firmware be used to load the new version on top of itself? It's a little like lifting yourself by reaching down and pulling up on your bootstraps.

Not ironically, that's almost exactly what happens: At your command (when you start the upgrade process), the Z5 shifts into a special mode in which it is no longer operating from its firmware but, rather, from a small piece of software called a *bootstrap loader*, a separate, protected software program that functions only at startup or when upgrading firmware. The loader's function is to look for firmware to launch or, when directed, to copy new firmware from a memory card to the internal memory space where the old firmware is located. Once the new firmware has replaced the old, you can "reboot" the camera using the new operating system.

Why Multiple Firmware Modules?

Your Nikon Z5's firmware is divided into multiple parts: C (for camera), L (for lens), and S (for strobe/Speedlight). There is additional firmware for the camera's FTZ adapter. Why chop the firmware up in the first place? You might have owned a previous Nikon camera that had an A and B firmware listing, located in the Firmware Version entry in the Setup menu. There's a good reason why the firmware was previously divided in twain. Each of the two modules was "in charge" of particular parts of the camera's operating system. So, when a bug was found, or a new feature added, it was possible, in many cases, to offer only an upgrade for either Firmware A or Firmware B, depending on which module was affected. Although mistakes in upgrading firmware are rare, you cut the opportunities for user errors in half when only one of the modules needs to be replaced.

So, what are Firmware L and Firmware S, found in some of the most current Nikon models like the Z5? The L firmware is a database of lens information that helps the camera integrate new lenses with its features, such as barrel and pincushion distortion, while the S firmware provides a similar database for strobes (or Speedlights, take your pick). Nikon regularly updates the C (camera) firmware to correct for mistakes or add features/support for new accessories, and the L and S modules to account for new lens and electronic flash introductions. Note that the strobe and FTZ adapter firmware will be shown in the Firmware Version menu *only* if you have an external dedicated flash unit installed and powered up or have attached the FTZ adapter (respectively).

WARNING Use a fully charged battery to ensure that you'll have enough power to operate the camera for the entire upgrade. Moreover, you should not turn off the camera while your old firmware is being overwritten. Don't open the memory card door or do anything else that might disrupt operation of the Z5 while the firmware is being installed.

Getting Ready

When it comes time to do an actual firmware upgrade for your Z5, you should double-check the instructions below against the recommended procedure that Nikon implements at that time. It should be very close to the steps I outline, but there may be some small differences.

The first thing to do is determine whether you need the current firmware update. Confirm the version number of your Nikon Z5's current firmware:

1. Turn on the Z5.
2. Press the MENU button and select `Firmware Version` from the Setup menu. The camera's firmware version will be displayed. If you have an external dedicated flash unit available, attach it and turn on the power.
3. Write down the Version numbers.
4. Turn off the Z5.

Next, go to the Nikon support site for your country; locate and download the firmware update. As I write this, the current firmware is Version 1.01.

If the version is later than the one you noted in your camera, click the firmware link in either the Windows or Macintosh columns (depending on your computer) to download the file. It will have a name like F-Z5-V101W.exe (Windows) or F-Z5-V101M.dmg (Macintosh). The auto-extracting file will deposit your firmware in a folder named Z5Update. The actual update files that you have extracted from the .exe or .dmg package will be named something like:

Z5_0101.bin

The final preparation you need to make is to decide whether you'd like to upgrade your firmware using a memory card reader, or by transferring the software to the Z5 using the USB cable. In either case, you'll need to format a memory card in the Z5. Then, perform one of the sets of steps in the sections that follow.

Updating from a Card Reader

To update from a card reader, use a reader connected to your computer with a USB cable. Then, follow these steps:

1. Insert a formatted memory card into the card reader. If you have been using Nikon Transfer or the "autoplay" features of your operating system to transfer images from your memory card to the computer, the automated transfer dialog box may appear. Close it.

2. The memory card will appear on your Macintosh desktop, or in the Computer/My Computer folders under Windows 10/Windows 8 or earlier releases.

3. Drag the firmware file to the memory card in Slot 1. Remember to copy the firmware to the *root* (top) directory of the memory card. The Z5 will be unable to find it if you place it in a folder.

Starting the Update

To perform the actual update, follow these steps:

1. With the memory card containing the firmware update software in Slot 1 in the camera, turn the camera on.

2. Press the MENU button and select Firmware Version in the Setup menu.

3. Select Update and press the multi selector button to the right.

4. When the firmware update screen appears, highlight Yes and press OK to begin the update.

5. The actual process may take a few minutes (from two to five). Be sure not to turn off the camera or perform any other operations while it is underway.

6. When the update is completed, the warning message will no longer be displayed on the screen. You can turn off the camera when the message disappears.

7. Press the MENU button and select Firmware Version in the Setup menu to view the current firmware number. If it matches the update, you've successfully upgraded that portion of the firmware.

8. A new choice will appear offering to delete the firmware files from your memory card. Do so. You can also simply reformat the memory card to return it to a "clean" condition.

Protecting Your LCD

The tilting 3.2-inch color LCD monitor on the back of your Nikon Z5 almost seems like a target for banging, scratching, and other abuse. The monitor itself is quite rugged, and a few errant knocks are unlikely to shatter the protective cover over the LCD, and scratches won't easily mar its tempered glass surface. However, if you want to be on the safe side, there are a number of protective products you can purchase to keep your LCD safe—and, in some cases, make it a little easier to view. Here's a quick overview of your options.

- **Plastic overlays.** The simplest solution (although not always the cheapest) is to apply a plastic overlay sheet or "skin" cut to fit your LCD. These adhere either by static electricity or through a light adhesive coating that's even less clingy than stick-it notes. You can cut down overlays made for PDAs or smartphones (although these can be pricey at up to $19.95 for a set of several sheets), or purchase overlays sold specifically for digital cameras. These products will do a good job of shielding your Z5's LCD screen from scratches and minor impacts but will not offer much protection from a good whack.

- **Acrylic/glass shields.** These scratch-resistant panels, laser cut to fit your camera perfectly, are my choice as the best protection solution, and what I use on my own Z5. At about $10–$15 each, they also happen to be the least expensive option as well. Although other vendors make some fine (and pricey) glass shields, I use the economical glass covers from GGS, available from a variety of sources, and shown in Figure 16.1. They attach flush and tight but allow the shield to be pried off and the adhesive removed easily if you want to remove or replace it. They don't attenuate your view of the LCD and are non-reflective enough for use under a variety of lighting conditions. I had to wait a while for 3.2-inch GGS shields to fit my Z5 to become available.

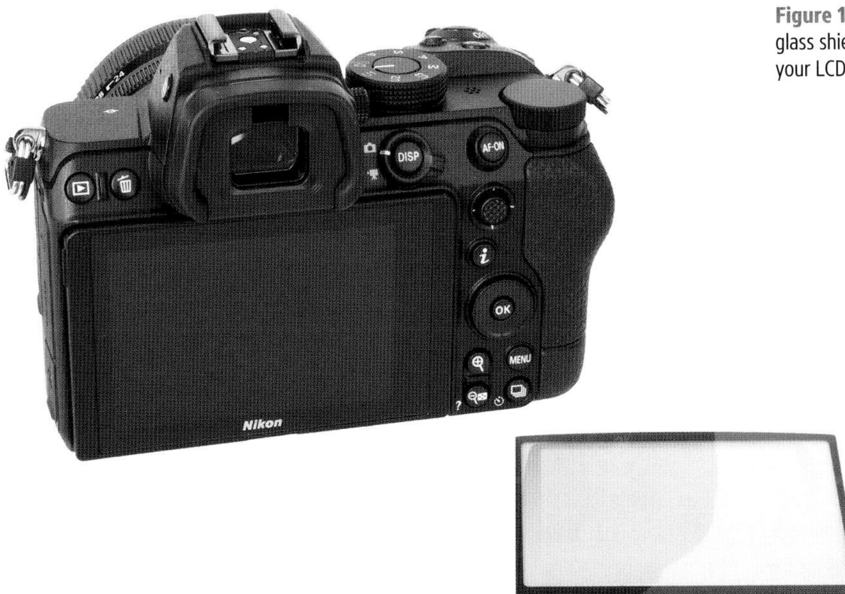

Figure 16.1 A tough glass shield can protect your LCD from scratches.

Troubleshooting Memory Cards

Sometimes good memory cards go bad. Sometimes good photographers can treat their memory cards badly. It's possible that a memory card that works fine in one camera won't be recognized when inserted into another. In the worst case, you can have a card full of important photos and find that the card seems to be corrupted and you can't access any of them. Don't panic! If these scenarios sound horrific to you, there are lots of things you can do to prevent them from happening, and a variety of remedies available if they do occur. You'll want to take some time—before disaster strikes—to consider your options.

All Your Eggs in One Basket?

The debate about whether it's better to use one large memory card or several smaller ones has been going on since even before there were memory cards. I can remember when computer users wondered whether it was smarter to install a pair of 200MB (not *gigabyte*) hard drives in their computer, or if they should go for one of those new-fangled 500MB models. By the same token, a few years ago the user groups were full of proponents who insisted that you ought to use 128MB memory cards rather than the huge 392MB versions. Today, with the huge file size of Z5 images, most of the arguments involve 64GB cards versus 128GB cards, or even 256GB (and larger) cards.

Why all the fuss? Are 64GB memory cards more likely to fail than 128GB cards? Are you risking all your photos if you trust your images to a larger card? Isn't it better to use several smaller cards, so that if one fails you lose only half as many photos? Or, isn't it wiser to put all your photos onto one larger card, because the more cards you use, the better your odds of misplacing or damaging one and losing at least some pictures?

In the end, the "eggs in one basket" argument boils down to statistics, and how you happen to use your Z5. The rationales can go both ways. If you have multiple smaller cards, you do increase your chances of something happening to one of them, so, arguably, you might be boosting the odds of losing some pictures. If all your images are important, the fact that you've lost 100 rather than 200 pictures isn't very comforting.

After all, the myth assumes that a damaged card will always be full before it becomes corrupted. Fortunately, memory cards don't magically wait until they are full before they fail. In a typical shooting session, it doesn't matter whether you've shot 12GB worth of pictures on a 64GB card or 12GB worth of pictures on a 128GB card. If either card fails, you've lost exactly the same number of images. Your risk increases *only* when you start shooting additional photos on the larger card. In the real world, most of us who use larger memory cards don't fill them up very often. We just like having the extra capacity there when we need it.

The myth also says that by using several smaller cards, you're spreading the risk around so that only some pictures will be lost in case of a failure. What is more important to you, your photographs or the members of your family? When going on vacation, do you insist on splitting your kin up and driving several smaller cars? Of course not.

If you shoot photojournalist-type pictures, you probably change memory cards when they're less than completely full in order to avoid the need to do so at a crucial moment. (When I shoot sports, my cards rarely reach 80 to 90 percent of capacity before I change them.) Using multiple smaller cards means you have to change them that more often, which can be a real pain when you're taking a lot of photos. As an example, if you use 16GB memory cards with a Nikon Z5 and shoot RAW+JPEG FINE*, you may get only a few dozen pictures on the card. That's not even twice the capacity of a 36-exposure roll of film (remember those?). In my book, I prefer keeping all my eggs in one basket, and then making very sure that nothing happens to that basket.

Preventive Measures

Here are some options for preventing loss of valuable images:

- **Interleaving.** One option is to *interleave* your shots. Say you don't shoot weddings, but you do go on vacation from time to time. Take 100 or so pictures on one card, or whatever number of images might fill about 25 percent of its capacity. Then, replace it with a different card and shoot about 25 percent of that card's available space. Repeat these steps with diligence (you'd have to be determined to go through this inconvenience), and, if you use four or more memory cards, you'll find your pictures from each location scattered among the different memory cards. If you lose or damage one, you'll still have *some* pictures from all the various stops on your trip on the other cards. That's more work than I like to do (I usually tote around a portable hard disk and copy the files to the drive as I go), but it's an option.

- **In-camera backup.** Fortunately, if you own a Nikon Z5, you don't need to restrict yourself to a single basket. Load your camera with two memory cards, then go to the Shooting menu and set Role Played by Card in Slot 2 to Backup, so that each shot you take is copied to both cards simultaneously. This will slow down your maximum shooting speed significantly (don't try this backup method when shooting sports), but for ordinary photography, this provides the peace of mind of knowing you're making a spare copy of each image right on the spot.

EXTREME BACKUP

I probably took the dual-card technique to the extreme recently while on a trip. I had my Z5 stocked with a pair of 64GB cards and was shooting in RAW+JPEG mode. I happened to be shooting three-exposure brackets, which I was going to process as HDR (high dynamic range) photos. With the camera set to copy to both cards at the same time, and using Continuous high, every time I pressed the shutter release, the Z5 took a three-shot set in both RAW+JPEG Fine (six pictures) and copied them to both cards (12 files in all). I managed the dubious feat of filling up 128GB of memory cards while pressing the shutter release just a few hundred times.

- **Transmit your images.** Another option is to transmit your images as they are shot over a network to your laptop, assuming a network and a laptop are available. You can use the Z5's built-in wireless capability and beam the images over to a computer as you shoot them.

- **External backup.** You can purchase external hard disk gadgets called Personal Storage Devices, which can copy files from your memory cards automatically. More expensive models have color LCD screens so you can review your images. I tend to prefer using a MacBook Air, like the one shown in Figure 16.2 (it fits in a pocket of my ScotteVest). I can store images on either computer's internal storage and make an extra backup copy to an external drive as well. Plus, I can access the Internet from Wi-Fi hotspots (including the one built into my iPhone), all using a very compact device. Lately, I've been backing up many images on my iPad, which has 256GB of storage—enough for short trips.

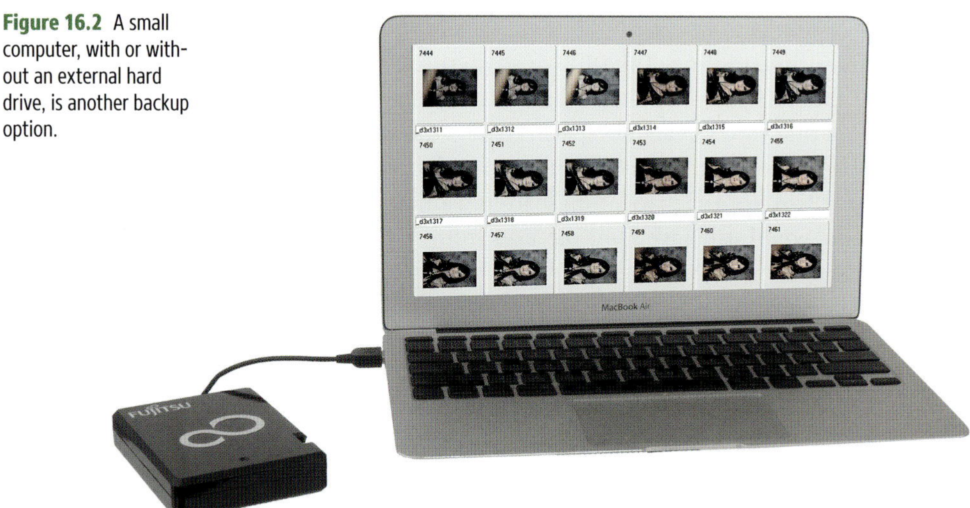

Figure 16.2 A small computer, with or without an external hard drive, is another backup option.

What Can Go Wrong?

There are lots of things that can go wrong with your memory card, but the ones that aren't caused by human stupidity are statistically very rare. Yes, a memory card's internal bit bin or controller can suddenly fail due to a manufacturing error or some inexplicable event caused by old age. However, if your card works for the first week or two that you own it, it should work forever. There's really not a lot that can wear out.

The typical memory card is rated for a Mean Time Between Failures of 1,000,000 hours of use. That's constant use 24/7 for more than 100 years! According to the manufacturers, they are good for 10,000 insertions in your camera, and should be able to retain their data (and that's without an external power source) for something on the order of 11 years. Of course, with the millions of cards in use, there are bound to be a few lemons here or there.

Given the reliability of solid-state memory compared to magnetic memory, though, it's more likely that your problems will stem from something that you do. Secure Digital and memory cards are small and easy to misplace if you're not careful. For that reason, it's a good idea to keep them in their original cases or a "card safe" offered by Gepe (www.gepe.com), Pelican (www.pelican.com), and others. Always placing your memory card in a case can provide protection from the second-most common mishap that befalls memory cards: the common household laundry. If you slip a card in a pocket, rather than a case or your camera bag often enough, sooner or later it's going to end up in the washing machine and probably the clothes dryer, too. There are plenty of reports of relieved digital camera owners who've laundered their memory cards and found they still worked fine, but it's not uncommon for such mistreatment to do some damage.

Memory cards can also be stomped on, accidentally bent, dropped into the ocean, chewed by pets, and otherwise rendered unusable in myriad ways. If the card is formatted in your computer with a memory card reader, your Z5 may fail to recognize it. Occasionally, I've found that a memory card used in one camera would fail if used in a different camera (until I reformatted it in Windows, and then again in the camera). Every once in a while, a card goes completely bad and—seemingly—can't be salvaged.

Another way to lose images is to do commonplace things with your card at an inopportune time. If you remove the card from the Z5 while the camera is writing images to the card, you'll lose any photos in the buffer and may damage the file structure of the card, making it difficult or impossible to retrieve the other pictures you've taken. The same thing can happen if you remove the memory card from your computer's card reader while the computer is writing to the card (say, to erase files you've already moved to your computer). You can avoid this by *not* using your computer to erase files on a memory card but, instead, always reformatting the card in your Z5 before you use it again.

What Can You Do?

Pay attention: If you're having problems, the *first* thing you should do is *stop* using that memory card. Don't take any more pictures. Don't do anything with the card until you've figured out what's wrong. Your second line of defense (your first line is to be sufficiently careful with your cards that you avoid problems in the first place) is to *do no harm* that hasn't already been done. Read the rest of this section and then, if necessary, decide on a course of action (such as using a data recovery service or software described later) before you risk damaging the data on your card further.

Now that you've calmed down, the first thing to check is whether you've actually inserted a card in the camera. If you've set the camera so that shooting without a card has been turned on, it's entirely possible (although not particularly plausible) that you've been snapping away with no memory card to store the pictures to, which can lead to massive disappointment later on. Of course, the –E- warning appears on the LCD when the camera is powered up, and the Demo message is superimposed on the review image after every shot (assuming you've enabled the Z5 to take photos when a card is not inserted), but maybe you're inattentive, or aren't using picture review. You can avoid all this by setting the Slot Empty Release Lock in the Setup menu to Release Locked and leaving it there.

Things get more exciting when the card itself is put in jeopardy. If you lose a card, there's not a lot you can do other than take a picture of a similar card and print up some Have You Seen This Lost Flash Memory? flyers to post on utility poles all around town.

If all you care about is reusing the card, and have resigned yourself to losing the pictures, try reformatting the card in your camera. You may find that reformatting removes the corrupted data and restores your card to health. Sometimes I've had success reformatting a card in my computer using a memory card reader (this is normally a no-no because your operating system doesn't understand the needs of your Z5), and *then* reformatting again in the camera.

If your memory card is not behaving properly, and you *do* want to recover your images, things get a little more complicated. If your pictures are very valuable, either to you or to others (for example, a wedding), you can always turn to professional data recovery firms. Be prepared to pay hundreds of dollars to get your pictures back, but these pros often do an amazing job. You wouldn't want them working on your memory card on behalf of the police if you'd tried to erase some incriminating pictures. There are many firms of this type, and I've never used them myself, so I can't offer a recommendation. Use a Google search to turn up a ton of them.

A more reasonable approach is to try special data recovery software you can install on your computer and use to attempt to resurrect your "lost" images yourself. They may not actually be gone completely. Perhaps your card's "table of contents" is jumbled, or only a few pictures are damaged in such a way that your camera and computer can't read some or any of the pictures on the card. Some of the available software was written specifically to reconstruct lost pictures, while other utilities are more general-purpose applications that can be used with any media, including floppy disks and hard disk drives. They have names like OnTrack, Photo Rescue 2, Digital Image Recovery, MediaRecover, Image Recall, and the aptly named Recover My Photos. I like the RescuePRO software that SanDisk supplies, especially since it originally came on a mini-CD that I was totally unable to erase by mistake, and more recently became downloadable from a URL SanDisk supplies with the memory card.

DIMINISHING RETURNS

Usually, once you've recovered any images on a memory card, reformatted it, and returned it to service, it will function reliably for the rest of its useful life. However, if you find a particular card going bad more than once, you'll almost certainly want to stop using it forever. See if you can get it replaced by the manufacturer if you can, but, in the case of memory card failures, the third time is never the charm.

Cleaning Your Sensor

Indeed, there's no avoiding dust. No matter how careful you are, some of it is going to settle on your camera and on the mounts of your lenses, eventually making its way inside your camera to settle in the interior chamber. As you take photos, airborne dust eventually comes to rest on the cover atop your sensor. There, dust and particles can show up in every single picture you take at a small enough aperture to bring the foreign matter into sharp focus. No matter how careful you are and how cleanly you work, eventually you will get some of this dust on your camera's sensor. Even the cleanest-working photographers using the Nikon Z5 are far from immune.

Fortunately, one of the Nikon Z5's most useful features is the automatic sensor cleaning system that reduces or eliminates the need to clean your camera's sensor manually. The sensor vibrates ultrasonically each time the Z5 is powered either on or off (or both, at your option), shaking loose any dust.

Although the automatic sensor cleaning feature operates when you power the camera up or turn it off (depending on the behavior you specify in the Setup menu), you can activate it manually at any time. Choose Clean Image Sensor from the Setup menu and select Clean Now. If you'd rather specify when automatic cleaning occurs, choose Clean at Shutdown. Or, select Cleaning Off (no automatic sensor cleaning will take place).

If some dust does collect on your sensor, you can often map it out of your images (making it invisible) using software techniques with the Image Dust Off Ref Photo feature in the Setup menu. Operation of this feature is described in Chapter 13.

Of course, even with the Nikon Z5's automatic sensor cleaning/dust resistance features, you may still be required to manually clean your sensor from time to time. This section explains the phenomenon and provides some tips on minimizing dust and eliminating it when it begins to affect your shots.

Dust the FAQs, Ma'am

Here are some of the most frequently asked questions about sensor dust issues.

Q. I see a bright or dark spot in the same place in all my photos. Is that sensor dust?

A. You've probably got either a "hot" pixel, a "dead" pixel, or one that is permanently "stuck" due to a defect in the sensor. A hot pixel is one that shows up as a bright spot only during long exposures as the sensor warms. These are often removed automatically if you use Long Exposure Noise Reduction or can disappear if you work with shorter exposures. A dead pixel is always dark and represents a defect in the sensor. A pixel stuck in the "on" position always appears in the image. Hot and stuck pixels show up as bright red, green, or blue pixels, usually surrounded by a small cluster of other improperly illuminated pixels, caused by the camera's interpolating the hot or stuck pixel into its surroundings, as shown in Figure 16.3. Hot, dead, and stuck pixels are likely to show up when they contrast with plain, evenly colored areas of your image.

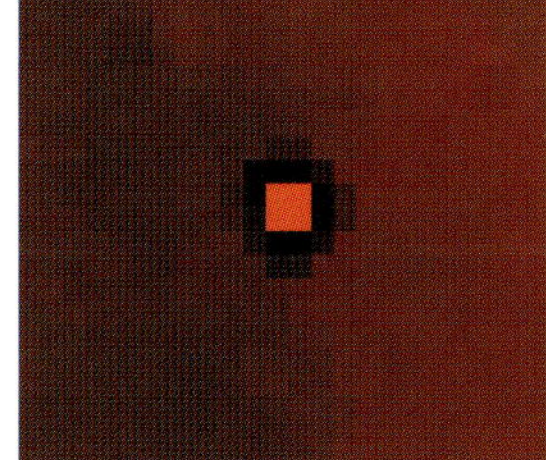

Figure 16.3 A stuck pixel is surrounded by improperly interpolated pixels created by the Z5's demosaicing algorithm.

Finding one or two hot or stuck pixels in your sensor is unfortunately fairly common. They can be "removed" by telling the Z5 to ignore them through a simple process called *pixel mapping.* If the bad pixels become bothersome, your Z5's pixel-mapping feature, discussed earlier, can remap your sensor's pixels without a trip to a service center.

Bad pixels can also show up on your camera's color LCD panel, but, unless they are abundant, the wisest course is to just ignore them.

Q. I see an irregular out-of-focus blob in the same place in my photos. Is that sensor dust?

A. Yes. Sensor contaminants can take the form of tiny spots, larger blobs, or even curvy lines if they are caused by minuscule fibers that have settled on the sensor. They'll appear out of focus because they aren't on the sensor surface but, rather, a fraction of a millimeter above it on the filter that covers the sensor. The smaller the f/stop used, the more in-focus the dust becomes. At large apertures, it may not be visible at all.

Q. I never see any dust on my sensor. What's all the fuss about?

A. Those who never have dust problems with their Nikon Z5 fall into one of four categories: those for whom the camera's automatic dust removal features are working well; those who seldom change their lenses and have clean working habits that minimize the amount of dust that invades their cameras in the first place; those who simply don't notice the dust (often because they don't shoot many macro photos or other pictures using the small f/stops that makes dust evident in their images); and those who are very, very lucky.

Identifying and Dealing with Dust

Sensor dust is less of a problem than it might be because it shows up only under certain circumstances. Indeed, you might have dust on your sensor right now and not be aware of it. The dust doesn't settle on the sensor itself. It settles on a protective filter a very tiny distance above the sensor, subjecting it to the phenomenon of *depth-of-focus.* Depth-of-focus is the distance the focal plane can be moved and still render an object in sharp focus. At f/2.8 to f/5.6 or even smaller, sensor dust, particularly if small, is likely to be outside the range of depth-of-focus and blur into an unnoticeable dot.

However, if you're shooting at f/16 to f/22 or smaller, those dust motes suddenly pop into focus. Forget about trying to spot them by peering directly at your sensor with the shutter open and the lens removed. The period at the end of this sentence, about .33mm in diameter, could block a group of pixels measuring 40 × 40 pixels (160 pixels in all!). Dust spots that are even smaller than that can easily show up in your images if you're shooting large, empty areas that are light colored. Dust motes are most likely to show up in the sky, as in Figure 16.4, or in white backgrounds of your seamless product shots and are less likely to be a problem in images that contain lots of dark areas and detail.

To see if you have dust on your sensor, take a few test shots of a plain, blank surface (such as a piece of paper or a cloudless sky) at small f/stops, such as f/22, and a few wide open. Open Photoshop or another image editor, copy several shots into a single document in separate layers, then flip back and forth between layers to see if any spots you see are present in all layers. You may have to boost contrast and sharpness to make the dust easier to spot.

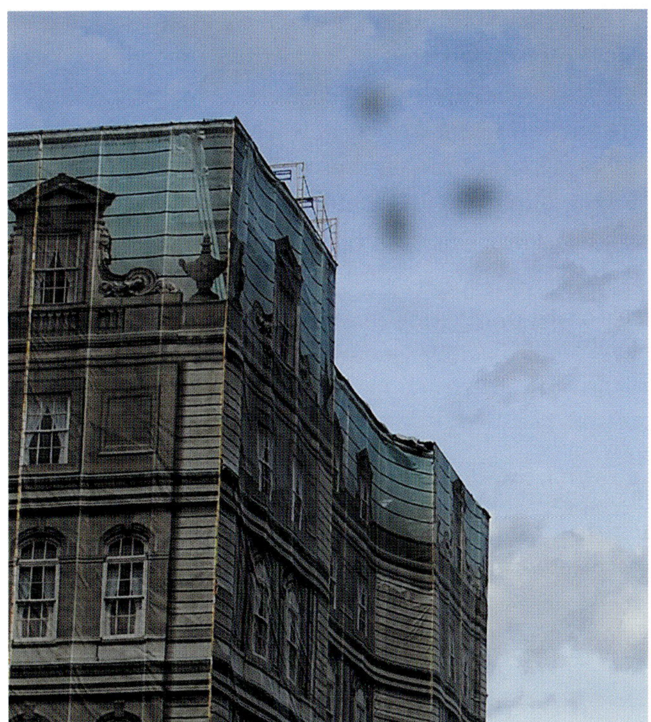

Figure 16.4 Only the dust spots in the sky are apparent in this shot.

Avoiding Dust

Of course, the easiest way to protect your sensor from dust is to prevent it from settling on the sensor in the first place. Here are my stock tips for eliminating the problem before it begins.

- **Clean environment.** Avoid working in dusty areas if you can do so. Hah! Serious photographers will take this one with a grain of salt, because it usually makes sense to go where the pictures are. Only a few of us are so paranoid about sensor dust (considering that it is so easily removed) that we'll avoid moderately grimy locations just to protect something that is, when you get down to it, just a tool. If you find a great picture opportunity at a raging fire, during a sandstorm, or while surrounded by dust clouds, you might hesitate to take the picture, but, with a little caution (don't remove your lens in these situations, and clean the camera afterward!), you can still shoot. However, it still makes sense to store your camera in a clean environment. One place cameras and lenses pick up a lot of dust is inside a camera bag. Clean your bag from time to time, and you can avoid problems.

- **Clean lenses.** There are a few paranoid types that avoid swapping lenses in order to minimize the chance of dust getting inside their cameras. It makes more sense just to use a blower or brush to dust off the rear lens mount of the replacement lens first, so you won't be introducing dust into your camera simply by attaching a new, dusty lens. Do this before you remove the current lens from your camera, and then avoid stirring up dust before making the exchange.

- **Work fast.** Minimize the time your camera is lensless and exposed to dust. That means having your replacement lens ready and dusted off, and a place to set down the old lens as soon as it is removed, so you can quickly attach the new lens.

- **Let gravity help you.** Face the camera downward when the lens is detached so any dust in the vestibule box will tend to fall away from the sensor. Turn your back to any breezes, indoor forced air vents, fans, or other sources of dust to minimize infiltration.

- **Protect the lens you just removed.** Once you've attached the new lens, quickly put the end cap on the one you just removed to reduce the dust that might fall on it.

- **Clean out the vestibule.** From time to time, remove the lens while in a relatively dust-free environment and use a blower bulb like the one shown in Figure 16.5 (*not* compressed air or a vacuum hose) to clean out the vestibule area. A blower bulb is generally safer than a can of compressed air, or a strong positive/negative airflow, which can tend to drive dust further into nooks and crannies.

- **Be prepared.** If you're embarking on an important shooting session, it's a good idea to clean your sensor *now*, rather than come home with hundreds or thousands of images with dust spots caused by flecks that were sitting on your sensor before you even started.

- **Clone out existing spots in your image editor.** Photoshop and other editors have a clone tool or healing brush you can use to copy pixels from surrounding areas over the dust spot or dead pixel. This process can be tedious, especially if you have lots of dust spots and/or lots of images to be corrected. The advantage is that this sort of manual fix-it probably will do the least damage to the rest of your photo. Only the damaged pixels will be affected.

- **Use filtration in your image editor.** A semi-smart filter like Photoshop's Dust & Scratches filter can remove dust and other artifacts by selectively blurring areas that the plug-in decides represent dust spots. This method can work well if you have many dust spots, because you won't need to patch them manually. However, any automated method like this has the possibility of blurring areas of your image that you didn't intend to soften.

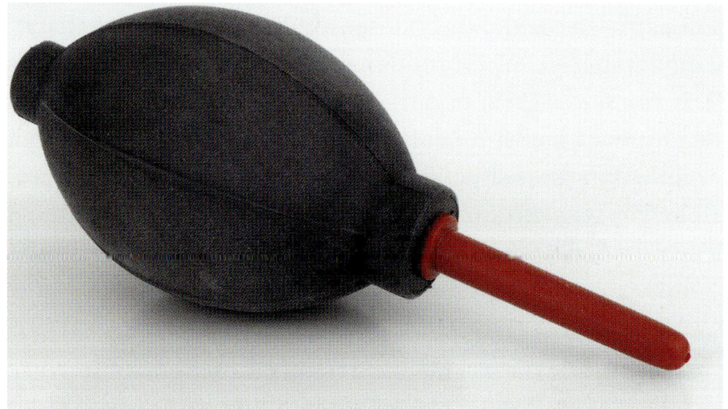

Figure 16.5 Use a sturdy blower bulb.

Sensor Cleaning

Those new to the concept of sensor dust hesitate before deciding to clean their camera themselves. Isn't it a better idea to pack up your Z5 and send it to a Nikon service center so their crack technical staff can do the job for you? Or, at the very least, shouldn't you let the friendly folks at your local camera store do it?

Of course, if you choose to let someone else clean your sensor, they will be using methods that are more or less identical to the techniques you would use yourself. None of these techniques are difficult, and the only difference between their cleaning and your cleaning is that they might have done it dozens or hundreds of times. If you're careful, you can do just as good a job.

Of course, vendors like Nikon won't tell you this, but it's not because they don't trust you. It's not that difficult for a real goofball to mess up a camera by hurrying or taking a shortcut. Perhaps the person uses the "Bulb" method of holding the shutter open and a finger slips, allowing the shutter curtain to close on top of a sensor cleaning brush. Or, someone tries to clean the sensor using masking tape, and ends up with goo all over its surface. If Nikon recommended *any* method that's mildly risky, someone would do it wrong, and then the company would face lawsuits from those who'd contend they did it exactly in the way the vendor suggested, so the ruined camera is not their fault.

You can see that vendors like Nikon tend to be conservative in their recommendations, and, in doing so, make it seem as if sensor cleaning is more daunting and dangerous than it really is. Some vendors recommend only dust-off cleaning, using reasonably gentle blasts of air, while condemning more serious scrubbing with swabs and cleaning fluids. However, these cleaning kits for the exact types of cleaning they recommended against are for sale in Japan only, where, apparently, your average photographer is more dexterous than those of us in the rest of the world. These kits are similar to those used by official repair staff to clean your sensor if you decide to send your camera in for a dust-up.

As I noted, sensors can be affected by dust particles that are much smaller than you might be able to spot visually on the surface of your lens. The filters that cover sensors tend to be fairly hard compared to optical glass. Cleaning the 24mm × 35.9mm sensor in your Nikon Z5 within the tight confines of the vestibule can call for a steady hand and careful touch. If your sensor's filter becomes scratched through inept cleaning, you can't simply remove it yourself and replace it with a new one.

There are three basic kinds of cleaning processes that can be used to remove dusty and sticky stuff that settles on your dSLR's sensor. All of these must be performed with the shutter locked open. I'll describe these methods and provide instructions for locking the shutter later in this section.

- **Air cleaning.** This process involves squirting blasts of air inside your camera with the shutter locked open. This works well for dust that's not clinging stubbornly to your sensor.
- **Brushing.** A soft, very fine brush is passed across the surface of the sensor's filter, dislodging mildly persistent dust particles and sweeping them off the imager.
- **Liquid cleaning.** A soft swab dipped in a cleaning solution such as ethanol is used to wipe the sensor filter, removing more obstinate particles.

Air Cleaning

Your first attempts at cleaning your sensor should always involve gentle blasts of air. Many times, you'll be able to dislodge dust spots, which will fall off the sensor and, with luck, out of the vestibule. Attempt one of the other methods only when you've already tried air cleaning and it didn't remove all the dust.

Here are some tips for doing air cleaning:

- **Use a clean, powerful air bulb.** Your best bet is bulb cleaners designed for the job, like the Giottos Rocket. Smaller bulbs, like those air bulbs with a brush attached sometimes sold for lens cleaning or weak nasal aspirators may not provide sufficient air or a strong enough blast to do much good.

- **Hold the camera upside down.** Then look up toward the sensor as you squirt your air blasts, increasing the odds that gravity will help pull the expelled dust downward, away from the sensor. You may have to use some imagination in positioning yourself. (See Figure 16.6, which illustrates how I clean my Nikon Z5.)

- **Never use air canisters.** The propellant inside these cans can permanently coat your sensor if you tilt the can while spraying. It's not worth taking a chance.

- **Avoid air compressors.** Super-strong blasts of air are likely to force dust under the sensor filter.

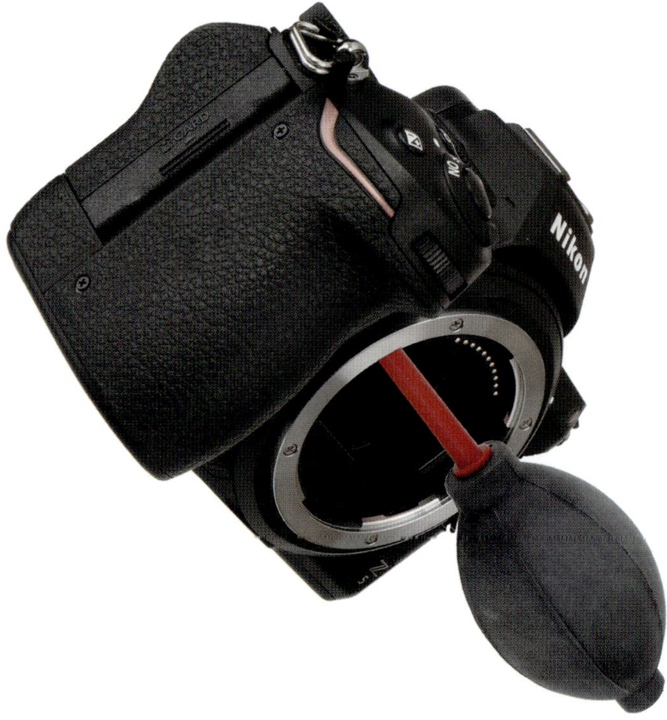

Figure 16.6 Hold the camera upside down and blow the dust off the sensor.

Brush Cleaning

If your dust is a little more stubborn and can't be dislodged by air alone, you may want to try a brush, charged with static electricity that can pick off dust spots by electrical attraction. One good, but expensive, option is the Sensor Brush sold at www.visibledust.com. You need one like the Arctic Butterfly shown in Figure 16.7, that can be stroked across the short dimension of your sensor.

Ordinary artist's brushes are much too coarse and stiff and have fibers that are tangled or can come loose and settle on your sensor. A good sensor-brush's fibers are resilient and described as "thinner than a human hair." Moreover, the brush has a non-conducting handle that reduces the risk of static sparks.

Brush cleaning is done with a dry brush by gently swiping the surface of the sensor filter with the tip. The dust particles are attracted to the brush particles and cling to them. You should clean the brush with compressed air before and after each use and store it in an appropriate air-tight container between applications to keep it clean and dust-free. Although these special brushes are expensive, one should last you a long time.

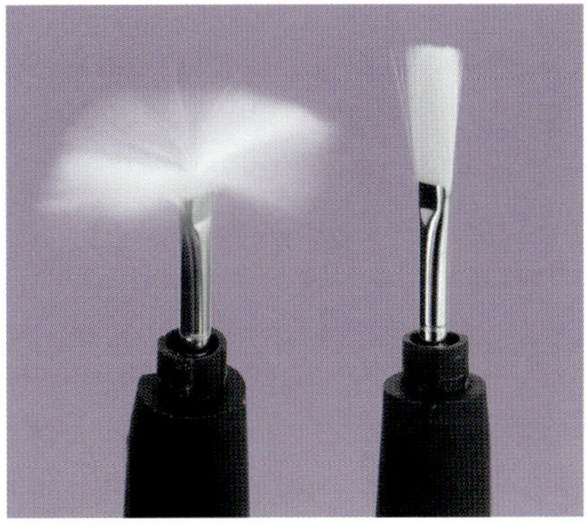

Figure 16.7 The motor in the Arctic Butterfly flutters the brush tips for a few minutes to charge them for picking up dust (left). Then, turn off the power and flick the tip above the surface of the sensor (right).

Liquid Cleaning

Unfortunately, you'll often encounter stubborn dust spots that can't be removed with a blast of air or flick of a brush. These spots may be combined with some grease or a liquid that causes them to stick to the sensor filter's surface. In such cases, liquid cleaning with a swab may be necessary. During my first clumsy attempts to clean my own sensor, I accidentally got my blower bulb tip too close to the sensor, and some sort of deposit from the tip of the bulb ended up on the sensor. I panicked until I discovered that liquid cleaning did a good job of removing whatever it was that took up residence on my sensor.

You can make your own swabs out of pieces of plastic (some use fast-food restaurant knives, with the tip cut at an angle to the proper size) covered with a soft cloth or Pec-Pad, as shown in Figure 16.8. However, if you've got the bucks to spend, you can't go wrong with good-quality commercial sensor-cleaning swabs, such as those sold by Photographic Solutions, Inc. (www.photosol.com).

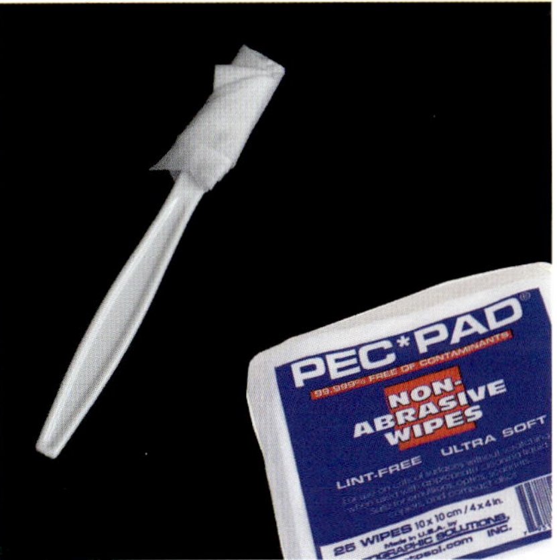

Figure 16.8 You can make your own sensor swab from a plastic knife that's been truncated.

You want a sturdy swab that won't bend or break so you can apply gentle pressure to the swab as you wipe the sensor surface. Use the swab with methanol (as pure as you can get it, particularly medical grade; other ingredients can leave a residue) or the Eclipse solution also sold by Photographic Solutions. Eclipse is quite a bit purer than even medical-grade methanol. A couple drops of solution should be enough, unless you have a spot that's extremely difficult to remove. In that case, you may need to use extra solution on the swab to help "soak" the dirt off.

Once you overcome your nervousness at touching your Z5's sensor, the process is easy. You'll wipe continuously with the swab in one direction, then flip it over and wipe in the other direction. You need to completely wipe the entire surface; otherwise, you may end up depositing the dust you collect at the far end of your stroke. Wipe; don't rub.

If you want a close-up look at your sensor to make sure the dust has been removed, you can pay $50 to $100 for a special sensor "microscope" with an illuminator. Or, you can do like I do and work with a plain-old Carson MiniBrite PO-55 illuminated 5X magnifier, as seen in Figure 16.9. It has a built-in LED and, held a few inches from the lens mount with the lens removed from your Z5, provides a sharp, close-up view of the sensor, with enough contrast to reveal any dust that remains. If you'd like to buy one for less than $10, I provide a link at my website, www.dslrguides.com/carson.

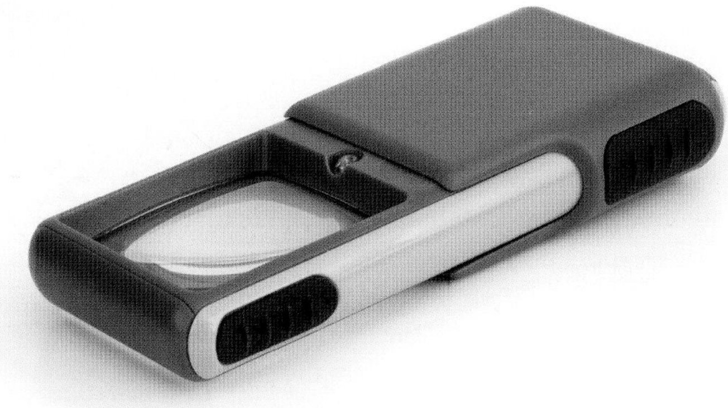

Figure 16.9 An illuminated magnifier like this Carson MiniBrite PO-55 can be used as a 'scope to view your sensor.

Index

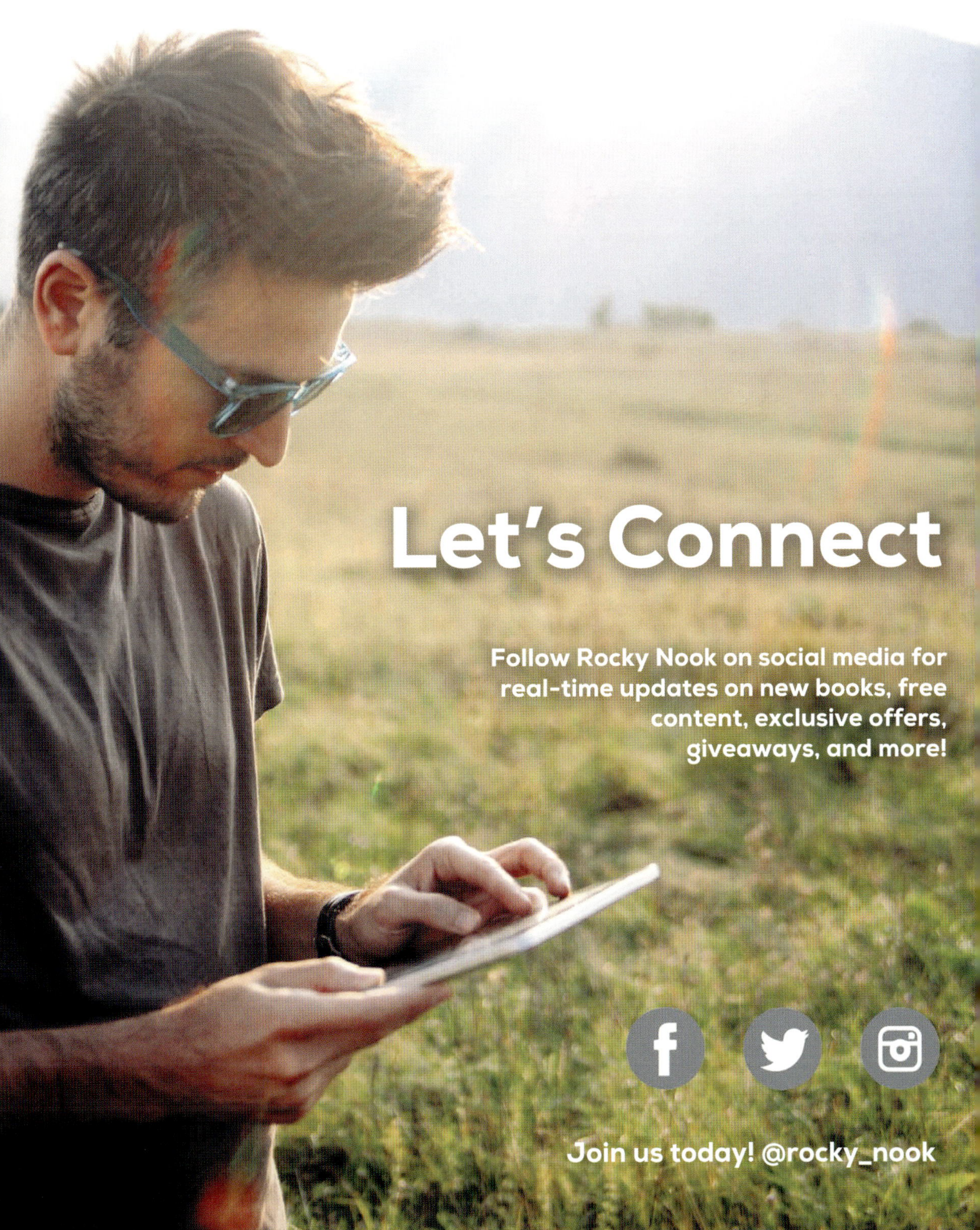

rockynook
Let's Connect
Follow Rocky Nook on social media for real-time updates on new books, free content, exclusive offers, giveaways, and more!
Join us today! @rocky_nook

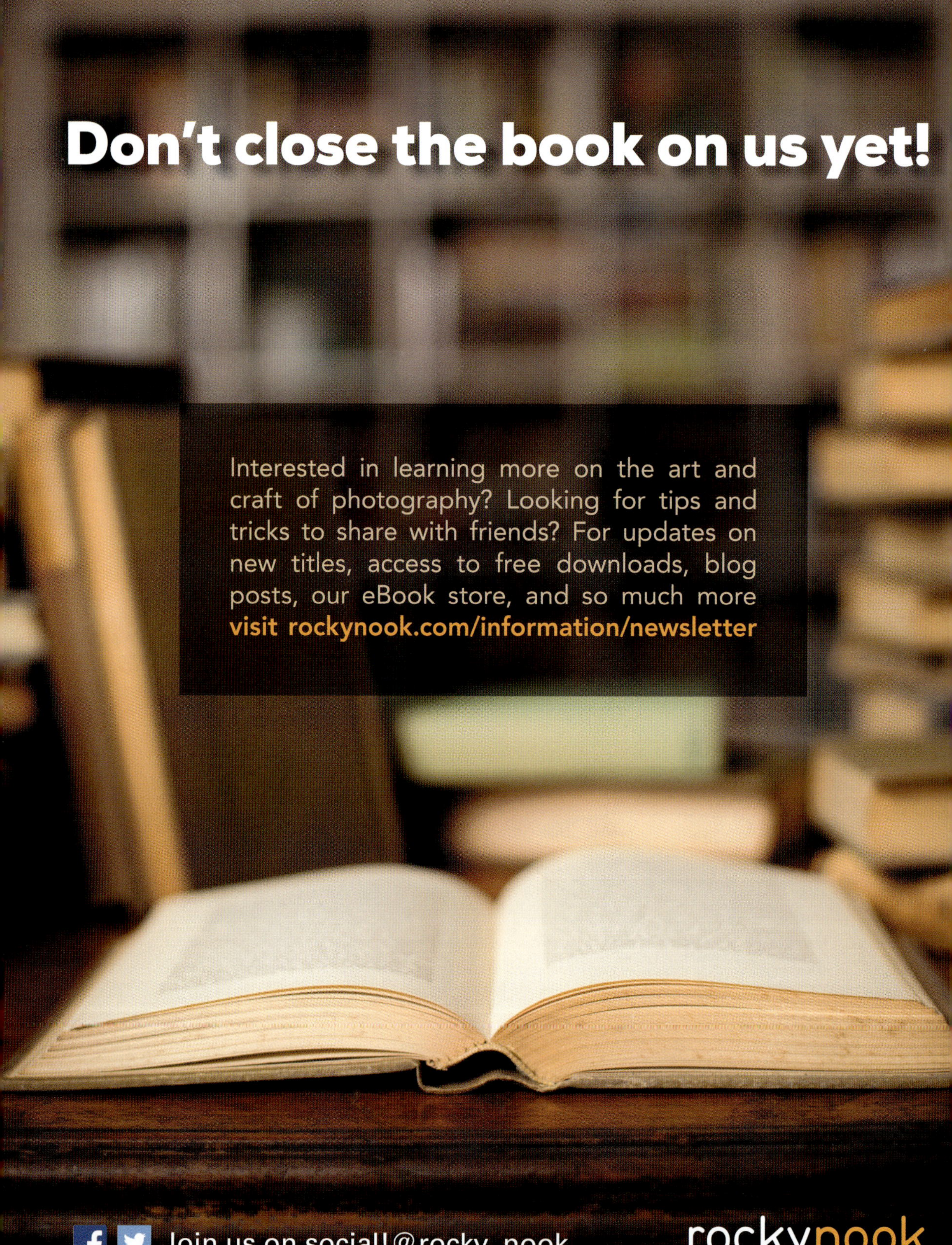

Don't close the book on us yet!

Interested in learning more on the art and craft of photography? Looking for tips and tricks to share with friends? For updates on new titles, access to free downloads, blog posts, our eBook store, and so much more visit rockynook.com/information/newsletter

Join us on social! @rocky_nook

rockynook